Perturbations, Optimization, and Statistics

Neural Information Processing Series

Michael I. Jordan and Thomas Dietterich, editors

Advances in Large Margin Classifiers, Alexander J. Smola, Peter L. Bartlett, Bernhard Schölkopf, and Dale Schuurmans, eds., 2000

Advanced Mean Field Methods: Theory and Practice, Manfred Opper and David Saad, eds., 2001

Probabilistic Models of the Brain: Perception and Neural Function, Rajesh P. N. Rao, Bruno A. Olshausen, and Michael S. Lewicki, eds., 2002

Exploratory Analysis and Data Modeling in Functional Neuroimaging, Friedrich T. Sommer and Andrzej Wichert, eds., 2003

Advances in Minimum Description Length: Theory and Applications, Peter D. Grünwald, In Jae Myung, and Mark A. Pitt, eds., 2005

Nearest-Neighbor Methods in Learning and Vision: Theory and Practice, Gregory Shakhnarovich, Piotr Indyk, and Trevor Darrell, eds., 2006

New Directions in Statistical Signal Processing: From Systems to Brains, Simon Haykin, José C. Príncipe, Terrence J. Sejnowski, and John McWhirter, eds., 2007

Predicting Structured Data, Gökhan Bakır, Thomas Hofmann, Bernhard Schölkopf, Alexander J. Smola, Ben Taskar, and S. V. N. Vishwanathan, eds., 2007

Toward Brain-Computer Interfacing, Guido Dornhege, José del R. Millán, Thilo Hinterberger, Dennis J. McFarland, and Klaus-Robert Müller, eds., 2007

Large-Scale Kernel Machines, Léon Bottou, Olivier Chapelle, Denis DeCoste, and Jason Weston, eds., 2007

Learning Machine Translation, Cyril Goutte, Nicola Cancedda, Marc Dymetman, and George Foster, eds., 2009

Dataset Shift in Machine Learning, Joaquin Quiñonero-Candela, Masashi Sugiyama, Anton Schwaighofer, and Neil D. Lawrence, eds., 2009

Optimization for Machine Learning, Suvrit Sra, Sebastian Nowozin, and Stephen J. Wright, eds., 2012

Practical Applications of Sparse Modeling, Irina Rish, Guillermo A. Cecchi, Aurelie Lozano, and Alexandru Niculescu-Mizil, eds., 2014

Advanced Structured Prediction, Sebastian Nowozin, Peter V. Gehler, Jeremy Jancsary, and Christoph H. Lampert, eds., 2014

Perturbations, Optimization, and Statistics, Tamir Hazan, George Papandreou, and Daniel Tarlow, eds., 2016

Perturbations, Optimization, and Statistics

Edited by Tamir Hazan, George Papandreou, and Daniel Tarlow

The MIT Press
Cambridge, Massachusetts
London, England

Library of Congress Cataloging-in-Publication Data

Names: Hazan, Tamir, editor. | Papandreou, George, editor. | Tarlow, Daniel, editor.

Title: Perturbations, optimization and statistics / edited by Tamir Hazan, George Papandreou, and Daniel Tarlow.

Description: Cambridge, MA : The MIT Press, [2016] | Series: Neural information processing series | Includes bibliographical references.

Identifiers: LCCN 2016023007 | ISBN 9780262035644 (hardcover : alk. paper) ISBN 9780262549943 (paperback)

Subjects: LCSH: Machine learning. | Perturbation (Mathematics) | Mathematical optimization.

Classification: LCC Q325.5 .P47 2016 | DDC 515/.392--dc23 LC record available at https://lccn.loc.gov/2016023007

Contents

Preface   ix

1 Introduction   1
Tamir Hazan, George Papandreou, and Daniel Tarlow
  1.1 Scope   1
  1.2 Regularization   4
  1.3 Modeling   9
  1.4 Roadmap 12
  1.5 References 14

2 Perturb-and-MAP Random Fields   17
George Papandreou and Alan L. Yuille
  2.1 Energy-Based Models: Deterministic vs. Probabilistic Approaches 19
  2.2 Perturb-and-MAP for Gaussian and Sparse Continuous MRFs   23
  2.3 Perturb-and-MAP for MRFs with Discrete Labels 28
  2.4 On the Representation Power of the Perturb-and-MAP Model 35
  2.5 Related Work and Recent Developments 38
  2.6 Discussion 40
  2.7 References 41

3 Factorizing Shortest Paths with Randomized Optimum Models   45
Daniel Tarlow, Alexander Gaunt, Ryan Adams,
and Richard S. Zemel
  3.1 Introduction 45
  3.2 Building Structured Models: Design Considerations 47
  3.3 Randomized Optimum Models (RandOMs) 48
  3.4 Learning RandOMs 54
  3.5 RandOMs for Image Registration 56
  3.6 Shortest Path Factorization 56
  3.7 Shortest Path Factorization with RandOMs 58

3.8 Experiments 63
3.9 Related Work 68
3.10 Discussion 70
3.11 References 70

4 Herding as a Learning System with Edge-of-Chaos Dynamics   73

Yutian Chen and Max Welling

4.1 Introduction 74
4.2 Herding Model Parameters 77
4.3 Generalized Herding 99
4.4 Experiments 109
4.5 Summary 118
4.6 Conclusion 120
4.8 References 123

5 Learning Maximum A-Posteriori Perturbation Models   127

Andreea Gane, Tamir Hazan, and Tommi Jaakkola

5.1 Introduction 128
5.2 Background and Notation 130
5.3 Expressive Power of Perturbation Models 131
5.4 Higher Order Dependencies 132
5.5 Markov Properties and Perturbation Models 134
5.6 Conditional Distributions 136
5.7 Learning Perturbation Models 141
5.8 Empirical Results 149
5.9 Perturbation Models and Stability 152
5.10 Related Work 155
5.11 References 156

6 On the Expected Value of Random Maximum A-Posteriori Perturbations   161

Tamir Hazan and Tommi Jaakkola

6.1 Introduction 161
6.2 Inference and Random Perturbations 164
6.3 Low-Dimensional Perturbations 169
6.4 Empirical Evaluation 182
6.5 References 188

7 A Poisson Process Model for Monte Carlo   193

Chris J. Maddison

7.1 Introduction 193
7.2 Poisson Processes 196
7.3 Exponential Races 203
7.4 Gumbel Processes 210
7.5 Monte Carlo Methods That Use Bounds 216
7.6 Conclusion 226
7.9 References 230

8 Perturbation Techniques in Online Learning and Optimization   233

Jacob Abernethy, Chansoo Lee, and Ambuj Tewari

8.1 Introduction 233
8.2 Preliminaries 235
8.3 Gradient-Based Prediction Algorithm 237
8.4 Generic Bounds 245
8.5 Experts Setting 247
8.6 Euclidean Balls Setting 252
8.7 The Multi-Armed Bandit Setting 254
8.9 References 262

9 Probabilistic Inference by Hashing and Optimization   265

Stefano Ermon

9.1 Introduction 265
9.2 Problem Statement and Assumptions 268
9.3 Approximate Model Counting via Randomized Hashing 270
9.4 Probabilistic Models and Approximate Inference: The WISH
     Algorithm 274
9.5 Optimization Subject to Parity Constraints 279
9.6 Applications 281
9.7 Open Problems and Research Challenges 282
9.8 Conclusion 284
9.9 References 285

10 Perturbation Models and PAC-Bayesian Generalization Bounds   289

Joseph Keshet, Subhransu Maji, Tamir Hazan, and Tommi Jaakkola

10.1 Introduction 290
10.2 Background 292
10.3 PAC-Bayesian Generalization Bounds 294
10.4 Algorithms 296
10.5 The Bayesian Perspective 298

10.6 Approximate Inference 301
10.7 Empirical Evaluation 302
10.8 Discussion 306
10.9 References 307

11 Adversarial Perturbations of Deep Neural Networks   **311**
David Warde-Farley and Ian Goodfellow
11.1 Introduction 312
11.2 Adversarial Examples 312
11.3 Adversarial Training 329
11.4 Generative Adversarial Networks 330
11.5 Discussion 338
11.6 References 339

12 Data Augmentation via Lévy Processes   **343**
Stefan Wager, William Fithian, and Percy Liang
12.1 Introduction 343
12.2 Lévy Thinning 349
12.3 Examples 361
12.4 Simulation Experiments 365
12.5 Discussion 368
12.6 Appendix: Proof of Theorem 12.4 369
12.7 References 371

13 Bilu-Linial Stability   **375**
Konstantin Makarychev and Yury Makarychev
13.1 Introduction 375
13.2 Stable Instances of Graph Partitioning Problems 380
13.3 Stable Instances of Clustering Problems 391
13.4 References 400

Preface

In nearly all machine learning tasks, decisions must be made given current knowledge (e.g., choose which label to predict). Perhaps surprisingly, always making what is believed to be the best decision is not always the best strategy, even when learning in a supervised learning setting. Recently, there is an emerging body of work on learning under different rules that apply perturbations to the decision and learning procedures. These methods provide simple and efficient learning rules with improved theoretical guarantees.

At the three highly successful workshops on Perturbations, Optimization, and Statistics at Advances in Neural Information Processing Systems (NIPS-2012, NIPS-2013, NIPS-2014), we looked at how injecting perturbations (whether it be random or adversarial "noise") into learning and inference procedures can be beneficial. The focus was on two angles: first, on how perturbations can be used to construct new types of probability models for structured data and, second, how perturbations affect the regularization and the generalization properties of learning algorithms.

This book is an expanded collection of the ideas presented at the workshops.

Tamir Hazan, George Papandreou, and Daniel Tarlow

April 2016

1 Introduction

Tamir Hazan   tamir.hazan@technion.ac.il
Technion
Haifa, Israel

George Papandreou   gpapan@google.com
Google Inc.
340 Main St., Los Angeles, CA 90291 USA

Daniel Tarlow   dtarlow@microsoft.com
Microsoft Research
Cambridge, UK

1.1 Scope

Modeling and regularization lie at the foundation of statistics and machine learning. They are avenues by which a practitioner can express assumptions that guide the learning process. Assumptions are critical, as without assumptions, learning is not possible. Without assumptions, a model will not be able to make nontrivial predictions beyond the set of examples that was used to train it. Assumptions can come in many forms. From the modeling perspective, assumptions describe the process by which data is generated and/or (soft) constraints on joint configurations of parameters and data that are plausible. Once a model is expressed, there is a large toolbox of methodologies for combining assumptions with observed data so that new predictions can be made and uncertainty can be quantified. Regularization is about expressing assumptions over which models are preferred to others so as to learn models that generalize beyond the training sample to novel settings.

There are strong connections between modeling and regularization. At a high level, they both narrow the space of possible hypotheses for how previously seen data relates to data that will be encountered in the future. At a lower level, they are often thought of interchangeably. For example, ℓ_2 regularization is commonly thought of both as a prior belief that parameters are distributed as zero-mean Gaussian distributions (probabilistic modeling assumption) and as a regularizer that controls model capacity so as to improve generalization (regularization assumption). More generally, we can think of estimating the maximum a posteriori (MAP) parameters in a Bayesian model as solving a regularized maximum likelihood problem, which gives a correspondence between the probabilistic modeling and regularization viewpoints. PAC-Bayesian generalization bounds further connect regularization and generalization to prior and posterior distributions in the probabilistic modeling setting.

While the foundations are still crucially important, machine learning is changing, primarily along two axes. First, the quality of systems being built is improving dramatically, enabled by easier access to larger data sets and computational power. Tasks that were considered infeasible only several years ago (e.g., real-time speech recognition and machine translation, plausible claims of beating human performance on nontrivial image classification tasks, systems that learn to play video games just by watching raw pixels on the screen, a professional-caliber Go player) are becoming reality. As the field progresses, we must revisit assumptions and recognize that certain assumptions of the past are crude in the modern light. These crude assumptions apply to both modeling (e.g., using a linear classifier with hand-crafted features for image classification) and regularization (e.g., ℓ_2 regularization for all parameters in a model). We must then look to models that either have higher model capacity or which are more carefully specified. Similarly, we must look for regularizers that give finer-grained preferences over which configurations of parameter should be preferred.

The second axis of change is that statistical machine learning systems are being applied in a broader range of domains than ever before, including biology, medicine, chemistry, marketing, archaeology, government, education, and programming languages. Along with these domains come new problems of different shapes. There is demand for machine learning systems that input or output highly structured objects like chemical molecules, scans of human bodies, paths that cars take through a city, essays, videos, computer programs, and DNA. As the field seeks to find success in this broad range of domains, the challenge is again about assumptions: what assumptions need to be made so that our learning systems correctly interpret and produce highly structured data? Making crude assumptions in highly structured domains can lead to a breakdown in learning. See Chapter 3 for an example.

So why are crude assumptions used? A key issue is that there is a conflict between making good assumptions and being able to efficiently compute: richer assumptions typically lead to harder computational problems. Consider modeling paths that salespeople take when visiting homes in a city under the assumption that each salesperson starts and ends at the same location and visits each home exactly once. A plausible parameterization of the problem would be to specify that there is an unknown cost associated with each road segment that connects the homes. A natural query is which route is most likely under the current setting of model parameters. However, this is the well-known Traveling Salesman problem, which is computationally hard to solve in the worst case. There is then a temptation to reformulate the problem with cruder assumptions.

Computational considerations do not just mean distinguishing between exponential and polynomial time algorithms. Often times, large datasets mean that computation must not only be efficient asymptotically, but it must be implemented in an optimized way. This may mean using specialized software like highly tuned combinatorial optimization algorithms or leveraging specialized hardware like Graphics Processing Units (GPUs), large scale distributed systems, and whatever powerful hardware is readily available. To scale learning systems up, we need to make use of the highly optimized computational primitives that current technology is capable of building.

With this background laid out, we can now state the central point of this book. This book is about how to build the fundamentals of modeling and regularization around highly optimized computational primitives. The philosophy is a departure from traditional viewpoints that focus on defining an aesthetically pleasing modeling and learning paradigm, then looking for efficient ways to compute the needed quantities, introducing approximations when intractable quantities arise. In this book, we seek to turn these considerations around: start with highly efficient computational primitives, and commit to using them as the core of the learning and inference procedure. Under this constraint, build the fundamentals of probabilistic modeling and regularization.

The key idea that ties together the work in this book is using *perturbations* to build these new foundations. Perturbations pair perfectly with efficient computational primitives, because they simply involve perturbing the inputs — either stochastically or adversarially — to the efficient computational routine. Consequently, no efficiency is lost when applying the computational routine to perturbed inputs. We can then ask what can be built upon this simple idea. Can we develop modeling and regularization paradigms upon a foundation of perturbations? How does such a paradigm relate to traditional paradigms? The results are surprisingly positive from both theoretical and empirical perspectives.

1.2 Regularization

Regularization is a fundamental concept in machine learning. Regularization constrains the learning process and prevents the learning algorithm from overfitting the data. Traditional machine learning approaches to classification, both in statistical machine learning and online learning, used the ℓ_2−norm as a regularizer. In recent years, novel perturbation methods were developed to regularize the learning process. In the following we describe these traditional approaches for classification. Subsequently, we describe how perturbation methods imply similar regularization properties. Regularization through perturbation is computationally appealing since it locally perturbs the learning process therefore it is easily integrated into complex learners such as structured predictors (e.g., Chapter 8 and Chapter 10) and deep learners (e.g., Chapter 11).

1.2.1 Statistical Machine Learning

Statistical machine learning utilizes non-asymptotic statistics in the form of generalization bounds. Such bounds measure the ability of a learning rule to generalize from a finite training dataset. Broadly, an algorithm generalizes well if its misclassification rate on a finite training dataset approaches to its expected misclassification error over all data instances in the world. To formalize this statement, we assume that the world consists of instance-label pairs, which we denote by (x, y). For example, the data-instance element $x \in R^d$ is an image and its label $y \in \{-1, +1\}$ indicates if the image contains a person or not. We assume that there is a distribution D that generates instance-label pairs and that the training sample S consists of m pairs $\{(x_1, y_1), ..., (x_m, y_m)\}$ that are sampled independently according to the distribution D. We say that a hyperplane $w \in R^d$ classifies a data-instance x according to sign, namely $y_w(x) = sign(\langle w, x \rangle)$. A hyperplane misclassifies a training pair (x_i, y_i) if $y_w(x_i) \neq y_i$. Therefore, the misclassification rate over the training set is

$$R_S(w) = \frac{1}{m} \sum_{i=1}^{m} 1[y_w(x_i) \neq y_i] \tag{1.1}$$

The function $1[y_w(x_i) \neq y_i]$ gets the value one if $y_w(x_i) \neq y_i$ and zero otherwise. $R_S(w)$ is said to be the zero-one empirical risk of the hyperplane w. The overall zero-one risk of a hyperplane w is its expected misclassification rate, with respect to the distribution D, namely:

$$R(w) = E_{(x,y) \sim D} 1[y_w(x) \neq y] \tag{1.2}$$

One of the earliest generalization bounds for classification considers separating hyperplanes, cf. (Mohri et al. (2012) Chapter 4 and Shalev-Shwartz and Ben-David (2014) Chapter 15). The classifying hyperplane is determined to maximize its distance from all training data points, namely its margin. For simplicity, assume that the world consists of separable data, i.e., there exists a hyperplane w that correctly labels all data with a margin α, namely $y\langle w, x \rangle \geq \alpha$.

Denote by w^s the hyperplane that maximizes the margin over the training dataset S

$$w^s = \arg\min_w \|w\|^2 \quad s.t. \quad \forall i \quad y_i \langle w, x_i \rangle \geq 1 \tag{1.3}$$

Assume that $\|x\| \leq 1$, then with probability of at least $1 - \delta$ over the draw of a training data set of size m holds

$$R(w^s) - R_S(w^s) \leq \sqrt{\frac{4/\alpha}{m}} + \sqrt{\frac{2 \log(2/\delta)}{m}} \tag{1.4}$$

A proof for this statement appears in (Shalev-Shwartz and Ben-David, 2014, Theorem 26.13).

The above bound holds for separable data thus it also satisfies a simpler form since $R_S(w^s) = 0$. In the non-separable case the program is infeasible and w^s does not exist. To learn non-separable data sets it is customary to relax the hard separability constraints by penalizing non-separable instances:

$$\min_w \frac{1}{2}\|w\|^2 + \sum_{i=1}^m \max\{0, 1 - y_i \langle w, x_i \rangle\}. \tag{1.5}$$

The function $\max\{0, 1 - y_i \langle w, x_i \rangle\}$ is called the hinge-loss since it a convex upper bound on the misclassification error. It penalizes points that are misclassified with respect to the margin. The regularization $\|w\|^2$ corresponds to the margin of the hyperplane, which is a global geometric concept. The data points that are closest to the hyperplane are called support vectors and the framework is widely known as the support vector machine (SVM).

Perturbation methods, specifically data perturbation and parameter perturbation, present other regularizations which are more local in nature. Therefore, regularization using perturbation methods is easier to apply.

Data perturbation amounts to shifting the data points during learning. This approach stems from robust optimization, a subarea of optimization that amounts to minimax learning—finding the minimizing parameters that separate the worst data perturbation under some restriction. Learning with data perturbation targets a classifier that gives the same result even if there are slight changes of the data points, e.g., the colors of an image. To enforce such a behavior there are random perturbations and adversarial perturbations, both related to SVMs in classification tasks, (Xu et al., 2009; Livni et al., 2012).

Random data perturbations consider an uncertainty in the data point measurement x_i using a probability distribution whose mean is x_i. To formalize the robust optimization program, define the set $\mathcal{P}(x_i)$ of all probability distribution $p_i(x)$ satisfying $E_{x \sim p_i}[x] = x_i$ and $E_{x \sim p_i} \|x - x_i\| = 1$. Then the following robust optimization program corresponds to the support vector machine program in Equation (1.5), (Livni et al., 2012):

$$\min_w \frac{1}{m} \sum_{i=1}^m \max_{p \sim \mathcal{P}(x_i)} E_{x \sim p}[\max\{0, 1 - y_i \langle w, x \rangle\}] \tag{1.6}$$

The above robust optimization program only consists of the hinge-loss that penalizes wrongly misclassified points. Although it does not explicitly use the ℓ_2-norm as regularization, this robust optimization program implicitly regularizes the learning by locally perturbing the training data. Therefore, in classification one can refrain from globally maximizing the margin from all data points and instead to locally perturb the data points (Livni et al., 2012).

Regularization can also be enforced using adversarial perturbation, which also leads to new generalization bounds (Xu et al., 2009). Both random and adversarial perturbations can generate margin-like behavior for linear classifiers, by implicitly enforcing the ℓ_2 regularization. The power of regularization through perturbation is in its locality. Therefore, they can be easily integrated into non-linear learners, such deep learners. Chapter 11 demonstrates regularization by data perturbation in deep learning.

Parameter perturbation amounts to shifting the parameters of the classifier. By doing so, parameter perturbation averages over infinitely many classifiers and obtain a robust prediction. This approach relates to Bayesian learning as it accounts for the uncertainty of the learning process by averaging predictions. By taking into account infinitely many predictions one stabilizes the learning process and augments the learning process with PAC-guarantees. A PAC-Bayesian generalization bound (McAllester, 2003; Germain et al., 2009; Seldin et al., 2012) asserts that with probability of at least $1 - \delta$ over the draw of a training data set of size m holds simultaneously for all distributions q

$$E_{w \sim q} R(w) - E_{w \sim q} R_S(w) \leq \frac{KL(q||p) + \log(1/\delta) + 1}{\sqrt{8m}} \tag{1.7}$$

$KL(q||p) = \int q(w) \log(q(w)/p(w))$ is the KL-divergence between distributions q, p. The distribution $q(w)$ is called a posterior distribution since it may be determined after seeing the training examples. For example, the expected value of $q(w)$ can be set to the empirical risk minimizer, e.g., w^s in Equation 1.3, and thus to encode the learning information. The distribution $p(w)$ is called the prior distribution since it is set before seeing the training data. If both the posterior and the prior distributions represent Gaussian random variables, the KL-divergence is the ℓ_2 regularization. Chapter 10 describes PAC-Bayesian generalization bounds and their applications to visual and language recognition tasks.

1.2.2 Online Learning

Online learning, or sequential prediction, is a game played between a learner and an omniscient adversary, also known as the environment. The game is played for T rounds. In each round t the learner predicts an element x_t from a predetermined set X.

Simultaneously, the environment decides on a loss function $f_t : X \to [0, 1]$ and the learner suffers a loss of $f_t(x_t)$. The performance of the learner is typically measured by her regret, defined as

$$\text{Regret} = \sum_{t=1}^{T} f_t(x_t) - \min_{x \in X} \sum_{t=1}^{T} f_t(x) \tag{1.8}$$

which the learner would like to minimize. The learner's regret is the difference between her cumulative loss over all T rounds and the cumulative loss of the best fixed $x \in X$ in hindsight. We say that a strategy of the learner *learns* a problem if it achieves a regret that is sublinear in T, namely Regret $\leq o(T)$.

The literature typically discusses two important special cases of online learning. The first of which is *prediction with expert advice*. Here, the learner has access to K experts. At every round, the learner chooses one expert and follows its advice; then the loss of the learner on this round is the loss that is associated with the expert that she chose. This can be formulated as following: the set $X = \{1, 2, \ldots, K\}$ is the set of K experts and each function f_t assigns an arbitrary loss between 0 and 1 to each expert.

The second special case that we consider is the one of *online convex optimization*. Here the set $X \subseteq \mathbb{R}^d$ is convex and the loss functions $f_1, \ldots, f_T$ are also convex. An important observation is that in general, any online learning problem can be formulated as an online convex optimization problem via randomization. For example take the setting of prediction with expert advice; by letting X be the $(K-1)$-dimensional probability simplex, we can associate every expert with a vertex of the simplex and think of the loss functions $f_1, \ldots, f_T$ as linear functions over X. On every round the learner selects $x_t \in X$ — a probability distribution over experts, and then randomly selects an expert by sampling from x_t. Since the learner is now randomized, we will measure her performance by her expected regret.

A first attempt at a learning algorithm is the Follow the Leader (FTL) algorithm. Denote the cumulative loss at time t by $F_t(x) = \sum_{\tau=1}^{t-1} f_\tau(x)$, then FTL involves picking x_t to be a minimizer of $F_t(x)$. FTL cannot achieve sublinear regret.[1] The problem with FTL is that greedy decisions may change too rapidly. If the environment changes the best $x \in X$ frequently throughout the game, then the learner must suffer high regret. If, on the other extreme, the learner always picks a single fixed $x \in X$, the environment can choose some other x as the best throughout the entire game, and once again the learner suffers high regret. Therefore, intuitively, the optimal strategy for the learner is one that interpolates between FTL and a strategy that picks a single fixed x.

There are several ways of stabilizing FTL to achieve such a strategy. The first of which is for the case of online convex optimization and is called Follow the Regularized Leader (FTRL). Here we assume that X is endowed with a convex regularizer $R : X \to \mathbb{R}$ and at every round t the learner predicts $x_t = \operatorname{argmin}_{x \in X} \eta F_t(x) + R(x)$, where $\eta > 0$ is a step-size parameter. Intuitively, if η is large then we expect x_t to be close to the minimizer of F_t and if η is small then we expect x_t to be close to the minimizer of R. Another possible algorithm is Follow the Perturbed Leader (FTPL). FTPL is the scheme of predicting an $x \in X$ that minimizes the perturbed cumulative loss, namely $x_t \in \operatorname{argmin}_{x \in X} \eta F_t(x) + \langle \Gamma, x \rangle$ where Γ is some random variable. Similarly to FTRL, η controls the size of the steps that x_t makes in expectation; if η is large then we expect $\mathbb{E}[x_t]$ to be close to the minimizer of F_t and if η is small then we expect $\mathbb{E}[x_t]$ to be close to the

---

1. Consider $X = [0,1]$, $f_1(x) = x/2$ and on other rounds $f_t(x) = |x - z_t|$, where $z_t = 0$ on odd rounds and $z_t = 1$ on even rounds. After an even number of rounds T, the best fixed $x \in X$ is $x = 1$ with a cumulative loss of $(T-1)/2$. On the other hand, with the exception of the first round, the learner plays $x = 1$ on odd rounds and $x = 0$ on even rounds and thus suffers a loss of 1 at every round. Then the regret of the learner is at least $(T-1)/2$ which is not sublinear in T.

fixed point of $\mathbb{E}[\operatorname{argmin}_{x\in X}\langle\Gamma,x\rangle]$. Chapter 8 presents the state-of-the-art in FTRL and FTPL.

1.3 Modeling

Structured prediction refers to a class of machine learning methods that describe systems of multiple inter-related variables. Structured prediction models are very popular in computer vision, speech recognition, natural language processing, computational biology, and other fields characterized by highly-dimensional state spaces with rich domain-specific structure.

Given an input vector of noisy measurements $\boldsymbol{x}$, our goal is to estimate the latent state output vector $\boldsymbol{y} = (y_1, \ldots, y_N)$. The elements of the state vector $y_i \in \mathcal{L}$ can take either continuous or discrete values from the label sets $\mathcal{L}$. In image processing applications such as image inpainting or deblurring the state vector $\boldsymbol{y}$ corresponds to a real-valued clean image that we wish to recover from its partial or degraded version $\boldsymbol{x}$. In computer vision applications such as image segmentation or labeling the state vector $\boldsymbol{y}$ corresponds to an assignment of image areas to different image segments or semantic object classes. In natural language processing, the state vector $\boldsymbol{y}$ may correspond to a syntactic parsing of a sentence $\boldsymbol{x}$.

Structured prediction is typically formulated as an optimization problem, either in terms of either energy minimization or utility maximization. The two viewpoints are equivalent and are roughly equally common in the literature. In this introductory Chapter we follow the former viewpoint but some of the other Chapters follow the latter viewpoint.

In the energy minimization framework, given a specific measurement $\boldsymbol{x}$, we quantify the quality of a particular interpretation $\boldsymbol{y}$ by means of a deterministic energy function $E(\boldsymbol{y}|\boldsymbol{x})$. We will often be working with energy functions of the form

$$E(\boldsymbol{y}|\boldsymbol{x};\boldsymbol{\theta}) = \langle\boldsymbol{\theta},\,\boldsymbol{\phi}(\boldsymbol{y},\boldsymbol{x})\rangle = \sum_{j=1}^{M}\theta_j\phi_j(\boldsymbol{y},\boldsymbol{x})\,, \tag{1.9}$$

where $\boldsymbol{\theta}\in\mathcal{R}^m$ is a vector of parameters and $\boldsymbol{\phi}(\boldsymbol{y},\boldsymbol{x})$ is a vector of features or potential functions extracted from the data. Sometimes, for notational convenience, we will be suppressing the dependence of the energy function or features on the measurements $\boldsymbol{x}$.

The energy function assigns lower energies to more preferable configurations, encouraging solutions $\boldsymbol{y}$ which are both compatible with local measurements $\boldsymbol{x}$ and satisfy domain-specific global constraints on $\boldsymbol{y}$, such as solution smoothness or syntactic validity. Fully specifying the energy function requires selecting both the features ϕ and parameters θ. Feature selection is usually informed by domain-specific considerations. Setting the parameters is typically done with the help of typical labeled training data, in the form of paired latent variable and measurement examples $(\boldsymbol{y}_k, \boldsymbol{x}_k)_{k=1}^{K}$. Such labeled training data allow us to tune the parameters θ so as the resulting model can faithfully represent real-world examples. Parameter learning plays a central role in both theory and practice of structured machine learning.

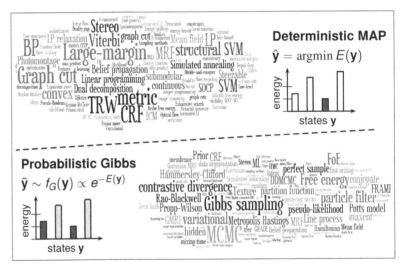

Figure 1.1: Deterministic energy minimization vs. probabilistic Gibbs modeling. Perturb-and-MAP attempts to bridge the gap between these two approaches.

As illustrated in Figure 1.1, there are two quite distinct ways to work with energy-based models. The first is entirely deterministic and amounts to finding a single most probable (MAP) configuration of minimum energy, $\hat{\boldsymbol{y}} = \operatorname{argmin}_{\boldsymbol{y}} E(\boldsymbol{y})$. The second class of methods is probabilistic, assigning to each state a Gibbs probability $f_G(\boldsymbol{y}) \propto e^{-E(\boldsymbol{y})}$. Their key advantage over MAP inference is that they also allow uncertainty quantification, which is particularly important when we interpret ambiguous data. The probabilistic framework also enables learning model parameters from training examples using maximum likelihood.

The fact that the energy function (1.9) couples together multiple variables induces a combinatorial nature to structure prediction problems. Both energy minimization and probabilistic inference in their general form require solving computationally intractable problems. However, several important families of energy functions involving both continuous and discrete-valued variables can be efficiently tackled with fast energy minimization algorithms, which can find exact or approximate solutions even for large scale problems involving millions of variables. On the other hand, probabilistic inference is considerably more difficult than optimization, since it requires capturing multiple solutions plausible under the posterior distribution instead of just a single MAP configuration. For example, submodular potentials, an important class of energy functions which favor solution smoothness, are amenable to fast optimization yet probabilistic inference under the induced Gibbs model is provably hard (Goldberg and Jerrum, 2007).

The observation that energy minimization is often computationally advantageous compared to sampling from the Gibbs distribution provides the key motivation for building probabilistic models on top of optimization problems, which constitutes one of the key themes of this volume. We introduce randomness to the optimization problem by randomly perturbing the parameter vector, followed by finding the minimizing assignment of the perturbed energy function. This Perturb-and-MAP technique (see Papandreou and Yuille (2011) and Chapter 2) establishes a link between the optimization and probabilistic inference approaches to energy-based modeling and allows us to repurpose the powerful computational arsenal of energy minimization algorithms for the task of probabilistic inference in structured prediction problems.

Two natural questions arise: Can the Perturb-and-MAP approach lead to probabilistic models that resemble their Gibbs counterparts? How to best design the perturbation process so as to minimize the mismatch between the two models?

It turns out that extreme value statistics (Gumbel and Lieblein, 1954), the field of statistics studying the properties of extrema of optimization problems, offers the right tools for tackling these questions. The *Gumbel* extreme value distribution is a continuous univariate distribution with log-concave density $g(z) = \exp(-(-z + e^z))$. We can efficiently draw independent Gumbel variates by transforming standard uniform samples by $u \to \log(-\log(u))$.[2] The Gumbel density naturally fits into the Perturb-and-MAP model, thanks to the following key property:

Lemma 1.1 (Gumbel Lemma). *Let* $(\theta_1, \ldots, \theta_m)$, *with* $\theta_n \in \mathbb{R}$, $n = 1, \ldots, m$. *We additively perturb them by* $\tilde{\theta}_n = \theta_n + \epsilon_n$, *with* ϵ_n *i.i.d. zero-mode Gumbel samples. Then:*

---

2. This is the min-stable version of the Gumbel distribution, appropriate for the energy minimization setup. In the dual utility maximization setup one needs to use the max-stable version of the Gumbel distribution. The latter has density $\tilde{g}(z) = \exp(-(z + e^{-z}))$ and can be sampled from by $u \to -\log(-\log(u))$.

(Min-Stability) The minimum of the perturbed parameters $\tilde{\theta}_{min} \triangleq \min_{n=1:m}\{\tilde{\theta}_n\}$ follows a Gumbel distribution with mode θ_0, where $e^{-\theta_0} = \sum_{n=1}^{m} e^{-\theta_n}$. Note that $\theta_0 = -\log Z$, where Z is the partition function.

(Arg-Min) The probability that $\tilde{\theta}_n$ is the minimum value is $\Pr\{\mathrm{argmin}(\tilde{\theta}_1,\ldots,\tilde{\theta}_m)=n\} = e^{-\theta_n}/e^{-\theta_0}$.

The *Gumbel Lemma* above plays such a central role in this book that we find it noteworthy to discuss some of its history. The *Min-Stability* property is a result of the study of asymptotic behavior of extreme value statistics, which was pioneered by Fisher and Tippett (1928) and Gnedenko (1943). A standard reference on extreme value theory is Gumbel and Lieblein (1954). To our knowledge, the *Arg-Min* property was discovered by mathematical psychologists (Luce, 1959; Yellott, 1977) and economists (McFadden, 1973) in the context of discrete choice theory. We refer the interested reader to Luce (1994) for a full historical discussion.

The Gumbel distribution gives an elegant exact solution to perturbation design for unstructured prediction models over discrete domains. A natural question to ask is if similar results are achievable in structured domains where enumeration of configurations is intractable, and in continuous domains. In the case of structured domains, lower dimensional perturbations that give rise to efficient algorithms can be employed (Chapter 2). The resulting Perturb-and-MAP models are no longer equivalent to their Gibbs counterparts. However, both experimental evidence and theoretical results presented in this volume suggest that this design choice has strong merits.

In the case of real-valued domains, it may not be immediately clear what the analog of Gumbel perturbations should be. However, the Gumbel Process (see Maddison et al. (2014) and Chapter 7) is a generalization of Gumbel perturbations in the discrete domains that has the analogous properties in real-valued domains. In real-valued domains (and in structured domains), the maximum perturbed value can no longer be found by enumeration. However, A* Sampling (Maddison et al., 2014) is an algorithm that uses bounds and A* search to solve this problem, which allows the exact optimum to be found in many instances. Kim et al. (2016) develops related ideas for the case of integer linear programs.

1.4   Roadmap

There are many research questions that arise upon adopting the perturbations viewpoint, and this book gives an overview of the state of the art.

Roughly, the work can be split into (a) the development of new perturbation models and learning algorithms, and (b) developing an understanding of perturbation models, and (c) developing and understanding new perturbation-based regularization techniques.

There are many recent modeling ideas that have arisen within the perturbations framework, many of which are developed in this book. Perturb & MAP (Chapter 2) and Randomized Optimum models (Chapter 3) define probabilistic models that include an efficient deterministic optimizer within the model definition. Herding (Chapter 4) develops a framework around chaotic deterministic sequences. In Chapter 10, randomized classifiers imply a modeling framework that is similar to P&M and RandOMs, but which is framed directly in terms of PAC-Bayesian generalization bounds. In Chapter 11, Generative Adversarial Networks use neural networks to map generic noise to a distribution over highly structured data like images.

Perturbation models often have the property that samples are efficient to generate, but evaluating likelihoods is difficult. This has led to a range of interesting learning procedures for these models. Chapter 3 describes how EM algorithms can take advantage of structure in combinatorial optimization algorithms to speed up learning. Chapter 5 develops an improved hard EM algorithm. Chapter 10 suggests biasing the perturbations in an importance sampling framework during learning in order to reduce the variance in a stochastic gradient-based learning algorithm. In Chapter 2, a learning algorithm is given that aims to directly match moments of model samples to moments of data. Chapter 11 suggests using a *discriminator* neural network to distinguish between samples from the model and data instances in such a way that the whole system is differentiable. Follow-up work (Li et al., 2015; Dziugaite et al., 2015) draws inspiration from statistical tests of whether two sets of samples are drawn from the same distribution in order to develop a training objective for perturbation models that again is based on matching moments. A related problem that arises in perturbation models is that conditioning on values of a subset of variables becomes trickier. This is one of the most important open problems in the area. Chapter 5 studies this problem and gives a condition under which simply fixing the observed value is correct, but much more study is needed here.

There has also been significant progress in understanding perturbation models and how they relate to traditional counterparts. In certain settings there are precise relationships between the perturbations viewpoint and traditional viewpoints, which are discussed in Chapter 5, Chapter 6, and Chapter 8. The perturbation viewpoint can lead to computational guarantees on problems which are provably hard in general (Chapter 13). The perturbations viewpoint can even lead to new algorithms for solving problems in the traditional setting, such as is the case with A* Sampling, which is discussed in Chapter 7.

Empirically, dropout (Srivastava et al., 2014) is perhaps the best known perturbation-based regularization technique, and it is credited for many gains in the performance of recent large-scale deep learning systems. Analytic understandings of perturbation-based regularization in neural networks were developed in Bishop (1995) and developed in the context of dropout by Wager et al. (2013). This gives an understanding of how dropout differs from ℓ_2 regularization, for example. Chapter 12 develops an extension of Wager et al. (2013), giving deeper understandings of dropout and a general framework for understanding dropout-like perturbations. Chapter 11 further studies perturbations in the context of deep neural networks, considering the effect of adversarial perturbations and using stochastic perturbations as the basis for a generative neural network model.

Put together, this book aims to introduce the reader to a new way of thinking about the fundamentals of statistical learning. While many connections are made and many ideas have been developed, we still believe there to be much more to discover in this space, and the hope is that this book is a launch pad that helps the interested researcher jump into this exciting area.

1.5   References

C. M. Bishop. Training with noise is equivalent to tikhonov regularization. *Neural computation*, 7(1):108–116, 1995.

G. K. Dziugaite, D. M. Roy, and Z. Ghahramani. Training generative neural networks via maximum mean discrepancy optimization. In *Proc. Int. Conf. on Uncertainty in Artificial Intelligence*, 2015.

R. A. Fisher and L. H. C. Tippett. Limiting forms of the frequency distribution of the largest or smallest member of a sample. *Mathematical Proceedings of the Cambridge Philosophical Society*, 24(02):180–190, April 1928. doi: 10.1017/S0305004100015681.

P. Germain, A. Lacasse, F. Laviolette, and M. Marchand. PAC-Bayesian learning of linear classifiers. In *ICML*, pages 353–360. ACM, 2009.

B. Gnedenko. Sur la distribution limite du terme maximum d'une serie aleatoire. *Annals of Mathematics*, 44(3):423–453, July 1943. doi: 10.2307/1968974.

L. Goldberg and M. Jerrum. The complexity of ferromagnetic ising with local fields. *Combinatorics Probability and Computing*, 16(1):43, 2007.

E. Gumbel and J. Lieblein. *Statistical theory of extreme values and some practical applications: a series of lectures*, volume 33. US Govt. Print. Office, 1954.

C. Kim, A. Sabharwal, and S. Ermon. Exact sampling with integer linear programs and random perturbations. In *Proc. 30th AAAI Conference on Artificial Intelligence*, 2016.

Y. Li, K. Swersky, and R. Zemel. Generative moment matching networks. In *Proc. Int. Conf. on Machine Learning*, 2015.

R. Livni, K. Crammer, A. Globerson, E.-I. Edmond, and L. Safra. A simple geometric interpretation of svm using stochastic adversaries. In *AISTATS*, pages 722–730, 2012.

R. Luce. Individual choice behavior. 1959.

R. D. Luce. Thurstone and sensory scaling: Then and now. 1994.

C. J. Maddison, D. Tarlow, and T. Minka. A* sampling. In Z. Ghahramani, M. Welling, C. Cortes, N. D. Lawrence, and K. Q. Weinberger, editors, *Advances in Neural Information Processing Systems 27*, pages 3086–3094. Curran Associates, Inc., 2014. URL `http://papers.nips.cc/paper/5449-a-sampling.pdf`.

D. McAllester. Simplified PAC-Bayesian margin bounds. *Learning Theory and Kernel Machines*, pages 203–215, 2003.

D. McFadden. Conditional logit analysis of qualitative choice behavior. 1973.

M. Mohri, A. Rostamizadeh, and A. Talwalkar. *Foundations of machine learning*. MIT press, 2012.

G. Papandreou and A. Yuille. Perturb-and-map random fields: Using discrete optimization to learn and sample from energy models. In *ICCV*, Barcelona, Spain, Nov. 2011. doi: 10.1109/ICCV.2011.

Y. Seldin, F. Laviolette, N. Cesa-Bianchi, J. Shawe-Taylor, and P. Auer. Pac-bayesian inequalities for martingales. *Information Theory, IEEE Transactions on*, 58(12):7086–7093, 2012.

S. Shalev-Shwartz and S. Ben-David. *Understanding machine learning: From theory to algorithms*. Cambridge University Press, 2014.

N. Srivastava, G. Hinton, A. Krizhevsky, I. Sutskever, and R. Salakhutdinov. Dropout: A simple way to prevent neural networks from overfitting. *The Journal of Machine Learning Research*, 15(1):1929–1958, 2014.

S. Wager, S. Wang, and P. S. Liang. Dropout training as adaptive regularization. In *Advances in neural information processing systems*, pages 351–359, 2013.

H. Xu, C. Caramanis, and S. Mannor. Robustness and regularization of support vector machines. *The Journal of Machine Learning Research*, 10:1485–1510, 2009.

J. I. Yellott. The relationship between Luce's choice axiom, Thurstone's theory of comparative judgment, and the double exponential distribution. *Journal of Mathematical Psychology*, 15(2), 1977.

2   Perturb-and-MAP Random Fields

George Papandreou   gpapan@google.com
Google Inc.
340 Main St., Los Angeles, CA 90291 USA

Alan L. Yuille   alan.yuille@jhu.edu
Johns Hopkins University
Baltimore, MD, 21218 USA

Probabilistic Bayesian methods such as Markov random fields are well suited for modeling structured data, providing a natural conceptual framework for capturing the uncertainty in interpreting them and automatically learning model parameters from training examples. However, Bayesian methods are often computationally too expensive for large-scale applications compared to deterministic energy minimization techniques.

This chapter presents an overview of the "Perturb-and-MAP" generative probabilistic random field model, which produces in a single shot a random sample from the whole field by first injecting noise into the energy function, then solving an optimization problem to find the least energy configuration of the perturbed system. Perturb-and-MAP random fields thus turn fast deterministic energy minimization methods into computationally efficient probabilistic inference machines and make Bayesian inference practically tractable for large-scale problems, as illustrated in challenging computer vision applications such as image inpainting and deblurring, image segmentation, and scene labeling.

We also present a new theoretical result. Specifically, we study the representation power of the Perturb-and-MAP model, showing that it is expressive enough to reproduce the sufficient statistics of arbitrary observed data.

Keywords: *MRF, energy minimization, Perturb-and-MAP, extreme value statistics, graph cuts, random sampling.*

Structured prediction models are typically built around an energy function, which assigns to each possible configuration vector $\boldsymbol{y} = (y_1, \ldots, y_N)$ a real-valued energy $E(\boldsymbol{y})$, with more preferable configurations getting lower energies. As explained in Chapter 1, one can approach energy-based problems in a purely deterministic fashion, which amounts to finding a single most probable (MAP) configuration of minimum energy, $\hat{\boldsymbol{y}} = \operatorname{argmin}_{\boldsymbol{y}} E(\boldsymbol{y})$. Alternatively, one can build probabilistic models around the energy function, assigning to each state a Gibbs probability $f_G(\boldsymbol{y}) \propto e^{-E(\boldsymbol{y})}$.

This chapter presents an overview of the Perturb-and-MAP method (Papandreou and Yuille, 2011a), which attempts to reduce probabilistic inference to an energy minimization problem, thus establishing a link between the optimization and probabilistic inference approaches to energy-based modeling, set up in Chapter 1. As illustrated in Figure 2.1, Perturb-and-MAP is a two-step generative process: (1) In a Perturb step, we inject additive random noise $N(\boldsymbol{y})$ into the system's energy function, followed by (2) a MAP step in which we find the minimum energy configuration of the perturbed system. By properly designing the noise injection process we can generate exact Gibbs samples from Gaussian MRFs and good approximate samples from discrete-label MRFs.

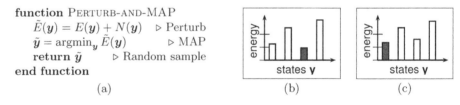

function PERTURB-AND-MAP
    $\tilde{E}(\boldsymbol{y}) = E(\boldsymbol{y}) + N(\boldsymbol{y})$ ▷ Perturb
    $\tilde{\boldsymbol{y}} = \operatorname{argmin}_{\boldsymbol{y}} \tilde{E}(\boldsymbol{y})$ ▷ MAP
    return $\tilde{\boldsymbol{y}}$ ▷ Random sample
end function

(a)   (b)   (c)

Figure 2.1: (a) The generic Perturb-and-MAP random sampling algorithm. (b) Original energies $E(\boldsymbol{y})$. (c) Perturbed energies $\tilde{E}(\boldsymbol{y})$. The MAP state $\hat{\boldsymbol{y}}$ and the Perturb-and-MAP sample $\tilde{\boldsymbol{y}}$ are shown shaded in (b) and (c), respectively.

While deterministic MAP inference summarizes the solution space into a single most probable estimate, Perturb-and-MAP gives other low energy states the chance to arise as random samples for some instantiations of the perturbation noise and is thus able to represent the whole probability landscape. Perturb-and-MAP follows a fundamentally different approach compared to other approximate probabilistic inference methods such as Markov Chain Monte-Carlo (MCMC) and Variational Bayes (VB), which are contrasted with Perturb-and-MAP in Figure 2.2. MCMC is broadly applicable and can provide very accurate results but is typically computationally very expensive for large scale problems. When the distribution has multiple modes, MCMC mixes slowly and becomes particularly ineffective because it moves in small steps through the state space. Crucially, Perturb-and-MAP generates samples in a single shot, completely bypassing the Markov Chain slow mixing problem, and thus has no difficulty in dealing with multimodal distributions. Variational Bayesian methods such as mean field or variational bounding approximate a complicated probability landscape with a simpler parametric distribution. VB is typically faster yet less accurate than MCMC, and also faces difficulties in the presence of multiple modes.

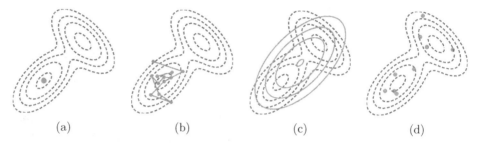

      (a)   (b)   (c)   (d)

Figure 2.2: Capturing a complicated probability landscape (in dashed lines) with standard approximate inference methods vs. Perturb-and-MAP. (a) Deterministic MAP. (b) Markov Chain Monte-Carlo. (c) Variational Bayes. (d) Perturb-and-MAP.

Perturb-and-MAP was initially developed for drawing exact random samples from Gaussian MRFs (Papandreou and Yuille, 2010). This efficient Gaussian sampling algorithm can also be used as sub-routine and considerably accellerate both MCMC and VB in applications involving continuous sparse potentials. We discuss these in Section 2.2. This line of research led to the development of Perturb-and-MAP for discrete MRFs (Papandreou and Yuille, 2011a), which we discuss in Section 2.3. We summarize some related work in Section 2.5.

2.1 Energy-Based Models: Deterministic vs. Probabilistic Approaches

2.1.1 Energies and Gibbs MRFs for Modeling Inverse Problems

Structured prediction for solving inverse problems is typically formulated in terms of energy functions. Given an input vector of noisy measurements x, our goal is to estimate the latent state output vector $y = (y_1, \ldots, y_N)$. The elements of the state vector $y_i \in \mathcal{L}$ can take either continuous or discrete values from the label set $\mathcal{L}$. As shown in Figure 2.3, in image processing applications such as image inpainting or deblurring the state vector y corresponds to a real-valued clean image that we wish to recover from its partial or degraded version $\boldsymbol{x}$. In computer vision applications such as image segmentation or labeling the state vector $\boldsymbol{y}$ corresponds to an assignment of image areas to different image segments or semantic object classes. Probabilistic Bayesian techniques offer a natural framework for combining the measurements with prior information in tackling such inverse problems.

(a)   (b)   (c)   (d)

Figure 2.3: In inverse modeling we use observations $\boldsymbol{x}$ (top row) to infer a latent interpretation $\boldsymbol{y}$ (bottom row). Image processing examples: (a) Inpainting. (b) Deblurring. Computer vision examples: (c) Figure-ground segmentation. (d) Scene labeling.

Given a specific measurement $\boldsymbol{x}$, we quantify a particular interpretation $\boldsymbol{y}$ by means of a *deterministic* energy function $E(\boldsymbol{y})$, where for notational convenience we are suppressing its dependence on the measurements $\boldsymbol{x}$. We will be working with energy functions of the general form

$$E(\boldsymbol{y}; \boldsymbol{\theta}) = \langle \boldsymbol{\theta}, \, \boldsymbol{\phi}(\boldsymbol{y}) \rangle = \sum_{j=1}^{M} \theta_j \phi_j(\boldsymbol{y}) \,, \tag{2.1}$$

where $\boldsymbol{\theta} \in \mathbb{R}^M$ is a real-valued parameter vector of length M, and $\boldsymbol{\phi}(\boldsymbol{y}) = (\phi_1(\boldsymbol{y}), \dots, \phi_M(\boldsymbol{y}))^T$ is a vector of potentials or "sufficient statistics". We can interpret θ_j as the weight assigned to the feature $\phi_j(\boldsymbol{y})$: we have many different design goals or sources of information (e.g., smoothness prior, measurements), each giving rise to some features, whose weighted linear combination constitutes the overall energy function. Each potential often depends on a small subset of the latent variables, which is made explicit in a factor graph representation of the energy function shown in Figure 2.4.

The Gibbs distribution is the standard way to induce a *probabilistic* model from the energy function. It defines a Markov random field whose probability

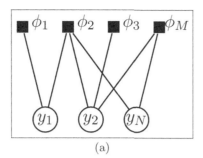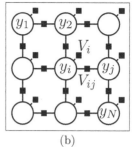

(a)   (b)

Figure 2.4: (a) The factor graph representation of the energy makes explicit which variables affect each potential. (b) A standard nearest neighbor 2-D grid MRF with unary and pairwise potentials, $\boldsymbol{\phi} = (\{V_i\}, \{V_{ij}\})$.

density/mass function has the exponential family form

$$f_G(\boldsymbol{y}; \boldsymbol{\theta}) = Z^{-1}(\boldsymbol{\theta}) \exp\left(-E(\boldsymbol{y}; \boldsymbol{\theta})\right), \tag{2.2}$$

where $Z(\boldsymbol{\theta}) = \sum_{\boldsymbol{y}} \exp\left(-E(\boldsymbol{y}; \boldsymbol{\theta})\right)$ is the partition function and summation over $\boldsymbol{y}$ should be interpreted as integration in the case of a continuous label space $\mathcal{L}$.

MAP inference in the Gibbs model, i.e., computing the most probable configuration, $\hat{\boldsymbol{y}} = \operatorname{argmax}_{\boldsymbol{y}} f_G(\boldsymbol{y})$, is equivalent to solving the energy minimization problem $\hat{\boldsymbol{y}} = \operatorname{argmin}_{\boldsymbol{y}} E(\boldsymbol{y})$. Thanks to powerful modern energy minimization algorithms, exact or high-quality approximate MAP inference can be performed efficiently for several important energy models. However, other key queries on the Gibbs model such as computing the marginals $f_G(y_i) = \sum_{\boldsymbol{y} \backslash y_i} f_G(\boldsymbol{y})$ or random sampling are computationally hard.

2.1.2   Probabilistic Parameter Learning from Training Examples

While we typically select the feature set $\boldsymbol{\phi}$ by hand, we can exercise much control on the behavior of the energy-based model by setting the parameters $\boldsymbol{\theta}$ to appropriate values. The high-level goal is to select the weight vector $\boldsymbol{\theta}$ in a way that the model assigns low energies to desirable configurations and high energies to "everything else".

When the number of parameters M is small, we can set them to reasonable values by hand. However, a more principled way is to automatically learn the parameters from a training set of K structured labeled examples $\{\boldsymbol{y}_k\}_{k=1}^{K}$. Discriminative learning criteria such as structured max-margin (Taskar et al., 2003; LeCun et al., 2007; Szummer et al., 2008; Koller and Friedman, 2009) are very powerful and described in detail in other chapters of this volume. Computationally, they are iterative and they typically require modified MAP inference at each parameter update step, which is computationally efficient for many energy models often used in practice.

In the probabilistic setting that is the focus of this chapter, maximum (penalized) likelihood (ML) is the natural criterion for learning the weights. Given the labeled training set $\{\boldsymbol{y}_k\}_{k=1}^K$, we fit the parameters $\boldsymbol{\theta}$ by maximizing the Gibbs log-likelihood function $L_G(\boldsymbol{\theta}) = -\log Z(\boldsymbol{\theta}) - (1/K)\sum_{k=1}^K E(\boldsymbol{y}_k; \boldsymbol{\theta})$, possibly also including an extra penalty term regularizing the weights. For fully observed models and energies of the form (2.1) the log-likelihood is a concave function of the weights $\boldsymbol{\theta}$ and thus the global maximum can be found by gradient ascent (Hinton and Sejnowski, 1983; Zhu et al., 1998; Koller and Friedman, 2009). The gradient is $\partial L_G/\partial \theta_j = \mathbb{E}_{\boldsymbol{\theta}}^G\{\phi_j(\boldsymbol{y})\} - \mathbb{E}_D\{\phi_j(\boldsymbol{y})\}$. Here $\mathbb{E}_{\boldsymbol{\theta}}^G\{\phi_j(\boldsymbol{y})\} \triangleq \sum_{\boldsymbol{y}} f_G(\boldsymbol{y}; \boldsymbol{\theta})\phi_j(\boldsymbol{y}) = -\partial(\log Z)/\partial \theta_j$ and $\mathbb{E}_D\{\phi_j(\boldsymbol{y})\} \triangleq (1/K)\sum_{k=1}^K \phi_j(\boldsymbol{y}_k)$ are, respectively, the expected sufficient statistics under the Gibbs model and the data distribution. Upon convergence, $\mathbb{E}_{\boldsymbol{\theta}}^G\{\phi_j(\boldsymbol{y})\} = \mathbb{E}_D\{\phi_j(\boldsymbol{y})\}$. Thus, ML estimation of the Gibbs model can be thought of as moment matching: random samples drawn from the trained model reproduce the sufficient statistics observed in the training data.

The chief computational challenge in ML parameter learning of the Gibbs model lies in estimating the model sufficient statistics $\mathbb{E}_{\boldsymbol{\theta}}^G\{\phi_j(\boldsymbol{y})\}$. Note that this inference step needs to be repeated at each parameter update step. The model sufficient statistics can be computed exactly in tree-structured (and low tree-width) graphs, but in general graphs one needs to resort to MCMC techniques for approximating them (Hinton and Sejnowski, 1983; Zhu et al., 1998; Hinton, 2002), an avenue considered too costly for many computer vision applications. Deterministic approximations such as variational techniques or loopy sum-product belief propagation do exist, but often are not accurate enough. Simplified criteria such as pseudo-likelihood (Besag, 1975) have been applied as substitutes to ML, but they can sometimes give results grossly different to ML.

Beyond model training, random sampling is very useful in itself, to reveal what are typical instances of the model – what the model has in its "mind" – and in applications such as texture synthesis (Zhu et al., 1998). Further, we might be interested not only in the global minimum energy configuration, but in the marginal densities or posterior means as well (Schmidt et al., 2010). In loopy graphs these quantities are typically intractable to compute, the only viable way being through sampling. Our Perturb-and-MAP random field model is designed specifically so as to be amenable to rapid sampling.

2.2 Perturb-and-MAP for Gaussian and Sparse Continuous MRFs

Gaussian Markov random fields (GMRFs) are an important MRF class describing continuous variables linked by quadratic potentials (Besag, 1974; Szeliski, 1990; Weiss and Freeman, 2001; Rue and Held, 2005). They are very useful both for modeling inherently Gaussian data and as building blocks for constructing more complex models.

2.2.1 Exact Gaussian MRF Sampling by Local Perturbations

We will be working with a GMRF defined by the energy function

$$E(\boldsymbol{y};\boldsymbol{\theta}) = \frac{1}{2}(\boldsymbol{F}\boldsymbol{y} - \boldsymbol{\mu}_0)^T \boldsymbol{\Sigma}_0^{-1}(\boldsymbol{F}\boldsymbol{y} - \boldsymbol{\mu}_0) = \frac{1}{2}\boldsymbol{y}^T \boldsymbol{J}\boldsymbol{y} - \boldsymbol{k}^T \boldsymbol{y} + (\text{const}) \quad (2.3)$$

where $\boldsymbol{J} = \boldsymbol{F}^T \boldsymbol{\Sigma}_0^{-1} \boldsymbol{F}$, $\boldsymbol{k} = \boldsymbol{F}^T \boldsymbol{\Sigma}_0^{-1} \boldsymbol{\mu}_0$. The energy can be cast in the generic inner product form of Equation (2.1) by defining the parameters $\boldsymbol{\theta} = (\boldsymbol{k}, \text{vec}(\boldsymbol{J}))$ and features $\boldsymbol{\phi}(\boldsymbol{y}) = (-\boldsymbol{y}, \frac{1}{2}\text{vec}(\boldsymbol{y}\boldsymbol{y}^T))$. We assume a diagonal matrix $\boldsymbol{\Sigma}_0 = \text{Diag}(\Sigma_1, \ldots, \Sigma_M)$, implying that the energy can be decomposed as a sum of M independent terms $E(\boldsymbol{y};\boldsymbol{\theta}) = \sum_{j=1}^{M} \frac{1}{2\Sigma_j}(\boldsymbol{f}_j^T \boldsymbol{y} - \mu_j)^2$, where $\boldsymbol{f}_j^T$ is the j-th row of the measurement matrix $\boldsymbol{F}$ and μ_j is the j-th entry of the vector $\boldsymbol{\mu}_0$.

The corresponding Gibbs distribution $f_G(\boldsymbol{y})$ is a multivariate Gaussian $\mathcal{N}(\boldsymbol{\mu}, \boldsymbol{\Sigma})$ with covariance matrix $\boldsymbol{\Sigma} = \boldsymbol{J}^{-1}$ and mean vector $\boldsymbol{\mu} = \boldsymbol{J}^{-1}\boldsymbol{k}$. The MAP estimate $\hat{\boldsymbol{y}} = \text{argmin}_{\boldsymbol{y}} \frac{1}{2}\boldsymbol{y}^T \boldsymbol{J}\boldsymbol{y} - \boldsymbol{k}^T \boldsymbol{y}$ under this Gaussian model coincides with the mean and amounts to solving the $N \times N$ linear system $\boldsymbol{J}\boldsymbol{\mu} = \boldsymbol{k}$. Solving this linear system with direct exact methods requires a Cholesky factorization of $\boldsymbol{J}$, whose complexity is $\mathcal{O}(N^2)$ for banded system matrices with tree-width $\mathcal{O}(\sqrt{N})$ arising in typical image analysis problems on 2-D grids. We can perform approximate MAP inference much faster using iterative techniques such as preconditioned conjugate gradients (Golub and Van Loan, 1996) or multigrid (Terzopoulos, 1988), whose complexity for many computer vision models is $\mathcal{O}(N^{3/2})$ or even $\mathcal{O}(N)$.

Standard algorithms for sampling from the Gaussian MRF also require a Cholesky factorization of $\boldsymbol{J}$ and thus have the same large time and memory complexity of direct system solvers. The following result though shows that we can draw *exact* GMRF samples by Perturb-and-MAP:

Proposition 2.1. *Assume that we replace the quadratic potential mean $\boldsymbol{\mu}_0$ by its perturbed version $\tilde{\boldsymbol{\mu}}_0 \sim \mathcal{N}(\boldsymbol{\mu}_0, \boldsymbol{\Sigma}_0)$, followed by finding the MAP of the perturbed model $\tilde{\boldsymbol{y}} = \boldsymbol{F}^T \boldsymbol{\Sigma}_0^{-1} \tilde{\boldsymbol{\mu}}_0$. Then $\tilde{\boldsymbol{y}}$ is an exact sample from the original GMRF $\mathcal{N}(\boldsymbol{\mu}, \boldsymbol{\Sigma})$.*

Proof. Since $\tilde{\boldsymbol{\mu}}_0$ is Gaussian, $\tilde{\boldsymbol{y}} = \boldsymbol{J}^{-1}\boldsymbol{F}^T\boldsymbol{\Sigma}_0^{-1}\tilde{\boldsymbol{\mu}}_0$ also follows a multivariate Gaussian distribution. It has mean $\mathbb{E}\{\tilde{\boldsymbol{y}}\} = \boldsymbol{\mu}$ and covariance matrix $\mathbb{E}\{(\tilde{\boldsymbol{y}} - \boldsymbol{\mu})(\tilde{\boldsymbol{y}} - \boldsymbol{\mu})^T\} = \boldsymbol{J}^{-1}\boldsymbol{F}^T\boldsymbol{\Sigma}_0^{-1}\boldsymbol{F}\boldsymbol{J}^{-1} = \boldsymbol{\Sigma}$. □

It is noteworthy that the algorithm only involves locally perturbing each potential separately, $\tilde{\mu}_j \sim \mathcal{N}(\mu_j, \Sigma_j)$, and turns any existing GMRF MAP algorithm into an effective random sampler.

As an example, we show in Figure 2.5 an image inpainting application in which we fill in the flat areas of an image given the values at its edges under a 2-D thin-membrane prior GMRF model (Terzopoulos, 1988; Szeliski, 1990; Malioutov et al., 2008), which involves pairwise quadratic potentials $V_{ij} = \frac{1}{2\Sigma}(y_i - y_j)^2$ between nearest neighbors connected as in Figure 2.4(b). We show both the posterior mean/MAP estimate and a random sample under the model, both computed in a fraction of a second by solving a Poisson equation by a $\mathcal{O}(N)$ multigrid solver originally developed for solving PDE problems (Terzopoulos, 1988).

Figure 2.5: Reconstructing an image from its value on edges under a nearest-neighbor Gaussian MRF model. (a) Masked image. (b) Posterior mean/MAP estimate $\hat{\boldsymbol{y}}$. (c) Random sample $\tilde{\boldsymbol{y}}$.

2.2.2 Efficient MCMC Inference in Conditionally Gaussian Models

Gaussian models have proven inadequate for image modeling as they fail to capture important aspects of natural image statistics such as the heavy tails in marginal histograms of linear filter responses. Nevertheless, much richer statistical image tools can be built if we also incorporate into our models latent variables or allow nonlinear interactions between multiple Gaussian fields and thus the GMRF sampling technique we describe here is very useful within this wider setting (Weiss and Freeman, 2007; Roth and Black, 2009; Papandreou et al., 2008).

In (Papandreou and Yuille, 2010) we discuss the integration of our GMRF sampling algorithm in a block-Gibbs sampling context, where the conditionally Gaussian continuous variables and the conditionally independent latent variables are sampled alternately. The most straightforward way to capture the heavy tailed histograms of natural images is to model each filter response with a Gaussian mixture expert, thus using a single discrete assignment variable at each factor (Papandreou et al., 2008; Schmidt et al., 2010). We show in Figure 2.6 an image inpainting example following this approach in which a wavelet domain hidden Markov tree model is used (Papandreou et al., 2008).

Figure 2.6: Filling in missing image parts from the ancient wall-paintings of Thera (Papandreou, 2009). Image inpainting with a wavelet domain model and block Gibbs sampling inference (Papandreou et al., 2008).

Efficient GMRF Perturb-and-MAP sampling can also be used in conjunction with Gaussian scale mixture (GSM) models for which the latent scale variable is continuous (Andrews and Mallows, 1974). We demonstrate this in the context of Bayesian signal restoration by sampling from the posterior distribution under a total variation (TV) prior, employing the GSM characterization of the Laplacian density. We show in Figure 2.7 an example of 1-D signal restoration under a TV signal model. The standard MAP estimator features characteristic staircasing artifacts (Nikolova, 2007). Block Gibbs sampling from the posterior distribution allows us to efficiently approximate the posterior mean estimator, which outperforms the MAP estimator in terms of mean square error/PSNR. Although individual posterior random samples are worse in terms of PSNR, they accurately capture the micro-texture of the original clean signal.

2.2.3 Variational Inference for Bayesian Compressed Sensing

Variational inference is increasingly popular for probabilistic inference in sparse models, providing the basis for many modern Bayesian compressed sensing methods. At a high level, variational techniques in this setting

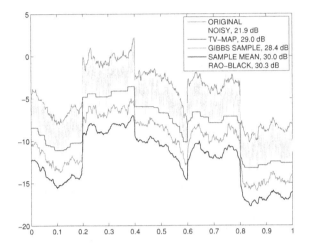

Figure 2.7: Signal denoising under a total variation prior model and alternative estimation criteria. From top to bottom, the graphs show: (a) Original latent clean signal, synthesized by adding Laplacian noise increments to a piece-wise constant signal. (b) Noisy version of the signal, corrupted by Gaussian i.i.d. noise. (c) MAP estimator under a TV prior model. (d) A single sample from the TV posterior Gibbs distribution. (e) Posterior mean estimator obtained by averaging multiple samples. (f) Rao-Blackwellized posterior mean estimator (Papandreou and Yuille, 2010).

typically approximate the true posterior distribution with a parameterized Gaussian which allows closed-form computations. Inference amounts to adjusting the variational parameters to make the fit as tight as possible (Wainwright and Jordan, 2008). Mostly related to our work are (Attias, 1999; Lewicki and Sejnowski, 2000; Girolami, 2001; Chantas et al., 2010; Seeger and Nickisch, 2011a). There exist multiple alternative criteria to quantify the fit quality, giving rise to approximations such as variational bounding (Jordan et al., 1999), mean field or ensemble learning, and, expectation propagation (EP) (Minka, 2001), as well as different iterative algorithms for optimizing each specific criterion. See (Bishop, 2006; Palmer et al., 2005) for further discussions about the relations among these variational approaches.

All variational algorithms we study in this chapter are of a double-loop nature, requiring Gaussian variance estimation in the outer loop and sparse point estimation in the inner loop (Seeger and Nickisch, 2011a; van Gerven et al., 2010; Seeger and Nickisch, 2011b). The ubiquity of the Gaussian variance computation routine is not coincidental. Variational approximations try to capture uncertainty in the intractable posterior distribution along the directions of sparsity. These are naturally encoded in the covariance matrix of the proxy Gaussian variational approximation. Marginal Gaussian variance computation is also required in automatic relevance determination algorithms for sparse Bayesian learning (MacKay, 1992) and relevance vector machine training (Tipping, 2001); the methods we review here could also be applied in that context.

It turns out that variance computation in large-scale Gaussian models is computationally challenging and a host of sophisticated techniques have been developed for this purpose, which often only apply to restricted classes of models (Schneider and Willsky, 2001; Sudderth et al., 2004; Malioutov et al., 2008).

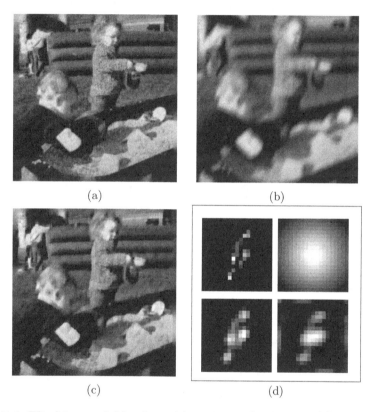

(a)   (b)

(c)   (d)

Figure 2.8: Blind image deblurring with variational inference. (a) Ground truth. (b) Blurred input image. (c) Estimated clean image. (d) Ground truth (top-left) and iteratively estimated blur kernel (clock-wise, starting from a diffuse Gaussian profile at top-right).

Perturb-and-MAP allows us to efficiently sample from the GMRF model and thus makes it practical to employ the generic sample-based estimator for computing Gaussian variances. More specifically, we repeatedly draw K independent GMRF samples $\{\tilde{\boldsymbol{y}}_k\}_{k=1}^K$ from which we can estimate the covariance matrix

$$\hat{\boldsymbol{\Sigma}} = \frac{1}{K} \sum_{k=1}^{K} (\tilde{\boldsymbol{y}}_k - \boldsymbol{\mu})(\tilde{\boldsymbol{y}}_k - \boldsymbol{\mu})^T \qquad (2.4)$$

This Monte-Carlo estimator, whose accuracy is independent of the problem size, is particularly attractive if only relatively rough variance estimates suffice, as is often the case in practice. We show in Figure 2.8 an example of applying this variational Bayesian estimation methodology in the problem of blind image deblurring (Papandreou and Yuille, 2011b).

2.3 Perturb-and-MAP for MRFs with Discrete Labels

2.3.1 Introduction

We now turn our attention to Markov random fields on discrete labels, which go back to the classic Ising and Potts models in statistical physics. Discrete-valued MRFs offer a natural and sound probabilistic modeling framework for a host of image analysis and computer vision problems involving discrete labels, such as image segmentation and labeling, texture synthesis, and deep learning (Besag, 1974; Geman and Geman, 1984; Zhu et al., 1998; Hinton, 2002; Koller and Friedman, 2009). Exact probabilistic inference and maximum likelihood model parameter fitting is intractable in general MRFs defined on 2-D domains and one has to employ random sampling schemes to perform these tasks (Geman and Geman, 1984; Hinton, 2002).

Recent powerful discrete energy minimization algorithms such as graph cuts, linear programming relaxations, or loopy belief propagation (Boykov et al., 2001; Kolmogorov and Zabih, 2004; Kolmogorov and Rother, 2007; Koller and Friedman, 2009) can efficiently find or well approximate the most probable (MAP) configuration for certain important classes of MRFs. They have had a particularly big impact on computer vision; for a recent overview, see the volume edited by Blake et al. (2011).

Our work on the Perturb-and-MAP discrete random field model has been motivated by the exact Gaussian MRF sampling algorithm described in Section 2.2. While the underlying mathematics and methods are completely different in the discrete setup, we have shown in (Papandreou and Yuille, 2011a) that the intuition of local perturbations followed by global optimization can also lead to powerful sampling algorithms for discrete label MRFs. Subsequent work by other groups, summarized in 2.5, has extended our results and explored related directions.

A surprising finding of our study has been the identification of a perturbation process from extreme value statistics which turns the Perturb-and-MAP model identical to its Gibbs counterpart even in the discrete setting. Although this perturbation is too expensive to be applicable in large-scale models, it nevertheless suggests low-order perturbations that result in perturbed energies that are effectively as easy to minimize as the original unperturbed one, while producing high-quality random samples.

Perturb-and-MAP endows discrete energy minimization algorithms such as graph cuts with probabilistic capabilities that allow them to support qualitatively new computer vision applications. We illustrate some of them in image segmentation and scene labeling experiments experiments: First, drawing several posterior samples from the model allows us to compute posterior marginal probabilities and quantify our confidence in the MAP solution. Second, efficient random sampling allows learning of MRF or CRF parameters using the moment matching rule, in which the model parameters are updated until the generated samples reproduce the (weighted) sufficient statistics of the observed data.

2.3.2 Model Definition and Weight Space Geometry

We assume a deterministic energy function which takes the inner product form of Equation (2.1), i.e., $E(\boldsymbol{y}; \boldsymbol{\theta}) = \langle \boldsymbol{\theta}, \boldsymbol{\phi}(\boldsymbol{y}) \rangle$, with y_i taking values in a discrete label set $\mathcal{L}$. A Perturb-and-MAP random sample is obtained by $\tilde{\boldsymbol{y}} = \operatorname{argmin}_{\boldsymbol{y}} E(\boldsymbol{y}; \boldsymbol{\theta} + \boldsymbol{\epsilon})$, where $\boldsymbol{\epsilon}$ is a real-valued random additive parameter perturbation vector. By construction, we can efficiently draw exact one-shot samples from the Perturb-and-MAP model by solving an energy minimization problem.

Thanks to the inner product form of the energy function, the Perturb-and-MAP model has a simple geometric interpretation in the parameter space. In particular, a state $\boldsymbol{y} \in \mathcal{L}^N$ will be minimizing the deterministic energy if, and only if, $E(\boldsymbol{y}; \boldsymbol{\theta}) \leq E(\boldsymbol{q}; \boldsymbol{\theta}), \forall \boldsymbol{q} \in \mathcal{L}^N$. This set of $|\mathcal{L}|^N$ linear inequalities defines a polyhedron $\mathcal{P}_{\boldsymbol{y}}$ in the weight space

$$\mathcal{P}_{\boldsymbol{y}} = \left\{ \boldsymbol{\theta} \in \mathbb{R}^M : \langle \boldsymbol{\theta}, \boldsymbol{\phi}(\boldsymbol{y}) - \boldsymbol{\phi}(\boldsymbol{q}) \rangle \leq 0, \forall \boldsymbol{q} \in \mathcal{L}^N \right\}. \tag{2.5}$$

Actually, $\mathcal{P}_{\boldsymbol{y}}$ is a polyhedral cone (Boyd and Vandenberghe, 2004), since $\boldsymbol{\theta} \in \mathcal{P}_{\boldsymbol{y}}$ implies $\alpha\boldsymbol{\theta} \in \mathcal{P}_{\boldsymbol{y}}$, for all $\alpha \geq 0$. These polyhedral cones are dually related to the marginal polytope $\mathcal{M} = \operatorname{conv}(\{\boldsymbol{\phi}(\boldsymbol{y})\}, \boldsymbol{y} \in \mathcal{L}^N)$, as illustrated in Figure 2.9; see (Wainwright and Jordan, 2008) for background on the marginal polytope. The polyhedra $\mathcal{P}_{\boldsymbol{y}}$ partition the weight space $\mathbb{R}^M$ into regions of influence of each discrete state $\boldsymbol{y} \in \mathcal{L}^N$. Under the Perturb-and-MAP model, $\boldsymbol{y}$ will be assigned to a particular state $\boldsymbol{y}$ if, and only

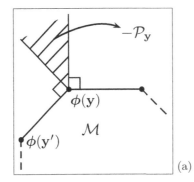 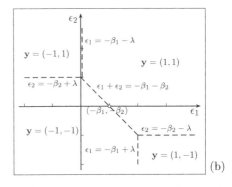

Figure 2.9: Perturb-and-MAP geometry. (a) The polyhedral cones $\mathcal{P}_{\boldsymbol{y}}$ are dual to the corner cones of the marginal polytope $\mathcal{M}$. (b) The Ising P-M model with $N = 2$ nodes and perturbations only in the unary terms, $\tilde{\beta}_i = \beta_i + \epsilon_i$, for parameter values $\beta_1 = -1$, $\beta_2 = 0$, and $\lambda = 1$. The ϵ-space is split into four polyhedra, with $\boldsymbol{y}(\epsilon) = \boldsymbol{y}$ iff $\epsilon \in \mathcal{P}_{\boldsymbol{y}} - \boldsymbol{\theta}$.

if, $\boldsymbol{\theta} + \epsilon \in \mathcal{P}_{\boldsymbol{y}}$ or, equivalently, $\epsilon \in \mathcal{P}_{\boldsymbol{y}} - \boldsymbol{\theta} \triangleq \{\epsilon \in \mathbb{R}^M : \boldsymbol{\theta} + \epsilon \in \mathcal{P}_{\boldsymbol{y}}\}$. In other words, if a specific instantiation of the perturbation ϵ falls in the shifted polyhedron $\mathcal{P}_{\boldsymbol{y}} - \boldsymbol{\theta}$, then the Perturb-and-MAP model generates $\boldsymbol{y}$ as sample.

We assume that perturbations are drawn from a density $f_{\epsilon}(\epsilon)$ which does not depend on the parameters $\boldsymbol{\theta}$. The probability mass of a state $\boldsymbol{y}$ under the Perturb-and-MAP model is then the weighted volume of the corresponding shifted polyhedron under the perturbation measure

$$f_{PM}(\boldsymbol{y}; \boldsymbol{\theta}) = \int_{\mathcal{P}_{\boldsymbol{y}} - \boldsymbol{\theta}} f_{\epsilon}(\epsilon) d\epsilon \,, \tag{2.6}$$

which is the counterpart of the Gibbs density in Equation (2.2). It is intractable (NP-hard) to compute the volume of general polyhedra in a high-dimensional space; see, e.g., (Ben-Tal et al., 2009, p. 29). However, for the class of perturbed energy functions which can be globally minimized efficiently, we can readily draw exact samples from the Perturb-and-MAP model, without ever explicitly evaluating the integrals in Equation (2.6).

2.3.3   Example: The Perturb-and-MAP Ising Model

Let us illustrate these ideas by considering the Perturb-and-MAP version of the classic Ising model. The Ising energy over the discrete "spins" $y_i \in \{-1, 1\}$ is defined as

$$E(\boldsymbol{y}; \boldsymbol{\theta}) = \frac{-1}{2} \sum_{i=1}^{N} \left(\beta_i y_i + \sum_{i'=i+1}^{N} \lambda_{ii'} y_i y_{i'} \right), \tag{2.7}$$

where β_i is the external field strength ($\beta_i > 0$ favors $y_i = 1$) and $\lambda_{ii'}$ is the coupling strength, with attractive coupling $\lambda_{ii'} > 0$ favoring the same spin for y_i and $y_{i'}$. This energy function can be written in the standard inner product form of Equation (2.1) with $\boldsymbol{\theta} = (\{\beta_i\}, \{\lambda_{ii'}\})^T$ and $\boldsymbol{\phi}(\boldsymbol{y}) = \frac{-1}{2}(\{y_i\}, \{y_i y_{i'}\})^T$. The MRF defined by Equation (2.2) is the Ising Gibbs random field.

Defining a Perturb-and-MAP Ising random field requires specifying the parameter perturbation density. In this example, we leave the binary term parameters $\lambda_{ii'}$ intact and only perturb the unary term parameters β_i. In particular, for each unary factor, we set $\tilde{\beta}_i = \beta_i + \epsilon_i$, with ϵ_i i.i.d. samples from the logistic distribution with density $l(z) = \frac{1}{4}\operatorname{sech}^2(\frac{z}{2})$. This corresponds to the order-1 Gumbel perturbation we discuss in Section 2.3.5 and ensures that if a particular node y_i is completely isolated, it will then follow the same Bernoulli distribution $\Pr\{y_i = 1\} = 1/(1 + e^{-\beta_i})$ as in the Gibbs case. The ϵ-space geometry in the case of two labels ($N = 2$) under the Ising energy $E(\boldsymbol{y}; \boldsymbol{\theta}) = -0.5(\beta_1 y_1 + \beta_2 y_2 + \lambda y_1 y_2)$ for a specific value of the parameters $\boldsymbol{\theta}$ and perturbations only to unary terms is depicted in Figure 2.9.

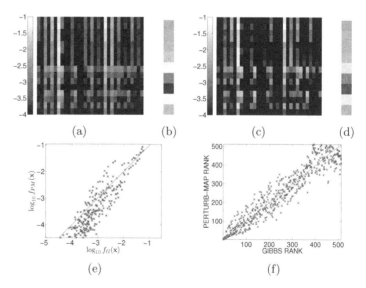

(a)   (b)   (c)   (d)

(e)   (f)

Figure 2.10: We compare the Gibbs (exact computation) and the Perturb-and-MAP (10^6 Monte-Carlo runs) models induced from an Ising energy on 3×3 grid, with β_i and $\lambda_{ii'}$ i.i.d. from $\mathcal{N}(0, 1)$. (a) Gibbs log-probabilities $\log_{10} f_G(\boldsymbol{y})$ for each of the 2^9 states, arranged as a $2^5 \times 2^4$ matrix. (b) Gibbs marginal probabilities $f_G(y_i = 1)$ for each of the 9 nodes. (c) Perturb-and-MAP log-probabilities $\log_{10} f_{PM}(\boldsymbol{y})$. (d) Perturb-and-MAP marginal probabilities $f_{PM}(y_i = 1)$. (e) Scatter-plot of state log probabilities under the two models. (f) Scatter-plot of states ranked by their probabilities under the two models.

We compare in Figure 2.10 the Gibbs and Perturb-and-MAP models for a small-scale Ising energy involving 9 variables on a 3×3 grid with 4-nearest neighbors connectivity and randomly generated parameters. The probability landscape (i.e., the probabilities of each of the 2^9 states) looks quite similar under the two models, see Figure 2.10 (a) and (c). The same holds for the corresponding marginal probabilities, shown in Figure 2.10 (b) and (d). To further compare the probability landscape under the two models, we show a scatter plot of their log probabilities in Figure 2.10(e), as well as a scatter plot of the states ranked by their probability in Figure 2.10(f). Perturb-and-MAP in this example is particularly close to Gibbs for the leading (most probable) states but tends to under-estimate the least probable states.

2.3.4 Parameter Estimation by Moment Matching

We would like to estimate the parameters $\boldsymbol{\theta}$ of the Perturb-and-MAP model from a labeled training set $\{\boldsymbol{y}_k\}_{k=1}^K$ by maximizing the log-likelihood

$$L_{PM}(\boldsymbol{\theta}) = (1/K) \sum_{k=1}^K \log f_{PM}(\boldsymbol{y}_k; \boldsymbol{\theta}) . \tag{2.8}$$

We can design the perturbations so as the Perturb-and-MAP log-likelihood L_{PM} is a concave function of $\boldsymbol{\theta}$. This ensures that the likelihood landscape is well-behaved and allows the use of local search techniques for parameter estimation, exactly as in the Gibbs case. Specifically, the following result is shown in (Papandreou and Yuille, 2011a):

Proposition 2.2. *If the perturbations $\boldsymbol{\epsilon}$ are drawn from a log-concave density $f_{\boldsymbol{\epsilon}}(\boldsymbol{\epsilon})$, the log-likelihood $L_{PM}(\boldsymbol{\theta})$ is a concave function of the energy parameters $\boldsymbol{\theta}$.*

The family of log-concave distributions (Boyd and Vandenberghe, 2004), i.e., $\log f_{\boldsymbol{\epsilon}}(\boldsymbol{\epsilon})$ is a concave function of $\boldsymbol{\epsilon}$, includes the Gaussian, the logistic, the Gumbel, and other commonly used distributions.

The gradient of $L_{PM}(\boldsymbol{\theta})$ is in general hard to compute. Motivated by the parameter update formula in the Gibbs case from Section 2.1.2, we opt for the moment matching learning rule, $\theta_j(t+1) = \theta_j(t) + r(t)\Delta\theta_j$, where

$$\Delta\theta_j = \mathbb{E}_{\boldsymbol{\theta}}^{PM}\{\phi_j(\boldsymbol{y})\} - \mathbb{E}_D\{\phi_j(\boldsymbol{y})\} . \tag{2.9}$$

Here $\mathbb{E}_{\boldsymbol{\theta}}^{PM}\{\phi_j(\boldsymbol{y})\} \triangleq \sum_{\boldsymbol{y}} f_{PM}(\boldsymbol{y}; \boldsymbol{\theta})\phi_j(\boldsymbol{y})$ is the expected sufficient statistic under the Perturb-and-MAP model for the current parameter values $\boldsymbol{\theta}$, which we can efficiently estimate by drawing exact samples from it. We typically adjust the learning rate by a Robbins-Monro type schedule, e.g.,

$r(t) = r_1/(r_2 + t)$. Figure 2.11 illustrates parameter learning by moment matching in a spatially homogeneous Ising energy model.

While the above moment matching rule was originally motivated by analogy to the Gibbs case (Papandreou and Yuille, 2011a), its fixed points do not need to be exact minima of the Perturb-and-MAP log-likelihood (2.8). Subsequent work has shown that moment matching performs gradient ascent for an objective function that lower bounds the Gibbs likelihood function (Hazan and Jaakkola, 2012). Moreover, this lower bound turns out to be concave even for perturbation densities $f_\epsilon(\epsilon)$ which are not log-concave.

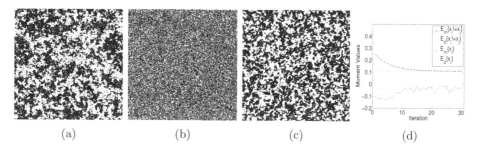

(a)   (b)   (c)   (d)

Figure 2.11: Perturb-and-MAP Ising random field parameter learning. The two model parameters, the global coupling strength λ and field strength β are fitted by moment matching. (a) Gibbs Ising model sample, used as training image. (b) Perturb-and-MAP Ising sample at initial parameter values. (c) Perturb-and-MAP Ising sample at final parameter values. (d) Model moments as they converge to training data moments.

2.3.5   Perturb-and-MAP Perturbation Design

Although any perturbation density induces a legitimate Perturb-and-MAP model, it is desirable to carefully design it so as the Perturb-and-MAP model approximates as closely as possible the corresponding Gibbs MRF. The Gibbs MRF has important structural properties that are not automatically satisfied by the Perturb-and-MAP model under arbitrary perturbations: (a) Unlike the Gibbs MRF, the Perturb-and-MAP model is not guaranteed to respect the state ranking induced by the energy, i.e., $E(\boldsymbol{y}) \leq E(\boldsymbol{y}')$ does not necessarily imply $f_{PM}(\boldsymbol{y}) \geq f_{PM}(\boldsymbol{y}')$, see Figure 2.10(f). (b) The Markov dependence structure of the Gibbs MRF follows directly from the support of the potentials $\phi_j(\boldsymbol{y})$, while the Perturb-and-MAP might give rise to longer-range probabilistic dependencies. (c) The maximum entropy distribution under moment constraints $\mathbb{E}\{\phi_j(\boldsymbol{y})\} = \bar{\phi}_j$ has the Gibbs form; the Perturb-and-MAP model trained by moment matching can reproduce these moments but will in general have smaller entropy than its Gibbs counterpart.

The *Gumbel* distribution arising in extreme value theory (Steutel and Van Harn, 2004) turns out to play an important role in our effort to design a perturbation mechanism that yields a Perturb-and-MAP model closely resembling the Gibbs MRF. We can use the Arg-Min aspect of the Gumbel Lemma 1.1 (p. 12) to construct a Perturb-and-MAP model that exactly replicates the Gibbs distribution, as follows. The Gibbs random field on N sites y_i, $i = 1, \ldots, N$, each allowed to take a value from the discrete label set $\mathcal{L}$, can be considered as a discrete distribution with $|\mathcal{L}|^N$ states. This can be made explicit if we enumerate $\{\boldsymbol{y}_j, j = 1, \ldots, \bar{M} = |\mathcal{L}|^N\}$ all the states and consider the maximal equivalent re-parameterization of Equation (2.1)

$$\bar{E}(\boldsymbol{y}; \bar{\boldsymbol{\theta}}) \triangleq \langle \bar{\boldsymbol{\theta}}, \bar{\boldsymbol{\phi}}(\boldsymbol{y}) \rangle = \langle \boldsymbol{\theta}, \boldsymbol{\phi}(\boldsymbol{y}) \rangle, \qquad (2.10)$$

where $\bar{\theta}_j = E(\boldsymbol{y}_j; \boldsymbol{\theta}) = \langle \boldsymbol{\theta}, \boldsymbol{\phi}(\boldsymbol{y}_j) \rangle$, $j = 1, \ldots, \bar{M}$, is the *fully-expanded* potential table and $\bar{\phi}_j(\boldsymbol{y})$ is the indicator function of the state $\boldsymbol{y}_j$ (i.e., equals 1, if $\boldsymbol{y} = \boldsymbol{y}_j$ and 0 otherwise). Using the Gumbel Lemma 1.1 we can show:

Proposition 2.3. *If we perturb each entry of the fully expanded $\mathcal{L}^N$ potential table with i.i.d. Gumbel noise samples $\epsilon_j, j = 1, \ldots, \bar{M}$, then the Perturb-and-MAP and Gibbs models coincide, i.e., $f_{PM}(\boldsymbol{y}; \boldsymbol{\theta}) = f_G(\boldsymbol{y}; \boldsymbol{\theta})$.*

This order-N perturbation is not practically applicable when N is large since it independently perturbs all $\bar{M} = |\mathcal{L}|^N$ entries of the fully expanded potential table and effectively destroys the local Markov structure of the energy function, rendering it too hard to minimize. Nevertheless, it shows that it is possible to design a Perturb-and-MAP model that exactly replicates the Gibbs MRF.

In practice, we employ low-order Gumbel perturbations. In our simplest order-1 design, we only add Gumbel noise to the unary potential tables. More specifically, for an energy function $E(\boldsymbol{y}) = \sum_{i=1}^{N} V_i(y_i) + \sum_j V_j(\boldsymbol{y}_j)$ which includes potentials $V_i(y_i)$ of order-1 and potentials $V_j(\boldsymbol{y}_j)$ of order-2 or higher, we add i.i.d. Gumbel noise to each of the $|\mathcal{L}|$ entries of each order-1 potential, while leaving the higher order potentials intact. This yields perturbed energies effectively as easy to minimize as the original unperturbed one, while producing random samples closely resembling Gibbs MRF samples. We can improve the Perturb-and-MAP sample quality by Gumbel perturbations of order-2 or higher, as described in (Papandreou and Yuille, 2011a). However, high order perturbations typically make the perturbed energy minimization problem harder to solve.

2.4 On the Representation Power of the Perturb-and-MAP Model

The moment matching parameter learning criterion in Section 2.3.4 leads us to the following fundamental question about the representation power of the Perturb-and-MAP model on MRFs with Discrete Labels: Is the model expressive enough to reproduce the statistics of arbitrary observed data?

More formally, let $\boldsymbol{\mu} \triangleq \mathbb{E}_D\{\boldsymbol{\phi}(\boldsymbol{y})\} = (1/K)\sum_{k=1}^{K}\boldsymbol{\phi}(\boldsymbol{y}_k)$ be the vector of sufficient statistics observed in a dataset $\{\boldsymbol{y}_k\}_{k=1}^{K}$. The set of all such possible sufficient statistics vectors for every realizable dataset forms the marginal polytope $\mathcal{M}$, which can also be expressed as the convex hull of all possible feature vectors, i.e., $\mathcal{M} = \text{conv}(\{\boldsymbol{\phi}(\boldsymbol{y})\}, \boldsymbol{y} \in \mathcal{L}^N) \subset \mathbb{R}^M$. We can then pose the representation power question mathematically as follows: Given a sufficient statistics vector $\boldsymbol{\mu} \in \mathcal{M}$, does a parameter vector $\boldsymbol{\theta} \in \mathbb{R}^M$ exist such that $\mathbb{E}_{\boldsymbol{\theta}}^{PM}\{\boldsymbol{\phi}(\boldsymbol{y})\} = \boldsymbol{\mu}$?

The answer to the representation power problem for the Gibbs distribution is positive. Specifically, for every $\boldsymbol{\mu} \in \text{ri}(\mathcal{M})$, there exists $\boldsymbol{\theta} \in \mathbb{R}^M$ such that $\mathbb{E}_{\boldsymbol{\theta}}^{G}\{\boldsymbol{\phi}(\boldsymbol{y})\} = \boldsymbol{\mu}$. Here $\text{ri}(\mathcal{M})$ denotes the relative interior of $\mathcal{M}$, which essentially includes every interior point in $\mathcal{M}$. Moreover, the corresponding Gibbs distribution has the largest entropy among all distributions satisfying the same moment matching constraints. We refer to Wainwright and Jordan (2008) for a detailed treatment of the classic Gibbs exponential family representation problem.

It turns out that the answer to the representation power problem for the Perturb-and-MAP model is also positive. We can prove this building on a key Theorem of Hazan and Jaakkola (2012) which associates Perturb-and-MAP moment matching with a maximization problem. We restate in our notation their Theorem 3:

Proposition 2.4. *Let* $\boldsymbol{\mu} \in \mathbb{R}^M$. *We define the maximization problem* $\max_{\boldsymbol{\theta} \in \mathbb{R}^M} J(\boldsymbol{\theta})$, *where*

$$J(\boldsymbol{\theta}) = \int f_{\boldsymbol{\epsilon}}(\boldsymbol{\epsilon}) \min_{\boldsymbol{y}} \langle \boldsymbol{\theta} + \boldsymbol{\epsilon}, \, \boldsymbol{\phi}(\boldsymbol{y}) \rangle d\boldsymbol{\epsilon} - \langle \boldsymbol{\theta}, \, \boldsymbol{\mu} \rangle. \tag{2.11}$$

If the perturbation density $f_{\boldsymbol{\epsilon}}(\boldsymbol{\epsilon})$ *is differentiable in* $\mathbb{R}^M$, *then (1)* $J(\boldsymbol{\theta})$ *is concave and differentiable in* $\mathbb{R}^M$ *and (2)* $\nabla J(\boldsymbol{\theta}) = \mathbb{E}_{\boldsymbol{\theta}}^{PM}\{\boldsymbol{\phi}(\boldsymbol{y})\} - \boldsymbol{\mu}$.

We are now ready to state and prove our Proposition on the representation power of Perturb-and-MAP.

Proposition 2.5. *If the perturbation density* $f_{\boldsymbol{\epsilon}}(\boldsymbol{\epsilon})$ *is differentiable in* $\mathbb{R}^M$, *then for every* $\boldsymbol{\mu} \in \text{ri}(\mathcal{M})$ *there exists a* $\boldsymbol{\theta} \in \mathbb{R}^M$ *such that* $\mathbb{E}_{\boldsymbol{\theta}}^{PM}\{\boldsymbol{\phi}(\boldsymbol{y})\} = \boldsymbol{\mu}$.

Proof. Based on Proposition 2.4, it suffices to show that there exists a $\boldsymbol{\theta} \in \mathbb{R}^M$ such that $\nabla J(\boldsymbol{\theta}) = \mathbf{0}$. Since $J(\boldsymbol{\theta})$ is concave and differentiable in $\mathbb{R}^M$, it suffices to show that it is coercive, i.e., $J(\boldsymbol{\theta}) \to -\infty$, when $\|\boldsymbol{\theta}\| \to +\infty$.

To show that, we start by recentering the feature vector to $\bar{\phi}(\boldsymbol{y}) \triangleq \phi(\boldsymbol{y}) - \boldsymbol{\mu}$, which allows us to express $J(\boldsymbol{\theta})$ without the linear ramp term dependence on $\boldsymbol{\theta}$:

$$J(\boldsymbol{\theta}) = \int f_{\boldsymbol{\epsilon}}(\boldsymbol{\epsilon}) \min_{\boldsymbol{y}} \langle \boldsymbol{\theta} + \boldsymbol{\epsilon}, \, \phi(\boldsymbol{y}) - \boldsymbol{\mu} \rangle d\boldsymbol{\epsilon} + \langle \bar{\boldsymbol{\epsilon}}, \, \boldsymbol{\mu} \rangle \,, \tag{2.12}$$

where $\bar{\boldsymbol{\epsilon}} = \int f_{\boldsymbol{\epsilon}}(\boldsymbol{\epsilon}) \boldsymbol{\epsilon} d\boldsymbol{\epsilon}$ is the perturbation mean. Next, let's write $\boldsymbol{\theta} = \|\boldsymbol{\theta}\| \hat{\boldsymbol{\theta}}$ and define $\boldsymbol{y}_{\boldsymbol{\theta}} = \operatorname{argmin}_{\boldsymbol{y}} \langle \boldsymbol{\theta}, \, \phi(\boldsymbol{y}) - \boldsymbol{\mu} \rangle$. Note that $\boldsymbol{y}_{\hat{\boldsymbol{\theta}}} = \boldsymbol{y}_{\boldsymbol{\theta}}$. Critically, $c_{\hat{\boldsymbol{\theta}}} \triangleq \langle \hat{\boldsymbol{\theta}}, \, \phi(\boldsymbol{y}_{\hat{\boldsymbol{\theta}}}) - \boldsymbol{\mu} \rangle < 0$ because $\boldsymbol{\mu} \in \operatorname{ri}(\mathcal{M})$. Then, since $f_{\boldsymbol{\epsilon}}(\boldsymbol{\epsilon}) \geq 0$ and $\int f_{\boldsymbol{\epsilon}}(\boldsymbol{\epsilon}) d\boldsymbol{\epsilon} = 1$, we can upper bound $J(\boldsymbol{\theta})$ as follows:

$$J(\boldsymbol{\theta}) \leq \int f_{\boldsymbol{\epsilon}}(\boldsymbol{\epsilon}) \langle \boldsymbol{\theta} + \boldsymbol{\epsilon}, \, \phi(\boldsymbol{y}_{\boldsymbol{\theta}}) - \boldsymbol{\mu} \rangle d\boldsymbol{\epsilon} + \langle \bar{\boldsymbol{\epsilon}}, \, \boldsymbol{\mu} \rangle \tag{2.13}$$

$$= \int f_{\boldsymbol{\epsilon}}(\boldsymbol{\epsilon}) \langle \boldsymbol{\theta}, \, \phi(\boldsymbol{y}_{\boldsymbol{\theta}}) - \boldsymbol{\mu} \rangle d\boldsymbol{\epsilon} + \langle \bar{\boldsymbol{\epsilon}}, \, \phi(\boldsymbol{y}_{\boldsymbol{\theta}}) - \boldsymbol{\mu} \rangle + \langle \bar{\boldsymbol{\epsilon}}, \, \boldsymbol{\mu} \rangle \tag{2.14}$$

$$= \langle \boldsymbol{\theta}, \, \phi(\boldsymbol{y}_{\boldsymbol{\theta}}) - \boldsymbol{\mu} \rangle + \langle \bar{\boldsymbol{\epsilon}}, \, \phi(\boldsymbol{y}_{\boldsymbol{\theta}}) \rangle \tag{2.15}$$

$$= \|\boldsymbol{\theta}\| \langle \hat{\boldsymbol{\theta}}, \, \phi(\boldsymbol{y}_{\hat{\boldsymbol{\theta}}}) - \boldsymbol{\mu} \rangle + \langle \bar{\boldsymbol{\epsilon}}, \, \phi(\boldsymbol{y}_{\hat{\boldsymbol{\theta}}}) \rangle \tag{2.16}$$

$$= c_{\hat{\boldsymbol{\theta}}} \|\boldsymbol{\theta}\| + \langle \bar{\boldsymbol{\epsilon}}, \, \phi(\boldsymbol{y}_{\hat{\boldsymbol{\theta}}}) \rangle \,. \tag{2.17}$$

Since $c_{\hat{\boldsymbol{\theta}}} < 0$, $J(\boldsymbol{\theta}) \leq c_{\hat{\boldsymbol{\theta}}} \|\boldsymbol{\theta}\| + \langle \bar{\boldsymbol{\epsilon}}, \, \phi(\boldsymbol{y}_{\hat{\boldsymbol{\theta}}}) \rangle \to -\infty$ as $\|\boldsymbol{\theta}\| \to +\infty$. $\square$

Our Proposition has been stated under the assumption that the perturbation density $f_{\boldsymbol{\epsilon}}(\boldsymbol{\epsilon})$ is differentiable in $\mathbb{R}^M$ but it also applies more generally whenever the function $J(\boldsymbol{\theta})$ is differentiable in $\mathbb{R}^M$.

2.4.1 Applications and Experiments

We present experiments with the Perturb-and-MAP model applied to image segmentation and scene labeling.

Our *interactive image segmentation* experiments have been performed on the Grabcut dataset which includes human annotated ground truth segmentations (Rother et al., 2004). The task is to segment a foreground object, given a relatively tight tri-map imitating user input obtained by a lasso or pen tool.

In our implementation we closely follow the CRF formulation of (Rother et al., 2011), using the same parameters for defining the image-based CRF terms and considering pixel interactions in a 8-neighborhood. We used our Perturb-and-MAP sampling algorithm with order-2 Gumbel perturbation and QPBO optimization (Kolmogorov and Rother, 2007) to learn the weights of the potentials – 5 weights in total, one for the unary and one for each of the 4 pairwise connections of the center pixel with its S, E, NE, SE neighbors. Using these parameters, we obtained a classification error rate of 5.6% with the global MAP decision rule. This is similar to the best results attainable with the particular CRF model and hand-tuned weights.

In Figure 2.12 we illustrate the ability of the Perturb-and-MAP model to produce soft segmentation maps. The soft segmentation map (average over 20 posterior samples) gives a qualitatively accurate estimate of the segmentation uncertainty, which could potentially be useful in guiding user interaction in an interactive segmentation application.

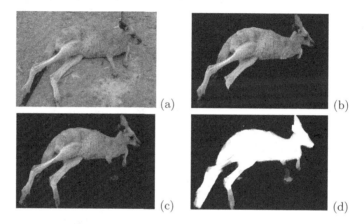

Figure 2.12: Interactive image segmentation results on the Grabcut dataset. Parameters learned by Perturb-and-MAP moment matching. (a) Original image. (b) Least energy MAP solution. (c) Soft Perturb-and-MAP segmentation. (d) The corresponding segmentation mask.

We next consider an application of Perturb-and-MAP random fields in *scene layout labeling* (Hoiem et al., 2007). We use the tiered layout model of (Felzenszwalb and Veksler, 2010), which allows exact global inference by efficient dynamic programming (Felzenszwalb and Veksler, 2010). The model has a relatively large number of parameters, making it difficult to hand tune. Training them with the proposed techniques illustrates our ability to effectively learn model parameters from labeled data.

We closely follow the evaluation approach of (Felzenszwalb and Veksler, 2010) in setting up the experiment: We use the dataset of 300 outdoor images (and the standard cross-validation splits into training/test sets) with ground truth from (Hoiem et al., 2007). Similarly to (Felzenszwalb and Veksler, 2010), we use five labels: T (sky), B (ground), and three labels for the middle region, L (facing left), R (facing right), C (front facing), while we exclude the classes "porous" and "solid". The unary scores are produced using classifiers that we trained using the dataset and software provided by Hoiem et al. (2007) following the standard five-fold cross-validation protocol.

We first fit the tiered scene model parameters (pairwise compatibility tables between the different classes) on the training data using Perturb-and-MAP moment matching (order-1 Gumbel perturbation). Weights are initialized as Potts CRF potentials and refined by moment matching rule; we separated the training set in batches of 10 images each and stopped after 50 epochs over the training set. We have measured the performance of the trained model in terms of average accuracy on the test set. We have tried two decision criteria, MAP (least energy configuration) and marginal MODE (i.e., assign each pixel to the label that appears most frequently in 20 random Perturb-And-Map conditional samples from the model), obtaining accuracy 82.7% and 82.6%, respectively. Our results are better than the unary-only baseline mean accuracy of 82.1% (Hoiem et al., 2007), and the MAP and MODE results of 82.1% and 81.8%, respectively, that we obtained with the hand-set weights of (Felzenszwalb and Veksler, 2010).

In Figure 2.13 we show some indicative examples of different scene layout labelings obtained by the unary-only, the tiered MAP, and the Perturb-and-MAP model. The uncertainty of the solution is indicated by entropy maps. The marginal mode and entropies shown are Monte Carlo estimates using 20 Perturb-and-MAP samples.

Figure 2.13: Tiered scene labeling results with pairwise potentials learned by our Perturb-and-MAP moment matching algorithm. Left to right: image; unary-only MAP; tiered MAP; one tiered Perturb-and-MAP sample; tiered Perturb-and-MAP marginal mode; tiered Perturb-and-MAP marginal entropy.

2.5   Related Work and Recent Developments

Studying the output sensitivity to input perturbations is omnipresent under many different guises not only in machine learning but also in optimization, signal processing, control, computer science, and theoretical psychology, among others. However, Perturb-and-MAP is unique in using random perturbations as the defining building block of a structured probabilistic model and setting the ambitious goal of replicating the Gibbs distribution using this approach.

To our knowledge, adding noise to the weighted edges of a graph so as to randomize the minimum energy configuration found by mincuts was first proposed by Blum et al. (2004) in the context of a submodular binary MRF energy arising in semi-supervised learning. Their goal was to break graph symmetries and allow the standard mincut algorithm to produce a different solution at each run. They interpret the relative frequency of each node receiving one or the other label as a confidence score for binary classification. However, beyond randomizing the deterministic mincut algorithm, they do not study the implied probabilistic model as a standalone object nor attempt to design the perturbation mechanism so as to approximate the corresponding Gibbs model. Indeed, the choice of perturbation distribution is not discussed at all in (Blum et al., 2004).

Herding (Welling, 2009) builds a deterministic dynamical system on the model parameters designed so as to reproduce the data sufficient statistics, which is similar in spirit to the moment-matching algorithm we use for learning. However, herding is still not a probabilistic model and cannot summarize the data into a concise set of model parameters.

As pointed out to us by McAllester (2012), Perturb-and-MAP is closely related to PAC-Bayes (McAllester, 1998) and PAC-Bayesian theorems such as those in (Germain et al., 2009) can be adapted to the Perturb-and-MAP setting. Model perturbations through the associated concept of stochastic Gibbs classifier play a key role to PAC-Bayesian theory, but PAC-Bayes typically aims at producing generalization guarantees for the deterministic classifier instead of capturing the uncertainty in the posterior distribution.

Averaging over multiple samples, Perturb-and-MAP allows efficiently estimating (sum-) marginal densities and thus quantifying the per-node solution uncertainty even in graphs with loops. Max-product belief propagation (Wainwright et al., 2005) and dynamic graph-cuts (Kohli and Torr, 2008) can compute max-marginals, which give some indication of the uncertainty in label assignments (Kohli and Torr, 2008) but cannot directly estimate marginal densities.

A number of different groups have followed up on our work (Papandreou and Yuille, 2011a) and further developed it in different directions. In their randomized optimum models, Tarlow et al. (2012) introduce variants of the Perturb-and-MAP model for discrete problems such as bi-partite matching and pursue maximum-likelihood learning of the model parameters using efficient MCMC algorithms.

The work in (Hazan and Jaakkola, 2012) has offered a better understanding of the Perturb-and-MAP moment matching learning rule, showing that it optimizes a well-defined concave lower bound of the Gibbs likelihood function. Moreover, they have shown how Perturb-and-MAP can be used for computing approximations to the partition function. This connection directly relates Perturb-and-MAP to the standard MRF inference problem and forms the basis of our study of the Perturb-and-MAP representation power presented in Section 2.4.

Another related partition function estimation algorithm is proposed in (Ermon et al., 2013). Interestingly, their method amounts to progressively introducing more random constraints, followed by energy minimization, in a randomized Constrain-and-MAP scheme.

While probabilistic random sampling allows one to explore alternative plausible solutions, Batra et al. (2012) propose to explicitly enforce diversity in generating a sequence of deterministic solutions.

The work in (Roig et al., 2013) is an excellent demonstration of how uncertainty quantification can yield practical benefits in a semantic image labeling setting. They employ Perturb-and-MAP to identify on the fly image areas with ambiguous labeling and only compute expensive features when their addition is likely to considerably decrease labeling entropy.

2.6 Discussion

This chapter has presented an overview of the Perturb-and-MAP method, which turns established deterministic energy minimization algorithms into efficient probabilistic inference machines. This is a promising new direction with many important open questions for both theoretical and application-driven research: (1) An in-depth systematic comparison of Perturb-and-MAP and more established approximate inference techniques such as MCMC or Variational Bayes is still lacking. (2) Unlike MCMC which allows trading off approximation quality with computation time by simply running the Markov chain for longer, there is currently no way to iteratively improve the quality of Perturb-and-MAP samples. (3) The modeling capacity of Perturb-and-MAP needs to be explored in several more computer vision and machine learning applications.

Acknowledgements

This work was done while both authors were affiliated with the Department of Statistics at the University of California, Los Angeles. It has been supported by the U.S. Office of Naval Research under MURI grant N000141010933; the NSF under award 0917141; the AFOSR under grant 9550-08-1-0489; and the Korean Ministry of Education, Science, and Technology, under the Korean National Research Foundation WCU program R31-10008. We would like to thank M. Welling, M. Seeger, T. Hazan, D. Tarlow, D. McAllester, A. Montanari, S. Roth, I. Kokkinos, M. Raptis, M. Ranzato, and C. Lampert for their feedback at various stages of this project.

2.7 References

D. Andrews and C. Mallows. Scale mixtures of normal distributions. *J. of Royal Stat. Soc. (Series B)*, 36(1):99–102, 1974.

H. Attias. Independent factor analysis. *Neural Computation*, 11:803–851, 1999.

D. Batra, P. Yadollahpour, A. Guzman-Rivera, and G. Shakhnarovich. Diverse m-best solutions in Markov random fields. In *Proc. European Conf. on Computer Vision*, 2012.

A. Ben-Tal, L. El Ghaoui, and A. Nemirovski. *Robust Optimization*. Princeton Univ. Press, 2009.

J. Besag. Spatial interaction and the statistical analysis of lattice systems. *J. of Royal Stat. Soc. (Series B)*, 36(2):192–236, 1974.

J. Besag. Statistical analysis of non-lattice data. *J. of Royal Stat. Soc. Series D (The Statistician)*, 24(3):179–195, 1975.

C. Bishop. *Pattern Recognition and Machine Learning*. Springer, 2006.

A. Blake, P. Kohli, and C. Rother, editors. *Markov Random Fields for Vision and Image Processing*. MIT Press, 2011.

A. Blum, J. Lafferty, M. Rwebangira, and R. Reddy. Semi-supervised learning using randomized mincuts. In *Proc. Int. Conf. on Machine Learning*, 2004.

S. Boyd and L. Vandenberghe. *Convex Optimization*. Cambridge Univ. Press, 2004.

Y. Boykov, O. Veksler, and R. Zabih. Fast approximate energy minimization via graph cuts. *IEEE Trans. Pattern Anal. Mach. Intell.*, 23(11):1222–1239, 2001.

G. Chantas, N. Galatsanos, R. Molina, and A. Katsaggelos. Variational Bayesian image restoration with a product of spatially weighted total variation image priors. *IEEE Trans. Image Process.*, 19(2):351–362, 2010.

S. Ermon, C. Gomes, A. Sabharwal, and B. Selman. Taming the curse of dimensionality: Discrete integration by hashing and optimization. In *Proc. Int. Conf. on Machine Learning*, 2013.

P. Felzenszwalb and O. Veksler. Tiered scene labeling with dynamic programming. In *Proc. IEEE Int. Conf. on Computer Vision and Pattern Recognition*, 2010.

S. Geman and D. Geman. Stochastic relaxation, Gibbs distributions, and the Bayesian restoration of images. *IEEE Trans. Pattern Anal. Mach. Intell.*, 6(6): 721–741, 1984.

P. Germain, A. Lacasse, F. Laviolette, and M. Marchand. PAC-Bayesian learning of linear classifiers. In *Proc. Int. Conf. on Machine Learning*, 2009.

M. Girolami. A variational method for learning sparse and overcomplete representations. *Neural Computation*, 13:2517–2532, 2001.

G. Golub and C. Van Loan. *Matrix Computations*. John Hopkins Press, 1996.

T. Hazan and T. Jaakkola. On the partition function and random maximum a-posteriori perturbations. In *Proc. Int. Conf. on Machine Learning*, 2012.

G. Hinton. Training products of experts by minimizing contrastive divergence. *Neural Computation*, 14(8):1771–1800, 2002.

G. Hinton and T. Sejnowski. Optimal perceptual inference. In *Proc. IEEE Int. Conf. on Computer Vision and Pattern Recognition*, 1983.

D. Hoiem, A. Efros, and M. Hebert. Recovering surface layout from an image. *Int. J. of Comp. Vis.*, 75(1):151–172, 2007.

M. Jordan, J. Ghahramani, T. Jaakkola, and L. Saul. An introduction to variational methods for graphical models. *Machine Learning*, 37:183–233, 1999.

P. Kohli and P. Torr. Measuring uncertainty in graph cut solutions. *Computer Vision and Image Understanding*, 112(1):30–38, 2008.

D. Koller and N. Friedman. *Probabilistic Graphical Models*. MIT Press, 2009.

V. Kolmogorov and C. Rother. Minimizing non-submodular functions with graph cuts – a review. *IEEE Trans. Pattern Anal. Mach. Intell.*, 29(7):1274–1279, 2007.

V. Kolmogorov and R. Zabih. What energy functions can be minimized via graph cuts? *IEEE Trans. Pattern Anal. Mach. Intell.*, 26(2):147–159, 2004.

Y. LeCun, S. Chopra, R. Hadsell, M. Ranzato, and F.-J. Huang. A tutorial on energy-based learning. In G. Bakir, T. Hofmann, B. Schölkopf, A. Smola, B. Taskar, and S. Vishwanathan, editors, *Predicting Structured Data*. MIT Press, 2007.

M. Lewicki and T. Sejnowski. Learning overcomplete representations. *Neural Computation*, 12:337–365, 2000.

D. MacKay. Bayesian interpolation. *Neural Computation*, 4(3):415–447, 1992.

D. Malioutov, J. Johnson, M. Choi, and A. Willsky. Low-rank variance approximation in GMRF models: Single and multiscale approaches. *IEEE Trans. Signal Process.*, 56(10):4621–4634, 2008.

D. McAllester. Some PAC-Bayesian theorems. In *Proc. Conf. on Learning Theory*, 1998.

D. McAllester. Connections between Perturb-and-MAP and PAC-Bayes. Personal communication, 2012.

T. Minka. Expectation propagation for approximate Bayesian inference. In *Proc. Int. Conf. on Uncertainty in Artificial Intelligence*, 2001.

M. Nikolova. Model distortions in Bayesian MAP reconstruction. *Inv. Pr. and Imag.*, 1(2):399–422, 2007.

J. Palmer, D. Wipf, K. Kreutz-Delgado, and B. Rao. Variational EM algorithms for non-Gaussian latent variable models. In *Proc. Advances in Neural Information Processing Systems*, 2005.

G. Papandreou. *Image Analysis and Computer Vision: Theory and Applications in the Restoration of Ancient Wall Paintings.* PhD thesis, NTUA, School of ECE, 2009.

G. Papandreou and A. Yuille. Gaussian sampling by local perturbations. In *Proc. Advances in Neural Information Processing Systems*, 2010.

G. Papandreou and A. Yuille. Perturb-and-MAP random fields: Using discrete optimization to learn and sample from energy models. In *Proc. IEEE Int. Conf. on Computer Vision*, 2011a.

G. Papandreou and A. Yuille. Efficient variational inference in large-scale Bayesian compressed sensing. In *Proc. IEEE Workshop on Information Theory in Computer Vision and Pattern Recognition (in conjunction with ICCV)*, 2011b.

G. Papandreou, P. Maragos, and A. Kokaram. Image inpainting with a wavelet domain hidden Markov tree model. In *Proc. IEEE Int. Conf. Acous., Speech, and Signal Processing*, 2008.

G. Roig, X. Boix, S. Ramos, R. de Nijs, and L. Van Gool. Active MAP inference in CRFs for efficient semantic segmentation. In *Proc. IEEE Int. Conf. on Computer Vision*, 2013.

S. Roth and M. Black. Fields of experts. *Int. J. of Comp. Vis.*, 82(2):205–229, 2009.

C. Rother, V. Kolmogorov, and A. Blake. Grabcut: Interactive foreground extraction using iterated graph cuts. In *Proc. ACM Int. Conference on Computer Graphics and Interactive Techniques*, pages 309–314, 2004.

C. Rother, V. Kolmogorov, Y. Boykov, and A. Blake. Interactive foreground extraction using graph cut. In *Advances in Markov Random Fields for Vision and Image Processing*. MIT Press, 2011.

H. Rue and L. Held. *Gaussian Markov random fields. Theory and Applications.* Chapman & Hall, 2005.

U. Schmidt, Q. Gao, and S. Roth. A generative perspective on MRFs in low-level vision. In *Proc. IEEE Int. Conf. on Computer Vision and Pattern Recognition*, 2010.

M. Schneider and A. Willsky. Krylov subspace estimation. *SIAM J. Sci. Comp.*, 22(5):1840–1864, 2001.

M. Seeger and H. Nickisch. Large scale Bayesian inference and experimental design for sparse linear models. *SIAM J. Imaging Sci.*, 4(1):166–199, 2011a.

M. Seeger and H. Nickisch. Fast convergent algorithms for expectation propagation approximate Bayesian inference. In *Proc. Int. Conf. on Artificial Intelligence and Statistics*, 2011b.

F. Steutel and K. Van Harn. *Infinite divisibility of probability distributions on the real line.* Dekker, 2004.

E. Sudderth, M. Wainwright, and A. Willsky. Embedded trees: Estimation of Gaussian processes on graphs with cycles. *IEEE Trans. Signal Process.*, 52(11):3136–3150, 2004.

R. Szeliski. Bayesian modeling of uncertainty in low-level vision. *Int. J. of Comp. Vis.*, 5(3):271–301, 1990.

M. Szummer, P. Kohli, and D. Hoiem. Learning CRFs using graph cuts. In *Proc. European Conf. on Computer Vision*, 2008.

D. Tarlow, R. Adams, and R. Zemel. Randomized optimum models for structured prediction. In *Proc. Int. Conf. on Artificial Intelligence and Statistics*, 2012.

B. Taskar, C. Guestrin, and D. Koller. Max-margin Markov networks. In *Proc. Advances in Neural Information Processing Systems*, 2003.

D. Terzopoulos. The computation of visible-surface representations. *IEEE Trans. Pattern Anal. Mach. Intell.*, 10(4):417–438, 1988.

M. Tipping. Sparse Bayesian learning and the relevance vector machine. *Journal of Machine Learning Research*, 1:211–244, 2001.

M. van Gerven, B. Cseke, F. de Lange, and T. Heskes. Efficient Bayesian multivariate fMRI analysis using a sparsifying spatio-temporal prior. *NeuroImage*, 50:150–161, 2010.

M. Wainwright and M. Jordan. Graphical models, exponential families, and variational inference. *Found. and Trends in Machine Learning*, 1(1-2):1–305, 2008.

M. Wainwright, T. Jaakkola, and A. Willsky. MAP estimation via agreement on trees: Message-passing and linear programming. *IEEE Trans. Inf. Theory*, 51(11):3697–3717, 2005.

Y. Weiss and W. Freeman. Correctness of belief propagation in Gaussian graphical models of arbitrary topology. *Neural Computation*, 13(10):2173–2200, 2001.

Y. Weiss and W. Freeman. What makes a good model of natural images? In *Proc. IEEE Int. Conf. on Computer Vision and Pattern Recognition*, 2007.

M. Welling. Herding dynamical weights to learn. In *Proc. Int. Conf. on Machine Learning*, 2009.

S. Zhu, Y. Wu, and D. Mumford. Filters, random fields and maximum entropy (FRAME): Towards a unified theory for texture modeling. *Int. J. of Comp. Vis.*, 27(2):107–126, 1998.

3   Factorizing Shortest Paths with Randomized Optimum Models

Daniel Tarlow   dtarlow@microsoft.com
Alexander Gaunt   t-algaun@microsoft.com
Microsoft Research
Cambridge, UK

Ryan Adams   rpa@seas.harvard.edu
Harvard University and Twitter
Cambridge, MA, USA

Richard S. Zemel   zemel@cs.toronto.edu
University of Toronto
Toronto, ON, Canada

Randomized Optimum Models (RandOMs) are probabilistic models that define distributions over structured outputs by making use of structured optimization procedures within the model definition. This chapter reviews RandOMs and develops a new application of RandOMs to the problem of factorizing shortest paths; that is, given observations of paths that users take to get from one node to another on a graph, learn edge-specific and user-specific trait vectors such that inner products of the two define user-specific edge costs, and the distribution of observed paths can be explained as users taking shortest paths according to noisy samples from their cost function.

3.1   Introduction

A broad challenge in statistics and machine learning is to build probabilistic models of structured data. This includes abstract structures like segmentations, colorings, matchings, and paths on graphs, and natural structures like images, text, source code, and chemical molecules. The main difficulty is that estimating the normalizing constant for commonly-used modeling distributions over these objects is often computationally hard. An interesting computational phenomenon is that in some cases where it is challenging to compute a sum over the entire space, it is efficient to find the maximum (or minimum). For example, the problem of computing a matrix permanent, which is #-P hard (Valiant, 1979), corresponds to computing a normalizing constant for a probabilistic model where the most probable configuration can be computed efficiently as a bipartite matching. More specifically, given an energy function $f(\cdot)$ over structures $\boldsymbol{y}$ (e.g., a path on a graph $\mathcal{G}$) from an output space $\mathcal{Y}$ (e.g., all paths on $\mathcal{G}$), the normalizing constant or *partition function* is $Z = \sum_{\boldsymbol{y} \in \mathcal{Y}} \exp\{-f(\boldsymbol{y})\}$. This chapter focuses on the case where the output space is a combinatorial set, by which we mean that membership can be tested efficiently but enumeration is intractable (Bouchard-Côté and Jordan, 2010); however, in principle, the output space could also be continuous. The corresponding optimization problem is to find the most probable structure: $\operatorname{argmin}_{\boldsymbol{y} \in \mathcal{Y}} f(\boldsymbol{y})$.

The typical approach for defining probability distributions over structured objects is to use a *Gibbs distribution*. That is, make sensible assumptions about the structure of an energy function $f(\boldsymbol{y})$ and combinatorial set $\mathcal{Y}$, and then define $p(\boldsymbol{y}) \propto 1\{\boldsymbol{y} \in \mathcal{Y}\} \exp\{f(\boldsymbol{y})\}$. For example, to define a model of foreground-background segmentations of an image with D pixels, a common choice might be $\boldsymbol{y} \in \{0, 1\}^D$ and to define an energy function according to a graph structure $\mathcal{G} = (\mathcal{V}, \mathcal{E})$ as

$$f(\boldsymbol{y}) = f(\boldsymbol{y}; g) = \sum_{i \in \mathcal{V}} g_i \cdot y_i + \sum_{ij \in \mathcal{E}} g_{ij} \cdot 1\{y_i = y_j\},$$

which encodes the assumption that there are node-specific costs g_i for each pixel i to be labeled 1 (foreground) and that edges in the graph encourage neighboring nodes to take on the same label with an edge-dependent cost for differing g_{ij}. A typical choice of edge structure would be a 4-connected grid, where there are edges between nearest neighbor pixels.

While the above assumptions are sensible, they immediately lead to computational difficulty. Consider making test-time predictions, which depend on $p(\boldsymbol{y})$ and therefore require the intractable Z. There are two common choices: (1) use approximate inference like belief propagation (see e.g., Koller and Friedman (2009)) to compute approximate marginals, or (2) use Markov chain Monte Carlo (MCMC) to draw approximate samples (see e.g., (Robert and Casella, 2013)). The focus of this chapter is on cases where the combinatorial structure of the object is important, so marginals do not suffice. The point of Randomized Optimum Models (RandOMs) is to provide an efficient alternative to MCMC at test time without sacrificing the well-founded probabilistic model.

The outline is as follows:

- Background on structured prediction, and design considerations for building probabilistic models of structured objects
- A review of RandOMs
- Shortest Path Factorization with RandOMs
- Experiments
- Related work
- Discussion

3.2 Building Structured Models: Design Considerations

Structured prediction is a large field, and there are many approaches for learning models of structured objects. This section describes a high level overview of the key considerations, with a bias towards probabilistic models of structured objects.

A key issue that affects the choice of model is what the utility function will be. That is, how will we evaluate the quality of a test-time output? Is the system going to be used by some downstream process, or is it going to be used to make a single prediction? In the former case, a natural output for the system is a probability distribution (e.g., a probability that a patient has cancer); in the latter case, the utility function needs to be considered by the system (e.g., how unpleasant the patient finds the treatment, and how much value they would place on being cured).

A second question is about the structure of the utility function, which is relevant even if the system is producing a probability distribution, because it has bearing on how the probability distribution should be represented. In a structured prediction setting, a key property of utility functions to consider is whether they are sensitive to high order structure or not. For example, if an image segmentation system is judged based on the number of pixel-level classifications that it gets correct, then the utility function depends only on low order statistics of the output probability distribution, i.e., it can be shown that the expected utility of a predictive distribution depends only on the marginal distributions of each pixel's label. In this case, representing a probability distribution over pixel labelings as a set of marginal distributions is perfectly reasonable. Even in cases where the utility function appears at first glance to have high order interactions, such as with the intersection-over-union measure that is common in evaluating image segmentations (Everingham et al., 2010), Nowozin (2014) has shown that marginal distributions contain enough information to make accurate utility-aware predictions.

However, there are cases where the utility function truly is high order, and in fact, these are very common cases. One might even argue that *most* natural utility functions over structured objects depend heavily on high order structure, and it is only computational convenience that leads to utility functions based on low order structure. Examples of utility functions that depend on high order structure include perceptual measures of the naturalness of an image or image segmentation when outputting images or pixel-wise labels (Movahedi and Elder, 2010; Lubin, 1998; Wang et al., 2004), measures of whether code compiles when outputting source code (Nguyen et al., 2014), measures of the meaningfulness of a generated sentence when outputting language, and measures of whether a driver could follow a path that is output by the model.

When the utility function has high order structure and we wish to directly output a single prediction, then in some cases max-margin learning (Taskar et al., 2004; Tsochantaridis et al., 2005) can be a good option. High order utility functions present challenges, but can sometimes be handled efficiently, such as in certain image segmentation settings (Tarlow and Zemel, 2012; Pletscher and Kohli, 2012).

When the utility function has high order structure and we wish to output a probability distribution, sample-based representations of the output distribution are the natural choice. This is the setting that motivates RandOMs, along with several other works, including some in this book, such as Perturb & MAP (Chapter 2), PAC-Bayesian perturbation models (Chapter 10), and MAP-perturbation models (Chapter 5); see Section 3.9 for a discussion of the similarities and differences between RandOMs and other works that focus on this regime. Our focus is to train models such that at test time, we can efficiently produce perfect samples from the model without resorting to MCMC or rejection sampling.

3.3   Randomized Optimum Models (RandOMs)

This section introduces notation and then develops the RandOM model.

RandOMs implicitly define a probability distribution over an output space $\mathcal{Y}$ via a generative procedure that includes a call to an algorithm that performs optimization over $\mathcal{Y}$. In the typical instantiation, $\mathcal{Y}$ is a combinatorial set and the optimization algorithm is a discrete optimization procedure.

3.3.1 Notation

Let $f_{\boldsymbol{w}} : \mathcal{Y} \to \mathbb{R}$ be a family of scoring functions indexed by $\boldsymbol{w} \in \mathbb{R}^P$, each of which maps a structure $\boldsymbol{y}$ to a real-valued cost. Let $\mathcal{Y}$ be the set of legal structures. For example, $\boldsymbol{w}$ may be node weights for a weighted vertex cover algorithm or edge costs for a graph cut algorithm, and $\mathcal{Y}$ would be the set of all vertex covers or the set of all graph cuts, respectively. In these cases, the individual dimensions of $\boldsymbol{w}$ might be costs of specific nodes or edges in some graph. A further description of f's dependence on $\boldsymbol{w}$ appears below.

It will then be useful to define $F : \mathbb{R}^P \to \mathcal{Y}$ as the function that executes an optimization algorithm given parameters $\boldsymbol{w}$ and returns a cost-minimizing configuration $\boldsymbol{y}^*$; i.e., $F(\boldsymbol{w}; \mathcal{Y}) = \text{argmin}_{\boldsymbol{y} \in \mathcal{Y}} f_{\boldsymbol{w}}(\boldsymbol{y})$. Also useful will be the *inverse set* $F^{-1}(\boldsymbol{y}; \mathcal{Y})$, which is defined as $F^{-1}(\boldsymbol{y}; \mathcal{Y}) = \{ \boldsymbol{w} \mid F(\boldsymbol{w}; \mathcal{Y}) = \boldsymbol{y} \}$. When the appropriate $\mathcal{Y}$ is clear from context, it will be dropped from the notation, resulting in $F(\boldsymbol{y})$ and $F^{-1}(\boldsymbol{y})$.

In some problems there is a notion of *legal* settings of $\boldsymbol{w}$. For example, a shortest path algorithm might reasonably assert that all edge costs should be non-negative, or a graph cut algorithm may assert that edge potentials are submodular. To handle these cases, the predicate $\mathcal{L} : \mathbb{R}^P \to \{0, 1\}$ will be used to indicate whether a $\boldsymbol{w}$ is legal.

3.3.2 RandOM Model

The key idea of RandOM models is to define probabilistic models where parameters $\boldsymbol{w}$ are latent variables. That is, a probabilistic model $p(\boldsymbol{y}; \psi)$ is defined via a distribution over $\boldsymbol{w}$, parameterized by ψ; the link between $\boldsymbol{y}$ and $\boldsymbol{w}$ values is a deterministic relationship that comes from running the optimization algorithm:

$$p(\boldsymbol{y}; \psi) \propto \int p(\boldsymbol{w}; \psi) \, 1\{F(\boldsymbol{w}) = \boldsymbol{y}\} \, 1\{\mathcal{L}(\boldsymbol{w})\} \, d\boldsymbol{w}. \tag{3.1}$$

The design space of distributions over $\boldsymbol{w}$ is large and flexible. Many variations are possible, such as conditioning on inputs $\mathbf{x}$:

$$p(\boldsymbol{y} \mid \mathbf{x}; \psi) \propto \int p(\boldsymbol{w} \mid \mathbf{x}; \psi) \, 1\{F(\boldsymbol{w}) = \boldsymbol{y}\} \, 1\{\mathcal{L}(\boldsymbol{w})\} d\boldsymbol{w}, \tag{3.2}$$

which is the form that was the focus of Tarlow et al. (2012). It would also be straightforward to treat ψ as random variables which themselves have prior distributions. The key to test-time tractability is that a sample from $p'(\boldsymbol{w}) \propto p(\boldsymbol{w})1\{\mathcal{L}(\boldsymbol{w})\}$ can be drawn efficiently. Given the sample of $\boldsymbol{w}$, the optimization algorithm can be executed to yield a sample $\boldsymbol{y}$; i.e., set $\boldsymbol{y} = F(\boldsymbol{w})$.

3.3.3 Constructing Conditional Random Field-Like f

This section describes a pattern for constructing $p(\boldsymbol{w} \mid \mathbf{x}; \psi)$ that parallels the energy function used in conditional random field (CRF) models. To illustrate how this works within the RandOM formulation, we focus on a pairwise CRF with binary variables, as would be used for the foreground-background segmentation example in the introduction.

To review, CRFs define distributions over $\mathcal{Y}$ via the Gibbs distribution. For pairwise CRFs with binary variables, the energy function $f(\boldsymbol{y})$ is constructed as a sum of unary and pairwise terms:

$$f(\boldsymbol{y}) = \sum_{i \in \mathcal{V}} g_i(y_i, \mathbf{x}; \psi) + \sum_{ij \in \mathcal{E}} g_{ij}(y_i, y_j, \mathbf{x}; \psi). \tag{3.3}$$

The $g(\cdot)$ terms are parameterized by weights ψ and can depend arbitrarily on the input $\mathbf{x}$, but have only local dependence on $\boldsymbol{y}$. The $g(\cdot)$ functions are usually constructed as a weighted sum of unary features and pairwise features. An example unary feature would be an affinity for the average color of image $\mathbf{x}$ around pixel i to class y_i. An example pairwise feature would be a cost for neighboring pixels i and j to take different classes with strength depending on the difference of appearance of the pixels.

Finally, the probability of a configuration is defined by the Gibbs distribution: $p(\boldsymbol{y}) \propto \exp\{-f(\boldsymbol{y})\}$.

3.3.3.1 *CRF Energy Functions in RandOM Notation*

First, a vector of *sufficient statistics* of $\boldsymbol{y}$ are chosen, denoted $\boldsymbol{\rho}(\boldsymbol{y}) = (\rho_p(\boldsymbol{y}))_{p=1}^{P}$ where $\rho_p : \mathcal{Y} \to \{0, 1\}$. Each $\rho_p(\cdot)$ is an indicator function that selects out some statistic of $\boldsymbol{y}$ that is relevant for the model. Example indicator functions are whether a particular subset of dimensions of $\boldsymbol{y}$ take on a particular joint configuration, or they could indicate whether the number of dimensions of y taking on a particular value (say a) is equal to some value (say b); i.e., $\rho_p(\boldsymbol{y}) = 1\{(\sum_i 1\{y_i = a\}) = b\}$.

As another example, in a pairwise graphical model, there are unary and pairwise sufficient statistics. The unary sufficient statistics are functions indicating if $y_i = a$ for each variable i and each possible value a. Pairwise sufficient statistics are defined over all edges and might indicate all joint configurations of a pair of neighboring variables, i.e.,

$(1\{y_i = 0 \wedge y_j = 0\}, \cdots, 1\{y_i = 1 \wedge y_j = 1\})$, or just whether neighboring variables take on the same label, i.e., $(1\{y_i = y_j\})$. There is flexibility in the choice of sufficient statistics. The main issue to be mindful of is that the choice of sufficient statistics can impact the tractability of the minimization problem, so some care must be taken. More examples of choices of sufficient statistics that lead to tractable optimization appear below.

Given a vector of sufficient statistics, the definition of $f_{\boldsymbol{w}}(\boldsymbol{y})$ is then simply that each dimension of $\boldsymbol{w}$ weights the sufficient statistic in the corresponding dimension:

$$f_{\boldsymbol{w}}(\boldsymbol{y}) = \boldsymbol{w}^\top \boldsymbol{\rho}(\boldsymbol{y}). \tag{3.4}$$

To produce an equivalent $f_{\boldsymbol{w}}$ using the RandOM formulation, define $p(\boldsymbol{w} \mid \mathbf{x}; \boldsymbol{\psi})$ to be a deterministic function of input $\mathbf{x}$ and parameters $\boldsymbol{\psi}$ as follows.

First, rewrite f as

$$f(\boldsymbol{y}) = \sum_{i \in \mathcal{V}} \sum_{\hat{y}_i} 1\{y_i = \hat{y}_i\} g_i(\hat{y}_i, \mathbf{x}; \boldsymbol{\psi}) \tag{3.5}$$

$$+ \sum_{ij \in \mathcal{E}} \sum_{\hat{y}_i, \hat{y}_j} 1\{y_i = \hat{y}_i \wedge y_j = \hat{y}_j\} g_{ij}(\hat{y}_i, \hat{y}_j, \mathbf{x}; \boldsymbol{\psi}). \tag{3.6}$$

Then it becomes clear that by defining sufficient statistics vector $\boldsymbol{\rho}(\boldsymbol{y})$ to be a concatenation of $(1\{y_i = a\})$ for all i and a with $(1\{y_i = 0 \wedge y_j = 0\}, 1\{y_i = 0 \wedge y_j = 1\}, 1\{y_i = 1 \wedge y_j = 0\}, 1\{y_i = 1 \wedge y_j = 1\})$ for all $ij \in \mathcal{E}$, and analogously defining $\boldsymbol{g}$ to be a vector of the $g_i(\cdot)$ or $g_{ij}(\cdot)$ functions corresponding to the entries of $\boldsymbol{\rho}(\boldsymbol{y})$, then setting $\boldsymbol{w} = \boldsymbol{g}$ ensures that $f(\boldsymbol{y}) = f_{\boldsymbol{w}}(\boldsymbol{y})$ for all $\boldsymbol{y}$.

Of course, if $\boldsymbol{w}$ is a deterministic function of $\mathbf{x}$ and $\boldsymbol{\psi}$, then the output distribution will be degenerate and assign nonzero probability to a single $\boldsymbol{y}$. Instead, to induce a meaningful distribution over outputs, $\boldsymbol{w}$ must be random. This is in contrast to CRFs, which define an energy function to be deterministically constructed from inputs, but then the distribution over $\boldsymbol{y}$ given the energy function is random.

3.3.3.2 Example: The Gibbs Distribution

As noted by Papandreou and Yuille (2011) and extended by Hazan and Jaakkola (2012), it is possible to leverage properties of Gumbel distributions in order to exactly represent the Gibbs distributions that arises in standard CRF models. While this connection is of theoretical interest, it is not a practical construction because it requires the set of sufficient statistics to be exponentially large, with one sufficient statistic for each possible configuration of $\boldsymbol{y}$. The connection is presented here for completeness. See Chapters 2, 6 and 7 for additional discussions of related issues.

A random variable G is said to have a Gumbel distribution with location $m \in \mathbb{R}$ if the CDF is $p(G < g) = \exp\left(-\exp(-g + m)\right)$. The key property of Gumbel distributions is that for a collection of independent Gumbels $G_1, \ldots, G_K$ with locations $m_1, \ldots, m_K$ respectively, the distribution of the maximum is also Gumbel-distributed but with location equal to the logsumexp of the locations, and the argmax is distributed according to the Gibbs distribution where m_k is the negative energy of configuration k. More precisely,

$$\max_k G_k \sim \text{Gumbel}\left(\log \sum_{k=1}^{K} \exp(m_k)\right), \text{ and} \tag{3.7}$$

$$\underset{k}{\text{argmax}}\, G_k \sim \frac{\exp(m_k)}{\sum_{k'=1}^{K} \exp(m_{k'})}. \tag{3.8}$$

Letting $p = 1, \ldots, |\mathcal{Y}|$ index all configurations and $\hat{\boldsymbol{y}}(p)$ be the pth configuration under this ordering, we can then let $\boldsymbol{\rho}(\boldsymbol{y}) = (1\{\boldsymbol{y} = \hat{\boldsymbol{y}}(p)\})_{p=1}^{|\mathcal{Y}|}$; i.e., there is one sufficient statistic for each $\hat{\boldsymbol{y}} \in \mathcal{Y}$ indicating whether $\boldsymbol{y}$ is exactly equal to $\hat{\boldsymbol{y}}(p)$. Finally, let $\bar{\boldsymbol{w}} = (-f(\hat{\boldsymbol{y}}(p)))_{p=1}^{|\mathcal{Y}|}$ be the vector that puts the negative energy of configuration p in dimension p, and let $-w_p \sim \text{Gumbel}(\bar{w}_p)$ for all p. Then

$$\underset{p}{\text{argmin}}\, \boldsymbol{w}^\top \boldsymbol{\rho}(\hat{\boldsymbol{y}}(p)) = \underset{p}{\text{argmax}} -w_p \sim \frac{\exp(\bar{w}_p)}{\sum_{p'} \exp(\bar{w}_{p'})} = \frac{\exp(-f(\hat{\boldsymbol{y}}(p)))}{\sum_{p'} \exp(-f(\hat{\boldsymbol{y}}(p')))}, \tag{3.9}$$

which shows the equivalence to the Gibbs distribution.

3.3.3.3 *Example: Bipartite Matching f*

The weighted perfect bipartite matching problem is defined in terms of a bipartite graph $\mathcal{G}$ with partite sets A and B with $J = |A| = |B|$. The only edges in $\mathcal{G}$ are between a node $v \in A$ and $v' \in B$; we will additionally assume that all possible edges exists, so there is an edge from each $v \in A$ to each $v' \in B$.

A perfect matching is a one-to-one mapping between nodes in A and nodes in B. Each edge (v, v') is assigned a cost $w_{vv'}$, and the cost of a matching is the sum of the costs of edges that are included in the matching.

To formalize this in terms of above notation, let $y_{vv'} \in \{0, 1\}$ be an indicator that edge (v, v') is used in a matching. Let $\boldsymbol{y}$ be an ordered list of indicators for each edge $\{y_{vv'} : v \in A, v' \in B\}$. Let $\boldsymbol{w}$ be an analogous ordered list $\{w_{vv'} : v \in A, v' \in B\}$ such that element p of $\boldsymbol{w}$ is the weight for edge being indicated by element p of $\boldsymbol{y}$. Finally, let $\mathcal{Y}$ be the set of binary vectors of length J^2 that correspond to valid matchings according to the encoding of $\boldsymbol{y}$ above. Then the cost of any matching $\boldsymbol{y} \in \mathcal{Y}$ is simply $f_{\boldsymbol{w}}(\boldsymbol{y}) = \boldsymbol{w}^{\top} \boldsymbol{y}$. (To match the general form in (3.4), $\boldsymbol{\rho}$ could be set to be the identity $\boldsymbol{\rho}(\boldsymbol{y}) = \boldsymbol{y}$, and then $f_{\boldsymbol{w}}(\boldsymbol{y}) = \boldsymbol{w}^{\top} \boldsymbol{\rho}(\boldsymbol{y})$ as above.)

3.3.3.4   Example: Shortest Paths f

An encoding of a shortest paths problem is similar. The shortest path problem is defined in terms of a weighted graph $\mathcal{G}$, and a start-end node pair (s, t). The combinatorial problem is to find the shortest path in $\mathcal{G}$ from s to t, where the cost of a path is a sum of the costs of the edges traversed by the path.

To encode an f function corresponding to this problem, let $\boldsymbol{y}$ be a vector of indicators of edges (as above), with dimension p indicating whether edge p is used in the path. Let $\boldsymbol{w}$ be the corresponding vector of edge costs. Then as in the bipartite matching case, $f_{\boldsymbol{w}}(\boldsymbol{y}) = \boldsymbol{w}^{\top} \boldsymbol{y}$.

The combinatorial set $\mathcal{Y} = \mathcal{Y}(s, t)$ is the set of all simple paths from s to t (i.e., paths with no repeating vertices).

3.3.4   Other Types of f

In all of the above examples, f has been defined as an inner product between $\boldsymbol{w}$ and a vector of sufficient statistics $\boldsymbol{\rho}(\boldsymbol{y})$. It is always possible to define $\boldsymbol{\rho}(\boldsymbol{y}) = (1\{\boldsymbol{y} = \hat{\boldsymbol{y}}\})_{\hat{\boldsymbol{y}} \in \mathcal{Y}}$, and thus if $f_{\boldsymbol{w}}(\boldsymbol{y}) = \boldsymbol{w}^{\top} \boldsymbol{\rho}(\boldsymbol{y})$ then each $\boldsymbol{y} \in \mathcal{Y}$ has an independent entry of $\boldsymbol{w}$ and all possible energy functions can be expressed; this is the equivalent of representing an energy function in a tabular form that assigns some cost to each configuration.

While such a construction is as flexible as possible, it does not mean that all interesting $f_{\boldsymbol{w}}(\boldsymbol{y})$ are of the form $\boldsymbol{w}^{\top} \boldsymbol{\rho}(\boldsymbol{y})$. Indeed, for $F(\boldsymbol{w})$ to be implemented efficiently, $\boldsymbol{w}$ must be represented in some compact form (such as edge costs in the above example), and each efficient combinatorial optimization routine expects an input of a particular form.

3.3.4.1   Example: Connected Components f

For example, consider the weighted connected components problem. Given a weighted graph $\mathcal{G}$, cut all edges with weight less than some parameter τ to get an unweighted graph $\mathcal{G}'$ that contains the uncut edges in $\mathcal{G}$, then partition the nodes into connected components; that is, two nodes v and v' are in the same connected component iff there is a path from v to v' in $\mathcal{G}'$.

For a given τ, the natural parameterization of the problem is to have one dimension of $\boldsymbol{w}$ to represent each edge cost in $\mathcal{G}$. There is some flexibility in how to represent $\boldsymbol{y}$, but one reasonable choice is to let $y_i \in \{1, \ldots, |\mathcal{V}|\}$ be equal to the smallest index j such that nodes i and j are in the same connected component. Then $\mathcal{Y}$ is the set of all $\boldsymbol{y}$ such that all nodes with a given label l are connected via edges where both endpoints are labeled l. One might then ask if there is some choice of sufficient statistics $\boldsymbol{\rho}$ such that $f_{\boldsymbol{w}}(\boldsymbol{y}) = \boldsymbol{w}^\top \boldsymbol{\rho}(\boldsymbol{y})$ and $\operatorname{argmin}_{\boldsymbol{y}} f_{\boldsymbol{w}}(\boldsymbol{y})$ gives the same output as the connected components algorithm described above. It turns out that this is not possible.

Lemma 3.1. *Let $G : \mathbb{R}^{|\mathcal{E}|} \to \mathcal{Y}$ be the function that maps $\boldsymbol{w}$ to the solution to the above weighted connected component problem with parameter τ. There is no choice of sufficient statistics $\boldsymbol{\rho}(\boldsymbol{y})$ such that for all $\boldsymbol{w}$, $\operatorname{argmin}_{\boldsymbol{y}} \boldsymbol{w}^\top \boldsymbol{\rho}(\boldsymbol{y}) = G(\boldsymbol{w}; \tau)$.*

Proof. (By contradiction). Suppose there were a choice of $\boldsymbol{\rho}(\boldsymbol{y})$ such that for all $\boldsymbol{w}$, $\operatorname{argmin}_{\boldsymbol{y}} \boldsymbol{w}^\top \boldsymbol{\rho}(\boldsymbol{y}) = G(\boldsymbol{w})$. Then $F^{-1}(\boldsymbol{y})$ is an intersection of halfspaces $\{\boldsymbol{w} : \boldsymbol{w}^\top \boldsymbol{\rho}(\boldsymbol{y}) \leq \boldsymbol{w}^\top \boldsymbol{\rho}(\boldsymbol{y}')\}$ for each $\boldsymbol{y}' \in \mathcal{Y}$, and is thus a convex set. However, $G^{-1}(\boldsymbol{y})$ is not a convex set, and thus F cannot be equivalent to G.

To see that $G^{-1}(\boldsymbol{y})$ is not a convex set, consider the fully connected graph on three vertices $1, 2, 3$ with edges $(1, 2), (1, 3), (2, 3)$ and $\tau = 1 - \epsilon$. Let $\boldsymbol{w}^A = (1, 1, 0)$, $\boldsymbol{w}^B = (0, 1, 1)$, and $\boldsymbol{y}^*$ be the configuration where all nodes belong to a single connected component. Clearly $\boldsymbol{w}^A \in G^{-1}(\boldsymbol{y}^*)$ and $\boldsymbol{w}^B \in G^{-1}(\boldsymbol{y}^*)$. However, consider $\boldsymbol{w}^C = \frac{1}{2}\boldsymbol{w}^A + \frac{1}{2}\boldsymbol{w}^B = (.5, 1, .5)$. $G(\boldsymbol{w}^C)$ assigns node 2 to its own connected component, and thus $\boldsymbol{w}^C \notin G^{-1}(\boldsymbol{y})$ and $G^{-1}(\cdot)$ is not always a convex set. $\square$

3.4 Learning RandOMs

There are two main approaches to learning RandOMs. Both are based on an Expectation Maximization (EM) algorithm (Dempster et al., 1977) with $\boldsymbol{w}$ as latent variables. A fully Bayesian treatment would also be straightforward, in which case the M step in the Monte Carlo EM variant would be replaced with an MCMC update, but this approach is not discussed further.

The difference between the two EM approaches is how distributions over $\boldsymbol{w}$ are estimated. In the Monte Carlo EM algorithm (MCEM) (Wei and Tanner,

1990), values of $\boldsymbol{w}$ are sampled from a posterior distribution over $\boldsymbol{w}$; in the Hard EM algorithm, a single most likely estimate of $\boldsymbol{w}$ is used.

In more detail, the EM algorithm can be understood as optimizing a single objective (Neal and Hinton, 1998) via an alternating maximization scheme. In the case of general RandOMs (3.1), the objective given a data set $\mathcal{D} = \{\boldsymbol{y}^{(n)}\}_{n=1}^{N}$ is $J(\psi, \{Q^{(n)}\}_{n=1}^{N})$

$$= \sum_{n=1}^{N} \mathbb{E}_{\hat{\boldsymbol{w}} \sim Q^{(n)}(\cdot)} \left[\log \left(p(\boldsymbol{y}^{(n)} \mid \hat{\boldsymbol{w}}) p(\hat{\boldsymbol{w}}; \psi) \right) - \log Q^{(n)}(\hat{\boldsymbol{w}}) \right] \qquad (3.10)$$

$$= \sum_{n=1}^{N} \mathbb{E}_{\hat{\boldsymbol{w}} \sim Q^{(n)}(\cdot)} \left[\log 1\{\boldsymbol{y}^{(n)} = F(\hat{\boldsymbol{w}})\} + \log p(\hat{\boldsymbol{w}}; \psi) - \log Q^{(n)}(\hat{\boldsymbol{w}}) \right].$$
$$(3.11)$$

EM algorithms alternate between maximizing J with respect to $\{Q^{(n)}\}_{n=1}^{N}$ (E step) and with respect to ψ (M step). Note that the E step is amenable to embarassingly parallel computation.

3.4.1   M Step

In both the MCEM and Hard EM algorithms, $Q^{(n)}(\cdot)$ is represented via a set of L samples $\hat{\boldsymbol{w}}^{(n1)}, \ldots, \hat{\boldsymbol{w}}^{(nL)}$. The M step is an incremental M step (Neal and Hinton, 1998), meaning that rather than updating ψ to optimality, an update is made that just increases J. Note that given fixed samples from $\{Q^{(n)}\}_{n=1}^{N}$ where each sample is in the corresponding inverse set $F^{-1}(\boldsymbol{y}^{(n)})$, the M step objective (dropping terms that do not depend on ψ) is

$$\sum_{n=1}^{N} \frac{1}{L} \sum_{l=1}^{L} \log p(\hat{\boldsymbol{w}}^{(nl)}; \psi). \qquad (3.12)$$

This is a standard maximum likelihood objective with parameters ψ and data $\boldsymbol{w}^{(nl)}$, which can be optimized with whatever standard optimizer is most appropriate for the specific form of $p(\boldsymbol{w}; \psi)$ that is chosen. For example, if $p(\boldsymbol{w}; \psi)$ is a neural network, then stochastic gradient ascent can be used.

3.4.2   Monte Carlo E Step

The optimal choice for $Q^{(n)}(\cdot)$ in the E step is to set it equal to the posterior distribution $p(\boldsymbol{w} \mid \boldsymbol{y}^{(n)}; \psi) \propto p(\boldsymbol{w}; \psi) 1\{F(\boldsymbol{w}) = \boldsymbol{y}^{(n)}\} \mathcal{L}(\boldsymbol{w})$. For most RandOMs, it does not appear possible to represent this posterior in closed form. Instead, in Monte Carlo EM, $Q^{(n)}(\cdot)$ is represented via a set of L samples from this posterior. In principle, any MCMC method can be used in the E step, but Slice Sampling (Neal, 2003) is particularly well suited to handle the structure of the problem, as will be discussed in more detail in Section 3.7.3.

3.4.3   Hard E Step

In the Hard EM algorithm, sampling from the posterior is replaced with a maximization step: $\hat{\boldsymbol{w}}$ is chosen so as to be the $\operatorname{argmax}_{\boldsymbol{w}} p(\boldsymbol{w}; \psi) 1\{F(\boldsymbol{w}) = \boldsymbol{y}^{(n)}\} \mathcal{L}(\boldsymbol{w})$. When $f_{\boldsymbol{w}}(\boldsymbol{y})$ is a linear function of $\boldsymbol{w}$ (as in (3.4)) and $p(\boldsymbol{w}; \psi)$ is a Gaussian distribution (log quadratic), then the argmax computation is a quadratic program (QP). More details of this approach appear in Tarlow et al. (2012). An improved Hard EM algorithm appears in Gane et al. (2014).

3.5   RandOMs for Image Registration

In Tarlow et al. (2012), RandOMs are applied to registration problems. The main application is deformable image registration in volumetric CT scans of human lungs. For each human subject in the data set, data consists of scans at different stages of the respiratory process that are annotated with landmarks. The problem is to take a pair of images with their associated landmarks and determine the correspondences between landmarks across the two images. To formulate this problem as a RandOM, $\mathcal{Y}$ is the set of all bipartite matchings with the first (second) partite set being landmarks in the first (second) image. The sufficient statistics indicate whether landmark i in the first image matches to landmark j in the second image, and $\boldsymbol{w}$ assigns a cost for each i, j pair. Features are extracted for each pair based on the difference in appearance of the volume around the landmarks, and parameters ψ weight the importance of different features.

Experimentally, RandOMs are compared against a Structural SVM approach (Taskar et al., 2004; Tsochantaridis et al., 2005) and Perturb & MAP (Papandreou and Yuille, 2011). Results show that RandOMs are competitive with the alternatives and perform best in terms of accuracy.

3.6   Shortest Path Factorization

This section introduces the problem studied in detail in this chapter.

The Shortest Path Factorization (SPF) problem is to observe a data set $\mathcal{D}$ of pairs of driver ids and paths $\mathcal{D} = \{(d_n, \boldsymbol{y}_n)\}_{n=1}^{N}$ where each $\boldsymbol{y}_n$ is a path through a graph $\mathcal{G} = (\mathcal{V}, \mathcal{E})$ and $d_n \in \{1, \ldots, D\}$ denotes the identity of the driver. The goal is to infer properties of the edges and drivers' preferences for edge properties under the assumption that drivers are taking shortest paths according to noisy copies of an underlying cost function. Given inferred driver preferences and edge costs, it is then possible to make predictions about the routes that will be taken by a driver on edges that have never been encountered by the driver before. For example, we can imagine learning from a driver traversing the streets of London and then make predictions about what routes the driver will prefer in Toronto. Alternatively, if city planners were considering changing road structures and they wanted to forecast how drivers would behave given a new road topology, a shortest path factorization model might be a good choice. In the factorization problem, we assume that driver-specific edge costs have a low-rank structure.

More specifically, paths are assumed to be shortest paths according to the driver's cost function. The cost function for a path is the sum of costs of edges on the path. Noise-free driver-specific edge costs are computed as the inner product of trait vector $\mathbf{U}_e \in \mathbb{R}^K$ for each edge e with a driver-specific preference vector $\mathbf{V}_d \in \mathbb{R}^K$ for each driver d. Noisy edge costs are drawn independently from Gaussian distributions with mean equal to the noise-free cost that are truncated to ensure that edge costs are non-negative.

The SPF problem is to infer $\mathbf{U}$ and $\mathbf{V}$ from the observations of paths. Intuitively, suppose that edges correspond to road segments, and drivers are members of the driving population. Paths are the routes that drivers take to get from home to work, from home to the grocery store, from a family member's house to the gas station, etc. The assumption is that there are a small number of traits that characterize each road segment. For example, real roads vary based on the average speed of traffic, start-stop frequency, the risk of traffic build-ups, their crowdedness, the scenery, the degree to which being an aggressive driver helps speed progress, etc. The degree to which a road segment e has such traits would be the kind of information stored in $\mathbf{U}_e$. The corresponding dimensions of $\mathbf{V}$ would then denote how important each of these traits is to each driver. Some drivers may be aggresive drivers concerned only about the total transit time, while others may prefer a minimal stress drive, even if it is slower. These different types of drivers could be represented via different $\mathbf{V}_d$ vectors. As in other matrix factorization-based algorithms like those used in recommendation systems (Rennie and Srebro, 2005; Salakhutdinov and Mnih, 2007), it is not assumed that the traits are given ahead of time. The assumption is simply that this low rank structure exists, and it is up to the learning algorithm to discover which edges and drivers have which traits.

3.7 Shortest Path Factorization with RandOMs

This section describes how to apply the RandOM formulation to the SPF problem.

3.7.1 Generative Model

The RandOM generative model for SPF given a graph $\mathcal{G} = (\mathcal{V}, \mathcal{E})$ is as follows:

$$\mathbf{U}_e \sim \text{Gaussian}(\mathbf{0}, \sigma^2 \mathbf{I}) \qquad\qquad \text{for each } e \in \mathcal{E} \qquad (3.13)$$

$$\mathbf{V}_d \sim \text{Gaussian}(\mathbf{0}, \sigma^2 \mathbf{I}) \qquad\qquad \text{for each } d = 1, \dots, D \qquad (3.14)$$

where σ^2 is a fixed variance.

Next sample each path conditional upon a driver d, a start node s, and an end node t. To sample each path:

$$w_e \sim \text{TruncGaussian}(\mathbf{U}_e^\top \mathbf{V}_d + b, 1) \qquad\qquad \text{for each } e \in \mathcal{E} \qquad (3.15)$$

$$\boldsymbol{y} = \text{ShortestPath}(s, t, \mathcal{G}, \boldsymbol{w}) \qquad\qquad\qquad (3.16)$$

where b is a fixed bias, $\text{TruncGaussian}(\mu, \sigma^2)$ is a Truncated Gaussian that is constrained to be greater than 0, and $\text{ShortestPath}(s, t, \mathcal{G}, \boldsymbol{w})$ returns the shortest path from s to t in $\mathcal{G}$ using edge costs given by $\boldsymbol{w}$.

3.7.2 Learning

The learning problem is to observe the data set $\mathcal{D}$ and infer parameters $\mathbf{U}$ and $\mathbf{V}$. Learning is done via MCEM.

The EM objective (Neal and Hinton, 1998) for a single data point $J(\mathbf{U}, \mathbf{V}, Q; \mathcal{D}_n)$ is

$$\mathbb{E}_{\hat{\boldsymbol{w}} \sim Q(\cdot)} \left[\log \left(p(\boldsymbol{y}_n \mid \boldsymbol{w}) p(\hat{\boldsymbol{w}} \mid \mathbf{U}, \mathbf{V}) p(\mathbf{U}) p(\mathbf{V}) \right) - \log Q(\hat{\boldsymbol{w}}) \right]. \qquad (3.17)$$

The EM algorithm alternates between performing E (expectation) steps and M (maximization) steps. In the E step, $\mathbf{U}$ and $\mathbf{V}$ are held fixed and $Q(\cdot)$ is updated to optimize J. Here there is a separate Q_n for each n. The standard result is that optimal choice for $Q_n(\cdot)$ is to set it equal to the posterior distribution

$$p(\boldsymbol{w} \mid \boldsymbol{y}_n, d_n, \mathbf{U}, \mathbf{V}) \propto 1\{\boldsymbol{y}_n = F(\boldsymbol{w})\} p(\boldsymbol{w} \mid \mathbf{U}, \mathbf{V}, d_n) \qquad (3.18)$$

$$= 1\{\boldsymbol{y}_n = F(\boldsymbol{w})\} \prod_{e \in \mathcal{E}} \mathrm{TruncGaussian}(w_e; \mathbf{U}_e^\top \mathbf{V}_{d_n}, 1).$$

$$(3.19)$$

In the M step, all $Q_n(\cdot)$ are held fixed, and J is optimized with respect to $\mathbf{U}$ and $\mathbf{V}$. The objective including all n is

$$\mathbf{U}, \mathbf{V} = \underset{\mathbf{U}', \mathbf{V}'}{\mathrm{argmax}} \sum_{n=1}^{N} \mathbb{E}_{\hat{\boldsymbol{w}} \sim Q_n(\cdot)} \left[\log\left(p(\hat{\boldsymbol{w}} \mid \mathbf{U}', \mathbf{V}') p(\mathbf{U}') p(\mathbf{V}')\right)\right]. \qquad (3.20)$$

These updates are not tractable to perform exactly, so instead an incremental MCEM algorithm is used (Neal and Hinton, 1998). In this variant, for each n, L samples $\hat{\boldsymbol{w}}^{(n1)}, \ldots, \hat{\boldsymbol{w}}^{(nL)}$ are drawn from (3.19) using a specialized slice sampler (described below). Then the M step objective is replaced with a Monte Carlo approximation:

$$\sum_{n=1}^{N} \frac{1}{L} \sum_{l=1}^{L} \left[\log\left(p(\hat{\boldsymbol{w}}^{(nl)} \mid \mathbf{U}, \mathbf{V}) p(\mathbf{U}) p(\mathbf{V})\right)\right], \qquad (3.21)$$

and $\mathbf{U}$ and $\mathbf{V}$ are updated using a small number of steps of gradient ascent.

3.7.3   Slice Sampling for the E Step

This section describes how to implement the Monte Carlo E step using a specialized slice sampler. The section begins by reviewing slice sampling, and then it describes how to combine slice sampling with combinatorial algorithms to obtain a fast sampler. This section describes a slice sampler tailored to the shortest paths problem, and it makes a general observation that may lead to minor improvements over Tarlow et al. (2012) for general RandOM slice samplers.

3.7.3.1   Review of Slice Sampling

Slice sampling (Neal, 2003) is a Markov Chain Monte Carlo (MCMC) method. It has favorable properties over alternatives like Metropolis Hastings in being less sensitive to parameters of a proposal distribution, and it has been shown to mix in polynomial time when run on log concave distributions (Lovász and Vempala, 2003). Tarlow et al. (2012) describe a specialization of slice sampling to RandOM models.

Slice sampling is used to draw samples from an unnormalized probability distribution $\tilde{p}(w)$. The basic idea is to sample uniformly from the region $R = \{(w, u) : 0 < u < \tilde{p}(w)\}$ using an MCMC algorithm that alternates between resampling w conditioned on u and resampling u conditioned on w so as to leave the distribution invariant.

The definition of R ensures that $\int p(w, u) du \propto \tilde{p}(w)$, so it is valid to jointly sample w and u, and then discard the u components of the sample. Starting from a current point w_0, the next point is chosen as follows:

■ Sample $u \sim \text{Uniform}(0, \tilde{p}(w_0))$ (note: this should all be implemented in log-space).

■ Sample w uniformly from the *slice*, $\{w' : \tilde{p}(w') > u\}$.

We say that w is *in the slice* if $\tilde{p}(w) > u$. The second step cannot always be implemented exactly, so Neal (2003) gives alternative updates that leave the uniform distribution over the slice invariant. The main suggestion is to do the following:

■ Construct a random initial interval $[w_l, w_r]$ such that $w_0 \in [w_l, w_r]$.

■ Step outwards by incrementing $w_l = w_l - \alpha$ until $\tilde{p}(w_l) < u$, where $\alpha \in \mathbb{R}_{>0}$ is a parameter that controls the speed at which the interval is expanded. Similarly, step outwards by incrementing $w_r = w_r + \alpha$ until $\tilde{p}(w_r) < u$. At this point, a contiguous section of the slice lies completely within the interval.

■ Step inwards by sampling $\hat{w} \sim \text{Uniform}(w_l, w_r)$. If $\hat{w}$ is in the slice, then finish and transition to $\hat{w}$. Otherwise, shrink the interval so that w_0 remains inside the interval and $\hat{w}$ is one of the endpoints. Repeat the stepping inwards step.

The above describes how to use slice sampling with a 1D w. To handle higher dimensions as will be needed when sampling $\boldsymbol{w} \in \mathbb{R}^P$, a standard approach is to choose a random direction $\Delta \in \mathbb{R}^P$ uniformly from the surface of a sphere centered at $\boldsymbol{w}$, and then to sample along the line defined by $\boldsymbol{w} + \lambda\Delta$ for $\lambda \in (-\infty, \infty)$.

3.7.3.2   *Specialization to General RandOMs*

This section gives guidance on how slice samplers should be implemented in general for RandOM models.

The problem is to perform one step of slice sampling on the MCEM posterior (e.g., (3.19)). We are given an initial $\boldsymbol{w}_0 \in F^{-1}(\boldsymbol{y})$ and a direction Δ, and would like to choose a λ that leaves the distribution invariant (i.e., do a slice sampling update). The key idea is to define three sub-slices.

- The *legal slice* $\{\lambda : \mathcal{L}(\boldsymbol{w} + \lambda\Delta)\}$.
- The *$\boldsymbol{y}$-slice* $\{\lambda : \boldsymbol{w} + \lambda\Delta \in F^{-1}(\boldsymbol{y})\}$.
- The *prior slice* $\{\lambda : p(\boldsymbol{w} + \lambda\Delta \mid \mathbf{U}, \mathbf{V}, d) > u\}$.

The slice is then the intersection of these three sub-slices.

There are then properties of the subslices that can be useful to improve efficiency.

Convexity.   The first source of efficiency is convexity, which can arise in all three types of sub-slice (but in any specific model may only arise in a subset of the sub-slices). For example:

1. If $\mathcal{L}(\boldsymbol{w})$ measures whether all dimensions of $\boldsymbol{w}$ are positive, then the legal slice is a convex set.

2. $F^{-1}(\boldsymbol{y})$ can be defined as $\{\boldsymbol{w} : f_{\boldsymbol{w}}(\boldsymbol{y}) \leq f_{\boldsymbol{w}}(\boldsymbol{y}')   \forall \boldsymbol{y}' \in \mathcal{Y}\}$. If $f_{\boldsymbol{w}}(\boldsymbol{y})$ is a CRF-like energy function as discussed in Section 3.3.3, then $f_{\boldsymbol{w}}(\boldsymbol{y})$ is a linear function of $\boldsymbol{w}$ (see (3.4)), so $F^{-1}(\boldsymbol{y})$ is an intersection of halfspaces and thus convex set, and the $\boldsymbol{y}$-slice is also a convex set.

3. If $p(\boldsymbol{w} \mid \ldots)$ is a log-concave distribution, then the prior slice is a convex set.

Convexity of the individual slices can be leveraged during the Stepping In phase of slice sampling. Since the initial point $\boldsymbol{w}_0$ will always be inside the slice and the interval resulting from the Stepping Out phase will always have endpoints outside the slice, convexity implies that there is a single transition point in between $\boldsymbol{w}_0$ and each endpoint where one leaves each convex sub-slice. For example, suppose for some $\hat{\lambda} > 0$, $\boldsymbol{w}_0 + \hat{\lambda}\Delta$ is in the $\boldsymbol{y}$-slice but not in the slice (maybe the point is not in the prior slice); it is then immediately known that $[0, \hat{\lambda}]$ is fully contained in the $\boldsymbol{y}$-slice, and there is no need for calling an expensive combinatorial algorithm for any later λ in this range that is encountered; it suffices to simply return `true`. When the union of the subslices is substantially different from the intersection, this can provide significant savings.

Combinatorial Algorithms for the $\boldsymbol{y}$-slice   The second type of efficiency comes from the combinatorial optimization view of $F(\boldsymbol{w})$ and the fact that a slice sampling step always starts with a setting of $\boldsymbol{w}_0$ that is in the $\boldsymbol{y}$-slice. This source of efficiency can be leveraged in addition to convexity structure if both are present. There are three ways of framing the problem of testing whether a particular $w \in F^{-1}(y)$:

1. Run a combinatorial optimization algorithm with weights w and check whether y is an argmin.

2. Suppose we have recently solved a combinatorial optimization algorithm with weights w'. Use a dynamic combinatorial optimization algorithm to update the solution to be the one for w, and check whether y is an argmin.

3. Suppose we have recently solved a combinatorial optimization algorithm with weights w' and that y was an argmin. Check whether the argmin changes given weights w.

Tarlow et al. (2012) shows how to use (2) to improve efficiency for bipartite matching RandOMs using dynamic combinatorial algorithms. The new observation here is that (3) can be more efficient than (2). Details for the shortest path case are given in the next section.

Ordering the Slices. The final suggestion is to test whether a point is in the slice by checking each of the sub-slices in order of least expensive to most expensive, and to short-circuit the computation as soon as a point is determined not to be in any of the sub-slices, since this implies that the point is not in the slice. This saves runs of the more expensive sub-slice computations and also makes the implementation more convenient by checking for legality of a point before calling the combinatorial optimization.

3.7.3.3   *Efficiently Handling the y-Slice with Shortest Path Trees*

Given a source node s in a weighted graph $\mathcal{G}$ with all edge costs > 0, we can run Dijkstra's algorithm to get a *shortest path tree*. A shortest path tree is represented via a pointer from each node $v \neq s$ to a parent $pa(v)$, and a cost $c(v)$ for each node. Such a structure is a shortest path tree if $c(v)$ represents the distance from s to v via the shortest path in $\mathcal{G}$ and if the last step in the shortest path from s to v is to go from v's parent to v. This implies $c(v) = c(pa(v)) + w_{pa(v),v}$, where w_{uv} is the cost of edge uv.

An interesting property of shortest path trees is that they can be verified more efficiently than they can be constructed. They can be constructed in $\mathcal{O}(|\mathcal{V}| \log |\mathcal{V}| + |\mathcal{E}|)$ time using Dijkstra's algorithm but verified in $\mathcal{O}(|\mathcal{E}|)$ time using a simple loop over edges (Cormen et al., Exercise 24.3-4 Solution).

To leverage this property within the slice sampler, we need a fast method for proposing a shortest path tree $\mathcal{T}(w)$ given a shortest path tree $\mathcal{T}(w_0)$. The new suggestion is to keep the parent structure of $\mathcal{T}(w)$ fixed and update the node costs $c(v)$ so that $c(v) = c(pa(v)) + w_{pa(v),v}$. By iterating over nodes in topological order, this can be done in one loop over nodes ($\mathcal{O}(|\mathcal{V}|)$ time). We can then run the verification algorithm on the newly proposed shortest path tree. If the verification algorithm succeeds, then we have proven that $\boldsymbol{w}$ is in the $\boldsymbol{y}$-slice. If the verification algorithm fails, then it is necessary to run a more expensive check (e.g., run Dijkstra's algorithm from scratch), since it is possible for the structure of the shortest path tree to change while leaving the shortest path from s to some target node v unchanged. However, perhaps there is a more efficient method for determining whether the shortest path has changed; this could be studied in future work. In general, the suggestion when working with RandOMs is to focus on the dynamic combinatorial verification problem (which returns true or false as to whether the argmin has changed) instead of focusing on the dynamic combinatorial optimization problem (which returns a full configuration).

The verification procedure is most useful in the Stepping Out phase of slice sampling. If α is chosen to be small, then it will induce small changes in $\boldsymbol{w}$ that do not affect the structure of the shortest path tree. In these cases, the above procedure provides a fast way of verifying that a particular λ remains in the $\boldsymbol{y}$-slice.

3.8   Experiments

3.8.1   Baseline Model

The goal in choosing a baseline model is to illustrate a common tradeoff when modelling structured data: models that ignore the combinatorial structure of the data can be appealing because they are often simpler to train, and sometimes a post-hoc cleanup step can enforce the combinatorial constraints (e.g., using rejection sampling). The baseline model adopts this philosophy.

The baseline model ignores the combinatorial structure of paths and produces a distribution that factorizes fully over the choice of each edge. More specifically, the approach follows 3-way factored models (Memisevic and Hinton, 2007; Krizhevsky et al., 2010; Kiros et al., 2014). There are three input components: the driver d, the start and end nodes s and t, and the edge identity e. Given the three inputs, the model produces a probability that edge e is used $p(u_e)$ in the shortest path from s to t. The goal of the model is to assign high probability to edges that are used on an observed path and low probability to edges that are not used. A training instance is then composed of the tuple (d, s, t, u_e^*).

More specifically, $p(u_e \mid d, s, t)$ is defined as

$$p(u_e \mid d, s, t) = \sigma\left(\mathbf{U}_e^\top \left(\mathbf{V}_d \oplus (\mathbf{T}_s + \mathbf{T}_t)\right)\right), \tag{3.22}$$

where $\sigma(\cdot)$ is the logistic sigmoid and $\oplus$ is either elementwise addition or multiplication for additive and multiplicative variants of the model, respectively. $\mathbf{U} \in \mathbb{R}^{|\mathcal{E}| \times K}$, $\mathbf{V} \in \mathbb{R}^{D \times K}$, and $\mathbf{T} \in \mathbb{R}^{|\mathcal{V}| \times K}$ are parameter matrices for edges, drivers, and nodes respectively. Subscripts select rows, so there is a K-dimensional real-valued representation vector for each entity. Note that the $\mathbf{T}$ parameters are needed so that the distribution over which edges are used is a function of the start and end points of the path. The training objective is then a standard maximum likelihood objective that can be optimized with gradient ascent.

3.8.2   Data

To test the RandOM model on the SPF problem we create a data set of N paths describing the routes of $D = 3$ drivers traversing a square grid graph with dimensions 3×6. We synthesize this data, by constructing $K = 2$ dimensional ground truth trait vectors $\mathbf{U}_{\mathrm{gt}}$ and $\mathbf{V}_{\mathrm{gt}}$ from which we generate noisy edge costs

$$w \sim \mathrm{TruncGaussian}(\mathbf{U}_{\mathrm{gt}}^\top \mathbf{V}_{\mathrm{gt}}, \eta^2), \tag{3.23}$$

where η sets the scale of the noise. For simplicity, we start by setting the elements of the trait vectors to be random numbers uniformly drawn from $[0, 1)$. Later, we will consider a more carefully crafted $\mathbf{U}_{\mathrm{gt}}$ designed to highlight differences between the baseline and RandOM models (see Section 3.8.4).

Using these edge costs we construct an element $(d_n, \boldsymbol{y}_n)$ in the data set by picking a random driver, $d_n \in \{1, 2, 3\}$, and random distinct nodes, s_n and t_n on the graph and then constructing the shortest path $\boldsymbol{y}_n$ from s_n to t_n according a sample from w_{e,d_n}.

3.8.3   Quantitative Results as a Function of Noise and Data Size

To measure the performance of the learned parameters $\mathbf{U}$ and $\mathbf{V}$, we draw 3×10^3 samples from the RandOM model to obtain Monte-Carlo estimates of $\log(p(\boldsymbol{y}_n \mid \mathbf{U}, \mathbf{V}, d_n))$ for each path $(d_n, \boldsymbol{y}_n)$ in the data. We report the "training score" as the average of these log probabilities over the training data and similarly compute a "test score" for 200 test paths not seen during training. If none of the Monte-Carlo samples match $\boldsymbol{y}_n$, we remove $\boldsymbol{y}_n$

from the evaluation procedure and separately report the proportion of such failures as the sampling failure rate.

For the baseline model, we compute the equivalent training and test scores using

$$p(\boldsymbol{y}_n \mid \mathbf{U}, \mathbf{V}, \mathbf{T}, d_n) = \prod_{e \in \boldsymbol{y}_n} p(u_e \mid d_n, s_n, t_n) \prod_{e \notin \boldsymbol{y}_n} (1 - p(u_e \mid d_n, s_n, t_n)).$$
(3.24)

We find that the baseline model assigns a significant probability to configurations of edges which do not correspond to valid paths between s_n and t_n. A simple fix for this is to reject these samples at test time until a valid path is produced, but this comes at a computational cost. The score of this rejection-sampled baseline is analytically computed on our small 3×6 node example by enumerating all valid paths, $\mathcal{Y}(s_n, t_n)$, between s_n and t_n and then evaluating

$$\frac{1}{N} \sum_{n=1}^{N} [\log (p(\boldsymbol{y}_n \mid \mathbf{U}, \mathbf{V}, \mathbf{T}, d_n)) - \log(A_n)],$$
(3.25)

where

$$A_n = \sum_{\boldsymbol{y} \in \mathcal{Y}(s_n, t_n)} p(\boldsymbol{y} \mid \mathbf{U}, \mathbf{V}, \mathbf{T}, d_n).$$
(3.26)

The average value of A_n is the typical acceptance rate for the rejection sampler which gives an indication the computational inefficiency of this method.

Figure 3.1(a) shows the convergence of the training and test scores during the training of a RandOM model on a data set of $N = 100$ paths generated with noise $\eta = 0.01$. We find that even after the scores have plateaued, the values of $\mathbf{U}$ and $\mathbf{V}$ continue to evolve, indicating a flat objective function near the chosen solution. At convergence, the RandOM model considerably

Model	Training Score	Test Score	Test Acceptance
Baseline ($\oplus$: multiply)	-8.035	-8.655	1.0
+Rejection	-0.389	-0.572	0.003
Baseline ($\oplus$: add)	-7.594	-8.369	1.0
+Rejection	-0.337	-0.542	0.003
RandOM	-0.097(0%)	-0.337(3.5%)	1.0

Table 3.1: Quantitative results for data size 100 and noise 0.01. Numbers in parentheses indicate the sample failure rate.

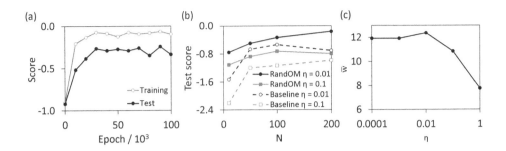

Figure 3.1: Performance of the RandOM model on the SPF problem. (a) Convergence of the training and test scores for a RandOM model trained on a data set with $N = 100$ and $\eta = 0.01$. (b) Comparison of the RandOM model with the baseline ($\oplus$: add) as a function of N for $\eta \in \{0.1, 0.01\}$. (c) The decay of the mean magnitude of the edge costs found by the RandOM model trained on $N = 100$ paths as the noise in the data set increases

outperforms the baseline models in predicting the shortest path taken by the drivers. This superiority remains true even with costly rejection sampling of the baseline model at test time (see table Table 3.1). We find that surprisingly few paths are required in the training data set for the RandOM model to achieve a good performance at test time (see Figure 3.1(b)), and for all parameters (N, η) we tested the RandOM model outperforms the baselines.

Besides inferring $\mathbf{U}$ and $\mathbf{V}$, we can also ask whether the RandOM model captures the noise in the training data. The RandOM model can represent variability in paths with a fixed standard deviation in (3.23) by changing the magnitude of $\boldsymbol{w}$; smaller (larger) values cause the fixed noise to have less (more) effect on which paths are chosen. Comparing (3.23) and (3.15), we expect the mean magnitude, $\bar{w}$, of the elements of $[\mathbf{U}^\top \mathbf{V} + b]$ to scale as η^{-1}. In Figure 3.1(c) we do not see this precise scaling, but we can correctly observe the decay of $\bar{w}$ with increasing η.

Here we have shown that the RandOM model quantitatively outperforms the baseline in a simple scenario. In the next section we describe a different scenario, which is engineered to highlight the key qualitative difference between the models.

3.8.4 Qualitative Results: Bias Resulting from Ignoring Combinatorial Structure

In the E step, the RandOM model only samples configurations of edge costs which are consistent with the shortest path structures observed in the data. The baseline model, in contrast, treats each edge independently,

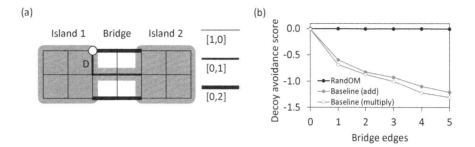

Figure 3.2: Biasing the baseline model. (a) By carefully arranging cheap, expensive and "impassable" edges (black lines), we implement a scenario resembling two islands linked by a bridge (grey outline). For the case illustrated the bridge contains 2 edges. We add the avoided decoy edge (D) and create a data set of paths starting at the circled node. (b) The score (representing the mean log probability oveer the test set of generating valid paths avoiding the decoy edge) for the RandOM model and baselines as a function of the bridge length.

and tries to learn to assign a high probability to edges used frequently in the training data (conditioning on the path start and end nodes). In this section we present an exaggerated scenario where the baseline's ignorance of the combinatorial structure in the data significantly hampers its performance.

We create a square grid graph that consists of three types of edge:

- "cheap" edges have feature vectors $[1, 0]$
- "expensive" edges have feature vectors $[0, 1]$
- "impassable" edges have feature vectors $[0, 2]$

The appropriate qualitative properties of these edges can be obtained by setting all driver feature vectors to $[v_n, 1]$, where $v_n \ll 1$. We build two separate "islands" of cheaply-linked nodes and connect these islands with impassable edges. Then we allow one path of expensive edges (a "busy bridge") to link the islands. Finally, we place a single "decoy" expensive edge on one of the islands which is never used in the ground truth paths due to it's cost (see Figure 3.2(a)). During training we give this carefully constructed $\mathbf{U}_{\text{gt}}$ to the models and only learn the remaining parameters.

If we observe drivers crossing from one island to the other, the baseline model will interpret the expensive edges on the bridge as being desirable, since they are used frequently. This bias means that the baseline will assign a significant probability for using the decoy edge even though this is inconsistent with the observed paths when correctly interpreting the constraints of the problem: if a driver is trying to get from one island to the other, there is no choice but to use the bridge, so the fact that the bridge is used should be irrelevant to determining the desirability of the decoy edge.

Instead, one should only look at whether the decoy edge is used or avoided, and in the data it is always avoided. The RandOM model correctly makes this inference and learns to avoid the decoy edge.

We generate a set of $N = 100$ training paths and separate set of 200 test paths on our engineered graph with edge cost noise $\eta = 0.01$. All paths start at one end of the decoy edge and finish at randomly chosen points on the graph.

Here we score the models by how often they produce samples which correctly avoid the decoy edge when trained on this data. For the RandOM model, the decoy avoidance score is computed as the average of Monte Carlo estimates of $\log\left(p(\boldsymbol{y} \in \mathcal{Y}_{\bar{D}}(s_n, t_n) \mid \mathbf{U}_{\text{gt}}, \mathbf{V}, d_n)\right)$ over the test set, where $\mathcal{Y}_{\bar{D}}(s_n, t_n)$ is the set of valid paths between s_n and t_n avoiding the decoy edge. For the baseline model, we again consider the case where invalid paths are rejected and compute the decoy avoidance score as

$$\frac{1}{N}\sum_n \left[\log\left(\sum_{\boldsymbol{y}\in\mathcal{Y}_{\bar{D}}(s_n,t_n)} p(\boldsymbol{y} \mid \mathbf{U}_{\text{gt}}, \mathbf{V}, \mathbf{T}, d_n)\right) - \log(A_n)\right]. \quad (3.27)$$

Figure 3.2(b) shows how these scores vary as we increase the length of the bridge between the islands. As the bridge extends there are more observations of drivers on expensive edges, which increasingly biases the baseline towards paths containing the decoy edge. In contrast, the RandOM model correctly interprets the shortest path structures in the data as indicating that the decoy edge is undesirable.

3.9   Related Work

There are several areas related to RandOMs. One place where there has been significant interest in perturbation-based models is in online learning, and in particular on Follow the Perturbed Leader algorithms (Kalai and Vempala, 2005). These algorithms have been applied to online learning in combinatorial settings such as shortest paths (Takimoto and Warmuth, 2003; Kalai and Vempala, 2005). See Chapter 8 for a detailed discussion of how perturbations are used and can be understood in the online learning setting.

For the purpose of semi-supervised learning, Blum et al. (2004) construct random graphs and find min-cuts that agree with labeled data. This leverages the idea of solving random combinatorial optimization problems, but no learning algorithm is presented. Perturb and MAP (P&M) (Papandreou and Yuille, 2011) learn structured models that involve a combinatorial optimization algorithm within the model definition, focusing on the case of using efficient minimum cut algorithms for image segmentation. The modelling formulation is very similar, although the RandOM formulation seems to extend more naturally to a broader range of models and optimization procedures. The main difference comes in the approach to learning. P&M proposes a moment-matching objective that is easy to optimize and that works well in practice, but the probabilistic underpinnings are less clear; i.e., learning is not directly maximizing the likelihood of observed data under the generative model. It is also not clear how, for example, P&M would be extended to a fully Bayesian treatment. Hazan and Jaakkola (2012) develops an understanding of how the expected score of the argmax configuration relates to the partition function of the more traditional Gibbs distribution. Gane et al. (2014) delves deeper into the correlation structure that results from using perturbation models with factorized perturbations.

There are other approaches to learning probabilistic structured prediction models to optimize high order utility functions. As mentioned previously, Gane et al. (2014) propose an improved Hard EM algorithm for the RandOM formulation that avoids a degeneracy that is heuristically worked around by Tarlow et al. (2012). Kim et al. (2015) employ an empirical risk minimization approach that directly minimizes expected losses in RandOM-like models using the combinatorial structure of the optimizer in order to do more efficient integration. Premachandran et al. (2014) propose a pragmatic approach of producing a set of diverse M-best proposals with combinatorial optimization algorithms (Batra et al., 2012), and then re-calibrating a probabilistic model over the proposals for use within a Bayesian decision theory-like decision procedure. The downside of this approach is that it is a two-stage procedure without a single objective function to optimize. For the shortest paths application, Ratliff et al. (2006) present a max-margin based approach that leverages efficient search procedure; however, there is no probabilistic interpretation.

A somewhat different line of work that shares the basic motivation is variational autoencoders (Kingma and Welling, 2014), generative adversarial networks (Goodfellow et al., 2014), and generative moment matching networks (Li et al., 2015). The generative adversarial networks and moment matching networks use different learning objectives from maximum likelihood. The commonality is that a generative model is built around highly efficient deterministic primitives; in these cases, rather than using a combinatorial optimization algorithm, these works use neural networks as the primitive. More precisely, if we let $\boldsymbol{w} = (\theta, \boldsymbol{u})$, where θ are neural network parameters and $\boldsymbol{u}$ is random noise, then we could define $F(\boldsymbol{w})$ to be the result of applying a neural network parameterized by θ to inputs $\boldsymbol{u}$. To make most sense in this analogy, the output should be a structured discrete object, such as a sentence. This formulation would apply equally if θ were a parameter or a random quantity as in Bayesian formulations of neural networks. The challenge with this direction is that in the RandOM formulation, $F^{-1}(\boldsymbol{y})$ is typically more structured than such a neural net formulation, which makes the sampling in the E step more plausibly effective. It is not immediately obvious, for example, how one would find a $\boldsymbol{w} = (\theta, \boldsymbol{u})$ such that $F(\boldsymbol{w}) = \boldsymbol{y}$ for a given a $\boldsymbol{y}$, much less sample from the space of such $\boldsymbol{w}$'s. However, if this could be done effectively then an MCEM algorithm analogous to the RandOM formulation would be a reasonable learning formulation.

3.10 Discussion

This chapter reviewed Randomized Optimum Models (RandOMs) and presented a new application of RandOMs to the problem of factorizing shortest paths into edge-specific and driver-specific trait vectors. The key computational challenge in RandOM formulations is developing a sampler for the E step of Monte Carlo EM. For this problem, slice sampling is particularly well-suited, and this chapter gives an additional illustration beyond Tarlow et al. (2012) about how to construct a slice sampler that takes advantage of the combinatorial structure in the problem. While it may be appealing to design simpler models that ignore the combinatorial structure present in the data (such as the baseline from Section 3.8.1), it is shown in Section 3.8.4 that this can lead to biases in the learned model that cause the wrong qualitative conclusions to be drawn from the observed data.

Looking forward, we would like to apply a similar formulation to models of highly structured natural data such as images and text, and to explore optimization routines beyond standard combinatorial optimization algorithms.

3.11 References

D. Batra, P. Yadollahpour, A. Guzman-Rivera, and G. Shakhnarovich. Diverse m-best solutions in markov random fields. In *Computer Vision–ECCV 2012*, pages 1–16. Springer, 2012.

A. Blum, J. Lafferty, M. R. Rwebangira, and R. Reddy. Semi-supervised learning using randomized mincuts. In *Proceedings of the twenty-first international conference on Machine learning*, page 13. ACM, 2004.

A. Bouchard-Côté and M. I. Jordan. Variational inference over combinatorial spaces. In *Advances in Neural Information Processing Systems*, pages 280–288, 2010.

T. H. Cormen, C. E. Leiserson, R. L. Rivest, and C. Stein. Introduction to algorithms.

A. P. Dempster, N. M. Laird, and D. B. Rubin. Maximum likelihood from incomplete data via the em algorithm. *Journal of the royal statistical society. Series B (methodological)*, pages 1–38, 1977.

M. Everingham, L. Van Gool, C. K. Williams, J. Winn, and A. Zisserman. The pascal visual object classes (voc) challenge. *International journal of computer vision*, 88(2):303–338, 2010.

A. Gane, T. Hazan, and T. Jaakkola. Learning with maximum a-posteriori perturbation models. In *Proceedings of the Seventeenth International Conference on Artificial Intelligence and Statistics*, pages 247–256, 2014.

I. Goodfellow, J. Pouget-Abadie, M. Mirza, B. Xu, D. Warde-Farley, S. Ozair, A. Courville, and Y. Bengio. Generative adversarial nets. In *Advances in Neural Information Processing Systems*, pages 2672–2680, 2014.

T. Hazan and T. Jaakkola. On the partition function and random maximum a-posteriori perturbations. *arXiv preprint arXiv:1206.6410*, 2012.

A. Kalai and S. Vempala. Efficient algorithms for online decision problems. *Journal of Computer and System Sciences*, 71(3):291–307, 2005.

A. Kim, K. Jung, Y. Lim, D. Tarlow, and P. Kohli. Minimizing expected losses in perturbation models with multidimensional parametric min-cuts. In *Proceedings of Uncertainty in Artificial Intelligence (UAI)*, 2015.

D. Kingma and M. Welling. Auto-encoding variational bayes. In *International Conference on Learning Representations*, 2014.

R. Kiros, R. Salakhutdinov, and R. Zemel. Multimodal neural language models. In *Proceedings of the 31st International Conference on Machine Learning (ICML-14)*, pages 595–603, 2014.

D. Koller and N. Friedman. *Probabilistic graphical models: principles and techniques.* 2009.

A. Krizhevsky, G. E. Hinton, et al. Factored 3-way restricted boltzmann machines for modeling natural images. In *International Conference on Artificial Intelligence and Statistics*, pages 621–628, 2010.

Y. Li, K. Swersky, and R. Zemel. Generative moment matching networks. *arXiv preprint arXiv:1502.02761*, 2015.

L. Lovász and S. Vempala. Hit-and-run is fast and fun. 2003.

J. Lubin. A human vision system model for objective image fidelity and target detectability measurements. In *Proc. EUSIPCO*, volume 98, pages 1069–1072, 1998.

R. Memisevic and G. Hinton. Unsupervised learning of image transformations. In *Computer Vision and Pattern Recognition, 2007. CVPR'07. IEEE Conference on*, pages 1–8. IEEE, 2007.

V. Movahedi and J. H. Elder. Design and perceptual validation of performance measures for salient object segmentation. In *Computer Vision and Pattern Recognition Workshops (CVPRW), 2010 IEEE Computer Society Conference on*, pages 49–56. IEEE, 2010.

R. M. Neal. Slice sampling. *Annals of Statistics*, 31(3):705–767, 2003.

R. M. Neal and G. E. Hinton. A new view of the EM algorithm that justifies incremental and other variants. In M. I. Jordan, editor, *Learning in Graphical Models*. Kluwer, Dordrecht, Netherlands, 1998.

A. T. Nguyen, T. T. Nguyen, and T. N. Nguyen. Migrating code with statistical machine translation. In *Companion Proceedings of the 36th International Conference on Software Engineering*, pages 544–547. ACM, 2014.

S. Nowozin. Optimal decisions from probabilistic models: the intersection-over-union case. In *Computer Vision and Pattern Recognition (CVPR), 2014 IEEE Conference on*, pages 548–555. IEEE, 2014.

G. Papandreou and A. Yuille. Perturb-and-MAP random fields: Using discrete optimization to learn and sample from energy models. In *Proceedings of the IEEE International Conference on Computer Vision*, 2011.

P. Pletscher and P. Kohli. Learning low-order models for enforcing high-order statistics. In *AISTATS*, 2012.

V. Premachandran, D. Tarlow, and D. Batra. Empirical minimum bayes risk prediction: How to extract an extra few% performance from vision models with just three more parameters. In *Computer Vision and Pattern Recognition (CVPR), 2014 IEEE Conference on*, pages 1043–1050. IEEE, 2014.

N. Ratliff, J. A. Bagnell, and M. Zinkevich. Maximum margin planning. In *International Conference on Machine Learning*, 2006.

J. D. Rennie and N. Srebro. Fast maximum margin matrix factorization for collaborative prediction. In *Proceedings of the 22nd international conference on Machine learning*, pages 713–719. ACM, 2005.

C. Robert and G. Casella. *Monte Carlo statistical methods*. Springer Science & Business Media, 2013.

R. Salakhutdinov and A. Mnih. Probabilistic matrix factorization. In *Advances in neural information processing systems*, pages 1257–1264, 2007.

E. Takimoto and M. K. Warmuth. Path kernels and multiplicative updates. *The Journal of Machine Learning Research*, 4:773–818, 2003.

D. Tarlow and R. Zemel. Structured output learning with high order loss functions. In *Artificial Intelligence and Statistics (AISTATS)*, 2012.

D. Tarlow, R. P. Adams, and R. S. Zemel. Randomized optimum models for structured prediction. In *Artificial Intelligence and Statistics (AISTATS)*, 2012.

B. Taskar, C. Guestrin, and D. Koller. Max-margin markov networks. In *Advances in Neural Information Processing Systems 16: Proceedings of the 2003 Conference*, volume 16, page 25. MIT Press, 2004.

I. Tsochantaridis, T. Joachims, T. Hofmann, and Y. Altun. Large margin methods for structured and interdependent output variables. *Journal of Machine Learning Research (JMLR)*, 6:1453–1484, 2005.

L. G. Valiant. The complexity of computing the permanent. *Theoretical computer science*, 8(2):189–201, 1979.

Z. Wang, A. C. Bovik, H. R. Sheikh, and E. P. Simoncelli. Image quality assessment: from error visibility to structural similarity. *Image Processing, IEEE Transactions on*, 13(4):600–612, 2004.

G. C. Wei and M. A. Tanner. A monte carlo implementation of the em algorithm and the poor man's data augmentation algorithms. *Journal of the American statistical Association*, 85(411):699–704, 1990.

4

Herding as a Learning System with Edge-of-Chaos Dynamics

Yutian Chen　　　　　　　　　yutianc@google.com
Google DeepMind
London, UK

Max Welling　　　　　　　　　m.welling@uva.nl
University of Amsterdam
Amsterdam, Netherlands

Herding defines a deterministic dynamical system at the edge of chaos. It generates a sequence of model states and parameters by alternating parameter perturbations with state maximizations, where the sequence of states can be interpreted as "samples" from an associated MRF model. Herding differs from maximum likelihood estimation in that the sequence of parameters does not converge to a fixed point and differs from an MCMC posterior sampling approach in that the sequence of states is generated deterministically. Herding may be interpreted as a "perturb and map" method where the parameter perturbations are generated using a deterministic nonlinear dynamical system rather than randomly from a Gumbel distribution. This chapter studies the distinct statistical characteristics of the herding algorithm and shows that the fast convergence rate of the controlled moments may be attributed to edge of chaos dynamics. The herding algorithm can also be generalized to models with latent variables and to a discriminative learning setting. The perceptron cycling theorem ensures that the fast moment matching property is preserved in the more general framework.

4.1 Introduction

The traditional view of a learning system is one where an initial parameter vector $\mathbf{w}_0$ is updated until some convergence criterion is met: $\mathbf{w}_0, \mathbf{w}_1, .., \mathbf{w}_T$ with (in theory) $T \to \infty$ and $\mathbf{w}_\infty = \mathbf{w}^*$ a fixed point of the updates. These updates usually maximize some objective such as the log-likelihood of the data. We can view this process as a dynamical system with a contractive map $\mathbf{w}_{t+1} = F_t(\mathbf{w}_t)$ which is designed to iterate to a fixed point. The map F_t can be either deterministic or stochastic. For instance, batch gradient descent is an example of a deterministic map while stochastic gradient descent is an example of a stochastic map. A natural question is whether the existence of a fixed point $\mathbf{w}^*$ is important, and whether meaningful learning systems can exist that do not converge to any fixed point but traverse an attractor set. To answer this question we can draw inspiration from Markov chain Monte Carlo (MCMC) procedures which generate samples from a posterior distribution $P(\mathbf{w}|\mathcal{D})$ (with $\mathcal{D}$ indicating the data). MCMC also generates a sequence of parameter values $\mathbf{w}_0, .., \mathbf{w}_T$ but one that does not converge to a fixed point. Rather the samples form an attractor set with a measure (density) equal to the posterior distribution. One can make meaningful predictions with MCMC chains by making predictions for every sampled model $\mathbf{w}_t$ separately and subsequently averaging the predictions. There is also evidence that learning in the brain is a dynamical process. For instance, Aihara and Matsumoto (1982) have described chaotic dynamics in the Hodgkin-Huxley equations for membrane dynamics and studied them experimentally in squid giant axons. Also, much evidence has now been accumulated that synapses are subject to fast dynamical processes such as postsynaptic depression and facilitation (Tsodyks et al., 1098).

Herding (Welling, 2009a) is perhaps the first learning dynamical system based on a deterministic map and with a nontrivial attractor (i.e. not a single fixed point). It emerged from taking the limit of infinite stepsize in the usual (maximum likelihood) updates for a Markov random field (MRF) model. It can be observed that in this limit the parameters will not converge to a fixed point but rather traverse a usually non-periodic trajectory in weight space. The information contained in the data is now stored in the trajectories (or the attractor) of this dynamical system, rather than in a point estimate of a collection of parameters. In fact it can be shown that this dynamical system is neither periodic (under some conditions) nor chaotic, a state which is associated with "edge of chaos" dynamics. As illustrated in this chapter, by slowly increasing the stepsize (or equivalently lowering the temperature) we will move from a standard MRF maximum likelihood learning system with a single fixed point, through a series of period doublings to a system on the edge of chaos. One can show that the attractor is sometimes fractal, and that the Lyapunov exponents of this system are equal to 0 implying that two nearby trajectories will eventually separate but only polynomially fast (and not exponentially fast as with chaotic systems). Many of the dynamical properties of this system are described by the theory of "piecewise isometries" (Goetz, 2000).

Herding can thus be viewed as a dynamical system that generates state-space samples $\mathbf{s}_1, .., \mathbf{s}_T$ that are highly similar to the samples that would be generated by a learned MRF model with the same features. The state-space samples satisfy the usual moment matching constraints that defines an MRF and can be used for making meaningful predictions. In a way, herding combines learning and inference in one dynamical system. However, the distribution from which herding generates samples is not identical to the associated MRF because while the same moment matching constraints are satisfied, the entropy of the herding samples is usually somewhat lower than the (maximal) entropy of the MRF. The sequence of samples in state space $\mathbf{s}_1, .., \mathbf{s}_T$ has very interesting properties. First, it forms an infinite memory sequence as every sample depends on all the previous samples and not just the most recent sample as in Markov sequences. It can be shown that the number of distinct subsequences of length T grows as $\mathcal{O}(\log(T))$ implying that their (topological) entropy vanishes. For simple systems these sequences can be identified with "low discrepancy sequences" and Sturmian sequences (Marston Morse, 1940). Probably related to this is the fact that Monte Carlo averages based on these sequences converge as $\mathcal{O}(1/T)$. This should be contrasted with random independent samples from the associated MRF distribution for which the convergence follows the usual $\mathcal{O}(1/\sqrt{T})$ rate. Herding sequences thus exhibit strong negative auto-correlations leading to the faster convergence of Monte Carlo averages. It is conjectured that this property is related to the edge of chaos characterization of herding, and that both stochastic systems (such as samplers) as well as fully chaotic systems will always generate samples that can at most result in $\mathcal{O}(1/\sqrt{T})$ convergence of Monte Carlo averages.

Similar to "perturb and map" (Papandreou and Yuille, 2011), the execution of the herding map requires one to compute the maximum a posteriori (MAP) state defined by the current parameter setting. While maximization is sometimes easier than computing the expectations required to update the parameters of an MRF, for complex models maximization can also be NP hard. A natural question is therefore if one can relax the requirement of finding the MAP state and get away with partial maximization to, say, a local maximum instead of the global maximum. The answer to this question comes from a theorem that was proven a long time ago in the context of Rosenblatt's perceptron (Rosenblatt, 1958) and is known as the "perceptron cycling theorem" (PCT) (Minsky and Papert, 1969). This theorem states precisely which conditions need to be fulfilled by herding at every iteration in order for the algorithm to satisfy the moment constraints. The PCT therefore allows us to relax the condition of finding the MAP state at every iteration, and as a side effect also allows us to run herding in an online setting or with stochastic minibatches instead of the entire dataset. A further relaxation of the herding conditions was described in Chen et al. (2014) where it was shown that herding with *inconsistent* moments as input (moments that can not be generated by a single joint probability distribution) still makes sense and generates the Euclidean projections of these moments on the marginal polytope.

Like MRF models can be extended to models with hidden variables and to discriminative models such as the conditional Markov random field (CRF) models, herding can also be generalized along these same dimensions. Herding with hidden variables was described in Welling (2009b) and shown to increase the ability of this dynamical system to represent complex dependencies. Conditional herding was described in Gelfand et al. (2010) and shown to be equivalent to the voted perceptron algorithm Freund and Schapire (1999) and to Collins' "voted HMM" Collins (2002) in certain special cases. The herding view allowed the extension of these discriminative models to include hidden variables.

Herding is related to (or has been connected to) a number of optimization, learning and inference methods. Herding has obvious similarities to the concept of "fast weights" introduced by Tieleman and Hinton (2009). Fast weights follow a dynamics that is designed to make the Markov chain embedded in a MRF learning process mix fast. A similar idea was used in Breuleux et al. (2011) to speed up the mixing rate of an (approximate) sampling procedure. By applying herding dynamics conditionally w.r.t. its parent-states for every variable in a graphical model yet another fast mixing sampling algorithm was developed, called "herded Gibbs" Bornn et al. (2013). Herding was extended in Chen et al. (2010) to a deterministic sampling algorithm in continuous state spaces (known as "kernel herding"). The view espoused in that paper led to an analysis of herding as a conditional gradient optimization algorithm (or Franke-Wolfe algorithm) in Bach et al. (2012) from which an improved convergence analysis emerged as well generalizations to versions of herding with non-uniform weights. In related work of Huszar and Duvenaud (2012) it was shown that an optimally weighted version of (kernel) herding is equivalent to Bayesian quadrature, again resulting in faster convergence. Harvey and Samadi (2014) focused on the convergence rate of herding with respect to the dimensionality of the feature vector and proposed a new algorithm that scaled near-optimally with the dimensionality.

Perhaps the method closest related to herding is "perturb and map" estimation, where the parameters of a MRF model are perturbed by sampling from a Gumbel distribution followed by maximization over the states. Like in herded Gibbs, the procedure is only "exact" if exponentially many parameters are perturbed. Herding is however different from perturb and map in that the perturbations are generated sequentially and deterministically.

This chapter is built on the results reported earlier in a series of conference papers Welling (2009a,b); Welling and Chen (2010); Chen et al. (2010); Gelfand et al. (2010). Our current understanding of herding is far from comprehensive but rather represents a first attempt to connect learning systems with the theory of nonlinear dynamical systems and chaos. We believe that it opens the door to many new directions of research with potentially surprising and exciting discoveries.

The chapter is organized as follows. In Section 4.2 we introduce the herding algorithm and study its statistical property as both a learning algorithm and a dynamical system. In Section 4.3 we provide a general condition for herding to satisfy the fast moment matching properties, under which the algorithm is extended for partially observed models and discriminative models. We evaluate the performance of the introduced algorithms empirically in Section 6.4. The chapter is concluded with a summary in Section 4.5 and a conclusion in Section 4.6.

4.2 Herding Model Parameters

4.2.1 The Maximum Entropy Problem and Markov Random Fields

Define $\mathbf{x} \in \mathcal{X}$ to be a random variable in the domain $\mathcal{X}$, and $\phi = \{\phi_\alpha(\mathbf{x})\}$ to be a set of feature functions of $\mathbf{x}$, indexed by α. In the maximum entropy problem (MaxEnt), given a data set of D observations $\mathcal{D} = \{\mathbf{x}_i\}_{i=1}^{D}$, we want to learn a probability distribution over $\mathbf{x}$, $P(\mathbf{x})$, such that the expected features, a.k.a. moments, match the average value observed in the data set, denoted by $\bar{\phi}_\alpha$. For the remaining degrees of freedom in the distribution we assume maximum ignorance which is expressed as maximum entropy. Mathematically, the problem is to find a distribution P such that:

$$P = \arg \max_{\mathcal{P}} \mathcal{H}(\mathcal{P}) \quad \text{s.t. } \mathbb{E}_{\mathbf{x} \sim \mathcal{P}}[\phi_\alpha(\mathbf{x})] = \bar{\phi}_\alpha, \ \forall \alpha \tag{4.1}$$

The dual form of the MaxEnt problem is known to be equivalent to finding the maximum likelihood estimate (MLE) of the parameters $\mathbf{w} = \{w_\alpha\}$ of a

Markov Random Field (MRF) defined on $\mathbf{x}$, each parameter associated with one feature ϕ_α:

$$\mathbf{w}_{\mathrm{MLE}} = \arg\max_{\mathbf{w}} P(\mathcal{D}; \mathbf{w}) = \arg\max_{\mathbf{w}} \prod_{i=1}^{D} P(\mathbf{x}_i; \mathbf{w}), \tag{4.2}$$

$$P(\mathbf{x}; \mathbf{w}) = \frac{1}{Z(\mathbf{w})} \exp\left(\sum_{\alpha} w_\alpha \phi_\alpha(\mathbf{x})\right), \tag{4.3}$$

where the normalization term $Z(\mathbf{w}) = \sum_{\mathbf{x}} \exp(\sum_{\alpha} w_\alpha \phi_\alpha(\mathbf{x}))$ is also called the partition function. The parameters $\{w_\alpha\}$ act as Lagrange multipliers to enforce the constraints in the primal form 4.1. Since they assign different weights to the features in the dual form, we will also called them "weights" below.

It is generally intractable to obtain the MLE of parameters because the partition function involves computing the sum of potentially exponentially many states. Take the gradient descent optimization algorithm for example. Denote the average log-likelihood per data item by

$$\ell(\mathbf{w}) \stackrel{\text{def}}{=} \frac{1}{D} \sum_{i=1}^{D} \log P(\mathbf{x}_i; \mathbf{w}) = \mathbf{w}^T \bar{\phi} - \log Z(\mathbf{w}) \tag{4.4}$$

The gradient descent algorithm searches for the maximum of ℓ with the following update step:

$$\mathbf{w}_{t+1} = \mathbf{w}_t + \eta(\bar{\phi} - \mathbb{E}_{\mathbf{x} \sim P(\mathbf{x}; \mathbf{w}_t)}[\phi(\mathbf{x})]) \tag{4.5}$$

Notice however that the second term in the gradient that averages over the model distribution, $\mathbb{E}_{P(\mathbf{x}; \mathbf{w})}[\phi(\mathbf{x})]$, is derived from the partition function and cannot be computed efficiently in general. A common solution is to approximate that quantity by drawing samples using Markov chain Monte Carlo (MCMC) at each gradient descent step. However, MCMC is known to suffer from slow mixing when the state distribution has multiple modes or variables are strongly correlated (Neal, 1993). Furthermore, we can usually afford to run MCMC for only a few iterations in the nested loop for the sake of efficiency (Neal, 1992; Tieleman, 2008), which makes it even harder to obtain an accurate estimate of the gradient.

Even when the MRF is well trained, it is usually difficult to apply the model to regular tasks such as inference, density estimation, and model selection, because all of those tasks require the computation of the partition function. One has to once more resort to running MCMC or other approximate inference methods during the prediction phase to obtain an approximation.

Is there a method to speed up the inference step that exists in both the training and test phases? The herding algorithm was proposed to address the slow mixing problem of MCMC and combine the execution of MCMC in both training and prediction phases into a single process.

4.2.2 Learning MRFs with Herding

When there exist multiple local modes in a model distribution, an MCMC sampler is prone to getting stuck in local modes and it becomes difficult to explore the state space efficiently. However, that is not a serious issue at the beginning of the MRF learning procedure as observed by, for example, Tieleman and Hinton (2009). This is because the parameters keep being updated with a large learning rate η at the beginning. Specifically, when the expected feature vector is approximated by a set of samples $\mathbb{E}_{P(\mathbf{x};\mathbf{w})}[\phi(\mathbf{x})] \approx \frac{1}{M} \sum_{m=1}^{M} \phi(\mathbf{x}_m)$ in the MCMC approach, after each update in Equation 4.5, the parameter $\mathbf{w}$ is translated along the direction that tends to reduce the inner product of $\mathbf{w}^T \phi(\mathbf{x}_m)$, and thereby reduces the state probability around the region of the current samples. This change in the state distribution helps the MCMC sampler escape local optima and mix faster.

This observation suggests that we can speed up the MCMC algorithm by updating the target distribution itself with a large learning rate. However, in order to converge to a point estimate of a model, η needs to be decreased using some suitable annealing schedule. But one may ask if we are necessarily interested in a fixed value for the model parameters? As discussed in the previous subsection, for many applications one needs to compute averages over the (converged) model which are intractable anyway. In that case, a sequence of samples to approximate the averages is all we need. It then becomes a waste of resources and time to nail down a single point estimate of the parameters by decreasing η when a sequence of samples is already available. We will actually kill two birds with one stone by obtaining samples during the training phase and reuse them for making predictions. The idea of the herding algorithm originates from this observation.

The herding algorithm proposed in Welling (2009a) can be considered as an algorithm that runs a gradient descent algorithm with a constant learning rate on an MRF in the zero-temperature limit. Define the distribution of an MRF with a temperature by replacing $\mathbf{w}$ with $\mathbf{w}/T$, where T is an artificial temperature variable. The log-likelihood of a model (multiplied by T) then becomes:

$$\ell_T(\mathbf{w}) = \mathbf{w}^T \bar{\phi} - T \log \left(\sum_{\mathbf{x}} \exp \left(\sum_{\alpha} \frac{w_\alpha}{T} \phi_\alpha(\mathbf{x}) \right) \right) \qquad (4.6)$$

When T approaches 0, all the probability is absorbed into the most probable state, denoted as $\mathbf{s}$, and the expectation of the feature vector, $\bar{\phi}$, equals that of state $\mathbf{s}$. The herding algorithm then consists of the iterative gradient descent updates in the limit, $T \to 0$, with a constant learning rate, η:

$$\mathbf{s}_t = \arg\max_{\mathbf{x}} \sum_{\alpha} w_{\alpha,t-1} \phi_{\alpha}(\mathbf{x}) \tag{4.7}$$

$$\mathbf{w}_t = \mathbf{w}_{t-1} + \eta(\bar{\phi} - \phi(\mathbf{s}_t)) \tag{4.8}$$

We usually set $\eta = 1$ except when mentioned explicitly because the herding dynamics is invariant to the learning rate as explained in Section 4.2.3. We treat the sequence of most probable states, $\{\mathbf{s}_t\}$, as a set of "samples" for herding and use it for inference tasks. At each iteration, we find the most probable state in the current model distribution deterministically, and update the parameter towards the average feature vector from the training data subtracted by the feature vector of the current sample. Compared to maintaining a set of random samples in the MCMC approach (see e.g. Tieleman, 2008), updating $\mathbf{w}$ with a single sample state facilitates updating the distribution at an even rate.

If we divide both sides of Equation 4.8 by T and redefine $\frac{\mathbf{w}}{T} \to \mathbf{w}'$ in both Equations 4.7-4.8,

$$\frac{\mathbf{w}_{t+1}}{T} = \frac{\mathbf{w}_t}{T} + \frac{\eta}{T}(\bar{\phi} - \mathbb{E}_{\mathbf{x} \sim P(\mathbf{x}; \frac{\mathbf{w}_t}{T})}[\phi(\mathbf{x})]) \tag{4.9}$$

we see that, after taking the limit $T \to \infty$, we can interpret herding as maximum likelihood learning with infinitely large stepsize and rescaled weights. The surprising observation is that the state sequence $\{\mathbf{s}_t\}$ generated by this process is still meaningful and can be interpreted as approximate samples from an MRF model with the correct moment constraints on the features $\phi(\mathbf{x})$.

One can obtain an intuitive impression of the dynamics of herding by looking at the change in the asymptotic behavior of the gradient descent algorithm as we decrease T in Equation 4.9 from a large value towards 0. Assume that we can compute the expected feature vector w.r.t. the model exactly. Given an initial value of $\mathbf{w}$, the gradient descent update equation 4.9 with a constant learning rate is a deterministic mapping in the parameter space. When T is large enough (η/T is small enough), the optimization process will converge and $\mathbf{w}/T$ will approach a single point which is the MLE. As T decreases below some threshold (η/T is above some threshold), the convergence condition is violated and the trajectory of $\mathbf{w}_t$ will move asymptotically into an oscillation between two points, that is,

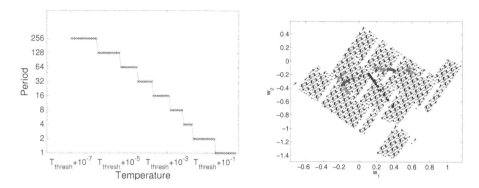

Figure 4.1: Attractor bifurcation for a model with 4 states and 2-dimensional feature vectors. Left: Asymptotic period of the weight sequence (i.e. size of the attractor set) repeatedly doubles as the temperature decreases towards a threshold value (right to left). $T_{thresh} \approx 0.116$ in this example. The dynamics transits from periodic to aperiodic at that threshold. Right: The evolution of the attractor set of the weight sequence. As the temperature decreases (from dark to light colors), the attractor set split from a single point to two points, then to four, to eight, etc. The black dot cloud in the background is the attractor set at $T = 0$.

the attractor set splits from a single point into two points. As T decreases further, the asymptotic oscillation period doubles from two to four, four to eight, etc, and eventually the process approaches an infinite period at another temperature threshold. Figure 4.1 shows an example of the attractor bifurcation phenomenon. The example model has 4 discrete states and each state is associated with 2 real valued features which are randomly sampled from $\mathcal{N}(0, 1)$. Starting from that second threshold, the trajectory of $\mathbf{w}$ is still bounded in a finite region as shown shortly in Section 4.3.1 but will not be periodic any more. Instead, we observe that the dynamics often converges to a fractal attractor set as shown in the right plot of Figure 4.1. The bifurcation process is observed very often in simulated models although it is not clear to us if it always happens for any discrete MRF. We discuss the dynamics related to this phenomenon in more detail in Section 4.2.6.

4.2.3 Tipi Function and Basic Properties of Herding

We will discuss a few distinguishing properties of the herding algorithm in this subsection. When we take the zero temperature limit in Equation 4.6, the log-likelihood function becomes

$$\ell_0(\mathbf{w}) = \mathbf{w}^T \bar{\boldsymbol{\phi}} - \max_{\mathbf{x}} \left[\mathbf{w}^T \boldsymbol{\phi}(\mathbf{x}) \right] \tag{4.10}$$

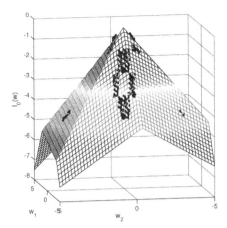

Figure 4.2: "Tipi function"(Welling, 2009a): the log-likelihood function at the zero temperature limit. The black dots show the attractor set of the sequence of $\mathbf{w}_t$.

This function has a number of interesting properties that justify the name "Tipi function"[1] (see Figure 4.2) (Welling, 2009a):

1. *ℓ_0 is continuous piecewise linear (C^0 but not C^1).* It is clearly linear in $\mathbf{w}$ as long as the maximizing state $\mathbf{s}$ does not change. However, changing $\mathbf{w}$ may in fact change the maximizing state in which case the gradient changes discontinuously.

2. *ℓ_0 is a concave, non-positive function of $\mathbf{w}$ with a maximum at $\ell_0(\mathbf{0}) = 0$.* This is true because the first term represents the average $\mathbb{E}_P[\mathbf{w}^T \boldsymbol{\phi}(\mathbf{x})]$ over some distribution P, while the second term is its maximum. Therefore, $\ell \leqq 0$. If we furthermore assume that $\boldsymbol{\phi}$ is not constant on the support of P then $\ell_0 < 0$ and the maximum at $\mathbf{w} = 0$ is unique. Concavity follows because the first term is linear and the second maximization term is convex.

3. *ℓ_0 is scale free.* This follows because $\ell_0(\beta\mathbf{w}) = \beta\ell_0(\mathbf{w}), \forall \beta \geq 0$ as can be easily checked. This means that the function has exactly the same structure at any scale of $\mathbf{w}$.

Herding runs gradient descent optimization on this Tipi function. There is no need to search for the maximum as $\mathbf{w} = 0$ is the trivial solution. However, the fixed learning rate will always result in a perpetual overshooting of the maximum and thus the sequence of weights will never converge to a fixed point. Every flat face of the Tipi function is associated with a state. An important property of herding is that the state sequence visited by the

---

1. A Tipi is a traditional native Indian dwelling.

gradient descent procedure satisfies the moment matching constraints in Equation 4.1, which will be discussed in details in Section 4.2.5. There are a few more properties of this procedure that are worth noticing.

Deterministic Nonlinear Dynamics

Herding is a deterministic nonlinear dynamical system. In contrast to the stochastic MLE learning algorithm based on MCMC, the two update steps in Equation 4.7 and 4.8 consist of a nonlinear deterministic mapping of the weights as illustrated in Figure 4.3. In particular it is not an MCMC procedure and it does not require random number generation.

The dynamics thus produces pseudo-samples that look random, but should not be interpreted as random samples. Although reminiscent of the Bayesian approach, the weights generated during this dynamics should not be interpreted as samples from some Bayesian posterior distribution. We will discuss the weakly chaotic behavior of the herding dynamics in detail in Section 4.2.6.

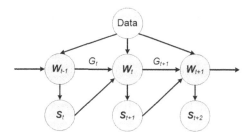

Figure 4.3: Herding as a nonlinear dynamical system.

Invariance to the Learning Rate

Varying the learning rate η does not change the behavior of the herding dynamics. The only effect is to change the scale of the invariant attractor set of the sequence $\mathbf{w}_t$. This actually follows naturally from the scale-free property of the Tipi function. More precisely, denote with $\mathbf{v}_t$ the standard herding sequence with $\eta = 1$ and $\mathbf{w}_t$ the sequence with an arbitrary learning rate. It is easy to see that if we initialize $\mathbf{v}_{t=0} = \frac{1}{\eta}\mathbf{w}_{t=0}$ and apply the respective herding updates for $\mathbf{w}_t$ and $\mathbf{v}_t$ afterwards, the relation $\mathbf{v}_t = \frac{1}{\eta}\mathbf{w}_t$ will remain true for all $t > 0$. In particular, the states $\mathbf{s}_t$ will be the same for both sequences. Therefore we simply set $\eta = 1$ in the herding algorithm.

Of course, if one initializes both sequences with arbitrary different values, then the state sequences will not be identical. However, if one accepts the conjecture that there is a unique invariant attractor set, then this difference can be interpreted as a difference in initialization which only affects the transient behavior (or "burn-in" behavior) but not the (marginal) distribution $P(\mathbf{s})$ from which the states $\mathbf{s}_t$ will be sampled.

Notice however that if we assign different learning rates $\{\eta_\alpha\}$ across the dimensions of the weight vector $\{w_\alpha\}$, it will change the distribution $P(\mathbf{s})$. While the moment matching constraints are still satisfied, we notice that the entropy of the sample distribution varies as a function of $\{\eta_\alpha\}$. In fact, changing the relative ratio of learning rates among feature dimensions is equivalent to scaling features with different factors in the greedy moment matching algorithm interpretation of Section 4.2.4. How to choose an optimal set of learning rates is still an open problem.

Negative Auto-correlation

A key advantage of the herding algorithm we observed in practice over sampling using a Markov chain is that the dynamical system mixes very rapidly over the attractor set. This is attributed to the fact that maximizations are performed on an ever changing model distribution as briefly mentioned at the beginning of this subsection. Let $\pi(\mathbf{x})$ be the distribution of training data $\mathcal{D}$, and $\mathbf{s}_t$ be the maximizing state at time t. The distribution of an MRF at time t with a regular temperature $T = 1$ is

$$P(\mathbf{x}; \mathbf{w}_{t-1}) \propto \exp(\mathbf{w}_{t-1}^T \boldsymbol{\phi}(\mathbf{x})) \tag{4.11}$$

After the weights are updated with Equation 4.8, the probability of the new model becomes

$$P(\mathbf{x}; \mathbf{w}_t) \propto \exp(\mathbf{w}_t^T \boldsymbol{\phi}(\mathbf{x})) = \exp((\mathbf{w}_{t-1} + \bar{\boldsymbol{\phi}} - \boldsymbol{\phi}(\mathbf{s}_t))^T \boldsymbol{\phi}(\mathbf{x}))$$

$$= \exp\left(\mathbf{w}_{t-1}^T \boldsymbol{\phi}(\mathbf{x}) + \sum_{\mathbf{y} \neq \mathbf{s}_t} \pi(\mathbf{y}) \boldsymbol{\phi}(\mathbf{y})^T \boldsymbol{\phi}(\mathbf{x}) - (1 - \pi(\mathbf{s}_t)) \boldsymbol{\phi}(\mathbf{s}_t)^T \boldsymbol{\phi}(\mathbf{x}) \right)$$

$$\tag{4.12}$$

Comparing Equation 4.12 with 4.11 we see that probable states (with large $\pi(\mathbf{x})$) are rewarded with an extra positive term $\pi(\mathbf{x}) \boldsymbol{\phi}(\mathbf{x})^T \boldsymbol{\phi}(\mathbf{x})$, *except* the most recently sampled state $\mathbf{s}_t$. This will have the effect (after normalization) that state $\mathbf{s}_t$ will have a smaller probability of being selected again. Imagine for instance that the sampler is stuck at a local mode. After drawing samples at that mode for a while, weights are updated to gradually reduce that mode and help the sampler escape it. The resulting negative auto-correlation would help mitigate the notorious problem of positive auto-correlation in most MCMC methods.

We illustrate the negative auto-correlation using a synthetic MRF with 10 discrete states, each associated with a 7-dimensional feature vector. The parameters of the MRF model are randomly generated from which the expected feature values are then computed analytically and fed into the herding algorithm to draw $T = 10^5$ samples. We define the auto-correlation of the sample sequence of discrete variables as follows:

$$R(t) = \frac{\frac{1}{T-t}\sum_{\tau=1}^{T-t}\mathbb{I}[s_\tau = s_{\tau+t}] - \sum_s \frac{1}{2}tP(s)^2}{1 - \sum_s \frac{1}{2}tP(s)^2} \tag{4.13}$$

where $\mathbb{I}$ is the indication function and $\frac{1}{2}tP$ is the empirical distribution of the 10^5 samples. It is easy to observe that $R(t=0) = 1$ and if the samples are independently distributed $R(t) = 0, \forall t > 0$ up to a small error due to the finite sample size. We run herding 100 times with different model parameters and show the mean and standard deviation of the auto-correlation in Figure 4.4. We can see that the auto-correlation is negative for neighboring samples, and converges to 0 as the time lag increases. This effect exists even if we use a local optimization algorithm when a global optimum is hard or expensive to be obtained. This type of "self-avoidance" is also shared with other sampling methods such as over-relaxation (Young, 1954), fast-weights PCD (Tieleman and Hinton, 2009) and adaptive MCMC (Salakhutdinov, 2010).

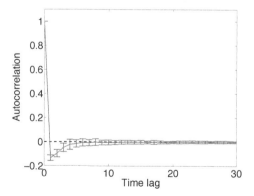

Figure 4.4: Negative auto-correlation of herding samples from a synthetic MRF.

4.2.4　Herding as a Greedy Moment Matching Algorithm

As herding does not obtain the MLE, the distribution of the generated samples does not provide a solution to the maximum entropy problem either. However, we observe that the moment matching constraints in Equation 4.1 are still respected, that is, when we compute the sampling average of the feature vector it will converge to the input moments. Furthermore, the negative auto-correlation in the sample sequence helps to achieve a convergence rate that is faster than what one would get from independently drawing samples or running MCMC at the MLE. Before providing any quantitative results, it would be easier for us to understand herding intuitively by taking a "dual view" of its dynamics where we remove weights $\mathbf{w}$ in favor of the states $\mathbf{x}$ (Chen et al., 2010).

Notice that the expression of $\mathbf{w}_T$ can be expanded recursively using the update Equation 4.8:

$$\mathbf{w}_T = \mathbf{w}_0 + T\bar{\phi} - \sum_{t=1}^{T} \phi(\mathbf{s}_t) \qquad (4.14)$$

Plugging 4.14 into Equation 4.7 results in

$$\mathbf{s}_{T+1} = \arg\max_{\mathbf{x}} \langle \mathbf{w}_0, \phi(\mathbf{x}) \rangle + T\langle \bar{\phi}, \phi(\mathbf{x}) \rangle - \sum_{t=1}^{T} \langle \phi(\mathbf{s}_t), \phi(\mathbf{x}) \rangle \qquad (4.15)$$

For ease of intuitive understanding of herding, we temporarily make the assumptions (which are not necessary for the propositions to hold in the next subsection):

1. $\mathbf{w}_0 = \bar{\phi}$
2. $\|\phi(\mathbf{x})\|_2 = R, \forall \mathbf{x} \in \mathcal{X}$

The second assumption is easily achieved, e.g. by renormalizing $\phi(\mathbf{x}) \leftarrow \frac{\phi(\mathbf{x})}{\|\phi(\mathbf{x})\|}$ or by choosing a suitable feature map ϕ in the first place. Given the first assumption, Equation 4.15 becomes

$$\mathbf{s}_{T+1} = \arg\max_{\mathbf{x}} \langle \bar{\phi}, \phi(\mathbf{x}) \rangle - \frac{1}{T+1} \sum_{t=1}^{T} \langle \phi(\mathbf{s}_t), \phi(\mathbf{x}) \rangle \qquad (4.16)$$

Combining the second assumption one can show that the herding update equation 4.16 is equivalent to greedily minimizing the squared error $\mathcal{E}_T^2$

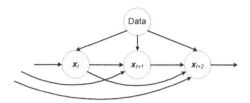

Figure 4.5: Herding as an infinite memory process on samples.

defined as

$$\mathcal{E}_T^2 \overset{\text{def}}{=} \left\| \bar{\phi} - \frac{1}{T} \sum_{t=1}^{T} \phi(\mathbf{s}_t) \right\|^2 \tag{4.17}$$

We therefore see that herding will generate pseudo-samples that greedily minimize the distance between the input moments and the sampling average of the feature vector at every iteration (conditioned on past samples). Note that the error function is unfortunately not submodular and the greedy procedure does not imply that the total collection of samples at iteration T is jointly optimal (see Huszar and Duvenaud (2012) for a detailed discussion). We also note that herding is an "infinite memory process" on $\mathbf{s}_t$ (as opposed to a Markov process) illustrated in Figure 4.5 because new samples depend on the entire history of samples generated thus far.

4.2.5 Moment Matching Property

With the dual view in the previous subsection, the distance between the moments and their sampling average in Equation 4.17 can be considered as the objective function for the herding algorithm to minimize. We discuss in this subsection under what condition and at what speed the moment constraints will be eventually satisfied.

Proposition 4.1 (Proposition 1 in Welling (2009a)). $\forall \alpha$, *if* $\lim_{\tau \to \infty} \frac{1}{\tau} w_{\alpha\tau} = 0$, *then* $\lim_{\tau \to \infty} \frac{1}{\tau} \sum_{t=1}^{\tau} \phi_\alpha(\mathbf{s}_t) = \bar{\phi}_\alpha$.

Proof. Following Equation 4.14, we have

$$\frac{1}{\tau} w_{\alpha\tau} - \frac{1}{\tau} w_{\alpha 0} = \bar{\phi}_\alpha - \frac{1}{\tau} \sum_{t=1}^{\tau} \phi_\alpha(\mathbf{s}_t) \tag{4.18}$$

Using the premise that the weights grow slower than linearly and observing that $w_{\alpha 0}$ is constant we see that the left hand term vanishes in the limit $\tau \to \infty$ which proves the result. $\qquad\square$

What this says is that under the very general assumption that the weights do not grow linearly to infinity (note that due to the finite learning rate they can not grow faster than linear either), the moment constraints will be satisfied by the samples collected from the combined learning/sampling procedure. In fact, we will show later that the weights are restricted in a bounded region, which leads to a convergence rate of $\mathcal{O}(1/\tau)$ as stated below.

Proposition 4.2. $\forall \alpha$, *if there exists a constant R such that $|w_{\alpha,t}| \leq R, \forall t$, then*

$$\left| \frac{1}{\tau} \sum_{t=1}^{\tau} \phi_\alpha(\mathbf{s}_t) - \bar{\phi}_\alpha \right| \leq \frac{2R}{\tau}.$$

The proof follows immediately Equation 4.18.

Note that if we want to estimate the expected feature of a trained MRF by a Monte Carlo method, the optimal standard deviation of the approximation error with independent and identically distributed (i.i.d.) random samples decays as $\mathcal{O}(\frac{1}{\sqrt{\tau}})$, where τ is the number of samples. (For positively autocorrelated MCMC methods this rate could be even slower.) Samples from herding therefore achieve a faster convergence rate in estimating moments than i.i.d. samples.

Recurrence of the Weight Sequence

It is important to ensure that the herding dynamics does not diverge to infinity. Welling (2009a) discovered an important property of herding, known as recurrence, that the sequence of the weights is confined in a ball in the parameter space. This property satisfies the premise of both Proposition 2.1 and 2.2. It was stated in a corollary of Proposition 4.3:

Proposition 4.3 (Proposition 2 in Welling (2009a)). $\exists \mathcal{R}$ *such that a herding update performed outside this radius will always decrease the norm $\|\mathbf{w}\|_2$.*

Corollary 4.4 (Corollary in Welling (2009a)). $\exists \mathcal{R}'$ *such that a herding algorithm initialized inside a ball with that radius will never generate weights $\mathbf{w}$ with norm $\|\mathbf{w}\|_2 > \mathcal{R}'$.*

However, there was a gap in the proof of Proposition 2 in Welling (2009a). We give the corrected proof below:

Proof of Proposition 4.3. Write the herding update equation 4.8 as $\mathbf{w}_t = \mathbf{w}_{t-1} + \nabla_{\mathbf{w}}\ell_0(\mathbf{w}_{t-1})$ (set $\eta = 1$). Expanding the squared norm of $\mathbf{w}_t$ leads to

$$\|\mathbf{w}_t\|_2^2 = \|\mathbf{w}_{t-1}\|_2^2 + 2\mathbf{w}_{t-1}^T\nabla_{\mathbf{w}}\ell_0(\mathbf{w}_{t-1}) + \|\nabla_{\mathbf{w}}\ell_0(\mathbf{w}_{t-1})\|_2^2$$
$$\implies \quad \delta\|\mathbf{w}\|_2^2 < 2\ell_0(\mathbf{w}_{t-1}) + \mathcal{B}^2 \tag{4.19}$$

where we define $\delta\|\mathbf{w}\|_2^2 = \|\mathbf{w}_t\|_2^2 - \|\mathbf{w}_{t-1}\|_2^2$. $\mathcal{B}$ is an upper bound of $\{\|\nabla_{\mathbf{w}}\ell_0(\mathbf{w})\|_2 : \mathbf{w} \in \mathcal{R}^{|\mathbf{w}|}\}$ introduced in Lemma 1 of Welling (2009a). That exists as long as the norm of the feature vector $\phi(\mathbf{x})$ is bounded in $\mathcal{X}$. We also use the fact that $\ell_0(\mathbf{w}) = \mathbf{w}^T\nabla_{\mathbf{w}}\ell_0(\mathbf{w})$.

Denote the unit hypersphere as $U = \{\mathbf{w}|\|\mathbf{w}\|_2^2 = 1\}$. Since ℓ_0 is continuous on U and U is a bounded closed set, ℓ_0 can achieve its supremum on U, that is, we can find a maximum point w^* on U where $\ell_0(\mathbf{w}^*) \geq \ell_0(\mathbf{w}), \forall \mathbf{w} \in U$.

Combining this with the fact that $\ell_0 < 0$ outside the origin, we know the maximum of ℓ_0 on U is negative. Now taking into account the fact that $\mathcal{B}$ is constant (i.e. does not scale with $\mathbf{w}$), there exists some constant $\mathcal{R}$ for which $\mathcal{R}\ell_0(\mathbf{w}^*) < -\mathcal{B}^2/2$. Together with the scaling property of ℓ_0, $\ell_0(\beta\mathbf{w}) = \beta\ell_0(\mathbf{w})$, we can prove that for any $\mathbf{w}$ with a norm larger than $\mathcal{R}$, ℓ_0 is smaller then $-\mathcal{B}^2/2$:

$$\ell_0(\mathbf{w}) = \|\mathbf{w}\|_2\ell_0(\mathbf{w}/\|\mathbf{w}\|_2) \leq \mathcal{R}\ell_0(\mathbf{w}^*) < -\mathcal{B}^2/2, \quad \forall\|\mathbf{w}\|_2 > R \tag{4.20}$$

The proof is concluded by plugging the inequality above in Equation 4.19.

$\square$

Corollary 4.4 proves the existence of a bound for $\|\mathbf{w}\|_2$ and thereby the constant R in Proposition 4.2. Harvey and Samadi (2014) further studied the value of R and proposed a variant of herding that obtained a near-optimal value for $R = O(\sqrt{d}\log^{2.5}\|\mathcal{X}\|)$ w.r.t. the dimensionality of the feature vector d and the size of a finite state space $\mathcal{X}$. The proposed algorithm has a polynomial time complexity in d and $\|\mathcal{X}\|$.

The Remaining Degrees of Freedom

Both the herding and the MaxEnt methods match the moments of the training data. But how does herding control the remaining degrees of freedom that are otherwise controlled by maximizing the entropy in the MaxEnt method? This is unfortunately still an open problem. Apart from some heuristics there is currently no principled way to enforce high entropy. In practice however, in discrete state spaces we usually observe that the sampling distribution from herding renders high entropy. We illustrate the behavior of herding in the example of simulating an Ising model in the next paragraph.

An Ising model is an MRF defined on a lattice of binary nodes, $G = (E, V)$, with biases and pairwise features. The probability distribution is expressed as

$$P(\mathbf{x}) = \frac{1}{Z} \exp \left(\beta \left(\sum_{(i,j) \in E} J_{i,j} x_i x_j + \sum_{i \in V} h_i x_i \right) \right), x_i \in \{-1, 1\}, \forall i \in V$$

$$(4.21)$$

where h_i is the bias parameter, $J_{i,j}$ is the pairwise parameter and $\beta \geq 0$ is the inverse temperature variable. When $h_i = 0$, $J_{i,j} = 1$ for all nodes and edges, and β is set at the inverse critical temperature, the Ising model is said to be at a critical phase where regular sampling algorithms fail due to long range correlations among variables. A special algorithm, the Swendsen-Wang algorithm (Swendsen and Wang, 1987), was designed to draw samples efficiently in this case. In order to run herding on the Ising model, we need to know the average features, $\bar{x}_i$ (0 in this case) and $\overline{x_i x_j}$ instead of the MRF parameters. So we first run the Swendsen-Wang algorithm to obtain an estimate of the expected cross terms, $\overline{x_i x_j}$, which are constant across all edges, and then run herding with weights for every node w_i and edge $w_{i,j}$. The update equations are:

$$\mathbf{s}_t = \underset{\mathbf{x}}{\text{argmax}} \sum_{(i,j) \in E} w_{(i,j),t-1} x_i x_j + \sum_{i \in V} w_{i,t-1} x_i \qquad (4.22)$$

$$w_{(i,j),t} = w_{(i,j),t-1} + \overline{x_i x_j} - s_{i,t} s_{j,t} \qquad (4.23)$$

$$w_{i,t} = w_{i,t-1} - s_{i,t} \qquad (4.24)$$

As finding the global optimum is an NP-hard problem we find a local maximum for $\mathbf{s}_t$ by coordinate descent.[2] Figure 4.6 shows a sample from an Ising model on an 100×100 lattice at the critical temperature. We do not observe qualitative difference between the samples generated by the Ising model (MaxEnt) and herding, which suggests that the sample distribution of herding may be very close to the distribution of the MRF. Furthermore, Figure 4.7 shows the distribution of the size of connected components in the samples. It is known that this distribution should obey a power law at the critical temperature. We find that samples from both methods exhibit the power law distribution with an almost identical exponent.

---

2. In Section 4.3.2 we show that the moment matching property still holds with a local search as long as the found state is better than the average.

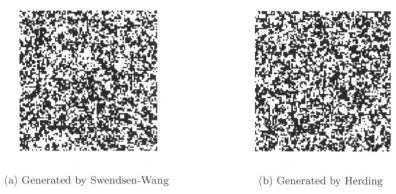

(a) Generated by Swendsen-Wang   (b) Generated by Herding

Figure 4.6: Sample from an Ising model on an 100×100 lattice at the critical temperature.

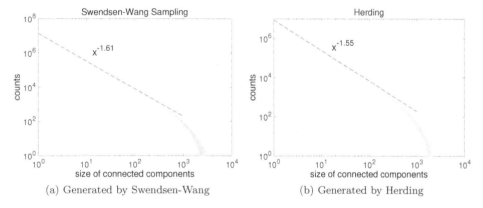

(a) Generated by Swendsen-Wang   (b) Generated by Herding

Figure 4.7: Histogram of the size of connected components in the samples of the Ising model at the critical temperature.

4.2.6   Learning Using Weak Chaos

There are two theoretical frameworks for statistical inference: the frequentist and the Bayesian paradigm. A frequentist assumes a true objective value for some parameter and tries to estimate its value from samples. Except for the simplest models, estimation usually involves an iterative procedure where the value of the parameter is estimated with increasing precision. In information theoretic terms, this means that more and more information from the data is accumulated in more decimal places of the estimate. With a finite data-set, this process should stop at some scale because there is not enough information in the data that can be transferred into the decimal places of the parameter. If we continue anyway, we will overfit to the dataset at hand. In a Bayesian setting we entertain a posterior distribution over parameters, the spread, or more technically speaking, entropy, of which determines the amount of information it encodes. In Bayesian estimation, the spread automatically adapts itself to the amount of available information in the data. In both cases, the learning process itself can be viewed as a dynamical system. For a frequentist this means a convergent series of parameter estimates indexed by the learning iteration $\mathbf{w}_1, \mathbf{w}_2, \ldots$. For a Bayesian running a MCMC procedure this means a stochastic process converging to some equilibrium distribution. Herding introduces a third possibility by encoding all the information in a deterministic nonlinear dynamical system. We focus on studying the weakly chaotic behavior of the herding dynamics in this subsection. The sequence of weights never converges but traces out a quasi-periodic trajectory on an attractor set which is often found to be of fractal dimension. In the language of iterated maps, $\mathbf{w}_{t+1} = F(\mathbf{w}_t)$, a (frequentist) optimization of some objective results in an attractor set that is a single point, Bayesian posterior inference results in a (posterior) probability distribution while herding will result in a (possibly fractal) attractor set which seems harder to meaningfully interpret as a probability distribution.

Example: Herding a Single Neuron

We first study an example of the herding dynamics in its simplest form and show its equivalence to some well-studied theories in mathematics. Consider a single (artificial) neuron, which can take on two distinct states: either it fires ($x = 1$) or it does not fire ($x = 0$). Assume that we want to simulate the activity of a neuron with an irrational firing rate, $\pi \in [0, 1]$, that is, the average firing frequency approaches $\lim_{T \to \infty} \frac{1}{T} \sum_{t=1}^{T} s_t = \pi$. We can achieve that by applying the herding algorithm with a one-dimensional feature $\phi(x) = x$ and feeding the input moment with the desired rate $\bar{\phi} = \pi$. Applying the update equations 4.7-4.8 we get the following dynamics:

$$s_t = \mathbb{I}(w_{t-1} > 0) \tag{4.25}$$

$$w_t = w_{t-1} + \pi - s_t \tag{4.26}$$

where $\mathbb{I}[\cdot]$ is the indicator function. With the moment matching property we can show immediately that the firing rate converges to the desired value π for any initial value of w. The update equations are illustrated in Figure 4.8. This dynamics is a simple type of interval translation mapping (ITM) problem in mathematics (Boshernitzan and Kornfeld, 1995). In a general ITM problem, the invariant set of the dynamics often has a fractal

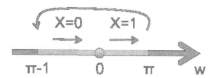

Figure 4.8: Herding dynamics for a single binary variable. At every iteration the weight is first increased by π. If w was originally positive, it is then depressed by 1.

dimension. But for this simple case, the invariant set is the entire interval $(\pi - 1, \pi]$ if π is an irrational number and a finite set if it is rational. As a neuron model, one can think of w_t as a "synaptic strength." At each iteration the synaptic strength increases by an amount π. When the synaptic strength rises above 0, the neuron fires. If it fires its synaptic strength is depressed by a factor 1. The value of w_0 only has some effect on the transient behavior of the resulting sequence $s_1, s_2, \ldots$.

It is perhaps interesting to note that by setting $\pi = \varphi$ with φ the golden mean $\varphi = \frac{1}{2}(\sqrt{5} - 1)$ and initializing the weights at $w_0 = 2\varphi - 1$, we exactly generate the "Rabbit Sequence": a well studied Sturmian sequence which is intimately related with Fibonacci numbers[3]). In Figure 4.9 we plot the weights (a) and the states (b) resulting from herding with the "Fibonacci neuron" model. For a proof, please see Welling and Chen (2010).

When initializing $w_0 = 0$, one may think of the synaptic strength as an error potential that keeps track of the total error so far. One can further show that the sequence of states is a discrete low discrepancy sequence (Angel et al., 2009) in the following sense:

Proposition 4.5. *If w is the weight of the herding dynamics for a single binary variable x with probability $P(x = 1) = \pi$, and $w_\tau \in (\pi - 1, \pi]$ at some step $\tau \geq 0$, then $w_t \in (\pi - 1, \pi], \forall t \geq \tau$. Moreover, for $T \in \mathbb{N}$, we have:*

$$\left| \sum_{t=\tau+1}^{\tau+T} \mathbb{I}[s_t = 1] - T\pi \right| \leq 1, \qquad \left| \sum_{t=\tau+1}^{\tau+T} \mathbb{I}[s_t = 0] - T(1 - \pi) \right| \leq 1 \qquad (4.27)$$

Proof. We first show that $(\pi - 1, \pi]$ is the invariant interval for herding dynamics. Denote the mapping of the weight in Equation 4.25 and 4.26 as

---

3. Imagine two types of rabbits: young rabbits (0) and adult rabbits (1). At each new generation the young rabbits grow up ($0 \to 1$) and old rabbits produce offspring ($1 \to 10$). Recursively applying these rules we produce the rabbit sequence: $0 \to 1 \to 10 \to 101 \to 10110 \to 10110101$ etc. The total number of terms of these sequences and incidentally also the total number of 1's (lagged by one iteration) constitutes the Fibonacci sequence: $1, 1, 2, 3, 5, 8, \ldots$.

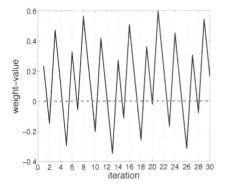
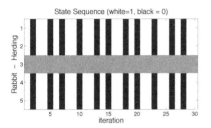

Figure 4.9: Sequence of weights and states generated by the "Fibonacci neuron" based on herding dynamics. Left: Sequence of weight values. Note that the state results by checking if the weight value is larger than 0 (in which case $s_t = 1$) or smaller than 0 (in which case $s_t = 0$). By initializing the weights at $w_0 = 2\varphi - 1$ and using $\pi = \varphi$, with φ the golden mean, we obtain the Rabbit sequence (see main text). Right: Top stripes show the first 30 iterates of the sequence obtained with herding. For comparison we also show the Rabbit sequence below it (white indicates 1 and black indicates 0). Note that these two sequences are identical.

$\mathcal{T}$. Then we can see that the interval $(\pi - 1, \pi]$ is mapped to itself as

$$\mathcal{T}(\pi-1, \pi] = \mathcal{T}(\pi-1, 0] \cup \mathcal{T}(0, \pi] = (2\pi-1, \pi] \cup (\pi-1, 2\pi-1] = (\pi-1, \pi] \quad (4.28)$$

Consequently when w_τ falls inside the invariant interval, we have $w_t \in (\pi - 1, \pi], \forall t \geq \tau$. Now summing up both sides of Equation 4.26 over t immediately gives us the first inequality in 4.27 as:

$$T\pi - \sum_{t=\tau+1}^{\tau+T} \mathbb{I}[s_t = 1] = w_{\tau+T} - w_\tau \in [-1, 1]. \quad (4.29)$$

The second inequality follows by observing that $\mathbb{I}[s_t = 0] = 1 - \mathbb{I}[s_t = 1]$. □

As a corollary of Proposition 4.5, when we initialize $w_0 = \pi - 1/2$, we can improve the bound of the discrepancy by a half.

Corollary 4.6. *If w is the weight of the herding dynamics in Proposition 4.5 and it is initialized at $w_0 = \pi - 1/2$, then for $T \in \mathbb{N}$, we have:*

$$\left| \sum_{t=\tau+1}^{\tau+T} \mathbb{I}[s_t = 1] - T\pi \right| \leq \frac{1}{2}, \quad \left| \sum_{t=\tau+1}^{\tau+T} \mathbb{I}[s_t = 0] - T(1 - \pi) \right| \leq \frac{1}{2} \quad (4.30)$$

The proof immediately follows Equation 4.29 by plugging $\tau = 0$ and $w_0 = \pi - 1/2$. In fact, setting $w_0 = \pi - 1/2$ corresponds to the condition in the greedy algorithm interpretation in Section 4.2.4. One can see this

by constructing an equivalent herding dynamics with a feature of constant
norm as:

$$\phi'(x) = \begin{cases} 1 & \text{if } x = 1 \\ -1 & \text{if } x = 0 \end{cases} \tag{4.31}$$

When initializing the weight at the moment $w'_0 = \bar{\phi}' = 2\pi - 1$, one
can verify that this dynamics generates the same sample sequence as the
original one and their weights are the same up to a constant factor of 2,
i.e. $w'_t = 2w_t, \forall t \geq 0$. The new dynamics satisfies the two assumptions in
Section 4.2.4 and therefore the sample sequences in both dynamical systems
greedily minimize the error of the empirical probability (up to a constant
factor):

$$\left| \frac{1}{T} \sum_{t=1}^{T} \phi'(x'_t) - (2\pi - 1) \right| = 2 \left| \frac{1}{T} \sum_{t=1}^{T} \mathbb{I}[x_t = 1] - \pi \right| \tag{4.32}$$

This greedy algorithm actually achieves the optimal bound one can get with
herding dynamics in the 1-neuron model, which is $1/2$.

Example: Herding a Discrete State Variable

The application of herding to a binary variable can be extended naturally
to a discrete state variables. Let x be a variable that can take one of the
D states, $\{0, 1, \ldots, D - 1\}$. Given any distribution over these D states in
the set $\pi \in \mathbb{R}^D, \sum_{d=0}^{D-1} \pi_d = 1$, we can run herding to simulate the activity
of the discrete variable. The feature function, $\phi(x)$, is defined as the 1-of-
D encoding of the discrete state, that is, a vector of D binary numbers, in
which all the numbers are 0 except for the element indexed by the value of x.
For example, for a variable with 4 states, the feature function of $\phi(x = 3)$ is
$[0, 0, 1, 0]$. It is easy to observe that the expected value of the feature vector
under the distribution π is exactly equal to π. Now, let us apply the herding
update equations with the feature map ϕ and input moment π:

$$s_t = \arg\max_x \mathbf{w}_{t-1}^T \phi(x) = \arg\max_x w_{x,t-1} \tag{4.33}$$

$$\mathbf{w}_t = \mathbf{w}_{t-1} + \pi - \phi(s_t) \tag{4.34}$$

The weight variables act similarly to the synaptic strength analogy in
the neuron model example. At every iteration, the state with the highest
potential gets activated, and then the corresponding weight is depressed
after activation. Applying Proposition 4.2, we know that the empirical
distribution of the samples converges to the input distribution at a faster

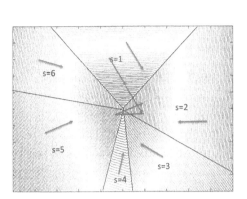

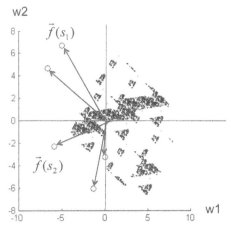

Figure 4.10: Cones in parameter space $\{w_1, w_2\}$ that correspond to the discrete states $s_1, ..., s_6$. Arrows indicate the translation vectors associated with the cones.

Figure 4.11: Fractal attractor set for herding with two parameters. The circles represent the feature-vectors evaluated at the states $s_1, ..., s_6$. Hausdorff dimension for this example is between 0 and 1.

rate than one would get from random sampling:

$$\left| \frac{1}{T} \sum_{t=1}^{T} \phi(s_t) - \boldsymbol{\pi} \right| = \mathcal{O}\left(\frac{1}{T}\right) \tag{4.35}$$

The dynamics of the weight vector is more complex than the case of a binary variable in the previous subsection. However, there are still some interesting observations one can make about the trajectory of the weights which we explain in the appendix.

Weak Chaos in the Herding Dynamics

Now let us consider herding in a general setting with D states and each state is associated with a K dimensional feature vector. The update equation for the weights 4.8 can be viewed as a series of translations in the parameter space, $\mathbf{w} \rightarrow \mathbf{w} + \rho(\mathbf{x})$, where each discrete state $\mathbf{x} \in \mathcal{X}$ corresponds to one translation vector (i.e. $\rho(\mathbf{x}) = \bar{\phi} - \phi(\mathbf{x})$). See Figure 4.10 for an example with $D = 6$ and $K = 2$. The parameter space is partitioned into cones emanating from the origin, each corresponding to a state according to Equation 4.7. If the current location of the weights is inside cone $\mathbf{x}$, then one applies the translation corresponding to that cone and moves along $\rho(\mathbf{x})$ to the next point. This system is an example of what is known as a piecewise translation (or piecewise isometry more generally) (Goetz, 2000).

It is clear that this system has zero Lyapunov exponents[4] everywhere (except perhaps on the boundaries between cones but since this is a measure zero set we will ignore these). As the evolution of the weights will remain bounded inside some finite ball the evolution will converge to some attractor set. Moreover, the dynamics is non-periodic in the typical case (more formally, the translation vectors must form an incommensurate (possibly over-complete) basis set; for a proof see Appendix B of Welling and Chen (2010)). It can often be observed that this attractor has fractal dimension (see Figure 4.11 for an example). All these facts point to the idea that herding is on the edge between full chaos (with positive Lyapunov exponents) and regular periodic behavior (with negative Lyapunov exponents). In fact, herding is an example of what is called "weak chaos", which is usually defined through its (topological) entropy discussed below. Finally, as we have illustrated in Figure 4.1, one can construct a sequence of iterated maps of which herding is the limit and which exhibits period doubling. This is yet another characteristic of systems that are classified as "edge of chaos". Whether the attractor set is of fractal dimension in general remains an open question. For the case of single neuron model, the attractor is the entire interval $(\pi - 1, \pi]$ if π is irrational but for systems with more states it remains unknown.

We will now estimate the entropy production rate of herding. This will inform us further of the properties of this system and how it processes information. From Figure 4.10 we see that the sequence $s_1, s_2, ...$ can be interpreted as the symbolic system of the continuous dynamical system defined for the parameters $\mathbf{w}$. A sequence of symbols (states) is sometimes referred to as an "itinerary." Every time $\mathbf{w}$ falls inside a cone we record its label which equals the state $\mathbf{x}$. The topological entropy for the symbolic system can be defined by counting the total number of subsequences of length T, which we will call $M(T)$. One may think of this as a dynamical language where the subsequences are called "words" and the topological entropy is thus related to the number of words of length T. More precisely, the topological entropy is defined as,

$$h = \lim_{T \to \infty} h(T) = \lim_{T \to \infty} \frac{\log M(T)}{T} \tag{4.36}$$

---

4. The Lyapunov exponent of a dynamical system is a quantity that characterizes the rate of separation of infinitesimally close trajectories. Quantitatively, two trajectories in phase space with initial separation $|\delta Z(0)|$ diverge (provided that the divergence can be treated within the linearized approximation) at a rate given by $|\delta Z(t)| \approx e^{\lambda t}|\delta Z(0)|$ where λ is the Lyapunov exponent.

It was rigorously proven in Goetz (2000) that $M(T)$ grows polynomially in T for general piecewise isometries, which implies that the topological entropy vanishes for herding. It is however interesting to study the growth of $M(T)$ as a function of T to get a sense of how chaotic its dynamics is.

For the simplest model of a single neruon with π being an irrational number, it turns out $M(T) = T + 1$, which is the absolute bare minimum for sequences that are not eventually periodic. It implies that our neuron model generates Sturmian sequences for irrational values of π which are precisely defined to be the non-eventually periodic sequences of minimal complexity (Lu and Wang, 2005). (For a proof, please see Welling and Chen (2010).)

To count the number of subsequences of length T for a general model, we can study the T-step herding map that results from applying herding T steps at a time. The original cones are now further subdivided into smaller convex polygons, each one labeled with the sequence $s_1, s_2, ..., s_T$ that the points inside the polygon will follow during the following T steps. Thus as we increase T, the number of these polygons will increase and it is exactly the number of those polygons which partition our parameter space that is equal to the number of possible subsequences. We first claim that every polygon, however small, will break up into smaller sub-pieces after a finite amount of time. This is proven in Welling and Chen (2010). In fact, we expect that in a typical herding system every pair of points will break up as well, which, if true, would infer that the diameter of the polygons must shrink. A partition with this property is called a *generating partition*. Based on some preliminary analysis and numerical simulations, we expect that the growth of $M(T)$ in the typical case (a.k.a. with an incommensurate translation basis, see Appendix B of Welling and Chen (2010)) is a polynomial function of the time, $M(T) \sim t^K$, where K is the number of dimensions (which is equal to the number of herding parameters). Since it has been rigorously proven that any piecewise isometry has a growth rate that must have an exponent less or equal than K (Goetz, 2000), this would mean that herding achieves the highest possible entropy within this class of systems with $H(T) = Th(T)$ for a sequence of length T (for T large enough) as:

$$H(T) = K \log(T) \tag{4.37}$$

This result should be understood in comparison with regular and random sequences. In a regular (constant or periodic) sequence, the number of subsequences is constant with respect to the length, i.e. $H(T) = \text{const}$. In contrast, the dominant part of the Kolmogorov-Sinai entropy of a random sequence (considering, e.g., a stochastic process) or a fully chaotic sequence grows linearly in time T, i.e. $H_{\text{ext}}(T) = hT$ due to the injected random noise.

4.3 Generalized Herding

The moment matching property in Proposition 4.1 and 4.2 requires only a mild condition on the L_2 norm of the dynamic weights. That grants us with great flexibility in modifying the original algorithm for more practical implementation as well as a larger spectrum of applications. Gelfand et al. (2010) provided a general condition on the recurrence of the weight sequence, from which we discuss how to generalize the herding algorithm in this section with two specific examples. Chen et al. (2014) described another extension of herding that violated the condition but it achieved the minimum matching distance instead in a constrained problem.

4.3.1 A General Condition for Recurrence — The Perceptron Cycling Theorem

The moment matching property of herding relies on the recurrence of the weight sequence (Corollary 4.4) whose proof again relies on the premise that the maximization is carried out exactly in the herding update equation 4.7. However, the number of model states is usually exponentially large (e.g. $|\mathcal{X}| = J^m$ when $\mathbf{x}$ is a vector of m discrete variables each with J values) and it is intractable to find a global maximum in practice. A local maximizer has to be employed instead. One wonders if the features averaged over samples will still converge to the input moments when the samples are suboptimal states? In this subsection we give a general and verifiable condition for the recurrence of the weight sequence based on the perceptron cycling theorem (Minsky and Papert, 1969), which consequently suggests that the moment matching property may still hold at the rate of $\mathcal{O}(1/T)$ even with a relaxed herding algorithm.

The invention of the perceptron (Rosenblatt, 1958) goes back to the very beginning of AI more than half a century ago. Rosenblatt's very simple, neurally plausible learning rule made it an attractive algorithm for learning relations in data: for every input $\mathbf{x}_i$, make a linear prediction about its label: $y_{i_t}^* = \text{sign}(\mathbf{w}_{t-1}^T \mathbf{x}_{i_t})$ and update the weights as,

$$\mathbf{w}_t = \mathbf{w}_{t-1} + \mathbf{x}_{i_t}(y_{i_t} - y_{i_t}^*). \tag{4.38}$$

A critical evaluation by Minsky and Papert (1969) revealed the perceptron's limited representational power. This fact is reflected in the behavior of

Rosenblatt's learning rule: if the data is linearly separable, then the learning rule converges to the correct solution in a number of iterations that can be bounded by $(R/\gamma)^2$, where R represents the norm of the largest input vector and γ represents the margin between the decision boundary and the closest data-case. However, "for data sets that are not linearly separable, the perceptron learning algorithm will never converge" (quoted from Bishop et al. (2006)).

While the above result is true, the theorem in question has something much more powerful to say. The "perceptron cycling theorem" (PCT) (Minsky and Papert, 1969) states that for the inseparable case the weights remain bounded and do not diverge to infinity. The PCT was initially introduced in Minsky and Papert (1969) but had a gap in the proof that was fixed in Block and Levin (1970).

Theorem 4.7 (Boundedness Theorem). *Consider a sequence of vectors* $\{\mathbf{w}_t\}$, $\mathbf{w}_t \in \mathbb{R}^D$, $t = 0, 1, \ldots$ *generated by the iterative procedure of Algorithm 4.1.*

Algorithm 4.1 Algorithm to generate the sequence $\{\mathbf{w}_t\}$.

V is a finite set of vectors in $\mathbb{R}^D$.
$\mathbf{w}_0$ is initialized arbitrarily in $\mathbb{R}^D$.
for $t = 0 \to T$ (T could be ∞) **do**
    $\mathbf{w}_{t+1} = \mathbf{w}_t + \mathbf{v}_t$, where $\mathbf{v}_t \in V$ satisfies $\mathbf{w}_t^T \mathbf{v}_t \leq 0$
end for

Then, $\|\mathbf{w}_t\| \leq \|\mathbf{w}_0\| + M, \forall t \geq 0$ *where* M *is a constant depending on* V *but not on* $\mathbf{w}_0$.

The theorem still holds when V is a finite set in a Hilbert space. The PCT leads to the boundedness of the perceptron weights where we identify $\mathbf{v}_t = \mathbf{x}_{i_{t+1}}(y_{i_{t+1}} - y_{i_{t+1}}^*)$, a finite set $V = \{\mathbf{x}_i(y_i - y_i^*)|y_i = \pm 1, y_i^* = \pm 1, i = 1, \ldots, N\}$ and observe

$$\mathbf{w}_t^T \mathbf{v}_t = \mathbf{w}_t^T \mathbf{x}_{i_{t+1}}(y_{i_{t+1}} - y_{i_{t+1}}^*) = |\mathbf{w}_t^T \mathbf{x}_{i_{t+1}}|(\text{sign}(\mathbf{w}_t^T \mathbf{x}_{i_{t+1}})y_{i_{t+1}} - 1) \leq 0 \quad (4.39)$$

When the data is linearly separable, Rosenblatt's learning rule will find a $\mathbf{w}$ such that $\mathbf{w}^T \mathbf{v}_i = 0, \forall i$ and the sequence of $\mathbf{w}_t$ converges. Otherwise, there always exists some $\mathbf{v}_i$ such that $\mathbf{w}^T \mathbf{v}_i < 0$ and PCT guarantees the weights are bounded.

The same theorem also applies to the herding algorithm by identifying $\mathbf{v}_t = \bar{\phi} - \phi(\mathbf{s}_{t+1})$ with $\mathbf{s}_{t+1}$ defined in Equation 4.7, a finite set $V =$

$\{\bar{\phi} - \phi(\mathbf{x}) | \mathbf{x} \in \mathcal{X}\}$, and observing that

$$\mathbf{w}_t^T \mathbf{v}_t = \mathbf{w}_t^T \bar{\phi} - \mathbf{w}_t^T \phi(\mathbf{s}_{t+1}) \leq 0 \qquad (4.40)$$

It is now easy to see that, in general, herding does not converge because under very mild conditions we can always find an $\mathbf{s}_{t+1}$ such that $\mathbf{w}_t^T \mathbf{v}_t < 0$. More importantly, the boundedness theorem (or PCT) provides a general condition for the recurrence property and hence the moment matching property of herding. Inequality 4.40 is easy to be verified at running time and does not require $\mathbf{s}_{t+1}$ to be the global optimum.

4.3.2   Generalizing the Herding Algorithm

PCT ensures that the average features from the samples will match the moments at a fast convergence rate as long as the algorithm we are running satisfies the following conditions:

1. The set V is finite,
2. $\mathbf{w}_t^T \mathbf{v}_t = \mathbf{w}_t^T \bar{\phi} - \mathbf{w}_t^T \phi(\mathbf{s}_t) \leq 0, \forall t$,

This set of mild conditions allows us to generalize the original herding algorithm easily.

Firstly, the PCT provides a theoretical justification for using a local search algorithm that performs partial maximization. For example, we may start the local search from the state we ended up in during the previous iteration (a so-called persistent chain (Younes, 1989; Neal, 1992; Yuille, 2004; Tieleman, 2008)). Or, one may consider contrastive divergence-like algorithms (Hinton, 2002), in which the sampling or mean field approximation is replaced by a maximization. In this case, maximizations are initialized on all data-cases and the weights are updated by the difference between the average over the data-cases minus the average over the $\{\mathbf{s}_i\}$ found after (partial) maximization. In this case, the set V is given by: $V = \{\bar{\phi} - \frac{1}{D} \sum_{i=1}^{D} \phi(\mathbf{s}_i) | \mathbf{s}_i \in \mathcal{X}, \forall i\}$. For obvious reasons, it is now guaranteed that $\mathbf{w}_t^T \mathbf{v}_t \leq 0$.

Secondly, we often use mini-batches of size $d < D$ in practice instead of the full data set. In this case, the cardinality of the set V is enlarged to, e.g., $|V| = C(d, D) J^m$, with $C(d, D)$ representing the "d choose D" ways to compute the sample mean $\bar{\phi}_{(d)}$ based on a subset of d data-cases. The negative term remains unaltered. Since the PCT still applies: $\left\| \frac{1}{\tau} \sum_{t=1}^{\tau} \bar{\phi}_{(d),t} - \frac{1}{\tau} \sum_{t=1}^{\tau} \phi(\mathbf{s}_t) \right\|_2 = \mathcal{O}(1/\tau)$. Depending on how the mini-batches are picked, convergence onto the overall mean $\bar{\phi}$ can be either

$\mathcal{O}(1/\sqrt{\tau})$ (random sampling with replacement) or $\mathcal{O}(1/\tau)$ (sampling without replacement which has picked all data-cases after $\lceil D/d \rceil$ rounds).

Besides changing the way we compute the positive and negative terms in $\mathbf{v}_t$, generalizing the definition of *features* will allow us to learn a much wider scope of models beyond the fully visible MRFs as discussed in the following sections.

4.3.3   Herding Partially Observed Random Field Models

The original herding algorithm only works for fully visible MRFs because in order to compute the average feature vector of the training data we have to observe the state of all the variables in a model. In this subsection, we generalize herding to partially observed MRFs (POMRFs) by dynamically imputing the value of latent variables in the training data during the run of herding. This extension allows herding to be applied to models with a higher representative capacity.

Consider a MRF with discrete random variables $(\mathbf{x}, \mathbf{z})$ where $\mathbf{x}$ will be observed and $\mathbf{z}$ will remain hidden. A set of feature functions is defined on $\mathbf{x}$ and $\mathbf{z}$, $\{\phi_\alpha(\mathbf{x}, \mathbf{z})\}$, each associated with a weight w_α. Given these quantities we can write the following Gibbs distribution,

$$P(\mathbf{x}, \mathbf{z}; \mathbf{w}) = \frac{1}{Z(\mathbf{w})} \exp \left(\sum_\alpha w_\alpha \phi_\alpha(\mathbf{x}, \mathbf{z}) \right) \qquad (4.41)$$

The log-likelihood function with a dataset $\mathcal{D} = \{\mathbf{x}_i\}_{i=1}^{D}$ is defined as

$$\ell(\mathbf{w}) = \frac{1}{D} \sum_{i=1}^{D} \log \left(\sum_{\mathbf{z}_i} \exp \left(\mathbf{w}^T \boldsymbol{\phi}(\mathbf{x}_i, \mathbf{z}_i) \right) \right) - \log Z(\mathbf{w}) \qquad (4.42)$$

Analogous to the duality relationship between MLE and MaxEnt for fully observed MRFs, we can write the log-likelihood of a POMRF as

$$\ell = \max_{\{Q_i\}} \min_R \frac{1}{D} \sum_{i=1}^{D} \mathcal{H}(Q_i) - \mathcal{H}(R) \qquad (4.43)$$

$$+ \sum_\alpha w_\alpha \left(\frac{1}{D} \sum_{i=1}^{D} \mathbb{E}_{Q_i(\mathbf{z}_i)}[\phi_\alpha(\mathbf{x}_i, \mathbf{z}_i)] - \mathbb{E}_{R(\mathbf{x}, \mathbf{z})}[\phi_\alpha(\mathbf{x}, \mathbf{z})] \right) \qquad (4.44)$$

where $\{Q_i\}$ are variational distributions on $\mathbf{z}$, and R is a variational distribution on $(\mathbf{x}, \mathbf{z})$. The dual form of MLE turns out as a minimax problem on

$\frac{1}{D} \sum_{i=1}^{D} \mathcal{H}(Q_i) - \mathcal{H}(R)$ with a set of constraints

$$\frac{1}{D} \sum_{i=1}^{D} \mathbb{E}_{Q_i(\mathbf{z}_i)}[\phi_\alpha(\mathbf{x}_i, \mathbf{z}_i)] = \mathbb{E}_{R(\mathbf{x},\mathbf{z})}[\phi_\alpha(\mathbf{x}, \mathbf{z})] \tag{4.45}$$

We want to achieve high entropy for the distributions $\{Q_i\}$ and R, and meanwhile the average feature vector on the training set with hidden variables marginalized out should match the expected feature w.r.t. to the joint distribution of the model. The weights $\mathbf{w}_\alpha$ act as Lagrange multipliers enforcing those constraints.

Similar to the derivation of herding for fully observed MRFs, we now introduce a temperature in Equation 4.42 by replacing $\mathbf{w}$ with $\mathbf{w}/T$. Taking the limit $T \to 0$ of $\ell_T \overset{\text{def}}{=} T\ell$, we see that the entropy terms vanish. For a given value of $\mathbf{w}$ and in the absence of entropy, the optimal distribution $\{Q_i\}$ and R are delta-peaks and their averages should be replace with maximizations, resulting in the objective,

$$\ell_0(\mathbf{w}) = \frac{1}{D} \sum_{i=1}^{D} \max_{\mathbf{z}_i} \mathbf{w}^T \phi(\mathbf{x}_i, \mathbf{z}_i) - \max_{\mathbf{s}} \mathbf{w}^T \phi(\mathbf{s}) \tag{4.46}$$

where we denote $\mathbf{s} = (\mathbf{x}, \mathbf{z})$.

Taking a gradient descent update on ℓ_0 with a fixed learning rate ($\eta = 1$) defines the herding algorithm on POMRFs (Welling, 2009b):

$$\mathbf{z}_{it}^* = \arg \max_{\mathbf{z}_i} \mathbf{w}_{t-1}^T \phi(\mathbf{x}_i, \mathbf{z}_i), \forall i \tag{4.47}$$

$$\mathbf{s}_t^* = \arg \max_{\mathbf{s}} \mathbf{w}_{t-1}^T \phi(\mathbf{s}) \tag{4.48}$$

$$\mathbf{w}_t = \mathbf{w}_{t-1} + \left[\frac{1}{D} \sum_{i=1}^{D} \phi(\mathbf{x}_i, \mathbf{z}_{it}^*) \right] - \phi(\mathbf{s}_t^*) \tag{4.49}$$

We use a superscript "*" to denote states obtained by maximization. These equations are similar to herding for the fully observed case, but different in the sense that we need to impute the unobserved variables $\mathbf{z}_i$ for every data-case separately through maximization. The weight update also consist of a positive "driving term," which is now a changing average over data-cases, and a negative term, which is identical to the corresponding term in the fully observed case.

Moment Matching Property

We can prove the boundedness of the weights with PCT by identifying $\mathbf{v}_t = \left[\frac{1}{D} \sum_{i=1}^{D} \phi(\mathbf{x}_i, \mathbf{z}_{i,t+1}^*) \right] - \phi(\mathbf{s}_{t+1}^*)$, a finite set $V = \{\mathbf{v}_t(\{\mathbf{z}_i\}, \mathbf{s}) | \mathbf{z}_i \in$

$\mathcal{X}_{\mathbf{z}}, \forall i, \mathbf{s} \in \mathcal{X}\}$, and observing the inequality

$$\mathbf{w}_t^T \mathbf{v}_t = \left[\frac{1}{D} \sum_{i=1}^{D} \mathbf{w}_t^T \boldsymbol{\phi}(\mathbf{x}_i, \mathbf{z}_{i,t+1}^*) \right] - \mathbf{w}_t^T \boldsymbol{\phi}(\mathbf{s}_{t+1}^*) \tag{4.50}$$

$$= \left[\frac{1}{D} \sum_{i=1}^{D} \max_{\mathbf{z}_i} \mathbf{w}_t^T \boldsymbol{\phi}(\mathbf{x}_i, \mathbf{z}_i) \right] - \max_{\mathbf{s}} \mathbf{w}_t^T \boldsymbol{\phi}(\mathbf{s}) \leq 0 \tag{4.51}$$

The last inequality holds because the second term maximizes over more variables than the first term. Again, we do not have to be able to solve the difficult optimization problems of Equation 4.47 and 4.48. Partial progress in the form of a few iterations of coordinate-wise descent is often enough to satisfy the condition in Equation 4.50 which can be checked easily.

Following a similar proof as Proposition 4.2, we obtain the fast moment matching property of herding on POMRFs:

Proposition 4.8. *There exists a constant R such that herding on a partially observed MRF satisfies*

$$\left| \frac{1}{\tau} \sum_{t=1}^{\tau} \frac{1}{D} \sum_{i=1}^{D} \phi_\alpha(\mathbf{x}_i, \mathbf{z}_{it}^*) - \frac{1}{\tau} \sum_{t=1}^{\tau} \phi_\alpha(\mathbf{s}_t^*) \right| \leq \frac{2R}{\tau}, \forall \alpha \tag{4.52}$$

Notice that besides a sequence of samples of the full state $\{\mathbf{s}_t^*\}$ that form the joint distribution in the herding algorithm, we also obtain a sequence of samples of the hidden variables $\{\mathbf{z}_{it}^*\}$ for every data case $\mathbf{x}_i$ that forms the conditional distribution of $P(\mathbf{z}_i | \mathbf{x}_i)$. Those consistencies in the limit of $\tau \to \infty$ in Proposition 4.8 are in direct analogy to the maximum likelihood problem of Equation 4.42 for which the following moment matching conditions hold at the MLE for all α,

$$\frac{1}{D} \sum_{i=1}^{D} \mathbb{E}_{P(\mathbf{z}_i | \mathbf{x}_i; \mathbf{w}_{\text{MLE}})}[\phi_\alpha(\mathbf{x}_i, \mathbf{z}_i)] = \mathbb{E}_{P(\mathbf{x}, \mathbf{z}; \mathbf{w}_{\text{MLE}})}[\phi_\alpha(\mathbf{x}, \mathbf{z})] \tag{4.53}$$

These consistency conditions alone are not sufficient to guarantee a good model. After all, the dynamics could simply ignore the hidden variables by keeping them constant and still satisfy the matching conditions. In this case the hidden and visible subspaces completely decouple, defeating the purpose of using hidden variables in the first place. Note that the same holds for the MLE consistency conditions alone. However, an MLE solution also strives for high entropy in the hidden states. We observe in practice that the herding dynamics usually also induces high entropy in the distributions for $\mathbf{z}$ avoiding the decoupling phenomenon described above.

The proof of the boundedness of weights depends on the assumption that
we can find the global maximum in Equation 4.48, which is an intractable
problem. Welling (2009b) also proposed a fully tractable herding variant
that was guaranteed to satisfy PCT.

Proposition 4.9. *Call $\mathcal{A}$ any tractable optimization algorithm to locate a
local maximum in the product $\mathbf{w}^T \phi(\mathbf{x}, \mathbf{z})$. This algorithm will be used to
compute both $\mathbf{z}_i^*$ and $\mathbf{s}^*$. Call $\mathcal{E}_{\mathcal{A}}(\mathbf{x}_i, \mathbf{w}) = -\mathbf{w}^T \phi(\mathbf{x}_i, \mathbf{z}_i^*)$ the energy of data-
case i (note that this definition depends on the algorithm $\mathcal{A}$). Assume that
given any initialization, $\mathcal{A}$ always return a state with an energy no larger
than its initial state. Then the following tractable herding algorithm will
remain in a compact region of weight space: Apply the usual herding updates
with the difference that the optimization for $\mathbf{s}^*$ is initialized at the state
$(\mathbf{x}_{i^*}, \mathbf{z}_{i^*}^*)$ which represents the data-case with lowest energy $\mathcal{E}_{\mathcal{A}}(\mathbf{x}_i, \mathbf{w})$.*

Proof. The proof is trivial using the PCT condition as:

$$\mathbf{w}_t^T \mathbf{v}_t = -\left[\frac{1}{D} \sum_{i=1}^{D} \mathcal{E}_{\mathcal{A}}(\mathbf{x}_i, \mathbf{w}_t) \right] + \mathcal{E}_{\mathcal{A}}(\mathbf{s}^*, \mathbf{w}_t) \tag{4.54}$$

$$\leq -\left[\frac{1}{D} \sum_{i=1}^{D} \mathcal{E}_{\mathcal{A}}(\mathbf{x}_i, \mathbf{w}_t) \right] + \mathcal{E}_{\mathcal{A}}(\mathbf{x}_{i^*}, \mathbf{w}_t) \leq 0 \tag{4.55}$$

□

4.3.4   Herding Discriminative Models

We have been talking about running herding dynamics in an unsupervised
learning setting. The idea of driving a nonlinear dynamical system to match
moments can also be applied to discriminative learning by incorporating
labels into the feature functions. Recalling the perceptron learning algorithm
in Section 4.3.1, the learning rule in Equation 4.38 can be reformulated in
herding style:

$$y_{i_t}^* = \underset{y \in \{-1, 1\}}{\operatorname{argmax}} \, \mathbf{w}_{t-1}^T (\mathbf{x}_{i_t} y) \tag{4.56}$$

$$\mathbf{w}_t = \mathbf{w}_{t-1} + \mathbf{x}_{i_t} y_{i_t} - \mathbf{x}_{i_t} y_{i_t}^* \tag{4.57}$$

where we identify the feature functions as $\phi_j(\mathbf{x}, y) = x_j y, j = 1, \ldots, m$,
use mini-batches of size 1 at every iteration, and do a partial maximization
of the full state $(\mathbf{x}, y)$ with the covariate $\mathbf{x}$ clamped at the input $\mathbf{x}_{i_t}$. The
PCT guarantees that the moments (correlation between covariates and la-
bels) $\mathbb{E}_{\mathcal{D}}[\mathbf{x}y]$ from the training data are matched with $\mathbb{E}_{\mathcal{D}_\mathbf{x} P(y^*|\mathbf{x})}[\mathbf{x}y^*]$ where
$p(y^*|x)$ is the model distribution implied by how the learning process gen-

erates y^* with the sequence of weights $\mathbf{w}_t$. The voted perceptron algorithm (Freund and Schapire, 1999) is an algorithm that runs exactly the same update procedure, applies the weights to make a prediction on the test data at every iteration $y^*_{\text{test},t}$, and obtains the final prediction by averaging over iterations $y^*_{\text{test}} = \text{sign}(\frac{1}{\tau}\sum_{t=1}^{\tau} y^*_{\text{test},t})$. This amounts to learning and predicting based on the conditional expectation $\mathbb{E}_{P(y^*|\mathbf{x})}[y^* = 1|\mathbf{x}_{\text{test}}]$ in the language of herding.

Let us now formulate the *conditional herding* algorithm in a more general way (Gelfand et al., 2010). Denote the complete state of a data-case by $(\mathbf{x}, \mathbf{y}, \mathbf{z})$ where $\mathbf{x}$ is the visible input variable, $\mathbf{y}$ is the label, and $\mathbf{z}$ is the hidden variable. Define a set of feature functions $\{\phi_\alpha(\mathbf{x}, \mathbf{y}, \mathbf{z})\}$ with associated weights $\{w_\alpha\}$. Given a set of training data-cases, $\mathcal{D} = \{\mathbf{x}_i, \mathbf{y}_i\}$, and a test set $\mathcal{D}_{\text{test}} = \{\mathbf{x}_{\text{test},j}\}$, we run the conditional herding algorithm to learn the correlations between the inputs and the labels and make predictions at the same time using the following update equations:

$$\mathbf{z}'_{it} = \underset{\mathbf{z}_i}{\text{argmax}}\ \mathbf{w}^T_{t-1}\phi(\mathbf{x}_i, \mathbf{y}_i, \mathbf{z}_i), \forall(\mathbf{x}_i, \mathbf{y}_i) \in \mathcal{D} \tag{4.58}$$

$$(\mathbf{y}^*_{it}, \mathbf{z}^*_{it}) = \underset{(\mathbf{y}_i, \mathbf{z}_i)}{\text{argmax}}\ \mathbf{w}^T_{t-1}\phi(\mathbf{x}_i, \mathbf{y}_i, \mathbf{z}_i), \forall\mathbf{x}_i \in \mathcal{D}_\mathbf{x} \tag{4.59}$$

$$\mathbf{w}_t = \mathbf{w}_{t-1} + \left[\frac{1}{D}\sum_{i=1}^{D}\phi(\mathbf{x}_i, \mathbf{y}_i, \mathbf{z}'_{it})\right] - \left[\frac{1}{D}\sum_{i=1}^{D}\phi(\mathbf{x}_i, \mathbf{y}^*_{it}, \mathbf{z}^*_{it})\right] \tag{4.60}$$

$$(\mathbf{y}^*_{\text{test},j,t}, \mathbf{z}^*_{\text{test},j,t}) = \arg\underset{(\mathbf{y}_j, \mathbf{z}_j)}{\max}\ \mathbf{w}^T_t\phi(\mathbf{x}_{\text{test},j}, \mathbf{y}_j, \mathbf{z}_j), \forall\mathbf{x}_{\text{test},j} \in \mathcal{D}_{\text{test}}$$
$$\tag{4.61}$$

In the positive term of Equation 4.60, we maximize over the hidden variables only, and in the negative term we maximize over both hidden variables and the labels. The last equation generates a sequence of labels, $\mathbf{y}^*_{\text{test},j,t}$, that can be considered as samples from the conditional distribution of the test input from which we obtain an estimate of the underlying conditional distribution:

$$P(\mathbf{y}|\mathbf{x}_{\text{test},j}) \approx \frac{1}{\tau}\sum_{t=1}^{\tau}\mathbb{I}(\mathbf{y}^*_{\text{test},j,t} = \mathbf{y}) \tag{4.62}$$

In general, herding systems perform better when we use normalized features: $\|\phi(\mathbf{x}, \mathbf{z}, \mathbf{y})\| = R,\ \forall(\mathbf{x}, \mathbf{z}, \mathbf{y})$. The reason is that herding selects states by maximizing the inner product $\mathbf{w}^T\phi$ and features with large norms will therefore become more likely to be selected. In fact, one can show that states inside the convex hull of the $\phi(\mathbf{x}, \mathbf{y}, \mathbf{z})$ are never selected. For binary (±1) variables all states live on the convex hull, but this need not be true in general, especially when we use continuous attributes $\mathbf{x}$. To remedy this, one can either normalize features or add one additional feature[5] $\phi_0(\mathbf{x}, \mathbf{y}, \mathbf{z}) = \sqrt{R_{\max}^2 - ||\phi(\mathbf{x}, \mathbf{y}, \mathbf{z})||^2}$, where $R_{\max} = \max_{\mathbf{x}, \mathbf{y}, \mathbf{z}} ||\phi(\mathbf{x}, \mathbf{y}, \mathbf{z})||$ with $\mathbf{x}$ only allowed to vary over the data-cases.

We may want to use mini-batches $\mathcal{D}_t$ instead of the whole training set for a more practical implementation, and the argument on the validity of using mini-batches in Section 4.3.2 applies here as well. It is easy to observe that Rosenblatts's perceptron learning algorithm is a special case of conditional herding when there are no hidden variables, $\mathbf{y}$ is a single binary variable, the feature function is $\phi = \mathbf{x}y$, and we use a mini-batch of size 1 at every iteration.

Compared to the herding algorithm on partially observed MRFs, the main difference is that we do partial maximization in Equation 4.59 with a clamped visible input $\mathbf{x}$ on every training data-case instead of a joint maximization on the full state. Notice that in this particular variant of herding, the sequence of updates may converge when all the training data-cases are correctly predicted, that is, $\mathbf{y}_{it}^* = \mathbf{y}_i, \forall i = 1, \ldots, D$ at some t. For an example, the convergence is guaranteed to happen for the percepton learning algorithm on a linearly separable data set. We adopt the strategy in the voted perceptron algorithm (Freund and Schapire, 1999) which stops herding when convergence occurs and uses the sequence of weights up to that point for prediction in order to prevent the converged weights from dominating the averaged prediction on the test data.

Clamping the input variables allows us to achieve the following moment matching property:

Proposition 4.10. *There exists a constant R such that conditional herding with the update equations 4.58-4.60 satisfies*

$$\left| \frac{1}{D} \sum_{i=1}^{D} \frac{1}{\tau} \sum_{t=1}^{\tau} \phi_\alpha(\mathbf{x}_i, \mathbf{y}_{it}^*, \mathbf{z}_{it}^*) - \frac{1}{D} \sum_{i=1}^{D} \frac{1}{\tau} \sum_{t=1}^{\tau} \phi_\alpha(\mathbf{x}_i, \mathbf{y}_i, \mathbf{z}_{it}') \right| \leq \frac{2R}{\tau}, \forall \alpha \quad (4.63)$$

The proof is straightforward by applying PCT where we identify

$$\mathbf{v}_t = \left[\frac{1}{D} \sum_{i=1}^{D} \phi(\mathbf{x}_i, \mathbf{y}_i, \mathbf{z}_{it}') \right] - \left[\frac{1}{D} \sum_{i=1}^{D} \phi(\mathbf{x}_i, \mathbf{y}_{it}^*, \mathbf{z}_{it}^*) \right], \quad (4.64)$$

the finite set $V = \{\mathbf{v}(\{\mathbf{z}_i'\}, \{\mathbf{y}_i^*\}, \{\mathbf{z}_i^*\}) | \mathbf{z}_i' \in \mathcal{X}_\mathbf{z}, \mathbf{y}_i^* \in \mathcal{X}_\mathbf{y}, \mathbf{z}_i^* \in \mathcal{X}_\mathbf{z}\}$, and observe the inequality $\mathbf{w}_t^T \mathbf{v}_t \leq 0$ because of the same reason as herding on POMRFs. Note that we require V to be of a finite cardinality, which in return requires $\mathcal{X}_\mathbf{y}$ and $\mathcal{X}_\mathbf{z}$ to be finite sets, but there is not any restriction on

---

5. If in test data this extra feature becomes imaginary we simply set it to zero.

the domain of the visible input variables $\mathbf{x}$. Therefore we can run conditional herding with input $\mathbf{x}$ as continuous variables.

Zero Temperature Limit of CRF

Consider a CRF with the probability distribution defined as

$$P(\mathbf{y}, \mathbf{z}|\mathbf{x}; \mathbf{w}) = \frac{1}{Z(\mathbf{w}, \mathbf{x})} \exp\left(\sum_{\alpha} w_\alpha \phi_\alpha(\mathbf{x}, \mathbf{y}, \mathbf{z})\right) \tag{4.65}$$

where $Z(\mathbf{w}, \mathbf{x})$ is the partition function of the conditional distribution. The log-likelihood function for a dataset $\mathcal{D} = \{\mathbf{x}_i, \mathbf{y}_i\}_{i=1}^{D}$ is expressed as

$$\ell(\mathbf{w}) = \frac{1}{D} \sum_{i=1}^{D} \left(\log \left(\sum_{\mathbf{z}_i} \exp\left(\mathbf{w}^T \phi(\mathbf{x}_i, \mathbf{y}_i, \mathbf{z}_i)\right)\right) - \log Z(\mathbf{w}, \mathbf{x}_i) \right) \tag{4.66}$$

Let us introduce the temperature T by replacing $\mathbf{w}$ with $\mathbf{w}/T$ and take the limit $T \to 0$ of $\ell_T \overset{\text{def}}{=} T\ell$. We then obtain the familiar piecewise linear Tipi function

$$\ell_0(\mathbf{w}) = \frac{1}{D} \sum_{i=1}^{D} \left(\max_{\mathbf{z}_i} \mathbf{w}^T \phi(\mathbf{x}_i, \mathbf{y}_i, \mathbf{z}_i) - \max_{\mathbf{y}_i, \mathbf{z}_i} \mathbf{w}^T \phi(\mathbf{x}_i, \mathbf{y}_i, \mathbf{z}_i) \right) \tag{4.67}$$

Running gradient descent updates on $\ell_0(\mathbf{w})$ immediately gives us the update equations of conditional herding 4.58-4.60.

Similar to the duality relationship between MLE on MRFs and the MaxEnt problem, MLE on CRFs is the dual problem of maximizing the entropy of the conditional distributions while enforcing the following constraints:

$$\frac{1}{D} \sum_{i=1}^{D} \mathbb{E}_{P(\mathbf{z}|\mathbf{x}_i, \mathbf{y}_i)} \left[\phi_\alpha(\mathbf{x}_i, \mathbf{y}_i, \mathbf{z})\right] = \frac{1}{D} \sum_{i=1}^{D} \mathbb{E}_{P(\mathbf{y}, \mathbf{z}|\mathbf{x}_i)} \left[\phi_\alpha(\mathbf{x}_i, \mathbf{y}, \mathbf{z})\right], \forall \alpha \tag{4.68}$$

When we run conditional herding, those constraints are satisfied with the moment matching property in Proposition 4.10, but how to encourage high entropy during the herding dynamics is again an open problem. We suggest some heuristics to achieve high entropy in the next experimental section. Note that there is a difference between MLE and conditional herding when making predictions. While the prediction of a CRF with MLE is made with the most probable label value at a point estimate of the parameters, conditional herding resorts to a majority voting strategy as in the voted perceptron algorithm. The regularization effect via averaging over predictions often provides more robust performance as shown later.

4.4 Experiments

We study the empirical performance of the herding algorithm introduced in Section 4.2 and the extension with hidden variables in Section 4.3.3 and for discriminative models in Section 4.3.4.

4.4.1 Herding with Fully Visible Models

In the following experiments we will determine the ability of herding to convert information about the average value of features in the training data into estimates of some quantities of interest. In particular the input to herding will be joint probabilities of pairs of variables (denoted H.XX) and sometimes triples of variables (denoted H.XXX) where all variables will be binary valued (which is easily relaxed).

In experiment I we will consider the quantity $P(k) = \mathbb{E}[\mathbb{I}[\sum_i X_i = k - 1]]$ which is the distribution of the total number of 1's across all attributes. This quantity involves all variables in the problem and cannot be directly estimated from the input which consists of pairwise information only. This experiment measures the ability of herding to generalize from local information to global quantities of interest. In total 100K samples were generated and used to estimate $P(k)$. The results were compared with the following two alternatives: 1) sampling 100K pseudo-samples from the single variable marginals and using them to estimate $P(k)$ (denoted "MARG"), 2) learning a fully connected, fully visible Boltzmann machine using the pseudo-likelihood method[6] (denoted PL), then sampling 200K samples from that model and using the last 100K to estimate $P(k)$.

In experiment II we will estimate a discriminant function for classifying one attribute (the label) given the values of other attributes. Our approach was simply to perform online learning of a logistic regression function after each pseudo-sample collected from herding. Again, local pairwise information is turned into a global discriminant function which is then compared with some standard classifiers learned directly from the data. In particular, we compared against Naive Bayes, 5-nearest neighbors, logistic regression and a fully observed, fully connected Boltzmann machine learned with pseudo likelihood on the joint space of attributes and labels. The learned model's conditional distribution of label given the remaining attributes was subsequently used for prediction.

We have used the following datasets in our experiments.

---

6. This method is close to optimal for this type of problem (Parise and Welling, 2005).

DATASET	H.XXX	H.XX	PL	MARG
BOWLING	5E-3	4.1E-2	1.2E-1	4.3E-1
ABELONE	8E-4	2.5E-3	2.2E-2	1.8E0
DIGITS	-	6.2E-2	3.3E-2	4E-1
NEWS	-	2.5E-2	1.9E-2	5E-1

Table 4.1: **Abelone/Digits/NewsGroups**: KL divergence between true (data) distribution and the estimates from 1) herding algorithm using all triplets, 2) herding with all pairs, 3) samples from pseudo-likelihood model and 4) samples from single marginals.

A) The "Bowling Data" set.[7] Each binary attribute represents whether a pin has fallen during two subsequent bowls. There are 10 pins and 298 games in total. This data was generated by P. Cotton to make a point about the modelling of company default dependency. Random splits of 150 train and 148 test instances were used for the classification experiments.

B) Abalone dataset.[8] We converted the dataset into binary values by subtracting the mean from all (8) attributes and labels and setting all obtained values to 0 if smaller than 0 and 1 otherwise. For the classification task we used random subsets of 2000 examples for training and the remaining 2177 for testing.

C) "Newsgroups-small"[9] prepared by S. Roweis. It has 100 binary attributes and $16,242$ instances and is highly sparse (4% of the values is 1). Random splits of $10,000$ train and $6,242$ test instances were used for the classification experiments.

D) Digits: 8×8 binarized handwritten digits. We used 1100 examples from the digit classes 3 and 5 respectively (a total of 2200 instances). The dataset contains 30% 1's. This dataset was split randomly in 1600 train and 600 test instances.

The results for experiment I are shown in Table 4.1 and Figure 4.12. Note that the herding algorithms are deterministic and repetition would have resulted in the same values.

We observe that herding is successful in turning local average statistics into estimates of global quantities. Providing more information such as joint probabilities over triplets does significantly improve the result (the triplet results for Digits and News took too long to run due to the large number of triplets involved). Also of interest is the fact that for the low dimensional

7. http://www.financialmathematics.com/wiki/Code:tenpin/data
8. Downloadable from UCI repository
9. Downloaded from: http://www.cs.toronto.edu/~roweis/data.html

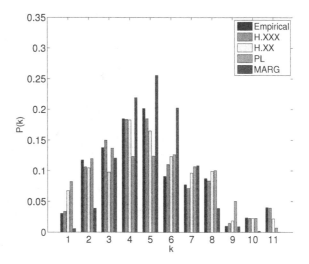

Figure 4.12: Estimates of $P(k)$ for the Bowling dataset. Each group of 5 bars represent the estimates for 1) ground truth, 2) herding with triples, 3) herding with pairs, 4) pseudo-likelihood, 5) marginals.

DATASET	H.XXY	PL	5NN	NB	LR
ABELONE	0.24 ± 0.004	0.24 ± 0.004	0.33 ± 0.1	0.27 ± 0.006	0.24 ± 0.004
BOWLING	0.23 ± 0.03	0.28 ± 0.06	0.32 ± 0.05	0.23 ± 0.03	0.23 ± 0.03
DIGITS	0.05 ± 0.01	0.06 ± 0.01	0.05 ± 0.01	0.09 ± 0.01	0.06 ± 0.02
NEWS	0.11 ± 0.005	0.04 ± 0.001	0.13 ± 0.006	0.12 ± 0.003	0.11 ± 0.004

Table 4.2: Average classification results averaged over 5 runs.

data H.XX outperformed PL but for the high-D datasets the opposite was true while both methods seem to leverage the same second order statistics (even though PL needs the actual data to learn its model).

The results for the classification experiment are shown in Table 4.2. On all tasks the online learning of a linear logistic regression classifier did just as well as running logistic regression on the original data directly. This implies that the herding algorithm generates the information necessary for classification and that the decision boundary can be learned online during herding. Interestingly, the PL procedure significantly outperformed all standard classifiers as well as herding on the Newsgroup data. This implies that a more sophisticated decision boundary is warranted for this data.

To see if the herding sequence contained the information necessary to estimate such a decision boundary we reran PL on the first 10,000 pseudo-

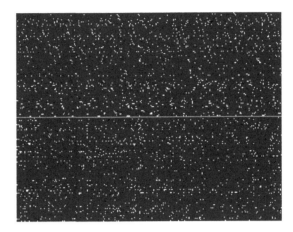

Figure 4.13: Top half: Sequence of 300 pseudo-samples generated from a herding algorithm for the "Newsgroup" dataset. White dots indicate the presence of certain word-types in documents (represented as columns). Bottom half: Newsgroup data (in random order). Data and pseudo-samples have the same first and second order statistics.

samples generated by herding resulting in an error of 0.04, answering the question in the affirmative. A plot of the herding pseudo-samples as compared to the original data is shown in Figure 1.

4.4.2 Herding with Hidden Variables

We studied generalized herding on the architecture of a restricted Boltzmann machine (Hinton, 2002) (RBM). We used features $\phi(x, z) = \{x_j, z_k, x_j z_k\}$, where j and k are indices of variables, and the $\{-1, +1\}$ representation because we found it worked significantly better than the $\{0, 1\}$ representation. To increase the entropy of the hidden units we left out the growth update for the features $\{z_k\}$ implying that $p(z_k = 1) \approx 0.5$. The intuition is the same as for bagging: we want to create a high diversity of (almost independent) ways to reconstruct the data because it will reduce the variance when making predictions. We observed that high entropy hidden representations automatically emerged when using a large number of hidden units. In contrast, for a small number of hidden units (say $K < 30$) there is a tendency for the system to converge on low entropy representations and the trick delivers some improvement.

We applied herding to the USPS Handwritten Digits dataset[10] which consists of 1100 examples of each digit 0 through 9 (totaling 11,000 ex-

---

10. Downloaded from `http://www.cs.toronto.edu/~roweis/data.html`

amples). Each image has 256 pixels and each pixel has a value between [1..256] which we turned into a binary representation through the mapping $x'_j = 2\Theta(\frac{x_j}{256} - 0.2) - 1$ with $\Theta(x > 0) = 1$ and 0 otherwise. Each digit class was randomly split into 700 train, 300 validation and 100 test examples. As benchmarks we used 1NN using Manhattan distance and multinomial logistic regression, both in pixel space.

We used two versions of herding, one where the maximization over **s** was initialized at the value from the previous time step (H) and one where we initialize at the data-case with the lowest energy (SH — the tractable algorithm). In both cases we ran herding for 2000 iterations for each class individually. During the second 1000 iterations we computed the energies for the training data in that class, as well as for all validation and test data across all classes. At each iteration we then used the training energies to standardize the validation and test energies by computing their Z-scores: $\mathcal{E}'_i = (\mathcal{E}_i - \mu_{\text{trn}})/\sigma_{\text{trn}}$ where μ_{trn} and σ_{trn} represent the mean and standard deviation of the energies of the training data at that iteration. The standardized energies for test and validation data were subsequently averaged over herding iterations (using online averaging). Once we have collected these average standardized energies across all digit classes we fit a multinomial logistic regression classifier to the validation data, using the 10 class-specific energies as features.

We also compared these results against models learned with contrastive divergence (Hinton, 2002) (CD) and persistent CD (Tieleman, 2008) (PCD). For both CD and PCD we first applied (P)CD learning for 1000 iterations in batch mode, using a stepsize of $\eta = 10^{-3}$. A momentum parameter of 0.9 and 1-step reconstructions were used for CD. No momentum and a single sample in the negative phase was used for PCD. In the second 1000 iterations we continued learning but also collected standardized validation and test energies as before which we subsequently used for classification. We have also experimented with chains of length 10 and found that it did not improved the results but became prohibitively inefficient. To improve efficiency we experimented with learning in mini-batches but this degraded the results significantly, presumably because the number of training examples used to standardize the energy scores became less reliable.

The results reported in Figure 4.14 show the classification results averaged across 4 runs with different splits and for different values of hidden units. Without trying to claim superior performance we merely want to make the case that herding can be leveraged to achieve state-of-the-art performance (note that USPS error rates are higher than MNIST error rates). We also see that the tractable version of herding did not perform as well as the herding using local optimization, which in turn performed equally well as learning a

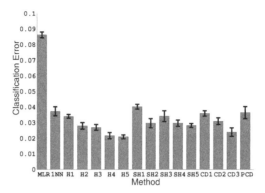

Figure 4.14: Classification results on USPS digits. 700 digits per class were used for training, 300 for validation and 100 for testing. Shown are average results over 4 different splits and their standard errors. From left to right: MLR (multinomial logistic regression), 1NN (1-nearest neighbor), H1-H5 (herding using local optimization with 50,100,250,500 and 1000 hidden units respectively), SH1-SH5 (safe, tractable herding from section 7 with 50,100,250,500 and 1000 hidden units respectively), CD1-CD3 (contrastive divergence with 50,100,250 hidden units respectively) and PCD (persistent CD with 500 hidden units).

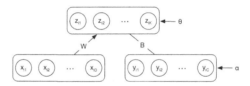

Figure 4.15: Discriminative Restricted Boltzmann Machine model of distribution $p(\mathbf{y}, \mathbf{z} | \mathbf{x})$.

model using CD. Persistent CD did not give very good results presumably because we did not use optimal settings for step-size, weight-decay etc.. It is finally interesting to observe that there does not seem to be any sign of over-fitting for herding. For the model with 1000 hidden units, the total number of real parameters involved is around 1.5 million which represents more capacity than the 1.5 million binary pixel values in the data.

4.4.3 Discriminative Herding

We studied the behavior of conditional herding on two artificial and four real-world data sets, comparing its performance to that of the voted perceptron (Freund and Schapire, 1999) and that of discriminative RBMs (Larochelle and Bengio, 2008). All the experiment results in this subsection are accredited to the authors of Gelfand et al. (2010).

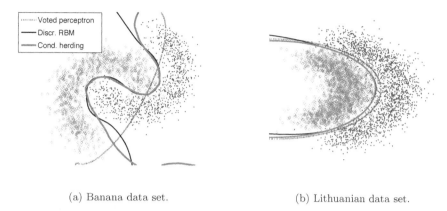

(a) Banana data set.   (b) Lithuanian data set.

Figure 4.16: Decision boundaries of VP, CH, and dRBMs on two artificial data sets.

We studied conditional herding in the discriminative RBM (dRBM) architecture illustrated in Figure 4.15, that is, we use the following parameterization

$$\mathbf{w}^T \phi(\mathbf{x}, \mathbf{y}, \mathbf{z}) = \mathbf{x}^T \mathbf{W} \mathbf{z} + \mathbf{y}^T \mathbf{B} \mathbf{z} + \boldsymbol{\theta}^T \mathbf{z} + \boldsymbol{\alpha}^T \mathbf{y}. \tag{4.69}$$

where $\mathbf{W}$, $\mathbf{B}$, $\boldsymbol{\theta}$ and $\boldsymbol{\alpha}$ are the weights, $\mathbf{z}$ is a binary vector and $\mathbf{y}$ is a binary vector in a 1-of-K scheme.

Per the discussion in Section 4.3.4, we added an additional feature $\phi_0(\mathbf{x}) = \sqrt{R_{\max}^2 - ||\mathbf{x}||^2}$ with $R_{\max} = \max_i ||\mathbf{x}_i||$ in all experiments.

Experiments on Artificial Data

To investigate the characteristics of the voted perceptron (VP), discriminative RBM (dRBM) and conditional herding (CH), we used the techniques discussed in Section 4.3.4 to construct decision boundaries on two artificial data sets: (1) the banana data set; and (2) the Lithuanian data set. We ran VP and CH for $1,000$ epochs using mini-batches of size 100. The decision boundary for VP and CH is located at the location where the sign of the prediction $\mathbf{y}_{\text{test}}^*$ changes. We used conditional herders with 20 hidden units. The dRBMs also had 20 hidden units and were trained by running conjugate gradients until convergence. The weights of the dRBMs were initialized by sampling from a Gaussian distribution with a variance of 10^{-4}. The decision boundary for the dRBMs is located at the point where both class posteriors are equal, i.e., where $p(y_{\text{test}}^* = -1|\tilde{\mathbf{x}}_{\text{test}}) = p(y_{\text{test}}^* = +1|\tilde{\mathbf{x}}_{\text{test}}) = 0.5$.

Plots of the decision boundary for the artificial data sets are shown in Figure 4.16. The results on the banana data set illustrate the representational advantages of hidden units. Since VP selects data points at random to update the weights, on the banana data set, the weight vector of VP tends to oscillate back and forth yielding a nearly linear decision boundary.[11] This happens because VP can regress on only $2+1 = 3$ fixed features. In contrast, for CH the simple predictor in the top layer can regress onto $M = 20$ hidden features. This prevents the same oscillatory behavior from occurring.

Experiments on Real-World Data

In addition to the experiments on synthetic data, we also performed experiments on four real-world data sets - namely, (1) the USPS data set, (2) the MNIST data set, (3) the UCI Pendigits data set, and (4) the 20-Newsgroups data set. The USPS data set consists of $11,000$, 16×16 grayscale images of handwritten digits ($1,100$ images of each digit 0 through 9) with no fixed division. The MNIST data set contains $70,000$, 28×28 grayscale images of digits, with a fixed division into $60,000$ training and $10,000$ test instances. The UCI Pendigits consists of 16 (integer-valued) features extracted from the movement of a stylus. It contains $10,992$ instances, with a fixed division into $7,494$ training and $3,498$ test instances. The 20-Newsgroups data set contains bag-of-words representations of $18,774$ documents gathered from 20 different newsgroups. Since the bag-of-words representation comprises of over $60,000$ words, we identified the $5,000$ most frequently occurring words. From this set, we created a data set of $4,900$ binary word-presence features by binarizing the word counts and removing the 100 most frequently occurring words. The 20-Newsgroups data has a fixed division into $11,269$ training and $7,505$ test instances. On all data sets with real-valued input attributes we used the 'normalizing' feature described above.

The data sets used in the experiments are multi-class. We adopted a 1-of-K encoding, where if $\mathbf{y}_i$ is the label for data point $\mathbf{x}_i$, then $\mathbf{y}_i = \{y_{i,1}, ..., y_{i,K}\}$ is a binary vector such that $y_{i,k} = 1$ if the label of the ith data point is k and $y_{i,k} = -1$ otherwise. Performing the maximization in Equation 4.59 is difficult when $K > 2$. We investigated two different procedures for doing so. In the first procedure, we reduce the multi-class problem to a series of binary decision problems using a one-versus-all scheme. The prediction on a test point is taken as the label with the largest online average. In the second procedure, we make predictions on all K labels jointly. To perform the maximization in Equation 4.59, we explore all states of $\mathbf{y}$ in a one-of-K encoding - i.e. one unit is activated and all others are inactive. This partial

---

11. On the Lithuanian data set, VP constructs a good boundary by exploiting the added 'normalizing' feature.

maximization is not a problem as long as the ensuing configuration satisfies $\mathbf{w}_t^T \mathbf{v}_t \leq 0$.[12] The main difference between the two procedures is that in the second procedure the weights $\mathbf{W}$ are shared amongst the K classifiers. The primary advantage of the latter procedure is its less computationally demanding than the one-versus-all scheme.

We trained the dRBMs by performing iterations of conjugate gradients (using 3 line searches) on mini-batches of size 100 until the error on a small held-out validation set started increasing (i.e., we employed early stopping) or until the negative conditional log-likelihood on the training data stopped coming down. Following Larochelle and Bengio (2008), we use L_2-regularization on the weights of the dRBMs; the regularization parameter was determined based on the generalization error on the same held-out validation set. The weights of the dRBMs were initialized from a Gaussian distribution with variance of 10^{-4}.

CH used mini-batches of size 100. For the USPS and Pendigits data sets CH used a burn-in period of $1,000$ updates; on MNIST it was $5,000$ updates; and on 20 Newsgroups it was $20,000$ updates. Herding was stopped when the error on the training set became zero.[13]

The parameters of the conditional herders were initialized by sampling from a Gaussian distribution. Ideally, we would like each of the terms in the energy function in Equation 4.69 to contribute equally during updating. However, since the dimension of the data is typically much greater than the number of classes, the dynamics of the conditional herding system will be largely driven by $\mathbf{W}$. To negate this effect, we rescaled the standard deviation of the Gaussian by a factor $1/M$ with M the total number of elements of the parameter involved (e.g. $\sigma_{\mathbf{W}} = \sigma/(\dim(\mathbf{x})\dim(\mathbf{z}))$ etc.). We also scale the learning rates $\boldsymbol{\eta}$ by the same factor so the updates will retain this scale during herding. The relative scale between $\boldsymbol{\eta}$ and σ was chosen by cross-validation. Recall that the absolute scale is unimportant (see Section 4.3.4 for details).

In addition, during the early stages of herding, we adapted the parameter update for the bias on the hidden units $\boldsymbol{\theta}$ in such a way that the marginal distribution over the hidden units was nearly uniform. This has the advantage that it encourages high entropy in the hidden units, leading to more useful dynamics of the system. In practice, we update $\boldsymbol{\theta}$ as

---

12. Local maxima can also be found by iterating over $y_{\text{test}}^{*,k}, z_{\text{test},j}^{*,k}$, but the proposed procedure is more efficient.

13. We use a fixed order of the mini-batches, so that if there are D data cases and the batch size is d, if the training error is 0 for $\lceil D/d \rceil$ iterations, the error for the whole training set is 0.

$\boldsymbol{\theta}_{t+1} = \boldsymbol{\theta}_t + \frac{\eta}{D_t} \sum_{i_t} (1 - \lambda) \langle \mathbf{z}_{i_t} \rangle - \mathbf{z}^*_{i_t}$, where i_t indexes the data points in the mini-batch at time t, D_t is the size of the mini-batch, and $\langle \mathbf{z}_{i_t} \rangle$ is the batch mean. λ is initialized to 1 and we gradually half its value every 500 updates, slowly moving from an entropy-encouraging update to the standard update for the biases of the hidden units.

VP was also run on mini-batches of size 100 (with a learning rate of 1). VP was run until the predictor started overfitting on a validation set. No burn-in was considered for VP.

The results of our experiments are shown in Table 4.3. In the table, the best performance on each data set using each procedure is typeset in boldface. The results reveal that the addition of hidden units to the voted perceptron leads to significant improvements in terms of generalization error. Furthermore, the results of our experiments indicate that conditional herding performs on par with discriminative RBMs on the MNIST and USPS data sets and better on the 20 Newsgroups data set. The 20 Newsgroups data is high dimensional and sparse and both VP and CH appear to perform quite well in this regime. Techniques to promote sparsity in the hidden layer when training dRBMs exist (see Larochelle and Bengio (2008)), but we did not investigate them here. It is also worth noting that CH is rather resilient to overfitting. This is particularly evident in the low-dimensional UCI Pendigits data set, where the dRBMs start to badly overfit with 500 hidden units, while the test error for CH remains level. This phenomenon is the benefit of averaging over many different predictors.

4.5   Summary

We introduce the herding algorithm in this chapter as an alternative to the maximum likelihood estimation for Markov random fields. It skips the parameter estimation step and directly converts a set of moments from the training data into a sequence of model parameters accompanied by a sequence of pseudo-samples. By integrating the intractable training and testing steps in the regular machine learning paradigm, herding provides a more efficient way of learning and predicting in MRFs.

We study the statistical properties of herding and show that herding dynamics introduces negative auto-correlation in the sample sequence which helps to speed up the mixing rate of the sampler in the state space. Quantitatively, the negative auto-correlation leads to a fast convergence rate of $\mathcal{O}(1/T)$ between the sampling statistics and the input moments. That is significantly faster than the rate of $\mathcal{O}(1/\sqrt{T})$ that an ideal random sampler would obtain for an MRF at MLE. This distinctive property of herding

One-Versus-All Procedure					
Data Set	**VP**	**Discriminative RBM**		**Conditional herding**	
		100	200	100	200
MNIST	7.69%	**3.57%**	3.58%	3.97%	3.99%
USPS	5.03% (0.4%)	3.97% (0.38%)	4.02% (0.68%)	3.49% (0.45%)	**3.35%** (0.48%)
UCI Pendigits	10.92%	5.32%	5.00%	3.37%	**3.00%**
20 Newsgroups	27.75%	34.78%	34.36%	29.78%	**25.96%**

Joint Procedure							
Data Set	**VP**	**Discriminative RBM**			**Conditional herding**		
		50	100	500	50	100	500
MNIST	8.84%	3.88%	2.93%	**1.98%**	2.89%	2.09%	2.09%
USPS	4.86% (0.52%)	3.13% (0.73%)	2.84% (0.59%)	4.06% (1.09%)	3.36% (0.48%)	3.07% (0.52%)	**2.81%** (0.50%)
UCI Pendigits	6.78%	3.80%	3.23%	8.89%	3.14%	**2.57%**	2.86%
20 Newsgroups	**24.89%**	–	30.57%	30.07%	–	25.76%	24.93%

Table 4.3: Generalization errors of VP, dRBMs, and CH on 4 real-world data sets. dRBMs and CH results are shown for various numbers of hidden units. The best performance on each data set is typeset in boldface; missing values are shown as '-'. The std. dev. of the error on the 10-fold cross validation of the USPS data set is reported in parentheses.

should also be attributed to its weak-chaotic behavior as a deterministic dynamic system, whose characteristics deserve its own interest for future research.

Experiments confirms that the information contained in the pseudo-samples of herding can be used for inference and prediction. It achieves comparable performance with traditional machine learning algorithms including the MRFs, even though the sampling distribution of herding does not guarantee the maximum entropy.

We further provide a general condition, PCT, for the fast moment matching property. That condition allows more practical implementations of herding. We also use it to derive extensions of the herding algorithm for a wider range of applications. As more flexible feature functions defined on both visible and latent variables can now be handled in the generalized algorithm, we apply herding to training partially observed MRFs. Experiments on the USPS dataset show a classification accuracy on par with the state-of-art training algorithms on the same model. Furthermore, we propose a discriminative learning variant of herding for supervised problems by including labelling information in the feature definition. The resulting conditional herding provides an alternative to training CRFs. Empirical evaluation shows competitive performance of herding compared with standard algorithms.

4.6 Conclusion

The view espoused in this chapter is that we can view learning as an iterated map: $\mathbf{w}_{t+1} = F(\mathbf{w}_t)$ and that we can study the properties of this map using the tools of nonlinear dynamics systems. The usual learning approaches based on point estimates form a contractive map where all of parameter space is eventually mapped to a point. In Bayesian approaches we seek to find a posterior distribution over parameters and the map should thus converge to a distribution (or measure). For MCMC for instance the map consists of convolving the current distribution with a kernel. Herding offers a third possibility where the attractor is neither a point, nor a measure in the usual sense, but rather a highly complex, possibly fractal set. Interestingly, the more recent approach "perturb and map" is related to herding in the sense that it consists of a sequence of perturbations of the parameters followed by an optimization over the state space. However, it is different from herding in the sense the perturbations are generated randomly and IID, while in herding the perturbations are deterministic and dynamic (i.e. depend on the previous parameters).

The surprising and powerful insight is that we can use a new set of tools from the mathematics literature to study these maps. For instance, it was shown in this chapter that herding dynamics is a special instance of the class of piecewise isometry maps, and should neither be classified as regular nor chaotic, but rather as what is known as "edge of chaos". We suspect that this type of dynamics has useful properties in the context of learning from data. For instance, it seems related to the fact that the certain empirical moments averages exhibit very fast convergence. This is supported by the observations that 1) piecewise isometries have vanishing topological entropy, 2) exhibit the "period doubling route to chaos" and 3) have vanishing Lyapunov exponents. We believe that these type of concepts from the field of nonlinear dynamical systems may one day play an important role in the field of machine learning.

Appendix:

Some Results on Herding in Discrete Spaces

The following proposition shows that the weight vectors move inside a $D-1$ dimensional subspace.

Proposition 4.11. *For any herding dynamics with D states and K dimensional feature vectors, the trajectory of the weight vector lies in a subspace of a dimension $K^* \leq \max\{D-1, K\}$. Also, there exists an equivalent herding dynamics with D states and K^* dimensional feature vectors, which generates the same sequence of samples.*

Proof. Let $\{\phi(x_d)\}_{d=0}^{D-1}$ be the set of D state feature vectors. Denote by Φ the subspace spanned of the set of $D-1$ vectors, $\{\phi(x_d) - \phi(x_0)\}_{d=1}^{D-1}$ in $\mathbb{R}^K$, and by $\Phi^\perp$ its complement. The dimension of Φ is apparently at most $\max\{D-1, K\}$. We want to construct a herding dynamics in Φ that generates the same sequence of states as the original dynamics.

Decompose the initial weight vector $\mathbf{w}_0$ and all the feature vectors into Φ and $\Phi^\perp$, denoting the component in Φ with a superscript $\|$ and in $\Phi^\perp$ with $\perp$. Then $\phi^\perp(x_d) = (\phi(x_d) - \phi(x_0) + \phi(x_0))^\perp = \phi^\perp(x_0), \forall d$ as $\phi(x_d) - \phi(x_0) \in \Phi$, and $\phi^\|(x_d) = \phi(x_d) - \phi^\perp(x_0), \forall d$. Consequently $\bar{\phi}^\| = \bar{\phi} - \phi^\perp(x_0)$ as $\bar{\phi}$ is a convex combination of the feature vectors.

Let us consider a new herding dynamics (denoted by a superscript *) with feature vectors $\{\phi^\|(x_d)\}_{d=0}^{D-1}$ and the moment $\bar{\phi}^\|$. We initialize with a weight vector $\mathbf{w}_0^* = \mathbf{w}_0^\|$. As Φ is closed with respect to the herding update in Equation 4.8 $\mathbf{w}_t^* \in \Phi, \forall t \geq 0$. Now we want to show that the set of samples $S_T^* \overset{\text{def}}{=} \{s_t^*\}_{t=1}^T$ is the same as $S_T \overset{\text{def}}{=} \{s_t\}_{t=1}^T$ for any $T \geq 0$.

Obviously this holds at $T = 0$ as $\mathbf{w}_0^* \in \Phi$ and $S_T^* = S_T = \emptyset$. Assume that $S_T^* = S_T$ holds for some $T \geq 0$. Following the recursive representation of $\mathbf{w}_T$ in Equation 4.14, we get

$$\mathbf{w}_T^* = \mathbf{w}_0^* + T\bar{\phi}^\| - \sum_{t=1}^T \phi^\|(\mathbf{s}_t) = \mathbf{w}_0 - \mathbf{w}_0^\perp + T\bar{\phi} - \sum_{t=1}^T \phi(\mathbf{s}_t) = \mathbf{w}_T - \mathbf{w}_0^\perp \quad (4.70)$$

The sample to be generated at iteration $T+1$ is computed as

$$\mathbf{s}_{T+1}^* = \arg\max_x (\mathbf{w}_T^*)^T \phi^\|(x) = \arg\max_x (\mathbf{w}_T)^T \phi(x) - (\mathbf{w}_0^\perp)^T \phi^\perp(x_0) = \mathbf{s}_{T+1}$$

$$(4.71)$$

Therefore, $S_{T+1}^* = S_{T+1}$, and consequently $S_T^* = S_T, \forall T \in [0, \infty)$ by induction. As a by-product of Equation 4.70, we observe that the trajectory

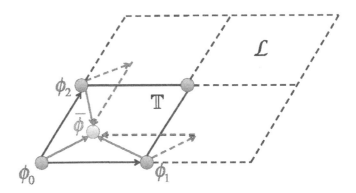

Figure 4.17: Example of the torus projection on herding dynamics with 3 states and 2-dimensional feature vectors. The red lines show the lattice and the torus (solid only) formed by $\phi(x_1) - \phi(x_0)$ and $\phi(x_2) - \phi(x_0)$, and the purple dashed arrows show that the herding dynamics corresponds to a constant rotation on the torus $\mathbb{T}^2$.

of the original herding dynamics $\{\mathbf{w}_t\}$ lies in the K^* dimensional affine subspace, $\mathbf{w}_0^\perp + \Phi$. $\square$

The proposition above suggests that the number of effective dimensions of the feature vector is upper-bounded by the number of states in the herding system. Also, the orthogonal component in the initial weight vector $\mathbf{w}_0^\perp$ does not affect the sequence of generated samples. In our example of sampling a D-valued discrete distribution with the 1-of-D encoding, the D feature vectors $\{\phi(x_d)\}_{d=1}^{D-1}$ are linearly independent with each other and hence we achieve the maximum number of feature dimensions $K^* = D - 1$. The affine subspace can be easily computed as $\{\mathbf{w} : \sum_{d=1}^{D} w_d = 1\}$. In the rest of this subsection, we will study the characteristics of a relatively more general type of herding dynamics with $D = K + 1$ states, whose feature vectors consist of a linearly independent set in the K dimensional feature space.

Let $\mathcal{L}$ be the lattice formed by the set of vectors $\{\phi(x_d) - \phi(x_0)\}_{d=1}^{K}$, and let $\mathbb{T}^K$ be the K dimensional torus $\mathbb{R}^K/\mathcal{L}$. A torus is a circular space with every pair of opposite edges connected with each other. See Figure 4.17 for an example of a 2D torus. Denote by $G : \mathbb{R}^K \to \mathbb{T}^K$ the canonical projection. For any point $u \in \mathbb{R}^K$, we have the property that $G(u + (\phi(x_d) - \phi(x_0))) = G(u), \forall d = 0, \ldots, K$. Let $\mathcal{T} : \mathbb{R}^K \to \mathbb{R}^K$ be the mapping of the herding dynamics in the feature space, which takes the form of a translation $\mathcal{T}(\mathbf{w}) = \mathbf{w} + \bar{\phi} - \phi(x(\mathbf{w}))$, where $x(\mathbf{w})$ is the sample to be generated by Equation 4.7. We can observe that the herding update on $\mathbf{w}$

corresponds a rotation on the torus:

$$
\begin{aligned}
G \circ \mathcal{T}(\mathbf{w}) &= G(\mathbf{w} + \bar{\phi} - \phi(x(\mathbf{w}))) \\
&= G(\mathbf{w} + (\bar{\phi} - \phi(x_0)) - (\phi(x(\mathbf{w})) - \phi(x_0))) \\
&= G(\mathbf{w}) + (\bar{\phi} - \phi(x_0)), \forall \mathbf{w} \in \mathbb{R}^K
\end{aligned}
\tag{4.72}
$$

where the translation operator in $\mathbb{T}^K$ in the last equation refers to a rotation in the torus. This is an interesting property of herding with a maximum number of feature dimensions as it suggests that no matter what sample the dynamics takes, the trajectory of $\mathbf{w}$ under the torus projection is driven by a constant rotation. Furthermore, if the set of elements in the translation vector $\bar{\phi} - \phi(x_0)$ is independent on rational numbers[14], the trajectory on $\mathbb{T}^K$ fills the entire torus, which leads to a non-fractal attractor set with a finite volume in the original feature space.

4.8   References

K. Aihara and G. Matsumoto. Temporally coherent organization and instabilities in squid giant axons. *Journal of theoretical biology*, 95(4):697–720, 1982.

O. Angel, A. E. Holroyd, J. B. Martin, and J. Propp. Discrete low-discrepancy sequences. *arXiv preprint arXiv:0910.1077*, 2009.

F. Bach, S. Lacoste-Julien, and G. Obozinski. On the equivalence between herding and conditional gradient algorithms. In J. Langford and J. Pineau, editors, *Proceedings of the 29th International Conference on Machine Learning (ICML-12)*, ICML '12, pages 1359–1366, New York, NY, USA, July 2012. Omnipress. ISBN 978-1-4503-1285-1.

C. M. Bishop et al. *Pattern Recognition and Machine Learning*, volume 1. springer New York, 2006.

H. Block and S. Levin. On the boundedness of an iterative procedure for solving a system of linear inequalities. *Proceedings of the American Mathematical Society*, 26(2):229–235, 1970.

L. Bornn, Y. Chen, N. de Freitas, M. Eskelin, J. Fang, and M. Welling. Herded Gibbs sampling. In *Proceedings of the International Conference on Learning Representations*, 2013.

M. Boshernitzan and I. Kornfeld. Interval translation mappings. *Ergodic Theory and Dynamical Systems*, 15(5):821–832, 1995.

O. Breuleux, Y. Bengio, and P. Vincent. Quickly generating representative samples from an rbm-derived process. *Neural Computation*, pages 1–16, 2011.

14. Independence of a set of numbers, $x_1, \ldots, x_K$, on rational numbers means that there does not exist a set of rational numbers $a_1, \ldots, a_K$ that are not all zeros, such that $\sum_{d=1}^K a_d x_d = 0$.

Y. Chen, A. Smola, and M. Welling. Super-samples from kernel herding. In *Proceedings of the Twenty-Sixth Conference Annual Conference on Uncertainty in Artificial Intelligence (UAI-10)*, pages 109–116, Corvallis, Oregon, 2010. AUAI Press.

Y. Chen, A. E. Gelfand, and M. Welling. *Advanced Structured Prediction*, chapter Herding for Structured Prediction, page 187. The MIT Press, 2014.

M. Collins. Discriminative training methods for hidden markov models: Theory and experiments with perceptron algorithms. In *Proceedings of the ACL-02 conference on Empirical methods in natural language processing-Volume 10*, page 8. Association for Computational Linguistics, 2002.

Y. Freund and R. Schapire. Large margin classification using the perceptron algorithm. *Machine learning*, 37(3):277–296, 1999.

A. Gelfand, Y. Chen, L. van der Maaten, and M. Welling. On herding and the perceptron cycling theorem. In J. Lafferty, C. K. I. Williams, J. Shawe-Taylor, R. Zemel, and A. Culotta, editors, *Advances in Neural Information Processing Systems 23*, pages 694–702, 2010.

A. Goetz. Dynamics of piecewise isometries. *Illinois Journal of Mathematics*, 44 (3):465–478, 2000.

N. Harvey and S. Samadi. Near-optimal herding. In *Proceedings of The 27th Conference on Learning Theory*, pages 1165–1182, 2014.

G. Hinton. Training products of experts by minimizing contrastive divergence. *Neural Computation*, 14:1771–1800, 2002.

F. Huszar and D. Duvenaud. Optimally-weighted herding is Bayesian quadrature. In *Proceedings of the Twenty-Eighth Conference Annual Conference on Uncertainty in Artificial Intelligence (UAI-12)*, pages 377–386, Corvallis, Oregon, 2012. AUAI Press.

H. Larochelle and Y. Bengio. Classification using discriminative restricted Boltzmann machines. In *Proceedings of the 25th International Conference on Machine learning*, pages 536–543. ACM, 2008.

K. Lu and J. Wang. Construction of Sturmian sequences. *J. Phys. A: Math. Gen.*, 38:2891–2897, 2005.

G. A. H. Marston Morse. Symbolic dynamics ii. sturmian trajectories. *American Journal of Mathematics*, 62(1):1–42, 1940. ISSN 00029327, 10806377. URL http://www.jstor.org/stable/2371431.

M. Minsky and S. Papert. *Perceptrons: An Introduction to Computational Geometry*, volume 1988. MIT press Cambridge, MA, 1969.

R. Neal. Connectionist learning of belief networks. *Articial Intelligence*, 56:71–113, 1992.

R. Neal. Probabilistic inference using Markov chain Monte Carlo methods. Technical Report CRG-TR-93-1, University of Toronto, Computer Science, 1993.

G. Papandreou and A. Yuille. Perturb-and-map random fields: Using discrete optimization to learn and sample from energy models. In *Proc. IEEE Int. Conf. on Computer Vision (ICCV)*, pages 193–200, Barcelona, Spain, Nov. 2011. doi: 10.1109/ICCV.2011.6126242.

S. Parise and M. Welling. Learning in Markov random fields: An empirical study. In *Joint Statistical Meeting*, volume 4, page 7, 2005.

F. Rosenblatt. The perceptron: A probabilistic model for information storage and organization in the brain. *Psychological Review*, 65(6):386–408, 1958.

R. Salakhutdinov. Learning deep Boltzmann machines using adaptive MCMC. In J. Fürnkranz and T. Joachims, editors, *Proceedings of the 27th International Conference on Machine Learning (ICML-10)*, pages 943–950, Haifa, Israel, June 2010. Omnipress. URL `http://www.icml2010.org/papers/441.pdf`.

R. H. Swendsen and J.-S. Wang. Nonuniversal critical dynamics in Monte Carlo simulations. *Physical Review Letters*, 58(2):80–88, 1987.

T. Tieleman. Training restricted Boltzmann machines using approximations to the likelihood gradient. In *Proceedings of the International Conference on Machine Learning*, volume 25, pages 1064–1071, 2008.

T. Tieleman and G. Hinton. Using fast weights to improve persistent contrastive divergence. In *Proceedings of the International Conference on Machine Learning*, volume 26, pages 1064–1071, 2009.

M. Tsodyks, K. Pawelzik, and H. Markram. Neural networks with dynamic synapses. *Neural Computation*, 10(4):821–835, 1098.

M. Welling. Herding dynamical weights to learn. In *Proceedings of the 21st International Conference on Machine Learning*, Montreal, Quebec, CAN, 2009a.

M. Welling. Herding dynamic weights for partially observed random field models. In *Proceedings of the Twenty-Fifth Conference Annual Conference on Uncertainty in Artificial Intelligence (UAI-09)*, pages 599–606, Corvallis, Oregon, 2009b. AUAI Press.

M. Welling and Y. Chen. Statistical inference using weak chaos and infinite memory. In *Proceedings of the Int'l Workshop on Statistical-Mechanical Informatics (IW-SMI 2010)*, pages 185–199, 2010.

L. Younes. Parametric inference for imperfectly observed Gibbsian fields. *Probability Theory and Related Fields*, 82:625–645, 1989.

D. Young. Iterative methods for solving partial difference equations of elliptic type. *Trans. Amer. Math. Soc*, 76(92):111, 1954.

A. Yuille. The convergence of contrastive divergences. In *Advances in Neural Information Processing Systems*, volume 17, pages 1593–1600, 2004.

5   Learning Maximum A-Posteriori Perturbation Models

Andreea Gane   `agane@csail.mit.edu`
Massachusetts Institute of Technology
Cambridge, MA

Tamir Hazan   `tamir.hazan@technion.ac.il`
Technion
Haifa, Israel

Tommi Jaakkola   `tommi@csail.mit.edu`
Massachusetts Institute of Technology
Cambridge, MA

Perturbation models are families of distributions induced from perturbations. They combine randomization of the parameters with maximization to draw unbiased samples. In this chapter, we describe randomization both as a modeling tool and as a means to enforce diversity and robustness in parameter learning. A perturbation model defined on the basis of low order statistics typically introduces high order dependencies in the samples. We analyze these dependencies and seek to estimate them from data. In doing so, we shift the modeling focus from the parameters of the potential function (base model) to the space of perturbations. We show how to estimate dependent perturbations over the parameters using a hard EM approach, cast in the form of inverse convex programs and illustrate the method on several computer vision problems.

5.1 Introduction

In applications that involve structured objects, such as object boundaries, textual descriptions, or speech utterances, the key problem is finding expressive yet tractable models. In these cases, the likely assignments are guided by potential functions over subsets of variables. The feasibility of inference is typically linked to the structure of the potential function and the tradeoff is between rich, faithful models defined on complex potential functions on one hand, and limited but manageable models on the other.

For instance, in natural language parsing, the goal is to return a dependency tree where arcs encode dependency relations, such as between a predicate and its subject. Whenever the interactions are of high order, computing the dependency tree corresponds to an NP-hard combinatorial optimization problem (McDonald and Satta, 2007), but when resorting to tractable formulations by limiting the type of interactions, the expressive power of the model is limited. In general, most realistic models for natural language parsing (Koo et al., 2010a), speech recognition (Rabiner and Juang, 1993) or image segmentation/captioning (Nowozin and Lampert, 2011; Fang et al., 2015) involve interactions between distant words in the sequence or large pixel neighborhoods.

Typical probabilistic models defined on structured potential functions make use of the Gibbs' distribution and its properties. Specifically, the structure of the potential function can be encoded as a graph that specifies conditional independencies (Markov properties) among the variables: two sets of vertices in the graph are conditionally independent when they are separated by observed vertices (e.g., Wainwright and Jordan (2008); Koller and Friedman (2009)). These assumptions are central for designing efficient exact or approximate inference techniques. Successful methods exploiting them include belief propagation (Pearl, 1988), Gibbs sampling (Geman and Geman, 1984), Metropolis-Hastings (Hastings, 1970) or Swendsen-Wang (Wang and Swendsen, 1987). In specific cases one can sample efficiently from a Markov random field model by constructing a rapidly mixing Markov chain (cf. (Jerrum and Sinclair, 1993; Jerrum et al., 2004a; Huber, 2003)). Such approaches do not extend to many practical cases where the values of the variables are strongly guided by both data (high signal) and prior knowledge (high coupling). Indeed, sampling in high-signal high-coupling regime is known to be provably hard (Jerrum and Sinclair, 1993; Goldberg and Jerrum, 2007).

Finding a single most likely assignment (MAP) structure is considerably easier than summing over the values of variables or drawing an unbiased sample. Substantial effort has gone into developing algorithms for recovering MAP assignments, either based on specific structural restrictions such as super-modularity (Kolmogorov, 2006) or by devising linear programming relaxations and successively refining them (Sontag et al., 2008; Werner, 2008). Furthermore, even when computing the MAP is provably hard, approximate techniques, such as loopy belief propagation (Murphy et al., 1999), tree reweighed message passing (Wainwright et al., 2005), local search algorithms (Zhang et al., 2014) or convex relaxations (Koo et al., 2010b) are often successful in recovering the optimal solutions (Koo et al., 2010a).

Recently, MAP inference has been combined with randomization to define new classes of probability models that are easy to sample from (Papandreou and Yuille, 2011; Tarlow et al., 2012; Hazan and Jaakkola, 2012; Hazan et al., 2013; Orabona et al., 2014; Maji et al., 2014). Each sample from these perturbation models involve randomization of Gibbs' potentials and finding the corresponding maximizing assignment. The models are shown to provide unbiased samples from the Gibbs distribution when perturbations are independent across assignments (Papandreou and Yuille, 2011; Tarlow et al., 2012) and have been applied to several applications where the base model is difficult to sample from: boundary annotation (Maji et al., 2014), image partitioning (Kappes et al., 2015), and others. Nonetheless, having a full account of the properties and power of perturbation models remains an open problem.

In this chapter, we describe and extend our work (Gane et al., 2014) on understanding and exploiting the expressive power of perturbation models. Specifically, the properties of the induced distribution are heavily governed by randomization. In contrast to Gibbs' distributions, low order potentials, after undergoing randomization and maximization, lead to high order dependencies in the induced distributions. Furthermore, we discuss conditioning, which is straightforward in Gibbs' distributions, but requires additional constraints on randomizations in perturbation models.

Finally, we explore the interplay between learning algorithms and tractability of inference procedures on complex potential functions by using dependent perturbations as a modeling tool. Perturbation models are latent variable models and we learn distributions over perturbations using a hard-EM approach. In the E-step, we use an inverse convex program to confine the randomization to the parameter polytope responsible for generating the observed answer. We illustrate the approach on several computer vision problems.

5.2   Background and Notation

In this chapter we are concerned with modeling distributions over structured objects $x \in \mathcal{X}$, such as image segmentations and keypoint matchings, where $\mathcal{X} = \mathcal{X}_1 \times \cdots \times \mathcal{X}_n$ is a discrete product space. We are scoring the possible assignments via a real valued potential function $\theta(x) = \theta(x_1, ..., x_n)$, where excluded configurations are implicitly encoded by setting $\theta(x) = -\infty$ whenever $x \notin dom(\theta)$. For instance, a foreground-background segmentation over an image of size $n \times m$ can be encoded by $x = (x_{ij})_{i\in[n], j\in[m]} \in \{0, 1\}^{n \times m}$, where $x_{ij} = 1$ denotes a foreground pixel at position (i, j). If we want to explicitly encode that a foreground object is always present, then $\theta(x) = -\infty$ whenever $x_{ij} = 0, \forall i \in [n], j \in [m]$.

Since dealing with arbitrary scoring functions is computationally intractable, $\theta(x)$ is typically defined as a sum of local potentials $\theta(x) = \sum_{\alpha \in \mathcal{A}} \theta_\alpha(x)$, where α denotes a small subset of variables (a factor) and $\mathcal{A}$ denotes the set of all such factors. In the image segmentation case, the set $\mathcal{A}$ may include local neighborhoods of the form $\{(i + d_i, j + d_j)|d_i, d_j \in \{+1, 0, -1\}\}$. In the following, we will often skip specifying $\mathcal{A}$ and write $\theta(x) = \sum_\alpha \theta_\alpha(x)$ for simplicity.

Traditionally, the potentials are mapped to the probability scale via the Gibbs' distribution:

$$p(x_1, ..., x_n) = \frac{1}{Z(\theta)} \exp(\theta(x_1, ..., x_n)) \tag{5.1}$$

Distributions defined in this manner have a number of desirable properties. For instance, the maximum-a-posteriory (MAP) prediction corresponds to the highest scoring assignment ($\hat{x} = \arg\max_x \theta(x)$), the set of conditional dependencies can be read from the structure of the potential function, and the model can be easily extended to handle partially observed data. Unfortunately, such distributions are challenging to learn and sample from, depending on how the potential function decomposes.

Our approach is based on randomizing potentials in Gibbs' distributions. We add a random function $\gamma : \mathcal{X} \to R$ to the potential function and draw samples by solving the resulting MAP prediction problem:

$$x^* = \arg\max_{x \in \mathcal{X}}\{\theta(x) + \gamma(x)\}. \tag{5.2}$$

The distribution induced by the samples is given by

$$\mathcal{P}(\hat{x}) = P_\gamma\Big[\hat{x} \in \arg\max_{x \in X}\{\theta(x) + \gamma(x)\}\Big] \tag{5.3}$$

and its properties are heavily dependent on the nature of randomization.

The simplest approach to designing the perturbation function γ is to associate an i.i.d. random variable $\gamma(x)$ for each $x \in \mathcal{X}$. The following result characterizes the induced distribution in this case, assuming that perturbations are Gumbel distributed. Specifically, due to the max-stability property of the Gumbel distribution, one can preserve the Markov properties of the Gibbs model. However, each realization x^* in this setup requires an independent draw of $\gamma(x)$, $x \in \mathcal{X}$, i.e., a high dimensional randomization.

Theorem 5.1. *(Gumbel and Lieblein, 1954) Let $\mathcal{X}$ be finite and let $\{\gamma(x), x \in \mathcal{X}\}$ be a collection of i.i.d. zero mean Gumbel distributed random variables, whose cumulative distribution functions is $F(t) = \exp(-\exp(-(t+c)))$ and $c \approx 0.5772$ is the Euler-Mascheroni constant. Then*

$$P_\gamma\Big[\hat{x} \in \arg\max_{x \in \mathcal{X}}\{\theta(x) + \gamma(x)\}\Big] = \frac{1}{Z(\theta)}\exp(\theta(\hat{x})) \tag{5.4}$$

Since perturbation models are useful only if they can be succinctly parametrized, our focus is on investigating *low-dimensional perturbations* which have the same structure as the potential function:

$$\mathcal{P}(\hat{x}) = P_\gamma\Big[\hat{x} \in \arg\max_{x \in X}\Big\{\sum_\alpha (\theta_\alpha(x_\alpha) + \gamma_\alpha(x_\alpha))\Big\}\Big] \tag{5.5}$$

In this case, each sample requires instantiating $\gamma_\alpha(x_\alpha)$ for each α and each assignment x_α, which is typically a much smaller set. Finally, since the noise function shares the structure of the potential function, the optimization algorithms designed for the original potential function remain applicable. We will often refer to the new (randomized) potential function as $\tilde{\theta}(x) = \sum_\alpha \tilde{\theta}_\alpha(x_\alpha)$, where $\tilde{\theta}_\alpha(x_\alpha) = \theta_\alpha(x_\alpha) + \gamma_\alpha(x_\alpha)$.

5.3   Expressive Power of Perturbation Models

Perturbation models were originally introduced as a way to approximate intractable Gibbs' distributions. In this chapter, we use perturbation models as a modeling tool, seeking to understand their properties, and how to estimate them from data.

The idea of specifying distributions over combinatorial objects by linking randomization and combinatorial optimization is not inherently limiting. At one extreme, the randomization may correspond to samples from the target distribution itself. Of course, the combination is advantageous only when both the randomization and the associated combinatorial problem are tractable. To this end, we focus on randomizing potentials in Gibbs' distributions whose MAP assignment can be obtained in polynomial time. The randomization we introduce will therefore have to respect how the potential functions decompose. For example, randomization of $\theta(x) = \sum_\alpha \theta_\alpha(x)$ should only directly affect individual terms $\theta_\alpha(x)$.

One of the key questions we address is how the resulting perturbation models differ from the associated Gibbs' models that they are based on. Gibbs' distributions are naturally understood in terms of Markov properties. Will these carry over to perturbation models as well? We will show that in contrast to Gibbs' distributions, low order potentials, after undergoing randomization and maximization, lead to high order dependencies in the induced distributions. Such induced dependences can be viewed as additional modeling power and specifically exploited and learned from data. Markov properties can be enforced in special cases such as with tailored perturbations in tree structured models, if desired.

Perturbation models yield simple mechanisms for drawing unbiased samples but they are cumbersome with respect to conditioning. Indeed, "plug-in" conditioning natural in Gibbs' distributions does not carry over to perturbation models. Conditioning requires care, restricting the randomization such that the setting of the observed variables are indeed obtained as part of maximizing assignments. We show how this can be done in simple examples.

5.4   Higher Order Dependencies

In this section, we show that perturbation models defined via low dimensional randomizations do not follow the Markov-type dependencies inherent in Gibbs distributions. We focus on perturbation models with tree structured potential functions and edge-based randomization, but the results can be generalized to more complex graphs.

The following theorem shows that when i.i.d. perturbations follow the edge structure of the potential function, we are able to capture dependencies above and beyond the initial structure.

Theorem 5.2. *Most perturbation models with tree structured potential functions and i.i.d. perturbation variables $\{\gamma_{ij}(x_i, x_j)\}$ indexed by $(i, j) \in E, (x_i, x_j) \in \mathcal{X}_i \times \mathcal{X}_j$ result in an induced model (5.5) that includes dependencies above and beyond the original tree structure.*

Proof. Consider a simple chain with three variables (x_1, x_2, x_3), potential function $\theta(x) = \theta_{12}(x_1, x_2) + \theta_{23}(x_2, x_3)$ and perturbations given by $\gamma(x) = \gamma_{12}(x_1, x_2) + \gamma_{23}(x_2, x_3)$. Let $\Gamma(\hat{x}_\alpha)$ be defined as

$$\Gamma(\hat{x}_\alpha) = \left\{ \gamma : \hat{x}_\alpha \in \underset{x \in X}{\arg\max}\{\theta(x) + \gamma(x)\} \right\} \tag{5.6}$$

and, similarly, for all subsets $\alpha, \beta \subseteq \{1, \ldots, n\}$, let

$$\Gamma(\hat{x}_\alpha | \hat{x}_\beta) = \left\{ \gamma : \ \hat{x}_\alpha \in \underset{x \in X, x_\beta = \hat{x}_\beta}{\arg \max} \{\theta(x) + \gamma(x)\} \right\} \tag{5.7}$$

be the set of perturbation assignments for which $\hat{x}_\alpha$ is optimal if we plug-in values $\hat{x}_\beta$.

We illustrate that $x_1 \perp\!\!\!\perp x_3 | x_2$ need not hold. To this end, consider probabilities:

$$\mathcal{P}(\hat{x}_i | \hat{x}_2) = P_\gamma \left(\Gamma(\hat{x}_i | \hat{x}_2) | \Gamma(\hat{x}_2) \right), \text{ for } i \in \{1, 3\}$$

Note that the set $\Gamma(\hat{x}_1 | \hat{x}_2)$ is governed by the constraint $\theta_{12}(\hat{x}_1, \hat{x}_2) + \gamma_{12}(\hat{x}_1, \hat{x}_2) \geq \max_{x_1} \{\theta_{12}(x_1, \hat{x}_2) + \gamma_{12}(x_1, \hat{x}_2)\}$ and similarly, $\Gamma(\hat{x}_3 | \hat{x}_2)$ is governed by an analogous constraint on γ_{23}. $\Gamma(\hat{x}_2)$, in contrast, involves inequalities that couple all the perturbation variables together: $\max_{x_1} \{\theta_{12}(x_1, \hat{x}_2) + \gamma_{12}(x_1, \hat{x}_2)\} + \max_{x_3} \{\theta_{23}(\hat{x}_2, x_3) + \gamma_{23}(\hat{x}_2, x_3)\} \geq \max_x \{\theta(x) + \gamma_{12}(x_1, x_2) + \gamma_{23}(x_2, x_3)\}$. Since in general these constraints cannot be decomposed as $(\gamma_{12}, \gamma_{23})$, the set is not a product space.

Consider the following example, where $x_i \in \{0, 1\}$ and $\theta_{12}(1, 1) = 1.9$, $\theta_{12}(0, 0) = 1.2$, $\theta_{12}(0, 1) = 1.1$, $\theta_{12}(1, 0) = 0$ and $\theta_{23}(a, b) = \theta_{12}(b, a), \forall a, b \in \{0, 1\}$. For $\hat{x}_2 = 1$, $\Gamma(\hat{x}_2)$ includes the constraint $\max\{1.9 + \gamma_{12}(1, 1), 1.1 + \gamma_{12}(0, 1)\} + \max\{1.9 + \gamma_{23}(1, 1), 1.1 + \gamma_{23}(1, 0)\} \geq \max\{1.2 + \gamma_{12}(0, 0), \gamma_{12}(1, 0)\} + \max\{1.2 + \gamma_{23}(0, 0), \gamma_{23}(0, 1)\}$. We argue that there exist i.i.d. perturbation distributions over $(\gamma_{12}, \gamma_{23})$ for which the constraint couples the two variables. In particular, if $\gamma_{12}(x_1, x_2) \sim U\{-1, 1\} \ \forall(x_1, x_2) \in \{0, 1\}^2$, $\gamma_{23}(x_2, x_3) \sim U\{-1, 1\} \ \forall(x_2, x_3) \in \{0, 1\}^2$ and U is the uniform distribution, then for $\gamma_{ij} = (\gamma_{ij}(1, 1), \gamma_{ij}(0, 1), \gamma_{ij}(0, 0), \gamma_{ij}(1, 0))$, the configurations $(\gamma_{12}, \gamma_{23}) \in \{((1, 1, -1, 1), (-1, 1, 1, 1)), ((1, 1, -1, 1), (1, 1, -1, 1)), ((-1, 1, 1, 1), (1, 1, -1, 1))\}$, are in $\Gamma(\hat{x}_2)$, but $((-1, 1, 1, 1), (-1, 1, 1, 1))$ is not, thus it cannot be a product space in this case.

As a result, γ_{12} and γ_{23} become dependent if we condition on $\hat{x}_2$ as the maximizing value. In other words, the indicator functions corresponding to $\Gamma(\hat{x}_1 | \hat{x}_2)$ and $\Gamma(\hat{x}_3 | \hat{x}_2)$ are also dependent if $\gamma \in \Gamma(\hat{x}_2)$. Whenever x_1 and x_3 depend non-trivially on the corresponding perturbation variables, we conclude that $x_1 \not\!\perp\!\!\!\perp x_3 | x_2$. This is typically the case.

$\square$

The key role of this theorem is to highlight how perturbation models might posses higher modeling power than their Gibbs counterparts. The choice of tree structured potential functions is often guided by computational reasons, rather than the need for conditional independence. Specifically, in a pose estimation application the goal is to relate a set of keypoints $x = (x_i)_{i \in [n]}$, where dimensions x_i are (pixel) locations arms, legs, body trunk or head and n is the total number of keypoints. A typical scoring function is $\theta(x) = \sum_{(i,j) \in E} \theta_{ij}(x_i, x_j)$, where the set of edges E includes pairs such as pair-trunk, arm-trunk, leg-trunk and the local scores $\theta_{ij}(x_i, x_j)$ depend on the distance between the keypoints. From the structure of $\theta(x)$, the Gibbs' distribution implies that the limbs locations are independent given the trunk. Perturbation models have the potential to capture additional long range dependencies between the parts without increasing the complexity of the scoring function.

5.5   Markov Properties and Perturbation Models

Given that typically low order perturbations lead to high order dependencies, we ask whether enforcing the Markov properties is possible in this case.

In the simplest case, whenever the Gibbs distribution is independent, it can indeed be represented using low order potentials. Specifically, recall that a probability distribution is independent whenever $p(x) = \prod_{i=1}^{n} p(x_i)$, where $p(x_i) = \sum_{x \setminus x_i} p(x)$ are its marginal probabilities. To show that the perturbation model matches the Gibbs distribution in this case we apply Theorem 6.1 for each dimension $i = 1, ..., n$ while setting $\theta_i(x_i) = \log p(x_i)$ and using i.i.d. perturbations $\gamma_i(x_i)$ that follow the Gumbel distribution.

In the following, we show that the tree structured potentials can also be randomized such that the induced distribution corresponds to the Gibbs' distribution.

5.5.1   Tree-Structured Perturbation Models

Distributions can be described by their conditional probabilities $p(x_1, ..., x_n) = \prod_{j=1}^{n} p(x_j | x_1, ..., x_{j-1})$, and in Markov random fields these conditional probabilities are simplified by their dependency graphs. Specifically, assume a tree structured MRF and let $\vec{E}$ be any directed version of the tree. For notational convenience, assume that the vertices $\{1, ..., n\}$ are topologically sorted and that there is an arc $(i \to j)$. Then $p(x_j | x_1, ..., x_{j-1}) = p(x_j | x_i)$. Furthermore, for a tree, specifying $\theta(x)$ is equivalent to specifying marginals probabilities $p(x_i)$, $i = 1, \ldots, n$, and $p(x_i, x_j)$, $(i, j) \in E$, which can be related as follows:

$$\theta_i(x_i) = \log p(x_i), \quad \theta_{ij}(x_i, x_j) = \log \frac{p(x_i, x_j)}{p(x_i)p(x_j)} \tag{5.8}$$

The following theorem shows that in this case, for any potential function there are low dimensional perturbation models that preserve these the independencies:

Theorem 5.3. *Consider the Gibbs distribution with a tree structured Markov random field. Then for any potential function*

$$\theta(x) = \sum_{i=1}^{n} \theta_i(x_i) + \sum_{(i,j) \in E} \theta_{ij}(x_i, x_j) \tag{5.9}$$

there are random variables $\{\gamma_{ij}(x_i, x_j)\}$ indexed by $(i,j) \in E, (x_i, x_j) \in \mathcal{X}_i \times \mathcal{X}_j$ such that

$$p(\hat{x}) = P_\gamma\Big[\hat{x} \in \underset{x \in \mathcal{X}}{\mathrm{argmax}}\{\theta(x) + \sum_{(i,j) \in E} \gamma_{ij}(x_i, x_j)\}\Big] \tag{5.10}$$

Proof. Let $\hat{\gamma}_{ij}(x_i, x_j)$ be i.i.d. random variables that follow the Gumbel distributions. Let $\vec{E}$ be a directed version of the tree and assume that the vertices $\{1, ..., n\}$ are topologically sorted and that there is an arc $(1 \to 2)$. Let $\gamma_{12}(x_1, x_2) = \hat{\gamma}_{12}(x_1, x_2)$ and for any other edge $(i \to j)$ define $\gamma_{ij}(x_i, x_j) =$

$$\hat{\gamma}_{ij}(x_i, x_j) - \max_{x'_j}\big\{\theta_{ij}(x_i, x'_j) + \theta_j(x'_j) + \hat{\gamma}_{ij}(x_i, x'_j)\big\} \tag{5.11}$$

Let $p(x_1, x_2) = \sum_{x \setminus \{x_1, x_2\}} p(x)$ be the marginal probabilities of Gibbs distribution. We begin by showing that

$$p(\hat{x}_1, \hat{x}_2) = P_\gamma\big[\hat{x}_1, \hat{x}_2 \in \underset{x \in \mathcal{X}}{\mathrm{argmax}}\{\theta(x) + \sum_{(i,j) \in \vec{E}} \gamma_{ij}(x_i, x_j)\}\big] \tag{5.12}$$

To this end, any sample $(\hat{x}_1, \hat{x}_2)$ from the induced marginal distribution is obtained by

$$
\begin{aligned}
\hat{x}_1, \hat{x}_2 &= \underset{x_1, x_2}{\mathrm{argmax}} \max_{x \setminus \{x_1, x_2\}} \big\{\theta(x) + \sum_{(i,j) \in \vec{E}} \gamma_{ij}(x_i, x_j)\big\} \\
&= \underset{x_1, x_2}{\mathrm{argmax}} \big\{\log p(x_1, x_2) + \gamma_{12}(x_1, x_2)\big\}
\end{aligned}
$$

where the equality follows from the definition of $\gamma_{ij}(x_i, x_j)$ that enforces $\max_{x_j}\{\theta_{ij}(x_i, x_j) + \theta_j(x_j) + \gamma_{ij}(x_i, x_j)\} = 0$, applied recursively to each leaf in the tree. Theorem 6.1 implies that marginal probabilities of the Gibbs distribution and the MAP perturbation distribution are the same since $\gamma_{12}(x_1, x_2)$ are independent Gumbel random variables.

To complete the proof we show that for every $(i \to j)$ the conditional probability of MAP perturbations is the same as the Gibbs. For that end, define for every $\alpha \subset \{1, .., n\}$ the subset of indexes $x_\alpha = (x)_{i \in \alpha}$, and $\Gamma(\hat{x}_\alpha)$ the set of perturbation assignments for which $\hat{x}_\alpha$ is optimal, as in (5.7). Recall the vertices are topologically ordered, thus we aim at showing that

$$p(x_j | x_i) = P_\gamma\Big(\Gamma(x_1, ..., x_j) | \Gamma(x_1, ..., x_{j-1})\Big) \tag{5.13}$$

By our construction, for any values of $x_1, ..., x_{j-1}$ the argument x_j is chosen to maximize $\theta_j(x_j) + \theta_{ij}(x_i, x_j) + \hat{\gamma}_{ij}(x_i, x_j)$. Since $\theta_j(x_j) + \theta_{ij}(x_i, x_j) = \log p(x_j|x_i)$ and $\hat{\gamma}_{ij}(x_i, x_j)$ are i.i.d. with zero mean Gumbel distribution, the result follows by applying Theorem 6.1. $\qquad\square$

The perturbation models may describe tree structured Gibbs distributions. Perhaps surprisingly, the random variables that enforce the Markov properties in this case are not independent nor identically distributed. This demonstrates the potential power of induced models when allowing dependent perturbation variables.

5.6   Conditional Distributions

Modeling and efficiently using conditional distributions are key issues in applications involving partially observed data. These include finding dense correspondences across images when only partial human annotations are provided, combining information from multiple predictors (semi-supervised learning) and so on. In Gibbs' models, regardless of the difficulty of inference calculations, conditioning is typically a straightforward operation, performed by plugging in the observed data. On the other hand, conditioning in perturbation models is a challenging open problem. In this case we cannot merely set the observed variables to their values. Instead, we must ensure that the observed values are selected via global maximization.

Specifically, for any subset of variables $x_\alpha, x_\beta, \alpha \cap \beta = \emptyset, \alpha, \beta \in V$, the conditional $\mathcal{P}(\hat{x}_\alpha | \hat{x}_\beta)$ is obtained by first sampling noise realizations that are consistent with observed data and maximizing the perturbed potential over the remaining variables:

$$\gamma \quad \sim \quad p(\gamma | \gamma \in \Gamma(\hat{x}_\beta)) \tag{5.14}$$

$$\hat{x}_\alpha \quad \leftarrow \quad \underset{x_\alpha}{\operatorname{argmax}} \max_{x_{V \setminus \alpha}} \tilde{\theta}(x) \tag{5.15}$$

Recall that $\Gamma(\hat{x}_\beta)$ is the set of perturbations for which the maximizing argument agrees with $\hat{x}_\beta$. The resulting distribution of $\hat{x}_\alpha$ is typically different from the one obtained by fixing the observed values $\hat{x}_\beta$ while maximizing over the remaining ones:

$$q(\hat{x}_\alpha | \hat{x}_\beta) = \Pr(\hat{x}_\alpha \in \underset{x_\alpha}{\operatorname{argmax}} \max_{x_{V \setminus \{\alpha, \beta\}}} \tilde{\theta}(x_{V \setminus \beta}, \hat{x}_\beta)) \tag{5.16}$$

To show how these two approaches may lead to different induced distributions, consider the example provided in the proof of Theorem 5.2. When conditioning on $\hat{x}_2$ in the three-variable chain $x_1 - x_2 - x_3$, the perturbation variables γ_{12} and γ_{23} become coupled and this is shown to imply conditional dependency between x_1 and x_3. However, in the distribution obtained by fixing the value of $\hat{x}_2$ and sampling γ_{12}, γ_{23} from their original (independent) distributions, x_1 and x_3 become independent. Therefore, the two distributions are in general not the same and in particular, the ability to perform conditioning by "plugging in" the observed variables is related to the higher order dependencies that arise with perturbation models.

In practice, the key difficulty for conditioning in perturbation models stems from dealing with the set $\Gamma(\hat{x}_\beta)$, which is often a union of (disparate) cones. This makes the posterior distribution $p(\gamma | \gamma \in \Gamma(\hat{x}_\beta))$ difficult to describe and sample from.

In the rest of this section, our aim is to characterize models for which we can perform conditioning with respect to a restricted subset of variables. We start by describing model constraints which ensure conditional independence (with respect to a single variable) in a three-variable chain. Furthermore, the conditions can be extended to enforce conditional independence in models whose potential functions decompose along the edges of the tree. We then show that when such conditions are met, we can perform conditioning on a single variable by fixing the observed variable to its value. While the conditions are restrictive, we show that there exist tree structured models which satisfy this set of conditions.

5.6.1   Max-marginals

We start by defining max-marginals since they arise when dealing with marginalization in perturbation models. For two adjacent nodes k and j, we define the max-sum message from j to k,

$$m_{j\to k}(x_k; \gamma) \ = \ \max_{x_j} \left\{ \tilde{\theta}_{jk}(x_j, x_k; \gamma) + \sum_{i \in N(j)\backslash k} m_{i \to j}(x_j; \gamma) \right\} \quad (5.17)$$

the corresponding maximizing assignment,

$$\hat{x}_{j \to k}(x_k; \gamma) \ = \ \arg\max_{x_j} \left\{ \tilde{\theta}_{jk}(x_j, x_k; \gamma) + \sum_{i \in N(j)\backslash k} m_{i \to j}(x_j; \gamma) \right\} \quad (5.18)$$

and the resulting max-marginal for node k, $m_k(x_k; \gamma)$, which sums over all the neighbors,

$$m_k(x_k; \gamma) \ = \ \sum_{j \in N(k)} m_{j \to k}(x_k; \gamma). \quad (5.19)$$

Furthermore, we use $m_{j \to k}(\gamma)$ to refer to the vector of messages from j to k, whose coordinates are the individual messages $m_{j \to k}(x_k; \gamma)$, and similarly we use $\hat{x}_{j \to k}(\gamma)$ for the vector of maximizing assignments.

Conditioning typically implies comparing differences of messages. To this end, we define for simplicity *normalized* messages and max-marginals by subtracting from each dimension the maximum over the vector of messages:

$$\bar{m}_{j \to k}(x_k, \gamma) \;=\; m_{j \to k}(x_k, \gamma) - \max_{x'_k} m_{j \to k}(x'_k; \gamma) \tag{5.20}$$

$$\bar{m}_k(x_k, \gamma) \;=\; m_k(x_k, \gamma) - \max_{x'_k} m_k(x'_k; \gamma) \tag{5.21}$$

After normalization, the difference of max-marginals is preserved $\bar{m}_k(x_k; \gamma) - \bar{m}_k(x'_k; \gamma) = m_k(x_k; \gamma) - m_k(x'_k; \gamma), \forall x_k, x'_k \in \mathcal{X}$, and the same is true for individual messages.

Note that the various quantities defined here are random variables induced by the perturbations γ and it makes sense to talk about their pairwise statistical dependency. One possible question is whether the messages $m_{j \to k}(x_k; \gamma)$ or $\bar{m}_{j \to k}(x_k; \gamma)$ are independent of the corresponding maximizing assignments $\hat{x}_{j \to k}(x_k; \gamma)$. Clearly this is true whenever the noise magnitudes are limited such that the maximizing assignments do not depend on the particular noise realizations. Similarly, the independence statement is trivially true whenever the individual messages or the normalized messages are constant with respect to perturbations (i.e. when randomizations "cancel out" regardless of the maximizing assignments). For instance, this is possible when perturbation variables are dependent, like in the proof of Theorem 5.3. One remaining open question is whether there are distributions of perturbations γ for which the statement is more generally true.

In the following we will show how the statistical dependency of max-marginals and maximizing assignments relate to conditional independency in perturbation models.

5.6.2 Conditional Independence

Since low-order perturbations typically give rise to dependencies that go beyond the structure of the potential function, one key question is whether any conditional independencies are maintained.

The first lemma claims that in a three-variable chain $x_1 - x_2 - x_3$, the conditional independence statement $x_1 \perp\!\!\!\perp x_3 | x_2$ holds if for at least one of the two neighbors, the normalized max-marginals are independent of the corresponding maximizing assignments.

Lemma 5.4. *Assume a chain structured model with 3 variables x_1, x_2, x_3, a randomized potential function of the form $\tilde{\theta}(x) = \tilde{\theta}_{12}(x_1, x_2) + \tilde{\theta}_{23}(x_2, x_3)$ such that $\tilde{\theta}_{12} \perp\!\!\!\perp \tilde{\theta}_{23}$, and the induced perturbation model $p(x)$.*

Then the independence statement $x_1 \perp\!\!\!\perp x_3 | x_2$ holds if one of the following statements holds:

$$\hat{x}_{1\to2}(x_2, \gamma) \quad \perp\!\!\!\perp \quad \bar{m}_{1\to2}(x_2', \gamma) \ \forall x_2, x_2' \tag{5.22}$$

$$\hat{x}_{3\to2}(x_2, \gamma) \quad \perp\!\!\!\perp \quad \bar{m}_{3\to2}(x_2', \gamma) \ \forall x_2, x_2' \tag{5.23}$$

Proof. When conditioning on $x_2 = \hat{x}_2$ we restrict the perturbations γ to the set $\Gamma(\hat{x}_2)$, defined via: $\mathbf{1}[\gamma \in \Gamma(\hat{x}_2)] =$ $\prod_{x_2 \in \mathcal{X}} \mathbf{1}[m_{1\to2}(\hat{x}_2; \gamma) + m_{3\to2}(\hat{x}_2; \gamma) \geq m_{1\to2}(x_2; \gamma) + m_{3\to2}(x_2; \gamma)].$ This can be more compactly written via max-marginals: $\mathbf{1}[\gamma \in \Gamma(\hat{x}_2)] =$ $\prod_{x_2 \in \mathcal{X}} \mathbf{1}[m_2(\hat{x}_2; \gamma) - m_2(x_2; \gamma) \geq 0] = \prod_{x_2 \in \mathcal{X}} \mathbf{1}[\bar{m}_2(\hat{x}_2; \gamma) - \bar{m}_2(x_2; \gamma) \geq 0].$

If condition (5.22) holds, then $\hat{x}_{1\to2}(\hat{x}_2; \gamma) \perp\!\!\!\perp \bar{m}_2(x_2', \gamma), \forall x_2'$, which implies $\hat{x}_{1\to2}(\hat{x}_2; \gamma) \perp\!\!\!\perp \bar{m}_2(\hat{x}_2; \gamma) - \bar{m}_2(x_2'; \gamma), \forall x_2'$ and finally $\hat{x}_{1\to2}(\hat{x}_2; \gamma) \perp\!\!\!\perp \mathbf{1}[\gamma \in \Gamma(\hat{x}_2)]$. Furthermore $\hat{x}_{1\to2}(\hat{x}_2; \gamma) \perp\!\!\!\perp \hat{x}_{3\to2}(\hat{x}_2; \gamma)$ from the independence of perturbations across edges and assignments. We can then show that

$$p(\hat{x}_1, \hat{x}_3 | \hat{x}_2) \tag{5.24}$$

$$= \ \Pr(\hat{x}_1, \hat{x}_3 \in \underset{x_1, x_3}{\operatorname{argmax}} \max_{x_2} \tilde{\theta}(x) | \gamma \in \Gamma(\hat{x}_2)) \tag{5.25}$$

$$= \ \Pr(x_1 \in \hat{x}_{1\to2}(\hat{x}_2; \gamma) \wedge x_3 \in \hat{x}_{3\to2}(\hat{x}_2; \gamma) | \gamma \in \Gamma(\hat{x}_2)) \tag{5.26}$$

$$= \ \Pr(x_3 \in \hat{x}_{3\to2}(\hat{x}_2; \gamma) | \gamma \in \Gamma(\hat{x}_2)) \Pr(x_1 \in \hat{x}_{1\to2}(\hat{x}_2; \gamma)) \tag{5.27}$$

$$= \ p(\hat{x}_1 | \hat{x}_2) p(\hat{x}_3 | \hat{x}_2) \tag{5.28}$$

$\square$

Intuitively, the independency between messages and the maximizing assignments is used to enforce that at least one of $\hat{x}_1$ or $\hat{x}_3$ is not affected by the joint constraints imposed to ensure that $\hat{x}_2$ is selected through global maximization.

In the following lemma, we show that under the same restrictions, we can condition on a single node by setting the observed variables to their values.

Lemma 5.5. *Assume a chain structured model with 3 variables x_1, x_2, x_3, a randomized potential function $\tilde{\theta}(x) = \tilde{\theta}_{12}(x_1, x_2) + \tilde{\theta}_{23}(x_2, x_3)$ such that $\tilde{\theta}_{12} \perp\!\!\!\perp \tilde{\theta}_{23}$, and the induced perturbation model $p(x)$.*

If $\hat{x}_{1\to2}(x_2, \gamma) \perp\!\!\!\perp \bar{m}_{1\to2}(x_2', \gamma), \forall x_2, x_2'$ and $\Gamma(\hat{x}_2) \neq \emptyset$, then $\Pr(x_1 = \hat{x}_{1\to2}(\hat{x}_2; \gamma)) = p(x_1 | \hat{x}_2)$. In other words, by fixing x_2 and perturbing the edge corresponding to x_1 only, we obtain the conditional distribution $p(x_1 | \hat{x}_2)$.

Furthermore, if for all $x_1, x_2, x_3, x_1', x_2', x_3'$ *we have:*

$$\hat{x}_{1\to 2}(x_2, \gamma) \quad \perp\!\!\!\perp \quad \bar{m}_{1\to 2}(x_2', \gamma) \text{ and } \Gamma(x_2) \neq \emptyset, \qquad (5.29)$$

$$\hat{x}_{2\to 1}(x_1, \gamma) \quad \perp\!\!\!\perp \quad \bar{m}_{2\to 1}(x_1', \gamma) \text{ and } \Gamma(x_1) \neq \emptyset, \qquad (5.30)$$

$$\hat{x}_{3\to 2}(x_2, \gamma) \quad \perp\!\!\!\perp \quad \bar{m}_{3\to 2}(x_2', \gamma) \text{ and } \Gamma(x_2) \neq \emptyset, \qquad (5.31)$$

$$\hat{x}_{2\to 3}(x_3, \gamma) \quad \perp\!\!\!\perp \quad \bar{m}_{2\to 3}(x_3', \gamma) \text{ and } \Gamma(x_3) \neq \emptyset, \qquad (5.32)$$

$$\hat{x}_{2\to\{1,3\}}(x_1, x_3, \gamma) \quad \perp\!\!\!\perp \quad \bar{m}_{2\to\{1,3\}}(x_1', x_3', \gamma) \text{ and } \Gamma(x_1, x_3) \neq \emptyset \qquad (5.33)$$

then we can condition by plugging in values for any $p(x_\alpha | x_\beta), \alpha \cap \beta = \emptyset$.

Proof. Using the same argument as above, we have that $\hat{x}_{1\to 2}(\hat{x}_2; \gamma) \perp\!\!\!\perp$ $\mathbf{1}[\gamma \in \Gamma(\hat{x}_2)]$, therefore $p(x_1 | \hat{x}_2) = \Pr(x_1 = \hat{x}_{1\to 2}(\hat{x}_2; \gamma) | \mathbf{1}[\gamma \in \Gamma(\hat{x}_2)]) = \Pr(x_1 = \hat{x}_{1\to 2}(\hat{x}_2; \gamma))$.

Furthermore, by applying this for possible subsets of variables in the chain $p(x_1|x_2)$, $p(x_2|x_1)$, $p(x_3|x_2)$, $p(x_2|x_3)$, $p(x_2|x_1, x_3)$ we obtain the set of conditions (5.29)-(5.33). □

We can easily extend these results to tree structured models and show that the restrictions on max-product messages provide a feasible method of conditioning on a single variable. One can ask whether there are any trees that satisfy the conditions above at every node and at every subset of nodes. The next lemma provides an example where the conditions hold at every node, but not at pairs of nodes.

Lemma 5.6. *There is a tree structured model for which the conditions of Lemma 5.5 hold for every node symmetrically. In this case, we can condition on every node by plugging in the fixed values.*

Proof. Consider a tree structured graphical model, with binary random variables in $\{-1, 1\}$ and with randomized potential function $\tilde{\theta}(x) = \sum_{(i,j)\in E} \tilde{\theta}_{ij} x_i x_j$. If node l is a leaf, then $m_{l\to k}(x_k; \gamma) = \max_{x_l \in \{-1,1\}} \{\tilde{\theta}_{lk} x_l x_k\} = |\tilde{\theta}_{lk}|$. In general, for any node k and any $l \in N(k)$, we have

$$m_{l\to k}(x_k; \gamma) = \sum_{e \in T(l;k)} |\tilde{\theta}_e| \qquad (5.34)$$

where $T(l; k)$ denotes the subtree rooted at node l and which does not contain k, $e \in T(l; k)$ is an edge in the subtree. Furthermore, the normalized messages and maximizing assignments are given by

$$\bar{m}_{l\to k}(x_k; \gamma) = 0 \qquad (5.35)$$

$$\hat{x}_{l\to k}(x_k; \gamma) = sgn(\tilde{\theta}_{lk} x_k) \qquad (5.36)$$

Since the normalized message is always equal to 0, we have $\hat{x}_{l \to k} \perp\!\!\!\perp \bar{m}_{l \to k}, \forall k, \forall l \in N(k)$ and therefore this model satisfies the conditions and we can do plug-in conditioning for any node k.

However, the two-variable conditions do not hold. Assume $n = 3$ and consider conditioning on x_1, x_3:

$$m_{2 \to 1,3}(x_1, x_3; \gamma) = |\tilde{\theta}_{12} x_1 + \tilde{\theta}_{23} x_3| \tag{5.37}$$

$$\bar{m}_{2 \to 1,3}(x_1, x_3; \gamma) = |\tilde{\theta}_{12} x_1 + \tilde{\theta}_{23} x_3| - \max_{x_1, x_3} |\tilde{\theta}_{12} x_1 + \tilde{\theta}_{23} x_3| \tag{5.38}$$

$$\hat{x}_{2 \to 1,3}(x_1, x_3; \gamma) = sgn(\tilde{\theta}_{12} x_1 + \tilde{\theta}_{23} x_3) \tag{5.39}$$

In this case, $\bar{m}_{2 \to 1,3}(\gamma)$ and $\hat{x}_{2 \to 1,3}(\gamma)$ will not be independent in general. $\quad\square$

In this section we provided a preliminary analysis of conditioning in perturbation models. In particular, we showed how max-marginals can provide sufficient conditions for conditional independencies with respect to single variables. Unfortunately the methods do not easily extend to conditioning on sets of variables, which remains an open question. Furthermore, we showed examples of perturbations which satisfy the restrictions in Lemma 5.4, which typically involve either the maximizing assignments or the messages to be constant with respect to perturbations. A further question to explore is whether there is a more general characterization of the type of perturbations that satisfy these restrictions.

5.7 Learning Perturbation Models

One of the most distinctive characteristics of perturbation models is that they give rise to dependencies that are not expressed in the base potential function. In the previous chapters we showed that such dependencies arise even when perturbations are independent across the different potential function terms, and across the local assignments within a term. Going a step further, if the perturbations are allowed to be coupled, then we can learn to create and enforce dependencies. This suggests that perturbation models have modeling capacity beyond their base Gibbs' distributions. For example, a tree-structured base model is itself rather restrictive but can be used to induce interactions of all orders in a perturbation setting.

In this section, our goal is to take advantage of this modeling power and learn perturbation models from data. Unlike Gibbs' models, the connection between the structure of the potential function and the properties of the induced distribution is less understood. To this end, we consider complex potential functions equipped with efficient algorithms for computing the maximizing assignment and with expressive dependent perturbations and rely on the learning algorithm to infer the optimal dependency structure.

For the rest of the chapter, we define perturbation models with respect to linear potential functions of the form $\theta(x, w) = w^T \phi(x)$, where w is a vector of parameters and $\phi(x)$ is a vector of features. For instance, for image segmentation, where the prediction is determined by binary variables per pixel location $x = (x_{ij})_{i \in [n], j \in [m]} \in \{0, 1\}^{n \times m}$, a possible feature may check whether neighboring pixels (i, j) and (k, l) are assigned the same class $\phi_{ij,kl}(x_{ij}, x_{kl}) = \mathbf{1}[x_{ij} = x_{kl}]$. In contrast to additive perturbations considered earlier, we define w directly as a random variable. The distribution $p(w; \eta)$ governs the randomization and η are the (hyper-)parameters we aim to learn. This includes the additive case as a special case by simply using $w = w_0 + \gamma$ where w_0 are fixed parameters and γ is a vector of random perturbations.

The induced distribution over the product space $\mathcal{X}$ is now given by:

$$\mathcal{P}(\hat{x}; \eta) = \int p(w; \eta)[[\hat{x} = \underset{x}{\arg\max} \, \theta(x; w)]] dw \qquad (5.40)$$

The goal is to learn the hyper-parameters η that maximize the induced log-likelihood of the data $\sum_{\hat{x} \in \mathcal{S}} \log \mathcal{P}(\hat{x}; \eta)$. This is a latent variable model with continuous hidden variables w. In principle, we could use the EM algorithm resulting in the following iterative updates

$$\eta^{(t+1)} = \underset{\eta}{\arg\max} \sum_{\hat{x} \in \mathcal{S}} E_{w \sim p(w|\hat{x}; \eta^{(t)})} \left[\log p(w; \eta) \right] \qquad (5.41)$$

Evaluating the expectation requires sampling from the inverse set $\Gamma(\hat{x})$. One way of approaching this issue is to use specialized MCMC algorithms. For instance, (Tarlow et al., 2012) uses a Slice Sampling algorithm which takes advantage of the structure of the problem to avoid fully recomputing the maximizing assignment at every step.

The second approach, which we pursue in this chapter, is to replace the expectation in the E-step with a maximization over w, obtaining a single point in the inverse set $\Gamma(\hat{x})$. This *hard-EM* algorithm is given by

$$\eta^{(t+1)} = \underset{\eta}{\arg\max} \sum_{\hat{x} \in \mathcal{S}} \underset{w \in \Gamma(\hat{x})}{\max} \log p(w; \eta) \qquad (5.42)$$

While this approach requires a single inner maximization, the problem remains challenging since the number of constraints specifying the inverse set can be exponential in the number of variables. For example, we might need to enforce $w^\top \phi(\hat{x}) \geq w^\top \phi(x)$ for every $x \in dom(\phi)$. However, we will show below that there are many problems of interest for which the inverse set can be described compactly.

5.7.1   Inverse Optimization

Optimization problems over discrete sets such as maximization of $w^\top \phi(x)$ over $x \in dom(\phi)$, can be cast as continuous optimization problems over the corresponding convex hull $conv(\{\phi(x) : x \in dom(\phi)\})$. The convex hull is a polytope defined by linear constraints $\{z : Az \leq b, z \geq 0\}$, and the vertexes of this polytope are exactly the statistics $\phi(x)$. Thus $w \in \Gamma(\hat{z})$ if and only if $\hat{z}$ is the maximizer of the linear objective $f(z) = w^\top z$ over the polytope. In many cases, the constraint matrix A is *totally unimodular*.

Naively one may verify that $\hat{z}$ is the maximizer by trying all the extreme points. More efficiently, we appeal to convex duality in order to maintain a certificate of optimality for $\hat{z}$. A dual certificate is a dual feasible solution that satisfies the complementary slackness constraints: if $\hat{z}_i > 0$ then the corresponding constraint on the dual variable y_i is satisfied with equality $[A^T y]_i = w_i$, and if $[A\hat{z}]_i < b_i$ then $y_i = 0$. Using the dual certificate, we can maintain the optimality of $\hat{z}$ while changing w. Specifically, we write the inner maximization problem in (5.42) as a convex program:

$$\max_{w,y} \quad \log p(w; \eta) \tag{5.43}$$

$$s.t. \quad A^T y \geq w, y \geq 0 \tag{5.44}$$

$$y_i = 0, \text{ for } i \in \{i | [A\hat{z}]_i < b\} \tag{5.45}$$

$$[A^T y]_j = w_j, \text{ for } j \in \{j | \hat{z}_j > 0\} \tag{5.46}$$

Such inverse linear programs have been used before in operations research. The goal is typically to find the parameter setting closest to a given w_0 while ensuring that $\hat{z}$ remains optimal. The distance is a weighted L_p norm, mostly L_1 and L_∞ norms (Ahuja and Orlin, 2001). Also see (Chatalbashev) for a related usage. In our case, $p(w; \eta)$ is a multivariate Gaussian and thus the resulting convex program is quadratic, solved using standard QP solvers.

When the linear program (LP) admits a compact representation, we can represent the inverse set compactly as well since there is a dual variable for every primal constraint. Cases of interest to us include bipartite matching, maximum spanning tree, and so on. When the LP formulation is a relaxation, the constraints (5.45-5.46) are tighter than necessary. The inverse program will return a point within a smaller set contained in the inverse set $\Gamma(\hat{x})$ (or the empty set).

We describe below a few examples that are relevant for our models.

Example 1: Image Matching

We start with an assignment problem. For a graph $G = (I \cup J, E, w), E \subseteq I \times J$ with edges weighted by w_{ij} and $|I| = |J| = n$, the goal is to find the maximum weight matching that assigns each element in I to exactly one element in J. Document ranking and key-point matching in images can be modeled as assignment problems.

By reweighing the edges, the optimal assignment can be formulated as a minimum cost matching problem, which can be computed in polynomial time using the Hungarian algorithm (Schrijver, 2003). Note that sampling and computing the partition function remain #P-complete (Valiant, 1979) though MCMC-based fully-polynomial approximation schemes exist (Jerrum et al., 2004b). In comparison, perturbation models rely only on the efficient polynomial time maximization.

The minimum cost matching can be obtained by minimizing a linear objective $f(z) = w^T z$ subject to constraints. The constraints ensure that each vertex is incident to exactly one edge in the matching $\sum_{k \in I} z_{kj} = 1, \sum_{k \in J} z_{ik} = 1$ (Schrijver, 2003). Using dual certificates, we can formulate the inverse problem, i.e., $\max_{w \in \Gamma(\hat{z})} \log p(w; \eta)$ as a convex program:

$$\max_{w,u,v} \quad \log p(w; \eta)$$
$$s.t. \quad u_i + v_j = w_{ij}, \ (i, j) \in \{(i, j) | \hat{z}_{ij} \neq 0\}$$
$$u_i + v_j \leq w_{ij}, \ (i, j) \in \{(i, j) | \hat{z}_{ij} = 0\}$$

where $\hat{z}$ is the observed assignment and u and v are dual variables. The compact description involves $2n^2$ constraints and $2n$ additional (dual) variables.

Example 2: Pose Estimation

In pose estimation, the human body is modeled as a tree-structured graphical model, where nodes correspond to body parts. The highest scoring labeling specifies the estimated locations for the parts (Yang and Ramanan, 2011). The tree structure is computationally appealing, but it assumes that limbs are independent given the body position. Perturbation models can capture longer range dependencies even when the potential function corresponds to a tree.

While inference and sampling in tree-structured models is easy, sampling from the inverse set is difficult. The constraints enforcing the solution $\hat{x}$ to be optimal extend beyond the tree structure. The MAP solution can be nevertheless cast as a maximization of a linear objective $f(\mu) = w^T \mu$ over the local polytope $\mathcal{M}_L(G) = \{\mu \geq 0 | \sum_{x_j} \mu_{i,j;x_i,x_j} = \mu_{i;x_i} \forall i, j, x_i,$

$\sum_{x_i} \mu_{i,j;x_i,x_j} = \mu_{j;x_j} \ \forall i, j, x_j, \ \sum_{x_i} \mu_{i;x_i} = 1 \ \forall i\}$. For trees, the solution $\hat{\mu}$ is integral and corresponds to the maximum assignment $\hat{x}$ (Fromer and Globerson, 2009b). In other words, $\hat{\mu}$ describes $\hat{x}$ in terms of local marginals. Using dual certificates, we can write the inverse problem as:

$$\max_{w} \quad \log p(w; \eta)$$

$$s.t. \quad y_i - \sum_j y'_{i,j;x_i} - \sum_j y''_{j,i;x_i} \geq w_{i;x_i}, \text{for } \hat{\mu}_{i;x_i} = 0$$

$$y_i - \sum_j y'_{i,j;x_i} - \sum_j y''_{j,i;x_i} = w_{i;x_i}, \text{for } \hat{\mu}_{i;x_i} > 0$$

$$y'_{i,j;x_i} + y''_{i,j;x_j} \geq w_{i,j;x_i,x_j}, \text{for } \hat{\mu}_{i,j;x_i,x_j} = 0$$

$$y'_{i,j;x_i} + y''_{i,j;x_j} = w_{i,j;x_i,x_j}, \text{for } \hat{\mu}_{i,j;x_i,x_j} > 0$$

where y, y', y'' are dual variables corresponding to the marginal constraints. The constraints are satisfied with equality when the corresponding marginals in $\hat{\mu}$ are non-zero.

Example 3: Image Segmentation

Image segmentation and other computer vision tasks can be modeled as energy minimization problems with sub-modular potentials. Minimum graph cuts are used as tools for finding the optimal assignments (Szeliski et al., 2007).

The s-t cut problem can be formulated as the following LP with $m + n$ variables and m constraints:

$$\min_{z} \quad w^T z$$

$$s.t. \quad z_j + z_{S,j} \geq 1 \quad (s, j) \in E$$

$$z_j - z_i + z_{i,j} \geq 0 \quad (i, j) \in E$$

$$-z_i + z_{i,T} \geq 1 \quad (i, T) \in E$$

For a graph $G = (V, E, w)$ with $|V| = n, |E| = m$ and edge costs given by w, the minimum s-t cut problem aims to find a subset of vertices S, with $s \in S$ and $t \in V \setminus S$, such that the cost of the cut (weight of the edges crossing S and $V \setminus S$) is minimized. The dual problem is maximum-flow, and we can solve the inverse problem via

$$\max_{w,y} \quad \log p(w;\eta)$$
$$\text{s.t.} \quad \sum_i y_{ik} = \sum_j y_{kj}, \ \forall k \neq s, k \neq t$$
$$0 \leq y_{ij} \leq w_{ij}, \forall i,j$$
$$y_{ij} = w_{ij}, \ \text{for } (i,j) \in \{(i,j)|\hat{z}_{ij} > 0\}$$

where y are the dual variables and $\hat{z}$ encodes the observed cut. We obtain a compact, polynomial size representation of the inverse problem, at the cost of introducing m additional variables. For image segmentation and for most examples we provide, the number of additional variables is at most the number of parameters w.

Example 4: Natural Language Parsing

Dependency parsing can be formulated as a maximum directed spanning tree problem over the words in the sentence (McDonald et al., 2005). Different interpretations of the sentence correspond to different parse trees. As a result, the target parse can be inherently ambiguous. Perturbation models can be used to efficiently sample high-scoring parse trees to represent candidate interpretations.

In this case, a polynomial size representation of the inverse problem can be obtained via LP formulation of the minimum cost directed tree problem. In a graph $G = (V, E, w)$, the primal LP involves minimizing a linear objective $\sum_{(i,j)\in E} w_{ij} z_{ij}$ subject to constraints ensuring that for every node $u \in V \setminus \{r\}$ there is an r-u flow $f^{(u)}$ of value 1 with $f_{ij}^{(u)} \leq z_{ij}$ (Schrijver, 2003). The feasible set is the projection of a high dimensional polytope in mn dimensions, governed by at most $n(2m + n)$ constraints. Here n and m are the length of the sentence and the number of edges, respectively. As a result, using the dual certificate approach (omitted), we can formulate the inverse problem with $O(mn)$ additional variables.

Example 5. Subset Selection

The subset selection problem appears in machine learning in the context of feature selection, video or text summarization, and others. The prevalence of the problem has lead to various modeling approaches, including budget-based formulations which are typically intractable even for MAP computations, and sub-modular formulations, which are often difficult to sample from. The sub-modular approaches are often optimized in this case via provable greedy approximations (Gygli et al., 2015) and the perturbation models can be defined as distributions of the (approximate) solution under perturbations of the parameters. In this section we will instead focus on the budget-based approaches and illustrate the inverse LP approach when the formulation is a relaxation.

Consider the task of selecting a fixed number of items (given by a budget B). Specifically, consider the scoring function $\theta(y) = \sum_\alpha \theta_\alpha(y_\alpha)$ where $y_i \in \{0, 1\}$ denotes the absence or presence of an item. In the context of video and text summarization, unary potentials may encode local information, such as the interestingness of the video chunk or sentence, pairwise potentials may encode the similarity between the two items and how far apart they are in the sequence, and so on. See (Gygli et al., 2015) for a range of objectives to consider for video summarization, and (Almeida and Martins, 2013) for text. The goal is to solve $\max_y \theta(y)$ s.t. $\sum_i L_i y_i \leq B$, where L_i is a weight associated with the selected item, e.g. number of frames in the video chunk or number of words in the sentence. Furthermore, we are interested in distributions over subsets, defined as $p(y) \propto \exp(\theta(y))$.

The optimization problem is in general intractable, as it includes the knapsack problem as a special case, and it can be approached by formulating an LP relaxation. For instance, (Almeida and Martins, 2013) use dual-decomposition for optimizing a knapsack objective for text summarization. Their coverage-based summarization model considers M possible sentence topics $(T_m)_{m=1}^M$ with associated relevance scores $w_m \geq 0$ and the goal is to select the subset of sentences that maximizes the overall relevance of the topics covered. Specifically, if $y \in \{0, 1\}^N$ and $u \in \{0, 1\}^M$ are binary vectors denoting the selected sentences and topics respectively, the integer optimization problem to be solved is given by:

$$\max_{u \in \{0,1\}, y \in \{0,1\}} \sum_{m=1}^{M} w_m u_m \tag{5.47}$$

$$s.t. \quad u_m \leq \sum_{i \in T_m} y_i, \quad \forall m \in \{1 \ldots M\} \tag{5.48}$$

$$\sum_{n=1}^{N} L_n y_n \leq B \tag{5.49}$$

After relaxing the integrality constraints and considering the dual, we introduce $(N + 2M + 1)$ new parameters: b and $(s_m)_{m=1}^N$ associated with the budget constraint and topic selection constraints, and $(\alpha_m)_{m=1}^M, (\beta_n)_{n=1}^N$ associated with the constraint of variables being less than 1. Finally, the optimality conditions lead to the following inverse problem:

$$\min_{w} \quad p(w; \eta) \tag{5.50}$$

$$s.t. \quad s_m + \alpha_m = w_m, \quad \forall m, u_m > 0 \tag{5.51}$$

$$s_m + \alpha_m \geq w_m, \quad \forall m, u_m = 0 \tag{5.52}$$

$$bL_n + \beta_n = \sum_{m: \; n \in T_m} s_m, \quad \forall n, y_n > 0 \tag{5.53}$$

$$bL_n + \beta_n \geq \sum_{m: \; n \in T_m} s_m, \quad \forall n, y_n = 0 \tag{5.54}$$

$$b, s, \alpha, \beta \geq 0 \tag{5.55}$$

5.7.2 Penalty-based Inverse Optimization

The inverse optimization framework provides a clean way of solving the inner maximization in (5.42) for many problems of interest. For completeness, we also provide examples where the size of the LP formulation is large relative to the number of parameters in w.

Consider learning a perturbation model over binary images of size $k \times k$, guided by a potential function $\theta(x; w) = \sum_{i=1}^{n} w_i x_i + \sum_{(i,j) \in E} w_{ij} x_i x_j$, $|E| = m$. For large k, it may be impractical to learn both unary and pairwise potentials resulting in $n + m$ parameters. We can instead estimate a subset of parameters, e.g. fix the higher-order potentials and learn n parameters for node potentials. Nonetheless, the min-cut inverse LP formulation in Example 3 adds additional variables for each edge and even for estimating a subset of parameters, the number of variables is given by $n + m$.

In many cases we must resort to constraints of the form $w^T \phi(\hat{x}) \geq w^T \phi(x), \forall x$. Assuming that the perturbations follow a multivariate Gaussian distribution, the inverse optimization problem is quadratic

$$\min_{w} (w - \mu)^T \Sigma^{-1} (w - \mu) + C \left[\max_{x} w^T \phi(x) - w^T \phi(\hat{x}) \right]$$

The objective is similar to structured SVM (Tsochantaridis et al., 2004) and a similar approach has been explored in (Tarlow et al., 2012). The problem can be solved using typical methods for structured SVMs, such as cutting-planes or gradient descent methods. We illustrate this in the experimental section using a sub-gradient descent with a decreasing step size.

Figure 5.1: First line: max-margin parameters and resulting segmentation, second line: the mean of the perturbation parameters, the average segmentation and the four images with the highest count.

5.8   Empirical Results

We conclude the chapter by presenting experiments demonstrating that perturbation models capture dependencies above and beyond the structure of the potential function. The first experiment explores an image segmentation task and illustrates the duality approach for learning perturbation models. While the potential function is formed of local pairwise potentials and implies long range conditional independencies, the experiment suggests that in the learned perturbation model various long range independencies do not hold. The second experiment shows an application of learning perturbation models in the context of image matching.

5.8.1   Image Segmentation

We selected four images from the Large Binary Image Database[1] representing basketball player silhouettes, with the goal of learning a model over the basketball player poses and showing that perturbation models are able to store multiple modes and sample from them.

We used an Ising model over labels $y_i \in \{+1, -1\}$ with potentials $\theta(y_i)$ encoding whether pixel i is foreground or background and $\theta(y_i, y_j)$ encouraging adjacent pixels to have the same labels. We assumed $\theta(y_i, y_j) = y_i y_j, \theta_i(y_i) = \gamma_i y_i$ and learned a distribution over the node parameters γ_i. Since the model contained node potentials only (resulting in 2500 parameters), we solved the inverse problem using the sub-gradient approach explained in the previous section. For each iteration of the hard-EM algorithm, we performed 3 iterations of the sub-gradient algorithm for each example, initialized with the point estimate from the previous hard-EM iteration. Since the setting is

---

1. http://www.lems.brown.edu/~dmc/

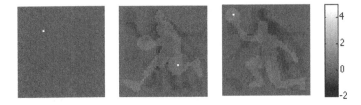

Figure 5.2: Correlations between a reference pixel (white) and the rest, as captured by the covariance matrix of the perturbation distribution. We show a pixel that is always off (so no correlations) and two pixels that are activated on different poses.

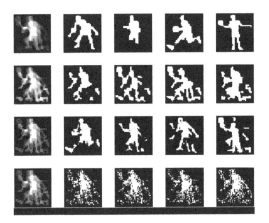

Figure 5.3: The average segmentation and samples from four models, one per line: perturbation model where the perturbations have unrestricted vs. diagonal covariance matrix and multivariate gaussian model with unrestricted vs. diagonal covariance matrix.

so simple, the hard-EM algorithm converged in less than 20 iterations. For computing the maximum likelihood estimates of η in the M-step we performed regularization by adding a constant c to the diagonal elements of the estimated covariance matrix (we set c to 0.1). We also implemented a structural SVM approach, using a similar stochastic sub-gradient algorithm.

In Figure 5.1, second line, we show in this order the mean of the perturbation parameters γ, the average segmentation from 10^4 samples and the four images with the highest count. In this case, the four images correspond to the four human poses we considered and images visually similar to them obtain a similar score. The first line shows the learned node parameters and the max-margin maximum weight configuration.

The potential function encodes only local interactions through the lattice structure, but the induced distribution shows longer range dependencies.

This is due to the correlations in the latent space as illustrated in Figure
5.2. For pixels that are always foreground or background the covariance
matrix reveals no correlations. The others have strong positive correlations
with pixels that are only activated on the same pose, and negative correlations with other poses. To further understand the perturbation models we
look at independent samples, Figure 5.3, where the perturbation distribution is a multivariate gaussian with unrestricted, resp. diagonal, covariance
matrix (first two lines). The second model captures few or no long-range
dependencies in this case.

Instead of perturbation models, one may learn a multivariate gaussian
model over the binary images and compute a sample image by thresholding
each pixel independently. We also show samples from these models in Figure
5.3, last two line, where the covariance matrix is unrestricted, resp. diagonal.
The latent space is capturing the long-range correlations, but the lack of
structure in the MAP solver results in visual artifacts.

5.8.2   Image Matching

We illustrate the LP duality approach for a matching task on images from the
Buffy Stickmen dataset[2]. Each frame is annotated with segment locations
for six body parts and we use the framework of (Yang and Ramanan, 2011)
to enlarge this set of locations such that we obtain 18 keypoints per image.
We select frames of the same person throughout an episode and from the
resulting set of all image pairs we randomly select two disjoint sets for
training and testing (15 train pairs and 23 test pairs). The set of keypoints
for an image pair serves as the ground truth for our matching experiments.

We represent the matching as a permutation of keypoints denoted by π,
and assume the following potential function, following (Volkovs and Zemel,
2012), $\theta(I, I', \pi; w) = \sum_{i,j} w^T (\psi(I, i) - \psi(I', j))^2$. The features $\psi(I, k)$ are
the SIFT descriptors evaluated keypoint k.

The inference problem can be formulated as an assignment problem, so
we learn the perturbation distribution using the hard-EM algorithm, and
computing the point estimate using the inverse optimization formulation.
In this case, the inverse problem becomes a quadratic program with 26
additional variables and 324 constraints corresponding to edges.

Figure 5.4 shows an example pair from the test set. We extract SIFT
features at scale 5 and we return the matching with the highest count after
1000 samples. In this case the perturbation model shows similar performance

---

2. http://www.robots.ox.ac.uk/~vgg/data/stickmen/

Figure 5.4: Example matching returned by the randomized MAP model. This is the matching with the highest count from 100 samples and has error equal to 4.

with SVM: the average error of the perturbation model after 1000 samples was equal to 8.47 while the average error of max margin was 8.69.

5.9 Perturbation Models and Stability

In the previous sections we showed how to estimate perturbation models from data and demonstrated their extended modeling power. To this end, we focused on base models where the MAP assignment can be evaluated efficiently even if the marginals (or the partition function) of the base Gibbs model is not feasible. Such models remain learnable within the perturbation framework, enriched by induced longer range dependencies.

The situation changes when the family of base potential functions no longer permits efficient MAP assignments. For instance, in section 5.7.1 we indicate how approximations can be used with inverse optimization. More generally, tractability may arise as a by-product of learning perturbation models. Indeed, while randomization is needed to introduce diversity in samples, maximizing the likelihood of the correct assignment also serves to carve out stable assignments. Stability, on the other hand, can be related to tractability. We start by describing various notions of stability and their relationship to the hardness of inference calculations.

The complex models we consider here are common in applications in natural language processing, computer vision and bioinformatics that involve clusters, parse trees, or arrangements. As a result, much of the work in structured prediction has focused on designing heuristics for inference, such as loopy belief propagation (Murphy et al., 1999), tree reweighed message passing (Wainwright et al., 2005), local search algorithms (Zhang et al., 2014) or convex relaxations (Koo et al., 2010b), and empirical results show that these methods are often successful in recovering the correct (target) solution (Koo et al., 2010b; Rush et al., 2010; Zhang et al., 2014). This suggests that the instances encountered during inference are much easier than indicated by their complexity class.

The success of the heuristics can be attributed to the additional structural properties that are present in the typical instances. For instance, if the target solution stands out amongst all other solutions in some manner, than we expect heuristic approaches to discover it in polynomial time.

In theoretical computer science, the relevant work has focused on identifying the interesting structural properties which can be exploited to design specialized new algorithms or to prove the correctness of current heuristics. Such properties include Bilu-Linial stability (Bilu et al., 2012; Awasthi et al., 2012; Bilu and Linial, 2012; Makarychev et al., 2014), approximation stability (Balcan and Liang, 2012), weak-deletion stability (Awasthi et al., 2012, 2010), and so on. For instance, the notion of Bilu-Linial γ-stability specifies that the optimal solution does not change upon multiplicative perturbations of the parameters of magnitude at most γ and in this case (Makarychev et al., 2014) showed that Max-Cut is tractable whenever $\gamma \geq \sqrt{n} \log \log n$ for some constant c.

In structured prediction, the additional properties that trigger the success of approximate inference procedures can be attributed to the learning algorithms used to estimate the parameters. For example, one of the common learning strategies is to maximize the margin between the target solution and potential candidates: $\theta(\hat{x}) - \theta(x) \geq \gamma \Delta(\hat{x}, x), \forall x$, where Δ is a distance measure between assignments, allowing a closer margin between similar assignments. This notion of stability (margin stability) has been empirically proven to produce tractable instances under various approximate inference algorithms (Finley and Joachims, 2008). Also, from the theoretical perspective, one can relate the notion of margin (additive) stability to the multiplicative stability mentioned above to provide weak guarantees, which suggests that explicitly enforcing the saliency of target solutions brings computational benefits for inference.

Even more concretely, the additive margins can be related to the empirical success of various linear programming relaxations approaches in machine learning. For instance, considering scoring functions of the form $\sum_\alpha \theta_\alpha(x_\alpha)$ on binary assignments $x \in \{0, 1\}^n$, the dual decomposition algorithm (Koo et al., 2010b; Sontag et al., 2011) has been successfully used for parsing with high order interactions, despite the theoretical intractability of the problem. To illustrate this, consider the optimality conditions for the resulting linear program. When most of the local potentials agree on the maximizing assignment, the relaxation is tight:

Lemma 5.7. *Assuming that a $(1-\delta)$ fraction of the components support the correct solution with a margin γ (i.e. for most α, $\theta_\alpha(x_\alpha^*) > \theta_\alpha(x_\alpha) + \gamma$), and the remaining δ fraction do not object by more than M (i.e. $\theta_\alpha(x_\alpha^*) > \theta_\alpha(x_\alpha) - M$) and $\delta \le \frac{\gamma}{\gamma+M}$, then the dual-decomposition algorithm returns the correct solution.*

Proof. Consider the binary structured prediction problem where the maximizing assignment is given by $\hat{x} = \arg\max_x \theta(x)$. We start by rewriting it as $\hat{x} = \arg\max_{x=x'} \sum_{i=1}^n \theta_i(x_i) + \sum_\alpha \theta_\alpha(x_\alpha')$, where we added constant unary potentials $\theta_i(x_i)$ for $i \in \{1 \ldots n\}$. Solving the optimization problem via dual decomposition involves computing

$$\hat{\delta} = \arg\min_\delta \Big\{ \max_x (\sum_i (\theta_i(x_i) - \sum_\alpha \delta_{i,\alpha}(x_i))) + \sum_\alpha \max_{x_\alpha'} (\theta_\alpha(x_\alpha') + \sum_i \delta_{i,\alpha}(x_i')) \Big\}$$

$$\hat{x} = \arg\max_x \Big\{ \sum_i (\theta_i(x_i) - \sum_\alpha \hat{\delta}_{i,\alpha}(x_i)) \Big\}$$

$$\hat{x}_\alpha' = \arg\max_{x_\alpha'} \Big\{ \theta_\alpha(x_\alpha') + \sum_i \hat{\delta}_{i,\alpha}(x_i') \Big\}$$

To show that a target assignment x^* is optimal, we find a dual witness δ^* such that: $\max_x (\sum_i (\theta_i(x_i) - \sum_\alpha \delta_{i,\alpha}^*(x_i))) + \sum_\alpha \max_{x_\alpha'} (\theta_\alpha(x_\alpha') + \sum_i \delta_{i,\alpha}^*(x_i')) \le \sum_i \theta_i(x_i^*) + \sum_\alpha \theta_\alpha(x_\alpha^*)$.

Define $\delta_{i,\alpha}^*(x_i^*) = 0$ and $\delta_{i,\alpha}^*(1-x_i^*) = \min_{x_\alpha'', \Delta(x_\alpha^*,x_\alpha'')>0} \frac{\theta_\alpha(x_\alpha^*)-\theta_\alpha(x_\alpha'')}{\Delta(x_\alpha^*,x_\alpha'')}$, where $\Delta(\cdot,\cdot)$ counts the number of dimension where the assignments disagree. Specifically, we design the dual witness δ^* such that it enforces local optimality of the target solution by increasing/decreasing the weight of the alternative local solutions.

With this choice of dual variables and an arbitrary assignment x_α', we have: $\theta_\alpha(x_\alpha') + \sum_i \delta_{i,\alpha}^*(x_i') = \theta_\alpha(x_\alpha') + \sum_{i,x_i' \ne x_i^*} \min_{x_\alpha'',\Delta(x_\alpha^*,x_\alpha'')>0} \frac{\theta_\alpha(x_\alpha^*)-\theta_\alpha(x_\alpha'')}{\Delta(x_\alpha^*,x_\alpha'')}$ $\le \theta_\alpha(x_\alpha') + \Delta(x_\alpha^*,x_\alpha') \frac{\theta_\alpha(x_\alpha^*)-\theta_\alpha(x_\alpha')}{\Delta(x_\alpha^*,x_\alpha')} = \theta_\alpha(x_\alpha^*)$. Therefore, all the modified local potentials select the target assignment via maximization and $\max_{x_\alpha'}\{\theta_\alpha(x_\alpha') + \sum_i \delta_{i,\alpha}^*(x_i')\} = \theta_\alpha(x_\alpha^*)$.

To conclude the proof we need to show that $\max_x \{\sum_i (\theta_i(x_i) - \sum_\alpha \delta_{i,\alpha}^*(x_i))\} \le \sum_i \theta_i(x^*)$. We have:

$$\sum_i (\theta_i(x_i) - \sum_\alpha \delta_{i,\alpha}^*(x_i)) = \sum_i \theta_i(x_i) - \sum_{i,x_i \ne x_i^*} \sum_\alpha \min_{x_\alpha'',\Delta(x_\alpha^*,x_\alpha'')>0} \frac{\theta_\alpha(x_\alpha^*)-\theta_\alpha(x_\alpha'')}{\Delta(x_\alpha^*,x_\alpha'')}$$

$$\le \sum_i \theta_i(x_i) - ((1-\delta)\gamma - \delta M)$$

where we used that $\theta_\alpha(x^*_\alpha) - \theta_\alpha(x''_\alpha) \geq \gamma$ for a $(1-\delta)$ fraction of the local potentials and $\theta_\alpha(x^*_\alpha) - \theta_\alpha(x''_\alpha) \geq -M$ for the rest.

If $((1-\delta)\gamma - \delta M \geq \max_x \sum_i(\theta_i(x_i) - \theta_i(x^*))$, then the target solution is optimal for the dual decomposition algorithm. Since θ_i were introduced as constant local potentials, we have that $\delta \leq \frac{\gamma}{\gamma+M}$ is sufficient to imply the optimality of the target solution.

$\square$

The observations in this section argue for enforcing stability with respect to perturbations of the parameters. In fact, dual-decomposition-based inference has been successfully applied in conjunction with simple learning algorithms which encourage local assignments to be consistent with the overall solution (Koo et al., 2010b).

Learning perturbation models is inherently tied to stability. Maximizing the probability that a perturbation model realizes a given answer also encourages the answer to be stable, carrying tractability benefits. Indeed, perturbation models can be tailored to achieve various notions of stability by designing appropriate (e.g. multiplicative) perturbations. Such variations can remain tractable even if the base model (as a class) is not.

5.10   Related Work

The Gibbs distribution plays a key role in many areas of computer science, statistics and physics. To learn more about its roles in machine learning we refer the interested reader to (Koller and Friedman, 2009; Wainwright and Jordan, 2008). The Gibbs distribution as well as its Markov properties can be realized from the statistics of high dimensional random MAP perturbations with the Gumbel distribution (see Theorem 6.1), (Papandreou and Yuille, 2011; Tarlow et al., 2012; Hazan and Jaakkola, 2012; Hazan et al., 2013). For comprehensive introduction to extreme value statistics we refer the reader to Kotz and Nadarajah (2000).

Recent work explores the different aspects of low dimensional MAP perturbation models (Papandreou and Yuille, 2010, 2011; Tarlow et al., 2012). Papandreou and Yuille (2010) describe sampling from the Gaussian distribution with random Gaussian perturbations. Papandreou and Yuille (2011) show empirically that MAP predictors with low dimensional perturbations share similar statistics as the Gibbs distribution. In our work we investigate the dependencies of such probability models. Specifically, we present non-i.i.d. low dimensional random perturbations that recover the Markov properties of tree structured Markov random fields. We also show that independent low dimensional perturbations may model long-range interactions. Tarlow et al. (2012) describe the Bayesian perspectives of these models and their efficient sampling procedures, as well as several learning techniques including hard-EM. In contrast, we focus on understanding the structure of the induced distribution and our learning approach is different. We use dual LPs in our hard-EM approach so as to obtain compact representations of the inverse polytope when possible, while Tarlow et al. (2012) focus on cutting plane approaches. When using cutting plane approaches for only a couple of iterations, the hard-EM estimates often fall outside the inverse polytope. Our dual LP approach alleviates this problem and in our experiments almost all estimates fall within the inverse polytope.

Our experiments show that we are able to sample from the modes of the distribution. Alternatively, one may use the M-best approach and its diverse-versions to recover such modes (Yanover and Weiss, 2004; Fromer and Globerson, 2009a; Batra, 2012; Mezuman et al., 2013; Batra et al., 2012; Guzman-Rivera et al., 2012). Finding the M-best carries a computational effort which extends beyond our learning approach whose complexity is as a 1-best solver. Alternatively, one may sample from determinantal point processes to retrieve the modes of the distributions (Kulesza and Taskar, 2012). This learning approach concerns problems that can be described by determinants while our approach is based on MRF potentials.

Acknowledgements

AG and TJ were partially supported by NSF grant #1524427

5.11 References

R. K. Ahuja and J. B. Orlin. Inverse optimization. In *Operations Research*, 2001.

M. B. Almeida and A. F. Martins. Fast and robust compressive summarization with dual decomposition and multi-task learning. In *ACL (1)*, pages 196–206, 2013.

P. Awasthi, A. Blum, and O. Sheffet. Clustering under natural stability assumptions. 2010.

P. Awasthi, A. Blum, and O. Sheffet. Center-based clustering under perturbation stability. *Information Processing Letters*, 112(1):49–54, 2012.

M. F. Balcan and Y. Liang. Clustering under perturbation resilience. In *Automata, Languages, and Programming*, pages 63–74. Springer, 2012.

D. Batra. An efficient message-passing algorithm for the m-best map problem. In *Conference on Uncertainty in Artificial Intelligence (UAI)*, 2012.

D. Batra, P. Yadollahpour, A. Guzman-Rivera, and G. Shakhnarovich. Diverse m-best solutions in markov random fields. In *ECCV*, 2012.

Y. Bilu and N. Linial. Are stable instances easy? *Combinatorics, Probability and Computing*, 21(05):643–660, 2012.

Y. Bilu, A. Daniely, N. Linial, and M. Saks. On the practically interesting instances of maxcut. *arXiv preprint arXiv:1205.4893*, 2012.

V. Chatalbashev. Inverse convex optimization.

H. Fang, S. Gupta, F. Iandola, R. K. Srivastava, L. Deng, P. Dollár, J. Gao, X. He, M. Mitchell, J. C. Platt, et al. From captions to visual concepts and back. In *Proceedings of the IEEE Conference on Computer Vision and Pattern Recognition*, pages 1473–1482, 2015.

T. Finley and T. Joachims. Training structural svms when exact inference is intractable. In *Proceedings of the 25th international conference on Machine learning*, pages 304–311. ACM, 2008.

M. Fromer and A. Globerson. An lp view of the m-best map problem. *Advances in Neural Information Processing Systems (NIPS)*, 22:567–575, 2009a.

M. Fromer and A. Globerson. An lp view of the m-best map problem. *Advances in Neural Information Processing Systems (NIPS)*, 2009b.

A. Gane, T. Hazan, and T. Jaakkola. Learning with maximum a-posteriori perturbation models. In *Proceedings of the Seventeenth International Conference on Artificial Intelligence and Statistics*, 2014.

S. Geman and D. Geman. Stochastic relaxation, gibbs distributions, and the bayesian restoration of images. *Pattern Analysis and Machine Intelligence, IEEE Transactions on*, 1984.

L. Goldberg and M. Jerrum. The complexity of ferromagnetic ising with local fields. *Combinatorics Probability and Computing*, 16(1):43, 2007.

E. Gumbel and J. Lieblein. *Statistical theory of extreme values and some practical applications: a series of lectures*, volume 33. US Govt. Print. Office, 1954.

A. Guzman-Rivera, P. Kohli, and D. Batra. Faster training of structural svms with diverse m-best cutting-planes. In *Discrete Optimization in Machine Learning Workshop (DISCML-NIPS)*, 2012.

M. Gygli, H. Grabner, and L. Van Gool. Video summarization by learning submodular mixtures of objectives. In *Proceedings of the IEEE Conference on Computer Vision and Pattern Recognition*, pages 3090–3098, 2015.

W. K. Hastings. Monte carlo sampling methods using markov chains and their applications. *Biometrika*, 57(1):97–109, 1970.

T. Hazan and T. Jaakkola. On the partition function and random maximum a-posteriori perturbations. *ICML*, 2012.

T. Hazan, S. Maji, and T. Jaakkola. On sampling from the gibbs distribution with random maximum a-posteriori perturbations. *Advances in Neural Information Processing Systems*, 2013.

M. Huber. A bounding chain for swendsen-wang. *Random Structures and Algorithms*, 2003.

M. Jerrum and A. Sinclair. Polynomial-time approximation algorithms for the ising model. *SIAM Journal on computing*, 22(5):1087–1116, 1993.

M. Jerrum, A. Sinclair, and E. Vigoda. A polynomial-time approximation algorithm for the permanent of a matrix with nonnegative entries. *Journal of the ACM (JACM)*, 51(4):671–697, 2004a.

M. Jerrum, A. Sinclair, and E. Vigoda. A polynomial-time approximation algorithm for the permanent of a matrix with nonnegative entries. *Journal of the ACM (JACM)*, 51(4):671–697, 2004b.

J. H. Kappes, P. Swoboda, B. Savchynskyy, T. Hazan, and C. Schnörr. Probabilistic correlation clustering and image partitioning using perturbed multicuts. In *Scale Space and Variational Methods in Computer Vision*, pages 231–242. Springer, 2015.

D. Koller and N. Friedman. *Probabilistic graphical models*. MIT press, 2009.

V. Kolmogorov. Convergent tree-reweighted message passing for energy minimization. *PAMI*, 2006.

T. Koo, A. Rush, M. Collins, T. Jaakkola, and D. Sontag. Dual decomposition for parsing with non-projective head automata. In *EMNLP*, 2010a.

T. Koo, A. M. Rush, M. Collins, T. Jaakkola, and D. Sontag. Dual decomposition for parsing with non-projective head automata. In *Proceedings of the 2010 Conference on Empirical Methods in Natural Language Processing*, pages 1288–1298. Association for Computational Linguistics, 2010b.

S. Kotz and S. Nadarajah. *Extreme value distributions: theory and applications*. World Scientific Publishing Company, 2000.

A. Kulesza and B. Taskar. Determinantal point processes for machine learning. *Foundations and Trends in Machine Learning*, 2012.

S. Maji, T. Hazan, and T. Jaakkola. Efficient boundary annotation using random map perturbations. In *Proceedings of the Seventeenth International Conference on Artificial Intelligence and Statistics*, 2014.

K. Makarychev, Y. Makarychev, and A. Vijayaraghavan. Bilu-linial stable instances of max cut and minimum multiway cut. In *Proceedings of the Twenty-Fifth Annual ACM-SIAM Symposium on Discrete Algorithms*, pages 890–906. SIAM, 2014.

R. McDonald and G. Satta. On the complexity of non-projective data-driven dependency parsing. In *Proceedings of the 10th International Conference on Parsing Technologies*, pages 121–132. Association for Computational Linguistics, 2007.

R. McDonald, F. Pereira, K. Ribarov, and J. Hajič. Non-projective dependency parsing using spanning tree algorithms. In *EMNLP*, 2005.

E. Mezuman, D. Tarlow, A. Globerson, and Y. Weiss. Tighter linear program relaxations for high order graphical models. In *Conference on Uncertainty in Artificial Intelligence (UAI)*, 2013.

K. P. Murphy, Y. Weiss, and M. I. Jordan. Loopy belief propagation for approximate inference: An empirical study. In *Proceedings of the Fifteenth conference on Uncertainty in artificial intelligence*, pages 467–475. Morgan Kaufmann Publishers Inc., 1999.

S. Nowozin and C. H. Lampert. Structured learning and prediction in computer vision. *Foundations and Trends® in Computer Graphics and Vision*, 6(3–4): 185–365, 2011.

F. Orabona, T. Hazan, A. Sarwate, and T. Jaakkola. On measure concentration of random maximum a-posteriori perturbations. In *ICML*, 2014.

G. Papandreou and A. Yuille. Gaussian sampling by local perturbations. In *Advances in Neural Information Processing Systems (NIPS)*, 2010.

G. Papandreou and A. Yuille. Perturb-and-map random fields: Using discrete optimization to learn and sample from energy models. In *ICCV*, 2011.

J. Pearl. *Probabilistic Reasoning in Intelligent Systems*. Morgan Kaufman, San Mateo, 1988.

L. Rabiner and B.-H. Juang. Fundamentals of speech recognition. 1993.

A. M. Rush, D. Sontag, M. Collins, and T. Jaakkola. On dual decomposition and linear programming relaxations for natural language processing. In *Proceedings of the 2010 Conference on Empirical Methods in Natural Language Processing*, pages 1–11. Association for Computational Linguistics, 2010.

A. Schrijver. *Combinatorial optimization: polyhedra and efficiency.* Springer, 2003.

D. Sontag, T. Meltzer, A. Globerson, T. Jaakkola, and Y. Weiss. Tightening LP relaxations for MAP using message passing. In *Conference on Uncertainty in Artificial Intelligence (UAI)*, 2008.

D. Sontag, A. Globerson, and T. Jaakkola. Introduction to dual decomposition for inference. *Optimization for Machine Learning*, 1:219–254, 2011.

R. Szeliski, R. Zabih, D. Scharstein, O. Veksler, V. Kolmogorov, A. Agarwala, M. Tappen, and C. Rother. A comparative study of energy minimization methods for markov random fields with smoothness-based priors. *IEEE Transactions on Pattern Analysis and Machine Intelligence*, pages 1068–1080, 2007.

D. Tarlow, R. Adams, and R. Zemel. Randomized optimum models for structured prediction. In *AISTATS*, 2012.

I. Tsochantaridis, T. Hofmann, T. Joachims, and Y. Altun. Support vector machine learning for interdependent and structured output spaces. In *ICML*, page 104. ACM, 2004.

L. Valiant. The complexity of computing the permanent. *Theoretical computer science*, 1979.

M. Volkovs and R. S. Zemel. Efficient sampling for bipartite matching problems. In *Advances in Neural Information Processing Systems (NIPS)*, 2012.

M. Wainwright and M. Jordan. Graphical models, exponential families, and variational inference. *Foundations and Trends in Machine Learning*, 2008.

M. J. Wainwright, T. S. Jaakkola, and A. S. Willsky. Map estimation via agreement on trees: message-passing and linear programming. *Information Theory, IEEE Transactions on*, 51(11):3697–3717, 2005.

J. Wang and R. Swendsen. Nonuniversal critical dynamics in monte carlo simulations. *Physical review letters*, 1987.

T. Werner. High-arity interactions, polyhedral relaxations, and cutting plane algorithm for soft constraint optimization (map-mrf). In *Computer Vision and Pattern Recognition (CVPR)*, 2008.

Y. Yang and D. Ramanan. Articulated pose estimation with flexible mixtures-of-parts. In *Computer Vision and Pattern Recognition (CVPR)*, 2011.

C. Yanover and Y. Weiss. Finding the m most probable configurations using loopy belief propagation. *Advances in Neural Information Processing Systems (NIPS)*, 2004.

Y. Zhang, T. Lei, R. Barzilay, and T. Jaakkola. Greed is good if randomized: New inference for dependency parsing. *EMNLP*, 2014.

6   On the Expected Value of Random Maximum A-Posteriori Perturbations

Tamir Hazan   tamir.hazan@technion.ac.il
Technion
Haifa, Israel

Tommi Jaakkola   tommi@csail.mit.com
Massachusetts Institute of Technology
Cambridge, MA

In this chapter we present how to perform high-dimensional structured inference that is based on optimization and random perturbations. This framework injects randomness to maximum a-posteriori (MAP) predictors by randomly perturbing its potential function. When the perturbations are of low dimension, sampling the perturb-max prediction is as efficient as MAP optimization. A classic result from extreme value statistics asserts that perturb-max operations generate unbiased samples from the Gibbs distribution using high-dimensional perturbations. Unfortunately, the computational cost of generating so many high-dimensional random variables can be prohibitive. In this work we show that the expected value of perturb-max inference with low dimensional perturbations can be used sequentially to generate unbiased samples from the Gibbs distribution. We also show that the expected value of the maximal perturbations is a natural bound on the entropy of such perturb-max models.

6.1   Introduction

Modern machine learning tasks in computer vision, natural language processing, and computational biology involve inference of high-dimensional models. Examples include scene understanding (Felzenszwalb and Zabih, 2011), parsing (Koo et al., 2010), and protein design (Sontag et al., 2008). In these settings inference involves finding likely structures that fit the data: objects in images, parsers in sentences, or molecular configurations in proteins. Each structure corresponds to an assignment of values to random variables and the preference of a structure is based on defining potential functions that account for interactions over these variables. Given the observed data, these preferences yield a *posterior probability distribution* on assignments known as the Gibbs distribution by exponentiating the potential functions. Contemporary high dimensional models that are used in machine learning incorporate local potential functions on the variables of the model that are derived from the data (signal) as well as higher order potential functions that account for interactions between the model variables and derived from domain-specific knowledge (coupling). The resulting posterior probability landscape is often "ragged" and in such landscapes Markov chain Monte Carlo (MCMC) approaches to sampling from the Gibbs distribution may become prohibitively expensive (Jerrum and Sinclair, 1993; Goldberg and Jerrum, 2007, 2012). By contrast, when no data terms (local potential functions) exist, MCMC approaches can be quite successful. These methods include Gibbs sampling (Geman and Geman, 1984), Metropolis-Hastings (Hastings, 1970) or Swendsen-Wang (Swendsen and Wang, 1987).

An alternative to sampling from the Gibbs distribution is to look for the *maximum a posteriori probability* (MAP) structure. Substantial effort has gone into developing optimization algorithms for recovering MAP assignments by exploiting domain-specific structural restrictions (Eisner, 1996; Boykov et al., 2001; Kolmogorov, 2006; Gurobi Optimization, 2015; Felzenszwalb and Zabih, 2011; Swoboda et al., 2013) or by linear programming relaxations (Wainwright et al., 2005b; Weiss et al., 2007; Sontag et al., 2008; Werner, 2008). MAP inference is nevertheless limiting when there are a number of alternative likely assignments. Such alternatives arise either from inherent ambiguities (e.g., in image segmentation or text analysis) or due to the use of computationally/representationally limited potential functions (e.g., super-modularity) aliasing alternative structures to have similar scores. For an illustration, see Figure 6.1.

Recently, several works have leveraged the current efficiency of MAP solvers to build (approximate) samplers for the Gibbs distribution, thereby avoiding the computational burden of MCMC methods (Papandreou and Yuille, 2011; Tarlow et al., 2012; Hazan et al., 2013; Ermon et al., 2013a,b,c, 2014; Maddison et al., 2014; Papandreou and Yuille, 2014; Gane and Tamir Hazan, 2014; Keshet et al., 2011; Kalai and Vempala, 2005). The relevant works have shown that one can represent the Gibbs distribution by

Figure 6.1: Comparing MAP inference and perturbation models. A segmentation is modeled by $x = (x_1, ..., x_n)$ where n is the number of pixels and $x_i \in \{0, 1\}$ is a discrete label relating a pixel to foreground ($x_i = 1$) or background ($x_i = 0$). $\theta(x)$ is the (super-modular) score of each segmentation. Left: original image. Middle: the MAP segmentation $\mathrm{argmax}_x \theta(x)$ recovered by the graph-cuts optimization algorithm (Boykov et al., 2001). Note that the "optimal" solution is inaccurate because thin and long objects (wings) are labeled incorrectly. Right: The marginal probabilities of the perturb-max model estimated using 20 samples (random perturbations of $\theta(x)$ followed by executing graph-cuts). The information about the wings is recovered by these samples. Estimating the marginal probabilities of the corresponding Gibbs distribution by MCMC sampling is slow in practice and provably hard in theory (Hazan et al., 2013; Goldberg and Jerrum, 2007).

calculating the MAP structure of a *randomly perturbed potential function*, whenever the perturbations follow the Gumbel distribution (Papandreou and Yuille, 2011; Tarlow et al., 2012). Unfortunately the total number of structures, and consequently the total number of random perturbations, is exponential in the structure's dimension. We call this a *perturb-max* approach.

In this work we perform high dimensional inference tasks using the expected value of perturb-max programs that are restricted to low dimensional perturbations. In this setting the number of random perturbations is linear is the structure's dimension and as a result statistical inference is as fast as computing the MAP structure, as illustrated in Figure 6.1. We also provide measure concentration inequalities that show the expected perturb-max value can be estimated with high probability using only a few random samples. This work simplifies and extends our previous works (Hazan and Jaakkola, 2012; Hazan et al., 2013; Maji et al., 2014; Orabona et al., 2014).

We begin by introducing the setting of high dimensional inference as well as the necessary background in extreme value statistics in Section 6.2. Subsequently, we develop high dimensional inference algorithms that rely on the expected MAP value of randomly perturbed potential function, while using only low dimensional perturbations. In Section 6.3.1 we propose a novel sampling algorithm and in Section 6.3.2 we derive bounds on the entropy that may be of independent interest.

6.2　Inference and Random Perturbations

We first describe the high dimensional statistical inference problems that motivate this work. These involve defining the potential function, the Gibbs distribution, and its entropy. Further background can be found in standard texts on graphical models (Wainwright and Jordan, 2008). We will then describe the MAP inference problem and describe how to use extreme value statistics to perform statistical inference while recovering the maximal structure of randomly perturbed potential functions (Kotz and Nadarajah, 2000) and (David and Nagaraja, 2003, pp.159–61). To do this we apply random perturbations to the potential function and use MAP solvers to produce a solution to the perturbed problem.

6.2.1　High Dimensional Models and Extreme Value Statistics

Statistical inference for high dimensional problems involve reasoning about the states of discrete variables whose configurations (assignments of values) describe discrete structures. Suppose that our model has n variables $\boldsymbol{x} = (x_1, x_2, \ldots, x_n)$ where each x_i takes values in a discrete set $\mathcal{X}_i$. Let $\mathcal{X} = \mathcal{X}_1 \times \mathcal{X}_2 \times \cdots \times \mathcal{X}_n$ so that $\boldsymbol{x} \in \mathcal{X}$. Let $\mathrm{Dom}(\theta) \subseteq \mathcal{X}$ be a subset of possible configurations and $\theta : \mathcal{X} \to \mathbb{R}$ be a potential function that gives a score to an assignment or structure $\boldsymbol{x}$. For convenience we define $\theta(\boldsymbol{x}) = -\infty$ for $\boldsymbol{x} \notin \mathrm{Dom}(\theta)$. The potential function induces a probability distribution on configurations $\boldsymbol{x} = (x_1, \ldots, x_n)$ via the Gibbs distribution:

$$p(\boldsymbol{x}) \overset{\Delta}{=} \frac{1}{Z(\theta)} \exp(\theta(\boldsymbol{x})) \qquad \text{where} \qquad Z(\theta) \overset{\Delta}{=} \sum_{\boldsymbol{x} \in \mathcal{X}} \exp(\theta(\boldsymbol{x})). \qquad (6.1)$$

The normalization constant $Z(\theta)$ is called the partition function. Sampling from the Gibbs distribution is often difficult because the partition function involves exponentially many terms (equal to the number of discrete structures in $\mathcal{X}$). In many cases, computing the partition function is in the complexity class $\#P$ (e.g., (Valiant, 1979)).

6.2.2　MAP Inference

In practical inference tasks, the Gibbs distribution is constructed given observed data. Thus we call its maximizing structure the maximum a-posteriori (MAP) prediction. We can express MAP inference problem in the same notation as Maximizing (6.1):

$$\mathbf{x}^* = \underset{\boldsymbol{x} \in \mathfrak{X}}{\operatorname{argmax}} \, \theta(\boldsymbol{x}). \tag{6.2}$$

Maximizing $\theta(\boldsymbol{x})$ is equivalent to maximizing $p(\boldsymbol{x})$. Methods for performing the optimization in (6.2) for high dimensional potential functions have been extensively researched in the last decade (Boykov et al., 2001; Sontag et al., 2008; Gurobi Optimization, 2015; Felzenszwalb and Zabih, 2011; Swoboda et al., 2013). These have been useful in many cases of practical interest in computer vision, such as foreground-background image segmentation with supermodular potential functions (e.g., (Kolmogorov and Zabih, 2004)), parsing and tagging (e.g., (Koo et al., 2010; Rush et al., 2010)), branch and bound for scene understanding and pose estimation (Schwing and Urtasun, 2012; Sun et al., 2012) and dynamic programming predictions for outdoor scene understanding (Felzenszwalb et al., 2010). Although the run-time of these solvers can be exponential in the number of variables, they are often surprisingly effective in practice, (Wainwright et al., 2005b; Globerson and Jaakkola, 2007; Sontag et al., 2008; Sontag and Jaakkola, 2008).

6.2.3   Inference and Extreme Value Statistics

Although MAP prediction is NP-hard in general, it is often simpler than sampling from the Gibbs distribution. Nevertheless, usually there are several values of $\boldsymbol{x}$ whose scores $\theta(\boldsymbol{x})$ are close to $\theta(\mathbf{x}^*)$ and we would like to sample these structures (see Figure 6.1). From such samples it is possible to estimate the amount of uncertainty in these models. A standard uncertainty measure is the entropy function:

$$H(p) = - \sum_{\boldsymbol{x} \in \mathfrak{X}} p(\boldsymbol{x}) \log p(\boldsymbol{x}) \tag{6.3}$$

Such statistical inference tasks usually resort to MCMC methods that tend to be slow to converge in many practical settings (Jerrum and Sinclair, 1993; Goldberg and Jerrum, 2007, 2012). Alternatively one can draw unbiased samples from the Gibbs distribution by perturbing the potential function and solving the perturbed MAP problem. The perturb-max approach adds a random function $\gamma : \mathfrak{X} \to \mathbb{R}$ to the potential function in (6.1) and solves the resulting MAP problem:

$$\mathbf{x}^\gamma = \underset{\boldsymbol{x} \in \mathfrak{X}}{\operatorname{argmax}} \left\{ \theta(\boldsymbol{x}) + \gamma(\boldsymbol{x}) \right\}. \tag{6.4}$$

The random function $\gamma(\cdot)$ associates a random variable to each $\boldsymbol{x} \in \mathfrak{X}$. The simplest approach to designing a perturbation function is to associate an independent and identically distributed (i.i.d.) random variable $\gamma(\boldsymbol{x})$ for each $\boldsymbol{x} \in \mathcal{X}$. In this case, the distribution of the perturb-max value $\theta(\boldsymbol{x}) + \gamma(\boldsymbol{x})$ has an analytic form. To verify this observation we denote by $F(t)$ the cumulative distribution function of $\gamma(\boldsymbol{x})$, namely, $F(t) = P[\gamma(\boldsymbol{x}) \leq t]$. The independence of $\gamma(\boldsymbol{x})$ across $\boldsymbol{x} \in \mathcal{X}$ implies that $\mathbb{P}_\gamma(\max_{\boldsymbol{x} \in \mathcal{X}} \{\theta(\boldsymbol{x}) + \gamma(\boldsymbol{x})\} \leq t) = \mathbb{P}_\gamma(\forall \boldsymbol{x} \in \mathcal{X} \ \{\theta(\boldsymbol{x}) + \gamma(\boldsymbol{x})\} \leq t) = \mathbb{P}_\gamma(\forall \boldsymbol{x} \in \mathcal{X} \ \{\theta(\boldsymbol{x}) + \gamma(\boldsymbol{x})\} \leq t) = \prod_{\boldsymbol{x} \in \mathcal{X}} F(t - \theta(\boldsymbol{x}))$. Unfortunately, the product of cumulative distribution functions usually is not a simple distribution.

The Gumbel distribution, the Fréchet distribution and the Weibull distribution, used in extremal statistics, are max-stable distributions. That is, the product $\prod_{\boldsymbol{x} \in \mathcal{X}} F(t - \theta(\boldsymbol{x}))$ can be described by their own cumulative distribution function $F(\cdot)$ (Fisher and Tippett, 1928; Gnedenko, 1943; Gumbel, 1954). In this work we focus on the Gumbel distribution with zero mean, which is described by its a double exponential cumulative distribution function

$$G(t) = \exp(-\exp(-(t + c))), \tag{6.5}$$

where $c \approx 0.5772$ is the Euler-Mascheroni constant. Throughout our work we use the max-stability of the Gumbel distribution as described in the following Theorem.

Theorem 6.1 (Max-stability of Gumbel perturbations (Fisher and Tippett, 1928; Gnedenko, 1943; Gumbel, 1954)). *Let $\gamma = \{\gamma(\boldsymbol{x}) : \boldsymbol{x} \in \mathcal{X}\}$ be a collection of i.i.d. Gumbel random variables whose commutative distribution function is given by $G(t) = P[\gamma(\boldsymbol{x}) \leq t] = \exp(-\exp(-(t + c)))$. Then the random variable $\max_{\boldsymbol{x} \in \mathcal{X}} \{\theta(\boldsymbol{x}) + \gamma(\boldsymbol{x})\}$ also has the Gumbel distribution whose mean is the log-partition function $Z(\theta)$.*

Proof. The proof is straightforward and we add it for completeness. By the independence assumption,

$$\mathbb{P}_\gamma \left(\max_{\boldsymbol{x} \in \mathcal{X}} \{\theta(\boldsymbol{x}) + \gamma(\boldsymbol{x})\} \leq t \right) = \prod_{x \in X} \mathbb{P}_{\gamma(\boldsymbol{x})} \left(\theta(\boldsymbol{x}) + \gamma(\boldsymbol{x}) \leq t \right).$$

The random variable $\theta(\boldsymbol{x}) + \gamma(\boldsymbol{x})$ follows the Gumbel distribution with mean $\theta(\boldsymbol{x})$. Therefore

$$\mathbb{P}_{\gamma(x)} \left(\theta(\boldsymbol{x}) + \gamma(\boldsymbol{x}) \leq t \right) = G(t - \theta(\boldsymbol{x})).$$

Lastly, the double exponential form of the Gumbel distribution yields the result:

$$\prod_{x \in X} G(t - \theta(\boldsymbol{x})) = \exp\left(-\sum_{\boldsymbol{x} \in \mathcal{X}} \exp\left(-(t - \theta(\boldsymbol{x}) + c)\right)\right)$$
$$= \exp\left(-\exp(-(t + c - \log Z(\theta)))\right)$$
$$= G(t - \log Z(\theta)).$$

$\square$

We can use the log-partition function to recover the moments of the Gibbs distribution. Thus the log-partition function characterizes the stability of the randomized MAP predictor $\mathbf{x}^\gamma$ in (6.4).

Corollary 6.2 (Sampling from perturb-max models (Luce, 1959; Ben-Akiva and Lerman, 1985; McFadden, 1974)). *Under the conditions of Theorem 6.1 the Gibbs distribution measures the stability of the perturb-max argument, namely*

$$\frac{\exp(\theta(\hat{\boldsymbol{x}}))}{Z(\theta)} = \mathbb{P}_\gamma\left(\hat{\boldsymbol{x}} = \operatorname*{argmax}_{\boldsymbol{x} \in \mathcal{X}} \{\theta(\boldsymbol{x}) + \gamma(\boldsymbol{x})\}\right), \tag{6.6}$$

Proof. From Theorem 6.1, we have $\log Z(\theta) = \mathbb{E}_\gamma[\max_{\boldsymbol{x} \in \mathcal{X}} \{\theta(\boldsymbol{x}) + \gamma(\boldsymbol{x})\}]$, so we can take the derivative with respect to some $\theta(\hat{\boldsymbol{x}})$. We note that by differentiating the left hand side we get the Gibbs distribution:

$$\frac{\partial \log Z(\theta)}{\partial \theta(\hat{\boldsymbol{x}})} = \frac{\exp(\theta(\hat{\boldsymbol{x}}))}{Z(\theta)}.$$

Differentiating the right hand side is slightly more involved: First, we can differentiate under the integral operator (cf. (Folland, 2013)) so

$$\frac{\partial}{\partial \theta(\hat{\boldsymbol{x}})} \int_{\mathbb{R}^{|\mathcal{X}|}} \max_{\boldsymbol{x} \in \mathcal{X}} \{\theta(\boldsymbol{x}) + \gamma(\boldsymbol{x})\} \, d\gamma = \int_{\mathbb{R}^{|\mathcal{X}|}} \frac{\partial}{\partial \theta(\hat{\boldsymbol{x}})} \max_{\boldsymbol{x} \in \mathcal{X}} \{\theta(\boldsymbol{x}) + \gamma(\boldsymbol{x})\} \, d\gamma.$$

The (sub)gradient of the max-function is the indicator function (an application of Danskin's theorem (Bertsekas et al., 2003)):

$$\frac{\partial}{\partial \theta(\hat{\boldsymbol{x}})} \max_{\boldsymbol{x} \in \mathcal{X}} \{\theta(\boldsymbol{x}) + \gamma(\boldsymbol{x})\} = \mathbf{1}\left(\hat{\boldsymbol{x}} = \operatorname*{argmax}_{\boldsymbol{x} \in \mathcal{X}} \{\theta(\boldsymbol{x}) + \gamma(\boldsymbol{x})\}\right).$$

The corollary then follows by applying the expectation to both sides of the last equation. $\square$

An alternative proof of the preceding corollary can be given by considering the probability density function $g(t) = G'(t)$ of the Gumbel distribution. This proof consists of two steps. First, the probability that

$\hat{x}$ maximizes $\theta(x) + \gamma(x)$ is $\int g(t - \theta(\hat{x})) \prod_{x \neq \hat{x}} G(t - \theta(x)) dt$. Second, $g(t - \theta(\hat{x})) = \exp(\theta(\hat{x})) \cdot \exp(-(t + c)) G(t - \theta(\hat{x}))$ therefore the probability that $\hat{x}$ maximizes $\theta(x) + \gamma(x)$ is proportional to $\exp(\theta(\hat{x}))$, i.e., it is the Gibbs distribution.

We can also use the random MAP perturbation to estimate the entropy of the Gibbs distribution.

Corollary 6.3. *Let $p(x)$ be the Gibbs distribution, defined in Equation (6.3). Under the conditions of Theorem 6.1,*

$$H(p) = \mathbb{E}_\gamma \left[\gamma(\mathbf{x}^\gamma) \right].$$

Proof. The proof consists of evaluating the entropy in Equation (6.3) and using Theorem 6.1 to replace $\log Z(\theta)$ with $\mathbb{E}_\gamma[\theta(\mathbf{x}^\gamma) + \gamma(\mathbf{x}^\gamma)]$. Formally,

$$
\begin{aligned}
H(p) &= - \sum_{x \in \mathcal{X}} p(x)\theta(x) + \mathbb{E}_\gamma[\theta(\mathbf{x}^\gamma) + \gamma(\mathbf{x}^\gamma)] \\
&= - \sum_{x \in \mathcal{X}} p(x)\theta(x) + \sum_{x \in \mathcal{X}} \theta(x)\mathbb{P}_\gamma(\mathbf{x}^\gamma = x) + \mathbb{E}_\gamma[\gamma(\mathbf{x}^\gamma)] \\
&= \mathbb{E}_\gamma[\gamma(\mathbf{x}^\gamma)],
\end{aligned}
$$

where in the last line we used Corollary 6.2, which says $\mathbb{P}_\gamma(\mathbf{x}^\gamma = x) = p(x)$. $\qquad\square$

A direct proof of the preceding corollary can be given by showing that $\mathbb{E}_\gamma \left[\gamma(\mathbf{x}^\gamma) \cdot 1[\hat{x} = \mathbf{x}^\gamma] \right] = -p(\hat{x}) \log p(\hat{x})$ while the entropy is then attained by summing over all $\hat{x}$, since $\sum_{\hat{x} \in \mathcal{X}} 1[\hat{x} = \mathbf{x}^\gamma] = 1$. To establish this equality we note that

$$\mathbb{E}_\gamma \left[\gamma(\mathbf{x}^\gamma) \cdot 1[\hat{x} = \mathbf{x}^\gamma] \right] = \int (t - \theta(\hat{x})) g(t - \theta(\hat{x})) \prod_{x \neq \hat{x}} G(t - \theta(x)) dt.$$

Using the relation between $g(t)$ and $G(t)$ and the fact that $\prod_{x \in X} G(t - \theta(x)) = G(t - \log Z(\theta))$ while changing the integration variable to $\hat{t} = t - \theta(\hat{x})$ we can rephrase this quantity as $\int t \exp(-(c+t)) G(t + \log p(\hat{x})) dt$. Again by using the relation between $g(t + \log p(\hat{x}))$ and $G(t + \log p(\hat{x}))$ we derive that $\mathbb{E}_\gamma \left[\gamma(\mathbf{x}^\gamma) \cdot 1[\hat{x} = \mathbf{x}^\gamma] \right] = p(\hat{x}) \int t g(t + \log p(\hat{x})) dt$ while the integral is now the mean of a Gumbel random variable with expected value of $-\log p(\hat{x})$.

The preceding derivations show that perturbing the potential function $\theta(x)$ and then finding the MAP estimate $\mathbf{x}^\gamma$ of the perturbed Gibbs distribution allows us to perform many core tasks for high-dimensional statistical inference by using i.i.d. Gumbel perturbations. The distribution of $\mathbf{x}^\gamma$ is $p(x)$, its expected maximum value is the log-partition function, and the expected maximizing perturbation is the entropy of $p(x)$. While theoretically appealing, these derivations are computationally intractable when dealing with high-dimensional structures. These derivations involve generating high-dimensional perturbations, namely $|\mathcal{X}|$ random variables in the image of $\gamma(\cdot)$, one for each structure in $\mathcal{X} = \mathcal{X}_1 \times \cdots \mathcal{X}_n$, which grows exponentially with n. The goal of this paper is to apply high-dimensional inference using max-solvers that involve a low-dimensional perturbation term. More specifically, we wish to involve only a linear (in n) number of random variables.

6.3   Low-Dimensional Perturbations

In this work we establish our high dimensional inference approaches by exploiting the structure of the partition function $Z(\theta)$. The partition function is a key quantity in these models – its gradient is the Gibbs distribution and the entropy is its Fenchel dual. It is well-known that computing $Z(\theta)$ for high-dimensional models is challenging because of the exponential size of $\mathcal{X}$. This complexity carries over to the perturb-max approach to estimating the log-partition function, which also involves generating an exponential number of Gumbel random variables. In this section we show that the log-partition function can be computed using low-dimensional perturbations in a sequence of expected max-value computations. This will give us some insight on performing high dimensional inference using low dimensional perturbations. In what follows we will use the notation x_i^j to refer to the tuple $(x_i, x_{i+1}, \ldots, x_j)$ for $i < j$, with $\mathbf{x} = x_1^n$.

The partition function has a self-reducible form. That is, we can compute it iteratively while computing partial partition functions of lower dimensions:

$$Z(\theta) = \sum_{x_1} \sum_{x_2} \cdots \sum_{x_n} \exp(\theta(x_1, ..., x_n)). \qquad (6.7)$$

For example, the partition function is the sum, over x_1, of partial partition functions $\sum_{x_2,\ldots,x_n} \exp(\theta(\boldsymbol{x}))$. Fixing $x_1, \ldots, x_i$, the remaining summations are partial partition functions $\sum_{x_{i+1},\ldots,x_n} \exp(\theta(\boldsymbol{x}))$. With this in mind, we can compute each partial partition function using Theorem 6.1 but with low-dimensional perturbations for each partial partition.

Theorem 6.4. *Let* $\{\gamma_i(x_i)\}_{x_i \in \mathcal{X}_i, i=1,\ldots,n}$, *be a collection of independent and identically distributed (i.i.d.) random variables following the Gumbel distribution, defined in Theorem 6.1. Define* $\gamma_i = \{\gamma_i(x_i)\}_{x_i \in \mathcal{X}_i}$. *Then*

$$\log Z = \mathbb{E}_{\gamma_1} \max_{x_1} \cdots \mathbb{E}_{\gamma_n} \max_{x_n} \left\{ \theta(\boldsymbol{x}) + \sum_{i=1}^{n} \gamma_i(x_i) \right\}. \qquad (6.8)$$

Proof. The result follows from applying Theorem 6.1 iteratively. Let $\theta_n(x_1^n) = \theta(x_1^n)$ and define

$$\theta_{i-1}(x_1^{i-1}) = \mathbb{E}_{\gamma_i} \max_{x_i}\{\theta_i(x_1^i) + \gamma_i(x_i)\} \qquad i = 2, 3, \ldots, n$$

If we think of x_1^{i-1} as fixed and apply Theorem 6.1 to $\theta_i(x_1^{i-1}, x_i)$, we see that from (6.7),

$$\theta_{i-1}(x_1^{i-1}) = \log \sum_{x_i} \exp(\theta_i(x_1^i)).$$

Applying this for $i = n$ to $i = 2$, we obtain (6.8).   □

The computational complexity of the alternating procedure in (6.8) is still exponential in n. For example, the inner iteration $\theta_{n-1}(x_1^{n-1}) = \mathbb{E}_{\gamma_n} \max_{x_n}\{\theta_n(x_1^n) + \gamma_n(x_n)\}$ needs to be estimated exponentially many times, i.e., for every $x_1^{n-1} = (x_1, ..., x_{n-1})$. Thus from computational perspective the alternating formulation in Theorem 6.4 is just as inefficient as the formulation in Theorem 6.1. Nevertheless, this is the building block that enables inference in high-dimensional problems using low dimensional perturbations and max-solvers. Specifically, it provides the means for a new sampling algorithm from the Gibbs distribution and bounds on the log-partition and entropy functions.

6.3.1 Sampling

In the following we use low dimensional perturbations to generate unbiased samples from the Gibbs distribution. Although Corollary 6.2 presents a method for sampling from the full Gibbs distribution using perturb-max operations, it requires exponentially many independent perturbations $\gamma(\boldsymbol{x})$, for each $\boldsymbol{x} \in X$. Here we rely on low-dimensional perturbations to draw samples from the Gibbs distribution.

Sampling from the Gibbs distribution is inherently tied to estimating the partition function. Assume we could have compute the partition function exactly, then we could have sample from the Gibbs distribution sequentially: for dimension $i = 1, ..., n$ sample x_i with probability which is proportional to $\sum_{x_{i+1}^n} \exp(\theta(\boldsymbol{x}))$. Unfortunately, direct computations of the partition function is #P-hard. Instead, we construct a family of self-reducible upper bounds which imitate the partition function behavior, namely by bounding the summation over its exponentiations.

Corollary 6.5. *Let $\{\gamma_i(x_i)\}$ be a collection of i.i.d. random variables, each following the Gumbel distribution with zero mean. Set $\theta_j(x_1^j) =$*

$\mathbb{E}_{\gamma} \left[\max_{x_{j+1}^n} \{ \theta(\boldsymbol{x}) + \sum_{i=j+1}^n \gamma_i(x_i) \} \right]$. *Then for every $j = 1, \ldots, n-1$ and every $\boldsymbol{x} = x_1^n$ the following inequality holds:*

$$\sum_{x_j} \exp\left(\theta_j(x_1^j) \right) \leq \exp\left(\theta_{j-1}(x_1^{j-1}) \right). \tag{6.9}$$

In particular, for $j = n$ we have $\sum_{x_n} \exp(\theta(x_1^n)) = \exp\left(\theta_{n-1}(x_1^{n-1}) \right)$.

Proof. The result is an application of the perturb-max interpretation of the partition function in Theorem 6.1. Intuitively, these bounds correspond to moving expectations outside the maximization operations in Theorem 6.4, each move resulting in a different bound. Formally, the left hand side can be expanded as

$$\mathbb{E}_{\gamma_j} \left[\max_{x_j} \mathbb{E}_{\gamma_{j+1}, \ldots, \gamma_n} \left[\max_{x_{j+1}^n} \left\{ \theta(x_1^n) + \sum_{i=j}^n \gamma_i(x_i) \right\} \right] \right], \tag{6.10}$$

while the right hand side is attained by alternating the maximization with respect to x_j with the expectation of $\gamma_{j+1}, \ldots, \gamma_n$. The proof then follows by exponentiating both sides. $\qquad\square$

We use these upper bounds for every dimension $i = 1, \ldots, n$ to sample from a probability distribution that follows a summation over exponential functions, with a discrepancy that is described by the upper bound. This is formalized below in Algorithm 6.1.

Algorithm 6.1 Unbiased sampling from Gibbs distribution using randomized prediction

---

Iterate over $j = 1, \ldots, n$, while keeping fixed $x_1, \ldots, x_{j-1}$. Set $\theta_j(x_1^j)$ as in Corollary 6.5.

1. $p_j(x_j) = \exp\left(\theta_j(x_1^j) \right) / \exp\left(\theta_{j-1}(x_1^{j-1}) \right)$
2. $p_j(r) = 1 - \sum_{x_j} p(x_j)$
3. Sample an element according to $p_j(\cdot)$. If r is sampled then reject and restart with $j = 1$. Otherwise, fix the sampled element x_j and continue the iterations.

Output: $x_1, \ldots, x_n$

When the potential function is decomposable, namely $\theta(\boldsymbol{x}) = \sum_i \theta_i(x_i)$, the upper bounds in Equation (6.9) are tight and the sampling algorithm never rejects and terminates after exactly n iterations.

We say the algorithm accepts if it terminates with an output $\boldsymbol{x}$. When we reject the discrepancy, the probability we accept a configuration $\boldsymbol{x}$ is the product of probabilities in all rounds. Since these upper bounds are self-reducible, i.e., for every dimension i we are using the same quantities that were computed in the previous dimensions $1, 2, \ldots, i-1$, we are sampling an accepted configuration proportionally to $\exp(\theta(\boldsymbol{x}))$, the full Gibbs distribution. This is summarized in the following theorem.

Theorem 6.6. *Let $p(\boldsymbol{x})$ be the Gibbs distribution defined in (6.1) and let $\{\gamma_i(x_i)\}$ be a collection of i.i.d. random variables following the Gumbel distribution with zero mean given in (6.5). Then*

$$\mathbb{P}\left(\text{Algorithm 6.1 accepts}\right) = Z(\theta) \Big/ \exp\left(\mathbb{E}_\gamma\left[\max_{\boldsymbol{x}}\{\theta(\boldsymbol{x}) + \sum_{i=1}^{n}\gamma_i(x_i)\}\right]\right).$$

Moreover, if Algorithm 6.1 accepts then it produces a configuration $\boldsymbol{x} = (x_1, \ldots, x_n)$ according to the Gibbs distribution:

$$\mathbb{P}\left(\text{Algorithm 6.1 outputs } \boldsymbol{x} \mid \text{Algorithm 6.1 accepts}\right) = \frac{\exp(\theta(\boldsymbol{x}))}{Z(\theta)}.$$

Proof. Set $\theta_j(x_1^j)$ as in Corollary 6.5. The probability of sampling a configuration $\boldsymbol{x} = (x_1, \ldots, x_n)$ without rejecting is

$$\prod_{j=1}^{n}\frac{\exp\left(\theta_j(x_1^j)\right)}{\exp\left(\theta_{j-1}(x_1^{j-1})\right)} = \frac{\exp(\theta(\boldsymbol{x}))}{\exp\left(\mathbb{E}_\gamma\left[\max_{\boldsymbol{x}}\{\theta(\boldsymbol{x}) + \sum_{i=1}^{n}\gamma_i(x_i)\}\right]\right)}.$$

The probability of sampling without rejecting is thus the sum of this probability over all configurations, i.e.,

$$\mathbb{P}(\text{Alg. 6.1 accepts}) = Z(\theta)\Big/\exp\left(\mathbb{E}_\gamma\left[\max_{\boldsymbol{x}}\left\{\theta(\boldsymbol{x}) + \sum_{i=1}^{n}\gamma_i(x_i)\right\}\right]\right).$$

Therefore conditioned on accepting a configuration, it is produced according to the Gibbs distribution. $\qquad\square$

Since acceptance/rejection follows the geometric distribution, the sampling procedure rejects k times with probability $(1 - \mathbb{P}(\text{Algorithm 6.1 accepts}))^k$. The running time of our Gibbs sampler is determined by the average number of rejections $1/\mathbb{P}(\text{Algorithm 6.1 accepts})$ and by taking the log-scale it is

$$\log\left(1/\mathbb{P}(\text{Alg. 6.1 accepts})\right) = \mathbb{E}_\gamma\left[\max_{\boldsymbol{x}}\left\{\theta(\boldsymbol{x}) + \sum_{i=1}^{n}\gamma_i(x_i)\right\}\right] - \log Z(\theta).$$

To be able to estimate the number of steps the sampling algorithm requires, we construct an efficiently computable lower bound to the log-partition function, that is based on perturb-max values.

Our suggested lower bound originates from the representation of the partition function by low-dimensional perturbations. It estimates each expected-max computation by its empirical average and then follows a model expansion to be able to compute this quantity with a single max-operation. Although the theory below requires exponentially many perturbations to have a tight bound, our experimental validation shows that our lower bounds is surprisingly tight using only a few random perturbations.

Corollary 6.7. *Let $\theta(\boldsymbol{x})$ be a potential function over $\boldsymbol{x} = (x_1, \ldots, x_n)$. We create multiple copies of x_i, namely $\tilde{\boldsymbol{x}}_i = \{x_{i,k_i} : k_i = 1, 2, \ldots, M_i\}$ for $i = 1, \ldots, n$, and define the extended potential function over $\tilde{\boldsymbol{x}} = (\tilde{\boldsymbol{x}}_1, \tilde{\boldsymbol{x}}_2, \ldots, \tilde{\boldsymbol{x}}_n)$:*

$$\hat{\theta}(\tilde{\boldsymbol{x}}) = \frac{1}{\prod_{i=1}^{n} M_i} \sum_{\{k_i\}=1}^{\{M_i\}} \theta(x_{1,k_1}, \ldots, x_{n,k_n}). \tag{6.11}$$

For i.i.d. perturbations $\gamma_{i,k_i}(x_{i,k_i})$ that distributed according to the Gumbel distribution with zero mean we define the extended perturbation model

$$\hat{\gamma}_i(\tilde{\boldsymbol{x}}_i) = \frac{1}{M_i} \sum_{k_i=1}^{M_i} \gamma_{i,k_i}(x_{i,k_i}). \tag{6.12}$$

Also, whenever θ is clear from the context we use the shorthand Z for $Z(\theta)$. Then

$$\mathbb{P}\left(\log Z \geq \max_{\tilde{\boldsymbol{x}}} \left\{ \hat{\theta}(\tilde{\boldsymbol{x}}) + \sum_{i=1}^{n} \hat{\gamma}_i(\tilde{\boldsymbol{x}}_i) \right\} - \epsilon n \right) \geq 1 - \sum_{i=1}^{n} \frac{\prod_{j=2}^{i} |\mathcal{X}_{j-1}| \pi^2}{6 M_i \epsilon^2}. \tag{6.13}$$

Proof. The proof consists of three steps:

- developing a measure concentration analysis for Theorem 6.1, which states that a single max-evaluation is enough to lower bound the expected max-value with high probability;

- using the self-reducibility of the partition function in Theorem 6.4 to show the partition function can be computed by iteratively applying low-dimensional perturbations;

- proving that these lower dimensional partition functions can be lower bounded uniformly (i.e., all at once) with a single measure concentration statement.

We first provide a measure concentration analysis of Theorem 6.1. Specifically, we estimate the deviation of the random variable $F = \max_{\boldsymbol{x} \in \mathcal{X}} \{\theta(\boldsymbol{x}) + \gamma(\boldsymbol{x})\}$ from its expected value using Chebyshev's inequality. For this purpose we recall Thoerem 6.1 which states that F is Gumbel-distributed and therefore its variance is $\pi^2/6$. Chebyshev's inequality then asserts that

$$\mathbb{P}_\gamma \left(|F - \mathbb{E}_\gamma [F]| \geq \epsilon \right) \leq \pi^2 / 6\epsilon^2. \tag{6.14}$$

Since we want this statement to hold with high probability for small epsilon we reduce the variance of the random variable while not changing its expectation by taking a sampled average of i.i.d. perturb-max values: Let $\hat{\boldsymbol{V}}(\gamma) = \max_{\boldsymbol{x}} \{\theta(\boldsymbol{x}) + \gamma(\boldsymbol{x})\}$. Suppose we sample M i.i.d. copies $\gamma_1, \gamma_2, \ldots, \gamma_M$ of γ with and generate the i.i.d. Gumbel-distributed values $F_j \overset{def}{=} F(\gamma_j)$. Since $\mathbb{E}_\gamma[F(\gamma)] = \log Z$, we can apply Chebyshev's inequality to the $\frac{1}{M} \sum_{i=1}^{M} \hat{\boldsymbol{V}}_j - \log Z$ to get

$$\mathbb{P} \left(\left| \frac{1}{M} \sum_{i=1}^{M} \hat{\boldsymbol{V}}_j - \log Z \right| \geq \epsilon \right) \leq \frac{\pi^2}{6M\epsilon^2}. \tag{6.15}$$

Using the explicit perturb-max notation and considering only the lower-side of the measure concentration bound: with probability at least $1 - \frac{\pi^2}{6M\epsilon^2}$ there holds:

$$\log Z \geq \frac{1}{M} \sum_{j=1}^{M} \max_{\boldsymbol{x} \in \mathcal{X}} \{\theta(\boldsymbol{x}) + \gamma_j(\boldsymbol{x})\} - \epsilon \tag{6.16}$$

To complete the first step, we wish to compute the summation over $M-$maximum values using a single maximization. For this we duplicate M copies of the variable $\boldsymbol{x}$ to the variables $\boldsymbol{x}_1, \boldsymbol{x}_2, \ldots, \boldsymbol{x}_M \in \mathcal{X}$:

$$\sum_{j=1}^{M} \max_{\boldsymbol{x} \in \mathcal{X}} \{\theta(\boldsymbol{x}) + \gamma_j(\boldsymbol{x})\} = \max_{\boldsymbol{x}_1, \boldsymbol{x}_2, \ldots, \boldsymbol{x}_M \in \mathcal{X}} \sum_{j=1}^{M} \{\theta(\boldsymbol{x}_j) + \gamma_j(\boldsymbol{x}_j)\} \tag{6.17}$$

For the remainder we use an argument by induction on n, the number of variables. Consider first the case $n = 2$ so that $\theta(\boldsymbol{x}) = \theta_{1,2}(x_1, x_2)$. The self-reducibility as described in Theorem 6.1 states that

$$\log Z = \log \left(\sum_{x_1} \exp \left[\log \left(\sum_{x_2} \exp(\theta_{1,2}(x_1, x_2)) \right) \right] \right) \tag{6.18}$$

As in the proof of Theorem 6.1, define $\theta_1(x_1) = \log(\sum_{x_2} \exp(\theta_{1,2}(x_1, x_2)))$. Thus we have $\log Z = \log \left(\sum_{x_1} \exp(\theta_1(x_1)) \right)$, which is a partition function for a single-variable model.

We wish to uniformly approximate $\theta_1(x_1)$ over all $x_1 \in \mathfrak{X}_1$. Fix $x_1 = a$ for some $a \in \mathfrak{X}_1$ and consider the single-variable model $\theta_{1,2}(a, x_2)$ over x_2 which has $\theta_1(a)$ as its log partition function. Then from Theorem 6.1, we have $\theta_1(a) = \mathbb{E}_{\gamma_2} \left[\max_{x_2} \{ \theta(a, x_2) + \gamma_2(x_2) \} \right]$. Applying Chebyshev's inequality in (6.15) to M_2 replicates of γ_2, we get

$$\mathbb{P} \left(\left| \frac{1}{M_2} \sum_{j=1}^{M_2} \max_{x_2} \{ \theta(a, x_2) + \gamma_{2,j}(x_2)] \} - \theta_1(a) \right| \geq \epsilon \right) \leq \frac{\pi^2}{6 M_2 \epsilon^2}.$$

Taking a union bound over $a \in \mathfrak{X}_1$ we have that with probability at least $1 - |\mathfrak{X}_1| \frac{\pi^2}{6 M_2 \epsilon^2}$

$$\left| \frac{1}{M_2} \sum_{j=1}^{M_2} \max_{x_2} \{ \theta(x_1, x_2) + \gamma_{2,j}(x_2)] \} - \theta_1(x_1) \right| \leq \epsilon \quad \forall x_1 \in \mathfrak{X}_1$$

This implies the following one-sided inequality with probability at least $1 - |\mathfrak{X}_1| \frac{\pi^2}{6 M_2 \epsilon^2}$ uniformly over $x_1 \in \mathfrak{X}_1$:

$$\theta_1(x_1) \geq \frac{1}{M_2} \sum_{j=1}^{M_2} \max_{x_2} \{ \theta(x_1, x_2) + \gamma_{2,j}(x_2)] \} - \epsilon. \tag{6.19}$$

Now note that the overall log partition function for the model $\theta(\boldsymbol{x}) = \theta_{1,2}(x_1, x_2)$ is a log partition function for a single variable model with potential $\theta_1(x_1)$, so $\log Z = \log(\sum_{x_1} \exp(\theta_1(x_1)))$. Again using Theorem 6.1, we have $\log Z = \mathbb{E}_{\gamma_1} \left[\max_{x_1} \{ \theta_1(x_1) + \gamma_1(x_1) \} \right]$, so we can apply Chebyshev's inequality to M_1 copies of γ_1 to get that with probability at least $1 - \frac{\pi^2}{6 M_1 \epsilon^2}$:

$$\log Z \geq \frac{1}{M_1} \sum_{k=1}^{M_1} \max_{x_1} \{ \theta_1(x_1) + \gamma_{1,k}(x_1) \} - \epsilon. \tag{6.20}$$

Plugging in (6.19) into (6.20), we get that with probability at least $1 - \frac{\pi^2}{6 M_1 \epsilon^2} - |\mathfrak{X}_1| \frac{\pi^2}{6 M_2 \epsilon^2}$ that $\log Z$ is lower bounded by

$$\frac{1}{M_1} \sum_{k=1}^{M_1} \max_{x_1} \left\{ \left(\frac{1}{M_2} \sum_{j=1}^{M_2} \max_{x_2} \{ \theta(x_1, x_2) + \gamma_{2,j}(x_2) \} \right) + \gamma_{1,k}(x_1) \right\} - 2\epsilon. \tag{6.21}$$

Now we pull the maximization outside the sum by introducing separate variables for each of the M_1 and M_2 summands, as in (6.17):

$$\frac{1}{M_1}\sum_{k=1}^{M_1}\max_{x_1}\left\{\left(\frac{1}{M_2}\sum_{j=1}^{M_2}\max_{x_2}\{\theta(x_1,x_2)+\gamma_{2,j}(x_2)\}\right)+\gamma_{1,k}(x_1)\right\}$$

$$=\frac{1}{M_1}\sum_{k=1}^{M_1}\max_{x_1}\left\{\left(\max_{\tilde{x}_2}\frac{1}{M_2}\sum_{j=1}^{M_2}\theta(x_1,x_{2,j})+\gamma_{2,j}(x_{2,j})\right)+\gamma_{1,k}(x_1)\right\}$$

$$=\max_{\tilde{x}_1}\max_{\tilde{x}_2}\frac{1}{M_1M_2}\sum_{k=1}^{M_1}\sum_{j=1}^{M_2}\theta(x_{1,k},x_{2,j})+\gamma_{2,j}(x_{1,k},x_{2,j})+\gamma_{1,k}(x_{1,k})$$

Note that in this bound we have to generate $|\mathcal{X}_1||\mathcal{X}_2|$ variables $\gamma_{2,j}(x_{1,k},x_{2,j})$, which will become inefficient as we add more variables. We can get an efficiently computable lower bound on this quantity by maximizing over a smaller set of variables: we use the same perturbation realization $\gamma_{2,j}(x_{2,j})$ for every value of $x_{1,k}$. Thus we have the lower bound

$$\log Z \geq \max_{\tilde{x}_1,\tilde{x}_2}\frac{1}{M_1M_2}\sum_{k=1}^{M_1}\sum_{j=1}^{M_2}(\theta(x_{1,k},x_{2,j})+\gamma_{2,j}(x_{2,j})+\gamma_{1,k}(x_{1,k}))-2\epsilon$$

with probability at least $1-\frac{\pi^2}{6M_1\epsilon^2}-|\mathcal{X}_1|\frac{\pi^2}{6M_2\epsilon^2}$.

Now suppose the result holds for models on $n-1$ variables and consider the model $\theta(x_1,x_2,\ldots,x_n)$ on n variables. Consider the 2-variable model $\theta(x_1,x_2^n)$ and define

$$\theta_1(x_1)=\log\left(\sum_{x_2^n}\exp(\theta(x_1,x_2^n))\right). \tag{6.22}$$

From the analysis of the 2-variable case, as in (6.20), we have that with probability at least $1-\frac{\pi^2}{6M_1\epsilon^2}$:

$$\log Z \geq \frac{1}{M_1}\sum_{k_1=1}^{M_1}\max_{x_1}\{\theta_1(x_1)+\gamma_{1,k_1}(x_1)\}-\epsilon. \tag{6.23}$$

but now for each value of x_1, the function $\theta_1(x_1)$ is a log partition function on the $n-1$ variables x_2^n so applying the induction hypothesis to $\theta_1(x_1)$, we have with probability at least

$$1-\frac{\pi^2}{6M_2\epsilon^2}-|\mathcal{X}_2|\frac{\pi^2}{6M_3\epsilon^2}-|\mathcal{X}_2||\mathcal{X}_3|\frac{\pi^2}{6M_4\epsilon^2}-\cdots-\prod_{j=2}^{n-1}|\mathcal{X}_j|\frac{\pi^2}{6M_n\epsilon^2}\tag{6.24}$$

we have

$$\theta_1(x_1) \geq \max_{\tilde{\boldsymbol{x}}_2^n} \left\{ \hat{\theta}(x_1, \tilde{\boldsymbol{x}}_2^n) + \sum_{i=2}^{n} \hat{\gamma}_i(\tilde{\boldsymbol{x}}_i) \right\} - \epsilon(n-1) \qquad (6.25)$$

Taking a union bound over all x_1, with probability at least

$$1 - \sum_{i=1}^{n} \left(\prod_{j=2}^{i} |\mathcal{X}_{j-1}| \right) \frac{\pi^2}{6 M_n \epsilon^2} \qquad (6.26)$$

we have

$$\log Z \geq \frac{1}{M_1} \sum_{k_1=1}^{M_1} \max_{x_1} \left\{ \max_{\tilde{\boldsymbol{x}}_2^n} \left\{ \hat{\theta}(x_1, \tilde{\boldsymbol{x}}_2^n) + \sum_{i=2}^{n} \hat{\gamma}_i(\tilde{\boldsymbol{x}}_i) \right\} + \gamma_{1,k_1}(x_1) \right\} - \epsilon n$$

$$\geq \max_{\tilde{\boldsymbol{x}}} \hat{\theta}(\tilde{\boldsymbol{x}}) + \sum_{i=1}^{n} \hat{\gamma}_i(\tilde{\boldsymbol{x}}_i) - \epsilon n$$

as desired.

$\square$

Despite the theory requires M_i is to exponentially large, it turns out that M_i may be very small to generate tight bounds (see Section 6.4).

6.3.2 Entropy Bounds

In the following we describe how to bound the entropy of high-dimensional models using perturb-max values. Estimating the entropy is an important building block in many machine learning applications. Corollary 6.3 applies the interpretation of Gibbs distribution as a perturb-max model (see Corollary 6.2) in order to define the entropy of Gibbs distributions using the expected value of the maximal perturbation. Unfortunately, this procedure requires exponentially many independent perturbations $\gamma(\boldsymbol{x})$, for every $\boldsymbol{x} \in \mathcal{X}$.

We again use low-dimensional perturbations to upper bound the entropy of perturb-max models. Accordingly, we extend our definition of perturb-max models as follows. Let $\mathcal{A}$ be a collection of subsets of $\{1, 2, \ldots, n\}$ such that $\bigcup_{\alpha \in \mathcal{A}} = \{1, 2, \ldots, n\}$. For each $\alpha \in \mathcal{A}$ generate a Gumbel perturbation $\gamma_\alpha(\boldsymbol{x}_\alpha)$ where $\boldsymbol{x}_\alpha = (x_i)_{i \in \alpha}$. We define the perturb-max models as

$$p(\hat{\boldsymbol{x}}; \theta) = \mathbb{P}_\gamma \left(\hat{\boldsymbol{x}} = \underset{\boldsymbol{x}}{\mathrm{argmax}} \left\{ \theta(\boldsymbol{x}) + \sum_{\alpha \in \mathcal{A}} \gamma_\alpha(\boldsymbol{x}_\alpha) \right\} \right). \qquad (6.27)$$

Our upper bound uses the duality between entropy and the log-partition function (Wainwright and Jordan, 2008) and then upper bounds the log-partition function with perturb-max operations.

Upper bounds for the log-partition function using random perturbations can be derived from the refined upper bounds in Corollary 6.5. However, it is simpler to provide an upper bounds that rely on Theorem 6.4. These bounds correspond to moving expectations outside the maximization operations. For example,

$$\log Z(\theta) \leq \mathbb{E}_\gamma \left[\max_{\boldsymbol{x}} \left\{ \theta(\boldsymbol{x}) + \sum_{i=1}^n \gamma_i(x_i) \right\} \right] \tag{6.28}$$

follows immediately from moving all the expectations in front (or equivalently, by Jensen's inequality). In this case the bound is a simple average of MAP values corresponding to models with only single node perturbations $\gamma_i(x_i)$, for every $i = 1, \ldots, n$ and $x_i \in \mathcal{X}_i$. If the maximization over $\theta(\boldsymbol{x})$ is feasible (e.g., due to super-modularity), it will typically be feasible after such perturbations as well. We generalize this basic result further below.

Corollary 6.8. *Consider a family of subsets $\alpha \in \mathcal{A}$ such that $\bigcup_{\alpha \in \mathcal{A}} \alpha = \{1, \ldots, n\}$, and let $\boldsymbol{x}_\alpha = \{x_i : i \in \alpha\}$. Assume that the random variables $\gamma_\alpha(\boldsymbol{x}_\alpha)$ are i.i.d. according to the Gumbel distribution, for every $\alpha, \boldsymbol{x}_\alpha$. Then*

$$\log Z(\theta) \leq \mathbb{E}_\gamma \left[\max_{\boldsymbol{x}} \left\{ \theta(\boldsymbol{x}) + \sum_{\alpha \in \mathcal{A}} \gamma_\alpha(\boldsymbol{x}_\alpha) \right\} \right].$$

Proof. If the subsets α are disjoint, then $\{\boldsymbol{x}_\alpha : \alpha \in \mathcal{A}\}$ simply defines a partition of the variables in the model. We can therefore use (6.28) over these grouped variables. In the general case, $\alpha, \alpha' \in \mathcal{A}$ may overlap. For each $\alpha \in \mathcal{A}$ generate an independent set of variables $\boldsymbol{x}'_\alpha$. We define a lifted configuration $\boldsymbol{x}' = \{\boldsymbol{x}'_\alpha : \alpha \in \mathcal{A}\}$ by lifting the potentials to $\theta'(\boldsymbol{x}')$ and including consistency constraints:

$$\theta'(\boldsymbol{x}') = \begin{cases} \theta(\boldsymbol{x}) & \text{if } \forall \alpha, i \in \alpha : x'_{\alpha,i} = x_i \\ -\infty & \text{otherwise} \end{cases} \tag{6.29}$$

Thus, $\log Z(\theta) = \log Z(\theta') = \sum_{\boldsymbol{x}'} \exp(\theta'(\boldsymbol{x}'))$ since inconsistent settings receive zero weight. Moreover,

$$\max_{\boldsymbol{x}'} \left\{ \theta'(\boldsymbol{x}') + \sum_{\alpha \in \mathcal{A}} \gamma_\alpha(\boldsymbol{x}'_\alpha) \right\} = \max_{\boldsymbol{x}} \left\{ \theta(\boldsymbol{x}) + \sum_{\alpha \in \mathcal{A}} \gamma_\alpha(\boldsymbol{x}_\alpha) \right\}$$

for each realization of the perturbation. This equality holds after expectation over γ as well. Now, given that the perturbations are independent for each lifted coordinate, the basic result in equation (6.28), guarantees that

$$\log Z(\theta) \leq \mathbb{E}_\gamma \left[\max_{\boldsymbol{x}'} \left\{ \theta'(\boldsymbol{x}') + \sum_{\alpha \in \mathcal{A}} \gamma_\alpha(\boldsymbol{x}'_\alpha) \right\} \right],$$

from which the result follows.   □

Establishing bounds on the log-partition function allows us to derive bounds on the entropy. For this we use the conjugate duality between the (negative) entropy and the log-partition function (Wainwright and Jordan, 2008). The entropy bound then follows from the log-partition bound.

Theorem 6.9. *Let* $p(\boldsymbol{x}; \theta)$ *be a perturb-max probability distribution in (10.19) and* $\mathcal{A}$ *be a collection of subsets of* $\{1, 2, \ldots, n\}$. *Let* $\boldsymbol{x}^\gamma$ *be the optimal perturb-max assignment using low dimensional perturbations:*

$$\boldsymbol{x}^\gamma = \operatorname*{argmax}_{\boldsymbol{x}} \left\{ \theta(\boldsymbol{x}) + \sum_{\alpha \in \mathcal{A}} \gamma_\alpha(\boldsymbol{x}_\alpha) \right\}.$$

Then under the conditions of Corollary 6.8, we have the following upper bound:

$$H(p) \leq \mathbb{E}_\gamma \left[\sum_{\alpha \in \mathcal{A}} \gamma_\alpha(\boldsymbol{x}_\alpha^\gamma) \right].$$

Proof. We use the characterization of the log-partition function as the conjugate dual of the (negative) entropy function (Wainwright and Jordan, 2008):

$$H(p) = \min_{\hat{\theta}} \left\{ \log Z(\hat{\theta}) - \sum_{\boldsymbol{x}} p(\boldsymbol{x}; \theta) \hat{\theta}(\boldsymbol{x}) \right\}.$$

For a fixed score function $\hat{\theta}(\boldsymbol{x})$, let $W(\hat{\theta})$ be the expected value of the low-dimensional perturbation:

$$W(\hat{\theta}) = \mathbb{E}_\gamma \left[\max_{\boldsymbol{x}} \left\{ \hat{\theta}(\boldsymbol{x}) + \sum_{\alpha \in \mathcal{A}} \gamma_\alpha(\boldsymbol{x}_\alpha) \right\} \right].$$

Corollary 6.8 asserts that $\log Z(\hat{\theta}) \leq W(\hat{\theta})$. Thus we can upper bound $H(p)$ by replacing $\log Z(\hat{\theta})$ with $W(\hat{\theta})$ in the duality relation:

$$H(p) \leq \min_{\hat{\theta}} \left\{ W(\hat{\theta}) - \sum_{\boldsymbol{x}} p(\boldsymbol{x}; \theta) \hat{\theta}(\boldsymbol{x}) \right\}$$

The minimum of the right hand side is attained whenever the gradient vanishes, i.e., whenever $\nabla W(\hat{\theta}) = p(\boldsymbol{x}; \theta)$. Since the derivatives of $W(\hat{\theta})$ are perturb-max models, and so is $p(\boldsymbol{x}; \theta)$, then the the minimum is attained for $\hat{\theta} = \theta$. Therefore, recalling that $\boldsymbol{x}^{\gamma}$ has distribution $p(\boldsymbol{x}; \theta)$ in (10.19):

$$\min_{\hat{\theta}} \left\{ W(\hat{\theta}) - \sum_{\boldsymbol{x}} p(\boldsymbol{x}; \theta) \theta(\boldsymbol{x}) \right\} = W(\theta) - \sum_{\boldsymbol{x}} p(\boldsymbol{x}; \theta) \theta(\boldsymbol{x}).$$

$$= \mathbb{E}_{\gamma} \left[\max_{\boldsymbol{x}} \left\{ \theta(\boldsymbol{x}) + \sum_{\alpha \in \mathcal{A}} \gamma_{\alpha}(\boldsymbol{x}_{\alpha}) \right\} \right] - \mathbb{E}_{\gamma} \left[\theta(\boldsymbol{x}^{\gamma}) \right]$$

$$= \mathbb{E}_{\gamma} \left[\theta(\boldsymbol{x}^{\gamma}) + \sum_{\alpha \in \mathcal{A}} \gamma_{\alpha}(\boldsymbol{x}_{\alpha}^{\gamma}) \right] - \mathbb{E}_{\gamma} \left[\theta(\boldsymbol{x}^{\gamma}) \right]$$

$$= \mathbb{E}_{\gamma} \left[\sum_{\alpha \in \mathcal{A}} \gamma_{\alpha}(\boldsymbol{x}_{\alpha}^{\gamma}) \right],$$

from which the result follows.   □

This entropy bound motivates the use of perturb-max posterior models. These models are appealing as they are uniquely built around prediction and as such they inherently have an efficient unbiased sampler. The computation of this entropy bound relies on MAP solvers. Thus computing these bounds is significantly faster than computing the entropy itself, whose computational complexity is generally exponential in n.

Using the linearity of expectation we may alternate summation and expectation. For simplicity, assume only local perturbations, i.e., $\gamma_i(x_i)$ for every dimension $i = 1, \ldots, n$. Then the preceding theorem bounds the entropy by summing the expected change of MAP perturbations $H(p) \leq \sum_i \mathbb{E}_{\gamma}[\gamma_i(x_i^{\gamma})]$. This bound resembles to the independence bound for the entropy $H(p) \leq \sum_i H(p_i)$, where $p_i(x_i) = \sum_{\boldsymbol{x} \setminus x_i} p(\boldsymbol{x})$ are the marginal probabilities (Cover and Thomas, 2012). The independence bound is tight whenever the joint probability $p(\boldsymbol{x})$ is composed of independent systems, i.e., $p(\boldsymbol{x}) = \prod_i p_i(x_i)$. In the following we show that the same holds for perturbation bounds.

Corollary 6.10. *Consider the setting in Theorem 6.9 and the independent probability distribution* $p(\boldsymbol{x}) = \prod_i p_i(x_i)$. *Then there is* $\theta(\boldsymbol{x})$ *for which*

$$H(p) = \mathbb{E}_\gamma \left[\sum_i \gamma_i(x_i^\gamma) \right]$$

while

$$\boldsymbol{x}^\gamma = \operatorname*{argmax}_{\boldsymbol{x}} \left\{ \theta(\boldsymbol{x}) + \sum_{i=1}^n \gamma_i(x_i) \right\}$$

Proof. Set $\theta_i(x_i) = \log p_i(x_i)$ and $\theta(\boldsymbol{x}) = \log p(\boldsymbol{x}) = \sum_i \theta_i(x_i)$. Consider the perturb-max model in (10.19) with $\mathcal{A} = \{\{i\} : i = 1, 2, \ldots, n\}$. Corollary 6.2 shows $p(\boldsymbol{x}) = p(\boldsymbol{x}; \theta)$. Broadly speaking, the statement then holds since $x_i^\gamma = \operatorname{argmax}_{x_i} \{\theta_i(x_i) + \gamma_i(x_i)\}$. Formally, $H(p) = \sum_i H(p_i)$ while $H(p_i) = \mathbb{E}_{\gamma_i}[\gamma_i(x_i^\gamma)]$ by Corollary 6.3.

□

There are two special cases for independent systems. First, the zero-one probability model, for which $p(\boldsymbol{x}) = 0$ except for a single configuration $p(\hat{\boldsymbol{x}}) = 1$. The entropy of such a probability distribution is 0 since the distribution if deterministic. In this case, the perturb-max entropy bound assigns $\boldsymbol{x}^\gamma = \hat{\boldsymbol{x}}$ for all random functions $\gamma = (\gamma_i(x_i))_{i,x_i}$. Since these random variables have zero mean, it follows that $\mathbb{E}_\gamma \left[\sum_i \gamma_i(\hat{x}_i) \right] = 0$. Another important case is for the uniform distribution, $p(\boldsymbol{x}) = 1/|\mathcal{X}|$ for every $\boldsymbol{x} \in \mathcal{X}$. The entropy of such a probability distribution is $\log |\mathcal{X}|$, as it has maximal uncertainty. Since our entropy bounds equals the entropy for minimal uncertainty and maximal uncertainty cases, this suggests that the perturb-max bound can be used as an alternative uncertainty measure.

Corollary 6.11. *Consider the setting of Theorem 6.9. Set*

$$U(p) = \mathbb{E}_\gamma \left[\sum_{\alpha \in \mathcal{A}} \gamma_\alpha(\boldsymbol{x}_\alpha^\gamma) \right]. \tag{6.30}$$

Then $U(p)$ *is an uncertainty measure, i.e., it is non-negative, it attains its minimal value for the deterministic distributions and its maximal value for the uniform distribution.*

Proof. Non-negativity follows from the non-negativity of entropy: $0 \leq H(p) \leq U(p)$. As argued above, $U(p)$ is 0 for deterministic p. To show that the uniform distribution maximizes $U(p)$ note that for the uniform distribution there exists a constant c such that $\theta(\boldsymbol{x}) = c$ for all $\boldsymbol{x} \in \mathcal{X}$. Suppose this distribution does not maximize $U(p)$. Then for two configurations $\boldsymbol{x}, \boldsymbol{x}' \in \mathcal{X}$ the corresponding $\theta(\cdot)$ satisfies $\theta(\boldsymbol{x}) < \theta(\boldsymbol{x}')$. Thus there are $\sum_\alpha \gamma_\alpha(x) > \sum_\alpha \gamma_\alpha(\hat{x}_\alpha)$ although $x^\gamma = \hat{x}$, a contradiction.

□

Using efficiently computable uncertainty measure allows us to extend the applications of perturb-max models to Bayesian active learning (Maji et al., 2014). The advantage of using the perturb-max uncertainty measure over the entropy function is that it does not require MCMC sampling procedures. Therefore, our approach well fits high dimensional models that currently dominate machine learning applications such as computer vision. Moreover, perturb-max uncertainty measure upper bounds the entropy thus reducing perturb-max uncertainty effectively reduces the entropy.

6.4   Empirical Evaluation

Statistical inference of high dimensional structures is closely related to estimating the partition function. Our proposed inference algorithms, both for sampling and inferring the entropy of high-dimensional structures, are derived from an alternative interpretation of the partition function as the expected value of the perturb-max value. We begin our empirical validation by computing the upper and lower bounds for the partition function computed as the expected value of a max-function and their measure concentration qualities. We then show that the perturb-max algorithm for sampling from the Gibbs distribution has a sub-exponential computational complexity. Subsequently, we evaluate the properties of the perturb-max entropy bounds. Lastly, we explore the deviation of the sample mean of the perturb-max value from its expectation.

We evaluate our approach on spin glass models, where each variable x_i represents a spin, namely $x_i \in \{-1, 1\}$. Each spin has a local field parameter θ_i which correspond to the local potential function $\theta_i(x_i) = \theta_i x_i$. The parameter θ_i represents data signal, which in the spin model is the preference of a spin to be positive or negative. Adjacent spins interact with couplings $\theta_{i,j}(x_i x_j) = \theta_{i,j} x_i x_j$. Whenever the coupling parameters are positive the model is called attractive as adjacent variables give higher values to positively correlated configurations. The potential function of a spin glass model is then

$$\theta(x_1, ..., x_n) = \sum_{i \in V} \theta_i x_i + \sum_{(i,j) \in E} \theta_{i,j} x_i x_j. \qquad (6.31)$$

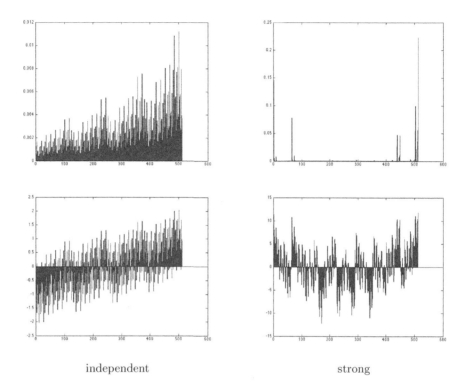

independent   strong

Figure 6.2: The probability (top row) and energy (bottom row) landscapes for all 512 configurations in a 3×3 spin glass system with strong local field, $\theta_i \in [-1, 1]$. When $\theta_{i,j} = 0$ the system is independent and one can observe the block pattern. As the coupling potentials get stronger the landscape get more ragged. By zooming one can see the ragged landscapes throughout the space, even for negligible configurations, which affect many local approaches. The random MAP perturbation directly targets the maximal configurations, thus performs well in these settings.

In our experiments we consider adjacencies of a grid-shaped model. We used low dimensional random perturbations $\gamma_i(x_i)$ since such perturbations do not affect the complexity of the MAP solver.

Evaluating the partition function is challenging when considering strong local field potentials and coupling strengths. The corresponding energy landscape is ragged, and characterized by a relatively small set of dominating configurations. An example of these energy and probability landscapes are presented in Figure 6.2.

First, we compared our bounds to the partition function on 10×10 spin glass models. For such comparison we computed the partition function exactly using dynamic programming (the junction tree algorithm). The local field parameters θ_i were drawn uniformly at random from $[-f, f]$, where $f \in \{0.1, 1\}$ reflects weak and strong data signal. The parameters $\theta_{i,j}$

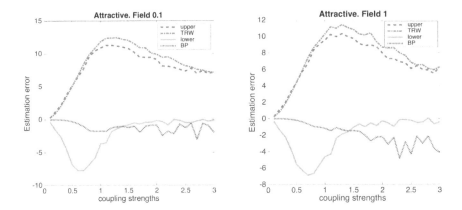

Figure 6.3: The attractive case. The (signed) difference of the different bounds and the log-partition function. These experiments illustrate our bounds on 10×10 spin glass model with weak and strong local field potentials and attractive coupling potentials. The plots below zero are lower bounds and plots above zero are upper bounds. We compare our upper bound (6.28) with the tree re-weighted upper bound. We compare our lower bound (Corollary 6.7) with the belief propagation result, whose stationary points are known to be lower bounds to the log-partition function for attractive spin-glass models.

were drawn uniformly from $[0, c]$ to obtain attractive coupling potentials. Attractive potentials are computationally favorable as their MAP value can be computed efficiently by the graph-cut algorithm (Boykov et al., 2001). First, we evaluate our upper bound in Equation (6.28) that holds in expectation with perturbations $\gamma_i(x_i)$. The expectation was computed using 100 random MAP perturbations, although very similar results were attained after only 10 perturbations. We compared this upper bound with the sum-product form of tree re-weighted belief propagation with uniform distribution over the spanning trees (Wainwright et al., 2005a). We also evaluate our lower bound that holds in probability and requires only a single MAP prediction on an expanded model, as described in Corollary 6.7. We estimate our probable bound by expanding the model to 1000×1000 grids, ignoring the discrepancy ϵ. We compared this lower bound to the belief propagation algorithm, whose stationary points are currently considered to be the tightest lower bounds for attractive spin glass models (Willsky et al., 2007; Ruozzi, 2012; Weller and Jebara, 2014). We computed the signed error (the difference between the bound and $\log Z$), averaged over 100 spin glass models, see Figure 6.3. One can see that the probabilistic lower bound is the tightest when considering the medium and high coupling domain, which is traditionally hard for all methods. Because the bound holds only with high probability probability it might generate a (random) estimate which is not

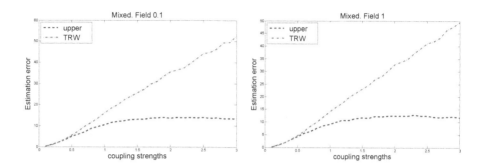

Figure 6.4: The (signed) difference of the different bounds and the log-partition function. These experiments illustrate our bounds on 10×10 spin glass model with weak and strong local field potentials and mixed coupling potentials. We compare our upper bound (6.28) with the tree re-weighted upper bound.

a proper lower bound. We can see that on average this does not happen. Similarly, our perturb-max upper bound is better than the tree re-weighted upper bound in the medium and high coupling domain. In the attractive setting, both our bounds use the graph-cuts algorithm and were therefore considerably faster than the belief propagation variants. Finally, the sum-product belief propagation lower bound performs well on average, but from the plots one can observe that its variance is high. This demonstrates the typical behavior of belief propagation, as it finds stationary points of the non-convex Bethe free energy, thus works well on some instances and does not converge or attains bad local minima on others.

We also compared our bound in the mixed case, where the coupling potentials may either be attractive or repulsive, namely $\theta_{ij} \in [-c, c]$. Recovering the MAP solution in mixed coupling domain is harder than the attractive domain. Therefore we could not test our lower bound in the mixed setting as it relies on expanding the model. We also omit the comparison to the sum-product belief propagation since it is no longer a lower bound in this setting. We evaluate the MAP perturbation value using MPLP (Sontag et al., 2008). One can verify that qualitatively the perturb-max upper bound is significantly better than the tree re-weighted upper bound. Nevertheless

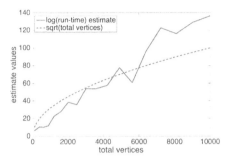

Figure 6.5: Estimating our unbiased sampling procedure complexity on spin glass models of varying sizes, ranging from 10×10 spin glass models to 100×100 spin glass models. The running time is the difference between our upper bound in Equation (6.28) and the log-partition function. Since the log-partition function cannot be computed for such a large scale model, we replaced it with its lower bound in Corollary 6.7.

it is significantly slower as it relies on finding the MAP solution, a harder task in the presence of mixed coupling strengths.

Next, we evaluate the computational complexity of our sampling procedure. Section 6.3.1 describes an algorithm that generates unbiased samples from the full Gibbs distribution. Focusing on spin glass models with strong local field potentials, it is well-known that one cannot produce unbiased samples from the Gibbs distributions in polynomial time (Jerrum and Sinclair, 1993; Goldberg and Jerrum, 2007, 2012). Theorem 6.6 connects the computational complexity of our unbiased sampling procedure to the gap between the log-partition function and its upper bound in (6.28). We use our probable lower bound to estimate this gap on large grids, for which we cannot compute the partition function exactly. Figure 6.5 suggests that in practice, the running time for this sampling procedure is sub-exponential.

Next we estimate our upper bounds for the entropy of perturb-max probability models that are described in Section 6.3.2. We compare them to marginal entropy bounds $H(p) \leq \sum_i H(p_i)$, where $p_i(x_i) = \sum_{x \setminus x_i} p(x)$ are the marginal probabilities (Cover and Thomas, 2012). Unlike the log-partition case which relates to the entropy of Gibbs distributions, it is impossible to use dynamic programming to compute the entropy of perturb-max models. Therefore we restrict ourselves to a 4×4 spin glass model to compare these upper bounds as shown in Figure 6.6. One can see that the MAP perturbation upper bound is tighter than the marginalization upper bound in the medium and high coupling strengths. We can also compare the marginal entropy bounds and the perturb-max entropy bounds to arbitrary grid sizes without computing the true entropy. Figure 6.6 shows that the larger the model the better the perturb-max bound.

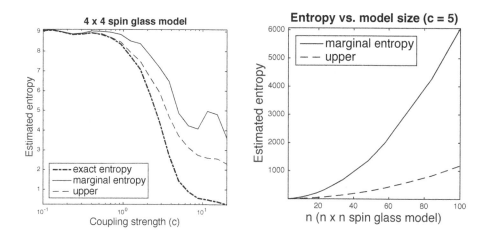

Figure 6.6: Estimating our entropy bounds (in Section 6.3.2) while comparing them to the true entropy and the marginal entropy bound. Left: comparison on small-scale spin models. Right: comparison on large-scale spin glass models.

Both our log-partition bounds as well as our entropy bounds hold in expectation. Thus we evaluate their measure concentration properties, i.e., how many samples are required to converge to their expected value. We evaluate our approach on a 100×100 spin glass model with $n = 10^4$ variables. The local field parameters θ_i were drawn uniformly at random from $[-1, 1]$ to reflect high signal. To find the perturb-max assignment for such a large model we restrict ourselves to attractive coupling setting, thus the parameters $\theta_{i,j}$ were drawn uniformly from $[0, c]$, where $c \in [0, 4]$ to reflect weak, medium and strong coupling potentials. Throughout our experiments we evaluate the expected value of our bounds with 100 different samples. We note that both our log-partition and the entropy upper bounds have the same gradient with respect to their random perturbations, thus their measure concentration properties are the same. In the following we only report the concentration of our entropy bounds; the same concentration occurs for our log-partition bounds.

Acknowledgements

TJ was partially supported by NSF grant #1524427

6.5   References

M. Ben-Akiva and S. R. Lerman. *Discrete Choice Analysis: Theory and Application to Travel Demand*, volume 9. MIT press, Cambridge, MA, USA, 1985.

D. P. Bertsekas, A. Nedić, and A. E. Ozdaglar. *Convex Analysis and Optimization.* Athena Scientific, Nashua, NH, USA, 2003.

Y. Boykov, O. Veksler, and R. Zabih. Fast approximate energy minimization via graph cuts. *IEEE Transactions on Pattern Analysis and Machine Intelligence*, 23(11):1222–1239, November 2001. doi: 10.1109/34.969114.

T. M. Cover and J. A. Thomas. *Elements of Information Theory.* John Wiley & Sons, Hoboken, NJ, USA, 2012.

H. A. David and H. N. Nagaraja. *Order Statistics.* John Wiley & Sons, Hoboken, NJ, USA, 3rd edition, 2003.

J. M. Eisner. Three new probabilistic models for dependency parsing: an exploration. In *Proceedings of the 16th Conference on Computational Linguistics (COLING '96)*, volume 1, pages 340–345. Association for Computational Linguistics, 1996. doi: 10.3115/992628.992688.

S. Ermon, C. Gomes, A. Sabharwal, and B. Selman. Taming the curse of dimensionality: Discrete integration by hashing and optimization. In S. Dasgupta and D. McAllester, editors, *Proceedings of The 30th International Conference on Machine Learning*, volume 28 of *JMLR: Workshop and Conference Proceedings*, pages 334–342, 2013a.

S. Ermon, C. Gomes, A. Sabharwal, and B. Selman. Optimization with parity constraints: From binary codes to discrete integration. In *Proceedings of the Twenty-Ninth Conference Annual Conference on Uncertainty in Artificial Intelligence (UAI-13)*, pages 202–211, Corvallis, Oregon, 2013b. AUAI Press.

S. Ermon, C. P. Gomes, A. Sabharwal, and B. Selman. Embed and project: Discrete sampling with universal hashing. In C. Burges, L. Bottou, M. Welling, Z. Ghahramani, and K. Weinberger, editors, *Advances in Neural Information Processing Systems 26 (NIPS 2013)*, pages 2085–2093. Curran Associates, Inc., 2013c.

S. Ermon, C. P. Gomes, A. Sabharwal, and B. Selman. Low-density parity constraints for hashing-based discrete integration. In E. P. Xing and T. Jebara, editors, *Proceedings of The 31st International Conference on Machine Learning*, volume 32 of *JMLR: Workshop and Conference Proceedings*, pages 271–279, 2014.

P. Felzenszwalb, R. Girshick, D. McAllester, and D. Ramanan. Object detection with discriminatively trained part based models. *IEEE Transactions on Pattern Analysis and Machine Intelligence*, 32(9):1627–1645, September 2010. doi: 10.1109/TPAMI.2009.167.

P. F. Felzenszwalb and R. Zabih. Dynamic programming and graph algorithms in computer vision. *Pattern Analysis and Machine Intelligence, IEEE Transactions on*, 33(4):721–740, April 2011. doi: 10.1109/TPAMI.2010.135.

R. A. Fisher and L. H. C. Tippett. Limiting forms of the frequency distribution of the largest or smallest member of a sample. *Mathematical Proceedings of the Cambridge Philosophical Society*, 24(02):180–190, April 1928. doi: 10.1017/S0305004100015681.

G. B. Folland. *Real Analysis: Modern Techniques and Their Applications.* John Wiley & Sons, New York, NY, USA, 2nd edition, 2013.

A. Gane and T. S. J. Tamir Hazan. Learning with maximum a-posteriori perturbation models. In S. Kaski and J. Corander, editors, *Proceedings of the Seventeenth International Conference on Artificial Intelligence and Statistics (AISTATS)*, volume 33 of *JMLR: Workshop and Conference Proceedings*, pages 247—256, 2014.

S. Geman and D. Geman. Stochastic relaxation, Gibbs distributions, and the Bayesian restoration of images. *IEEE Transactions on Pattern Analysis and Machine Intelligence*, PAMI-6(6):721–741, November 1984. doi: 10.1109/TPAMI. 1984.4767596.

A. Globerson and T. S. Jaakkola. Fixing max-product: Convergent message passing algorithms for MAP LP-relaxations. In J. Platt, D. Koller, Y. Singer, and S. Roweis, editors, *Advances in Neural Information Processing Systems 20*, volume 21, pages 553–560. Curran Associates, Inc., 2007.

B. Gnedenko. Sur la distribution limite du terme maximum d'une serie aleatoire. *Annals of Mathematics*, 44(3):423–453, July 1943. doi: 10.2307/1968974.

L. A. Goldberg and M. Jerrum. The complexity of ferromagnetic Ising with local fields. *Combinatorics Probability and Computing*, 16(1):43, January 2007. doi: 10.1017/S096354830600767X.

L. A. Goldberg and M. Jerrum. Approximating the partition function of the ferromagnetic potts model. *Journal of the ACM (JACM)*, 59(5):25, 2012.

E. J. Gumbel. *Statistical theory of extreme values and some practical applications: a series of lectures*. Number 33 in National Bureau of Standards Applied Mathematics Series. US Govt. Print. Office, Washington, DC, USA, 1954.

Gurobi Optimization. Gurobi optimizer documentation, 2015.

W. K. Hastings. Monte Carlo sampling methods using Markov chains and their applications. *Biometrika*, 57(1):97–109, April 1970. doi: 10.1093/biomet/57.1.97.

T. Hazan and T. Jaakkola. On the partition function and random maximum a-posteriori perturbations. In *The 29th International Conference on Machine Learning (ICML 2012)*, 2012.

T. Hazan, S. Maji, and T. Jaakkola. On sampling from the Gibbs distribution with random maximum a-posteriori perturbations. In C. Burges, L. Bottou, M. Welling, Z. Ghahramani, and K. Weinberger, editors, *Advances in Neural Information Processing Systems 26*, pages 1268–1276. Curran Associates, Inc., 2013.

M. Jerrum and A. Sinclair. Polynomial-time approximation algorithms for the Ising model. *SIAM Journal on computing*, 22(5):1087–1116, October 1993. doi: 10.1137/0222066.

A. Kalai and S. Vempala. Efficient algorithms for online decision problems. *Journal of Computer and System Sciences*, 71(3):291–307, October 2005. doi: 10.1016/j.jcss.2004.10.016.

J. Keshet, D. McAllester, and T. Hazan. PAC-Bayesian approach for minimization of phoneme error rate. In *Proceedings of the 2011 IEEE International Conference on Acoustics, Speech and Signal Processing (ICASSP)*, pages 2224–2227, 2011. doi: 10.1109/ICASSP.2011.5946923.

V. Kolmogorov. Convergent tree-reweighted message passing for energy minimization. *IEEE Transactions on Pattern Analysis and Machine Intelligence*, 28(10): 1568–1583, October 2006. doi: 10.1109/TPAMI.2006.200.

V. Kolmogorov and R. Zabih. What energy functions can be minimized via graph cuts? *IEEE Transactions on Pattern Analysis and Machine Intelligence*, 26(2): 147–159, February 2004. doi: 10.1109/TPAMI.2004.1262177.

T. Koo, A. Rush, M. Collins, T. Jaakkola, and D. Sontag. Dual decomposition for parsing with non-projective head automata. In *Proceedings of the 2010 Conference on Empirical Methods in Natural Language Processing (EMNLP '10)*, pages 1288–1298, 2010.

S. Kotz and S. Nadarajah. *Extreme value distributions: theory and applications.* Imperial College Press, London, UK, 2000.

R. D. Luce. *Individual Choice Behavior: A Theoretical Analysis.* John Wiley and Sons, New York, NY, USA, 1959.

C. Maddison, D. Tarlow, and T. Minka. A* sampling. In Z. Ghahramani, M. Welling, C. Cortes, N. Lawrence, and K. Weinberger, editors, *Advances in Neural Information Processing Systems 27*, pages 2085–2093. Curran Associates, Inc., 2014.

S. Maji, T. Hazan, and T. Jaakkola. Active boundary annotation using random MAP perturbations. In S. Kaski and J. Corander, editors, *Proceedings of the Seventeenth International Conference on Artificial Intelligence and Statistics (AISTATS)*, volume 33 of *JMLR: Workshop and Conference Proceedings*, pages 604–613, 2014.

D. McFadden. Conditional logit analysis of qualitative choice behavior. In P. Zarembka, editor, *Frontiers in Econometrics*, chapter 4, pages 105–142. Academic Press, New York, NY, USA, 1974.

F. Orabona, T. Hazan, A. Sarwate, and T. Jaakkola. On measure concentration of random maximum a-posteriori perturbations. In E. P. Xing and T. Jebara, editors, *Proceedings of The 31st International Conference on Machine Learning*, volume 32 of *JMLR: Workshop and Conference Proceedings*, page 1, 2014.

G. Papandreou and A. Yuille. Perturb-and-MAP random fields: Using discrete optimization to learn and sample from energy models. In *Proceedings of the 2011 IEEE International Conference on Computer Vision (ICCV)*, pages 193–200, Barcelona, Spain, November 2011. doi: 10.1109/ICCV.2011.6126242.

G. Papandreou and A. Yuille. Perturb-and-MAP random fields: Reducing random sampling to optimization, with applications in computer vision. In S. Nowozin, P. V. Gehler, J. Jancsary, and C. H. Lampert, editors, *Advanced Structured Prediction*, chapter 7, pages 159–186. MIT Press, Cambridge, MA, USA, 2014.

N. Ruozzi. The Bethe partition function of log-supermodular graphical models. In F. Pereira, C. Burges, L. Bottou, and K. Weinberger, editors, *Advances in Neural Information Processing Systems 25*, pages 117–125. Curran Associates, Inc., 2012.

A. Rush, D. Sontag, M. Collins, and T. Jaakkola. On dual decomposition and linear programming relaxations for natural language processing. In *Proceedings of the 2010 Conference on Empirical Methods in Natural Language Processing (EMNLP '10)*, pages 1–11, 2010.

A. G. Schwing and R. Urtasun. Efficient exact inference for 3D indoor scene understanding. In *Computer Vision – ECCV 2012 : 12th European Conference on Computer Vision*, volume 7577 of *Lecture Notes in Computer Science*, chapter 22, pages 299–313. Springer, Berlin, Germany, 2012. doi: 10.1007/978-3-642-33783-3.

D. Sontag and T. S. Jaakkola. New outer bounds on the marginal polytope. In J. Platt, D. Koller, Y. Singer, and S. Roweis, editors, *Advances in Neural Information Processing Systems 20*, pages 1393–1400. Curran Associates, Inc., 2008.

D. Sontag, T. Meltzer, A. Globerson, T. Jaakkola, and Y. Weiss. Tightening LP relaxations for MAP using message passing. In *Proceedings of the Twenty-Fourth Conference Annual Conference on Uncertainty in Artificial Intelligence (UAI-08)*, pages 503–510, Corvallis, Oregon, USA, 2008. AUAI Press.

M. Sun, M. Telaprolu, H. Lee, and S. Savarese. An efficient branch-and-bound algorithm for optimal human pose estimation. In *Proceedings of the 2012 IEEE Conference on Computer Vision and Pattern Recognition (CVPR)*, pages 1616–1623, Providence, RI, 2012. doi: 10.1109/CVPR.2012.6247854.

R. H. Swendsen and J.-S. Wang. Nonuniversal critical dynamics in Monte Carlo simulations. *Physical Review Letters*, 58(2):86–88, January 1987. doi: 10.1103/PhysRevLett.58.86.

P. Swoboda, B. Savchynskyy, J. Kappes, and C. Schnörr. Partial optimality via iterative pruning for the Potts model. In *Scale Space and Variational Methods in Computer Vision: 4th International Conference*, volume 7893 of *Lecture Notes in Computer Science*, chapter 40, pages 477–488. Springer, Berlin, Germany, 2013. doi: 10.1007/978-3-642-38267-3.

D. Tarlow, R. P. Adams, and R. S. Zemel. Randomized optimum models for structured prediction. In N. Lawrence and M. Girolami, editors, *Proceedings of the Fifteenth International Conference on Artificial Intelligence and Statistics*, volume 22 of *JMLR: Workshop and Conference Proceedings*, pages 1221–1229, 2012.

L. G. Valiant. The complexity of computing the permanent. *Theoretical computer science*, 8(2):189–201, 1979. doi: 10.1016/0304-3975(79)90044-6.

M. Wainwright and M. Jordan. Graphical models, exponential families, and variational inference. *Foundations and Trends in Machine Learning*, 1(1-2):1–305, 2008. doi: 10.1561/2200000001.

M. J. Wainwright, T. S. Jaakkola, and A. S. Willsky. A new class of upper bounds on the log partition function. *IEEE Transactions on Information Theory*, 51(7):2313–2335, July 2005a. doi: 10.1109/TIT.2005.850091.

M. J. Wainwright, T. S. Jaakkola, and A. S. Willsky. MAP estimation via agreement on trees: Message-passing and linear programming. *IEEE Transactions on Information Theory*, 51(11):3697–3717, November 2005b. doi: 10.1109/TIT.2005.856938.

Y. Weiss, C. Yanover, and T. Meltzer. MAP estimation, linear programming and belief propagation with convex free energies. In *Proceedings of the Twenty-Third Conference Conference on Uncertainty in Artificial Intelligence (2007)*, pages 416–425, Corvallis, Oregon, USA, 2007. AUAI Press.

A. Weller and T. Jebara. Clamping variables and approximate inference. In Z. Ghahramani, M. Welling, C. Cortes, N. Lawrence, and K. Weinberger, editors, *Advances in Neural Information Processing Systems 27*, pages 909–917. Cur, 2014.

T. Werner. High-arity interactions, polyhedral relaxations, and cutting plane algorithm for soft constraint optimisation (MAP-MRF). In *Proceedings of the 2008 IEEE Conference on Computer Vision and Pattern Recognition (CVPR)*, pages 1–8, 2008. doi: 10.1109/CVPR.2008.4587355.

A. S. Willsky, E. B. Sudderth, and M. J. Wainwright. Loop series and Bethe variational bounds in attractive graphical models. In J. Platt, D. Koller, Y. Singer, and S. Roweis, editors, *Advances in Neural Information Processing Systems 20*, pages 1425–1432. Curran Associates, Inc., 2007.

7   A Poisson Process Model for Monte Carlo

Chris J. Maddison   cmaddis@cs.toronto.edu
University of Toronto
Toronto, Canada

Simulating samples from arbitrary probability distributions is a major research program of statistical computing. Recent work has shown promise in an old idea, that sampling from a discrete distribution can be accomplished by perturbing and maximizing its mass function. Yet, it has not been clearly explained how this research project relates to more traditional ideas in the Monte Carlo literature. This chapter addresses that need by identifying a Poisson process model that unifies the perturbation and accept-reject views of Monte Carlo simulation. Many existing methods can be analyzed in this framework. The chapter reviews Poisson processes and defines a Poisson process model for Monte Carlo methods. This model is used to generalize the perturbation trick to infinite spaces by constructing Gumbel processes, random functions whose maxima are located at samples over infinite spaces. The model is also used to analyze A* sampling and OS*, two methods from distinct Monte Carlo families.

7.1   Introduction

The simulation of random processes on computers is an important tool in scientific research and a subroutine of many statistical algorithms. One way to formalize this task is to return samples from some distribution given access to a density or mass function and to a pseudorandom number generator that returns independent uniform random numbers. "Monte Carlo methods", a phrase originally referring to the casinos of Monte Carlo, is a catchall for algorithms that solve this problem. Many Monte Carlo methods exist for specific distributions or classes of distributions (Walker, 1977; Devroye, 1986), but there are a few generic principles. One principle is to simulate a Markov chain whose stationary distribution is the distribution of interest. Work on these Markov chain Monte Carlo methods has exploded over the past few decades, because of their efficiency at sampling from complex distributions in high dimensions. Their downside is that convergence can be slow and detecting convergence is hard. A second principle is propose samples from a tractable distribution and accept them according to a correction factor. These accept-reject Monte Carlo methods are the workhorses of modern statistical packages, but their use is restricted to simple distributions on low dimensional spaces.

Recently, a research program has developed around another principle for sampling from discrete distributions, the so called "Gumbel-Max trick". The trick proceeds by simulating a random function $G : \{1, \ldots, m\} \to \mathbb{R}$ whose maximum is located at a sample. Sampling therefore reduces to finding the state that maximizes G. This trick has the same complexity as better known methods, but it has inspired research into approximate methods and extensions. Methods that abandon exactness for efficiency have considered introducing correlated G with a variety of applications (Papandreou and Yuille, 2011; Tarlow et al., 2012; Hazan et al., 2013). Chen and Ghahramani (2015) consider bandit algorithms for optimizing G over low dimensional spaces when function evaluation is expensive. Maddison et al. (2014) generalized G with Gumbel processes, random functions over infinite spaces whose maxima occur at samples of arbitrary distributions, and introduced A* sampling, a branch and bound algorithm that executes a generalized Gumbel-Max trick. Kim et al. (2016) introduced a related branch and bound algorithm tailored to discrete distributions and successfully sampled from a large fully connected attractive Ising model. Taken together, this view of simulation as a maximization problem is a promising direction, because it connects Monte Carlo research with the literature on optimization. Yet, its relationship to more established methods has not been clearly expressed. This chapter addresses that need by identifying a model that jointly explains both the accept-reject principle and the Gumbel-Max trick.

As a brief introduction, we cover a simple example of an accept-reject algorithm and the Gumbel-Max trick shown in Figure 7.1. Suppose we are given a positive function $f : \{1, \ldots, m\} \to \mathbb{R}^+$, which describes the unnormalized mass of a discrete random variable I,

$$\mathbb{P}(I \in B) = \sum_{i \in B} \frac{f(i)}{\sum_{j=1}^{m} f(j)}, \quad B \subseteq \{1, \ldots, m\}. \tag{7.1}$$

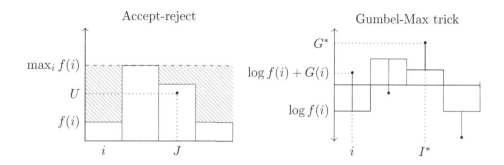

Figure 7.1: Two simple Monte Carlo methods for a discrete distribution described by positive function f via (7.1). The left hand plot shows the first accepted sample J in an accept-reject scheme; note that $U < f(J)$. The right hand plot shows a sample I^* in the Gumbel-Max trick; I^* is the state that achieves the maximum $G^* = \max_i \log f(i) + G(i)$.

The following algorithms return an integer with the same distribution as I. The accept-reject algorithm is,

1. Sample J uniformly from $\{1, \ldots, m\}$, U uniformly from $[0, \max_{i=1}^{m} f(i)]$,
2. If $U < f(J)$, return J, else go to 1.

We can intuitively justify it by noticing that accepted pair (J, U) falls uniformly under the graph of $f(i)$, Figure 7.1. The sample J, which is accepted or rejected, is often called a *proposal*. The Gumbel-Max trick proceeds by optimizing a random function,

1. For $i \in \{1, \ldots m\}$ sample an independent Gumbel random variable $G(i)$.
2. Find and return $I^* = \text{argmax}_{i=1}^{m} \log f(i) + G(i)$.

Because the random values $\log f(i) + G(i)$ can be seen as a perturbed negative energy function, the function G is often called a *perturbation*. Uniform and Gumbel random variables are included among the standard distributions of statistical computing packages. So these algorithms, while inefficient, are simple to program.

Considering their apparent differences and the fact that they have been studied in distinct literatures, it is surprising that both algorithms can be unified under the same theoretical framework. The framework rests on the study of Poisson processes, a random object whose value is a countable set of points in space (Kingman, 1992; Daley and Vere-Jones, 2007). The central idea is to define a specific Poisson process, called an exponential race, which models a sequence of independent samples arriving from some distribution. Then we identify two operations, corresponding to accept-reject and the

Gumbel-Max trick, which modify the arrival distribution of exponential races. In this view a Monte Carlo method is an algorithm that simulates the first arrival of an exponential race, and many existing algorithms fall into this framework.

Section 7.2 reviews Poisson processes and studies the effect of operations on their points. Section 7.3 introduces exponential races and studies the accept-reject and perturb operations. In Section 7.4 we construct Gumbel processes from exponential races and study the generalized Gumbel-Max trick. In Section 7.5 we analyze A* sampling and OS* (Dymetman et al., 2012) and show how they use perturb and accept-reject operations, respectively, to simulate the first arrival of an exponential race. All of our Poisson process results are either known or elementary extensions; the correctness and behaviour of the Monte Carlo methods that we study have all been established elsewhere. Our contribution is in identifying a theory that unifies two distinct literatures and in providing a toolset for analyzing and developing Monte Carlo methods.

7.2   Poisson Processes

7.2.1   Definition and Properties

A Poisson process is a random countable subset $\Pi \subseteq \mathbb{R}^n$. Many natural processes result in a random placement of points: the stars in the night sky, cities on a map, or raisins in oatmeal cookies. A good generic mental model to have is the plane $\mathbb{R}^2$ and pinpricks of light for all points in Π. Unlike most natural processes, a Poisson process is distinguished by

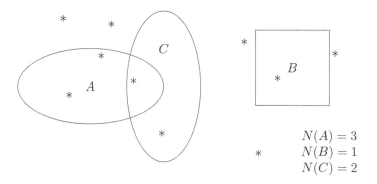

$$N(A) = 3$$
$$N(B) = 1$$
$$N(C) = 2$$

Figure 7.2: The set of $*$ is a realization of a Poisson process in the plane. Counts in sets A, B, C are marginally Poisson and are independent for disjoint sets.

its complete randomness; the number of points in disjoint subsets are independent random variables, see Figure 7.2. In this section we review a general Poisson process theory culminating in two theorems, which describe how they behave under the generic operations of removing or relocating their points. In the next section we restrict our view to a specific Poisson process and two specific operations, which correspond to accept-reject and Gumbel-Max. Our study is situated in $\mathbb{R}^n$ for intuition, but these results generalize naturally; for more information, the ideas of this section are adapted from the general treatment in Kingman (1992). Readers familiar with that treatment can safely skip this section

To identify a realization of a random countable set $\Pi \subseteq \mathbb{R}^n$, we use counts of points in subsets $B \subset \mathbb{R}^n$,

$$N(B) = \#(\Pi \cap B).$$

where $N(B) = \infty$ if B is infinite, see Figure 7.2 again. Counts are nonnegative and additive, so for any realization of Π $N(B)$ satisfies

1. (*Nonnegative*) $N(B) \geq 0$,
2. (*Countably additive*) For disjoint $B_i \subseteq \mathbb{R}^n$, $N(\cup_{i=1}^{\infty} B_i) = \sum_{i=1}^{\infty} N(B_i)$.

Set functions from subsets of $\mathbb{R}^n$ to the extended reals $\mathbb{R} \cup \{\infty, -\infty\}$ that are nonnegative and countably additive are called measures. Measure theory is a natural backdrop for the study of Poisson processes, so we briefly mention some basic concepts. In general measures μ assign real numbers to subsets with the same consistency that we intuitively expect from measuring lengths or volumes in space. If $\mu(\mathbb{R}^n) = 1$, then μ is a probability distribution. Because it is not possible to define a measure consistently for all possible subsets, the subsets $B \subseteq \mathbb{R}^n$ are restricted here and throughout the chapter to be from the Borel sets, a nice measurable family of subsets. The Borel sets contain almost any set of interest, so for our purposes it is practically unrestricted. Integration of some function $f : \mathbb{R}^n \to \mathbb{R}$ with respect to some measure μ naturally extends Riemann integration, which we can think about intuitively as the area under the graph of $f(x)$ weighted by the instantaneous measure $\mu(dx)$. When a measure is equal to the integral of a nonnegative function $f : \mathbb{R}^n \to \mathbb{R}^{\geq 0}$ with respect to μ, we say f is the *density* with respect to μ.

The Poisson process receives its name from the marginal distribution of counts $N(B)$. $N(B)$ is Poisson distributed on the nonnegative integers parameterized by a rate, which is also its expected value.

Definition 7.1 (Poisson random variable). *N is a Poisson distributed random variable on $k \in \{0, 1, \ldots\}$ with nonnegative rate $\lambda \in \mathbb{R}^{\geq 0}$ if*

$$\mathbb{P}(N = k) = \exp(-\lambda)\frac{\lambda^k}{k!}.$$

This is denoted $N \sim \mathrm{Poisson}(\lambda)$. $N \sim \mathrm{Poisson}(0)$ and $N \sim \mathrm{Poisson}(\infty)$ are the random variables whose values are 0 and ∞ with probability one. If $N \sim \mathrm{Poisson}(\lambda)$, then $\mathbb{E}(N) = \lambda$.

The Poisson distribution is particularly suited to modelling random counts, because it is countably additive in the rate.

Lemma 7.1. *If $N_i \sim \mathrm{Poisson}(\lambda_i)$ independent with $\lambda_i \in \mathbb{R}^{\geq 0}$, then*

$$\sum_{i=1}^{\infty} N_i \sim \mathrm{Poisson}\left(\sum_{i=1}^{\infty} \lambda_i\right).$$

Proof. (Kingman, 1992). Let $S_m = \sum_{i=1}^{m} N_i$ and assume $\lambda_i > 0$ without loss of generality. Then for S_2,

$$\begin{aligned}
\mathbb{P}(S_2 = k) &= \sum_{r=0}^{k} \mathbb{P}(N_1 = r, N_2 = k - r) \\
&= \sum_{r=0}^{k} \exp(-\lambda_1)\frac{\lambda_1^r}{r!} \exp(-\lambda_2)\frac{\lambda_2^{k-r}}{(k-r)!} \\
&= \frac{\exp(-\lambda_1 - \lambda_2)}{k!} \sum_{r=0}^{k} \binom{k}{r} \lambda_1^r \lambda_2^{k-r} \\
&= \frac{\exp(-\lambda_1 - \lambda_2)}{k!} (\lambda_1 + \lambda_2)^k.
\end{aligned}$$

By induction Lemma 7.1 also holds for S_m. For infinite sums the events $\{S_m \leq k\}$ are nonincreasing. Thus,

$$\mathbb{P}(S_\infty \leq k) = \lim_{m \to \infty} \mathbb{P}(S_m \leq k) = \sum_{j=1}^{k} \lim_{m \to \infty} \exp\left(-\sum_{i=1}^{m} \lambda_i\right) \frac{(\sum_{i=1}^{m} \lambda_i)^j}{j!}.$$

$\square$

Because expectations distribute over infinite sums of positive random variables, the Poisson rate $\mu(B) = \mathbb{E}(N(B))$ must also be a measure.

Instead of starting with a definition of Poisson processes, we work backwards from an algorithmic construction. Algorithm 7.1 is a procedure that realizes a Poisson process Π for a specified mean measure μ. Algorithm 7.1 iterates through a partition $\{B_i\}_{i=1}^{\infty}$ of $\mathbb{R}^n$. For each B_i it first decides the number of points to place in Π by sampling a Poisson with rate given by

---

Algorithm 7.1 A Poisson process Π with σ-finite nonatomic mean measure μ

Let $\{B_i\}_{i=1}^{\infty}$ be a partition of $\mathbb{R}^n$ with $\mu(B_i) < \infty$
$\Pi = \emptyset$
for $i = 1$ to ∞ **do**
    $N_i \sim \text{Poisson}(\mu(B_i))$
    for $j = 1$ to N_i **do**
        $X_{ij} \sim \mu(\cdot \cap B_i)/\mu(B_i)$
        $\Pi = \Pi \cup \{X_{ij}\}$
    end for
end for

---

the measure, $N_i \sim \text{Poisson}(\mu(B_i))$. Then, it places N_i points by sampling independently from the probability distribution proportional to μ restricted to B_i. Normally, $X \sim \mathcal{D}$ is just a statement about the marginal distribution of X. In the context of an Algorithm box we also implicitly assume that it implies independence from all other random variables. We should note that Algorithm 7.1 operates on volumes and samples from μ. This is not an issue, if we think of it as a mathematical construction. It would be an issue, if we set out to simulate Π on a computer.

Algorithm 7.1 will occasionally have pathological behaviour, unless we restrict μ further. First, we require that each subset B_i of the partition has finite measure; if $\mu(B_i) = \infty$, then Algorithm 7.1 will stall when it reaches B_i and fail to visit all of $\mathbb{R}^n$. If a partition $\{B_i\}_{i=1}^{\infty}$ with $\mu(B_i) < \infty$ exists for measure μ, then μ is called σ-finite. Second, we want the resulting counts $N(B_i)$ to match the number of points placed N_i. This can be ensured if all of the points X_{ij} are distinct with probability one. It is enough to require that $\mu(\{x\}) = 0$ for all singleton sets $x \in \mathbb{R}^n$. This kind of measure is known as nonatomic.

The crucial property of the sets Π produced by Algorithm 7.1 is that the number of points $N(A_j)$ that fall in *any* finite collection $\{A_j\}_{j=1}^{m}$ of disjoint sets are independent Poisson random variables. Clearly, the counts $N(B_i)$ for the partitioning sets of Algorithm 7.1 are independent Poissons; it is not obvious that this is also true for other collections of disjoint sets. To show this we study the limiting behaviour of $N(B)$ by counting the points placed in $B_i \cap B$ and summing as Algorithm 7.1 iterates over $\mathbb{R}^n$.

Theorem 7.2. *Let $\Pi \subseteq \mathbb{R}^n$ be the subset realized by Algorithm 7.1 with σ-finite nonatomic mean measure μ and $A_1, \ldots A_m \subseteq \mathbb{R}^n$ disjoint. $N(B) = \#(\Pi \cap B)$ for $B \subseteq \mathbb{R}^n$ satisfies*

1. $N(A_j) \sim \text{Poisson}(\mu(A_j))$,

2. $N(A_j)$ *are independent.*

Proof. Adapted from Kingman (1992). Let B_i be the partition of Algorithm 7.1 with $\mu(B_i) > 0$ without loss of generality. With probability one,

$$N(A_j) = N(\cup_{i=1}^{\infty} B_i \cap A_j) = \sum_{i=1}^{\infty} N(B_i \cap A_j).$$

Consider the array of $N(B_i \cap A_j)$ for $i \in \{1, 2, \ldots\}$ and $j \in \{1, \ldots, m\}$. The rows are clearly independent. Thus, by Lemma 7.1 it is enough to show

1. $N(B_i \cap A_j) \sim \text{Poisson}(\mu(B_i \cap A_j))$,
2. $N(B_i \cap A_j)$ for $j \in \{1, \ldots, m\}$ are independent,

Let A_0 be the complement of $\cup_{i=1}^{m} A_i$. Because μ is nonatomic, each point is distinct with probability one. Thus,

$$\mathbb{P}(N(B_i \cap A_0) = k_0, \ldots, N(B_i \cap A_m) = k_m | N_i = k) =$$
$$\frac{k!}{k_0! \ldots k_m!} \prod_{j=0}^{m} \frac{\mu(B_i \cap A_j)^{k_j}}{\mu(B_i)^{k_j}}$$

with $k_0 = k - \sum_{j=1}^{m} k_j$. Now,

$$\mathbb{P}(N(B_i \cap A_1) = k_1, \ldots, N(B_i \cap A_m) = k_m) =$$
$$\sum_{k=\sum_j k_j}^{\infty} \exp(-\mu(B_i)) \frac{\mu(B_i)^k}{k!} \frac{k!}{k_0! \ldots k_m!} \prod_{j=0}^{m} \frac{\mu(B_i \cap A_j)^{k_j}}{\mu(B_i)^{k_j}}$$
$$\sum_{k_0=0}^{\infty} \prod_{j=0}^{m} \exp(-\mu(B_i \cap A_j)) \frac{\mu(B_i \cap A_j)^{k_j}}{k_j!}$$
$$= \prod_{j=1}^{m} \exp(-\mu(B_i \cap A_j)) \frac{\mu(B_i \cap A_j)^{k_j}}{k_j!}.$$

finishes the proof. □

Notice that the partition in Algorithm 7.1 has an indistinguishable effect on the eventual counts $N(B)$. In fact there may be entirely different algorithms that realize random subsets indistinguishable from Π. This motivates the standard definition for deciding whether a random process is Poisson.

Definition 7.2 (Poisson process). *Let μ be a σ-finite nonatomic measure on $\mathbb{R}^n$. A random countable subset $\Pi \subseteq \mathbb{R}^n$ is a Poisson process with mean measure μ if*

1. *For $B \subseteq \mathbb{R}^n$, $N(B) \sim \text{Poisson}(\mu(B))$.*
2. *For $A_1, \ldots A_m \subseteq \mathbb{R}^n$ disjoint, $N(A_j)$ are independent.*

Algorithm 7.1 together with Theorem 7.2 is an existence proof for Poisson processes. Poisson processes are generic models for procedures that place points completely randomly in space. In later sections we specialize them to model the sequence of points considered by Monte Carlo methods.

7.2.2 Mapping and Thinning a Poisson Process

We are ultimately interested in understanding how the operations of accept-reject and the Gumbel-Max trick modify distributions. They are special cases of more generic operations on the points $X \in \Pi$ of a Poisson process, which modify its measure. Accept-reject corresponds to the stochastic removal of points based on their location. The Gumbel-Max trick corresponds to the deterministic relocation of points. Here we study those operations in some generality.

The stochastic removal of points $X \in \Pi$ is called thinning. To count the number of points that remain after thinning, we need their joint distribution before thinning. If we restrict our attention to one of the subsets B_i of the partition in Algorithm 7.1, then the distribution is clear: conditioned on $N(B_i) = k$, each point is distributed identically and independently (i.i.d.) as μ restricted to B_i. This property turns out to be true for any subset $B \subseteq \mathbb{R}^n$ of finite measure.

Lemma 7.3. *Let $\Pi \subseteq \mathbb{R}^n$ be a Poisson Process with σ-finite nonatomic mean measure μ and $B \subseteq \mathbb{R}^n$ with $0 < \mu(B) < \infty$. Given $N(B) = k$, each $X_i \in \Pi \cap B$ for $i \in \{1, \ldots k\}$ is i.i.d. as,*

$$X_i \,|\, \{N(B) = k\} \sim \mu(\cdot \cap B)/\mu(B). \tag{7.2}$$

Proof. The proof is uninformative, so we leave it to the Appendix. □

Intuitively, this result ought to be true, because we could have realized Π via Algorithm 7.1 with B as one of the partitioning sets.

Now suppose we remove points $X \in \Pi$ independently with probability $1 - \rho(X)$, where $\rho : \mathbb{R}^n \to [0, 1]$ is some integrable function. For B with finite measure, given $N(B)$ the probability of keeping $X \in \Pi \cap B$ is

$$\mathbb{P}(\text{keep } X \,|\, N(B) = k) = \mathbb{E}(\rho(X) \,|\, N(B) = k) = \int_B \frac{\rho(x)}{\mu(B)} \mu(dx). \tag{7.3}$$

By summing over the value of $N(B)$, we can derive the marginal distribution over the number of remaining points. This is the basic strategy of the Thinning Theorem.

Theorem 7.4 (Thinning). *Let $\Pi \subseteq \mathbb{R}^n$ be a Poisson Process with σ-finite nonatomic mean measure μ and $S(x) \sim \text{Bernoulli}(\rho(x))$ an independent*

Bernoulli random variable for $x \in \mathbb{R}^n$ with integrable $\rho : \mathbb{R}^n \to [0, 1]$, then

$$\text{thin}(\Pi, S) = \{X : X \in \Pi \ and \ S(X) = 1\} \tag{7.4}$$

is a Poisson process with mean measure

$$\mu^*(B) = \int_B \rho(x)\mu(dx). \tag{7.5}$$

Proof. Originally from Lewis and Shedler (1979). Let $B \subseteq \mathbb{R}^n$. Define,

$$N^*(B) = \#(\text{thin}(\Pi, S) \cap B)$$

$N^*(B)$ clearly satisfies the independence property and the result is trivial for $\mu(B) = 0$. For $0 < \mu(B) < \infty$,

$$\mathbb{P}(N^*(B) = k) = \sum_{j=k}^{\infty} \mathbb{P}(N(B) = j)\mathbb{P}(k \ of \ S(X_i) = 1 | N(B) = j).$$

Let $\bar{\mu}^*(B) = \mu(B) - \mu^*(B)$. By (7.3),

$$= \sum_{j=k}^{\infty} \exp(-\mu(B))\frac{\mu(B)^j}{j!}\binom{j}{k}\frac{\mu^*(B)^k}{\mu(B)^k}\frac{\bar{\mu}^*(B)^{j-k}}{\mu(B)^{j-k}}$$

$$= \exp(-\mu^*(B))\frac{\mu^*(B)^k}{k!}\sum_{j=k}^{\infty}\exp(-\bar{\mu}^*(B))\frac{\bar{\mu}^*(B)^{j-k}}{(j-k)!}$$

$$= \exp(-\mu^*(B))\frac{\mu^*(B)^k}{k!}.$$

For $\mu(B) = \infty$, partition B into subsets with finite measure. The countable additivity of integrals of nonnegative functions and of Poisson random variables (Lemma 7.1) finishes the proof. □

A measurable function $h : \mathbb{R}^n \to \mathbb{R}^n$ that relocates points $X \in \Pi$ is easy to analyze if it is 1-1, because it will not relocate two distinct points to the same place. The key insight is that we can count the points relocated to $B \subseteq \mathbb{R}^n$ by counting in the preimage $h^{-1}(B)$; the so-called Mapping Theorem.

Theorem 7.5 (Mapping). *Let $\Pi \subseteq \mathbb{R}^n$ be a Poisson process with σ-finite nonatomic mean measure μ and $h : \mathbb{R}^n \to \mathbb{R}^n$ a measurable 1-1 function, then*

$$h(\Pi) = \{h(X) : X \in \Pi\}$$

is a Poisson process with mean measure

$$\mu^*(B) = \mu(h^{-1}(B)) \tag{7.6}$$

Proof. Adapted from Kingman (1992). h is 1-1, therefore

$$\#(\{h(X) : X \in \Pi\} \cap B) = \#\{X \in \Pi : X \in h^{-1}(B)\} \sim \text{Poisson}(\mu(h^{-1}(B))) \quad (7.7)$$

Pre-images preserve disjointness, so the independence property is guaranteed. 1-1 functions map partitions of the domain to partitions of the range, so μ^* is still σ-finite.   □

7.3 Exponential Races

7.3.1 Definition and First Arrivals Distribution

In this section we specialize the Poisson process to model the sequence of points considered by accept-reject and the Gumbel-Max trick. We call the model an exponential race as a reference to a classical example. An exponential race (occasionally race for short) is a Poisson process in $\mathbb{R}^+ \times \mathbb{R}^n$, which we interpret as points in $\mathbb{R}^n$ ordered by an arrival time in the positive reals $\mathbb{R}^+$. The ordered points of an exponential race have a particularly simple distribution; the location in $\mathbb{R}^n$ of each point is i.i.d. according to some arrival distribution and the rate at which points arrive in time depends stochastically on the normalization constant of that arrival distribution. The Thinning and Mapping Theorems of Poisson processes have corresponding lemmas for exponential races, which describe operations that modify the arrival distribution of an exponential race. The ultimate value of this model is that a variety of apparently disparate Monte Carlo methods can be interpreted as procedures that simulate an exponential race. In Section 7.5 we present Monte Carlo methods which produce samples from intractable distributions by operating on the simulation of an exponential race with a tractable distribution. In this section we define an exponential race for an arbitrary finite nonzero measure P, discuss strategies for simulating exponential races when P is tractable, and derive two operations that modify the arrival distribution of exponential races.

For motivation we review the traditional exponential race example (see Durrett, 2012). Imagine instantaneous flashes of light arriving in time at m distinct points p_j scattered in $\mathbb{R}^2$. Suppose the arrival times of the flashes at each p_j are determined by independent Poisson processes $\Pi_j \subseteq \mathbb{R}^+$ with mean measure $\lambda_j((0,t]) = \lambda_j t$ and $\lambda_j > 0$, see Figure 7.3. The question is which point will get the first flash of light and how long do we need to wait? The first arrival at p_j is after time t iff $\Pi_j \cap (0,t]$ is empty,

$$\mathbb{P}(T_j > t) = \mathbb{P}(\#(\Pi_j \cap (0,t]) = 0) = \exp(-\lambda_j t). \quad (7.8)$$

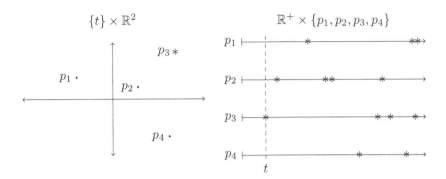

Figure 7.3: The realization of an exponential race with points arriving at $p_j \in \mathbb{R}^2$. The left hand plot shows the location of arrivals in the plane $\mathbb{R}^2$ and the first arrival at time t at p_3. The right hand plot shows future arrival times at the four points.

(7.8) is the complementary cumulative distribution function of an exponential random variable, which we briefly review.

Definition 7.3 (Exponential random variable). *E is an exponential random variable distributed on positive $t \in \mathbb{R}^+$ with nonnegative rate $\lambda \in \mathbb{R}^{\geq 0}$ if*

$$\mathbb{P}(E > t) = \exp(-\lambda t). \tag{7.9}$$

This is denoted $E \sim \mathrm{Exp}(\lambda)$ and $E \sim \mathrm{Exp}(0)$ is the random variable whose value is ∞ with probability one. If $E \sim \mathrm{Exp}(1)$, then $E/\lambda \sim \mathrm{Exp}(\lambda)$.

Thus, the location and time of the first arrival is determined by the minimum of m exponential random variables. For exponential random variables this is particularly easy to analyze; the minimum is an exponential random variable with rate $\sum_{j=1}^{m} \lambda_j$ and it is achieved at the jth variable with probability proportional to the rate λ_j. Surprisingly, these values are independent.

Lemma 7.6. *Let $E_j \sim \mathrm{Exp}(\lambda_j)$ independent with nonnegative $\lambda_j \in \mathbb{R}^{\geq 0}$. If*

$$E^* = \min_{1 \leq j \leq m} E_j \ and \ J^* = \operatorname*{argmin}_{1 \leq j \leq m} E_j, \tag{7.10}$$

and at least one $\lambda_j > 0$ then

1. *The density of E_j with $\lambda_j > 0$ is $\lambda_j \exp(-\lambda_j t)$ for $t \in \mathbb{R}^+$,*
2. *$E^* \sim \mathrm{Exp}(\sum_{j=1}^{m} \lambda_j)$,*
3. *$\mathbb{P}(J^* = k) \propto \lambda_k$,*
4. *E^* is independent of J^*.*

Proof. 1. The derivative of $1 - \exp(-\lambda_j t)$ is $\lambda_j \exp(-\lambda_j t)$.

2., 3., 4. Note that with probability 1 the E_j will be distinct, so

$$\mathbb{P}(J^* = k, E^* > t) = \mathbb{P}(\cap_{j \neq k}\{E_j > E_k > t\})$$
$$= \int_t^\infty \lambda_k \exp(-\lambda_k x) \prod_{j \neq k} \exp(-\lambda_j x)\, dx$$
$$= \frac{\lambda_k}{\sum_{j=1}^m \lambda_j} \int_t^\infty (\sum_{j=1}^m \lambda_j) \exp(-\sum_{j=1}^m \lambda_j x)\, dx$$
$$= \frac{\lambda_k}{\sum_{j=1}^m \lambda_j} \exp(-\sum_{j=1}^m \lambda_j t).$$

This finishes the lemma. □

The extension of exponential races to arbitrary distributions on $\mathbb{R}^n$ is straightforward. The m Poisson processes of the example are together a single Poisson process on $\mathbb{R}^+ \times \mathbb{R}^n$ with mean measure $(\lambda \times P)((0,t] \times B) = \sum_{j=1}^m t\lambda_j 1_B(p_j)$. $\lambda \times P$ is the product measure on $\mathbb{R}^+ \times \mathbb{R}^n$, where each is respectively equipped with $\lambda((0,t]) = t$ and $P(B) = \sum_j \lambda_j 1_B(p_j)$. Extending this idea to an arbitrary finite measure P (not just the discrete measures) is the key idea behind exponential races. Notice that P in our example is atomic, which is fine, because the product measure $\lambda \times P$ is not atomic. On the other hand, we want the points arriving in $\mathbb{R}^n$ to correspond to the probability distribution $P(\cdot)/P(\mathbb{R}^n)$, so we will require that P is finite, $P(\mathbb{R}^n) < \infty$, and nonzero, $0 < P(\mathbb{R}^n)$. Also, in contrast to Poisson processes, exponential races have a natural ordering in time.

Definition 7.4 (Exponential race). *Let P be a finite nonzero measure on $\mathbb{R}^n$. A random countable subset $R \subseteq \mathbb{R}^+ \times \mathbb{R}^n$ is an exponential race with measure P if the following hold*

1. *R is a Poisson process with mean measure $\lambda \times P$.*

2. *R is totally ordered by time, the first coordinate.*

If $R = \{(T_i, X_i)\}_{i=1}^\infty$, then we assume the enumeration corresponds to the ordering so that $i < j$ implies $T_i < T_j$.

We can realize an exponential race with a slight modification of Algorithm 7.1; use the partition of rectangles $B_i = (i-1, i] \times \mathbb{R}^n$, and sort points by their time variable. This is not the most direct characterization, so instead we derive the joint distribution of the first m ordered points in Theorem 7.7. The distribution of the countably infinite set R is completely described by the joint distribution of the first m points for all finite m. The proof of Theorem 7.7 shows that the locations X_i are independently distributed as $P(\cdot)/P(\mathbb{R}^n)$ and the interarrival times $T_i - T_{i-1}$ are independent and exponentially distributed with rate $P(\mathbb{R}^n)$. This theorem is the cornerstone of this chapter, because it suggest a strategy for proving the correctness of Monte Carlo methods; if we can prove that the output of an algorithm (T, X) is the first arrival of an exponential race with measure P, then Theorem 7.7 guarantees that the location X is a sample from $P(\cdot)/P(\mathbb{R}^n)$.

Theorem 7.7. *Let P be a finite nonzero measure on $\mathbb{R}^n$, $X_i \sim P(\cdot)/P(\mathbb{R}^n)$ independent, and $E_i \sim \mathrm{Exp}(P(\mathbb{R}^n))$ independent, then first m points $\{(T_i, X_i)\}_{i=1}^m$ of any exponential race $R \subseteq \mathbb{R}^+ \times \mathbb{R}^n$ with measure P have the same joint distribution as*

$$\{(\sum\nolimits_{j=1}^i E_j, X_i)\}_{i=1}^m.$$

Proof. Let $T(t, B)$ be the time of the first arrival in B after time $t \geq 0$,

$$T(t, B) = \min\{T_i : (T_i, X_i) \in R \cap (t, \infty) \times B\}. \tag{7.11}$$

$R \cap ((t, s + t] \times B)$ is finite with probability one for all $s > 0$, so (7.11) is well defined. $T(t, B) - t$ is an exponential random variable, because

$$\mathbb{P}(T(t, B) - t > s) = \mathbb{P}(N((t, s + t] \times B) = 0) = \exp(-P(B)s).$$

$T(t, B)$ and $T(t, B^c)$ are independent, by Poisson process independence.

We proceed by induction. The event $\{T_1 > s, X_1 \in B\}$ is equivalent to $\{T(0, B^c) > T(0, B) > s\}$. $P(B) > 0$ or $P(B^c) > 0$, so by Lemma 7.6,

$$\mathbb{P}(T_1 > s, X_1 \in B) = \mathbb{P}(T(0, B^c) > T(0, B) > s) = \exp(-sP(\mathbb{R}^n))\frac{P(B)}{P(\mathbb{R}^n)}.$$

Now, assume Theorem 7.7 holds for k. The event

$$\{T_i = t_i, X_i = x_i\}_{i=1}^k$$

is completely described by counts in $(0, t_k] \times \mathbb{R}^n$ and thus independent of

$$\{T(t_k, B^c) > T(t_k, B) > s + t_k\}$$

Thus

$$
\begin{aligned}
\mathbb{P}(T_{k+1} - T_k > s, X_{k+1} \in B | \{T_i = t_i, X_i = x_i\}_{i=1}^k) \\
= \mathbb{P}(T(t_k, B^c) > T(t_k, B) > s + t_k | \{T_i = t_i, X_i = x_i\}_{i=1}^k) \\
= \mathbb{P}(T(t_k, B^c) > T(t_k, B) > s + t_k) \\
= \exp(-sP(\mathbb{R}^n))\frac{P(B)}{P(\mathbb{R}^n)}
\end{aligned}
$$

concludes the proof. $\square$

7.3.2 Simulating an Exponential Race with a Tractable Measure

If Q is a tractable finite nonzero measure on $\mathbb{R}^n$, that is we have a procedure for computing $Q(\mathbb{R}^n)$ and sampling from $Q(\cdot)/Q(\mathbb{R}^n)$, then Theorem 7.7 suggests Algorithm 7.2 for simulating an exponential race R with measure Q. Algorithm 7.2 simulates the points of an exponential race in order of arrival time. It does not terminate, but we can think of it as a coroutine or generator, which maintains state and returns the next arrival in $\mathbb{R}$ each time it is invoked. As a simple example consider the uniform measure $Q((a,b]) = b - a$ on $[0,1]$. Algorithm 7.2 for this Q simulates a sequence of arrivals $\{(T_i, X_i)\}_{i=1}^{\infty}$ with arrival location $X_i \sim \text{Uniform}[0,1]$ and interarrival time $T_{i+1} - T_i \sim \text{Exp}(1)$, see the left hand plot of Figure 7.4.

As with the initial discrete example, in which we constructed an exponential race from m independent Poisson processes, this is not the only approach. More generally, if $\{B_i\}_{i=1}^{m}$ is any finite partition of $\mathbb{R}^n$ such that $Q(\cdot \cap B_i)$ is tractable, then we can simulate R by simulating m independent exponential races R_i with measure $Q(\cdot \cap B_i)/Q(B_i)$ via Algorithm 7.2 and sorting the result $\cup_{i=1}^{m} R_i$. This can be accomplished lazily and efficiently with a priority queue data type, which prioritizes the races R_i according to which arrives next in time. It also possible to split the races R_i online by partitioning B_i and respecting the constraint imposed by the arrivals already generated in B_i. We highlight a particularly important variant, which features in A* sampling in Section 7.5. Consider an infinitely deep tree in which each node is associated with a subset $B \subseteq \mathbb{R}^n$. If the root is $\mathbb{R}^n$ and the children of each node form a partition of the parent, then we call this a space partitioning tree. We can realize an exponential race over a space partitioning tree by recursively generating arrivals (T, X) at each node B. Each location X is sampled independently from $Q(\cdot \cap B)/Q(B)$, and each time T is sampled by adding an independent $\text{Exp}(Q(B))$ to the parent's arrival time. The arrivals sorted by time over the realization of the tree form a exponential race. See Figure 7.4.

Algorithm 7.2 An exponential race R with finite nonzero measure Q

$R = \emptyset$
$T_0 = 0$
for $i = 1$ to ∞ **do**
$\quad E_i \sim \text{Exp}(Q(\mathbb{R}^n))$
$\quad X_i \sim Q(\cdot)/Q(\mathbb{R}^n)$
$\quad T_i = T_{i-1} + E_i$
$\quad R = R \cup \{(T_i, X_i)\}$
end for

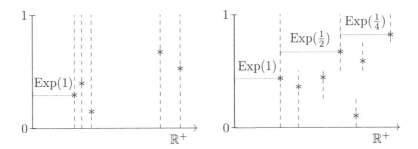

Figure 7.4: Two methods for simulating an exponential race. The left hand plot shows the first arrivals of a uniform exponential race on $[0, 1]$ simulated by Algorithm 7.2. The right hand plot shows the first arrivals of an exponential race simulated over a space partitioning tree. Dashed lines dominate the set in which an arrival is first.

7.3.3 Transforming an Exponential Race with Accept-Reject and Perturb

Most finite nonzero measures P on $\mathbb{R}^n$ are not tractable. Monte Carlo methods accomplish their goal of sampling from intractable distributions by transforming samples of tractable distributions. In this subsection we present accept-reject and perturb operations, which transform a realization of an exponential race with measure Q into a realization of an exponential race with a distinct measure P. In practice Q will be tractable and P intractable, so that simulating an exponential race with an intractable measure can be accomplished by simulating the points of an exponential race with a tractable measure, for example via Algorithm 7.2, and transforming it with accept-reject or perturb operations. The accept-reject and perturb operations are named after their respective literatures, accept-reject corresponds to rejection sampling and perturb corresponds to the Gumbel-Max trick. The correspondence between the perturb operation and the Gumbel-Max trick may not be obvious, so we discuss this in Section 7.4.

Let Q and P be finite nonzero measures in $\mathbb{R}^n$. We assume that they have densities g and f with respect to some base measure μ,

$$Q(B) = \int_B g(x)\mu(dx) \qquad P(B) = \int_B f(x)\mu(dx). \tag{7.12}$$

We assume that g and f have the same support and their ratio is bounded,

$$\text{supp}(f) = \text{supp}(g) \qquad \frac{f(x)}{g(x)} \leq M \text{ for all } x \in \text{supp}(g) \tag{7.13}$$

where $\text{supp}(g) = \{x \in \mathbb{R}^n : g(x) \neq 0\}$. The assumption $\text{supp}(f) = \text{supp}(g)$ can be softened here and throughout the chapter to $\text{supp}(f) \subseteq \text{supp}(g)$, but it complicates the analysis. The accept-reject strategy is to realize more points than needed from an exponential race with measure $MQ(\cdot)$ and stochastically *reject* points with probability equal to the ratio of instantaneous rates of arrival, $f(x)/(g(x)M)$. The perturbation strategy is to realize just the points needed from an exponential race with measure Q, but to *perturb* the arrival times according to the transformation $t \to tg(x)/f(x)$ for all points arriving at x.

Before we present the proofs, consider the following intuition. Imagine taking a long exposure photograph of the plane as instantaneous flashes arrive according to an exponential race with measure Q. The rate at which points arrive will determine the intensity of a heat map with regions receiving more points brighter than those receiving fewer. Over time the relative intensities will correspond to the probability distribution proportional to Q. If someone were just ahead of us in time and stochastically discarded points that arrived in B or delayed points in B relative to points in B^c, then our perception of the likelihood of B would change. Mired in time, we would not be able to distinguish whether points were discarded, reordered, or the true measure Q was in fact different.

The correctness of these operations on an exponential race can be justified as special cases of the Thinning and Mapping Theorems.

Lemma 7.8 (Accept-Reject). *Let Q and P be finite nonzero measures on $\mathbb{R}^n$ under assumptions (7.12) and (7.13). If $R \subseteq \mathbb{R}^+ \times \mathbb{R}^n$ is an exponential race with measure $MQ(\cdot)$ and* $\text{accept}(t,x) \sim \text{Bernoulli}(\rho(t,x))$ *is i.i.d. for all (t,x) with probability*

$$\rho(t,x) = \frac{f(x)}{g(x)M},$$

then $\text{thin}(R, \text{accept})$*, from (7.4), is an exponential race with measure P.*

Proof. By the Thinning Theorem, the mean measure of $\text{thin}(R, \text{accept})$ is

$$\iint_B \frac{f(x)}{g(x)M} g(x)M\mu(dx)\lambda(dt) = \iint_B f(x)\mu(dx)\lambda(dt) = (\lambda \times P)(B).$$

for $B \subseteq \mathbb{R}^+ \times \text{supp}(g)$. The subsampled (T_i, X_i) are in order and thus an exponential race with measure P. $\square$

Lemma 7.9 (Perturbation). *Let Q and P be finite nonzero measures on $\mathbb{R}^n$ under assumptions (7.12) and (7.13). If $R \subseteq \mathbb{R}^+ \times \mathbb{R}^n$ is an exponential* *race with measure Q and*

$$\text{perturb}(t, x) = \left(t\frac{g(x)}{f(x)}, x \right),$$

then $\text{sort}(\text{perturb}(R))$ *is an exponential race with measure* P *where* sort *totally orders points by the first coordinate, time.*

Proof. perturb is 1-1 on $\text{supp}(f)$, so the Mapping Theorem applies. It is enough to check the mean measure of $\text{perturb}(R)$ on subsets of the form $B = (0, s] \times A$ for $s \in \mathbb{R}^+$ and $A \subseteq \text{supp}(g)$,

$$\iint\limits_{h^{-1}(B)} g(x)\lambda(dt)\mu(dx) = \int\limits_A g(x)s\frac{f(x)}{g(x)}\mu(dx) = (\lambda \times P)(B).$$

Thus, sorting $\text{perturb}(T_i, X_i)$ forms an exponential race with measure P. $\square$

7.4   Gumbel Processes

7.4.1   Definition and Construction

The central object of the Gumbel-Max trick is a random function over a finite set whose values are Gumbel distributed. Gumbel valued functions over a finite choice set are extensively studied in random choice theory, where there is a need for a statistical model of utility (Yellott, 1977 for example). The extension to Gumbel valued functions over continuous spaces has been explored in random choice theory (Malmberg, 2013) and in the context of Monte Carlo simulation (Maddison et al., 2014). Following Maddison et al. (2014) we will refer to this class of Gumbel valued functions on $\mathbb{R}^n$ as Gumbel processes. Gumbel processes underpin the recent interest in perturbation based Monte Carlo methods, because their maxima are located at samples from probability distributions, see also (Papandreou and Yuille, 2011; Tarlow et al., 2012; Hazan et al., 2013; Chen and Ghahramani, 2015; Kim et al., 2016). In this section we clarify the connection between Gumbel processes and our development of exponential races. We will show that the value of a Gumbel process at $x \in \mathbb{R}^n$ can be seen as the log transformed time of the first arrival at x of some exponential race. This has the advantage of simplifying their construction and connecting the literature on the Gumbel-Max trick to our discussion. Related constructions have also been considered in the study of extremal processes (Resnick, 2007). In this subsection we define and construct Gumbel processes. In the next subsection we discuss their simulation and present a generalized Gumbel-Max trick derived from the Perturbation Lemma.

The Gumbel distribution dates back to the statistical study of extrema and rare events (Gumbel and Lieblein, 1954). The Gumbel is a member of a more general class of extreme value distributions. A central limit theorem exists for these distributions — after proper renormalization the maximum of an i.i.d. sample of random variables converges to one of three possible extreme value distributions (Gedenko, 1948). The Gumbel is parameterized by a location $\mu \in \mathbb{R}$.

Definition 7.5 (Gumbel random variable). *G is a Gumbel distributed random variable on $\mathbb{R}$ with location $\mu \in \mathbb{R}$ if*

$$\mathbb{P}(G \leq g) = \exp(-\exp(-g + \mu))$$

This is denoted $G \sim \text{Gumbel}(\mu)$ and $G \sim \text{Gumbel}(-\infty)$ is the random variable whose value is $-\infty$ with probability one. If $G \sim \text{Gumbel}(0)$, then $G + \mu \sim \text{Gumbel}(\mu)$.

The Gumbel distribution has two important properties for our purposes. The distribution of the maximum of independent Gumbels is itself a Gumbel — a property known as max-stability — and the index of the maximum follows the Gibbs distribution: if $G(i) \sim \text{Gumbel}(\mu_i)$, then

$$\max_{1 \leq i \leq m} G(i) \sim \text{Gumbel}(\log \sum_{i=1}^{m} \exp(\mu_i)) \quad \operatorname*{argmax}_{1 \leq i \leq m} G(i) \sim \frac{\exp(\mu_i)}{\sum_{i=1}^{m} \exp(\mu_i)}.$$

The Gumbel-Max trick of the introduction for sampling from a discrete distribution with mass function $f : \{1, \ldots, m\} \to \mathbb{R}^+$ is explained by taking $\mu_i = \log f(i)$. It is informative to understand these properties through the Gumbel's connection to the exponential distribution.

Lemma 7.10. *If $E \sim \text{Exp}(\lambda)$ with nonnegative rate $\lambda \in \mathbb{R}^{\geq 0}$, then*

$$-\log E \sim \text{Gumbel}(\log \lambda).$$

Proof. $\mathbb{P}(-\log E \leq g) = \mathbb{P}(E \geq \exp(-g)) = \exp(-\exp(-g + \log \lambda))$ □

Therefore the distribution of the maximum and argmaximum of Gumbels is explained by Lemma 7.6, because passing a maximization through $-\log$ becomes a minimization.

A Gumbel process $G : \mathbb{R}^n \to \mathbb{R} \cup \{-\infty\}$ is a Gumbel valued random function. Their characterizing property is that the maximal values of a Gumbel process over the subsets $B \subseteq \mathbb{R}^n$ are marginally Gumbel distributed with a location that scales logarithmically with the volume of B according to some finite nonzero measure P,

$$\max_{x \in B} G(x) \sim \text{Gumbel}(\log P(B))$$

Implicit in this claim is the assertion that the maximizations $\max_{x \in B} G(x)$ are well-defined — the maximum exists — for all $B \subseteq \mathbb{R}^n$.

Definition 7.6 (Gumbel process). *Let P be a finite nonzero measure on $\mathbb{R}^n$, $G : \mathbb{R}^n \to \mathbb{R} \cup \{-\infty\}$ a random function, and*

$$G^*(B) = \max_{x \in B} G(x). \tag{7.14}$$

G is a Gumbel process with measure P if

1. *For $B \subseteq \mathbb{R}^n$, $G^*(B) \sim \text{Gumbel}(\log P(B))$.*

2. *For $A_1, \ldots, A_m$ are disjoint, $G^*(A_i)$ are independent.*

Note, the event that $\text{argmax}_{x \in \mathbb{R}^n} G(x)$ lands in $B \subseteq \mathbb{R}^n$ depends on which of $G^*(B)$ or $G^*(B^c)$ is larger. Following this reasoning one can show that the argmax over $\mathbb{R}^n$ is distributed as $P(\cdot)/P(\mathbb{R}^n)$.

The study of Gumbel processes can proceed without reference to exponential races, as in Maddison et al. (2014), but our construction from exponential races is a convenient shortcut that allows us to import results from Section 7.3. Consider the function that reports the arrival time of the first arrival at $x \in \mathbb{R}^n$ for an exponential race R with measure P,

$$T(x) = \min\{T_i : (T_i, x) \in R\}$$

This function is almost surely infinite at all x, but for any realization of R it will take on finite value at countably many points in $\mathbb{R}^n$. Moreover, the minimum of $T(x)$ over subsets $B \subseteq \mathbb{R}^n$ is well-defined and finite for sets with positive measure $P(B) > 0$; it is exponentially distributed with rate $P(B)$. In this way we can see that $-\log T(x)$ is Gumbel process, Figure 7.5.

Theorem 7.11. *Let $R \subseteq \mathbb{R}^+ \times \mathbb{R}^n$ be an exponential race with measure P.*

$$G(x) = -\log \min\{T_i : (T_i, x) \in R\} \tag{7.15}$$

is a Gumbel process with measure P.

Proof. First, for $x \in \mathbb{R}^n$

$$\min\{T_i : (T_i, x) \in R\} = T(0, \{x\}),$$

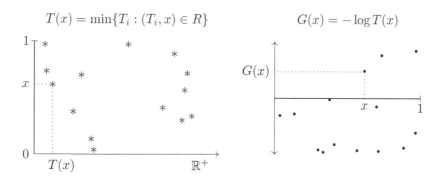

$$T(x) = \min\{T_i : (T_i, x) \in R\} \qquad\qquad G(x) = -\log T(x)$$

Figure 7.5: Constructing a uniform Gumbel process $G : \mathbb{R}^n \to \mathbb{R} \cup \{-\infty\}$ on $[0, 1]$ with an exponential race. The left hand plot shows the first arrivals $*$ of a uniform exponential race R. The right hand plot shows $G(x)$ set to $-\log$ the time $T(x)$ of the first arrival at x. The graph of $G(x)$ extends downwards to $-\infty$ taking on finite value at all points in $[0, 1]$ that have arrivals and $-\infty$ for all points with no arrivals.

where $T(0, B)$ is the first arrival time in subset $B \subseteq \mathbb{R}^n$ defined in (7.11) from Theorem 7.7. Thus $G^*(B)$ of (7.14) is well defined, because

$$G^*(B) = \max_{x \in B} -\log \min\{T_i : (T_i, x) \in R\} = -\log T(0, B).$$

$G^*(B)$ inherits the independence properties from Poisson process independence. Finally, Lemma 7.10 gives us the marginal distribution of $G^*(B)$. $\square$

7.4.2   Simulating a Gumbel Process and the Gumbel-Max Trick

Gumbel processes are relevant to Monte Carlo simulation in the same sense that we motivated exponential races — if we can simulate the maximum value of a Gumbel process with measure P, then its location is a sample from the distribution $P(\cdot)/P(\mathbb{R}^n)$. Maddison et al. (2014) gave an algorithm for simulating Gumbel processes with tractable measures and a generalized Gumbel-Max trick for transforming their measure. We present those results derived from our results for exponential races.

The Gumbel process G from construction (7.15) has value $-\infty$ everywhere except at the countably many arrival locations of an exponential race. Therefore, for tractable measures Q we could adapt Algorithm 7.2 for exponential races to simulate $G(x)$. The idea is to initialize $G(x) = -\infty$ everywhere and iterate through the points (T_i, X_i) of an exponential race R setting $G(X_i) = -\log T_i$. To avoid reassigning values of $G(x)$ we refine space as in Section 7.3.2 by removing the locations generated so far. Algorithm 7.3 implements this procedure, although it is superficially different from our

---

Algorithm 7.3 A Gumbel process with finite measure Q

Initialize $G(x) = -\infty$ for all $x \in \mathbb{R}^n$.
$(\Omega_1, G_0, i) = (\mathbb{R}^n, \infty, 1)$
while $Q(\Omega_i) > 0$ **do**
    $G_i \sim \text{TruncGumbel}(\log Q(\Omega_i), G_{i-1})$
    $X_i \sim Q(\cdot \cap \Omega_i)/Q(\Omega_i)$
    $G(X_i) = G_i$ % assign $G(x)$ at X_i to G_i
    $\Omega_{i+1} = \Omega_i - \{X_i\}$
    $i = i + 1$
end while

---

description. In particular the value $G(X_i)$ is instead set to a truncated Gumbel $G_i \sim \text{TruncGumbel}(\log Q(\Omega_i), G_{i-1})$, a Gumbel random variable with location $\log Q(\Omega_i)$ whose domain is truncated to $(-\infty, G_{i-1}]$. The connection to Algorithm 7.2 can be derived by decomposing the arrival times $T_i = \sum_{j=1}^i E_j$ for $E_j \sim \text{Exp}(Q(\Omega_j))$ and then considering the joint distribution of $G_i = -\log(\sum_{j=1}^i E_j)$. A bit of algebraic manipulation will reveal that

$$G_i \,|\, G_{i-1} \sim \text{TruncGumbel}(\log Q(\Omega_i), G_{i-1})$$

Thus, translating between procedures for simulating Gumbel processes and procedures for simulating exponential races is as simple as replacing chains of truncated Gumbels with partial sums of exponentials.

For continuous measures removing countably many points from the sample space has no effect, and in practice the removal line of Algorithm 7.3 can be omitted. For those and many other measures Algorithm 7.3 will not terminate; instead it iterates through the infinitely many finite values of $G(x)$ in order of their rank. For discrete measures with finite support Algorithm 7.3 will terminate once every atom has been assigned a value.

Finally, for simulating Gumbel processes with intractable measures P the Perturbation Lemma of exponential races justifies a generalized Gumbel-Max trick. The basic insight is that multiplication by the ratio of densities $g(x)/f(x)$ becomes addition in log space.

Lemma 7.12 (Gumbel-Max trick). *Let Q and P be finite nonzero measures on $\mathbb{R}^n$ with densities g and f under assumptions (7.12) and (7.13). If $G: \mathbb{R}^n \to \mathbb{R} \cap \{-\infty\}$ is a Gumbel process with measure Q, then*

$$G'(x) = \begin{cases} \log f(x) - \log g(x) + G(x) & x \in \text{supp}(g) \\ -\infty & \text{otherwise} \end{cases}$$

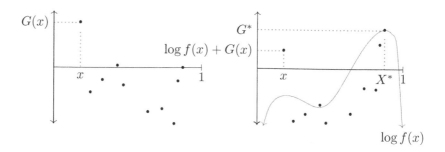

Figure 7.6: A continuous Gumbel-Max trick. The left hand plot shows the maximal values of a uniform Gumbel process $G(x)$ on $[0,1]$. The right hand plot shows the result of perturbing $\log f(x)$ with $G(x)$. Notice that the ordering of values changes, and X^* is now the location of the maximum $G^* = \max_x \log f(x) + G(x)$. Therefore, X^* is a sample from the distribution with density proportional to $f(x)$.

is a Gumbel process with measure P. In particular for $G^* = \max_{x \in \mathbb{R}^n} G'(x)$ and $X^* = \mathrm{argmax}_{x \in \mathbb{R}^n} G'(x)$,

$$G^* \sim \mathrm{Gumbel}(\log P(\mathbb{R}^n)) \qquad X^* \sim P(\cdot)/P(\mathbb{R}^n)$$

Proof. Arguing informally, this follows from the Perturbation Lemma applied to our construction (7.15) of Gumbel processes. For $x \in \mathrm{supp}(g)$

$$\log f(x) - \log g(x) + G(x) = -\log \min\{T_i g(x)/f(x) : (T_i, x) \in R\}.$$

See Maddison et al. (2014) for a formal proof. □

When Q is the counting measure on $\{1, \ldots, m\}$, Lemma 7.12 exactly describes the Gumbel-Max trick of the introduction. This brings full circle the connection between accept-reject and the Gumbel-Max trick.

A Gumbel process is not profoundly different from an exponential race, but the difference of perspective — a function as opposed to a random set — can be valuable. In particular consider the following generalization of a result from Hazan and Jaakkola of this book. Let $G : \mathbb{R}^n \to \mathbb{R} \cup \{-\infty\}$ be a Gumbel process with measure P whose density with respect to μ is f. If $G^* = \max_{x \in \mathbb{R}^n} G(x)$ and $X^* = \mathrm{argmax}_{x \in \mathbb{R}^n} G(x)$, then

$$\mathbb{E}(G^*) = \log P(\mathbb{R}^n) + \gamma \qquad \mathbb{E}(-\log f(X^*) + G^*) = H(f) + \gamma,$$

where $H(f)$ is the entropy of a probability distribution with probability density function proportional to f and γ is the Euler-Mascheroni constant. Therefore the representation of probability distributions through Gumbel processes gives rise to a satisfying and compact representation of some of their important constants.

7.5   Monte Carlo Methods That Use Bounds

7.5.1   Rejection Sampling

In this section we present practical Monte Carlo methods that use bounds on the ratio of densities to produce samples from intractable distributions. We show how these methods can be interpreted as algorithms that simulate the first arrival of an exponential race. The basic strategy for proving their correctness is to argue that they perform accept-reject or perturb operations on the realization of an exponential race until they have provably produced the first arrival of the transformed race. We start by discussing the traditional rejection sampling and a related perturbation based method. Then we study OS* (Dymetman et al., 2012), an accept-reject method, and A* sampling (Maddison et al., 2014), a perturbation method. These algorithms have all been introduced elsewhere in the literature, so for more information we refer readers to the original papers.

Throughout this section our goal is to draw a sample from the probability distribution proportional to some measure P with density f with respect to some base measure μ. We assume, as in the Accept-Reject and Perturbation Lemmas, access to a tractable proposal distribution proportional to a measure Q with density g with respect to μ such that f and g have the same support and the ratio $f(x)/g(x)$ is bounded by some constant M. For example consider the sample space $\{0,1\}^n$ whose elements are bit vectors of length n. A proposal distribution might be proportional to the counting measure Q, which counts the number of configurations in a subset $B \subseteq \{0,1\}^n$. Sampling from $Q(\cdot)/Q(\{0,1\}^n)$ is as simple as sampling n independent Bernoulli(1/2).

Rejection sampling is the classic Monte Carlo method that uses bound information. It proposes (X, U) from Q and Uniform[0, 1], respectively, and accepts X if $U \leq f(X)/(g(X)M)$. The algorithm terminates at the first acceptance and is normally justified by noticing that it samples uniformly from the region under the graph of $f(x)$ by rejecting points that fall between $g(x)M$ and $f(x)$, see the left hand graph on Figure 7.7 for an intuition. The acceptance decision also corresponds exactly to the accept-reject operation on exponential races, so we can interpret it as an procedure on the points of an exponential race. We call this procedure **REJ** for short,

> **for** $(T_i, X_i) \in R$ simulated by Algorithm 7.2 with measure $MQ(\cdot)$ **do**
> $U_i \sim$ Uniform[0, 1].
>   **if** $U_i < f(X_i)/(g(X_i)M)$ **then return** (T_i, X_i)
>   **end if**
> **end for**

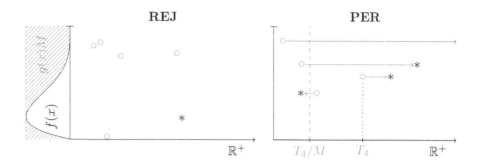

Figure 7.7: Algorithms **REJ** and **PER** for measure P on $[0,1]$ with proposal measure Q. The densities of Q and P are shown on the left hand side as densities over $x \in [0,1]$. ∘ are arrivals of the race with measure Q, ∗ of the race with measure P. Both plots show the proposals considered until the first acceptance. For **PER** opaque solid lines represent the perturb operation. T_4 is the fourth arrival from the race with measure Q. T_4/M is the lower bound on all future arrivals, and thus all ∗ points to the left of T_4/M are in order.

The Accept-Reject Lemma guarantees that the returned values (T, X) will be the first arrival of an exponential race with measure P, and Theorem 7.7 guarantees that X is a sample from $P(\cdot)/P(\mathbb{R}^n)$. This is the basic flavour of the arguments of this section.

The Perturbation Lemma has a corresponding procedure, which uses the bound M to provably return the first arrival of a perturbed exponential race. It is shown on the right hand side of Figure 7.7, and we call it **PER**.

> $(T^*, X^*) = (\infty, \text{null})$
> **for** $(T_i, X_i) \in R$ simulated by Algorithm 7.2 with measure Q **do**
>   **if** $T^* > T_i g(X_i)/f(X_i)$ **then**
> $T^* = T_i g(X_i)/f(X_i)$
> $X^* = X_i$
>   **end if**
>   **if** $T_{i+1}/M \geq T^*$ **then return** (T^*, X^*)
>   **end if**
> **end for**

In this procedure (T_i, X_i) iterates in order through the arrivals of an exponential race with measure Q. The perturbed times $T_i g(X_i)/f(X_i)$ will form a race with measure P, but not necessarily in order. (T^*, X^*) are variables that track the earliest perturbed arrival so far, so T^* is an upper bound on the eventual first arrival time for the race with measure P. T_{i+1} is the arrival time of the next point in the race with measure Q and M bounds the contribution of the perturbation, so T_{i+1}/M is a lower bound on the remaining perturbed arrivals. When T^* and T_{i+1}/M cross, (T^*, X^*) is guaranteed to be the first arrival of the perturbed race.

REJ and **PER** can turned into generators for iterating through all of the arrivals of an exponential race with measure P as opposed to just returning the first. For **REJ** it is as simple as replacing **return** with **yield**, so that each time the generator is invoked it searches until the next acceptance and returns. For **PER** we must store every perturbed arrival until its eventual order in the race with measure P is determined. This can be accomplished with a priority queue $\mathcal{U}$, which prioritizes by earliest arrival time,

$\mathcal{U} = \text{minPriorityQueue}()$
for $(T_i, X_i) \in R$ simulated by Algorithm 7.2 with measure Q **do**
  $\mathcal{U}.\text{pushWithPriortiy}(T_i g(X_i)/f(X_i), X_i)$
  if $T_{i+1}/M \geq \min \mathcal{U}$ **then yield** $\mathcal{U}.\text{pop}()$
  end if
end for

$\mathcal{U}$ takes the place of T^* and X^* in **PER**. The highest priority arrival on $\mathcal{U}$ will be the earliest of the unordered perturbed arrivals and T_{i+1}/M is a lower bound on all future perturbed arrivals. When $T_{i+1}/M \geq \min \mathcal{U}$, the earliest arrival on $\mathcal{U}$ is guaranteed to be the next arrival. It is informative to think of the generator version of **PER** via Figure 7.7. The lower bound T_{i+1}/M is a bound across space that advances rightward in time, every arrival to the left of T_{i+1}/M is in order and every arrival to the right is unordered.

Consider the number of iterations until the first acceptance in **REJ** and **PER**. At first it seems that both algorithms should have different runtimes. **REJ** is obviously memoryless, and it seems wasteful — no information accumulates. On the other hand **PER** accumulates the earliest arrival and its termination condition depends on a history of arrivals. Unfortunately, both algorithms have the same geometric distribution over the number of arrivals considered. Arguing informally, the lower bound T_{i+1}/M of **PER** plotted over the iterations will form a line with slope $(MQ(\mathbb{R}^n))^{-1}$. **PER** terminates when this line crosses the first arrival time of the perturbed race. The first arrival of a race with measure P occurs at $P(\mathbb{R}^n)^{-1}$ in expectation, so we expect the crossing point to occur on average at $MQ(\mathbb{R}^n)/P(\mathbb{R}^n)$ iterations. This is the same as the expected runtime of **REJ**.

Lemma 7.13. *Let $K(\mathbf{REJ})$ and $K(\mathbf{PER})$ be the number of proposals considered by the rejection and perturbation sampling algorithms. Then*

$$\mathbb{P}(K(\mathbf{REJ}) > k) = \mathbb{P}(K(\mathbf{PER}) > k) = (1 - \rho)^k \text{ with } \rho = \frac{P(\mathbb{R}^n)}{Q(\mathbb{R}^n)M}.$$

Thus $K(\mathbf{REJ})$ and $K(\mathbf{PER})$ are geometric random variable with

$$\mathbb{E}(K(\mathbf{REJ})) = \mathbb{E}(K(\mathbf{PER})) = \frac{1}{\rho}$$

Proof. The probability of accepting a proposal at any iteration of **REJ** is

$$\mathbb{E}(f(X_i)/(g(X_i)M)) = \int \frac{f(x)}{g(x)M}\frac{g(x)}{Q(\mathbb{R}^n)}\mu(dx) = \rho.$$

Each decision is independent, so the probability of k rejections is $(1-\rho)^k$.

PER exceeds k iterations if $T_i g(X_i)/f(X_i) > T_{k+1}/M$ for all $i \leq k$. Because the X_i are i.i.d.,

$$\mathbb{P}(K(\mathbf{PER}) > k \mid \{T_i = t_i\}_{i=1}^{k+1}) = \prod_{i=1}^{k} \mathbb{P}(t_i/t_{k+1} > f(X)/(g(X)M)),$$

where $X \sim Q(\cdot)/Q(\mathbb{R}^n)$. Given $T_{k+1} = t_{k+1}$ the T_i for $i \leq k$ are i.i.d. $T_i \sim \text{Uniform}(0, t_{k+1})$ by Lemma 7.3. Thus $T_i/T_{k+1} \sim \text{Uniform}(0,1)$ i.i.d.

$$\mathbb{P}(K(\mathbf{PER}) > k) = \prod_{i=1}^{k} \mathbb{P}(U > f(X)/(g(X)M)) = (1-\rho)^k$$

finishes the proof. $\square$

7.5.2 Adaptive Bounds

Lemma 7.13 is disappointing, because it suggests that reasoning about perturbations is as inefficient as discarding proposals. The problem is fundamentally that information carried in the bound M about the discrepancy between $g(x)$ and $f(x)$ is static throughout the execution of both algorithms. Considering a contrived scenario will illustrate this point. Suppose that for every failed proposal we are given a tighter bound $M_{i+1} < M_i$ from some oracle. Both **REJ** and **PER** can be adapted to take advantage of these adaptive bounds simply by dropping in M_i wherever M appears.

In this case **PER** is distinguished from **REJ**. **REJ** makes an irrevocable decision at each iteration. In contrast **PER** simply pushes up the lower bound T_{i+1}/M_i without erasing its memory, bringing it closer to accepting the earliest arrival so far. Indeed, the probability of this oracle rejection sampling exceeding k proposals is

$$\mathbb{P}(K(\mathbf{OREJ}) > k) = \prod_{i}(1-\rho_i) \text{ where } \rho_i = P(\mathbb{R}^n)/(Q(R^n)M_i).$$

On the other hand, the probability of this oracle perturbation sampling exceeding k proposals is

$$\mathbb{P}(K(\mathbf{OPER}) > k) = \prod_{i=1}^{k} \mathbb{P}(U > f(X)/(g(X)M_k)) = (1 - \rho_k)^k,$$

or the probability of rejecting k proposals *as if* the M_kth bound was known all along. By tracking the earliest arrival so far **OPER** makes efficient use of adaptive bound information, reevaluating all points in constant time.

7.5.3   OS* Adaptive Rejection Sampling and A* Sampling

The difference between **REJ** and **PER** exposed by considering adaptive bounds motivates studying OS* and A* sampling, Monte Carlo methods that use realistic adaptive bounds. Both methods iteratively refine a partition $\{B_i\}_{i=1}^{m}$ of $\mathbb{R}^n$, which allows them to use regional bounds $M(B_i)$, where $f(x)/g(x) \leq M(B_i)$ for $x \in B_i$. As with **REJ** and **PER**, OS* and A* sampling are only distinguished by how they use this information. OS* reasons about accept-reject operations, A* sampling about perturb operations. In contrast to the relationship between **REJ** and **PER**, A* sampling makes more efficient use of proposal samples than OS*.

OS* and A* sampling must compute volumes and samples of subsets under the proposal measure Q. It will be possibly intractable to consider any possible $B_i \subseteq \mathbb{R}^n$, so a user must implicitly specify a nice family $\mathcal{F}$ of subsets that is closed under a user-specified refinement function $\mathrm{split}(B, x)$. Hyperrectangles are a simple example. All together, the user must provide,

1. finite nonzero measure P with a method for computing the density $f(x)$.

2. finite nonzero proposal measure Q with methods for sampling restricted to $B \in \mathcal{F}$, computing measures of $B \in \mathcal{F}$, and computing the density $g(x)$.

3. partitioning set function $\mathrm{split}(B, x) \subseteq \mathcal{F}$ for $B \in \mathcal{F}$ that partitions B.

4. bounding set function $M(B)$ for $B \in \mathcal{F}$, $f(x)/g(x) \leq M(B)$ for $x \in B$.

Specific examples, which correspond to experimental examples, are given in the Appendix.

OS* (**OS*** for short) is in a family of adaptive rejection sampling algorithms, which use the history of rejected proposals to tighten the gap between the proposal density and the density of interest. The name adaptive rejection sampling (ARS) is normally reserved for a variant that assumes $\log f(x)$ is concave (Gilks and Wild, 1992). Accept-reject decisions are independent, so any adaptive scheme is valid as long as the rejection rate is not growing too quickly (Casella et al., 2004). Our proof of the correctness

---

Algorithm 7.4 OS* adaptive rejection sampling for P with proposal Q

$\mathcal{P}_0 = \{\mathbb{R}^n\}$
$T_0 = 0$
for $i = 1$ to ∞ **do**
    $B_i \sim \mathbb{P}(B) \propto Q(B)M(B)$ for $B \in \mathcal{P}_{i-1}$
    $X_i \sim Q(\cdot \cap B_i)/Q(B_i)$
    $E \sim \text{Exp}(\sum_{B \in \mathcal{P}_{i-1}} M(B)Q(B))$
    $T_i = T_{i-1} + E$
    $U_i \sim \text{Uniform}[0, 1]$
    if $U_i < f(X_i)/(g(X_i)M(B_i))$ **then**
        return (T_i, X_i)
    else
        $\mathcal{C} = \text{split}(B_i, X_i)$
        $\mathcal{P}_i = \mathcal{P}_{i-1} - \{B_i\} + \mathcal{C}$
    end if
end for

---

appeals to exponential races, and it works for a wider range of adaptive schemes than just **OS***.

In more detail, **OS*** begins with the proposal density $g(x)$ and a partition $\mathcal{P}_0 = \{\mathbb{R}^n\}$. At every iteration it samples from the distribution with density proportional to $\sum_{B \in \mathcal{P}_{i-1}} g(x)M(B)1_B(x)$ in a two step procedure, sampling a subset $B \in \mathcal{P}_{i-1}$ with probability proportional to $Q(B)M(B)$, and then sampling a proposal point X from the distribution with density $g(x)$ restricted to B. If X is rejected under the current proposal, then P_{i-1} is refined by splitting B with the user specified $\text{split}(B, X)$. There is a choice of when to refine and which subset $B \in \mathcal{P}_{i-1}$ to refine, but for simplicity we consider just the form the splits the subset of the current proposal. **OS*** continues until the first acceptance, see Algorithm 7.4.

Theorem 7.14 (Correctness of OS*). *Let $K(\mathbf{OS}^*)$ be the number of proposal samples considered before termination. Then*

$$\mathbb{P}(K(\mathbf{OS}^*) > k) \leq (1 - \rho)^k \ \text{where} \ \rho = \frac{P(\mathbb{R}^n)}{Q(\mathbb{R}^n)M(\mathbb{R}^n)}$$

and upon termination the return values (T, X) of OS* are independent and

$$T \sim \text{Exp}(P(\mathbb{R}^n)) \quad X \sim \frac{P(\cdot)}{P(\mathbb{R}^n)}.$$

Proof. The situation is complicated, because the proposals $\{(T_i, X_i)\}_{i=1}^{\infty}$ of **OS*** are not an exponential race. Instead, we present an informal argument derived from a more general thinning theorem, Proposition 14.7.I. in Daley and Vere-Jones (2007). Let $g_i(x)$ be the proposal density at iteration i,

$$g_i(x) = \sum_{B \in \mathcal{P}_{i-1}} g(x)M(B)1_B(x).$$

Clearly, $g_i(x)$ depends on the history of proposals so far and $f(x) \leq g_i(x) \leq g(x)M(\mathbb{R}^n)$ for all i. Let R be an exponential race with measure $M(\mathbb{R}^n)Q(\cdot)$ and $U_j \mathrm{Uniform}[0,1]$ i.i.d. for each $(T_j, X_j) \in R$. Consider the following adaptive thinning procedure, subsample all points of R that satisfy $U_j \leq g_i(X_j)/(g(X_j)M(\mathbb{R}^n))$ where $g_i(X_j)$ is defined according to the refinement scheme in **OS***, but relative to the history of *points subsampled from R in the order of their acceptance*. It is possible to show that the sequence of accepted points $\{(T_i, X_i, U_i)\}_{i=1}^\infty$ have the same marginal distribution as the sequence of proposals in **OS***.

Thus, we can see **OS*** and **REJ** as two separate procedures on the same realization of R. For the termination result, notice that **REJ** considers at least as many points as **OS***. For partial correctness, the points (T_i, X_i, U_i) such that $U_i < f(X_i)/g_i(X_i)$ are exactly the subsampled points that would have resulted from thinning R directly with probability $f(x)/(g(x)M(\mathbb{R}^n))$. Thus, by the Accept-Reject Lemma, the returned values (T, X) will be the first arrival of an exponential race with measure P. $\square$

A* sampling (**A***for short) is a branch and bound routine that finds the first arrival of a perturbed exponential race. It follows **PER** in principle by maintaining a lower bound on all future perturbed arrivals. The difference is that **A*** maintains a piecewise constant lower bound over a partition of space that it progressively refines. On every iteration it selects the subset with smallest lower bound, samples the next arrival in that subset, and refines the subset unless it can terminate. It continues refining until the earliest perturbed arrival is less than the minimum of the piecewise constant lower bound. The name A* sampling is a reference to A* search (Hart et al., 1968), which is a path finding algorithm on graphs that uses a best-first criteria for selecting from heuristically valued nodes on the fringe of a set of visited nodes. A* sampling was originally introduced by Maddison et al. (2014) as an algorithm that maximizes a perturbed Gumbel process. We define it over an exponential race for the sake of consistency. Usually, it is better to work with a Gumbel process to avoid numerical issues.

In more detail, **A*** searches over a simulation of an exponential race organized into a space partitioning tree, as in the right hand plot of Figure 7.4, for the first arrival of the perturbed race. The tree is determined by the splitting function $\mathrm{split}(B, x)$. Each node v of the tree is associated with a subset $B_v \subseteq \mathbb{R}^n$ and an arrival (T_v, X_v) from an exponential race with measure Q. **A*** iteratively expands a subtree of internal visited nodes, taking

---

Algorithm 7.5 A* sampling for P with proposal Q

$\mathcal{L}, \mathcal{U} = \text{minPriorityQueue}(), \text{minPriorityQueue}()$
$T_1 \sim \text{Exp}(Q(\mathbb{R}^n))$
$\mathcal{L}.\text{pushWithPriority}(T_1/M(\mathbb{R}^n), \mathbb{R}^n)$
for $i = 1$ to ∞ **do**
$\quad (T_i/M(B_i), B_i) = \mathcal{L}.\text{pop}()$
$\quad X_i \sim Q(\cdot \cap B)/Q(B_i)$
$\quad \mathcal{U}.\text{pushWithPriority}(T_i g(X_i)/f(X_i), X_i)$
$\quad E \sim \text{Exp}(Q(B_i))$
$\quad T = T_i + E$
$\quad$**if** $\min(\min \mathcal{L}, T/M(B_i)) < \min \mathcal{U}$ **then**
$\quad\quad \mathcal{C} = \text{split}(B_i, X_i)$
$\quad\quad$**while** $\mathcal{C} \neq \emptyset$ **do**
$\quad\quad\quad C \sim \mathbb{P}(C) \propto Q(C)$ for $C \in \mathcal{C}$
$\quad\quad\quad \mathcal{L}.\text{pushWithPriority}(T/M(C), C)$
$\quad\quad\quad \mathcal{C} = \mathcal{C} - \{C\}$
$\quad\quad\quad E \sim \text{Exp}(\sum_{C \in \mathcal{C}} Q(C))$
$\quad\quad\quad T = T + E$
$\quad\quad$**end while**
$\quad$**else**
$\quad\quad \mathcal{L}.\text{pushWithPriority}(T/M(B_i), B_i)$
$\quad$**end if**
$\quad$**if** $\min \mathcal{L} \geq \min \mathcal{U}$ **then**
$\quad\quad$**return** $\mathcal{U}.\text{pop}()$
$\quad$**end if**
end for

---

and visiting one node from the current fringe at each iteration. The fringe $\mathcal{L}$ of the visited subtree is always a partition of $\mathbb{R}^n$. Each subset $B \in \mathcal{L}$ is associated with the arrival time T of the next arrival of the race with measure Q in B. Therefore $T/M(B)$ is a lower bound on all future perturbed arrivals in B. $\mathcal{L}$ is implemented with a priority queue that prioritizes the subset B with the lowest regional bound $T/M(B)$. As **A*** expands the set of visited nodes the lower bound $\min \mathcal{L}$ increases.

$\mathcal{L}$ is initialized with the root of the tree $\{(T_1/M(\mathbb{R}^n), \mathbb{R}^n)\}$. At the start of an iteration **A*** removes and visits the subset $(T_i/M(B_i), B_i)$ with lowest lower bound on $\mathcal{L}$. Visiting a subset begins by realizing a location X_i from $Q(\cdot \cap B_i)/Q(B_i)$ and pushing the perturbed arrival $(T_i g(X_i)/f(X_i), X_i)$ onto another priority queue $\mathcal{U}$. $\mathcal{U}$ prioritizes earlier arrivals by the perturbed arrival times $T_i g(X_i)/f(X_i)$. In this way **A*** decreases the upper bound $\min \mathcal{U}$ at each iteration.

A* attempts to terminate by simulating the next arrival time $T > T_i$ in B_i of the race with measure Q. If $\min \mathcal{U} \leq \min(\min \mathcal{L}, T/M(B_i))$, then the top of $\mathcal{U}$ will not be superseded by future perturbed arrivals and it will be the first arrival of the perturbed race. If termination fails, **A*** refines the the partition by splitting B_i into a partition split(B_i, X_i) of children. Arrival times for each of the children are assigned respecting the constraints of the exponential race in B_i. Each child C is pushed onto $\mathcal{L}$ prioritized by its lower bound $T/M(C)$. Because the lower bounds have increased there is a second opportunity to terminate before continuing. $\mathbf{A}^*$ checks if $\min \mathcal{U} \leq \min \mathcal{L}$, and otherwise continues, see Algorithm 7.5. As with **PER**, $\mathbf{A}^*$ can be turned into a generator for iterating in order through the points of the perturbed race by replacing the **return** statement with a **yield** statement in Algorithm 7.5.

Theorem 7.15 (Correctness of A* sampling). *Let $K(\mathbf{A}^*)$ be the number of proposal samples considered before termination. Then*

$$\mathbb{P}(K(\mathbf{A}^*) > k) \leq (1 - \rho)^k \text{ where } \rho = \frac{P(\mathbb{R}^n)}{Q(\mathbb{R}^n)M(\mathbb{R}^n)}$$

and upon termination the return values (T, X) of A sampling are independent and*

$$T \sim \text{Exp}(P(\mathbb{R}^n)) \quad X \sim \frac{P(\cdot)}{P(\mathbb{R}^n)}.$$

Proof. Adapted from Maddison et al. (2014). The proposals are generated lazily in a space partitioning tree. If $\{(T_i, X_i)\}_{i=1}^{\infty}$ are the arrivals at every node of the infinite tree sorted by increasing T_i, then (T_i, X_i) forms an exponential race with measure Q.

For the termination result, each node v of the tree can be associated with a subset B_v and a lower bound $T_v/M(B_v)$. One of the nodes will contain the first arrival of the perturbed process with arrival time T^*. $\mathbf{A}^*$ visits at least every node v with $T_v/M(B_v) > T^*$. If $M(B)$ is replaced with a constant $M(\mathbb{R}^n)$, then this can only increase the number of visited nodes. The last step is to realize that $\mathbf{A}^*$ searching over a tree with constant bounds $M(\mathbb{R}^n)$ searches in order of increasing T_v, and so corresponds to a realization of **PER**. The distribution of runtimes of **PER** is given in Lemma 7.13.

For partial correctness, let (T, X) be the return values with highest priority on the upper bound priority queue $\mathcal{U}$. The arrival time of unrealized perturbed arrivals is bounded by the lower bound priority queue $\mathcal{L}$. At termination T is less than the top of the lower bound priority queue. So no unrealized points will arrive before (T, X). By Lemma 7.9 (T, X) is the first arrival of an exponential race with measure P. $\qquad \square$

P	Q	Ω	N	$\bar{K}(\mathbf{OS}^*)$	$\bar{K}(\mathbf{A}^*)$
clutter posterior	prior	$\mathbb{R}$	6	9.34	7.56
clutter posterior	prior	$\mathbb{R}^2$	6	38.3	33.0
clutter posterior	prior	$\mathbb{R}^3$	6	130	115
robust Bayesian regression	prior	$\mathbb{R}$	10	9.36	6.77
robust Bayesian regression	prior	$\mathbb{R}$	100	40.6	32.2
robust Bayesian regression	prior	$\mathbb{R}$	1000	180	152
fully connected Ising model	uniform	$\{-1,1\}^5$	-	4.37	3.50
fully connected Ising model	uniform	$\{-1,1\}^{10}$	-	19.8	15.8

Table 7.1: Comparing $\mathbf{A}^*$ and $\mathbf{OS}^*$. Clutter and robust Bayesian regression are adapted from Maddison et al. (2014) and the Ising model from Kim et al. (2016). Ω is the support of the distribution; N is the number of data points; and $\bar{K}(\mathbf{OS}^*)$ and $\bar{K}(\mathbf{A}^*)$ are averaged over 1000 runs. More information in the Appendix.

7.5.4 Runtime of A* Sampling and OS*

$\mathbf{A}^*$ and $\mathbf{OS}^*$ are structurally similar; both search over a partition of space and refine it to increase the probability of terminating. They will give practical benefits over rejection sampling if the bounds $M(B)$ shrink as the volume of B shrinks. In this case the bound on the probability of rejecting k proposals given in Theorems 7.14 and 7.15 can be very loose, and $\mathbf{OS}^*$ and $\mathbf{A}^*$ can be orders of magnitude more efficient than rejection sampling. Still, these methods scale poorly with dimension.

The cost of running $\mathbf{A}^*$ and $\mathbf{OS}^*$ will be dominated by computing the ratio of densities $f(x)/g(x)$ and computing bounds $M(B)$. Because the number of bound computations is within a factor of 2 of the number of density computations, the number of evaluations of $f(x)/g(x)$ (equivalently number of proposals) is a good estimate of complexity. Table 7.1 presents a summary of experimental evidence that $\mathbf{A}^*$ makes more efficient use of density computations across three different problems. For each problem the full descriptions of P, Q, $M(B)$, and $\mathrm{split}(B,x)$ are found in the Appendix.

The dominance of $\mathbf{A}^*$ in experiments is significant, because it has access to the same information as $\mathbf{OS}^*$. There are at least two factors that may give $\mathbf{A}^*$ this advantage. First, if all lower bounds increase sharply after some exploration $\mathbf{A}^*$ can retroactively take advantage of that information, as in Section 7.5.2. Second, $\mathbf{A}^*$ can take advantage of refined bound information on the priority queue $\mathcal{L}$ before proposing the next sample. Still, the difference in search strategy and termination condition may counteract these advantages, so a rigorous theory is needed to confirm exactly the sense in which $\mathbf{A}^*$ and $\mathbf{OS}^*$ differ. We refer readers to Maddison et al. (2014) for more detailed experiments.

7.6 Conclusion

The study of Poisson processes is traditionally motivated by their application to natural phenomenon, and Monte Carlo methods are developed specifically for them (Ripley, 1977; Geyer and Møller, 1994). We considered the inverse relationship, using Poisson processes to better understand Monte Carlo methods. We suspect that this general perspective holds value for future directions in research.

Monte Carlo methods that rely on bounds are not suitable for most high dimensional distributions. Rejection sampling scales poorly with dimensionality. Even for A* sampling there are simple examples where adaptive bounds become uninformative in high dimensions, such as sampling from the uniform hypersphere when using hyperrectangular search subsets. Still, specialized algorithms for limited classes of distributions may be able to take advantage of conditional independence structure to improve their scalability.

Another direction is to abandon the idea of representing arbitrary distributions, and study the class of distributions represented by the maxima of combinations of lower order Gumbel processes. This is the approach of the perturbation models studied in Papandreou and Yuille; Gane et al.; Hazan and Jaakkola; Tarlow et al.; and Keshet at al. of this book. In these models a Gumbel process over a discrete space is replaced by sums of independent Gumbel processes over discrete subspaces. The maxima of these models form a natural class of distributions complete with their own measures of uncertainty. An open direction of inquiry is developing efficient algorithms for optimizing their continuous counterparts.

Our study of Poisson processes and Monte Carlo methods was dominated by the theme of independence; the points of an exponential race arrive as independent random variables and accept-reject or perturb do not introduce correlations between the points of the transformed race. Continuing in this direction it is natural to investigate whether other Poisson process models or other operations on an exponential race could be used to define a new class of Monte Carlo methods. In a separate direction the Markov Chain Monte Carlo (MCMC) methods produce a sequence of correlated samples whose limiting distribution is the distribution of interest. The theory of point processes includes a variety of limit theorems, which describe the limiting distribution of random countable sets (Daley and Vere-Jones, 2007). It would be interesting to see whether a point process treatment of MCMC bears fruit, either in unifying our proof techniques or inspiring new algorithms.

Acknowledgements

We would like to thank Daniel Tarlow and Tom Minka for the ideas, discussions, and support throughout this project. Thanks to the other editors Tamir Hazan and George Papandreou. Thanks to Jacob Steinhardt, Yee Whye Teh, Arnaud Doucet, Christian Robert for comments on the draft. Thanks to Sir J.F.C. Kingman for encouragement. This work was supported by the Natural Sciences and Engineering Research Council of Canada.

Appendix: Proof of Lemma 7.3

Proof. The lemma is trivial satisfied for $k = 0$. For $k > 0$ and $B_i \subseteq B$ we will express

$$\mathbb{P}(\{X_i \in B_i\}_{i=1}^k | N(B) = k) \qquad (7.16)$$

in terms of counts. The difficulty lies in the possible overlap of B_is, so we consider 2^k sets of the form

$$A_j = B_1^* \cap B_2^* \cap \ldots \cap B_k^*$$

where $*$ is blank or a complement, and A_1 is interpreted as $B \cap B_1^c \cap \ldots \cap B_k^c$. The A_j are a disjoint partition of B,

$$B_i = \cup_{j \in I(i)} A_j, \quad B = \cup_{j=1}^{2^k} A_j,$$

where $I(i) \subseteq \{1, \ldots, 2^k\}$ is some subset of indices. Let $\mathcal{I} = I(1) \times I(2) \times \ldots \times I(k)$, so that each $s \in \mathcal{I}$ is a vector indices $(s_1, s_2, \ldots, s_k)$ associated with the disjoint events $\{X_i \in A_{s_i}\}_{i=1}^k$. Thus,

$$\mathbb{P}(\{X_i \in B_i\}_{i=1}^k | N(B) = k) = \sum_{s \in \mathcal{I}} \mathbb{P}(\{X_i \in A_{s_i}\}_{i=1}^k | N(B) = k).$$

For $s \in \mathcal{I}$, let $n_j(s) = \#\{i : s_i = j\}$ be the number of indices in s equal to j and notice that $\sum_{j=1}^{2^k} n_j(s) = k$. To relate the probability if specific numbering $\{X_i \in A_{s_i}\}_{i=1}^k$ with counts $\{N(A_j) = n_j(s)\}_{j=1}^{2^k}$, we discount by all ways of the arranging k points that result in the same counts.

$$\mathbb{P}(\{X_i \in A_{s_i}\}_{i=1}^k | N(B) = k) = \frac{\prod_{j=1}^{2^k} n_j(s)!}{k!} \frac{\mathbb{P}(\{N(A_j) = n_j(s)\}_{j=1}^{2^k})}{\mathbb{P}(N(B) = k)}$$

$$= \frac{\prod_{j=1}^{2^k} \mu(A_j)^{n_j(s)}}{\mu(B)^k}.$$

Thus (7.16) is equal to

$$\sum_{s \in \mathcal{I}} \frac{\prod_{j=1}^{2^k} \mu(A_j)^{n_j(s)}}{\mu(B)^k} = \prod_{i=1}^k \frac{\sum_{j \in I(i)} \mu(A_j)}{\mu(B)} = \prod_{i=1}^k \frac{\mu(B_i)}{\mu(B)}$$

□

Appendix: Experimental Details

Clutter Posterior

This example is taken exactly from Maddison et al. (2014). The clutter problem (Minka, 2001) is to estimate the mean $\theta \in \mathbb{R}^n$ of a Normal distribution under the assumption that some points are outliers. The task is to sample from the posterior P over w of some empirical sample $\{(x_i)\}_{i=1}^N$.

$$f_i(\theta) = \frac{0.5 \exp(-0.5 \|\theta - x_i\|^2)}{(2\pi)^{n/2}} + \frac{0.5 \exp(-0.5 \|x_i\|^2/100^2)}{100^n (2\pi)^{n/2}}$$

$$\log g(\theta) = -\frac{\|\theta\|^2}{8} \quad \log f(\theta) = \log g(\theta) + \sum_{i=1}^N \log f_i(\theta)$$

$$(a, b] = \{y : a_d < y_d \le b_d\} \text{ for } a, b \in \mathbb{R}^n$$

$$M((a, b]) = \prod_{i=1}^N f_i(x^*(a, b, x_i)) \quad x^*(a, b, x)_d = \begin{cases} a_d & \text{if } x_d < a_d \\ b_d & \text{if } x_d > b_d \\ x_d & \text{o.w.} \end{cases}$$

$$\text{split}((a, b], x) = \{(a, b] \cap \{y : y_s \le x_s\}, (a, b] \cap \{y : y_s > x_s\}\}$$

$$\text{where } s = \underset{d}{\text{argmax}} \, b_d - a_d$$

Our dataset was 6 points $x_i \in \mathbb{R}^n$ of the form $x_i = (a_i, a_i, \ldots, a_i)$ for $a_i \in \{-5, -4, -3, 3, 4, 5\}$.

Robust Bayesian Regression

This example is an adaption from Maddison et al. (2014) with looser bounds. The model is a robust linear regression $y_i = wx_i + \epsilon_i$ where the noise ϵ_i is distributed as a standard Cauchy and w is a standard Normal. The task is to sample from the posterior P over w of some empirical sample $\{(x_i, y_i)\}_{i=1}^N$.

$$\log g(w) = -\frac{w^2}{8}$$

$$\log f(w) = \log g(w) - \sum_{i=1}^N \log(1 + (wx_i - y_i)^2)$$

$$M((a,b]) = \prod_{i=1}^N M_i((a,b]) \quad M_i((a,b]) = \begin{cases} \exp(a) & \text{if } y_i/x_i < a \\ \exp(b) & \text{if } y_i/x_i > b \\ \exp(y_i/x_i) & \text{o.w.} \end{cases}$$

$$\text{split}((a,b], x) = \{(a,x], (x,b]\}$$

The dataset was generated by setting $w^* = 2$; $x_i \sim \text{Normal}(0,1)$ and $y_i = wx_i + \epsilon$ with $\epsilon \sim \text{Normal}(0, 0.1^2)$ for $i \leq N/2$; and $x_i = x_{i-N/2}$ and $y_i = -y_{i-N/2}$ for $i > N/2$.

Attractive Fully Connected Ising Model

This is an adaptation of Kim et al. (2016). The attractive fully connected Ising model is a distribution over $x \in \{-1, 1\}^n$ described by parameters $w_{ij} \sim \text{Uniform}[0, 0.2]$ and $f_i \sim \text{Uniform}[-1, 1]$.

$$\log g(x) = 0$$

$$\log f(x) = \sum_i f_i x_i + \sum_{i<j\leq n} w_{ij} x_i x_j$$

We considered subsets of the form $B = \{x : x_i = b_i, i \in I\}$ where $I \subseteq \{1, \ldots, n\}$ and $b_i \in \{0, 1\}$. We split on one of the unspecified variables x_i by taking variable whose linear program relaxation was closest to 0.5.

$$\text{split}(B, x) = \{B \cap \{x : x_i = 0\}, B \cap \{x : x_i = 1\}\}$$

$\log M(B)$ is computed by solving a linear program relaxation for the following type of integer program. Let $b_i \in \{0, 1\}$ for $1 \leq i \leq n$ and $b_{ijkl} \in \{0, 1\}$ for $1 \leq i < j \leq n$ and $k, l \in \{0, 1\}$.

$$\min_x \sum_i -f_i b_i + f_i(1 - b_i) + \sum_{1\leq i<j\leq n} \sum_{k,l\in\{0,1\}} (-1)^{kl+(1-l)(1-k)} w_{ij} b_{ijkl}$$

subject to the constraints for $1 \leq i < j \leq n$,

$$\sum_{l \in \{0,1\}} b_{ij0l} = 1 - b_i \qquad \sum_{k \in \{0,1\}} b_{ijk0} = 1 - b_j$$

$$\sum_{l \in \{0,1\}} b_{ij1l} = b_i \qquad \sum_{k \in \{0,1\}} b_{ijk1} = b_j$$

as the subsets B narrowed we just solved new linear programs with constants for the fixed variables.

7.9   References

G. Casella, C. P. Robert, and M. T. Wells. *Generalized Accept-Reject sampling schemes*, volume 45 of *Lecture Notes–Monograph Series*. Institute of Mathematical Statistics, 2004.

Y. Chen and Z. Ghahramani. Scalable Discrete Sampling as a Multi-Armed Bandit Problem. *ArXiv e-prints*, June 2015.

D. J. Daley and D. Vere-Jones. *An Introduction to the Theory of Point Processes, Volume II: General Theory and Structure*. Springer, 2007.

L. Devroye. *Non-Uniform Random Variate Generation*. Springer, 1986.

R. Durrett. *Essentials of Stochastic Processes*. Springer, 2012.

M. Dymetman, G. Bouchard, and S. Carter. The OS* Algorithm: a Joint Approach to Exact Optimization and Sampling. *arXiv preprint arXiv:1207.0742*, 2012.

B. Gedenko. On a local limit theorem of the theory of probability. *Uspekhi Mat. Nauk*, 3, 1948.

C. J. Geyer and J. Møller. Simulation procedures and likelihood inference for spatial point processes. *Scandinavian Journal of Statistics*, 1994.

W. R. Gilks and P. Wild. Adaptive rejection sampling for Gibbs sampling. *Applied Statistics*, 1992.

E. J. Gumbel and J. Lieblein. *Statistical Theory of Extreme Values and Some Practical Applications: a Series of Lectures*. US Govt. Print. Office, 1954.

P. Hart, N. Nilsson, and B. Raphael. A Formal Basis for the Heuristic Determination of Minimum Cost Paths. *Systems Science and Cybernetics, IEEE Transactions on*, 4(2), 1968.

T. Hazan, S. Maji, and T. Jaakkola. On Sampling from the Gibbs Distribution with Random Maximum A-Posteriori Perturbations. In *NIPS*. 2013.

C. Kim, A. Sabharwal, and S. Ermon. Exact Sampling with Integer Linear Programs and Random Perturbations. In *AAAI*, 2016.

J. Kingman. *Poisson Processes*. Oxford University Press, 1992.

P. A. W. Lewis and G. S. Shedler. Simulation of nonhomogeneous poisson processes by thinning. *Naval Research Logistics Quarterly*, 26(3), 1979.

C. J. Maddison, D. Tarlow, and T. Minka. A* Sampling. In *NIPS*. 2014.

H. Malmberg. Random Choice over a Continuous Set of Options. 2013.

T. P. Minka. Expectation propagation for approximate Bayesian inference. In *UAI*, 2001.

G. Papandreou and A. Yuille. Perturb-and-MAP Random Fields: Using Discrete Optimization to Learn and Sample from Energy Models. In *ICCV*, 2011.

S. I. Resnick. *Extreme Values, Regular Variation and Point Processes*. Springer, 2007.

B. D. Ripley. Modelling Spatial Patterns. *Journal of the Royal Statistical Society. Series B (Methodological)*, 1977.

D. Tarlow, R. P. Adams, and R. S. Zemel. Randomized Optimum Models for Structured Prediction. In *AISTATS*, 2012.

A. J. Walker. An efficient method for generating discrete random variables with general distributions. *ACM Transactions on Mathematical Software*, 3(3), 1977.

J. I. Yellott. The relationship between Luce's choice axiom, Thurstone's theory of comparative judgment, and the double exponential distribution. *Journal of Mathematical Psychology*, 15(2), 1977.

8 Perturbation Techniques in Online Learning and Optimization

Jacob Abernethy
University of Michigan
Ann Arbor, MI

jabernet@umich.edu

Chansoo Lee
University of Michigan
Ann Arbor, MI

chansool@umich.edu

Ambuj Tewari
University of Michigan
Ann Arbor, MI

tewaria@umich.edu

In this chapter we give a new perspective on so-called perturbation methods *that have been applied in a number of different fields, but in particular for adversarial online learning problems. We show that the classical algorithm known as Follow The Perturbed Leader (FTPL) can be viewed through the lens of* stochastic smoothing, *a tool that has proven popular within convex optimization. We prove bounds on regret for several online learning settings, and provide generic tools for analyzing perturbation algorithms. We also consider the so-called* bandit *setting, where the feedback to the learner is significantly constrained, and we show that near-optimal bounds can be achieved as long as a simple condition on the perturbation distribution is met.*

8.1 Introduction

In this chapter we will study the problem of *online learning* with the goal of *minimizing regret*. A learner must iteratively play a sequence of actions, where each action is based on the data received up to the previous iteration. We consider learning in a potentially adversarial environment, where we avoid making any stochastic assumptions about the sequence of data. The goal of the learner is to suffer as little regret as possible, where regret is defined as the difference between the learner's loss and the loss of the best fixed action in hindsight. The key to developing optimal algorithms is *regularization*, which may be interpreted either as *hedging* against bad future events, or similarly can be seen as avoiding *overfitting* to the observed data. In this paper, we focus on regularization techniques for online linear optimization problems where the learner's action is evaluated on a linear reward function.

In the present chapter, we will mostly focus on learning settings where our learner's decisions are chosen from a convex subset of $\mathbb{R}^N$, and where the "data" we observe arrives in the form of a (bounded) vector $g \in \mathbb{R}^N$, and the costs/gains will be linear in each. Specifically, the gain (equiv., reward) received on a given round, when the learner plays action w and Nature chooses vector g, is the inner product $\langle w, g \rangle$. Generally we will use the the symbol G to refer to the *cumulative gain vector* up to a particular time period.

The algorithm commonly known as Follow the Regularized Leader (FTRL) selects an action w on a given round by solving an explicit optimization problem, where the objective combines a "data fitness" term along with a regularization *via penalty function*. More precisely, FTRL selects an action by optimizing $\text{argmax}_w \langle w, G \rangle - \mathcal{R}(w)$ where $\mathcal{R}$ is a strongly convex penalty function; a well-studied choice for $\mathcal{R}$ is the well-known ℓ_2-regularizer $\| \cdot \|_2^2$. The regret analysis of FTRL reduces to the analysis of the second-order behavior of the penalty function (Shalev-Shwartz, 2012), which is well-studied due to the powerful convex analysis tools. In fact, regularization via penalty methods for online learning in general are very well understood. Srebro et al. (2011) proved that Mirror Descent, a regularization via penalty method, achieves a nearly optimal regret guarantee for a general class of online learning problems, and McMahan (2011) showed that FTRL is equivalent to Mirror Descent under some assumptions.

Follow the Perturbed Leader (FTPL), on the other hand, uses implicit regularization *via perturbations*. At every iteration, FTPL selects an action by optimizing $\text{argmax}_w \langle w, G + z \rangle$ where G is the observed data and z is some random noise vector, often referred to as a "perturbation" of the input. The early FTPL analysis tools lacked a generic framework and relied substantially on clever algebra tricks and heavy probabilistic analysis (Kalai and Vempala, 2005; Devroye et al., 2013; van Erven et al., 2014). This was in contrast to the elegant and simple convex analysis techniques that provided the basis for studying FTRL and proving tight bounds.

This book chapter focuses on giving a new perspective on perturbation methods and on providing a new set of analysis tools for controlling the regret of FTPL. In particular, we show that the results hinge on certain *second-order properties* of stochastically-smoothed convex functions. Indeed, we show that both FTPL and FTRL naturally arise as *smoothing operations* of a non-smooth potential function and the regret analysis boils down to understanding the *smoothness* as defined in Section 8.3. This new unified analysis framework recovers known (near-)optimal regret bounds and provides tools for controlling regret.

An interesting feature of our analysis framework is that we can directly apply existing techniques from the optimization literature, and conversely, our new findings in online linear optimization may apply to optimization theory. In Section 8.4, a straightforward application of the results on Gaussian smoothing by Nesterov (2011) and Duchi et al. (2012) gives a generic regret bound for an arbitrary online linear optimization problem. In Section 8.5 and 8.6, we improve this bound for the special cases that correspond to canonical online linear optimization problems; we analyze the so-called "experts setting" (Section 8.5) and we also look at the case where the decision set is the Euclidean ball (Section 8.6). Finally, in Section 8.7, we turn our attention to the *bandit setting* where the learner has limited feedback. For this case, we show that the perturbation distribution has to be chosen quite carefully, and indeed we show that near-optimal regret can be obtained as long as the perturbation distribution has a *bounded hazard rate* function.

8.2 Preliminaries

8.2.1 Convex Analysis

For this preliminary discussion, assume we are given an arbitrary norm $\|\cdot\|$. Throughout the chapter we will utilize various norms, such as the $\ell_1, \ell_2, \ell_\infty$, and the spectral norm of a matrix. In addition, we will often use $\|\cdot\|_*$ to refer to the *dual norm* of $\|\cdot\|$, defined as $\|\mathbf{z}\|_* = \max_{\mathbf{y}:\|\mathbf{y}\|\leq 1}\langle\mathbf{y},\mathbf{z}\rangle$.

Assume we are given f a differentiable, closed, and proper convex function whose domain is $\text{dom } f \subseteq \mathbb{R}^N$. We say that f is *L-Lipschitz* with respect to a norm $\|\cdot\|$ when f satisfies $|f(x) - f(y)| \leq L\|x - y\|$ for all $x, y \in \text{dom}(f)$.

The *Bregman divergence* $D_f(y, x)$ is the gap between $f(y)$ and the linear approximation of $f(y)$ around x. Formally, $D_f(y, x) = f(y) - f(x) - \langle\nabla f(x), y - x\rangle$. We say that f is β-*strongly convex* with respect to a norm

$\|\cdot\|$ if we have $D_f(y,x) \geq \frac{\beta}{2}\|y-x\|^2$ for all $x, y \in \text{dom } f$. Similarly, f is said to be β-*strongly smooth* with respect to a norm $\|\cdot\|$ if we have $D_f(y,x) \leq \frac{\beta}{2}\|y-x\|^2$ for all $x, y \in \text{dom } f$.

The Bregman divergence measures how fast the gradient changes, or equivalently, how large the second derivative is. In fact, we can bound the Bregman divergence by analyzing the local behavior of Hessian, as the following adaptation of Abernethy et al. (2013, Lemma 4.6) shows.

Lemma 8.1. *Let f be a twice-differentiable convex function with $\text{dom } f \subseteq \mathbb{R}^N$. Assume that the eigenvalues of $\nabla^2 f(x)$ all lie in the range $[a, b]$ for every $x \in \text{dom } f$. Then, $a\|v\|^2/2 \leq D_f(x+v, x) \leq b\|v\|^2/2$ for any $x, x + v \in \text{dom } f$.*

The *Fenchel conjugate* of f is defined as $f^\star(G) = \sup_{w \in \text{dom}(f)}\{\langle w, G \rangle - f(w)\}$, and it is a dual mapping that satisfies $f = (f^\star)^\star$. If f is differentiable and strictly convex we also have $\nabla f^\star \in \text{dom}(f)$. One can also show that the notions of strong convexity and strong smoothness are dual to each other. That is, f is β-strongly convex with respect to a norm $\|\cdot\|$ if and only if $f^\star$ is $\frac{1}{\beta}$-strongly smooth with respect to the dual norm $\|\cdot\|_\star$. For more details and proofs, readers are referred to an excellent survey by Shalev-Shwartz (2012).

8.2.2   Online Linear Optimization

Let $\mathcal{X}$ and $\mathcal{Y}$ be convex and closed subsets of $\mathbb{R}^N$. The online linear optimization (OLO) is defined to be the following repeated game between two entities that we call the *learner* and the *adversary*:

On round $t = 1, \ldots, T$,

- the learner plays $w_t \in \mathcal{X}$;
- the adversary reveals $g_t \in \mathcal{Y}$;
- the learner receives a reward[1] $\langle w_t, g_t \rangle$.

We say $\mathcal{X}$ is the *decision set* and $\mathcal{Y}$ is the *reward set*. Let $G_t = \sum_{s=1}^t g_s$ be the cumulative reward. The learner's goal is to minimize the (external)

---

1. Our somewhat less conventional choice of maximizing the reward instead of minimizing the loss was made so that we directly analyze the convex function $\max(\cdot)$ without cumbersome sign changes.

regret, defined as:

$$\text{Regret} = \underbrace{\max_{w \in \mathcal{X}} \langle w, G_T \rangle}_{\text{baseline potential}} - \sum_{t=1}^{T} \langle w_t, g_t \rangle. \tag{8.1}$$

The *baseline potential function* $\Phi(G) := \max_{w \in \mathcal{X}} \langle w, G \rangle$ is the comparator term against which we define the regret, and it coincides with the *support function* of $\mathcal{X}$. For a bounded compact set $\mathcal{X}$, the support function of $\mathcal{X}$ is positively homogeneous, subadditive, and Lipschitz continuous with respect to any norm $\| \cdot \|$, where the Lipschitz constant is equal to $\sup_{x \in \mathcal{X}} \|x\|_*$. For more details and proofs, readers are referred to Rockafellar (1997, Section 13) or Molchanov (2005, Appendix F).

8.3 Gradient-Based Prediction Algorithm

Follow the Leader (FTL) style algorithms select the next action $w_t \in \mathcal{X}$ via an optimization problem: given the cumulative reward vector G_{t-1}, an FTL style algorithm selects $w_t = \text{argmax}_{w \in \mathcal{X}} f(w, G_{t-1})$. The most simple algorithm, FTL, does not incorporate any perturbation or regularization into the optimization, and uses the objective $f(w, G) = \langle w, G \rangle$. Unfortunately FTL does not enjoy non-trivial regret guarantees in many scenarios, due to the inherent instability of vanilla linear optimization—that is, since the the optimal solution can fluctuate with small changes in the input. There are a couple of ways to induce stability in FTL. Follow the Regularized Leader (FTRL) sets $f(w, G) = \langle w, G \rangle - \mathcal{R}(w)$ where $\mathcal{R}$ is a strongly convex regularizer providing stability to the solution. Follow the Perturbed Leader (FTPL) sets $f(w, G) = \langle w, G + z \rangle$ where z is a random vector. The randomness in z imparts stability to the (expected) move of the FTPL algorithm.

We now proceed to show that a common property shared by all such algorithms is that the action w_t is exactly the *gradient* of some scalar-valued potential function $\widetilde{\Phi}_t$ evaluated at G_{t-1}. (For the remainder of the paper we will use the notation $\widetilde{\Phi}$ to refer to a modification of the baseline potential Φ). This perspective gives rise to what we call the Gradient-based Prediction Algorithm (GBPA), presented in Algorithm 1. In the following Section we give a full regret analysis of this algorithm. We note that Cesa-Bianchi and Lugosi (2006, Theorem 11.6) presented a similar algorithm, but our formulation eliminates all dual mappings.

Algorithm 1: Gradient-Based Prediction Algorithm (GBPA)

Input: $\mathcal{X}, \mathcal{Y} \subseteq \mathbb{R}^N$
Require: convex potentials $\widetilde{\Phi}_1, \ldots, \widetilde{\Phi}_T : \mathbb{R}^N \to \mathbb{R}$, with $\nabla \widetilde{\Phi}_t(G) \in \mathcal{X}$, $\forall G$
Initialize: $G_0 = 0$
for $t = 1$ *to* T **do**
$\quad$ The learner plays $w_t = \nabla \widetilde{\Phi}_t(G_{t-1})$
$\quad$ The adversary reveals $g_t \in \mathcal{Y}$
$\quad$ The learner receives a reward of $\langle w_t, g_t \rangle$
$\quad$ Update the cumulative gain vector: $G_t = G_{t-1} + g_t$

8.3.1 GBPA Analysis

We begin with a generic result on the regret of GBPA in the full-information setting.

Lemma 8.2 (GBPA Regret). *Let* Φ *be the baseline potential function for an online linear optimization problem. The regret of the GBPA can be decomposed as follows:*

$$
\text{Regret} = \sum_{t=1}^{T} \left(\underbrace{\left(\widetilde{\Phi}_t(G_{t-1}) - \widetilde{\Phi}_{t-1}(G_{t-1}) \right)}_{\text{overestimation penalty}} + \underbrace{D_{\widetilde{\Phi}_t}(G_t, G_{t-1})}_{\text{divergence penalty}} \right)
$$
$$
+ \underbrace{\Phi(G_T) - \widetilde{\Phi}_T(G_T)}_{\text{underestimation penalty}}, \tag{8.2}
$$

where $\widetilde{\Phi}_0 \equiv \Phi$.

Proof. We note that since $\widetilde{\Phi}_0(0) = 0$,

$$
\begin{aligned}
\widetilde{\Phi}_T(G_T) &= \sum_{t=1}^{T} \widetilde{\Phi}_t(G_t) - \widetilde{\Phi}_{t-1}(G_{t-1}) \\
&= \sum_{t=1}^{T} \left(\left(\widetilde{\Phi}_t(G_t) - \widetilde{\Phi}_t(G_{t-1}) \right) + \left(\widetilde{\Phi}_t(G_{t-1}) - \widetilde{\Phi}_{t-1}(G_{t-1}) \right) \right) \\
&= \sum_{t=1}^{T} \left(\left(\langle \nabla \widetilde{\Phi}_t(G_{t-1}), g_t \rangle + D_{\widetilde{\Phi}_t}(G_t, G_{t-1}) \right) \right. \\
&\qquad\qquad \left. + \left(\widetilde{\Phi}_t(G_{t-1}) - \widetilde{\Phi}_{t-1}(G_{t-1}) \right) \right),
\end{aligned}
$$

where the last equality holds because:

$$
\widetilde{\Phi}_t(G_t) - \widetilde{\Phi}_t(G_{t-1}) = \langle \nabla \widetilde{\Phi}_t(G_{t-1}), g_t \rangle + D_{\widetilde{\Phi}_t}(G_t, G_{t-1}). \tag{8.3}
$$

We now have

$$\text{Regret} := \Phi(G_T) - \sum_{t=1}^{T} \langle w_t, g_t \rangle$$

$$= \Phi(G_T) - \sum_{t=1}^{T} \langle \nabla \widetilde{\Phi}_t(G_{t-1}), g_t \rangle$$

$$= \Phi(G_T) - \widetilde{\Phi}_T(G_T) + \sum_{t=1}^{T} D_{\widetilde{\Phi}_t}(G_t, G_{t-1}) + \widetilde{\Phi}_t(G_{t-1}) - \widetilde{\Phi}_{t-1}(G_{t-1}),$$

which completes the proof. $\qquad\square$

We point out a couple of important facts about Lemma 8.2:

1. If $\widetilde{\Phi}_1 \equiv \cdots \equiv \widetilde{\Phi}_T$, then the overestimation penalty sums up to $\widetilde{\Phi}_1(0) - \widetilde{\Phi}(0) = \widetilde{\Phi}_T(0) - \widetilde{\Phi}(0)$.

2. If $\widetilde{\Phi}_t$ is β-strongly smooth with respect to $\|\cdot\|$, the divergence penalty at t is at most $\frac{\beta}{2}\|g_t\|^2$.

One source of regret is the Bregman divergence of $\widetilde{\Phi}_t$; since g_t is not known until playing w_t, the GBPA always ascends along the gradient that is one step behind. The adversary can exploit this and play g_t to induce a large *gap* between $\widetilde{\Phi}_t(G_t)$ and the linear approximation of $\widetilde{\Phi}_t(G_t)$ around G_{t-1}. The learner can reduce this gap by choosing a *smooth* $\widetilde{\Phi}_t$ whose gradient changes slowly.

The learner, however, cannot achieve low regret by choosing an arbitrarily smooth $\widetilde{\Phi}_t$, because the other source of regret is the difference between $\widetilde{\Phi}_t$ and Φ. In short, the GBPA achieves low regret if the potential function $\widetilde{\Phi}_t$ gives a favorable tradeoff between the two sources of regret. This tradeoff is captured by the following definition of *smoothing parameters*, adapted from Beck and Teboulle (2012, Definition 2.1).

Definition 8.1. *Let f be a closed proper convex function. A collection of functions $\{\tilde{f}_\eta : \eta \in \mathbb{R}_+\}$ is said to be an η-smoothing of f with smoothing parameters $(\alpha, \beta, \|\cdot\|)$, if for every $\eta > 0$:*

1. There exists α_1 (underestimation bound) and α_2 (overestimation bound) such that

$$\sup_{G \in \text{dom}(f)} f(G) - \tilde{f}_\eta(G) \leq \alpha_1 \eta \quad and \quad \sup_{G \in \text{dom}(f)} \tilde{f}_\eta(G) - f(G) \leq \alpha_2 \eta \quad (8.4)$$

with $\alpha_1 + \alpha_2 = \alpha$.

2. $\tilde{f}_\eta$ is $\frac{\beta}{\eta}$-strongly smooth with respect to $\|\cdot\|$.

We say α is the deviation parameter, *and β is the* smoothness parameter.

A straightforward application of Lemma 8.2 gives the following statement:

Corollary 8.3. *Let Φ be the baseline potential for an online linear optimization problem. Suppose $\{\widetilde{\Phi}_\eta\}$ is an η-smoothing of Φ with parameters $(\alpha, \beta, \|\cdot\|)$. Then, the GBPA run with $\widetilde{\Phi}_1 \equiv \cdots \equiv \widetilde{\Phi}_T \equiv \widetilde{\Phi}_\eta$ enjoys the following regret bound,*

$$\text{Regret} \leq \alpha\eta + \frac{\beta}{2\eta} \sum_{t=1}^{T} \|g_t\|^2. \tag{8.5}$$

Choosing η to optimize the bound gives $\text{Regret} \leq \sqrt{2\alpha\beta \sum_{t=1}^{T} \|g_t\|^2}$.

In OLO, we often consider the settings where the reward vectors $g_1, \ldots, g_t$ are constrained in norm, i.e., $\|g_t\| \leq r$ for all t. In such settings, the regret grows in $O(r\sqrt{\alpha\beta T})$ for the optimal choice of η. The product $\alpha\beta$ of the devation and smoothness parameters is, therefore, at the core of the GBPA regret analysis.

An important smoothing technique for this chapter is *stochasting smoothing*, which is the convolution of a function with a probability density function.

Definition 8.2 (Stochastic Smoothing). *Let $f : \mathbb{R}^N \to \mathbb{R}$ be a function. We define $\tilde{f}(\cdot; \mathcal{D}_\eta)$ to be the* stochastic smoothing *of f with distribution $\mathcal{D}$ and scaling parameter $\eta > 0$. The function value at G is obtained as:*

$$\tilde{f}(G; \mathcal{D}_\eta) := \mathbb{E}_{z' \sim \mathcal{D}_\eta}[f(G + z')] = \mathbb{E}_{z \sim \mathcal{D}}[f(G + \eta z)], \tag{8.6}$$

where we adopt the convention that if z has distribution $\mathcal{D}$ then the distribution of ηz is denoted by $\mathcal{D}_\eta$.

Notes on estimation penalty If the perturbation used has mean zero, it follows from Jensen's inequality that the stochastic smoothing will overestimate the convex function Φ. Hence, for mean zero perturbations, the underestimation penalty is always non-positive. When the scaling parameter η_t changes every iteration, the overestimation penalty becomes a sum of T terms. The following lemma shows that we can collapse them into one since the baseline potential Φ in OLO problems is sub-additive: $\Phi(G+H) \leq \Phi(G) + \Phi(H)$.

Lemma 8.4. *Let $\Phi : \mathbb{R}^N \to \mathbb{R}$ be a baseline potential function of an OLO problem. Let $\mathcal{D}$ be a continuous distribution with zero mean and support $\mathbb{R}^N$. Consider the GBPA with $\widetilde{\Phi}_t(G) = \widetilde{\Phi}(G; \mathcal{D}_{\eta_t})$ for $t = 0, \ldots, T$ where $(\eta_1, \ldots, \eta_T)$ is a non-decreasing sequence of non-negative numbers. Then* *the overestimation penalty has the following upper bound,*

$$\sum_{t=1}^{T} \widetilde{\Phi}_t(G_{t-1}) - \widetilde{\Phi}_{t-1}(G_{t-1}) \leq \eta_T \mathbb{E}_{u \sim \mathcal{D}}[\Phi(u)], \tag{8.7}$$

and the underestimation penalty is non-positive which gives gives a regret bound of

$$\text{Regret} \leq \eta_T \mathbb{E}_{u \sim \mathcal{D}}[\Phi(u)] + \sum_{t=1}^{T} D_{\widetilde{\Phi}_t}(G_t, G_{t-1}). \tag{8.8}$$

Proof. By virtue of the fact that Φ is a support function, it is also subadditive and satisfies the triangle inequality. Hence we can see that, for any $0 < \eta' \leq \eta$,

$$\begin{aligned}
\widetilde{\Phi}(G; \mathcal{D}_\eta) - \widetilde{\Phi}(G; \mathcal{D}_{\eta'}) &= \mathbb{E}_{u \sim \mathcal{D}}[\Phi(G + \eta u) - \Phi(G + \eta' u)] \\
&\leq \mathbb{E}_{u \sim \mathcal{D}}[\Phi((\eta - \eta')u)] = (\eta - \eta')\mathbb{E}_{u \sim \mathcal{D}}[\Phi(u)],
\end{aligned}$$

where the final line follows from the positive homogeneity of Φ. Since we implicitly assume that $\widetilde{\Phi}_0 \equiv \Phi$ we can set $\eta_0 = 0$. We can then conclude that

$$\sum_{t=1}^{T} \widetilde{\Phi}_t(G_{t-1}) - \widetilde{\Phi}_{t-1}(G_{t-1}) \leq \left(\sum_{t=1}^{T} \eta_t - \eta_{t-1}\right)\mathbb{E}_{u \sim \mathcal{D}}[\Phi(u)] = \eta_T \mathbb{E}_{u \sim \mathcal{D}}[\Phi(u)], \tag{8.9}$$

which completes the proof. $\qquad\square$

8.3.2 Understanding Follow the Perturbed Leader via Stochastic Smoothing

The technique of *stochastic smoothing* has been well-studied in the optimization literature for gradient-free optimization algorithms (Glasserman, 1991; Yousefian et al., 2010) and accelerated gradient methods for non-smooth optimizations (Duchi et al., 2012).

One very useful property of stochastic smoothing is that as long as $\mathcal{D}$ has a support over $\mathbb{R}^N$ and has a differentiable probability density function μ, $\tilde{f}$ is always differentiable. To see this, we use the change of variable technique:

$$\tilde{f}(G; \mathcal{D}) = \int f(G + z)\mu(z)\,dz = \int f(\tilde{G})\mu(\tilde{G} - G)\,d\tilde{G}, \tag{8.10}$$

and it follows that

$$\nabla_G \tilde{f}(G; \mathcal{D}) = -\int f(\tilde{G}) \nabla_G \mu(\tilde{G} - G) \, d\tilde{G},$$
$$\nabla_G^2 \tilde{f}(G; \mathcal{D}) = \int f(\tilde{G}) \nabla_G^2 \mu(\tilde{G} - G) \, d\tilde{G}. \tag{8.11}$$

This change of variable trick leads to the following useful expressions for the first and second derivatives of $\tilde{f}$ in case the density $\mu(G)$ is proportional to $\exp(-\nu(G))$ for a sufficiently smooth ν.

Lemma 8.5 (Exponential Family Smoothing). *Suppose $\mathcal{D}$ is a distribution over $\mathbb{R}^N$ with a probability density function μ of the form $\mu(G) = \exp(-\nu(G))/Z$ for some normalization constant Z. Then, for any twice-differentiable ν, we have*

$$\nabla \tilde{f}(G) = \mathbb{E}[f(G + z)\nabla_z \nu(z)], \tag{8.12}$$
$$\nabla^2 \tilde{f}(G) = \mathbb{E}[f(G + z)\left(\nabla_z \nu(z)\nabla_z \nu(z)^T - \nabla_z^2 \nu(z)\right)].$$

Furthermore, if f is convex, we have

$$\nabla^2 \tilde{f}(G) = \mathbb{E}[\nabla f(G + z)\nabla_z \nu(z)^T].$$

Proof. If ν is twice-differentiable, $\nabla \mu = -\mu \cdot \nabla \nu$ and $\nabla^2 \mu = \left(\nabla \nu \nabla \nu^T - \nabla^2 \nu\right)\mu$. Plugging these in (8.11) and using the substitution $z = \tilde{G} - G$ immediately gives the first two claims of the lemma. For the last claim, we first directly differentiate the expression for $\nabla \tilde{f}$ in (8.12) by swapping the expectation and gradient. This is justified because f is convex (and is hence differentiable almost everywhere) and μ is absolutely continuous w.r.t. Lebesgue measure everywhere (Bertsekas, 1973, Proposition 2.3). □

Let $\mathcal{D}$ be a probability distribution over $\mathbb{R}^N$ with a well-defined density everywhere. Consider the GBPA run with a stochastic smoothing of the baseline potential:

$$\forall t, \widetilde{\Phi}_t(G) = \widetilde{\Phi}(G; \mathcal{D}_{\eta_t}) = \mathbb{E}_{z \sim \mathcal{D}}\left[\max_{w \in \mathcal{X}} \langle w, G + \eta_t z\rangle\right]. \tag{8.13}$$

Then, from the convexity of $G \mapsto \max_{w \in \mathcal{X}} \langle w, G + \eta_t z\rangle$ (for any fixed z), we can swap the expectation and gradient (Bertsekas, 1973, Proposition 2.2) and evaluate the gradient at $G = G_{t-1}$ to obtain

$$\nabla \widetilde{\Phi}_t(G_{t-1}) = \mathbb{E}_{z \sim \mathcal{D}}\left[\underset{w \in \mathcal{X}}{\operatorname{argmax}} \langle w, G_{t-1} + \eta_t z\rangle\right]. \tag{8.14}$$

Taking a single random sample of argmax inside expectation is equivalent to the decision rule of FTPL (Hannan, 1957; Kalai and Vempala, 2005); the

GBPA on a stochastically smoothed potential can thus be seen as playing the *expected action* of FTPL. Since the learner gets a linear reward in online linear optimization, the regret of the GBPA on a stochastically smoothed potential is equal to the *expected regret* of FTPL. For this reason, we will use the terms FTPL and GBPA with stochastic smoothing interchangably.

8.3.3 Connection between FTPL and FTRL via Duality

We have been discussing a method of smoothing out an objective (potential) function by taking the average value of the objective over a set of nearby "perturbed" points. Another more direct method of smoothing the objective function is via a regularization penalty. We can define the *regularized potential* as follows:

$$\widetilde{\Phi}(G) = \mathcal{R}^\star(G) = \max_{w \in \mathcal{X}} \{ \langle w, G \rangle - \mathcal{R}(w) \} \tag{8.15}$$

where $\mathcal{R} : \mathcal{X} \to \mathbb{R}$ is some strictly convex function. This technique has been referred to as "inf-conv" smoothing of Φ with $\mathcal{R}^*$. The connection between regularization and smoothing is further developed by Abernethy et al. (2014), and the terminology draws from the work of Beck and Teboulle (2012) among others. The class of FTRL algorithms can be viewed precisely as an instance of GBPA where the potential is chosen according to Eqn. (8.15). This follows because of the following fact, which is a standard result of Fenchel duality:

$$\nabla f^\star(\theta) = \arg\max_x \langle x, \theta \rangle - f(x), \tag{8.16}$$

under the condition that f is differentiable and strictly convex (Rockafellar, 1997). In other words, if we consider $f(\cdot)$ to be the regularizer for an FTRL function, then solution to the FTRL objective corresponds directly with the gradient of the potential function $f^\star(\cdot)$.

Now that we have see that FTRL and FTPL can be viewed as a certain type of smoothing operation, a natural question one might ask is: to what extent are stochastic smoothing and inf-conv smoothing related? That is, can we view FTRL and FTPL as really two sides of the same coin? The answer here is "partially yes" and "partially no":

1. When $\mathcal{X}$ is 1-dimensional then (nearly) every instance of FTRL can be seen as a special case of FTPL, and vice versa. In other words, stochastic smoothing and inf-conv smoothing are effectively one and the same, and we describe this equivalence in detail below.

2. For problems of dimension larger than 1, every instance of FTPL can be described as an instance of FTRL. More precisely, if we have a distribution $\mathcal{D}_\eta$ which leads to a stochastically smoothed potential $\widetilde{\Phi}(\cdot) = \widetilde{\Phi}(\cdot; \mathcal{D}_\eta)$, then we can always write the gradient of $\widetilde{\Phi}(\cdot)$ as the solution of an FTRL optimization. That is,

$$\nabla\widetilde{\Phi}(G, \mathcal{D}_\eta) = \arg\max_{x\in\mathcal{X}}\langle x, \theta\rangle - \mathcal{R}(x) \quad \text{where} \quad \mathcal{R}(x) := \widetilde{\Phi}^\star(x), \quad (8.17)$$

and we recall that $\widetilde{\Phi}^\star$ denotes the Fenchel Conjugate. In other words, the perturbation $\mathcal{D}$ induces an implicit regularizer defined as the cojugate of $\mathbb{E}_{z\sim\mathcal{D}}[\max_{g\in\mathcal{X}}\langle g, G\rangle]$

3. In general, however, stochastic smoothing is not as general as inf-conv smoothing. FTPL is in some sense less general than FTRL, as there are examples of regularizers that can not be "induced" via a specific perturbation. One particular case is given by Hofbauer and Sandholm (2002).

We now given a brief description of the equivalence between stochastic smoothing and inf-conv smoothing for the 1-dimensional case.

On the near-equivalence between FTRL and FTPL in one dimension. Consider a one-dimensional online linear optimization prediction problem where the player chooses an action w_t from $\mathcal{X} = [0, 1]$ and the adversary chooses a reward g_t from $\mathcal{Y} = [0, 1]$. This can be interpreted as a two-expert setting; the player's action $w_t \in \mathcal{X}$ is the probability of following the first expert and g_t is the net excess reward of the first expert over the second. The baseline potential for this setting is $\widetilde{\Phi}(G) = \max_{w\in[0,1]} wG$.

Let us consider an instance of FTPL with a continuous distribution $\mathcal{D}$ whose cumulative density function (cdf) is $F_\mathcal{D}$. Let $\widetilde{\Phi}$ be the smoothed potential function (Equation 8.13) with distribution $\mathcal{D}$. Its derivative is

$$\widetilde{\Phi}'(G) = \mathbb{E}[\arg\max_{w\in\mathcal{Y}} w(G + u)] = \mathbb{P}[u > -G] \quad (8.18)$$

because the maximizer is unique with probability 1. Notice, crucially, that the derivative $\widetilde{\Phi}'(G)$ is exactly the expected solution of our FTPL instance. Moreover, by differentiating it again, we see that the second derivative of $\widetilde{\Phi}$ at G is exactly the pdf of $\mathcal{D}$ evaluated at $(-G)$.

We can now precisely define the mapping from FTPL to FTRL. Our goal is to find a convex regularization function $\mathcal{R}$ such that $\mathbb{P}(u > -G) = \arg\max_{w\in\mathcal{X}} (wG - \mathcal{R}(w))$. Since this is a one-dimensional convex optimization problem, we can differentiate for the solution. The characterization of

$\mathcal{R}$ is:

$$\mathcal{R}(w) - \mathcal{R}(0) = -\int_0^w F_{\mathcal{D}}^{-1}(1 - z)\mathrm{d}z. \tag{8.19}$$

Note that the cdf $F_{\mathcal{D}}(\cdot)$ is indeed invertible since it is a strictly increasing function.

The inverse mapping is just as straightforward. Given a regularization function $\mathcal{R}$ well-defined over $[0, 1]$, we can always construct its Fenchel conjugate $\mathcal{R}^\star(G) = \sup_{w \in \mathcal{X}} \langle w, G \rangle - \mathcal{R}(w)$. The derivative of $\mathcal{R}^\star$ is an increasing convex function, whose infimum is 0 at $G = -\infty$ and supremum is 1 at $G = +\infty$. Hence, $\mathcal{R}^\star$ defines a cdf, and an easy calculation shows that this perturbation distribution exactly reproduces FTRL corresponding to $\mathcal{R}$.

8.4 Generic Bounds

In this section, we show how the general result in Corollary 8.3, combined with stochastic smoothing results from the existing literature, painlessly yield regret bounds for two generic settings: one in which the learner/adversary sets are bounded in ℓ_1/ℓ_∞ norms and another in which they are bounded in the standard Euclidean (i.e., ℓ_2) norm.

8.4.1 ℓ_1/ℓ_∞ Geometry

With slight abuse of notation, we will use $\|\mathcal{X}\|$ to denote $\sup_{x \in \mathcal{X}} \|x\|$ where $\|\cdot\|$ is a norm and $\mathcal{X}$ is a set of vectors.

Theorem 8.6. *Consider GBPA run with a potential* $\widetilde{\Phi}_t(G) = \widetilde{\Phi}(G; \mathcal{D}_\eta)$ *where* $\mathcal{D}$ *is the uniform distribution on the unit* ℓ_∞ *ball. Then we have,*

$$\text{Regret} \leq \frac{1}{2\eta}T\|\mathcal{X}\|_\infty\|\mathcal{Y}\|_1^2 + \eta\frac{\|\mathcal{X}\|_\infty N}{2}. \tag{8.20}$$

Choosing η *to optimize the bound gives* $\text{Regret} \leq \|\mathcal{X}\|_\infty\|\mathcal{Y}\|_1\sqrt{NT}$.

Proof. The baseline potential function Φ is $\|\mathcal{X}\|_\infty$-Lipschitz with respect to $\|\cdot\|_1$. Also note that $\|g_t\|_1 \leq \|\mathcal{Y}\|_1$. Now, by Corollary 8.3, it suffices to prove that the stochastic smoothing of Φ with the uniform distribution on the unit ℓ_∞ ball is an η-smoothing with parameters

$$\left(\frac{\|\mathcal{X}\|_\infty N}{2}, \|\mathcal{X}\|_\infty, \|\cdot\|_1\right). \tag{8.21}$$

These smoothing parameters have been shown to hold by Duchi et al. (2012, Lemma E.1). □

FTPL with perturbations drawn from the uniform distribution over the hypercube was considered by Kalai and Vempala (2005). The above theorem gives essentially the same result as their Theorem 1.1(a). The proof above not only uses our general smoothing based analysis but also yields better constants.

8.4.2 Euclidean Geometry

In this section, we will use a generic property of Gaussian smoothing to derive a regret bound that holds for any arbitrary online linear optimization problem.

Theorem 8.7. *Consider GBPA run with a potential $\widetilde{\Phi}_t(G) = \widetilde{\Phi}(G; \mathcal{D}_\eta)$ where $\mathcal{D}$ is the uniform distribution on the unit ℓ_2 ball. Then we have,*

$$\text{Regret} \leq \frac{1}{2\eta}T\sqrt{N}\|\mathcal{X}\|_2\|\mathcal{Y}\|_2^2 + \eta\|\mathcal{X}\|_2. \tag{8.22}$$

If we choose $\mathcal{D}$ to be the standard multivariate Gaussian distribution, then we have,

$$\text{Regret} \leq \frac{1}{2\eta}T\|\mathcal{X}\|_2\|\mathcal{Y}\|_2^2 + \eta\sqrt{N}\|\mathcal{X}\|_2. \tag{8.23}$$

In either case, optimizing over η we get $\text{Regret} \leq \|\mathcal{X}\|_2\|\mathcal{Y}\|_2 N^{1/4}\sqrt{2T}$.

Proof. The baseline potential function Φ is $\|\mathcal{X}\|_2$-Lipschitz with respect to $\|\cdot\|_2$. Also note that $\|g_t\|_2 \leq \|\mathcal{Y}\|_2$. Duchi et al. (2012, Lemma E.2) show that the stochastic smoothing of Φ with the uniform distribution on the Euclidean unit ball is an η-smoothing with parameters

$$\left(\|\mathcal{X}\|_2, \|\mathcal{X}\|_2\sqrt{N}, \|\cdot\|_1\right). \tag{8.24}$$

Further, Duchi et al. (2012, Lemma E.3) shows that the stochastic smoothing of Φ with the standard Gaussian distribution is an η-smoothing with parameters

$$\left(\|\mathcal{X}\|_2\sqrt{N}, \|\mathcal{X}\|_2, \|\cdot\|_1\right). \tag{8.25}$$

The result now follows from Corollary 8.3. □

We are not aware of a previous result for FTPL of generality comparable to Theorem 8.7 above. However, Rakhlin et al. (2012) prove a regret bound for $4\sqrt{2}\sqrt{T}$ when $\mathcal{X}, \mathcal{Y}$ are unit balls of the ℓ_2 norm. Their FTPL algorithm, however, draws $T - t$ samples from the uniform distribution over the unit *sphere*. In contrast, we will show that, for this special case, a dimension independent $O(\sqrt{T})$ bound can be obtained via an FTPL algorithm using a single Gaussian perturbation per time step (see Theorem 8.10 below).

8.5 Experts Setting

Now we apply the GBPA analysis framework to the classical online learning problem of the *hedge setting*, or often referred to as *prediction with expert advice*[2]. Here we assume a learner is presented with a set of fixed actions, and on each round must (randomly) select one such action. Upon commiting to her choice, the learner then receives a vector of gains (or losses), one for each action, where the ith gain (loss) value is the reward (cost) for selecting action i. The learner's objective is to continually update the sampling distribution over actions in order to accumulate an expected gain (loss) that is not much worse than the gain (loss) of the optimal fixed action.

The important piece to note about this setting is that it may be cast as an instance of an OLO problem. To see this, we set $\mathcal{X} = \Delta^N \overset{\text{def}}{=} \{w \in \mathbb{R}^N : \sum_i w_i = 1, w_i \geq 0 \; \forall i\}$, the N-dimensional probability simplex, and we set $\mathcal{Y} = \{g \in \mathbb{R}^N : \|g\|_\infty \leq 1\}$, a set of bounded gain vectors. We may define the baseline potential function therefore as

$$\Phi(G) = \max_{w \in \mathcal{X}} \langle w, G \rangle = \max_{i=1,\dots,N} G_i = G_{i^*(G)} \tag{8.26}$$

where $i^*(G) := \min\{i : G_i = \max_j G_j\}$ (We need the outer $\min\{\cdot\}$ to define i^* in order to handle possible ties; in such cases we select the lowest index). In our framework we have used language of maximizing gain, in contrast to the more common theme of minimizing loss. However, the loss-only setting can be easily obtained by simply changing the domain $\mathcal{Y}$ to contain only vectors with negative-valued coordinates.

---

2. The use of the term "expert" is historical and derives from an early version of the problem where one was given advice (a prediction) from a set of experts (Littlestone and Warmuth, 1994), and the learner's goal is to aggregate this advice. In the version we discuss here, proposed by Freund (1997), a more appropriate intuition is to imagine the task of choosing among a set of "actions" that each receive a "gain" or "loss" on every round.

8.5.1 The Exponential Weights Algorithm, and the Equivalence of Entropy Regularization and Gumbel Perturbation

The most well-known and widely used algorithm in the experts setting is the *Exponential Weights Algorithm* (EWA), often referred to as the *Multiplicative Weights Algorithm* and strongly related to the classical *Weighted Majority Algorithm* (Littlestone and Warmuth, 1994). On round t, EWA specifies a set of unnormalized weights based on the cumulative gains thus far,

$$\tilde{w}_{t,i} := \exp(\eta G_{t-1,i}) \qquad i = 1, \ldots, N, \tag{8.27}$$

where $\eta > 0$ is a parameter. The learner's distribution on this round is then obtained by normalizing $\tilde{w}_t$

$$w_{t,i} := \frac{\tilde{w}_{t,i}}{\sum_{j=1}^{N} \tilde{w}_{t,j}} \qquad i = 1, \ldots, N. \tag{8.28}$$

More recent perspectives of EWA have relied on an alternative interpretation via an optimization problem. Indeed the weights obtained in Eqn. 8.28 can be equivalently obtained as follows,

$$w_t = \operatorname*{argmax}_{w \in \Delta^N} \left\{ \langle \eta G_{t-1}, w \rangle - \sum_{i=1}^{N} w_i \log w_i \right\}. \tag{8.29}$$

We have cast the exponential weights algorithm as an instance of FTRL where the regularization function $\mathcal{R}$ corresponds to the *negative entropy function*, $\mathcal{R}(w) := \sum_i w_i \log w_i$. Applying Lemma 8.2 one can show that EWA obtains a regret of order $\sqrt{T \log N}$.

A third interpretation of EWA is obtained via the notion of stochastic smoothing (perturbations) using the *Gumbel distribution*:

$$\mu(z) := e^{-(z + e^{-z})} \qquad \text{is the PDF of the standard Gumbel; and}$$

$$\Pr(Z \leq z) = e^{-e^{-z}} \qquad \text{is the CDF of the standard Gumbel.}$$

The Gumbel distribution has several natural properties, including for example that it is *max-stable*: the maximum value of several Gumbel-distributed random variables is itself distributed according to a Gumbel distribution[3]. But another nice fact is that the distribution of the maximizer of N fixed values perturbed with Gumbel noise leads to an exponentially-weighted distribution. Precisely, if we have a values $v_1, \ldots, v_N$, and we draw n IID sam-

---

3. Above we only defined the standard Gumbel, but in general the Gumbel has both a scaling and shift parameter.

ples $Z_1, \ldots, Z_N$ from the standard Gumbel, then a straightforward calculus exercise gives that

$$\Pr\left[v_i + Z_i = \max_{j=1,\ldots,N} \{v_j + Z_j\}\right] = \frac{\exp(v_i)}{\sum_{j=1,\ldots,N} \exp(v_j)} \qquad i = 1, \ldots, N \quad (8.30)$$

What we have just arrived at is that EWA is indeed an instance of FTPL with Gumbel-distributed noise. This was described by Adam Kalai in personal communication, and later Warmuth (2009) expanded it into a short note available online. However, the result appears to be folklore in the area of probabilistic choice models, and it is mentioned briefly by Hofbauer and Sandholm (2002).

8.5.2 Experts Bounds via Laplacian, Gaussian, and Gumbel Smoothing

We will now apply our stochastic smoothing analysis to derive bounds on a class of algorithms for the Experts Setting using three different perturbations: the *Exponential, Gaussian,* and *Gumbel*. The latter noise distribution generates an algorithm which is equivalent to EWA, as discussed above, but we prove the same bound using new tools. Note, however that we use a mean-zero Gumbel whereas the standard Gumbel has mean 1.

The key lemma for the GBPA analysis is Lemma 8.2, which decomposes the regret into overestimation, underestimation, and divergence penalty. By Lemma 8.4, the underestimation is less than or equal to 0 and the overestimation penalty is upper-bounded by $\mathbb{E}_{z \sim \mathcal{D}}\left[\max_{i=1,\ldots,N} z_i\right]$. This expectation for commonly used distributions $\mathcal{D}$ is well-studied in extreme value theory.

In order to upper bound the divergence penalty, it is convenient to analyze the Hessian matrix, which has a nice structure in the experts setting. We will be especially interested in bounding the trace of this Hessian.

Lemma 8.8. *Let Φ be the baseline potential for the N-experts setting, and $\mathcal{D}$ be a continuous distribution with a differentiable probability density function. We will consider the potential $\widetilde{\Phi}(G) = \widetilde{\Phi}(G; \mathcal{D}_\eta)$. If for some constant β we have a bound $\mathrm{Tr}(\nabla^2 \widetilde{\Phi}(G)) \leq \beta/\eta$ for every G, then it follows that*

$$D_{\widetilde{\Phi}}(G + g, G) \leq \beta \|g\|_\infty^2 / \eta. \tag{8.31}$$

Proof. The Hessian exists because μ is differentiable (Equation 8.11). Let H denote the Hessian matrix of the stochastic smoothing of Φ, i.e., $H(\cdot) = \nabla^2 \widetilde{\Phi}(\cdot; \mathcal{D}_\eta)$. First we claim two properties on H:

1. Diagonal entries are non-negative and off diagonal entries are non-positive.

2. Each row or column sums up to 0.

All diagonal entries of H are non-negative because $\widetilde{\Phi}$ is convex. Note that $\nabla_i \widetilde{\Phi}$ is the probability that the i-th coordinate of $G + z$ is the maximum coordinate, and an increase in the j-th of G where $j \neq i$ cannot increase that probability; hence, the off-diagonal entries of H are non-positive. To prove the second claim, note that the gradient $\nabla \widetilde{\Phi}$ is a probability vector, whose coordinates always sum up to 1. Thus, each row (or each column) must sum up to 0.

By Taylor's theorem in the mean-value form, we have $D_{\widetilde{\Phi}}(G + g, G) = \frac{1}{2} g^T \nabla^2 \widetilde{\Phi}(\tilde{G}) g$ where $\tilde{G}$ is some convex combination on G and $G + g$. Now we have

$$D_{\widetilde{\Phi}}(G + g, G) \leq \frac{1}{2} \|\nabla^2 \widetilde{\Phi}(\tilde{G})\|_{\infty \to 1} \|g\|_\infty^2, \tag{8.32}$$

where $\|M\|_{\infty \to 1} := \sup_{u \neq 0} \|Mv\|_1 / \|v\|_\infty$. Finally note that, for any M, $\|M\|_{\infty \to 1} \leq \sum_{i,j} |M_{i,j}|$. We can now conclude the proof by noting that the sum of absolute values of the entries of $\nabla^2 \widetilde{\Phi}(\tilde{G})$ is upper bounded by twice its trace given the two properties of the Hessian above. $\square$

The above result will be very convenient in proving bounds on the divergence penalty associated with different noise distributions. In particular, assume we have a noise distribution with exponential form, then IID sample $z = (z_1, \ldots, z_n)$ has density $\mu(z) \propto \prod_i \exp(-\nu(z_i))$. Now applying Lemma 8.5 we have a nice expression for the diagonal Hessian values:

$$
\begin{aligned}
\nabla_{ii}^2 \widetilde{\Phi}(G; \mathcal{D}_\eta) &= \frac{1}{\eta} \mathop{\mathbb{E}}_{(z_1, \ldots, z_n) \sim \mu} \left[\nabla_i \Phi(G + \eta z) \frac{d}{dz_i} \nu(z_i) \right] \\
&= \frac{1}{\eta} \mathop{\mathbb{E}}_{(z_1, \ldots, z_n) \sim \mu} \left[\mathbf{1}\{i = i^*(G + \eta z)\} \frac{d\nu(z_i)}{dz_i} \right].
\end{aligned} \tag{8.33}
$$

The above formula now gives us a natural bound on the trace of the Hessian for the three distributions of interest.

▪ **Laplace:** For this distribution we have $\nu(z) = |z| \implies \frac{d\nu(z)}{dz} = \text{sign}(z)$, where the sign function returns $+1$ if the argument is positive, -1 if the argument is negative, and 0 otherwise. Then we have

$$
\begin{aligned}
\text{Tr}(\nabla^2 \widetilde{\Phi}(G)) &= \frac{1}{\eta} \mathop{\mathbb{E}}_{(z_1, \ldots, z_n) \sim \mu} \left[\sum_{i=1}^N \mathbf{1}\{i = i^*(G + \eta z)\} \frac{d\nu(z_i)}{dz_i} \right] \\
&= \frac{1}{\eta} \mathop{\mathbb{E}}_z \left[\sum_{i=1}^N \mathbf{1}\{i = i^*(G + \eta z)\} \text{sign}(z_i) \right] \\
&\leq \frac{1}{\eta} \mathop{\mathbb{E}}_z \left[\sum_{i=1}^N \mathbf{1}\{i = i^*(G + \eta z)\} \right] = \frac{1}{\eta}.
\end{aligned}
$$

- **Gumbel:** Here, using zero-mean Gumbel, we have $\nu(z) = z + 1 + e^{-z-1} \implies \frac{d\nu(z)}{dz} = 1 - e^{-z-1}$. Applying the same arguments we obtain

$$\mathrm{Tr}(\nabla^2 \widetilde{\Phi}(G)) = \frac{1}{\eta} \mathbb{E}_z \left[\sum_{i=1}^N \mathbf{1}\{i = i^*(G + \eta z)\}(1 - e^{-z_i - 1}) \right]$$

$$\leq \frac{1}{\eta} \mathbb{E}_z \left[\sum_{i=1}^N \mathbf{1}\{i = i^*(G + \eta z)\} \right] = \frac{1}{\eta}.$$

- **Gaussian:** Here we have $\nu(z) = \frac{z^2}{2} \implies \frac{d\nu(z)}{dz} = z$. Bounding the sum of diagonal Hessian terms requires a slightly different trick:

$$\mathrm{Tr}(\nabla^2 \widetilde{\Phi}(G)) = \frac{1}{\eta} \mathbb{E}_z \left[\sum_{i=1}^N \mathbf{1}\{i = i^*(G + \eta z)\} z_i \right]$$

$$= \frac{1}{\eta} \mathbb{E}_z \left[z_{i^*(G+\eta z)} \right] \leq \frac{1}{\eta} \mathbb{E}_z [\max_i z_i] \leq \frac{\sqrt{2 \log N}}{\eta}.$$

where the last inequality follows according to moment generating function arguments given below.

To obtain regret bounds, all that remains is a bound on the overestimation penalty. As we showed in Lemma 8.4, the overestimation penalty is upper bounded as $\eta \mathbb{E}_{z \sim \mathcal{D}}[\Phi(z)] = \eta \mathbb{E}[\max_i z_i]$. We can bound this quantity using moment generating functions. Let $s > 0$ be some parameter and notice

$$s\mathbb{E}[\max_i z_i] \leq \log \mathbb{E}[\exp(s \max_i z_i)] \leq \log \sum_i \mathbb{E}[\exp(s z_i)] \leq \log N + \log m(s) \quad (8.34)$$

where $m(s)$ is the *moment generating function*[4] (mgf) of the distribution $\mathcal{D}$ (or an upper bound thereof). The statement holds for any positive choice of s in the domain of $m(\cdot)$, hence we have

$$\mathbb{E}_{z \sim \mathcal{D}}[\Phi(z)] \leq \inf_{s > 0} \frac{\log N + \log m(s)}{s}. \quad (8.35)$$

- **Laplace:** The mgf of the standard Laplace is $m(s) = \frac{1}{1-s}$. Choosing $s = \frac{1}{2}$ gives us that $\mathbb{E}[\max_i z_i] \leq 2 \log 2N$.

- **Gumbel:** The mgf of the mean-zero Gumbel is $m(s) = \Gamma(1 - s)e^{-s}$. Choosing $s = 1/2$ gives that $\mathbb{E}[\max_i z_i] \leq 2 \log 2N$ since $m(0.5) < 2$.

- **Gaussian:** The mgf of the standard Gaussian is $m(s) = \exp(s^2/2)$. Choosing $s = \sqrt{2 \log N}$ gives $\mathbb{E}[\max_i z_i] \leq \sqrt{2 \log N}$.

Theorem 8.9. *Let Φ be the baseline potential for the experts setting. Suppose we GBPA run with $\widetilde{\Phi}_t(\cdot) = \widetilde{\Phi}(\cdot; \mathcal{D}_\eta)$ for all t where the mean-zero*

---

4. The mgf of a distribution $\mathcal{D}$ is the function $m(s) := \mathbb{E}_{X \sim \mathcal{D}}[\exp(sX)]$.

distribution $\mathcal{D}$ is such that $\mathbb{E}_{z \sim \mathcal{D}}[\Phi(z)] \leq \alpha$ and $\forall G, \mathrm{Tr}(\nabla^2 \widetilde{\Phi}(G)) \leq \beta/\eta$. Then we have

$$\text{Regret} \leq \eta\alpha + \frac{\beta T}{\eta}. \tag{8.36}$$

Choosing η to optimize the bound gives $\text{Regret} \leq 2\sqrt{\alpha\beta T}$. In particular, for Laplace, (mean-zero) Gumbel and Gaussian perturbations, the regret bound becomes $2\sqrt{2T \log 2N}$, $2\sqrt{2T \log 2N}$ and $2\sqrt{2T \log N}$ respectively.

Proof. Result follows by plugging in bounds into Lemma 8.2. Mean-zero perturbations imply that the underestimation penalty is zero. The overestimation penalty is bounded by $\eta\alpha$ and the divergence penalty is bounded by $\beta T/\eta$ because of Lemma 8.8 and the assumption that $\|g_t\|_\infty \leq 1$. Our calculations above showed that for the Laplace, (mean-zero) Gumbel and Gaussian perturbations, we have $\alpha = 2\log 2N$, $2\log 2N$ and $\sqrt{2\log N}$ respectively. Furthermore, we have $\beta = 1, 1$ and $\sqrt{2\log N}$ respectively. $\square$

8.6   Euclidean Balls Setting

The Euclidean balls setting is where $\mathcal{X} = \mathcal{Y} = \{x \in \mathbb{R}^N : \|x\|_2 \leq 1\}$. The baseline potential function is $\Phi(G) = \max_{w \in \mathcal{X}} \langle w, G \rangle = \|G\|_2$. We show that the GBPA with Gaussian smoothing achieves a minimax optimal regret (Abernethy et al., 2008) up to a constant factor.

Theorem 8.10. *Let Φ be the baseline potential for the Euclidean balls setting. The GBPA run with $\widetilde{\Phi}_t(\cdot) = \widetilde{\Phi}(\cdot; \mathcal{N}(0, I)_{\eta_t})$ for all t has regret at most*

$$\text{Regret} \leq \eta_T \sqrt{N} + \frac{1}{2\sqrt{N}} \sum_{t=1}^T \frac{1}{\eta_t} \|g_t\|_2^2. \tag{8.37}$$

If the algorithm selects $\eta_t = \sqrt{\sum_{s=1}^T \|g_s\|_2^2/(2N)}$ for all t, we have

$$\text{Regret} \leq \sqrt{2 \sum_{t=1}^T \|g_t\|_2^2}. \tag{8.38}$$

If the algorithm selects η_t adaptively according to $\eta_t = \sqrt{(1 + \sum_{s=1}^{t-1} \|g_s\|_2^2))/N}$, we have

$$\text{Regret} \leq 2\sqrt{1 + \sum_{t=1}^T \|g_t\|_2^2} \tag{8.39}$$

Proof. The proof is mostly similar to that of Theorem 8.9. In order to apply Lemma 8.2, we need to upper bound (i) the overestimation and underestimation penalty, and (ii) the Bregman divergence.

The Gaussian smoothing always overestimates a convex function, so it suffices to bound the overestimation penalty. Furthermore, it suffices to consider the fixed η_t case due to Lemma 8.1. The overestimation penalty can be upper-bounded as follows:

$$\widetilde{\Phi}_T(0) - \widetilde{\Phi}(0) = \mathbb{E}_{u \sim \mathcal{N}(0,I)} \|G + \eta_T u\|_2 - \|G\|_2$$
$$\leq \eta_T \mathbb{E}_{u \sim \mathcal{N}(0,I)} \|u\|_2 \leq \eta_T \sqrt{\mathbb{E}_{u \sim \mathcal{N}(0,I)} \|u\|_2^2} = \eta_T \sqrt{N}.$$

The first inequality is from the triangle inequality, and the second inequality is from the concavity of the square root.

For the divergence penalty, note that the upper bound on $\max_{v:\|g\|_2=1} g^T (\nabla^2 \widetilde{\Phi}) g$ is exactly the maximum eigenvalue of the Hessian, which we bound in Lemma 8.11. The final step is to apply Lemma 8.1. $\qquad\square$

Lemma 8.11. *Let Φ be the baseline potential for the Euclidean balls setting. Then, for all $G \in \mathbb{R}^N$ and $\eta > 0$, the Hessian matrix of the Gaussian smoothed potential satisfies*

$$\nabla^2 \widetilde{\Phi}(G; \mathcal{N}(0,I)_\eta) \preceq \frac{1}{\eta \sqrt{N}} I. \tag{8.40}$$

Proof. The Hessian of the Euclidean norm $\nabla^2 \Phi(G) = \|G\|_2^{-1} I - \|G\|_2^{-3} G G^T$ diverges near $G = 0$. Expectedly, the maximum curvature is at origin even after Gaussian smoothing (See Appendix 8.8.1). So, it suffices to prove

$$\nabla^2 \widetilde{\Phi}(0) = \mathbb{E}_{u \sim \mathcal{N}(0,I)}[\|u\|_2 (uu^T - I)] \preceq \sqrt{\frac{1}{N}} I, \tag{8.41}$$

where the Hessian expression is from Lemma 8.5.

By symmetry, all off-diagonal elements of the Hessian are 0. Let $Y = \|u\|^2$, which is Chi-squared with N degrees of freedom. So,

$$\mathrm{Tr}(\mathbb{E}[\|u\|_2 (uu^T - I)]) = \mathbb{E}[\mathrm{Tr}(\|u\|_2 (uu^T - I))] = \mathbb{E}[\|u\|_2^3 - N\|u\|_2]$$
$$= \mathbb{E}[Y^{\frac{3}{2}}] - N\mathbb{E}[Y^{\frac{1}{2}}]$$

Using the Chi-squared moment formula (Simon, 2002, p. 13):

$$\mathbb{E}[Y^k] = \frac{2^k \Gamma(\frac{N}{2} + k)}{\Gamma(\frac{N}{2})}, \tag{8.42}$$

the above becomes:

$$\frac{2^{\frac{3}{2}} \Gamma(\frac{3}{2} + \frac{N}{2})}{\Gamma(\frac{N}{2})} - \frac{N 2^{\frac{1}{2}} \Gamma(\frac{1}{2} + \frac{N}{2})}{\Gamma(\frac{N}{2})} = \frac{\sqrt{2} \Gamma(\frac{1}{2} + \frac{N}{2})}{\Gamma(\frac{N}{2})}. \tag{8.43}$$

From the log-convexity of the Gamma function,

$$\log \Gamma \left(\tfrac{1}{2} + \tfrac{N}{2} \right) \leq \tfrac{1}{2} \left(\log \Gamma \left(\tfrac{N}{2} \right) + \log \Gamma \left(\tfrac{N}{2} + 1 \right) \right) = \log \Gamma \left(\tfrac{N}{2} \right) \sqrt{\tfrac{N}{2}}. \quad (8.44)$$

Exponentiating both sides, we obtain

$$\Gamma \left(\tfrac{1}{2} + \tfrac{N}{2} \right) \leq \Gamma \left(\tfrac{N}{2} \right) \sqrt{\tfrac{N}{2}}, \quad (8.45)$$

which we apply to Equation 8.43 and get $\mathrm{Tr}(\nabla^2 \widetilde{\Phi}(0)) \leq \sqrt{N}$. To complete the proof, note that by symmetry, each entry must have the same expected value, and hence it is bounded by $\sqrt{1/N}$. $\qquad \square$

8.7 The Multi-Armed Bandit Setting

Let us introduce the adversarial multi-armed bandit (MAB) setting. The MAB problem is a variation of the loss-only experts setting (Section 8.5) with $\mathcal{X} = \Delta^N$ and $\mathcal{Y} = [-1, 0]^N$. The two main differences are that (a) that learner is required to playing randomly, sampling an action $i_t \in \{1, \ldots, N\}$ according to w_t and then suffering loss/gain g_{t,i_t}, and (b) the learner then observes *only the scalar value* g_{t,i_t}, she receives no information regarding the losses/gains for the unplayed actions, i.e. the values $g_{t,j}$ for $j \neq i_t$ remain unobserved. Note that, while g_t is assumed to take only negative values, we will continue to refer to these quantities as *gains*.

This limited-information feedback makes the bandit problem much more challenging than the full-information setting we studied in Section 8.5, where the learner was given the entire g_t on each round. In the adversarial MAB problem the learner is indeed required to play randomly; it can be shown that a deterministic strategy will lead to linear regret in the worst case. Hence our focus will be on the *expected* regret over the learner's randomization, and we will assume that the sequence of gains are fixed in advance and thus non-random. While the present book chapter will explore this area, other work has considered the problem of obtaining high-probability bounds (Auer et al., 2003), as well as bounds that are robust to adaptive adversaries (Abernethy and Rakhlin, 2009).

The MAB framework is not only mathematically elegant, but useful for a wide range of applications including medical experiment design (Gittins, 1996), automated poker playing strategies (Van den Broeck et al., 2009), and hyperparameter tuning (Pacula et al., 2012). For the survey of work on MAB, see Bubeck and Cesa-Bianchi (2012).

8.7.1 Gradient-Based Prediction Algorithms for the Multi-Armed Bandit

We give a generic template for constructing MAB strategies in Algorithm 2, and we emphasize that this template can be viewed as a bandit reduction to the (full information) GBPA framework. Randomization is used for making decisions and for *estimating* the losses via importance sampling.

Algorithm 2: GBPA Template for Multi-Armed Bandits.

Require: fixed convex potential $\widetilde{\Phi} : \mathbb{R}^N \to \mathbb{R}$, with $\nabla \widetilde{\Phi} \subset \text{interior}(\Delta^N)$.
Require: Adversary selects (hidden) seq. of loss vectors $g_1, \ldots, g_T \in [-1, 0]^N$
Initialize: $\hat{G}_0 = 0$
for $t = 1$ to T **do**

   Sampling: Learner chooses i_t according to dist. $p(\hat{G}_{t-1}) = \nabla \widetilde{\Phi}(\hat{G}_{t-1})$
   Cost: Learner "gains" g_{t,i_t}, and observes this value
   Estimation: Learner produces estimate of gain vector, $\hat{g}_t := \frac{g_{t,i_t}}{p_{i_t}(\hat{G}_{t-1})} \mathbf{e}_{i_t}$
   Update: $\hat{G}_t = \hat{G}_{t-1} + \hat{g}_t$

Nearly all proposed methods have relied on this particular algorithmic blueprint. For example, the EXP3 algorithm of Auer et al. (2003) proposed a more advanced version of the Exponential Weights Algorithm (discussed in Section 8.5) to set the sampling distribution $p(\hat{G}_{t-1})$, where the only real modification is to include a small probability of uniformly sampling the arms.[5] But EXP3 more or less fits the template we propose in Algorithm 2 when we select $\widetilde{\Phi}(\cdot) = \mathbb{E}_{z \sim \text{Gumbel}} \Phi(G + \eta z)$. We elaborated on the connection between EWA and Gumbel perturbations in Section 8.5.

Lemma 8.12. *The baseline potential for this setting is $\Phi(G) \equiv \max_i G_i$ so that we can write the expected regret of GBPA($\widetilde{\Phi}$) as*

$$\mathbb{E}\text{Regret}_T = \Phi(G_T) - \mathbb{E}[\sum_{t=1}^{T} \langle \nabla \widetilde{\Phi}(\hat{G}_{t-1}), g_t \rangle]. \tag{8.46}$$

---

5. One of the conclusions we may draw from this section is that the uniform sampling of EXP3 is not necessary when we are only interested in expected-regret bounds and we focus on negative gains (that is, where $\hat{g}_t \in [-1, 0]^N$). It has been suggested that the uniform sampling may be necessary in the case of positive gains, although this point has not been resolved to the authors' knowledge.

Then, the expected regret of GBPA($\widetilde{\Phi}$) can be written as:

$$\mathbb{E}\mathrm{Regret}_T \leq \mathbb{E}_{i_1,\dots,i_T}\left[\underbrace{\Phi(\hat{G}_T) - \widetilde{\Phi}(\hat{G}_T)}_{\text{underestimation penalty}} + \sum_{t=1}^{T}\underbrace{\mathbb{E}_{i_t}[D_{\widetilde{\Phi}}(\hat{G}_t, \hat{G}_{t-1})|\hat{G}_{t-1}]}_{\text{divergence penalty}}\right]$$

$$+ \underbrace{\widetilde{\Phi}(0) - \Phi(0)}_{\text{overestimation penalty}} \tag{8.47}$$

where the expectations are over the sampling of $i_t, t = 1, \dots, T$.

Proof. Let $\widetilde{\Phi}$ be a valid convex function for GBPA. Consider GBPA($\widetilde{\Phi}$) run on the loss sequence $g_1, \dots, g_T$. The algorithm produces a sequence of estimated losses $\hat{g}_1, \dots, \hat{g}_T$. Now consider GBPA-FI($\widetilde{\Phi}$), which is GBPA($\widetilde{\Phi}$) run with the full information on the deterministic loss sequence $\hat{g}_1, \dots, \hat{g}_T$ (there is no estimation step, and the learner updates $\hat{G}_t$ directly). The regret of this run can be written as

$$\Phi(\hat{G}_T) - \sum_{t=1}^{T}\langle \nabla\widetilde{\Phi}(\hat{G}_{t-1}), \hat{g}_t\rangle \tag{8.48}$$

and $\Phi(G_T) \leq \mathbb{E}[\Phi(\hat{G}_T)]$ by the convexity of Φ. $\qquad\square$

8.7.2   Implementation of Perturbation Methods

It is clear that $\nabla\widetilde{\Phi}$ is in the probability simplex, and note that

$$\frac{\partial\widetilde{\Phi}}{\partial G_i} = \mathbb{E}_{Z_1,\dots,Z_N}\mathbf{1}\{G_i + Z_i > G_j + Z_j, \forall j \neq i\}$$

$$= \mathbb{E}_{\tilde{G}_{j^*}}[\mathbb{P}_{Z_i}[Z_i > \tilde{G}_{j^*} - G_i]] = \mathbb{E}_{\tilde{G}_{j^*}}[1 - F(\tilde{G}_{j^*} - G_i)] \tag{8.49}$$

where $\tilde{G}_{j^*} = \max_{j\neq i} G_j + Z_j$ and F is the cdf of Z_i. The unbounded support condition guarantees that this partial derivative is non-zero for all i given any G. So, $\widetilde{\Phi}(G; \mathcal{D})$ satisfies the requirements of Algorithm 2.

The sampling step of the bandit GBPA (Framework 2) with a stochastically smoothed function (Equation 8.13) can be implemented efficiently: we need not evaluate the full expectation (Equation 8.14) and instead rely on but a single random sample. On the other hand, the estimation step is challenging since generally there is no closed-form expression[6] for $\nabla\widetilde{\Phi}$.

To address this issue, Neu and Bartók (2013) proposed Geometric Resampling (GR). GR uses an iterative resampling process to estimate $\nabla\widetilde{\Phi}$.

---

6. A case where we find a natural closed form solution occurs when the perturbation is chosen to be Gumbel, as we know this corresponds to the EXP3 algorithm which relies on exponential weighting of $\tilde{G}$.

They showed that if we stop after M iterations, the extra regret due to the estimation bias is at most $\frac{NT}{eM}$ (additive term). That is, all our GBPA regret bounds in this section hold for the corresponding FTPL algorithm with an extra additive $\frac{NT}{eM}$ term.. This term, however, does not affect the asymptotic regret rate as long as $M = \sqrt{NT}$, because the lower bound for any algorithm is of the order $\sqrt{NT}$.

8.7.3 Differential Consistency

Recall that for the full information experts setting, if we have a uniform bound on the trace of $\nabla^2 \widetilde{\Phi}$, then we immediately have a finite regret bound. In the bandit setting, however, the regret (Lemma 8.12) involves terms of the form $D_{\widetilde{\Phi}}(\hat{G}_{t-1} + \hat{g}_t, \hat{G}_{t-1})$, where the incremental quantity $\hat{g}_t$ can scale as large as *the inverse of the smallest probability* of $p(\hat{G}_{t-1})$. These inverse probabilities are essentially unavoidable, because unbiased estimates of a quantity that is observed with only probability p must necessarily involve fluctuations that scale as $O(1/p)$.

Therefore, we need a stronger notion of smoothness that counters the $1/p$ factor in $\|\hat{g}_t\|$. We propose the following definition which bounds $\nabla^2 \widetilde{\Phi}$ in correspondence with $\nabla \widetilde{\Phi}$.

Definition 8.3 (Differential Consistency). *For constant $C > 0$, we say that a convex function $f(\cdot)$ is C-differentially-consistent if for all $G \in (-\infty, 0]^N$,*

$$\nabla^2_{ii} f(G) \leq C \nabla_i f(G). \tag{8.50}$$

In other words, the rate in which we decrease p_i should approach 0 as p_i approaches 0. This guarantees that the algorithm reduces the rate of exploration slowly enough. We later show that smoothings obtaining using perturbations with bounded hazard rate satisfy the differential consistency property introduced above (see Lemma 8.15).

We now prove a generic bound that we will use in the following two sections, in order to derive regret guarantees.

Theorem 8.13. *Suppose $\widetilde{\Phi}$ is C-differentially-consistent for constant $C > 0$. Then divergence penalty at time t in Lemma 8.12 can be upper bounded as:*

$$\mathbb{E}_{i_t}[D_{\widetilde{\Phi}}(\hat{G}_t, \hat{G}_{t-1})|\hat{G}_{t-1}] \leq \frac{NC}{2}. \tag{8.51}$$

Proof. For the sake of clarity, we drop the t subscripts on $\hat{G}$ and $\hat{g}$; we use $\hat{G}$ to denote the cumulative estimate $\hat{G}_{t-1}$, $\hat{g}$ to denote the marginal estimate $\hat{g}_t = \hat{G}_t - \hat{G}_{t-1}$, and g to denote the true loss g_t.

Note that by definition of Algorithm 2, $\hat{g}$ is a sparse vector with one non-zero (and negative) coordinate with value $\hat{g}_{i_t} = g_{t,i_t}/\nabla_{i_t}\widetilde{\Phi}(\hat{G})$. Plus, i_t is conditionally independent given $\hat{G}$. Now we can expand the expectation as

$$\mathbb{E}_{i_t}[D_{\widetilde{\Phi}}(\hat{G}+\hat{g},\hat{G})|\hat{G}] = \sum_i \mathbb{P}[i_t = i]\mathbb{E}[D_{\widetilde{\Phi}}(\hat{G}+\hat{g},\hat{G})|\hat{G}, i_t = i]$$

$$= \sum_i \nabla_i\widetilde{\Phi}(\hat{G})\mathbb{E}[D_{\widetilde{\Phi}}(\hat{G}+\hat{g},\hat{G})|\hat{G}, i_t = i]. \quad (8.52)$$

For each term in the sum on the right hand side, the conditional expectation given $\hat{G}$ is now,

$$\mathbb{E}[D_{\widetilde{\Phi}}(\hat{G}+\hat{g},\hat{G})|\hat{G}, i_t = i] = D_{\widetilde{\Phi}}\left(\hat{G}+\frac{g_i}{\nabla_i\widetilde{\Phi}(\hat{G})}\mathbf{e}_i,\hat{G}\right) = \frac{g_i^2}{2(\nabla_i\widetilde{\Phi}(\hat{G}))^2}\nabla_{ii}^2\widetilde{\Phi}(J_i)(8.53)$$

where J_i is some vector on the line segment joining $\hat{G}$ and $\hat{G}+\frac{g_i}{\nabla_i\widetilde{\Phi}(\hat{G})}\mathbf{e}_i$. Using differential consistency, we have $\nabla_{ii}^2\widetilde{\Phi}(J_i) \leq C\nabla_i\widetilde{\Phi}(J_i)$. Note that J_i agrees with $\hat{G}$ in all coordinates except coordinate i where it is at most $\hat{G}_i$. Note that this conclusion depends crucially on the *loss-only assumption* that $g_i \leq 0$. Convexity of $\widetilde{\Phi}$ guarantees that ∇_i is a non-decreasing function of coordinate i. Therefore, $\nabla_i\widetilde{\Phi}(J_i) \leq \nabla_i\widetilde{\Phi}(\hat{G})$. This means that

$$\mathbb{E}[D_{\widetilde{\Phi}}(\hat{G}+\hat{g},\hat{G})|\hat{G}, i_t = i] \leq C\frac{g_i^2}{2(\nabla_i\widetilde{\Phi}(\hat{G}))^2}\nabla_i\widetilde{\Phi}(\hat{G}) \leq \frac{C}{2\nabla_i\widetilde{\Phi}(\hat{G})}, \quad (8.54)$$

since $g_i^2 \leq 1$. Plugging this into (8.52), we get

$$\mathbb{E}_{i_t}[D_{\widetilde{\Phi}}(\hat{G}+\hat{g},\hat{G})|\hat{G}] \leq \sum_i \nabla_i\widetilde{\Phi}(\hat{G})\frac{C}{2\nabla_i\widetilde{\Phi}(\hat{G})} = \frac{NC}{2}. \quad \square \quad (8.55)$$

8.7.4   Hazard Rate Analysis

Despite the fact that perturbation-based multi-armed bandit algorithms provide a natural randomized decision strategy, they have seen little applications mostly because they are hard to analyze. But one should expect general results to be within reach: as we mentioned above, the EXP3 algorithm can be viewed through the lens of perturbations, where the noise is distributed according to the Gumbel distribution. Indeed, an early result of Kujala and Elomaa (2005) showed that a near-optimal MAB strategy comes about through the use of exponentially-distributed noise, and the same perturbation strategy has more recently been utilized in the work of Neu and Bartók (2013) and Kocák et al. (2014). However, a more general understanding of perturbation methods has remained elusive. For example, would Gaussian noise be sufficient for a guarantee? What about, say, the Weibull distribution?

In this section, we show that the performance of the GBPA($\widetilde{\Phi}(G; \mathcal{D})$) can be characterized by the *hazard function* of the smoothing distribution $\mathcal{D}$. The hazard rate is a standard tool in survival analysis to describe failures due to aging; for example, an increasing hazard rate models units that deteriorate with age while a decreasing hazard rate models units that improve with age (a counter intuitive but not illogical possibility). To the best of our knowledge, the connection between hazard rates and design of adversarial bandit algorithms has not been made before.

Definition 8.4 (Hazard rate function). *Assume we are given a distribution $\mathcal{D}$ whose PDF is given by f and whose CDF is given by F. The hazard rate function of $\mathcal{D}$ is*

$$h_{\mathcal{D}}(x) := \frac{f(x)}{1 - F(x)}. \tag{8.56}$$

We will write $\sup h_{\mathcal{D}}$ to mean the supremal value obtained by $h_{\mathcal{D}}$ on its domain; we drop the subscript $\mathcal{D}$ when it is clear.

For the rest of the section, we assume that $F(x) < 1$ for all finite x, so that $h_{\mathcal{D}}$ is well-defined everywhere. This assumption is for the clarity of presentation but is not strictly necessary.

Theorem 8.14. *The regret of the GBPA for multi-armed bandits (Algorithm 2) with $\widetilde{\Phi}(G) = \mathbb{E}_{Z_1,\ldots,Z_n \sim D} \max_i \{G_i + \eta Z_i\}$ is at most:*

$$\underbrace{\eta \mathbb{E}_{Z_1,\ldots,Z_n \sim D} \left[\max_i Z_i \right]}_{\text{overestimation penalty}} + \underbrace{\frac{N \sup h_{\mathcal{D}}}{\eta} T}_{\text{divergence penalty}} \tag{8.57}$$

Proof. Due to the convexity of Φ, the underestimation penalty is nonpositive. The overestimation penalty is clearly at most $\mathbb{E}_{Z_1,\ldots,Z_n \sim D}[\max_i Z_i]$, and Lemma 8.15 proves the $N(\sup h_{\mathcal{D}})$ upper bound on the divergence penalty.

It remains to prove the tuning parameter η. Suppose we scale the perturbation Z by $\eta > 0$, i.e., we add ηZ_i to each coordinate. It is easy to see that $\mathbb{E}[\max_{i=1,\ldots,n} \eta X_i] = \eta \mathbb{E}[\max_{i=1,\ldots,n} X_i]$. For the divergence penalty, let F_η be the CDF of the scaled random variable. Observe that $F_\eta(t) = F(t/\eta)$ and thus $f_\eta(t) = \frac{1}{\eta} f(t/\eta)$. Hence, the hazard rate scales by $1/\eta$, which completes the proof. $\quad\square$

Lemma 8.15. *Consider implementing GBPA with potential function*

$$\widetilde{\Phi}(G) = \mathbb{E}_{Z_1,\ldots,Z_n \sim D} \max_i \{G_i + \eta Z_i\}. \tag{8.58}$$

The divergence penalty on each round is at most $N(\sup h_{\mathcal{D}})$.

Distribution	$\sup_x h_{\mathcal{D}}(x)$	$\mathbb{E}[\max_{i=1}^N Z_i]$	Parameters
Gumbel$(\mu = 1, \beta = 1)$	1 as $x \to 0$	$\log N + \gamma_0$	N/A
Frechet $(\alpha > 1)$	at most 2α	$N^{1/\alpha}\Gamma(1 - 1/\alpha)$	$\alpha = \log N$
Weibull$(\lambda = 1, k \leq 1)$	k at $x = 0$	$O((\frac{1}{k})!(\log N)^{\frac{1}{k}})$	$k = 1$
Pareto$(x_m = 1, \alpha)$	α at $x = 0$	$\alpha N^{1/\alpha}/(\alpha - 1)$	$\alpha = \log N$
Gamma$(\alpha \geq 1, \beta)$	β as $x \to \infty$	$\log N + (\alpha - 1) \log \log N - \log \Gamma(\alpha) + \beta^{-1}\gamma_0$	$\beta = \alpha = 1$

Table 8.1: *Distributions that give $O(\sqrt{TN \log N})$ regret FTPL algorithm.* The parameterization follows Wikipedia pages for easy lookup. We denote the Euler constant (≈ 0.58) by γ_0. Please see Abernethy et al. (2015) for a full description.

Proof. Recall the gradient expression in Equation 8.49. We upper bound the i-th diagonal entry of the Hessian, as follows. First, let where $\tilde{G}_{j^*} = \max_{j \neq i}\{G_j + Z_j\}$ which is a random variable independent of Z_i. Now,

$$
\begin{aligned}
\nabla_{ii}^2 \widetilde{\Phi}(G) &= \frac{\partial}{\partial G_i}\mathbb{E}_{\tilde{G}_{j^*}}[1 - F(\tilde{G}_{j^*} - G_i)] = \mathbb{E}_{\tilde{G}_{j^*}}\left[\frac{\partial}{\partial G_i}(1 - F(\tilde{G}_{j^*} - G_i))\right] \\
&= \mathbb{E}_{\tilde{G}_{j^*}} f(\tilde{G}_{j^*} - G_i) \\
&= \mathbb{E}_{\tilde{G}_{j^*}}[h(\tilde{G}_{j^*} - G_i)(1 - F(\tilde{G}_{j^*} - G_i))] \qquad (8.59) \\
&\leq (\sup h)\mathbb{E}_{\tilde{G}_{j^*}}[1 - F(\tilde{G}_{j^*} - G_i)] \\
&= (\sup h)\nabla_i \widetilde{\Phi}(G).
\end{aligned}
$$

We have just established that $\widetilde{\Phi}$ is differentially consistent with parameter $C = \sup h$. We apply Theorem 8.13 and the proof is complete. $\square$

Corollary 8.16. *Algorithm 2 run with $\widetilde{\Phi}$ that is obtained by smoothing Φ using any of the distributions in Table 8.1 (restricted to a certain range of parameters), combined with Geometric Resampling with $M = \sqrt{NT}$, has an expected regret of order $O(\sqrt{TN \log N})$.*

Table 8.1 provides the two terms we need to bound. More details on these distributions and their relation to stochastic smoothing can be found in Abernethy et al. (2015).

Acknowledgements

We would like to thank Elad Hazan and Gergely Neu for many helpful and insightful conversations on this work. The research was supported by NSF CAREER Awards IIS-1453304 and IIS-1452099, as well as NSF grants IIS-1421391 and IIS-1319810.

Appendix: Detailed Proofs

8.8.1 Proof That the Origin Is the Worst Case (Lemma 8.11)

Proof. Let $\Phi(G) = \|G\|_2$ and η be a positive number. By continuity of eigenvectors, it suffices to show that the maximum eigenvalue of the Hessian matrix of the Gaussian smoothed potential $\widetilde{\Phi}(G; \eta, \mathcal{N}(0, I))$ is decreasing in $\|G\|$ for $\|G\| > 0$.

By Lemma 8.5, the gradient can be written as follows:

$$\nabla\Phi(G; \eta, \mathcal{N}(0, I)) = \frac{1}{\eta}\mathbb{E}_{u\sim\mathcal{N}(0,I)}[u\|G + \eta u\|] \tag{8.60}$$

Let u_i be the i-th coordinate of the vector u. Since the standard normal distribution is spherically symmetric, we can rotate the random variable u such that its first coordinate u_1 is along the direction of G. After rotation, the gradient can be written as

$$\frac{1}{\eta}\mathbb{E}_{u\sim\mathcal{N}(0,I)}\left[u\sqrt{(\|G\| + \eta u_1)^2 + \sum_{k=2}^{N}\eta^2 u_k^2}\right]$$

which is clearly independent of the coordinates of G. The pdf of standard Gaussian distribution has the same value at $(u_1, u_2, \ldots, u_n)$ and its sign-flipped pair $(u_1, -u_2, \ldots, -u_n)$. Hence, in expectation, the two vectors cancel out every coordinate but the first, which is along the direction of G. Therefore, there exists a function α such that $\mathbb{E}_{u\sim\mathcal{N}(0,I)}[u\|G + \eta u\|] = \alpha(\|G\|)G$.

Now, we will show that α is decreasing in $\|G\|$. Due to symmetry, it suffices to consider $G = te_1$ for $t \in \mathbb{R}^+$, without loss of generality. For any $t > 0$,

$$\alpha(t) = \mathbb{E}[u_1\sqrt{(t + \eta u_1)^2 + u_{\text{rest}}^2}]/t$$

$$= \mathbb{E}_{u_{\text{rest}}}[\mathbb{E}_{u_1}[u_1\sqrt{(t + \eta u_1)^2 + b^2}|u_{\text{rest}} = b]]/t$$

$$= \mathbb{E}_{u_{\text{rest}}}[\mathbb{E}_{a=\eta|u_1|}[a\left(\sqrt{(t + a)^2 + b^2} - \sqrt{(t - a)^2 + B}\right)|u_{\text{rest}} = b]]/t$$

Let $g(t) = \left(\sqrt{(t + a)^2 + B} - \sqrt{(t - a)^2 + B}\right)/t$. Take the first derivative with respect to t, and we have:

$$g'(t) = \frac{1}{t^2}\left(\sqrt{(t - a)^2 + b^2} - \frac{t(t - a)}{\sqrt{(t + a)^2 + b^2}} - \sqrt{(t + a)^2 + b^2} + \frac{t(t - a)}{\sqrt{(t + a)^2 + b^2}}\right)$$

$$= \frac{1}{t^2}\left(\frac{a^2 + b^2 - at}{\sqrt{(t - a)^2 + b^2}} - \frac{a^2 + b^2 + at}{\sqrt{(t + a)^2 + b^2}}\right)$$

$$\left((a^2+b^2)-at\right)^2\left((t+a)^2+b^2\right)-\left((a^2+b^2)+at\right)^2\left((t-a)^2+b^2\right) = -4ab^2t^3 < 0$$

because t, η, u', B are all positive. So, $g(t) < 0$, which proves that α is decreasing in G.

The final step is to write the gradient as $\nabla(\widetilde{\Phi}; \eta, \mathcal{N}(0, I))(G) = \alpha(\|G\|)G$ and differentiate it:

$$\nabla^2 f_\eta(G) = \frac{\alpha'(\|G\|)}{\|G\|}GG^T + \alpha(\|G\|)I \qquad (8.61)$$

The Hessian has two distinct eigenvalues $\alpha(\|G\|)$ and $\alpha(\|G\|)+\alpha'(\|G\|)\|G\|$, which correspond to the eigenspace orthogonal to G and parallel to G, respectively. Since α' is negative, α is always the maximum eigenvalue and it decreases in $\|G\|$. $\qquad\square$

8.9   References

J. Abernethy and A. Rakhlin. Beating the Adaptive Bandit with High Probability. In *Proceedings of Conference on Learning Theory (COLT)*, 2009.

J. Abernethy, P. L. Bartlett, A. Rakhlin, and A. Tewari. Optimal Stragies and Minimax Lower Bounds for Online Convex Games. In *Proceedings of Conference on Learning Theory (COLT)*, 2008.

J. Abernethy, Y. Chen, and J. W. Vaughan. Efficient Market Making via Convex Optimization, and a Connection to Online Learning. *ACM Transactions on Economics and Computation*, 1(2):12, 2013.

J. Abernethy, C. Lee, A. Sinha, and A. Tewari. Online Linear Optimization via Smoothing. In *Proceedings of Conference on Learning Theory (COLT)*, 2014.

J. Abernethy, C. Lee, and A. Tewari. Fighting bandits with a new kind of smoothness. In *Advances in Neural Information Processing Systems 28*, 2015. to appear.

P. Auer, N. Cesa-Bianchi, Y. Freund, and R. E. Schapire. The Nonstochastic Multiarmed Bandit Problem. *SIAM Journal of Computuataion*, 32(1):48–77, 2003. ISSN 0097-5397.

A. Beck and M. Teboulle. Smoothing and First Order Methods: A Unified Framework. *SIAM Journal on Optimization*, 22(2):557–580, 2012.

D. P. Bertsekas. Stochastic optimization problems with nondifferentiable cost functionals. *Journal of Optimization Theory and Applications*, 12(2):218–231, 1973. ISSN 0022-3239.

S. Bubeck and N. Cesa-Bianchi. Regret analysis of stochastic and nonstochastic multi-armed bandit problems. *arXiv preprint arXiv:1204.5721*, 2012.

N. Cesa-Bianchi and G. Lugosi. *Prediction, learning, and games*. Cambridge University Press, 2006. ISBN 978-0-521-84108-5.

L. Devroye, G. Lugosi, and G. Neu. Prediction by Random-Walk Perturbation. In *Proceedings of Conference on Learning Theory (COLT)*, 2013.

J. Duchi, P. L. Bartlett, and M. J. Wainwright. Randomized Smoothing for Stochastic Optimization. *SIAM Journal on Optimization*, 22(2):674–701, 2012. doi: 10.1137/110831659.

Y. Freund. A Decision-Theoretic Generalization of On-Line Learning and an Application to Boosting. *Journal of Computer and System Sciences*, 55(1):119–139, 1997. ISSN 0022-0000. doi: http://dx.doi.org/10.1006/jcss.1997.1504.

J. Gittins. Quantitative methods in the planning of pharmaceutical research. *Drug Information Journal*, 30(2):479–487, 1996.

P. Glasserman. *Gradient Estimation Via Perturbation Analysis*. Kluwer international series in engineering and computer science: Discrete event dynamic systems. Springer, 1991. ISBN 9780792390954.

J. Hannan. Approximation to Bayes risk in repeated play. *Contributions to the Theory of Games*, 3:97–139, 1957.

J. Hofbauer and W. H. Sandholm. On the global convergence of stochastic fictitious play. *Econometrica*, 70(6):2265–2294, 2002.

A. T. Kalai and S. Vempala. Efficient algorithms for online decision problems. *Journal of Computer and System Sciences*, 71(3):291–307, 2005.

T. Kocák, G. Neu, M. Valko, and R. Munos. Efficient learning by implicit exploration in bandit problems with side observations. In *Proceedings of Neural Information Processing Systems (NIPS)*, pages 613–621. Curran Associates, Inc., 2014.

J. Kujala and T. Elomaa. On following the perturbed leader in the bandit setting. In *Algorithmic Learning Theory*, pages 371–385. Springer, 2005.

N. Littlestone and M. K. Warmuth. The Weighted Majority Algorithm. *Information and Computation*, 108(2):212–261, 1994.

H. B. McMahan. Follow-the-Regularized-Leader and Mirror Descent: Equivalence Theorems and L1 Regularization. In *AISTATS*, pages 525–533, 2011.

I. S. Molchanov. *Theory of random sets*. Probability and its applications. Springer, New York, 2005. ISBN 1-85233-892-X.

Y. Nesterov. Random Gradient-Free Minimization of Convex Functions. *ECORE Discussion Paper*, 2011.

G. Neu and G. Bartók. An efficient algorithm for learning with semi-bandit feedback. In *Algorithmic Learning Theory*, pages 234–248. Springer, 2013.

M. Pacula, J. Ansel, S. Amarasinghe, and U.-M. OReilly. Hyperparameter tuning in bandit-based adaptive operator selection. In *Applications of Evolutionary Computation*, pages 73–82. Springer, 2012.

S. Rakhlin, O. Shamir, and K. Sridharan. Relax and randomize: From value to algorithms. In *Advances in Neural Information Processing Systems*, pages 2141–2149, 2012.

R. Rockafellar. *Convex Analysis*. Convex Analysis. Princeton University Press, 1997. ISBN 9780691015866.

S. Shalev-Shwartz. Online Learning and Online Convex Optimization. *Foundations and Trends in Machine Learning*, 4(2):107–194, feb 2012. ISSN 1935-8237.

M. K. Simon. *Probability distributions involving Gaussian random variables: A handbook for engineers and scientists*. Springer Science & Business Media, 2002.

N. Srebro, K. Sridharan, and A. Tewari. On the Universality of Online Mirror Descent. In *Proceedings of Neural Information Processing Systems (NIPS)*, pages 2645–2653, 2011.

G. Van den Broeck, K. Driessens, and J. Ramon. Monte-Carlo tree search in poker using expected reward distributions. In *Advances in Machine Learning*, pages 367–381. Springer, 2009.

T. van Erven, W. Kotlowski, and M. K. Warmuth. Follow the Leader with Dropout Perturbations. 2014.

M. Warmuth. A perturbation that makes "Follow the leader" equivalent to "Randomized Weighted Majority". http://classes.soe.ucsc.edu/cmps290c/Spring09/lect/10/wmkalai-rewrite.pdf, 2009. Accessed: March 19, 2016.

F. Yousefian, A. Nedić, and U. V. Shanbhag. Convex nondifferentiable stochastic optimization: A local randomized smoothing technique. In *Proceedings of American Control Conference (ACC), 2010*, pages 4875–4880, June 2010.

9   Probabilistic Inference by Hashing and Optimization

Stefano Ermon
Stanford University
Stanford, CA, USA

`ermon@cs.stanford.edu`

Probabilistic inference is one of the central problems of statistical machine learning. To date, only a handful of distinct methods have been developed, most notably Monte Carlo sampling, decomposition, and variational methods. In this chapter, a different approach based on random projections and optimization is introduced. This new approach provides provable guarantees on the accuracy, can leverage modern optimization technology and outperforms traditional methods in a range of domains, in particular those involving combinations of probabilistic and deterministic dependencies among the variables.

Keywords: *probabilistic inference; universal hashing; optimization*

9.1   Introduction

Many problems in machine learning and statistics involve the computation of high-dimensional integrals, where one has to consider a large number of possible scenarios (or states of the world), and weight them by their probability. For example, this computation is needed to evaluate (posterior) probabilities, average over ensembles of models, and more generally to compute expectations. Computing expectations with respect to high dimensional probability distributions is known to be intractable in the worst-case (Roth, 1996), and is a key computational challenge in computer science (Dyer et al., 1991; Simonovits, 2003; Cai and Chen, 2010). Intuitively, the difficulty arises because the number of possible states scales exponentially with the number of variables, a phenomenon traditionally known as the *curse of dimensionality* (Bellman, 1961).

In this chapter, we focus on discrete probability distributions and revisit the problem of *approximately* computing expectations. This problem encompasses several important probabilistic inference tasks, such as computing marginal probabilities or normalization constants in undirected graphical models, which are in turn cornerstones for parameter and structure learning (Wainwright and Jordan, 2008; Koller and Friedman, 2009). Standard approaches in this context are Monte Carlo sampling methods (Andrieu et al., 2003; Jerrum and Sinclair, 1997; Madras, 2002) and variational techniques (Wainwright and Jordan, 2008). Sampling techniques approximate complex distributions using a small number of representative states, while variational methods approximate complex models using families of tractable distributions (Jordan et al., 1999; Wainwright and Jordan, 2008). Monte Carlo techniques, invented many decades ago (1950s), are still the most widely used, and are the workhorse of statistical inference. While these techniques have been successfully applied to a wide range of domains, they typically do not provide tight guarantees on the accuracy of the results.

The key idea behind Markov Chain Monte Carlo (MCMC) is that one can answer queries about complex statistical models by drawing a relatively small set of samples (typical scenarios) from the underlying probability distribution and calculate statistics of interest by averaging over the samples. The key difficulty is that to draw proper samples, one needs to set up a Markov Chain over the entire state space which has to reach an equilibrium distribution. For many statistical models of interest, reaching the equilibrium distribution will require exponential time Madras (2002). In practice, the approach will therefore only give approximate answers. Unfortunately, there is generally little or no information on the quality of the approximation. In fact, the Markov Chain may completely miss important parts of the state space because the chain gets trapped in less relevant areas of the state space.

In this chapter, we review a new family of approximate inference algorithms based on randomized hashing and modern optimization techniques (Gomes et al., 2006a; Chakraborty et al., 2013b; Ermon et al., 2013c; Achlioptas and Jiang, 2015). These algorithms are a promising alternative to variational and sampling methods and yield with high probability *provably accurate results* assuming access to an optimization oracle. Specifically, these randomized schemes can compute partition functions or marginal probabilities providing an approximately correct answer (within a factor of $1 + \epsilon$ of the true value for any desired $\epsilon > 0$) with high probability (at least $1 - \delta$ for any desired $\delta > 0$).

With this new approach, statistics of interest are also computed by considering only a small set of representative states (samples) from the model. However, these samples are not drawn at random from the underlying probability distribution using a Markov Chain, rather *they are very particular states that can be discovered solving a constrained optimization problem.* More specifically, these special states are obtained by randomly projecting the original high-dimensional space to a lower-dimensional one (using universal hash functions) and then using optimization to look for extreme, high-weight states (configurations or states that are the most likely) in the projected subspace. Quite surprisingly, it is possible to show that a small collection of such extreme states is representative of the overall probability distribution and can be used to estimate normalization constants and marginal probabilities for the original statistical model *with provable accuracy guarantees.* Because current optimization tools can handle large problems, often with a million or more variables, it is possible to quickly "hunt down" these special states and answer queries much more accurately than with other methods (Ermon et al., 2013c).

From a computational complexity perspective, the inference problems we consider are complete for the #P complexity class (Valiant, 1979), a set of problems encapsulating the entire Polynomial Hierarchy and believed to be significantly harder than NP. The key idea behind the techniques we will describe is to reduce a #P inference problem to a small number (quasi-polynomial in the number of variables) of instances of a NP-equivalent[1] combinatorial optimization problem defined on the same space and subject to randomly generated parity constraints. The rationale behind this approach is that although combinatorial optimization is intractable in the worst case, it has witnessed great success in the past 50 years in fields such as Mixed Integer Programming (MIP) and propositional Satisfiability Testing (SAT). Problems such as computing a Maximum a Posteriori (MAP) assignment, although NP-hard, can in practice often be approximated or solved exactly fairly efficiently (Park, 2002; Ravikumar and Lafferty, 2006; Riedel, 2008; Sontag et al., 2008). In fact, modern solvers can exploit structure in real-world problems and prune large portions of the search space, often dramatically reducing the runtime. In contrast, in a #P counting problem such as computing a marginal probability, one may need to consider contributions of an exponentially large number of items.

We begin with a general formulation of the inference problems we consider, and discuss two important special cases, namely model counting and

---

1. As hard as the hardest problem in NP, but not harder.

the computation of the partition function of undirected graphical models. We introduce a new class of probabilistic inference methods based on universal hashing and optimization, and discuss their formal properties. We then highlight some interesting connections with error correcting codes and decoding problems from information theory, and finally we conclude with some open research questions. This chapter is based on and reviews work that previously appeared in (Ermon et al., 2013c,b, 2014; Zhao et al., 2016).

9.2   Problem Statement and Assumptions

We follow the setup of (Ermon et al., 2013c). Let Σ be a (large) but finite set, e.g., the set of all possible assignments to the variables in a model. Let $w : \Sigma \to \mathbb{R}^+$ be a non-negative function that assigns a weight to each element of Σ. We wish to (approximately) compute the total weight of the set, defined as the following discrete integral or "partition function"

$$W = \sum_{\sigma \in \Sigma} w(\sigma) \tag{9.1}$$

We assume w is given as input and that it can be compactly represented and stored, for instance in a factored form as the product of conditional probabilities tables.

Assumption: We assume that we have access to an *optimization oracle* that can solve the following constrained optimization problem

$$\max_{\sigma \in \Sigma} \; w(\sigma) 1_{\{\mathcal{C}\}}(\sigma) \tag{9.2}$$

where $1_{\{\mathcal{C}\}} : \Sigma \to \{0,1\}$ is an indicator function for a compactly represented subset $\mathcal{C} \subseteq \Sigma$, i.e., $1_{\{\mathcal{C}\}}(\sigma) = 1$ if $\sigma \in \mathcal{C}$ and 0 otherwise. $\mathcal{C}$ might be compactly specified using a small number of constraints. For concreteness, we discuss our setup and assumptions in the context of constraint satisfaction problems and probabilistic graphical models. We shall discuss the application of our method in two specific contexts:

9.2.1   Counting Satisfying Assignments

Let V be a set of 0/1 (Boolean) variables, where $|V| = n$, and let $\Sigma = \{0,1\}^n$ be the set of all possible assignments to these variables. The weight function w is defined using a logical formula F in clausal normal form. A formula F is said to be in clausal normal form (CNF) form if it is a logical conjunction of a set of clauses $C_1, \cdots, C_m$. A clause C is a logical disjunction of a set of (possibly negated) variables, such as for example $(x_1 \vee \neg x_2 \vee x_3)$. A variable assignment $\sigma \in \Sigma$ can be seen as a mapping that assigns a value in $\{0, 1\}$ to each variable in V. We say that σ satises a clause C_i if at least one literal (a variable, possibly negated) of clause C_i takes value 1. For example, $(x_1 = 0, x_2 = 0, x_3 = 0)$ satisfies $(x_1 \vee \neg x_2 \vee x_3)$. We define the weight $w(\sigma)$ to be 1 if all the clauses $C_1, \cdots, C_m$ are satisfied by σ, and 0 otherwise.

Satisfiability Testing (SAT) is the problem of deciding if there exists a variable assignment that satisfies all the clauses $C_1, \cdots, C_m$. Equivalently, it is the problem of deciding if there exists at least one variable assignment σ with weight 1, i.e., such that F evaluates to TRUE. This is the canonical NP-complete problem (Garey and Johnson, 2002). While SAT is believed to be intractable in the worst-case, SAT solvers have shown great success in the past 20 years, and can routinely handle large problems with hundreds of thousands of variables arising in a wide range of application domains (Biere et al., 2009; Vardi, 2014).

Computing the total weight W as in (9.1), which is the total number of satisfying assignments, is known as #-SAT and is the canonical #-P complete problem (Valiant, 1979). The problem of counting the number of solutions of a constraint satisfaction problem is clearly more general and believed to be harder than the problem of deciding if at least one solution exists.

In the context of constraint satisfaction problems, our main assumption is that we can check if there exists a satisfying assignment in a compactly represented subset $\mathcal{C} \subseteq \Sigma$. Note that if $\mathcal{C}$ can be represented *compactly* using a set of constraints (clauses), then queries like (9.2) are in NP and can be answered by invoking a SAT solver. In particular, it is sufficient to consider the conjunction of the original formula F and the constraints defining $\mathcal{C}$ as input for the SAT solver.

9.2.2 Inference in Graphical Models

We now consider the strictly more general case of discrete probabilistic graphical models. Given a graphical model, we let $\Sigma = \mathcal{X}$ be the set of all possible configurations (variable assignments). Define a weight function $w : \mathcal{X} \to \mathbb{R}^+$ that assigns to each configuration a score proportional to its probability: $w(x) = \prod_{\alpha \in \mathcal{I}} \psi_\alpha(\{x\}_\alpha)$. Z may then be rewritten as

$$Z = \sum_{x \in \mathcal{X}} w(x) = \sum_{x \in \mathcal{X}} \prod_{\alpha \in \mathcal{I}} \psi_\alpha(\{x\}_\alpha) \tag{9.3}$$

Computing Z is typically intractable because it involves a sum over an exponential number of configurations, and is often the most challenging inference task for many families of graphical models. Computing Z is needed for many inference and learning tasks, such as evaluating the likelihood of data for a given model, computing marginal probabilities, and parameter estimation (Wainwright and Jordan, 2008).

In the context of graphical models inference, we assume access to an optimization oracle that can answer Maximum a Posteriori (MAP) queries, namely, solve the following constrained optimization problem

$$\arg\max_{x \in \mathcal{X}} \; p(x \mid x \in \mathcal{C}) \tag{9.4}$$

that is, we can find the most likely state (and its weight) given some evidence $\mathcal{C}$.

9.3   Approximate Model Counting via Randomized Hashing

The problem of counting the number of solutions of a constraint satisfaction problem (e.g., #-SAT defined in section 9.2.1) is clearly more general and believed to be harder than the problem of deciding if at least one solution exists. What about the problem of *approximately* counting the number of solutions? Surprisingly, *approximate model counting* can be formally reduced (in a probabilistic sense) to the problem of deciding if a solution exists or not, i.e., to SAT.

The problem of approximately computing the number of solutions of a formula, assuming access to an oracle that can answer queries in NP (such as a SAT solver), was originally considered by Stockmeyer (1985). This landmark paper introduced a randomized scheme that can estimate the number of solutions of a formula F within a factor of $(1 + \epsilon)$ of the true value for any desired $\epsilon > 0$, and succeeds with probability at least $(1 - \delta)$ for any desired $\delta > 0$. This algorithm runs in polynomial time and invokes the NP-oracle a number of times that is at most polynomial in the number of variables of the formula. Stockmeyer's work therefore established an important result in computational complexity theory, namely that #P can be approximated in BPP^{NP}. BPP^{NP} refers to algorithms that have bounded-error probabilistic polynomial time and access to an NP-oracle (Sipser, 2006). Informally, this results states that *approximate model counting* is not harder than deciding if a solution exists or not.

The intuition behind the algorithm is as follows. Let $S \subseteq \Sigma$ be the set of solutions to a Boolean formula F. Stockmeyer (1985) showed that one can reliably estimate $|S|$ by repeating the following simple process: randomly partition Σ into 2^m cells, select one of these cells, and compute whether S has at least one element in this cell (this can be accomplished with a query

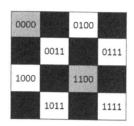

Figure 9.1: Pictorial representation, for $\Sigma = \{0,1\}^4$ and variables x_1, x_2, x_3, x_4. Solutions $S = \{(0,0,0,0), (0,0,1,0), (1,1,0,0), (1,0,1,0)\}$ shown in green. Middle panel: the space is partitioned into 2 cells, based on the parity of $x_3 \oplus x_4$. Two solutions are left in the chosen cell, corresponding to the assignments satisfying $x_3 \oplus x_4 = 0$. Right panel: after partitioning again based on the parity of $x_2 \oplus x_3$, only solution $(0,0,0,0)$ is left.

to an NP oracle, e.g., invoking a SAT solver). The idea to estimate $|S|$ is to define progressively smaller cells, until the cells become so small that no element of S can be found inside a (randomly) chosen cell. The intuition is that the larger $|S|$ is, the smaller the cells will have to be, and we can use this information to estimate $|S|$ reliably.

Based on this intuition, we give a hashing-based approximate counting procedure (Algorithm 9.1, ApproxModelCount), which relies on an NP oracle $\mathcal{O}_S$ to check whether S has an element in the cell. It is adapted from the SPARSE-WISH algorithm of Ermon et al. (2014). The correctness of the approach relies crucially on how the space is randomly partitioned into cells. To achieve strong worst-case (probabilistic) guarantees, the algorithm relies on *universal hash functions*, a powerful concept from theoretical computer science (Vadhan, 2011; Goldreich, 2011).

Definition 9.1. *A family of functions* $\mathcal{H} = \{h : \{0,1\}^n \to \{0,1\}^m\}$ *is strongly universal (pairwise independent) if the following two conditions hold when h is chosen uniformly at random from $\mathcal{H}$. 1) $\forall x \in \{0,1\}^n$, the random variable $H(x)$ is uniformly distributed in $\{0,1\}^m$. 2) $\forall x_1, x_2 \in \{0,1\}^n$ $x_1 \neq x_2$, the random variables $H(x_1)$ and $H(x_2)$ are independent.*

Statistically optimal functions can be constructed by considering the family $\mathcal{H}^{full}$ of all possible functions from $\{0,1\}^n$ to $\{0,1\}^m$. It is easy to verify that this is a family of *fully* independent functions. However, functions from this family require $m2^n$ bits to be specified, making this construction not very useful for large n. On the other hand, *pairwise independent* hash functions can be specified compactly, using a number of bits linear in n. They are generally based on modular arithmetic constraints of the form $Ax = b \mod 2$, referred to as parity or XOR constraints. Note that by the properties of modular arithmetic, $Ax = b \mod 2$ is equivalent to $Ax + b = 0$

Algorithm 9.1 ApproxModelCount $(F, \mathcal{O}_S, \Delta)$

1:   Let S denote the set of solutions to the input formula F
2:   $T \leftarrow \left\lceil \frac{\log(1/\Delta)}{\alpha} \log n \right\rceil$
3:   $i = 0$
4:   **while** $i \leq n$ **do**
5:      **for** $t = 1, \cdots, T$ **do**
6:         Sample hash function $h^i_{A,b} : \Sigma \rightarrow \{0,1\}^i$, i.e.
7:           sample uniformly $A \in \{0,1\}^{i \times n}$, $b \in \{0,1\}^i$
8:         Let $S(h^i_{A,b}) = |\{x \in S \mid Ax \equiv b \pmod 2\}|$
9:         $w^t_i \leftarrow \mathbb{I}[S(h^i_{A,b}) \geq 1]$, using $\mathcal{O}_S$ to check if $\{x \in S \mid Ax \equiv b \pmod 2\}$ is empty
10:      **end for**
11:      **if** $\text{Median}(w^1_i, \cdots, w^T_i) < 1$ **then**
12:         break
13:      **end if**
14:      $i = i + 1$
15:   **end while**
16:   Return $\lfloor 2^{i-1} \rfloor$

---

mod 2, and simply means that Ax is congruent to b modulo 2. This is also written as $Ax \equiv b \pmod 2$.

Proposition 9.1. *Let* $A \in \{0,1\}^{m \times n}$, $b \in \{0,1\}^m$. *The family* $\mathcal{H} = \{h_{A,b}(x) : \{0,1\}^n \rightarrow \{0,1\}^m\}$ *where* $h_{A,b}(x) = Ax + b \mod 2$ *is a family of pairwise independent hash functions.*

Relying on pairwise independence, it is possible to show that Approx-ModelCount provides with high probability an accurate estimate of the true model count, as summarized by the following property:

Theorem 9.2. *For any* $\Delta > 0$, *positive constant* $\alpha \leq 0.0042$, *Approx-ModelCount makes* $\Theta(n \ln n \ln 1/\delta)$ *queries to the NP oracle* $\mathcal{O}_S$ *and, with probability at least* $(1 - \Delta)$, *outputs a 16-approximation of* $|S|$, *the number of solutions of a formula* F.

Proof. **Sketch:** Given any solution $x \in S$, it is easy to see that at iteration i, $P[Ax \equiv b \pmod 2] = \left(\frac{1}{2}\right)^i$ because of the uniformity property of Definition 9.1. By linearity of expectation, $E[S(h^i_{A,b})] = \frac{|S|}{2^i}$. In expectation, the While loop should therefore break for $i \approx \log |S|$, i.e., when the corresponding expected number of "surviving" solutions is less than 1. When this happens, the algorithm provides an accurate estimate for $|S|$. The challenge is to show that the expected behavior is actually the typical behavior. This follows from pairwise independence. In fact, because the hash function family is pairwise independent, $S(h^i_{A,b})$ is the sum of pairwise independent random variables (one for each element of S, corresponding to whether that solution satisfies the random constraints or not). Therefore, the variance of $S(h^i_{A,b})$ is just the sum of the individual variances, and can be shown to be "small" compared to the mean. By standard concentration inequalities, $S(h^i_{A,b})$ will take a value close to its mean reasonably often. Taking the median over T runs guarantees an accurate estimate with high probability.   □

The proof follows from the analysis in the original paper (Stockmeyer, 1985); similar analysis and derivations can be found in Achlioptas and Jiang (2015); Ermon et al. (2013c); Chakraborty et al. (2013b); Gomes et al. (2006a).

9.3.1   Improving the Approximation Factor

Given a κ-approximation algorithm such as Algorithm 9.1 and any $\epsilon > 0$, it is possible to design a $(1 + \epsilon)$-approximation algorithm with the following construction. Let $\ell = \log_{1+\epsilon} \kappa$. Define a new set of configurations $\Sigma^\ell = \Sigma \times \Sigma \times \cdots \times \Sigma$, and a new weight function $w' : \Sigma^\ell \to \mathbb{R}$ as $w'(\sigma_1, \cdots, \sigma_\ell) = w(\sigma_1)w(\sigma_2)\cdots w(\sigma_\ell)$.

Proposition 9.3. *Let* $\widehat{W}$ *be a* κ*-approximation of* $\sum_{\sigma' \in \Sigma^\ell} w'(\sigma')$*. Then* $\widehat{W}^{1/\ell}$ *is a* $\kappa^{1/\ell}$*-approximation of* $\sum_{\sigma \in \Sigma} w(\sigma)$*.*

To see why this holds, observe that $W' = \sum_{\sigma' \in \Sigma^\ell} w'(\sigma') = \left(\sum_{\sigma \in \Sigma} w(\sigma)\right)^\ell = W^\ell$. Since $\frac{1}{\kappa} W' \leq \widehat{W} \leq \kappa W'$, we obtain that $\widehat{W}^{1/\ell}$ must be a $\kappa^{1/\ell} = 1 + \epsilon$ approximation of W.

Note that this construction requires running Algorithm 9.1 on an enlarged problem with ℓ times more variables. Although the number of optimization queries grows polynomially with ℓ, increasing the number of variables might significantly increase the runtime. Other techniques to improve the approximation factor of the basic algorithm can be found in (Chakraborty et al., 2013b). The idea is to estimate the size of $S(h^i_{A,b})$ in line 9 of Algorithm 9.1 using multiple calls to the NP-oracle, rather than just checking if the set is empty or not. For example, one could check if $S(h^i_{A,b})$ contains at least k elements. The threshold k is referred to as a *pivot*. This reduces the variance and can be used to improve the accuracy (but requires more invocations of the NP-oracle).

9.3.2   Practical Implementations and Extensions

In practice, line 9 in Algorithm 9.1 is implemented using a SAT solver as an NP-oracle. In a model counting application, this is accomplished by adding to the original formula i parity constraints, and checking the satisfiability of the augmented formula. Note that a naive encoding of a parity constraint over p variables would require 2^{p-1} clauses of length p, ruling out half of the 2^p possible assignments (the ones with the wrong parity). Each constraint can however be represented compactly introducing $O(p)$ extra variables with a standard Tseitin transformation (Tseitin, 1983). For example $x_1 \oplus x_2 \oplus x_3 \oplus x_4 = 0$ can be written as $\{x_1 \oplus x_2 = z_1, x_2 \oplus x_3 = z_2, z_1 \oplus z_2 = 0\}$. See also (Feldman et al., 2005) for compact encodings of the so-called parity polytope using linear inequalities.

The first practical implementation of these ideas is from Gomes et al. (2006b,a), who used a SAT solver as an NP-oracle and demonstrated the practical feasibility of an approach similar to Algorithm 9.1. Their algorithm was able to leverage decades of research and engineering in SAT solving technology for approximate model counting, and resulted in huge improvements over competing techniques (Sang et al., 2004). More recently, Chakraborty et al. (2013a); Ivrii et al. (2015) also studied the problem and provided several practical improvements. Chakraborty et al. (2013a) introduced the use of *pivots*, where an NP oracle is used in line 9 of Algorithm 9.1 to check the existence of at least $k > 1$ solutions ($k = 1$ corresponds to Algorithm 9.1), to improve the accuracy of the estimated model count.

Note that although we only discussed the problem of counting the number of solutions, similar ideas can also be used to construct approximate solution *sampling* schemes, with provable guarantees on the quality of the samples (Gomes et al., 2006a; Chakraborty et al., 2013a; Ermon et al., 2013a). This is to be expected, as counting and sampling are known to be self-reducible (Jerrum and Sinclair, 1997). More surprising is the fact that, given access to an NP-oracle, it is possible to construct *exact sampling* schemes; in contrast, it is believed that *exact counting* cannot be done in polynomial time, even with access to an NP-oracle. This is consistent with the fact a Monte Carlo estimate based on *exact samples* would only provide an approximation for the corresponding counting problem, not an exact solution. The first *exact sampling* scheme based on an NP-oracle was introduced by Bellare et al. (2000). The algorithm uses hash functions to partition the space into cells, as the algorithms described in this Chapter, in conjunction with rejection sampling. However, it requires k-wise independent hash functions for $k > 2$ (as opposed to pairwise independence, as in Proposition 9.1), and as far as we know, has never been used in practice.

9.4 Probabilistic Models and Approximate Inference: The WISH Algorithm

The approximate model counter presented in the previous section is not applicable to counting problems involving general weight functions, such as the one arising in discrete graphical models for computing the partition function (cf. section 9.2.2). If the weight function $w(\sigma)$ is such that $\frac{\max_\sigma w(\sigma)}{\min_{\sigma:w(\sigma)\neq 0} w(\sigma)}$ is small, then the hashing-based algorithm of Chakraborty et al. (2014) can be applied. Intuitively, these weight functions are "close" to being constant on a subset of the states, and zero elsewhere. This is close to the unweighted model counting problem described in Section 9.3, where the weight function is 1 on a subset of the states (the set of solutions), and zero elsewhere. Typical models in machine learning, however, are unlikely to satisfy this restriction. For example, if the weight function is log-linear the weight function can have huge variability.

An alternative algorithm, which can handle general weight functions and is based on universal hashing and combinatorial optimization, was introduced by Ermon et al. (2013c). We start with the intuition behind the algorithm, which is called **W**eighted-**I**ntegrals-And-**S**ums-By-**H**ashing (WISH).

Computing W as defined in Equation (9.1) is challenging because the sum has an exponentially large number of terms, i.e., $|\Sigma| = 2^n$ when there are n binary variables. Let us define the *tail distribution* of weights as $G(u) \triangleq |\{\sigma \mid w(\sigma) \geq u\}|$. Note that G is a non-increasing step function, changing values at no more than 2^n points. Then W may be rewritten as $\int_{\mathbb{R}^+} G(u)\mathrm{d}u$, i.e., the total *area* A under the $G(u)$ vs. u curve:

$$\int_{\mathbb{R}^+} G(u)\mathrm{d}u = \int_{\mathbb{R}^+}\int_u^\infty g(t)\mathrm{d}t\mathrm{d}u = \int_{\mathbb{R}^+}\int_0^t g(t)\mathrm{d}u\mathrm{d}t = \int_{\mathbb{R}^+} tg(t)\mathrm{d}t = W \quad (9.5)$$

This is a well known relationship between the mean of a random variable taking only non-negative values and its cumulative distribution function. One way to approximate W is to (implicitly) divide this area A into either *horizontal* or *vertical* slices (see Figure 9.2), approximate the area in each slice, and sum up. Note that a similar approach based on estimating "quantiles" is also used in nested sampling (Skilling et al., 2006).

Suppose we had an efficient procedure to estimate $G(u)$ given any u. This could in principle be done using Algorithm 9.1, ApproxModelCount, as estimating $G(u)$ is an unweighted counting problem.[2] Then it is not hard to see that one could create enough slices by dividing up the x-axis, estimate $G(u)$ at these points, and estimate the area A using quadrature. However, the natural way of doing this to any degree of accuracy would require a number of slices that grows at least logarithmically with the weight range on the x-axis, which is undesirable, and estimating the weight range itself would require access to an optimization oracle.

---

2. Note however that representing $\{\sigma \mid w(\sigma) \geq u\}$ in a compact form using a clausal normal form is non-trivial. A more expressive language such as Integer Linear Programming would be more practical.

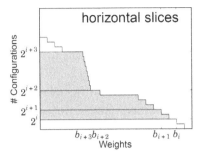 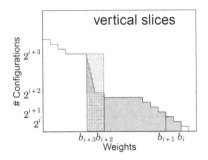

Figure 9.2: Horizontal vs. vertical slices for integration. Riemann vs. Lebesgue integrals of a function. The area under the curve between b_{i+3} and b_{i+2} is no larger than the area marked with a diagonal pattern, and at least as large as the area marked with a grid pattern. The area marked with a diagonal pattern is exactly twice as large as the area marked with a grid pattern because of the geometric binning of the y axis.

Alternatively, one could split the y-axis, i.e., the $G(u)$ value range $[0, 2^n]$, at geometrically growing values $1, 2, 4, \cdots, 2^n$, i.e., into bins of sizes $1, 1, 2, 4, \cdots, 2^{n-1}$. Let $b_0 \geq b_1 \geq \cdots \geq b_n$ be the weights of the configurations at the split points. In other words, b_i is the 2^i-th quantile of the weight distribution. Unfortunately, despite the monotonicity of $G(u)$, the area in the horizontal slice defined by each bin is difficult to bound, as b_i and b_{i+1} could be arbitrarily far from each other. However, the area in the *vertical* slice defined by b_i and b_{i+1} must be bounded between $2^i(b_i - b_{i+1})$ and $2^{i+1}(b_i - b_{i+1})$, i.e., within a factor of 2. Thus, summing over the lower bound for all such slices and the left-most slice, the total area A must be within a factor of 2 of $\sum_{i=0}^{n-1} 2^i(b_i - b_{i+1}) + 2^n b_n = b_0 + \sum_{i=1}^{n} 2^{i-1} b_i$. Of course, we don't know b_i. But if we could approximate each b_i within a factor of p, we would get a $2p$-approximation to the area A, i.e., to W.

WISH provides an efficient way to realize this strategy, using a combination of randomized hash functions and an optimization oracle to approximate the b_i values with high probability. Note that this method allows us to compute the partition function W (or the area A) by estimating weights b_i at $n + 1$ carefully chosen points, which is "only" an optimization problem.

The key insight to compute the b_i values is as follows. Suppose we apply to configurations in Σ a randomly sampled pairwise independent hash function with 2^m buckets and use an optimization oracle to compute the weight w_m of a *heaviest* configuration in a fixed (arbitrary) bucket. If we repeat this process T times and consistently find that $w_m \geq w^*$, then we can infer by the properties of hashing that at least 2^m configurations (globally) are likely to have weight at least w^*. By the same token, if there were in fact at least 2^{m+c} configurations of a heavier weight $\hat{w} > w^*$ for some $c > 0$, there is a

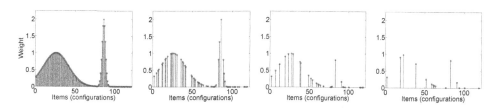

Figure 9.3: Visualization of the "thinning" effect of random parity constraints, after adding 0, 1, 2, and 3 parity constraints. Leftmost plot shows the original function to integrate. The optimal solution (subject to constraints) is shown in red.

good chance that the optimization oracle will find $w_m \geq \hat{w}$ and we would not underestimate the weight of the 2^m-th heaviest configuration. As we will see shortly, this process, using pairwise independent hash functions to keep variance low, allows us to estimate b_i accurately with only $T = O(\ln n)$ samples.

Algorithm 9.2 WISH $(w : \Sigma \to \mathbb{R}^+, n = \log_2 |\Sigma|, \Delta, \alpha)$

1: $T \leftarrow \left\lceil \frac{\ln(n/\delta)}{\alpha} \right\rceil$
2: **for** $i = 0, \cdots, n$ **do**
3:     **for** $t = 1, \cdots, T$ **do**
4:        Sample hash function $h^i_{A,b} : \Sigma \to \{0,1\}^i$, i.e.
5:          sample uniformly $A \in \{0,1\}^{i \times n}$, $b \in \{0,1\}^i$
6:        $w^t_i \leftarrow \max_\sigma w(\sigma)$ subject to $A\sigma \equiv b \pmod 2$
7:     **end for**
8:     $M_i \leftarrow \text{Median}(w^1_i, \cdots, w^T_i)$
9: **end for**
10: Return $M_0 + \sum_{i=0}^{n-1} M_{i+1} 2^i$

The pseudocode of WISH is shown as Algorithm 9.2. It is parameterized by the weight function w, the dimensionality n, a correctness parameter $\Delta > 0$, and a constant $\alpha > 0$. Notice that the algorithm requires solving only $\Theta(n \ln n / \Delta)$ optimization instances (MAP inference) to compute a sum defined over 2^n items. In the following section, we formally prove that the output is a constant factor approximation of W with probability at least $1 - \delta$ (probability over the choice of hash functions). Figure 9.3 shows the working of the algorithm. As more and more random parity constraints are added in the outer loop of the algorithm ("levels" increasing from 1 to n), the configuration space is (pairwise-uniformly) thinned out and the optimization oracle selects the heaviest (in red) of the surviving configurations. The final output is a weighted sum over the median of T such modes obtained at each level. Note that if the weight function w takes values in $\{0, 1\}$, then WISH essentially becomes `ApproxModelCount`.

In analogy with Theorem 9.2, it is possible to show that Algorithm 9.2 provides a constant factor approximation to the partition function. The complete proof can be found in Ermon et al. (2013c).

Theorem 9.4. *For any $\delta > 0$ and positive constant $\alpha \leq 0.0042$, Algorithm 9.2 makes $\Theta(n \ln n / \delta)$ MAP queries and, with probability at least $(1 - \delta)$, outputs a 16-approximation of $W = \sum_{\sigma \in \Sigma} w(\sigma)$.*

Proof. **Sketch:** The challenge is to show that w_i^t on Line 6 is "close" to b_i, the 2^i-th quantile of the weight distribution. Because of the earlier discussion and the geometric intuition in Figure 9.2, this implies the estimate of Z is accurate (within a constant factor). To show that w_i^t on Line 6 is "close" to b_i, we need to show that w_i^t is neither too large ($w_i^t \leq b_{i-2}$), nor too small ($w_i^t \geq b_{i+2}$).

Let's first consider the set S of the 2^{i-2} assignments with largest weight. The intuition is the same as in the proof sketch of Theorem 9.2. Given a configuration $x \in S$, it is easy to see that at iteration i, $P[Ax \equiv b \pmod 2] = \left(\frac{1}{2}\right)^i$ because of the uniformity property from Definition 9.1. By linearity of expectation, $E[S(h_{A,b}^i)] = \frac{|S|}{2^i} = \frac{1}{4}$. In expectation, no element of S "survives" at iteration i. Because of the constraints $A\sigma \equiv b \pmod 2$, it follows that $w_i^t \leq b_{i-2}$, that is, the optimal value cannot be too large because all the "heavy" configurations (i.e., the set S) have been ruled out by the constraints.

Let's now consider the set S of the 2^{i+2} assignments with largest weight. As before, by linearity of expectation, $E[S(h_{A,b}^i)] = \frac{|S|}{2^i} = 4$. In expectation, a few elements of S "survive" at iteration i. It follows that $w_i^t \geq b_{i+2}$, that is, the optimal value cannot be too small.

Leveraging pairwise independence to control the variance, as in the proof sketch of Theorem 9.2, it is possible to show that this is the typical behavior, and taking a Median on Line 8 guarantees that the estimate is accurate with high probability. $\square$

As in the model counting case, Proposition 9.3 can be used to boost the accuracy to a $(1 + \epsilon)$ approximation.

9.4.1   Further Approximations

While in practical applications MAP inference problems can often be solved quickly (Weiss et al., 2007), there are cases where solving to optimality is beyond reach. When the instances defined in the inner loop are not solved to optimality, Algorithm 9.2 still provides approximate *lower bounds* on W with high probability. Similarly, if one has access to upper bounds to the values of the optimization instances, e.g., from linear programming relaxations, the output of the algorithm using these upper bounds is an *approximate upper bound* with high probability.

Theorem 9.5. *Let $\widetilde{w}_i^t$ be suboptimal solutions for the optimization problems in Algorithm 9.1, i.e., $\widetilde{w}_i^t \leq w_i^t$. Let $\widetilde{W}$ be the output of Algorithm 9.1 with these suboptimal solutions. Then, for any $\delta > 0$, with probability at least $1-\delta$, $\frac{\widetilde{W}}{16} \leq W$. Similarly, let $\widehat{w}_i^t$ be upper bounds for the optimization problems in Algorithm 9.1, i.e., $\widehat{w}_i^t \geq w_i^t$. Let $\widehat{W}$ be the output of Algorithm 9.1 using these upper bounds. Then, for any $\delta > 0$, with probability at least $1 - \delta$, $\widehat{W} \geq \frac{W}{16}$. Further, if $\widehat{w}_i^t \geq \frac{1}{L} w_i^t$ for some $L > 0$, then with probability at least $1 - \delta$, $\widehat{W}$ is a $16L$-approximation to W.*

The output is always an approximate lower bound, even if the optimization is stopped early. The lower bound is monotonically non-decreasing over time, and is guaranteed to eventually reach within a constant factor of W. We thus have an *anytime* algorithm. Furthermore, each of the optimization instances can be solved independently, allowing natural massive *parallelization*.

9.5 Optimization Subject to Parity Constraints

The parity constraints used to implement universal hash functions (as in Proposition 9.1) are simple linear equations over a finite field. The space $\mathcal{C} = \{x : Ax = b \bmod 2\} = \{x : Ax \equiv b \pmod{2}\}$ has a nice geometric interpretation as the translated nullspace of the random matrix A, which is a finite dimensional vector space, with operations defined on the field $\mathbb{F}(2)$ (arithmetic modulo 2). Despite this apparent simplicity, optimizing (or searching) over $\mathcal{C} \subseteq \Sigma$ can be harder in practice than optimizing over the entire domain Σ.

Although from a worst-case perspective checking satisfiability of a formula augmented with parity constraints remains in NP (i.e., it does not become harder), a key question is whether the augmented formula is easier or harder to solve than the original one *in practice*. Similarly, a key question in the weighted case if how much harder an optimization problem of the form $\max_\sigma w(\sigma)$ becomes after adding parity constraints of the form $Ax \equiv b \pmod{2}$.

Empirically, the number and the length of the parity constraints added appear to have a significant effect on the runtime of modern combinatorial search and optimization solvers (Gomes et al., 2007; Ermon et al., 2013b; Soos et al., 2009). The construction in Proposition 9.1 involves parity constraints of average length $n/2$ where n is the number of variables. This is because each row of the matrix A from Proposition 9.1 is generated by sampling i.i.d. n Bernoulli random variables with parameter $1/2$. Short parity constraints, involving a smaller number of variables, appear to be much easier to handle in practice (Gomes et al., 2007; Ermon et al., 2014; Ivrii et al., 2015; Achlioptas and Jiang, 2015). For example, a parity constraint of length one (involving a single variable) simply clamps that variable to a particular value. In many cases, fixing a variable to a particular value simplifies a (combinatorial) optimization problem. A parity constraint of length k (involving k variables), on the other hand, is more difficult to deal with. In particular, we can only propagate such a constraint (inferring something about the variables involved) after $k - 1$ variables have been set. For example, given a parity constraint $x \oplus y \oplus z = 0$, knowing that $x = 0$ does not tell us anything about the possible values y or z can take (both $y = 0, z = 0$ and $y = 1, z = 1$ are valid assignments). Only knowing the value of x and y can we determine z. Furthermore, from a theoretical perspective, parity constraints are known to be fundamentally difficult for the resolution proof system underlying SAT solvers (cf. exponential scaling of Tseitin tautologies (Tseitin, 1968)). A natural question, therefore, is whether *short parity constraints* (involving a small number of variables, less than $n/2$ as the construction from Proposition 9.1) can be used and still provide rigorous guarantees on the accuracy.

A natural way to construct hash functions based on short parity constraints is similar to the one from Proposition 9.1, except that each variable is added to each constraint with probability $p < 1/2$. This results in parity constraints of average length np. When $p \ll 1/2$, the statistical guarantees of these hash functions are much weaker than those from Proposition 9.1. For example, they are clearly not pairwise independent. Although they still divide the space "uniformly" into cells, the resulting variance can be too high to be useful for counting. To see this, consider partitioning the space (as in Figure 9.1) using a parity constraint of length 1, i.e., based on the value of a single variable. Clearly, this divides the space evenly, however, the two halves might behave very differently. For example, one half might contain a lot of solutions, while the other one very few. These weak statistical properties can lead to extremely inaccurate counts.

Ermon et al. (2014) proposed a new family of hash functions that are weaker than pairwise independent, but have good enough statistical properties to be used for approximate counting (preserving the formal accuracy guarantees of Algorithms 9.1 and 9.2). Crucially, these hash functions can be implemented using sparser (and empirically easier to solve) parity constraints. Zhao et al. (2016) provide an analysis of the optimal asymptotic constraint length required for obtaining high-confidence approximations to model counts and partition functions. Surprisingly, for formulas with n variables, when $i = \Theta(n)$ parity constraints are added, a constraint length of $\Theta(\log n)$ is both necessary and sufficient. This is a significant improvement over standard long XORs, which have length $\Theta(n)$. Constraints of logarithmic length can, for instance, be encoded efficiently with a polynomial number of clauses. The proofs leverage ideas and results from the theory of error correcting codes. In fact, there is an intimate connection and a correspondence between universal hash functions and (binary) codes, where one can construct hash functions from binary codes and vice versa. We refer the reader to (Stinson, 1996) for an in depth discussion of the relationships between hash functions, error correcting codes and combinatorial designs.

An alternative approach towards using short parity constraints is taken in (Ivrii et al., 2015), where it is shown that under certain conditions we only need to add constraints over a subset of the original variables (the so called *independent set variables*). This approach often results in much shorter XORs, and can potentially be combined with the techniques proposed in (Ermon et al., 2014). Another very insightful perspective on the use of short parity constraints for probabilistic inference and discrete integration can be found in (Achlioptas and Jiang, 2015). In particular, Achlioptas and Jiang (2015) show how to develop local search techniques that explore $\mathcal{C}$ leveraging its algebraic structure, i.e., the fact that it is a (translated) linear subspace for which one can easily construct a basis.

9.6 Applications

The approximate inference and counting techniques described in this chapter are a generic alternative to MCMC and variational techniques, and can be applied to any *discrete* probabilistic or constraint-based model. Whenever the problems are within reach of existing optimization/search techniques, these approaches provide strong accuracy guarantees and tend to outperform traditional approximate inference methods (variational and sampling based). A detailed comparison of the various techniques is beyond the scope of this Chapter. Experimental results comparing hashing-based techniques to variational methods such as mean field, belief propagation, tree-reweighted belief propagation, and sampling techniques such as Gibbs sampling and annealed importance sampling (Neal, 2001) can be found in (Ermon et al., 2013c,b,a, 2014; Hadjis and Ermon, 2015; Zhao et al., 2016). For example, on clique structured Ising models the WISH algorithm provides partition function estimates that are between 20 and 100 orders of magnitude more accurate than mean field, belief propagation, and tree-reweighted belief propagation (Ermon et al., 2013c). The benchmarks considered range from Ising models and restricted Boltzmann machines to constraint satisfaction problems arising in hardware and software verification. The improvements are particularly evident on domains with a combination of soft probabilistic dependencies and hard deterministic constraints, as these tend to be difficult[3] for traditional inference methods (Ermon et al., 2013c). Clearly, however, there is also a wide range of domains where traditional techniques, even though without formal worst-case guarantees, do provide accurate answers. Sampling and variational approximations are often much faster in these cases. Further, there exist instances that are too difficult for existing optimization techniques (consistently with worst-case hardness results). In these cases, one can only obtain bounds on the quantities of interest (such as the one from Proposition 9.5), that can however be very loose.

Random testing is an important tool in simulation-based verification, where a model of the system is simulated using random test stimuli in order to uncover bugs or undesired behavior (Naveh et al., 2007). These stimuli need to be sampled uniformly or near-uniformly from the space of all valid stimuli, which is often specified using a set of constraints. The hashing-based techniques described in this chapter have been shown to be very effective for this problem in (Chakraborty et al., 2013a; Ermon et al., 2013a). Hashing-based techniques have also been shown to be effective at analyzing contingency tables in statistics, i.e., tables that capture the (multivariate) frequency distribution of several random variables. Several statistical tests, such as Fisher's exact test (Fisher, 1954) which tests contingency tables for homogeneity of proportion, involve counting problems that can be solved using the techniques discussed in this chapter (Zhao et al., 2016). Finally, similar techniques have also been applied to challenging probabilistic reasoning problems involving routing and planning decisions on road networks (Belle et al., 2015). For example, they have been used to estimate the probability distribution of travel time over all possible routes that satisfy some given constraints, e.g., of the "traveling salesman" type.

9.7   Open Problems and Research Challenges

The new paradigm for inference and counting presented in this chapter is a rich research area with a number of exciting directions that remain to

---

3. For example, deterministic constraints create regions of probability zero that break the ergodicity assumptions of Markov Chain Monte Carlo methods.

be explored. This is not unlike traditional MCMC and variational methods, for which countless extensions and variations tailored to specific applications have been developed in the past decades. A few examples are provided below.

The main open challenge is how to further improve scalability. On the optimization side, the techniques described in this chapter will certainly benefit from future advances in optimization and search technology, a field that is progressing rapidly (researchers jokingly call this the "Moore's Law for SAT" (Vardi, 2014)). On the hashing side, there is great potential for developing new families of hash functions that are more "friendly" to the optimizers. While sparse parity constraints and related ensembles show significant promise, it is likely that there exist other, completely different, classes of hash functions that might be much more efficient in practice.

Perhaps the most interesting counting problems are those where the corresponding decision problem is in NP, e.g., problems involving the permanent of a matrix or matchings in graphs. For example, counting the number of possible perfect matchings in a graph is known to be #-P complete, even though (maximum) matchings can be found in polynomial time (Jerrum and Sinclair, 1997). It is an open problem whether there exist interesting counting problems where the corresponding "projected" optimization problem (subject to parity constraints) remains in NP. If such problems exist, then these counting strategies would lead to new, potentially more efficient classes of FPRAS algorithms.

Traditional approximate inference methods, namely variational and sampling techniques, can be applied both to discrete and continuous models. It is not clear how hashing-based techniques can be extended to continuous random variables (without essentially discretizing the space). In particular, an extension would likely leverage continuous (non-convex) optimization to solve MAP inferece problems, however, it is not obvious what is the right notion of a random projection for a continuous space. Some interesting first steps in this direction are presented in (Belle et al., 2015). Some of the ideas and methods based on Gumbel perturbations and A* sampling (Hazan and Jaakkola, 2012; Maddison et al., 2014) might also be useful. The randomized hash functions used in this Chapter can be seen as a type of discrete random perturbation that can only take two values (leaving the weight unchanged, or setting it to zero respectively). It would be interesting to know if other types of perturbations besides universal hash functions and Gumbels are possible. Furthermore, approaches based on Gumbel perturbations (Hazan and Jaakkola, 2012; Maddison et al., 2014) typically require fully i.i.d. perturbations, just like the fully independent hash family $\mathcal{H}^{full}$ defined in Section 9.3. It would be interesting to know if weaker independence assumptions (e.g., pairwise independence) can be made on the Gumbel perturbations.

An interesting question is whether hashing-based techniques can be combined with traditional inference methods to yield stronger accuracy guarantees, or can be used to "verify" the results provided by other methods, providing certificates of accuracy. Some preliminary results in this direction can be found in (Zhu and Ermon, 2015; Hsu et al., 2016), where it is shown that mean field methods combined with random projections (implemented with universal hash functions) provide tight approximations with high probability. It is likely that similar ideas might be applicable to MCMC methods as well.

9.8   Conclusion

Making inferences about complex, high-dimensional statistical models is a fundamental reasoning problem in AI and machine learning. This chapter discussed a new approach to tackle these problems based on randomized hashing, which can be though of as a type of random perturbation, and optimization. These recently developed techniques provide strong accuracy guarantees on the quality of the results and complement previous approaches such as MCMC and variational techniques.

We introduced a randomized algorithm that, with high probability, gives a constant-factor approximation of a general discrete integral defined over an exponentially large set. The counting or integration problem is reduced to a small number of instances of a combinatorial optimization problem subject to parity constraints used to implement a hash function. In the context of graphical models, we showed how to approximately compute the normalization constant, or partition function, using a small number of MAP queries. The algorithm can leverage directly fast, off-the-shelf combinatorial optimization techniques in a black-box fashion. Further, it is massively parallelizable, allowing it to directly leverage the increasing availability of large compute clusters, and can be used in an anytime fashion trading off runtime for accuracy.

The combinatorial optimization problems that arise in this scheme have been investigated both from a theoretical and empirical perspective. In particular, they have deep connections with the max-likelihood decoding problem in information theory, and some techniques and ideas originally developed in that context can be used to make the optimization problems more tractable in practice. The new method works well on a variety of challenging application domains, and is particularly well suited to deal with models that incorporate complex, deterministic dependencies or constraints among the variables. These constraints assign zero probability to assignments that violate them, and can be challenging for traditional sampling schemes, as they can lead to very inefficient importance sampling schemes and break the ergodicity of MCMC methods. In the presence of hard deterministic constraints, even finding a single assignment with non-zero probability can be difficult. The techniques presented in this chapter, however, can leverage the reasoning power of state-of-the-art constraint optimization technology such as SAT solvers and handle a combination of deterministic and probabilistic constraints.

The approaches presented in this chapter are relatively new, and a number of extensions are possible. These include new methods to quickly approximate or bound the solution to optimization problems subject to parity constraints, the use of different classes of hash functions that are more amenable to optimization, and extensions to models with continuous random variables.

9.9   References

D. Achlioptas and P. Jiang. Stochastic integration via error-correcting codes. In *Proc. Uncertainty in Artificial Intelligence*, 2015.

C. Andrieu, N. de Freitas, A. Doucet, and M. I. Jordan. An introduction to MCMC for machine learning. *Machine learning*, 50(1-2):5–43, 2003.

M. Bellare, O. Goldreich, and E. Petrank. Uniform generation of NP-witnesses using an NP-oracle. *Information and Computation*, 163(2):510–526, 2000.

V. Belle, G. Van den Broeck, and A. Passerini. Hashing-based approximate probabilistic inference in hybrid domains. In *Proceedings of the 31st Conference on Uncertainty in Artificial Intelligence (UAI)*, 2015.

R. Bellman. *Adaptive control processes: A guided tour*. Princeton University Press, Princeton, NJ, 1961.

A. Biere, M. Heule, H. van Maaren, and T. Walsh. Handbook of satisfiability. frontiers in artificial intelligence and applications, vol. 185, 2009.

J. Cai and X. Chen. A decidable dichotomy theorem on directed graph homomorphisms with non-negative weights. In *Proc. of the 51st Symposium on Foundations of Computer Science (FOCS)*, 2010.

S. Chakraborty, K. Meel, and M. Vardi. A scalable and nearly uniform generator of SAT witnesses. In *Proc. of the 25th International Conference on Computer Aided Verification (CAV)*, 2013a.

S. Chakraborty, K. Meel, and M. Vardi. A scalable approximate model counter. In *Proc. of the 19th International Conference on Principles and Practice of Constraint Programming (CP)*, pages 200–216, 2013b.

S. Chakraborty, D. J. Fremont, K. S. Meel, S. A. Seshia, and M. Y. Vardi. Distribution-aware sampling and weighted model counting for sat. In *Twenty-Eighth AAAI Conference on Artificial Intelligence*, 2014.

M. Dyer, A. Frieze, and R. Kannan. A random polynomial-time algorithm for approximating the volume of convex bodies. *Journal of the ACM*, 38(1):1–17, 1991.

S. Ermon, C. P. Gomes, A. Sabharwal, and B. Selman. Embed and project: Discrete sampling with universal hashing. In *Advances in Neural Information Processing Systems (NIPS)*, pages 2085–2093, 2013a.

S. Ermon, C. P. Gomes, A. Sabharwal, and B. Selman. Optimization with parity constraints: From binary codes to discrete integration. In *Proc. of the 29th Conference on Uncertainty in Artificial Intelligence (UAI)*, 2013b.

S. Ermon, C. P. Gomes, A. Sabharwal, and B. Selman. Taming the curse of dimensionality: Discrete integration by hashing and optimization. In *Proc. of the 30th International Conference on Machine Learning (ICML)*, 2013c.

S. Ermon, C. P. Gomes, A. Sabharwal, and B. Selman. Low-density parity constraints for hashing-based discrete integration. In *Proc. of the 31st International Conference on Machine Learning (ICML)*, pages 271–279, 2014.

J. Feldman, M. J. Wainwright, and D. R. Karger. Using linear programming to decode binary linear codes. *Information Theory, IEEE Transactions on*, 51(3): 954–972, 2005.

R. Fisher. *Statistical Methods for Research Workers*. Oliver and Boyd, 1954.

M. R. Garey and D. S. Johnson. *Computers and intractability*, volume 29. WH freeman New York, 2002.

O. Goldreich. Randomized methods in computation. *Lecture Notes*, 2011.

C. P. Gomes, A. Sabharwal, and B. Selman. Near-uniform sampling of combinatorial spaces using XOR constraints. In *Advances in Neural Information Processing Systems (NIPS)*, 2006a.

C. P. Gomes, A. Sabharwal, and B. Selman. Model counting: A new strategy for obtaining good bounds. In *Proc. of the 21st National Conference on Artificial Intelligence (AAAI)*, pages 54–61, 2006b.

C. P. Gomes, J. Hoffmann, A. Sabharwal, and B. Selman. Short XORs for model counting: From theory to practice. In *Theory and Applications of Satisfiability Testing (SAT)*, pages 100–106, 2007.

S. Hadjis and S. Ermon. Importance sampling over sets: A new probabilistic inference scheme. In *UAI*, 2015.

T. Hazan and T. Jaakkola. On the partition function and random maximum a-posteriori perturbations. In *Proc. of the 29th International Conference on Machine Learning (ICML)*, 2012.

L.-K. Hsu, T. Achim, and S. Ermon. Tight variational bounds via random projections and I-projections. *Conference on Artificial Intelligence and Statistics*, 2016.

A. Ivrii, S. Malik, K. S. Meel, and M. Y. Vardi. On computing minimal independent support and its applications to sampling and counting. *Constraints*, pages 1–18, 2015.

M. Jerrum and A. Sinclair. The Markov chain monte carlo method: An approach to approximate counting and integration. In *Approximation Algorithms for NP-hard Problems*, pages 482–520. PWS Publishing, Boston, MA, 1997.

M. I. Jordan, Z. Ghahramani, T. Jaakkola, and L. Saul. An introduction to variational methods for graphical models. *Machine learning*, 37(2):183–233, 1999.

D. Koller and N. Friedman. *Probabilistic graphical models: principles and techniques*. MIT Press, 2009.

C. J. Maddison, D. Tarlow, and T. Minka. A* sampling. In *Advances in Neural Information Processing Systems*, pages 3086–3094, 2014.

N. Madras. *Lectures on Monte Carlo Methods*. American Mathematical Society, 2002.

Y. Naveh, M. Rimon, I. Jaeger, Y. Katz, M. Vinov, E. Marcu, and G. Shurek. Constraint-based random stimuli generation for hardware verification. *AI Magazine*, 28(3):13, 2007.

R. M. Neal. Annealed importance sampling. *Statistics and Computing*, 11(2):125–139, 2001.

J. Park. Using weighted MAX-SAT engines to solve MPE. In *Proc. of the 18th National Conference on Artificial Intelligence (AAAI)*, pages 682–687, 2002.

P. Ravikumar and J. Lafferty. Quadratic programming relaxations for metric labeling and Markov random field MAP estimation. In *Proc. of the 23rd International Conference on Machine Learning (ICML)*, pages 737–744, 2006.

S. Riedel. Improving the accuracy and efficiency of MAP inference for Markov Logic. In *Proc. of the 24th Conference on Uncertainty in Artificial Intelligence (UAI)*, pages 468–475, 2008.

D. Roth. On the hardness of approximate reasoning. *Artificial Intelligence*, 82(1): 273–302, 1996.

T. Sang, F. Bacchus, P. Beame, H. Kautz, and T. Pitassi. Combining component caching and clause learning for effective model counting. In *Theory and Applications of Satisfiability Testing (SAT)*, 2004.

M. Simonovits. How to compute the volume in high dimension? *Mathematical programming*, 97(1):337–374, 2003.

M. Sipser. *Introduction to the Theory of Computation*, volume 2. Thomson Course Technology Boston, 2006.

J. Skilling et al. Nested sampling for general bayesian computation. *Bayesian analysis*, 1(4):833–859, 2006.

D. Sontag, T. Meltzer, A. Globerson, T. Jaakkola, and Y. Weiss. Tightening LP relaxations for MAP using message passing. In *Proc. of the 24th Conference on Uncertainty in Artificial Intelligence (UAI)*, pages 503–510, 2008.

M. Soos, K. Nohl, and C. Castelluccia. Extending SAT solvers to cryptographic problems. In *Theory and Applications of Satisfiability Testing (SAT)*, 2009.

D. R. Stinson. On the connections between universal hashing, combinatorial designs and error-correcting codes. In *Congressus Numerantium*, pages 7–28, 1996.

L. Stockmeyer. On approximation algorithms for #P. *SIAM Journal on Computing*, 14(4):849–861, 1985.

G. S. Tseitin. On the complexity of derivation in the propositional calculus. In A. O. Slisenko, editor, *Studies in Constructive Mathematics and Mathematical Logic, Part II*. 1968.

G. S. Tseitin. On the complexity of derivation in propositional calculus. In *Automation of reasoning*, pages 466–483. Springer, 1983.

S. Vadhan. Pseudorandomness. *Foundations and Trends in Theoretical Computer Science*, 2011.

L. Valiant. The complexity of enumeration and reliability problems. *SIAM Journal on Computing*, 8(3):410–421, 1979.

M. Y. Vardi. Boolean satisfiability: theory and engineering. *Communications of the ACM*, 57(3):5, 2014.

M. J. Wainwright and M. I. Jordan. Graphical models, exponential families, and variational inference. *Foundations and Trends in Machine Learning*, 1(1-2):1–305, 2008.

Y. Weiss, C. Yanover, and T. Meltzer. MAP estimation, linear programming and belief propagation with convex free energies. In *Proc. of the 23rd Conference on Uncertainty in Artificial Intelligence (UAI)*, 2007.

S. Zhao, S. Chaturapruek, A. Sabharwal, and S. Ermon. Closing the gap between short and long XORs for model counting. In *Proc. 30th AAAI Conference on Artificial Intelligence (AAAI-16)*, 2016.

M. Zhu and S. Ermon. A hybrid approach for probabilistic inference using random projections. In *Proceedings of the 32nd International Conference on Machine Learning (ICML-15)*, pages 2039–2047, 2015.

10 Perturbation Models and PAC-Bayesian Generalization Bounds

Joseph Keshet
Bar-Ilan University
Ramat-Gan, Israel

joseph.keshet@biu.ac.il

Subhransu Maji
University of Massachusetts Amherst
Amherst, MA

smaji@cs.umass.edu

Tamir Hazan
Technion
Haifa, Israel

tamir.hazan@technion.ac.il

Tommi Jaakkola
Massachusetts Institute of Technology
Cambridge, MA

tommi@csail.mit.edu

In this chapter we explore the generalization power of perturbation models. Learning parameters that minimize the expected task loss of perturbation models amounts to minimizing PAC-Bayesian generalization bounds. We provide an elementary derivation of PAC-Bayesian generalization bounds, while focusing on their Bayesian components, namely their predictive probabilities and their posterior distributions. We connect their predictive probabilities to perturbation models and their posterior distributions to the smoothness of the PAC-Bayesian bound. Consequently, we derive algorithms that minimize PAC-Bayesian generalization bounds using stochastic gradient descent and explore their effectiveness on speech and visual recognition tasks.

10.1 Introduction

Learning and inference in complex models drives much of the research in machine learning applications ranging from computer vision to natural language processing to computational biology (Blake et al., 2004; Rush and Collins; Sontag et al., 2008). Each such task has its own measure of performance, such as the intersection-over-union score in visual object segmentation, the BLEU score in machine translation, the word error rate in speech recognition, the NDCG score in information retrieval, and so on. The *inference* problem in such cases involves assessing the likelihood of possible structured-labels, whether they be objects, parsers, or molecular structures. Given a training dataset of instances and labels, the *learning* problem amounts to estimation of the parameters of the inference engine, so as to minimize the desired measure of performance, or *task loss*.

The structures of labels are specified by assignments of random variables, and the likelihood of the assignments are described by a potential function. Usually it is only feasible to infer the most likely or maximum a-posteriori (MAP) assignment, rather than sampling according to their likelihood. Indeed, substantial effort has gone into developing inference algorithms for predicting MAP assignments, either based on specific parametrized restrictions such as super-modularity (e.g., Boykov et al., 2001) or by devising approximate methods based on linear programming relaxations (e.g., Sontag et al., 2008).

Learning the parameters of the potential function greatly influences the prediction accuracy. In supervised settings, the learning algorithm is provided with training data which is composed of pairs of data instances and their labels. For example, data instances can be images or sentences and their labels may be the foreground-background segmentation of these images or the correct translations of these sentences. The goal of the learning procedure is to find the potential function for which its MAP prediction for a training data instance is the same as its paired training label. The goodness of fit between the MAP predicted label and the training label is measured by a loss function. Unfortunately, the prediction function is non-smooth as well as non-convex and direct task loss minimization is hard in practice (McAllester et al., 2010).

To overcome the shortcomings of direct task loss minimization, the task loss function is replaced with a surrogate loss function. There are various surrogate loss functions, some of them are convex (and non-smooth), while others are smooth (and non-convex). The structured hinge loss, a convex upper bound to the task loss, is the surrogate loss function used both in

max-margin Markov models (Taskar et al., 2004) and in structural SVMs
(Tsochantaridis et al., 2006). Unfortunately, the error rate of the structured
hinge loss minimizer does not converge to the error rate of the Bayesian
optimal linear predictor in the limit of infinite training data, even when the
task loss is the 0-1 loss (McAllester, 2006; Tewari and Bartlett, 2007). The
structured ramp loss (Do et al., 2008) is another surrogate loss function
that proposes a tighter bound to the task loss than the structured hinge
loss. In contrast to the hinge loss, the structured ramp loss was shown to be
strongly consistent (McAllester and Keshet, 2011). In general both the hinge
loss and the structured ramp loss functions require the task loss function
to be decomposable in the size of the output label. Decomposable task
loss functions are required in order to solve the loss-augmented inference
that is used within the training procedure (Ranjbar et al., 2013), and
evaluation metrics like intersection-over-union or word error rate, which are
not decomposable, need to be approximated when utilized in these training
methods.

Conditional random fields (Lafferty et al., 2001) utilize the negative log-
likelihood as a surrogate loss function. Minimizing this loss amounts to maximizing the log-likelihood of the conditional Gibbs distribution of the training
data. While this is a convex function with a nice probabilistic properties, it
is unrelated to the task loss, and hence not expected to optimize the risk.
Alternatively, one may integrate the task loss function by minimizing the
expected loss, while averaging with respect to the Gibbs distribution (Gimpel and Smith, 2010). This approach is computationally appealing since it
effortlessly deals with non-decomposable loss functions, while shifting the
computational burden to sampling from the Gibbs distribution. Unfortunately, sampling from the Gibbs distribution is provably hard (Jerrum and
Sinclair, 1993; Goldberg and Jerrum, 2007)

Recently, several works (Keshet et al., 2011; Papandreou and Yuille, 2011;
Tarlow et al., 2012) have constructed probability models through MAP
predictions. These "perturb-max" models describe the robustness of the
MAP prediction to random changes of its parameters. Therefore, one can
draw unbiased samples from these distributions using MAP predictions.
Interestingly, when using perturbation models to compute the expected loss
minimization one would ultimately minimize PAC-Bayesian generalization
bounds (McAllester, 2003; Langford and Shawe-Taylor, 2002; Seeger, 2003;
Catoni, 2007; Germain et al., 2009; Keshet et al., 2011; Seldin et al., 2012).

This chapter explores the Bayesian aspects that emerge from PAC-
Bayesian generalization bounds. We focus on their predictive probability
models, which turn to be perturbation models as well as on PAC-Bayesian
posterior distributions. We also focus on its algorithmic aspects, both of the

predictive probability and the posterior distribution, so that they could be used to minimize the risk bound efficiently. We demonstrate the effectiveness of minimizing these bounds on visual and speech recognition problems.

10.2   Background

Learning complex models typically involves reasoning about the states of discrete variables whose labels (assignments of values) specify the discrete structures of interest. The learning task which we consider in this work is to fit parameters w that produce the most accurate prediction $y \in \mathcal{Y}$ for a given object x. Structures of labels are conveniently described by a discrete product space $\mathcal{Y} = \mathcal{Y}_1 \times \cdots \times \mathcal{Y}_n$. We describe the potential of relating a label y to an object x with respect to the parameters w by real valued functions $\theta(y; x, w)$. Maximum a-posteriori prediction amounts to compute the best scoring label:

$$\text{(MAP predictor)} \qquad \hat{y}_w(x) = \arg\max_y \ \theta(y; x, w), \qquad (10.1)$$

where $y = (y_1, ..., y_n)$.

We measure the goodness of fit by a loss function $L : \mathcal{Y} \times \mathcal{Y} \to [0, 1]$. The loss of the MAP predictor for an object-label pair is $L(\hat{y}_w(x), y)$. We assume that the object-label pairs in the world are distributed according to an unknown distribution $\mathcal{D}$. The risk of the MAP predictor that is parametrized by w, denoted by $R(w)$ is the expected loss

$$R(w) = \mathbb{E}_{(x,y)\sim\mathcal{D}}\Big[L(\hat{y}_w(x), y)\Big] \qquad (10.2)$$

Our goal is to learn the parameters w and consequently their predictor $\hat{y}_w(x)$ which minimizes the risk, that is,

$$w^* = \arg\min_w \ \mathbb{E}_{(x,y)\sim\mathcal{D}}\Big[L(\hat{y}_w(x), y)\Big]. \qquad (10.3)$$

Since the distribution $\mathcal{D}$ is unknown, we use a training dataset S of independent and identically distributed (i.i.d.) samples of pairs (x, y) from $\mathcal{D}$. We then define the empirical risk to be

$$R_S(w) = \mathbb{E}_{(x,y)\sim S}\Big[L(\hat{y}_w(x), y)\Big] = \frac{1}{|S|}\sum_{(x,y)\in S} L(\hat{y}_w(x), y) \qquad (10.4)$$

A direct minimization of the empirical risk is computationally unappealing as it is a non-smooth and non-convex function of w. Alternatively, the loss function in the empirical risk is replaced with a surrogate loss, and an additional regularization term is added to avoid overfitting of the parameters and add stability. The objective of the learning procedure is therefore

$$w^* = \arg\min_w \; \mathbb{E}_{(x,y)\sim S}\Big[L(\hat{y}_w(x),y)\Big] + \lambda\,\Omega(w), \tag{10.5}$$

where $\Omega(w)$ is a regularization function and λ is a trade-off parameter.

It is possible to decrease the empirical risk by upper bounding the task loss function with a convex surrogate, as applied in structured-SVM that is governed by the hinge-loss:

$$L_{hinge}(x,y,w) = \max_{\hat{y}\in Y} \; \{L(\hat{y},y) + \theta(\hat{y};x,w) - \theta(y;x,w)\} \tag{10.6}$$

It is straightforward to verify that the hinge-loss $L_{hinge}(x,y,w)$ upper bounds the task loss $L(\hat{y}_w(x),y)$ since

$$L(\hat{y}_w(x),y) \le L(\hat{y}_w(x),y) + \theta(\hat{y}_w(x);x,w) - \theta(y;x,w) \le L_{hinge}(x,y,w).$$

Moreover, the hinge-loss is a convex function of w as it is a maximum of linear functions of w. The hinge-loss leads to "loss adjusted inference" since computing its value requires more than just MAP inference $\hat{y}_w(x)$. In particular, when the loss function is more involved than the MAP prediction, as happens in computer vision problems (e.g., PASCAL VOC loss) or language processing tasks (e.g., BLEU loss), learning with structured-SVMs is computationally hard.

The prediction $\hat{y}_w(x)$ as well as "loss adjusted inference" rely on the potential structure to compute the MAP assignment. Potential functions are conveniently described by a family R of subsets of variables $r \subset \{1,...,n\}$, called cliques. We denote by y_r the set of labels that correspond to the clique r, namely $(y_i)_{i\in r}$ and consider the following potential functions $\theta(y;x,w) = \sum_{r\in R}\theta_r(y_r;x,w)$. Thus, MAP prediction can be formulated as an integer linear program:

$$b^* \in \arg\max_{b_r(y_r)} \sum_{r,y_r} b_r(y_r)\theta_r(y_r;x,w) \tag{10.7}$$

$$s.t. \quad b_r(y_r) \in \{0,1\}, \quad \sum_{y_r} b_r(y_r) = 1, \quad \sum_{y_s\setminus y_r} b_s(y_s) = b_r(y_r) \quad \forall r \subset s$$

The correspondence between MAP prediction and integer linear program solutions is $(\hat{y}_w(x))_i = \arg\max_{y_i} b_i^*(y_i)$. Although integer linear program solvers provide an alternative to MAP prediction, they may be restricted to problems of small size. This restriction can be relaxed when one replaces the integral constraints $b_r(y_r) \in \{0,1\}$ with nonnegative constraints $b_r(y_r) \ge 0$. These linear program relaxations can be solved efficiently using different convex max-product solvers, and whenever these solvers produce an integral solution it is guaranteed to be the MAP prediction (Sontag et al., 2008).

A substantial effort has been invested to solve this integer linear program in some special cases, particularly when $|r| \leq 2$. In this case, the potential function corresponds to a standard graph: $\theta(y; x, w) = \sum_{i \in V} \theta_i(y_i; x, w) + \sum_{i,j \in E} \theta_{i,j}(y_i, y_j; x, w)$. If the graph has no cycles, MAP prediction can be computed efficiently using the belief propagation algorithm (Pearl, 1988). There are cases where MAP prediction can be computed efficiently for graph with cycles.

10.3 PAC-Bayesian Generalization Bounds

The PAC-Bayesian generalization bound asserts that the overall risk of predicting w can be estimated by the empirical risk over a finite training set. This is essentially a measure concentration theorem: the expected value (risk) can be estimated by its (empirical) sampled mean. Given an object-label sample $(x, y) \sim \mathcal{D}$, the loss function $L(\hat{y}_w(x), y)$ turns out to be a bounded random variable in the interval $[0, 1]$. In the following we assume that the training data $S = \{(x_1, y_1), ..., (x_m, y_m)\}$ is sampled i.i.d. from the distribution $\mathcal{D}$, and is denoted by $S \sim \mathcal{D}^m$. The measure concentration of a sampled average is then described by the moment generating function, also known as the Hoeffding lemma:

$$\mathbb{E}_{S \sim \mathcal{D}^m} \left[\exp \left(\sigma \left(R(w) - R_S(w) \right) \right) \right] \leq \exp(\sigma^2/8m), \tag{10.8}$$

for all $\sigma \in \mathbb{R}$.

We average over all possible parameters and therefore take into account all possible predictions $\hat{y}_w(x)$:

Lemma 10.1. *Let $L(\hat{y}, y) \in [0, 1]$ be a bounded loss function. Let $p(w)$ be any probability density function over the space of parameters. Then, for any positive number $\sigma > 0$ holds*

$$\mathbb{E}_{S \sim \mathcal{D}^m} \mathbb{E}_{w \sim p} \left[\exp \left(\sigma(R(w) - R_S(w)) \right) \right] \leq \exp(\sigma^2/8m) \tag{10.9}$$

The above bound measures the expected (exponentiated) risk of Gibbs predictors. Gibbs predictors $\hat{y}_w(x)$ are randomized predictors, determined by $w \sim p$. The probability distribution $p(w)$ is determined before seeing the training data and is therefore considered to be a prior distribution over the parameters. $p(w)$ may be any probability distribution over the space of parameters and it determines the amount of influence of any parameter w to the overall expected risk. Therefore when computing the expected risk it also takes into account the desired parameters w^*, which are intuitively the risk minimizer. For example, the prior distribution may be the centered normal distribution $p(w) \propto \exp(\|w\|^2/2)$. Since a centered normal distribution is defined for every w, it also assigns a weight to w^*. However, the centered normal distribution rapidly decays outside of a small radius around the center, and if the desired parameters w^* are far from the center, the above expected risk bound only consider a negligible part of it.

The core idea of PAC-Bayesian theory is to shift the Gibbs classifier to be centered around the desired parameters w^*. Since these parameters are unknown, the PAC-Bayesian theory applies to all possible parameters u. Such bounds are called uniform.

Lemma 10.2. *Consider the setting of Lemma 10.1. Let $q_u(w)$ be any probability density function over the space of parameters with expectation u. Let $D_{\mathrm{KL}}(q_u\|q) = \int q_u(w) \log(q_u(w)/p(w))dw$ be the KL-divergence between two distributions. Then, for any set $S = \{(x_1, y_1), ..., (x_m, y_m)\}$ the following holds simultaneously for all u:*

$$\mathbb{E}_{w \sim p}\Big[\exp\big(R(w) - R_S(w)\big)\Big] \geq \exp\Big(\mathbb{E}_{w \sim q_u}[R(w) - R_S(w)] - D_{\mathrm{KL}}(q_u\|p)\Big) \tag{10.10}$$

Proof. The proof includes two steps. The first step transfers the prior $p(w)$ to the posterior $q_u(w)$. To simplify the notation we omit the subscript of the posterior distribution, writing it as $q(w)$.

$$\mathbb{E}_{w \sim p}\Big[\exp\big(R(w) - R_S(w)\big)\Big] = \mathbb{E}_{w \sim q}\Big[\frac{p(w)}{q(w)} \exp\big(R(w) - R_S(w)\big)\Big] \tag{10.11}$$

We move the ratio $p(w)/q(w)$ to the exponent, thus the right hand-side equals

$$\mathbb{E}_{w \sim q}\Big[\exp\big(R(w) - R_S(w) - \log\frac{q(w)}{p(w)}\big)\Big] \tag{10.12}$$

The second step of the proof uses the convexity of the exponent function to derive a lower bound to this quantity with

$$\exp\Big(\mathbb{E}_{w \sim q}[R(w) - R_S(w)] - \mathbb{E}_{w \sim q}[\log(q(w)/p(w))]\Big). \tag{10.13}$$

The proof then follows from the definition of the KL-divergence as the expectation of $\log(q(w)/p(w))$. $\qquad\square$

We omit σ from Lemma 10.2 to simplify the notation. The same proof holds for $\sigma(R(w) - R_S(w))$, for any positive σ. The lemma holds for any S, thus also holds in expectation, i.e., when taking expectations on both sides of the inequality. Combining both lemmas above we get

$$\mathbb{E}_{S \sim \mathcal{D}^m} \left[\exp \left(\mathbb{E}_{w \sim q_u}[\sigma(R(w) - R_S(w))] - D_{\mathrm{KL}}(q_u \| p)] \right) \right] \leq \exp(\sigma^2/8m) \quad (10.14)$$

This bound holds uniformly (simultaneously) for all u and particularly to the (empirical) risk minimizer w^*. This bound holds in expectation over the samples of training sets. It implies a similar bound that holds in high probability via Markov inequality:

Theorem 10.3. *Consider the setting of the above Lemmas. Then, for any $\delta \in (0, 1]$ and for any real number $\lambda > 0$, with a probability of at least $1 - \delta$ over the draw of the training set, the following holds simultaneously for all u*

$$\mathbb{E}_{w \sim q_u}\left[R(w)\right] \leq \mathbb{E}_{w \sim q_u}\left[R_S(w)\right] + \lambda D_{\mathrm{KL}}(q_u \| p)$$
$$+ \frac{1}{\lambda \cdot 8m} + \lambda \log \frac{1}{\delta} \quad (10.15)$$

Proof. Markov inequality asserts that $Pr[Z \leq EZ/\delta] \geq 1 - \delta$. The theorem follows by setting $Z = \exp\left(\mathbb{E}_{w \sim q_u}[\lambda(R(w) - R_S(w))] - D_{\mathrm{KL}}(q_u \| p)]\right)$ and using Equation (10.14). □

The above bound is a standard PAC-Bayesian bound that appears in various versions in the literature (McAllester, 2003; Langford and Shawe-Taylor, 2002; Seeger, 2003; Catoni, 2007; Seldin, 2009; Germain et al., 2009; Keshet et al., 2011; Seldin et al., 2012).

10.4   Algorithms

Recall that our goal is to find the parameters that minimize the risk as in Equation (10.3). As we stated in (10.5), the empirical risk can be replaced by a surrogate loss function and a regularization term. In our case, the training objective is defined as follows

$$w^* = \arg\min_u \; \mathbb{E}_{w \sim q_u}\left[R_S(w)\right] + \lambda D_{\mathrm{KL}}(q_u \| p), \quad (10.16)$$

where $D_{\mathrm{KL}}(q_u \| p)$ is the regularization term, λ is the regularization parameter, and the surrogate loss is the generalized probit loss defined as

$$\mathbb{E}_{w \sim q_u}\left[L(\hat{y}_w(x), y)\right], \quad (10.17)$$

and can be derived from the linearity of the expectation and Equation (10.4). Note that the minimizer of the objective in Equation (10.16) is also the minimizer of the right-hand side of the bound in Equation (10.15).

We now turn to show that whenever the posterior distributions have smooth probability density functions $q_u(w)$, the perturbation probability model is a smooth function of u. Thus the randomized risk bound can be minimized with gradient methods to approach the desired u.

Theorem 10.4. *Assume $q_u(w)$ is a smooth function of its parameters, then the PAC-Bayesian bound is a smooth function of u:*

$$\nabla_u \mathbb{E}_{w \sim q_u}\Big[R_S(w)\Big] = \frac{1}{m} \sum_{(x,y) \in S} \mathbb{E}_{w \sim q_u}\Big[\nabla_u[\log q_u(w)]L(y_w(x), y)\Big]$$

Moreover, the KL-divergence is a smooth function of w and its gradient takes the form:

$$\nabla_u D_{\mathrm{KL}}(q_u || p) = \mathbb{E}_{w \sim q_u}\Big[\nabla_u[\log q_u(w)]\Big(\log(q_u(w)/p(w)) + 1\Big)\Big]$$

Proof. $\mathbb{E}_{w \sim q_u} R_S(w) = \frac{1}{m} \sum_{i=1}^{m} \int q_u(w) L(\hat{y}_w(x_i), y_i) dw$. Since $q_u(w)$ is a probability density function and $L(\hat{y}, y) \in [0, 1]$ we can differentiate under the integral (cf. Folland, 1999, Theorem 2.27). The gradient is

$$\nabla_u \mathbb{E}_{w \sim q_u}\Big[R_S(w)\Big] = \frac{1}{m} \sum_{i=1}^{m} \int \nabla_u q_u(w) L(\hat{y}_w(x), y) dw. \tag{10.18}$$

Using the identity $\nabla_u q_u(w) = q_u(w) \nabla_u \log(q_u(w))$ the first part of the proof follows. The second part of the proof follows in the same manner, while noting that $\nabla_u(q_u(w) \log q_u(w)) = (\nabla_u q_u(w))(\log q_u(w) + 1)$. $\square$

The gradient of the randomized empirical risk is governed by the gradient of the log-probability density function of its corresponding posterior model. For example, Gaussian model with mean w and identity covariance matrix has the probability density function $q_u(w) \propto \exp(-\|w - u\|^2/2)$, thus the gradient of its log-density is the linear moment of w, i.e., $\nabla_u[\log q_u] = w - u$.

Taking any smooth distribution $q_u(w)$, we can find the parameters u by descending along the stochastic gradient of the PAC-Bayesian generalization bound. The gradient of the randomized empirical risk is formed by two expectations, over the sample points and over the posterior distribution. Computing these expectations is time consuming, thus we use a single sample $\nabla_u[\log q_u(w)]L(y_w(x), y)$ as an unbiased estimator for the gradient. Similarly we estimate the gradient of the KL-divergence with an unbiased estimator which requires a single sample of $\nabla_u[\log q_u(w)](\log(q_u(w)/p(w))+1)$. This approach, called stochastic approximation or online gradient descent, amounts to use of the stochastic gradient update rule, where η is the learning rate. Next, we explore different posterior distributions from computational perspectives. Specifically, we show how to learn the posterior model so as to ensure the computational efficiency of its MAP predictor.

10.5   The Bayesian Perspective

PAC-Bayesian theory has a strong Bayesian ingredient. It integrates over uncertainty of its parameters using the posterior distribution. This important aspect guarantees a uniform generalization bound, over all possible posterior parameters. As a consequence of this theory, a new predictive distribution emerges, the perturbation model, that connects the posterior distribution to the task loss.

10.5.1   Predictive Distribution

The PAC-Bayesian risk give rise to novel distribution models that involve optimization and perturbation. The risk averages over all parameters. $\mathbb{E}_{w\sim q_u}[R(w)] = \mathbb{E}_{w\sim q_u}[L(\hat{y}_w(x), y)]$. To reveal the underlying Bayesian model we aggregate all parameters w that result in the same prediction

$$p(y|x; u) = \mathbb{P}_{w\sim q_u}[y = \hat{y}_w(x)] \tag{10.19}$$

This novel probability distribution measures how much stable a prediction is under random perturbation of the parameters. The appealing property of this distribution is that unlike the Gibbs distribution, it is easy to draw unbiased samples for as long as optimizing is easy. Since this perturbation model is defined by perturbation and optimization it is also called perturb-max or perturb-and-map model.

10.5.2   Posterior Distribution

The posterior distribution accounts for the space of parameters that can be learned. The ability to efficiently apply MAP predictors is key to the success of the learning process. Although MAP predictions are NP-hard in general, there are posterior models for which they can be computed efficiently. For example, whenever the potential function corresponds to a graphical model with no cycles, MAP prediction can be efficiently computed for any learned parameters w.

Learning unconstrained parameters with random MAP predictors provides some freedom in choosing the posterior distribution. In fact, Theorem 10.4

suggests that one can learn any posterior distribution by performing gradient descent on its risk bound, as long as its probability density function is smooth. We show that for unconstrained parameters, additive posterior distributions simplify the learning problem, and the complexity of the bound (i.e., its KL-divergence) mostly depends on its prior distribution.

Corollary 10.5. *Let $q_0(w)$ be a smooth probability density function with zero mean and set the posterior distribution using additive shifts $q_u(w) = q_0(w - u)$. Let $H(q) = -\mathbb{E}_{w \sim q}[\log q(w)]$ be the entropy function. Then*

$$D_{\mathrm{KL}}(q_u || p) = -H(q_0) - \mathbb{E}_{w \sim q_0}[\log p(w + u)]$$

In particular, if $p(w) \propto \exp(-\|w\|^2)$ is Gaussian then $\nabla_u D_{\mathrm{KL}}(q_u || p) = u$

Proof: $D_{\mathrm{KL}}(q_u || p) = -H(q_u) - \mathbb{E}_{w \sim q_u}[\log p(w)]$. By a linear change of variable $\hat{w} = w - u$ it follows that $H(q_u) = H(q_0)$ thus $\nabla_u H(q_u) = 0$. Similarly $\mathbb{E}_{w \sim q_u}[\log p(w)] = \mathbb{E}_{w \sim q_0}[\log p(w + w)]$. Finally, if $p(w)$ is Gaussian then $\mathbb{E}_{w \sim q_0}[\log p(w + u)] = -u^2 - \mathbb{E}_{w \sim q_0}[w^2]$. $\square$

This result implies that every additively-shifted smooth posterior distribution may consider the KL-divergence penalty as the square regularization when using a Gaussian prior $p(w) \propto \exp(-\|w\|^2)$. This generalizes the standard claim on Gaussian posterior distributions (Langford and Shawe-Taylor, 2002), for which $q_0(w)$ are Gaussians. Thus one can use different posterior distributions to better fit the randomized empirical risk without increasing the computational complexity over Gaussian processes.

Learning unconstrained parameters can be efficiently applied to tree structured graphical models. This, however, is restrictive. Many practical problems require more complex models, with many cycles. For some of these models linear program solvers give efficient, although sometimes approximate, MAP predictions. For supermodular models there are specific solvers, such as graph-cuts, that produce fast and accurate MAP predictions. In the following we show how to define posterior distributions that guarantee efficient predictions, thus allowing efficient sampling and learning.

MAP predictions can be computed efficiently in important practical cases, e.g., supermodular potential functions satisfying $\theta_{i,j}(-1, -1; x, w) + \theta_{i,j}(1, 1; x, w) \geq \theta_{i,j}(-1, 1; x, w) + \theta_{i,j}(1, -1; x, w)$. Whenever we restrict ourselves to symmetric potential function $\theta_{i,j}(y_i, y_j; x, w) = w_{i,j} y_i y_j$, supermodularity translates to nonnegative constraint on the parameters $w_{i,j} \geq 0$. In order to model posterior distributions that allow efficient sampling we define models over the constrained parameter space. Unfortunately, the additive posterior models $q_u(w) = q_0(w - u)$ are inappropriate for this purpose, as they have a positive probability for negative w values and would generate non-supermodular models.

To learn constrained parameters one requires posterior distributions that respect these constraints. For nonnegative parameters we apply posterior distributions that are defined on the nonnegative real numbers. We suggest the incorporation of the parameters of the posterior distribution in a multiplicative manner into a distribution over the nonnegative real numbers. For any distribution $q_\alpha(w)$ we determine a posterior distribution with parameters u as $q_u(w) = q_\alpha(w/u)/u$. We show that multiplicative posterior models naturally provide log-barrier functions over the constrained set of nonnegative numbers. This property is important to the computational efficiency of the bound minimization algorithm.

Corollary 10.6. *For any probability distribution $q_\alpha(w)$, let $q_{\alpha,u}(w) = q_\alpha(w/u)/u$ be the parametrized posterior distribution. Then*

$$D_{\mathrm{KL}}(q_{\alpha,u}\|p) = -H(q_\alpha) - \log u - \mathbb{E}_{w\sim q_\alpha}[\log p(uw)]$$

Define the Gamma function $w(\alpha) = \int_0^\infty w^{\alpha-1}\exp(-w)$. If $p(w) = q_\alpha(w) = w^{\alpha-1}\exp(-w)/w(\alpha)$ have the Gamma distribution with parameter α, then $\mathbb{E}_{w\sim q_\alpha}[\log p(uw)] = (\alpha-1)\log u - \alpha u$. Alternatively, if $p(w)$ are truncated Gaussians then $\mathbb{E}_{w\sim q_\alpha}[\log p(uw)] = -\frac{\alpha}{2}u^2 + \log\sqrt{\pi/2}$.

Proof: The entropy of multiplicative posterior models naturally implies the log-barrier function:

$$-H(q_{\alpha,u}) \stackrel{\hat{w}=w/u}{=} \int q_\alpha(\hat{w})\Big(\log q_\alpha(\hat{w}) - \log u\Big)d\hat{w} = -H(q_\alpha) - \log u.$$

Similarly, $\mathbb{E}_{w\sim q_{\alpha,u}}[\log p(w)] = \mathbb{E}_{w\sim q_\alpha}[\log p(uw)]$. The special cases for the Gamma and the truncated normal distribution follow by a direct computation. $\square$

The multiplicative posterior distribution would provide the barrier function $-\log u$ as part of its KL-divergence. Thus the multiplicative posterior effortlessly enforces the constraints of its parameters. This property suggests that using multiplicative rules is computationally favorable. Interestingly, using a prior model with Gamma distribution adds to the barrier function a linear regularization term $\|u\|_1$ that encourages sparsity. On the other hand, a prior model with a truncated Gaussian adds a square regularization term which drifts the nonnegative parameters away from zero. A computational disadvantage of the Gaussian prior is that its barrier function cannot be controlled by a parameter α.

10.6 Approximate Inference

We may use the flexibility of Bayesian models to extend perturbation models beyond MAP prediction, as in the case of approximate inference. MAP prediction can be phrased as an integer linear program, stated in Equation (10.7). The computational burden of integer linear programs can be relaxed when one replaces the integral constraints with nonnegative constraints. This approach produces approximate MAP predictions. An important learning challenge is to extend the predictive distribution of perturbation models to incorporate approximate MAP solutions. Approximate MAP predictions are are described by the feasible set of their linear program relaxations which is usually called the local polytope:

$$L(R) = \left\{ b_r(y_r) : b_r(y_r) \geq 0, \sum_{y_r} b_r(y_r) = 1, \forall r \subset s \sum_{y_s \backslash y_r} b_s(y_s) = b_r(y_r) \right\}$$

Linear program solutions are usually the extreme points of their feasible polytope. The local polytope is defined by a finite set of equalities and inequalities, thus it has a finite number of extreme points. The predictive distribution that is defined in Equation (10.19) can be effortlessly extended to the finite set of the local polytope's extreme points. This approach has two flaws. First, linear program solutions might not be extreme points, and decoding such a point usually requires additional computational effort. Second, without describing the linear program solutions one cannot incorporate loss functions that take the structural properties of approximate MAP predictions into account when computing the randomized risk.

Theorem 10.7. *Consider approximate MAP predictions that arise from relaxation of the MAP prediction problem in Equation (10.7).*

$$\arg \max_{b_r(y_r)} \sum_{r, y_r} b_r(y_r) \theta_r(y_r; x, w) \quad s.t. \quad b \in L(R)$$

Then any optimal solution b^* is described by a vector $\tilde{y}_w(x)$ in the finite power sets over the cliques $\tilde{\mathcal{Y}} \subset \times_r 2^{\mathcal{Y}_r}$:

$$\tilde{y}_w(x) = (\tilde{y}_{w,r}(x))_{r \in \mathcal{R}} \qquad where \qquad \tilde{y}_{w,r}(x) = \{y_r : b_r^*(y_r) > 0\}$$

Moreover, if there is a unique optimal solution b^* then it corresponds to an extreme point in the local polytope.

Proof: The program is convex over a compact set, thus strong duality holds. Fixing the Lagrange multipliers $\lambda_{r \to s}(y_r)$ that correspond to the marginal constraints $\sum_{y_s \backslash y_r} b_s(y_s) = b_r(y_r)$, and considering the probability constraints as the domain of the primal program, we derive the dual program

$$\sum_r \max_{y_r} \left\{ \theta_r(y_r; x, w) + \sum_{c:c \subset r} \lambda_{c \to r}(y_c) - \sum_{p:p \supset r} \lambda_{r \to p}(y_r) \right\}$$

Lagrange optimality constraints (or equivalently, Danskin Theorem) determine the primal optimal solutions $b_r^*(y_r)$ to be probability distributions over the set $\arg \max_{y_r} \{ \theta_r(y_r; x, w) + \sum_{c:c \subset r} \lambda_{c \to r}^*(y_c) - \sum_{p:p \supset r} \lambda_{r \to p}^*(y_r) \}$ that satisfy the marginalization constraints. Thus $\tilde{y}_{w,r}(x)$ is the information that identifies the primal optimal solutions, i.e., any other primal feasible solution that has the same $\tilde{y}_{w,r}(x)$ is also a primal optimal solution. $\square$

This theorem extends Proposition 3 in Globerson and Jaakkola (2007) to non-binary and non-pairwise graphical models. The theorem describes the discrete structures of approximate MAP predictions. Thus we are able to define posterior distributions that use efficient, although approximate, predictions while taking into account their structures. To integrate these posterior distributions to randomized risk we extend the loss function to $L(\tilde{y}_w(x), y)$. One can verify that the results in Section 10.3 follow through, e.g., by considering loss functions $L : \tilde{\mathcal{Y}} \times \tilde{\mathcal{Y}} \to [0, 1]$ while the training examples labels belong to the subset $\mathcal{Y} \subset \tilde{\mathcal{Y}}$.

10.7   Empirical Evaluation

We presents two sets of experiments. The first set is a phoneme recognizer when the loss is frame error rate (Hamming distance) and phoneme error rate (normalized edit distance). The second set of experiments is an interactive image segmentation.

10.7.1   Phonetic Recognition

We evaluated the proposed method on the TIMIT acoustic-phonetic continuous speech corpus (Lamel et al., 1986). The training set contains 462 speakers and 3696 utterances. We used the core test set of 24 speakers and 192 utterances and a development set of 50 speakers and 400 utterances as defined in (Sha and Saul, 2007) to tune the parameters. Following the common practice (Lee and Hon, 1989), we mapped the 61 TIMIT phonemes into 48 phonemes for training, and further collapsed from 48 phonemes to 39 phonemes for evaluation. We extracted 12 MFCC features and log energy with their deltas and double deltas to form 39-dimensional acoustic feature vectors. The window size and the frame size were 25 msec and 10 msec, respectively.

Method	Frame error rate	Phoneme error rate
HMM (Cheng et al., 2009)	39.3%	42.0%
HMM (Keshet et al., 2006)	35.1%	40.9%
KSBSC (Keshet et al., 2006)	-	45.1%
PA (Crammer, 2010)	30.0%	33.4%
DROP (Crammer, 2010)	29.2%	31.1%
PAC-Bayes 1-frame	**27.7%**	**30.2%**
Online LM-HMM (Cheng et al., 2009)	25.0%	30.2%
Batch LM-HMM (Sha and Saul, 2007)	-	28.2%
CRF, 9-frames, MLP (Morris and Fosler-Lussier, 2008)	-	29.3%
PAC-Bayes 9-frames	**26.5%**	**28.6%**

Table 10.1: Reported results on TIMIT core test set.

Similar to the output and transition probabilities in HMMs, our implementation has two sets of potentials. The first set of potential captures the confidence of a phoneme based on the acoustic. For each phoneme we define a potential function that is a sum over all acoustic features corresponding to that phoneme. Rather than sum the acoustic features directly, we sum them mapped through an RBF kernel. The kernel is approximated using the Taylor expansion of order 3. Below we report results with a context window of 1 frame and a context window of 9 frames.

The second set of potentials captures the duration of each phoneme and the transition between phonemes. For each pair of phonemes $p, q \in P$ we define the potential as a sum over all transitions between phoneme p and q.

We applied the algorithm as discussed in Section 10.4 where we set the parameters over a development set. The probit expectation was approximated by a mean over 1000 samples. The initial weight vector was set to averaged weight vector of the Passive-Aggressive (PA) algorithm Crammer et al. (2006), which was trained with the same set of parameters and with 100 epochs as described in Crammer (2010).

Table 10.1 summarizes the results and compare the performance of the proposed algorithm to other algorithms for phoneme recognition. Although the algorithm aims at minimizing the phoneme error rate, we also report the frame error rate, which is the fraction of misclassified frames. A common practice is to split each phoneme segment into three (or more) states. Using such a technique usually improves performance (see for example Mohamed and Hinton (2010); Sung and Jurafsky (2010); Schwartz et al. (2006)). Here we report results on approaches which treat the phoneme as a whole, and defer the issues of splitting into states in our algorithm for future work. In

Method	Grabcut loss	PASCAL loss
Our method	**7.77%**	**5.29%**
Structured SVM (Hamming loss)	9.74%	6.66%
Structured SVM (all-zero loss)	7.87%	5.63%
GMMRF (Blake et al., 2004)	7.88%	5.85%
Perturb-and-MAP (Papandreou and Yuille, 2011)	8.19%	5.76%

Table 10.2: Learning the Grabcut segmentations using two different loss functions. Our learned parameters outperform structured SVM approaches and Perturb-and-MAP moment matching

the upper part of the table (above the line), we report results on approaches which make use of context window of 1 frame. The first two rows are two HMM systems taken from Keshet et al. (2006) and Cheng et al. (2009) with a single state corresponding to our setting. KSBSC Keshet et al. (2006) is a kernel-based recognizer trained with the PA algorithm. PA and DROP Crammer (2010) are online algorithms which use the same setup and feature functions described here. Online LM-HMM Cheng et al. (2009) and Batch LM-HMM Sha and Saul (2007) are algorithms for large margin training of continuous density HMMs. Below the line, at the bottom part of the table, we report the results with a context of 9 frames. CRF Morris and Fosler-Lussier (2008) is based on the computation of local posteriors with MLPs, which was trained on a context of 9 frames. We can see that our algorithm outperforms all algorithms except for the large margin HMMs. The difference between our algorithm and the LM-HMM algorithm might be in the richer expressive power of the latter. Using a context of 9 frames the results of our algorithm are comparable to LM-HMM.

10.7.2 Image Segmentation

We perform experiments on an interactive image segmentation. We use the Grabcut dataset proposed by Blake et al. (2004) which consists of 50 images of objects on cluttered backgrounds and the goal is to obtain the pixel-accurate segmentations of the object given an initial "trimap" (see Figure 10.1). A trimap is an approximate segmentation of the image into regions that are well inside, well outside and the boundary of the object, something a user can easily specify in an interactive application.

A popular approach for segmentation is the GrabCut approach (Boykov et al., 2001; Blake et al., 2004). We learn parameters for the "Gaussian Mixture Markov Random Field" (GMMRF) formulation of Blake et al. (2004) using a potential function over foreground/background segmentations $Y = \{-1, 1\}^n$: $\theta(y; x, w) = \sum_{i \in V} \theta_i(y_i; x, w) + \sum_{i,j \in E} \theta_{i,j}(y_i, y_j; x, w)$. The

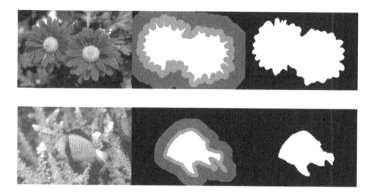

Figure 10.1: Two examples of image (*left*), input "trimap" (*middle*) and the final segmentation (*right*) produced using our learned parameters.

local potentials are $\theta_i(y_i; x, w) = w_{y_i} \log P(y_i|x)$, where w_{y_i} are parameters to be learned while $P(y_i|x)$ are obtained from a Gaussian mixture model learned on the background and foreground pixels for an image x in the initial trimap. The pairwise potentials are $\theta_{i,j}(y_i, y_j; x, w) = w_a \exp(-(x_i - x_j)^2)y_iy_j$, where x_i denotes the intensity of image x at pixel i, and w_a are the parameters to be learned for the angles $a \in \{0, 90, 45, -45\}°$. These potential functions are supermodular as long as the parameters w_a are nonnegative, thus MAP prediction can be computed efficiently with the graph-cuts algorithm. For these parameters we use multiplicative posterior model with the Gamma distribution. The dataset does not come with a standard training/test split so we use the odd set of images for training and even set of images for testing. We use stochastic gradient descent with the step parameter decaying as $\eta_t = \frac{\eta}{t_o+t}$ for 250 iterations.

We use two different loss functions for training/testing our approach to illustrate the flexibility of our approach for learning using various task specific loss functions. The "GrabCut loss" measures the fraction of incorrect pixel labels in the region specified as the boundary in the trimap. The "PASCAL loss", which is commonly used in several image segmentation benchmarks, measures the ratio of the intersection and union of the foregrounds of ground truth segmentation and the solution.

As a comparison we also trained parameters using moment matching of MAP perturbations (Papandreou and Yuille, 2011) and structured SVM. We use a stochastic gradient approach with a decaying step size for 1000 iterations. Using structured SVM, solving loss-augmented inference $\max_{\hat{y} \in Y}\{L(y, \hat{y}) + \theta(y; x, w)\}$ with the Hamming loss can be efficiently done using graph-cuts. We also consider learning parameters with all-zero loss function, i.e., $L(y, \hat{y}) \equiv 0$. To ensure that the weights remain non-negative we project the weights into the non-negative side after each iteration.

Table 10.2 shows the results of learning using various methods. For the GrabCut loss, our method obtains comparable results to the GMMRF framework of Blake et al. (2004), which used hand-tuned parameters. Our results are significantly better when PASCAL loss is used. Our method also outperforms the parameters learned using structured SVM and Perturb-and-MAP approaches. In our experiments the structured SVM with the Hamming loss did not perform well – the loss augmented inference tended to focus on maximum violations instead of good solutions which causes the parameters to change even though the MAP solution has a low loss (a similar phenomenon was observed in Szummer et al. (2008). Using the all-zero loss tends to produce better results in practice as seen in Table 10.2. Figure 10.1 shows some sample images, the input trimap, and the segmentations obtained using our approach.

10.8   Discussion

Learning complex models requires one to consider non-decomposable loss functions that take into account the desirable structures. We suggest the use of the Bayesian perspectives to efficiently sample and learn such models using random MAP predictions. We show that any smooth posterior distribution would suffice to define a smooth PAC-Bayesian risk bound which can be minimized using gradient decent. In addition, we relate the posterior distributions to the computational properties of the MAP predictors. We suggest multiplicative posterior models to learn supermodular potential functions that come with specialized MAP predictors such as the graph-cut algorithm. We also describe label-augmented posterior models that can use efficient MAP approximations, such as those arising from linear program relaxations. We did not evaluate the performance of these posterior models, and further exploration of such models is required.

The results here focus on posterior models that would allow for efficient sampling using MAP predictions. There are other cases for which specific posterior distributions might be handy, e.g., learning posterior distributions of Gaussian mixture models. In these cases, the parameters include the covariance matrix, thus would require to sample over the family of positive definite matrices.

Acknowledgements

TJ was partially supported by NSF grant #1524427

10.9 References

A. Blake, C. Rother, M. Brown, P. Perez, and P. Torr. Interactive image segmentation using an adaptive gmmrf model. In *ECCV 2004*, pages 428–441. 2004.

Y. Boykov, O. Veksler, and R. Zabih. Fast approximate energy minimization via graph cuts. *PAMI*, 2001.

O. Catoni. PAC-Bayesian supervised classification: the thermodynamics of statistical learning. *arXiv preprint arXiv:0712.0248*, 2007.

C.-C. Cheng, F. Sha, and L. K. Saul. A fast online algorithm for large margin training of continuous-density hidden Markov models. In *Interspeech*, 2009.

K. Crammer. Efficient online learning with individual learning-rates for phoneme sequence recognition. In *Proc. ICASSP*, 2010.

K. Crammer, O. Dekel, J. Keshet, S. Shalev-Shwartz, and Y. Singer. Online passive aggressive algorithms. *Journal of Machine Learning Research*, 7, 2006.

C. Do, Q. Le, C.-H. Teo, O. Chapelle, and A. Smola. Tighter bounds for structured estimation. In *Proceedings of NIPS (22)*, 2008.

G. Folland. Real analysis: Modern techniques and their applications, john wiley & sons. *New York*, 1999.

P. Germain, A. Lacasse, F. Laviolette, and M. Marchand. PAC-Bayesian learning of linear classifiers. In *ICML*, pages 353–360. ACM, 2009.

K. Gimpel and N. Smith. Softmax-margin crfs: Training log-linear models with cost functions. In *Human Language Technologies: The 2010 Annual Conference of the North American Chapter of the Association for Computational Linguistics*, pages 733–736. Association for Computational Linguistics, 2010.

A. Globerson and T. S. Jaakkola. Fixing max-product: Convergent message passing algorithms for MAP LP-relaxations. *Advances in Neural Information Processing Systems*, 21, 2007.

L. Goldberg and M. Jerrum. The complexity of ferromagnetic ising with local fields. *Combinatorics Probability and Computing*, 16(1):43, 2007.

M. Jerrum and A. Sinclair. Polynomial-time approximation algorithms for the ising model. *SIAM Journal on computing*, 22(5):1087–1116, 1993.

J. Keshet, S. Shalev-Shwartz, S. Bengio, Y. Singer, and D. Chazan. Discriminative kernel-based phoneme sequence recognition. In *Interspeech*, 2006.

J. Keshet, D. McAllester, and T. Hazan. PAC-Bayesian approach for minimization of phoneme error rate. In *ICASSP*, 2011.

J. Lafferty, A. McCallum, and F. Pereira. Conditional random fields: Probabilistic models for segmenting and labeling sequence data. In *International Conference of Machine Learning*, pages 282–289, 2001.

L. Lamel, R. Kassel, and S. Seneff. Speech database development: Design an analysis of the acoustic-phonetic corpus. In *DARPA Speech Recognition Workshop*, 1986.

J. Langford and J. Shawe-Taylor. PAC-Bayes & margins. *Advances in neural information processing systems*, 15:423–430, 2002.

K.-F. Lee and H.-W. Hon. Speaker independent phone recognition using hidden markov models. *IEEE Trans. Acoustic, Speech and Signal Proc.*, 37(2):1641–1648, 1989.

D. McAllester. Simplified PAC-Bayesian margin bounds. *Learning Theory and Kernel Machines*, pages 203–215, 2003.

D. McAllester. Generalization bounds and consistency for structured labeling. In B. Schölkopf, A. J. Smola, B. Taskar, and S. Vishwanathan, editors, *Predicting Structured Data*, pages 247–262. MIT Press, 2006.

D. McAllester and J. Keshet. Generalization bounds and consistency for latent structural probit and ramp loss. In *Proceeding of NIPS*, 2011.

D. McAllester, T. Hazan, and J. Keshet. Direct loss minimization for structured prediction. *Advances in Neural Information Processing Systems*, 23:1594–1602, 2010.

A. Mohamed and G. Hinton. Phone recognition using restricted boltzmann machines. In *Proc. ICASSP*, 2010.

J. Morris and E. Fosler-Lussier. Conditional random fields for integrating local discriminative classifiers. *IEEE Trans. on Acoustics, Speech, and Language Processing*, 16(3):617–628, 2008.

G. Papandreou and A. Yuille. Perturb-and-map random fields: Using discrete optimization to learn and sample from energy models. In *ICCV*, Barcelona, Spain, Nov. 2011. doi: 10.1109/ICCV.2011.

J. Pearl. *Probabilistic Reasoning in Intelligent Systems: Networks of Plausible Inference*. Morgan Kaufmann Publishers, 1988.

M. Ranjbar, T. Lan, Y. Wang, S. Robinovitch, Z.-N. Li, and G. Mori. Optimizing nondecomposable loss functions in structured prediction. *IEEE Trans. Pattern Analysis and Machine Intelligence*, 35(4):911–924, 2013.

A. Rush and M. Collins. A tutorial on dual decomposition and lagrangian relaxation for inference in natural language processing.

P. Schwartz, P. Matejka, and J. Cernocky. Hierarchical structures of neural networks for phoneme recognition. In *Proc. ICASSP*, 2006.

M. Seeger. Pac-bayesian generalisation error bounds for gaussian process classification. *The Journal of Machine Learning Research*, 3:233–269, 2003.

Y. Seldin. *A PAC-Bayesian Approach to Structure Learning*. PhD thesis, 2009.

Y. Seldin, F. Laviolette, N. Cesa-Bianchi, J. Shawe-Taylor, and P. Auer. Pac-bayesian inequalities for martingales. *Information Theory, IEEE Transactions on*, 58(12):7086–7093, 2012.

F. Sha and L. K. Saul. Comparison of large margin training to other discriminative methods for phonetic recognition by hidden Markov models. In *Proc. ICASSP*, 2007.

D. Sontag, T. Meltzer, A. Globerson, T. Jaakkola, and Y. Weiss. Tightening LP relaxations for MAP using message passing. In *Conf. Uncertainty in Artificial Intelligence (UAI)*, 2008.

Y.-H. Sung and D. Jurafsky. Hidden conditional random fields for phone recognition. In *Proc. ASRU*, 2010.

M. Szummer, P. Kohli, and D. Hoiem. Learning crfs using graph cuts. In *Computer Vision–ECCV 2008*, pages 582–595. Springer, 2008.

D. Tarlow, R. Adams, and R. Zemel. Randomized optimum models for structured prediction. In *AISTATS*, pages 21–23, 2012.

B. Taskar, C. Guestrin, and D. Koller. Max-margin Markov networks. *Advances in neural information processing systems*, 16:51, 2004.

A. Tewari and P. Bartlett. On the consistency of multiclass classification methods. *Journal of Machine Learning Research*, 8:1007–1025, 2007.

I. Tsochantaridis, T. Joachims, T. Hofmann, and Y. Altun. Large margin methods for structured and interdependent output variables. *Journal of Machine Learning Research*, 6(2):1453, 2006.

11   Adversarial Perturbations of Deep Neural Networks

David Warde-Farley   wardefar@iro.umontreal.ca
Montreal Institute for Learning Algorithms, Université de Montréal
Montreal, QC, Canada

Ian Goodfellow   goodfellow@google.com
Google, Inc.
Mountain View, CA, USA

This chapter provides a review of a body of recent work on the topic of adversarial examples *and* generative adversarial networks. *Adversarial examples are examples created via worst-case perturbation of the input to a machine learning model. Adversarial examples have become a useful tool for the analysis and regularization of deep neural networks for classification. In the generative adversarial networks framework, the task of probabilistic modeling is reduced to the task of predicting worst-case perturbations of the input to a deep neural network. A discriminator network learns to recognize real data and reject fake samples, while a generator network learns to emit samples that deceive the discriminator. The GAN framework provides an alternative to maximum likelihood. The new framework has many advantageous computational properties, and is better suited than maximum likelihood to the task of generating realistic samples. More generally, games may be designed to have equilibria that direct learning algorithms to accomplish other goals, such as domain adaptation or preservation of privacy.*

11.1   Introduction

The past several years have given rise to two related lines of inquiry in deep learning research that view the training of neural networks through the lens of an adversarial game. The first body of work centers on the surprising result that discriminative classifiers are often highly sensitive to very small perturbations in the input space. This finding has led to algorithms designed to increase classifier robustness, to these perturbations and more generally, by exploiting these "adversarial examples". The second body of work frames generative model training as an adversarial game, pitting a sample generation process against a classifier trained to discriminate synthesized examples from training data.

This chapter describes how to construct adversarial perturbations in Section 11.2, then describes how to use the resulting adversarial examples to improve the robustness of a classifier in Section 11.3. Finally, Section 11.4 describes more sophisticated games in which one network is trained to generate inputs that deceive another network. These games between two machine learning models can be used for generative modeling, privatization of data, domain adaptation, and other applications.

11.2   Adversarial Examples

Neural networks have enjoyed much recent success in various application domains, owing to their ability to learn rich, non-linear parametric mappings from large amounts of data. While the general principles of training such networks via gradient descent are now well understood, a fully principled account of the internal representations they learn to compute remains elusive. As the commercial and industrial adoption of neural network technology hastens, the search for these insights becomes ever more important. Efforts to better understand how neural networks parameterize the input-output mappings they learn have yielded surprising results.

Szegedy et al. (2014b) discovered that small changes to the input of a neural network can have large, surprising effects on its output. For example, a well-chosen perturbation of pixels in the input to an image classifier can completely alter the class predicted by the network; in extreme cases, such as the one illustrated in Figure 11.1, the difference between the original and perturbed examples is imperceptible to a human observer. This surprising sensitivity to small perturbations has been found to exist not only in neural networks but also in more traditional machine learning methods, such as

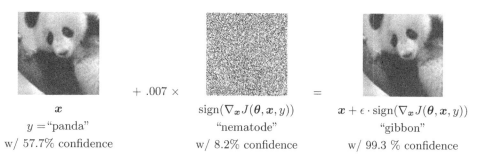

$$x \qquad\qquad\qquad \text{sign}(\nabla_{\boldsymbol{x}} J(\boldsymbol{\theta}, \boldsymbol{x}, y)) \qquad x + \epsilon \cdot \text{sign}(\nabla_{\boldsymbol{x}} J(\boldsymbol{\theta}, \boldsymbol{x}, y))$$

$y =$ "panda"   "nematode"   "gibbon"

w/ 57.7% confidence   w/ 8.2% confidence   w/ 99.3 % confidence

Figure 11.1: An example of an adversarial perturbation of an ImageNet example, where the perturbation is so small that it is imperceptible to a human observer despite changing the model's classification of the input. The model assigns higher confidence to the incorrect classification of the adversarial example that it assigned to the correct classification of the original image. The model in this example is GoogLeNet (Szegedy et al., 2014a). Figure reproduced with permission from Goodfellow et al. (2014b).

linear and nearest neighbor classifiers. In-domain examples that have been altered in this fashion are known as *adversarial examples*.

Adversarial examples are interesting from many different perspectives. First, they demonstrate that machine learning methods do not yet truly understand the tasks they are asked to perform, even though these methods often achieve human level performance (or better) on a test set consisting of naturally occurring inputs. Improving performance on adversarial examples therefore naturally implies achieving a deeper understanding of the underlying task. To this end, improvements in classification of adversarial examples can indeed lead to improvements on the original, non-adversarial classification task, as described in Section 11.3. Second, adversarial examples also have important implications for computer security, discussed in Section 11.2.1. Adversarial examples suggest that contemporary machine learning algorithms deployed against artificial perception tasks are performing fundamentally different computations than the human perceptual system, as discussed in Section 11.2.2. Finally, adversarial examples are interesting because they present a major difficulty for certain forms of model-based optimization. In scenarios where automated classification is useful but the major task of interest is a search for examples with desirable properties (e.g. drug design), one might be tempted to employ a well-performing differentiable classifier and perform gradient ascent with respect to the input. However, the existence and relative abundance of adversarial examples suggests this approach will most often be fruitless.

11.2.1   Cross-Model, Cross-Dataset Generalization and Security

A shocking property of adversarial examples, discovered by Szegedy et al. (2014b), is that a specific input point $\tilde{x}$ that was designed to deceive one model (model A) will often also deceive another model, model B. When model B has a different architecture than model A, this is called *cross-model generalization* of adversarial examples. When model B was trained on a different training set than model A, this is called *cross-dataset generalization*. It is not fully understood why this happens, but Section 11.2.3 offers some intuitive justification.

Both Szegedy et al. (2014b) and Goodfellow et al. (2014b) present several experiments demonstrating the transfer rate between various model families and subsets of the training set. Additional experimental results unique to this chapter are presented in Table 11.1, using the same adversarial example generation procedure as Goodfellow et al. (2014b). The crafting model for the majority of these experiments was a maxout neural network of the same architecture employed for the permutation-invariant MNIST task in Goodfellow et al. (2013a). Additionally, transfer between a smoothed, differentiable version of nearest neighbor classification and conventional nearest neighbor is examined, where the prediction of the smoothed nearest neighbor classifier predicts a probability for class i via the formula

$$y_i(\boldsymbol{x}) = \frac{1}{N} \sum_{n=1}^{N} w_n y_i^{(n)} \tag{11.1}$$

where $y_i^{(n)}$ is equal to 1 if training example n has class i and 0 otherwise, and w_n is the softmax-normalized squared Euclidean distance from the test example $\boldsymbol{x}$ to training example $\boldsymbol{x}^{(n)}$,

$$w_n = \frac{\exp\left(-\|\boldsymbol{x} - \boldsymbol{x}^{(n)}\|^2\right)}{\sum_{m=1} \exp\left(-\|\boldsymbol{x} - \boldsymbol{x}^{(m)}\|^2\right)} \tag{11.2}$$

These results show that there is a non-trivial error rate even when the adversarial examples are crafted to fool a neural network, then deployed against an extremely different machine learning model such as nearest neighbor classification. Because these models are so different from each other, nearest neighbor has a lower error rate on the transferred adversarial examples than has usually been reported previously, but the error rate remains significant. These results also show that models that are not differentiable (such as nearest neighbor) can easily be attacked using cross model transfer from a differentiable model (maxout networks or smoothed nearest neighbor).

Crafting model	Target model	Error rate
Maxout network	Nearest neighbor	25.3%
Smoothed nearest neighbor	Nearest neighbor	47.2%
Maxout network	ReLU network	47.2%
Maxout network	Tanh network	99.3%
Maxout network	Softmax regression	88.9%

Table 11.1: Results of additional cross-model adversarial transfer experiments. The maxout crafting model is identical in architecture to that employed for the permutation-invariant MNIST task by Goodfellow et al. (2013a). The ReLU and Tanh neural networks each contained two layers of 1,200 hidden units each. All nerual networks were trained with dropout (Srivastava et al., 2014).

Cross-model, cross-dataset generalization of adversarial examples implies that adversarial examples pose a security risk even under a threat model where the attacker does not have access to the target's model definition, model parameters, or training set. The attacker can prepare a training set (for the same task), train a model on their own training set, craft adversarial examples that deceive their own model, and then deploy these adversarial examples against the target system.

Attacks that leverage cross-model and cross-dataset generalization of adversarial examples have been acknowledged as a theoretical possibility since the work of Szegedy et al. (2014b) introduced these effects. Papernot et al. (2016a) provided the first practical demonstration of attacks based on adversarial examples in a realistic scenario: they trained a classifier for the MNIST dataset using the MetaMind API, wherein the model parameters reside on MetaMind's servers and its definition is not disclosed to the user. By training another model locally and crafting adversarial examples that fooled it, the authors were able to successfully fool the model they had trained via the MetaMind API. This suggests that modern machine learning methods require new defenses before they can be safely used in situations where they might face an actual adversary.

11.2.2 Adversarial Examples and the Human Brain

It is natural to wonder whether the human brain is vulnerable to adversarial examples. At first glance, it seems difficult to test, because there is no known method for obtaining a description of the brain as a differentiable model in the form used by adversarial example construction algorithms. However, the cross-model, cross-dataset generalization property of adversarial examples suggests that if the brain were even remotely similar to modern machine learning algorithms, it should be fooled by the same images that fool machine learning models. So far this seems not to be the case.

However, the brain can be easily fooled by many illusions; see Robinson (2013) for a review. For example, optical illusions in which one line appears to be longer than another despite both lines being the same length can be interpreted as adversarial examples for the line length regression task.

Audible and visible stimuli can also cause a range of beneficial or detrimental involuntary side effects in human observers, ranging from pain relief to seizures. Many of these effects rely on synchronizing the temporal frequency of a visual stimulus to the temporal frequency of changes in brain activity measured by EEG. This might be analogous to adversarial example construction techniques that match a spatial pattern of inputs to the spatial distribution of neural network weights. See Frederick et al. (2005) for a useful review of the effects of audible and visible stimuli constructed using information from EEG.

11.2.3   The Linearity Hypothesis

When Szegedy et al. (2014b) discovered the existence of adversarial examples, their cause was unknown. Initially, they were suspected to be caused by neural networks being highly complex, non-linear models that can assign very random classifications to test set inputs.

Goodfellow et al. (2014b) argued that these explanations failed to explain two important experimental observations. First, adversarial examples affect some very simple models, such as shallow linear classifiers, just as much as they affect deep models. Model complexity and overfitting would therefore not seem to be the primary problem. Second, adversarial examples can consistently fool models other than the one from which they are initially derived, as described in Section 11.2.1. If adversarial examples were just a manifestation of overfitting, then different models should respond to each adversarial example differently. Goodfellow et al. (2014b) demonstrated, to the contrary, that distinct models not only mislabel the same adversarial examples, but also mislabel them with the same class.

Goodfellow et al. (2014b) introduced *the linearity hypothesis*, which predicts that most adversarial examples affecting current machine learning models arise due to the model behaving extremely linearly as a function of its inputs. To confirm this hypothesis, Goodfellow et al. (2014b) demonstrated that adversarial attacks against linear approximations of deep models are highly successful, and introduced visualizations showing that the *logits* (i.e. the inputs to a final softmax output layer) of a deep neural network classifier are piecewise linear with large pieces as a function of the input to the model.

This hypothesis is based on the observation that modern deep networks are based on components that have been designed to be extremely linear, such as rectified linear units (Jarrett et al., 2009; Glorot et al., 2011). Though deep neural networks are very nonlinear as a function of their parameters, they can nonetheless be very linear as a function of their inputs. Deep rectifier networks divide input space into several regions, with the output of the rectified linear layers being linear within each region. These regions are often extremely large, especially compared to the size of perturbations used to construct adversarial examples.

To understand why linear functions are highly vulnerable to adversarial examples, consider the output of a regression model $f(\boldsymbol{x}) = \boldsymbol{w}^\top \boldsymbol{x}$. If the input is perturbed by $\epsilon \cdot \mathrm{sign}(\boldsymbol{w})$, then the output increases by $\epsilon \|\boldsymbol{w}\|_1$. When $\boldsymbol{w}$ is high dimensional, the increase in the output can be extremely large. In other words, linear functions can add up very many tiny pieces of evidence to reach an extreme conclusion. If $\boldsymbol{x}$ has large feature values that are not closely aligned with $\boldsymbol{w}$, it will have less of an effect on the output than a perturbation consisting of many small values that are all closely aligned to $\boldsymbol{w}$.

Even in low dimensional spaces, linear functions behave in ways that seem disadvantageous for machine learning. A logistic regression model applied to a one-dimensional input space that classifies an input of $x = -1$ as belonging to the negative class and an input of $x = 1$ as belonging to the positive class must classify an input of $x = 2$ as belonging to the positive class with extremely high confidence, even if no value as large as 2 occurred in the training set. Larger values of x result in more confidence, even if they are even farther from examples that were seen at training time.

Because neural networks are parameterized in terms of linear components, they are biased toward learning functions that make wild predictions when extrapolating far from previously seen inputs. In high-dimensional spaces, even small perturbations of each input can take the input vector very far in Euclidean distance from the starting point. This explains the majority of adversarial examples affecting modern neural networks.

It is natural to wonder how adversarial examples are distributed throughout space. For example, one could imagine that they are rare and occur in small, fine pockets that must be found with careful search procedures. The linearity hypothesis predicts instead that adversarial examples occupy large volumes of space. If the cost function $J(\boldsymbol{x}, y)$ increases in a roughly linear fashion in direction $\boldsymbol{d}$, then an adversarial example $\tilde{\boldsymbol{x}} = \boldsymbol{x} + \boldsymbol{\eta}$ will be misclassified so long as $\boldsymbol{\eta}^\top \boldsymbol{d}$ is large. The linearity hypothesis thus predicts that a hyperplane where $\boldsymbol{\eta}^\top \boldsymbol{d} = C$ for some constant C divides the space $\mathbb{R}^n$ into two half-spaces. The original input $\boldsymbol{x}$ is correctly classified, and a large region of points on the same side of the hyperplane as x are also classified the same as x. On the opposite side of the hyperplane, nearly all points have a different classification.

Goodfellow et al. (2014b) provided a variety of sources of indirect evidence for the linearity hypothesis. This chapter introduces some visualizations that show the resulting half-spaces of adversarial examples more directly. These visualizations are called *church window plots* due to their resemblance to stained glass windows. These plots show two-dimensional cross sections of the classification function, exploring input space near test set examples. Figure 11.2 shows cross sections exploring the adversarial direction defined by the fast gradient sign method and a random direction. Figure 11.3 shows cross sections exploring two random orthogonal directions. Figure 11.4 shows cross sections exploring two adversarial directions, with the first defined by the fast gradient sign method and the second defined by the component of the gradient that is orthogonal to the first direction.

11.2.4 Crafting Adversarial Examples

Several different methods of crafting adversarial examples are available. When adversarial examples were first discovered, they were generated with general purpose methods that make no assumption about the underlying cause of adversarial examples, but that are expensive and require multiple iterations. Later, inexpensive methods based on linearity assumptions were developed. Most adversarial example crafting techniques require training set labels, but *virtual adversarial examples* remove this requirement. Specialized methods provide fast methods of attacking classifiers specifically or crafting perturbations that change as few input dimensions as possible.

Let $x \in \mathbb{R}^n$ be a vector of input features (usually the pixels of an image) and y be an integer specifying the desired output class of the model. Let f be the classification function learned by the model, so that $f(x)$ is an integer giving the model's prediction. Let $J(x, y)$ be the cost used to train the model.

The goal of adversarial example crafting is to find an input point $\tilde{x} = x + \eta$ that causes the model to perform poorly. Different methods of crafting adversarial examples use different criteria to determine how poorly the model behaves, different approaches to limit the size of η, and different approximations to optimize the chosen criterion. In all cases, the goal is to find a perturbation η to be small enough that an ideal classifier (usually approximated by human judgment) would still assign class y to $\tilde{x}$. Guaranteeing that $\tilde{x}$ truly belongs to the same class as x is a subtle point, discussed further in Section 11.2.5.

Figure 11.2: *Church window plots* applied to a convolutional network trained on CIFAR-10. The convolutional network is that of Goodfellow et al. (2013b). Each cell in the 10×10 grid in the figure is a different church window plot corresponding to a different CIFAR-10 test example. Here the model is viewed as a function $f : \mathbb{R}^n \to \{1, \dots, 10\}$. At coordinate (h, v) within the plot, the pixel is drawn with a unique shade (in the book, the pixel is printed with a unique grayscale shade indicating the class, while on a computer monitor, each pixel may be displayed with a unique color indicating the class) for each class, indicating the class output by $f(\boldsymbol{x} + h\boldsymbol{u}^{(1)} + v\boldsymbol{u}^{(2)})$, where $\boldsymbol{u}^{(1)}$ and $\boldsymbol{u}^{(2)}$ are orthogonal unit vectors that span a 2-D subspace of $\mathbb{R}^n$. The correct class for each example, given by the test set label, is always plotted as white. To aid visibility, a black contour is drawn around the boundary of each class region. The horizontal coordinate h within the plot begins at $-\epsilon$ on the left side of the plot and increases to ϵ on the right side of the plot. The vertical coordinate v spans the same range, beginning at $-\epsilon$ at the top of the plot. The center of the plot thus corresponds to the classification of the unperturbed input $\boldsymbol{x}$. In all cases these visualizations use .25 for ϵ, which corresponds to large perturbations on our preprocessing of CIFAR-10. Such large perturbations seriously degrade the quality of the image but do not prevent a human observer from recognizing the class. In this figure, $\boldsymbol{u}^{(1)}$ is the direction defined by a fast technique for finding adversarial examples discussed later in this section, while $\boldsymbol{u}^{(2)}$ is a direction chosen uniformly at random among those orthogonal to $\boldsymbol{u}^{(1)}$. From this figure, one can see that the adversarial direction usually roughly divides space into a half-space of correct classification and incorrect classification, with the test example usually lying on the correct side but somewhat near the decision boundary. One can also see that in these cross-sections, the decision boundaries have simple, roughly linear, shapes.

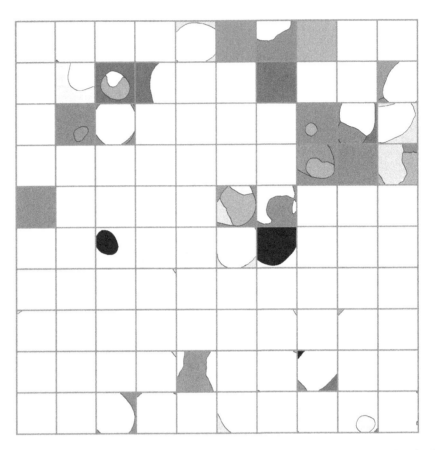

Figure 11.3: Church window plots with both basis directions chosen randomly. See Figure 11.2 for a description of church window plots. In this plot, one can see that random directions rarely cause the class to change. Many authors mistakenly speak of "adversarial noise." This figure illustrates that noise actually does not change the classification very often compared to adversarial directions of perturbation. The empirical observation that noise is less harmful than adversarial directions dates back to Szegedy et al. (2014b), but the church window plots make the mechanism clear. The classification decision is sensitive mostly to a small subspace of adversarial directions that are unlikely to be chosen randomly.

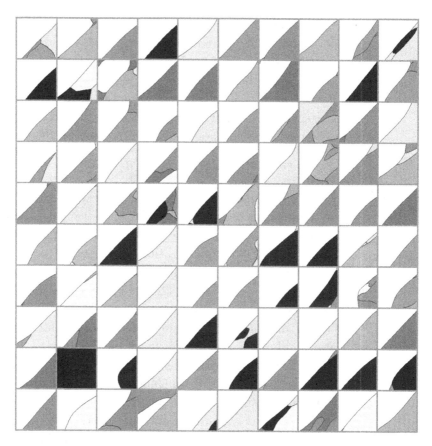

Figure 11.4: Church window plots with both basis directions chosen adversarially. See Figure 11.2 for a description of church window plots. In this plot, the first direction is the one given by the fast gradient sign method (Equation 11.6) and the second direction is the component of the gradient that is orthogonal to the first direction. One can still see linear decision boundaries within this subspace. From this one can see that adversarial examples do not lie in small pockets whose exact coordinates are difficult to find. Instead, adversarial examples may be found by moving in any direction that has large dot product with the gradient.

Different methods of crafting adversarial examples quantify poor model performance in different ways. Some methods are explicitly designed to cause the model to label $\tilde{x}$ as belonging to class $\tilde{y}$, where $\tilde{y} \neq y$. Other methods make use of the cost function $J(x, y)$ used to train the model, and seek a perturbation that results in a large (ideally, maximal) value of $J(\tilde{x}, y)$.

Szegedy et al. (2014b) introduced the first method for crafting adversarial examples. This method was based on solving the optimization problem

$$\eta = \underset{\eta}{\operatorname{argmin}} \lambda ||\eta||_2^2 + J(x + \eta, \tilde{y}) \text{ subject to } (x + \eta) \in [0, 1]^n, \quad (11.3)$$

where $\tilde{y}$ is an incorrect class of the attacker's choice. The initial experiments on adversarial examples used box-constrained L-BFGS to accomplish the minimization, but in principle any gradient-based optimization algorithm would suffice. The minimization was repeated multiple times with different values of λ in order to find the smallest η that resulted in successfully causing $f(x + \eta) = \tilde{y}$. This method is extremely effective, finds very small perturbations, and can cause the model to output specific, desired classes, and makes no assumptions about the structure of the model, but is also highly expensive, requiring multiple calls to an iterative optimization procedure for each example.

Szegedy et al. (2014b) included a constraint that $(x + \eta) \in [0, 1]^n$. This constraint ensures that the adversarial example has the same range of pixel values as the original data, and that it lies within the domain of the original function. Later authors frequently omitted this constraint for simplicity, because the perturbations η are typically small and thus do not move the input significantly far outside the original domain.

For the cost functions that are used to train neural network classifiers, such as $J(x, y) = -\log P(y \mid x)$, a model that is linear over wide regions of its input domain also yields a cost that is approximately linear over wide regions of the input domain. This motivated the development of a fast adversarial example generation scheme based on a linear approximation of the cost function. The method of Szegedy et al. (2014b) fixes a desired target class and minimizes the size of η. The method of Goodfellow et al. (2014b) simplifies the problem by fixing the allowed size of η and maximizing the cost incurred by the perturbation:

$$\eta = \underset{\eta}{\operatorname{argmax}} J(x + \eta, y) \text{ subject to } ||\eta||_\infty \leq \epsilon, \quad (11.4)$$

where ϵ is a hyperparameter chosen by the attacker, specifying the maximum desired pertubation size. The use of the max norm $||\eta||_\infty$ is motivated in Section 11.2.5, but this method could also work with other norms, including the L^2 norm. Solving Equation 11.4 requires iterative optimization in general. To obtain a fast, closed-form solution, Goodfellow et al. (2014b) replaced J with a first-order Taylor series approximation:

$$\boldsymbol{\eta} = \operatorname*{argmax}_{\boldsymbol{\eta}} J(\boldsymbol{x}, y) + \boldsymbol{\eta}^\top \boldsymbol{g} \text{ subject to } ||\boldsymbol{\eta}||_\infty \le \epsilon. \qquad (11.5)$$

where $\boldsymbol{g} = \nabla_{\boldsymbol{x}} J(\boldsymbol{x}, y)$. The solution to Equation 11.5 is given by

$$\boldsymbol{\eta} = \epsilon \cdot \operatorname{sign}(\boldsymbol{g}) \qquad (11.6)$$

This is called the *fast gradient sign method* of generating adversarial examples. The method has the advantage of being extremely fast compared to the L-BFGS method (computing the gradient once instead of hundreds of times), making adversarial example generation feasible for use within the inner loop of a learning algorithm, as described in Section 11.3. The method has some disadvantages, namely that its justification rests on the linearity hypothesis. In some cases, when the linear approximation poorly represents the function, this method requires larger perturbations than other methods. In extreme cases, such as when a model has been explicitly trained to resist the fast gradient sign method, the fast gradient sign method might cease to find adversarial examples while the L-BFGS method continues to do so. The L-BFGS method was also designed to cause the model to predict a specific class $\tilde{y}$ chosen by the attacker. While the fast gradient sign method as outlined above does not allow for the specification of a target class, it can be trivially extended to this setting by following the gradient of $\log P(\tilde{y} \mid \boldsymbol{x})$ rather than $J(\boldsymbol{x}, y)$. Finally, the fast gradient sign method is highly general because it is based on maximizing J. This allows it to be applied to models other than classifiers. For example, it can be used to find inputs to an autoencoder that incur high reconstruction error.

Both the L-BFGS method and the fast gradient sign method rely on access to the true class label y. Miyato et al. (2015) devised a way to remove this requirement. After a model has been at least partially trained, it is usually able to provide mostly accurate labels. Therefore, rather than making a perturbation intended to reduce the probability of the label provided in the training set, the attacker can make a perturbation intended to make the model change its prediction. *Virtual adversarial examples* are thus designed to approximately maximize

$$D_{\mathrm{KL}}\left(p(y \mid \boldsymbol{x}) \| p(y \mid \boldsymbol{x} + \boldsymbol{\eta})\right) \qquad (11.7)$$

with respect to $\boldsymbol{\eta}$, under appropriate constraints on $\boldsymbol{\eta}$. The ability to construct adversarial examples without access to ground truth labels enables the use of adversarial examples for semi-supervised learning, described in Section 11.3.1.

Other specialized methods of crafting adversarial examples provide different benefits. Huang et al. (2015) introduced an attack specialized for classifiers. While the fast gradient sign method linearizes the **cost function**, the attack of Huang et al. (2015) linearizes the **model**. Under the linear approximation of the model, it is possible to solve for the smallest perturbation that yields a change in the output class in closed form. By more tightly modeling the problem of changing the output class, this method is able to achieve class changes with smaller perturbation sizes than the fast gradient sign method.

Most methods of crafting adversarial examples change many input dimensions, each by a small amount. Papernot et al. (2016b) introduced a different approach, that changes few input dimensions, but may change each one by a large amount.

Finally, Sabour et al. (2015) showed that it is possible to construct adversarial examples that cause the model to assign a hidden representation to $\tilde{x}$ that closely resembles the hidden representation of a different example x'. For example, an image of farm equipment may be perturbed so that it has approximately the same hidden representation as an image of a bird. This is a stronger condition than perturbing the image to take on a specific class. For example, when the image of farm equipment is perturbed to have the same hidden representation as the image of a bird, the hidden representation may be decoded to obtain the same color of bird standing in the same location with the same pose—it is not just the concept of the output class "bird" that is imposed on the adversarial example.

11.2.5   Ensuring That Class Changes Are Mistakes

One subtle point when constructing adversarial examples is that the perturbation η must not change the *true* class of the input – that is, the adversarial example should be such that for the task at hand, it would still be desirable that a classifier assign it the same class as it would the original. If η is "too large", an adversarial perturbation could subtract the true identifying characteristics of the original class identity and replace them with the true identifying characteristics of another class, yielding an adversarial example $\tilde{x}$ that truly does belong to a different class $\tilde{y}$. In other words, it is sometimes correct for the classifier to change its class output when the input changes. Adversarial examples must be crafted in such a way that it remains a mistake for the class output to change.

So far there is no general principle determining how to tell whether the class should change for an arbitrary new input, and it seems that if such a principle were known there would no longer be a need for machine learning classifiers. Instead, Goodfellow et al. (2014b) advocate devising a set of sufficient conditions that guarantee that a perturbation $\boldsymbol{\eta}$ will not change the class for a particular application area. For the specific application of object recognition in images, Goodfellow et al. (2014b) suggests that a perturbation $\boldsymbol{\eta}$ that does not change any specific pixel by more than some amount ϵ cannot change the output class. The value of ϵ should be chosen based on knowledge of the task. For example, on the MNIST dataset, the input values are typically normalized to lie in the range $[0, 1]$. The images are of written digits, typically displayed as white digits on a black background. The information content of each pixel is thus roughly binary. Consequently, ϵ may be chosen to be quite large for this task. An ϵ of .25 turns a white pixel with value 1.0 into a bright gray pixel with value .75, which may still easily be recognized as carrying the same semantics as a white pixel. Because some pixels in the original data are gray, perturbations larger than .25 become difficult for human observers to classify. For other object recognition datasets, one might choose ϵ to be small enough that the change to a pixel is imperceptible to a human observer, or to be small enough that a change to the 32 bit floating point encoding of the input does not change the 8 bit representation used to store the images on disk. This principle of ensuring that no pixel changes by more than some negligible amount motivates the use of the max norm to constrain the size of $\boldsymbol{\eta}$ in Equation 11.4. Figure 11.5 provides some illustrations showing how the max norm can be superior to the L^2 norm for ensuring that perturbations do not alter the true class.

The use of the max norm to constrain $\boldsymbol{\eta}$ is of course a sufficient condition for preventing a class change when the task is object recognition. One could imagine other tasks where no norm of $\boldsymbol{\eta}$ provides a useful restriction on the perturbation. For example, consider a regression task where the true output should be $\boldsymbol{d}^\top \boldsymbol{x}$. Then any perturbation that has non-zero dot product with $\boldsymbol{d}$ will change the true output that the regression model should return. The norm of the perturbation is not relevant for this hypothetical task, but rather the direction.

11.2.6 Rubbish Class Examples

Adversarial examples are closely related to the idea of rubbish class examples (LeCun et al., 1998). Rubbish class examples are pathological inputs that do not belong to any class encountered during training. For example, an image where the pixels are drawn from a uniform distribution usually does not belong to any class of images of objects. Ideally, one would like a classifier that assigns normalized probabilities to various output classes to report a uniform distribution over output classes when presented with such an input.

Figure 11.5: Examples of perturbations, illustrating that an L^2 perturbation can behave unpredictable, while a perturbation subject to a max norm constraint can be guaranteed to preserve the object class. The grid on the left shows the result of L^2-constrained perturbation while the grid on the right shows the result of max norm-constrained perturbation. Within each grid, each row shows a the results of a single perturbation. Each row of three images consists of (left to right) an image of input x, an image of a perturbation η, and an image of a resulting perturbed input, $\tilde{x} = x + \eta$.

In the grid on the left, three different perturbations are shown. From top to bottom, the first perturbation causes the true class to change from 3 to 7 (the pertubation is just the difference between an example 7 and an example 3 from the dataset), the second perturbation causes no change, and the final perturbation causes the class to change from 3 to the rubbish class. All three of these perturbations have the same L^2 norm.

In the grid on the right, see three new perturbations that still have the same L^2 norm as the first three, but that have been modified to obey a max norm constraint. These perturbations were constructed by taking the sign of the corresponding perturbation on the left, assigning zero entries to be -1 or 1 randomly, and multiplying by a scaling factor. Randomly replacing zero entries with -1 or 1 is necessary to increase the perturbation size enough to maintain the same L^2 norm as the perturbation on the left. None of the max norm constrained perturbations change the class.

All six perturbations shown have the same L^2 norm but yield different outcomes. This suggests that the L^2 norm is not a useful way of constraining η while constructing adversarial examples for object recognition. The max norm provides a sufficient (but not necessary) condition that guarantees an adversarial example will not change the true underlying class.

The perturbations used in this visualization are relatively small, with an L^2 norm of roughly 4 for all six perturbations and a max norm of roughly 0.14 for the perturbations on the right. When using the max norm constraint, it is possible to construct adversarial examples with max norm .25. Such perturbations have a L^2 norm of 7.

Similarly, a model that reports an independent probability estimate for the detection of each class should preferably indicate that no classes are present. However, both formulations are easily fooled into reporting that a specific class is present with high probability simply by using Gaussian noise as input to the model (Goodfellow et al., 2014b). Nguyen et al. (2014) demonstrated that large, state of the art convolutional networks can also be fooled using rich, structured images generated by genetic algorithms. Because rubbish class examples do not correspond to small perturbations of a realistic input example, they are beyond the scope of this chapter.

11.2.7 Defenses

To date, the most effective strategy for defending against adversarial examples is to explicitly train the model on them, as described in Section 11.3.

Many traditional regularization strategies such as weight decay, ensemble methods, and so on, are not viable defenses. Regularization strategies can fail in two different ways. Some of them reduce the error rate of the model on the test set, but do not reduce the error rate of the model on adversarial examples. Others reduce the sensitivity of the model to adversarial perturbation, but only have a significant effect if they are applied so powerfully (e.g., with such a large weight decay coefficient) that they cause the performance of the model to seriously degrade on the validation set. The failure of some traditional regularization strategies to provide a defense against adversarial examples is discussed by Szegedy et al. (2014b) and the failure of many more traditional regularization strategies is discussed by Goodfellow et al. (2014b). In summary, most traditional neural network regularization techniques have been tested and do not provide a viable defense.

In addition to these traditional methods, some new methods have been devised to defend against adversarial examples. However, none of these methods are yet very effective. For even the best methods, the error rate on adversarial examples remains noticeably higher than on unperturbed examples.

Gu and Rigazio (2014) trained a denoising autoencoder, where the noise corruption process was the adversarial example generation process. In other words, the autoencoder is trained with adversarial example to predict the corresponding unperturbed example as output. The goal was to use the autoencoder as a preprocessing step before applying a classifier, in order to make the classifier resistant to adversarial examples. Unfortunately, the combination of the autoencoder and the classifier then becomes vulnerable to a different class of adversarial examples that the autoencoder has not been trained to resist. Gu and Rigazio (2014) reported that the combined system was vulnerable to adversarial examples with smaller perturbation size than the original classifier. The authors of this chapter speculate that this can be explained by the linearity hypothesis; the autoencoder is still built mostly out of linear components. If one views the classifier as being roughly a product of matrices, then the autoencoder simply introduces two more matrix factors into this product. If these matrices have any singular values that are larger than one, then they amplify adversarial perturbations in the corresponding directions.

Papernot et al. (2015) introduced an approach called *defensive distillation*. First, a teacher model is trained to maximize the likelihood of the training set labels:

$$\boldsymbol{\theta}^{(t)*} = \operatorname{argmax} \sum_{i=1}^{m} \log p^{(t)}\left(y^{(i)} \mid \boldsymbol{x}^{(i)}; \boldsymbol{\theta}^{(t)}\right). \tag{11.8}$$

The teacher model is then used to provide soft targets for a second network, called the student network. The student network is trained not just to predict the same class as the teacher network, but to predict the same probability distribution over classes:

$$\boldsymbol{\theta}^{(s)*} = \operatorname*{argmin}_{\boldsymbol{\theta}^{(s)}} \sum_{i=1}^{m} D_{\mathrm{KL}}\left(p^{(t)}\left(y^{(i)} \mid \boldsymbol{x}^{(i)}; \boldsymbol{\theta}^{(t)}\right) \| p^{(s)}\left(y^{(i)} \mid \boldsymbol{x}^{(i)}; \boldsymbol{\theta}^{(s)}\right)\right) \tag{11.9}$$

This technique noticeably reduces the vulnerability of a model to adversarial examples but does not completely resolve the problem.

As an original contribution of this chapter, an experimental observation shows that a simpler method than defensive distillation also has a beneficial effect. Rather than training a teacher network to provide soft targets, it is possible to simply modify the targets from the training set to be soft, e.g., for a k class problem, replace a target value of 1 for the correct class with a target value of .9, and for the incorrect classes replace the target of 0 with a target of $\frac{1}{10k}$. This technique is called *label smoothing* and is a component of some state of the art object recognition systems (Szegedy et al., 2015). The label smoothing experiment was based on a near-replication of the MNIST classifier of Goodfellow et al. (2013a). This classifier is a feedforward network with two hidden layers consisting of maxout units, trained with dropout (Srivastava et al., 2014). The model was trained on only on the first 50,000 examples and was not re-trained on the validation set, so the test error rate was higher than in the original investigation of Goodfellow et al. (2013a). The model obtained an error rate of 1.28% on the MNIST test set. The error rate of the model on adversarial examples on the MNIST test set using the fast gradient sign method (Equation 11.6) with $\epsilon = .25$ was 99.97%.

A second instantiation of exactly the same model was trained using label smoothing. The error on the test set dropped to 1.17%, and the error rate on the adversarially perturbed test set dropped to 33.0%. This error rate indicates a significant remaining vulnerability but it is a vast improvement over the pre-smoothing adversarial example error rate.

The linearity hypothesis can explain the effectiveness of label smoothing. Without label smoothing, a softmax classifier is trained to make infinitely confident predictions on the training set. This encourages the model to learn large weights and strong responses. When values are pushed outside the areas where training data concentrates, the model makes even more extreme predictions when extrapolating linearly. Label smoothing penalizes the model for making overly confident predictions on the training set, forcing it to learn either a more non-linear function or a linear function with smaller slope. Extrapolations by the label-smoothed model are consequently less extreme.

11.3   Adversarial Training

Adversarial training corresponds to the process of explicitly training a model to correctly label adversarial examples. In other words, given a training example x with label y, the training set may be augmented with an adversarial example $\tilde{x}$ that is still associated with training label y. Szegedy et al. (2014b) proposed this method, but were unable to generate large amounts of adversarial examples due to reliance on the expensive L-BFGS method of crafting adversarial examples. Goodfellow et al. (2014b) introduced the fast gradient sign method and showed that it enabled practical adversarial training. In their approach, the model is trained on a minibatch consisting of both unmodified examples from the training set and adversarially perturbed versions of the same examples. Crucially, the adversarial perturbation is recomputed using the latest version of the model parameters every time a minibatch is presented. Adversarial training can be interpreted as a minimax game,

$$\theta^* = \operatorname*{argmin}_{\theta} \mathbb{E}_{x,y} \max_{\eta} \left[J(x, y, \theta) + J(x + \eta, y) \right], \tag{11.10}$$

with the learning algorithm as the minimizing player and a fixed procedure (such as L-BFGS or the fast gradient sign method) as the maximizing player.

Goodfellow et al. (2014b) found that adversarial training on MNIST reduced both the test set error rate and the adversarially perturbed test set error rate of a maxout network. The reduction in error rate on the unperturbed test set is presumably due to adversarial training forcing the model to learn a more parsimonious function that can explain a wide variety of adversarial examples with a small number of parameters.

Training with the fast gradient sign method means that the model is selectively resistant to adversarial examples that were constructed with this method. However, some resistance to other forms of adversarial examples is achieved. Goodfellow et al. (2014b) reported that their maxout network had an error rate of 18% on the MNIST test set when perturbed by the fast gradient sign method with $\epsilon = .25$. This chapter introduces the observation that using gradient descent on the true model to find the best perturbation with max norm less than .25 increases the error rate to 97%. However, this does not mean that adversarial training with the fast gradient sign method was ineffective. If the max norm constraint is tightened to $\epsilon = .1$, then the error rate of the adversarially trained maxout network falls to 22%. Without adversarial training, the error rate at this perturbation magnitude is 79%. Adversarial training with the fast gradient sign method thus confers robustness to other types of perturbation, but with a smaller perturbation size than was used for training.

11.3.1   Virtual Adversarial Training

Miyato et al. (2015) extended adversarial training to the semi-supervised setting by introducing the virtual adversarial example construction technique, which allows the construction of adversarial examples when no class label is available. This approach allows the model to be trained to have a highly robust classification function in the neighborhood of unlabeled examples. This technique improved the state of the art on semi-supervised learning on the MNIST dataset, outperforming much more complicated methods based on training generative models of unlabeled examples.

11.4   Generative Adversarial Networks

The generative adversarial network (GAN) framework introduced in Goodfellow et al. (2014a) phrases the problem of estimating a generative model in terms of a sample generation process $G : \mathbb{R}^d \to \mathbb{R}^n$, which takes as its argument a random variate $\boldsymbol{z} \sim p(\boldsymbol{z})$; $p(\boldsymbol{z})$ is often chosen from some simple family such as an isotropic Gaussian distribution, or a uniform distribution on $[-1, 1]^d$. $G(\cdot)$ is a machine parameterized by Θ_G which learns to map a sample from the base distribution $p(\boldsymbol{z})$ to a corresponding sample from an implicitly defined distribution $p_g(\boldsymbol{x})$. The combined procedure of drawing a sample $\boldsymbol{z}$ from $p(\boldsymbol{z})$ and applying G to $\boldsymbol{z}$ is referred to as the *generator*.

In contrast with many existing generative modeling frameworks, GANs may be trained without an explicit algebraic representation of $p_{\text{model}}(x)$, tractable or otherwise. The GAN framework is compatible with some models that explicitly define a probability distribution—any directed graphical model whose sampling process is compatible with stochastic backpropagation (Williams, 1992; Kingma and Welling, 2014; Rezende et al., 2014) may be used as a GAN generator—but the framework does not require explicit specification of any conditional or marginal distributions, only the sample generation process. In frameworks based on explicit specification of probabilities it is typical to maximize the empirical expectation of $\log p_{\text{model}}(\boldsymbol{x})$, applying Monte Carlo or variational approximations if faced with intractable terms (often in the form of a normalizing constant). Instead, GANs are trained to match the data distribution indirectly with the help of a *discriminator*, i.e. a binary classifier $D : \mathbb{R}^n \to [0, 1]$, parameterized by Θ_D, whose output represents a calibrated probability estimate that a given example was sampled from $p_{\text{data}}(\boldsymbol{x})$. The conditional log likelihood of the discriminator, on a balanced dataset of real and synthetic examples, is (in the usual fashion) *maximized* with respect to the parameters of D, but simultaneously *minimized* with respect to the parameters of G.

11.4.1   Adversarial Networks in Theory and Practice

The joint training procedure for the generator G and the discriminator D can be viewed as a two-player, continuous minimax game with a certain value function. In their introduction of the GAN framework, Goodfellow et al. (2014a) proved that the GAN training criterion has a unique global optimum in the space of distributions represented by G and D, wherein the distribution sampled by the generator exactly matches that of the data generating process, and the discriminator D is completely unable to distinguish real data from synthetic. It can also be proved, under certain assumptions, that the game converges to this optimum if G is improved at every round and D is chosen to be the ideal discriminator between $p_g(\boldsymbol{x})$ and $p_{\text{data}}(\boldsymbol{x})$, i.e. $D^\star(\boldsymbol{x}) = p_{\text{data}}(\boldsymbol{x})/(p_{\text{data}}(\boldsymbol{x}) + p_g(\boldsymbol{x}))$.

Goodfellow (2014) advanced the theoretical understanding of the GAN training criterion and its relationship to other distinguishability-based learning criteria. In particular, *noise-contrastive estimation (NCE)* (Gutmann and Hyvarinen, 2010) can be viewed as a variant of the GAN criterion wherein the generator is fixed, and the discriminator is a generatively parameterized classifier that learns an explicit model of $p(\boldsymbol{x})$ as a side effect of discriminative training, while a variant of noise contrastive estimation employing (a copy of) the learned generative model is shown to be equivalent, in expectation, to maximum likelihood. Perhaps most importantly, Goodfellow (2014) noted a subtlety of theoretical results outlined above, pointing out that they are significantly weakened by the setting in which GANs are typically optimized in practice.

Optimization of the generator and discriminator necessarily takes place in the space of parameterized families of functions, and the cost surface in the space of these parameters may have symmetries and other pathologies that imply non-uniqueness of the optima as well as practical difficulties locating them. One does not typically have analytical access to $p_g(\boldsymbol{x})$ and certainly not to $p_{\text{data}}(\boldsymbol{x})$, and must attempt to infer the optimal discriminator from data and samples. It is often prohibitively expensive to fully optimize the parameters of D after every change in the parameters of G – therefore, in practice, one settles for a parameter update aimed at improving D, such as one or more stochastic gradient steps. This means that the generator's role in the minimax game of minimizing with respect to $p_g(\boldsymbol{x})$ given a *maximum* of the value function with respect to D, is instead *minimizing a lower bound* on the correct objective. It is not at all clear whether the minimization of this lower bound improves the quantity of interest or simply loosens the bound.

Note that Goodfellow et al. (2014a) optimize a slightly different but equivalent criterion than described above. Let $D(x) = p\,(\boldsymbol{x}$ is data $\mid \boldsymbol{x})$, the discriminator's estimate that a given sample $\boldsymbol{x}$ comes from the data. Rather than minimize

$$\mathbb{E}_{\boldsymbol{z} \sim p(\boldsymbol{z})} \log\left(1 - D(G(\boldsymbol{z}))\right) \qquad\qquad (11.11)$$

(a term that already appears in the training criterion for the discriminator) with respect to the parameters of G, one can instead maximize $\mathbb{E}_{\boldsymbol{z} \sim p(\boldsymbol{z})} \log\left(D(G(\boldsymbol{z}))\right)$; this criterion was found to work better in practice. The motivation for this lies in the fact that early in training, when G is producing samples that look nothing at all like data, the discriminator D can quickly learn to distinguish the two, and $\log\left(1 - D(G(\boldsymbol{z}))\right)$ can quickly saturate to zero. The derivative of the per-sample objective contains a factor of $(1 - D(G(\boldsymbol{z})))^{-1}$, thus scaling the gradients which G receives via backpropagation to have very small magnitude. Pushing upward on $\log(D(G(\boldsymbol{z}))$ yields a multiplicative factor of $D(G(\boldsymbol{z}))^{-1}$ instead, resulting in gradients with a more favourably scaled magnitude if $D(G(\boldsymbol{z}))$ is small.

As G and D are both parameterized learners, the balance between the respective modeling capacities (and effective capacities during learning) can have a profound effect on the learning dynamics and the success of generative learning. In particular, the discriminator must be sufficiently flexible to reliably model the difference between the data distribution and the generated distribution, as the latter gradually tends towards reproducing the statistical structure of the former. At the same time, the discriminator must not become too effective too quickly, or else the gradients it provides the generator will be uninformative: no small change in the generated sample will move it significantly closer to the discriminator's decision boundary.

11.4.2 Generator Collapses

Note that in theory, a perfectly optimal discriminator could exploit any subtle mismatch between $p_{\mathrm{data}}(\boldsymbol{x})$ and $p_g(\boldsymbol{x})$ to give itself a better-than-chance ability to correctly distinguish real and synthetic examples; the generator could then use the gradients obtained from this optimal discriminator to correct its misallocations of probability mass. In practice, when using richly parameterized neural networks for generation and discrimination, the objective functions used to train the generator are non-convex and (due to the dependence between the learning tasks for the generator and the discriminator) highly nonstationary; it is impractical and even theoretically intractable to globally optimize the discriminator prior to each change in the generator. A failure mode for the training criterion therefore manifests when the generator learns to place too much probability mass on a subregion of the data distribution. In the most extreme cases, a generator could elect to place all of its mass on a single point, perfectly reproducing a single training example. A well-trained discriminator can quickly learn to exploit this and confidently classify every other point in the training set correctly. This presents a problem for generator learning, in that the gradients the generator receives are entirely with respect to a single synthetic example, most local perturbations of which will result in gradients that point back towards the singularity. To date, strategies to mitigate this type of failure are an active area of research. Radford et al. (2015) noted that the judicious use of batch normalization (Ioffe and Szegedy, 2015) appears, empirically, to prevent these kinds of collapses to a large degree.

11.4.3 Sample Fidelity and Learning the Objective Function

Machine learning problems are classically posed in terms of an objective function that is a fixed function of the parameters given a training set, often the log likelihood of training data under some parametric model. Viewed from the perspective of the generator G, the GAN training procedure does not involve a single, fixed objective function: G's objective is defined at any moment by the discriminator D, the parameters of which are being continually adapted to both the data and to the current state of G. This can be considered a *learned objective function*, whereby the objective function for G is *automatically* adapted to the data distribution being estimated. The inductive bias for G is characterized by the family of functions from which D is chosen: G is optimized so as to elude detection via any statistical difference between p_g and p_{data} that D can learn to detect.

It is this property that is arguably responsible for the perceived visual quality of generated samples of GANs trained on natural images. Models trained via objective functions involving reconstruction terms, such as the variational autoencoder (Kingma and Welling, 2014; Rezende et al., 2014), implicitly commit to a static definition of sample plausibility. In the case of conditionally Gaussian likelihood, this takes the form of mean squared error, which is a particularly poor perceptual metric for natural image pixel intensities: it considers all perturbations of a given magnitude equivalent, without regard for the fact that changes in luminance which blur out sharp edges decrease the plausibility of the sample as a natural image much more than minor shifts in chroma across the entire image. While one popular approach in the case of models of natural images, and in many other domains, is to design the static objective so as to mitigate the mismatch between training criterion and the statistical properties of the domain, the solution offered by GANs is in some sense more universal: train D to detect and exploit any difference it can between the distributions of samples and real data, train G to outwit this new discriminator, and repeat. This often results in generated samples that more closely match human conceptions of saliency, illustrated in Figure 11.6 in an application to parameterized image generation, where an adversarial loss allows the model to accurately extrapolate the presence of ears, a visually salient feature which a model trained with mean squared error sees fit to discard.

11.4.4   Extensions and Refinements

Since the initial introduction of generative adversarial networks, the framework has been extended in several notable directions. Many of these rely on a straightforward extension to the *conditional* setting, where the generator and discriminator receive additional contextual inputs, first explored by Mirza and Osindero (2014). For example, in the aforementioned work, the authors train a class-conditional generator on the MNIST handwritten digits by feeding the network an additional input consisting of a "one-hot" vector indicating the desired class. The discriminator is fed the generated or real image as well as the class label (the assigned label if the image is real, the desired label if the image is generated). Through training, the discriminator learns that in the presence of a given class label, the image should

Ground Truth   MSE   Adversarial

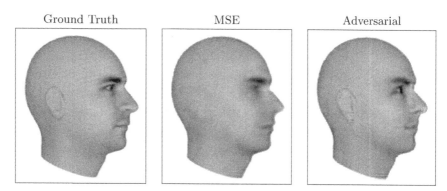

Figure 11.6: Predictive generative networks provide an example of how a learned cost function can correspond more closely to human intuition for which aspects of the data are salient and important to model than a fixed, hand-designed cost function such as mean squared error. These images show the results when predictive generative networks are trained to generate images of 3-D models of human heads at specified viewing angles. *(Left)* An example output frame from the test set. This is the target image that the model is expected to predict. *(Center)* When trained using mean squared error, the model fails to predict the presence of ears. Ears are not salient under the mean squared error loss because they do not cause a major change in brightness for a large enough number of pixels. *(Right)* When trained using a combination of mean squared error and adversarial loss, the model successfully predicts the presence of ears. Because ears have a repeated, predictable structure, they are highly salient to the discriminator network. Future research work may discover better ways of determining which aspects of the input should be considered salient. Figures reproduced with permission from Lotter et al. (2015).

resemble instances of that class from the training data. Likewise, in order to succeed at fooling the discriminator, the generator must learn to use the class label input to inform the characteristics of its generated sample.

In pursuit of more realistic models of natural images, Denton et al. (2015) introduced a hierarchical model, dubbed LAPGAN, which interleaved conditional GAN generators with spatial upsampling in a Laplacian pyramid (Burt et al., 1983). The first generator, either class-conditional or traditional, is trained to generate a small thumbnail image. A fixed upsampling and blurring is performed and a second conditional generator, conditioned on the newly upsampled image, is trained to reproduce the *difference* between the image at the current resolution and the upsampled thumbnail. This process is iterated, with subsequent conditional generators predicting residuals at ever higher resolutions.

Also in the space of natural image generation, Radford et al. (2015) leveraged recent advances in the design and training of discriminative convolutional networks to successfully train a single adversarial pair to generated realistic images of relatively high resolution. These generator networks employ "fractionally strided convolutions", otherwise recognizable as the transpose operation of "valid"-mode strided convolution commonly used when backpropagating gradients through a strided convolutional layer, to learn their own upsampling operations. The authors identify a set of architectural constraints on the generator and discriminator which allow for relatively stable training, including the elimination of downsampling in favour of strided convolution in the discriminator, the use of the bounded tanh() function at the generator output layer, careful application of batch normalization (Ioffe and Szegedy, 2015) and the use of rectified linear units (Jarrett et al., 2009; Glorot et al., 2011) and leaky rectified linear units (Maas et al., 2013) throughout the generator and discriminator, respectively. Inspired by recent work on word embeddings (e.g. Mikolov et al. (2013)), the authors also interrogate the latent representations, i.e. samples from $p(z)$, and find that they obey surprising arithmetic properties when trained on a dataset of faces as shown in Figure 11.7.

11.4.5 Hybrid Models

A recent body of work has examined the combination of the adversarial network training criterion with other formalisms, notably autoencoders. Larsen et al. (2015) combine a GAN with a variational autoencoder (VAE) (Kingma and Welling, 2014; Rezende et al., 2014), dispensing with the VAE's reconstruction error term in favor of an squared error expressed in the space of the discriminator's hidden layers, combining the resulting modified VAE

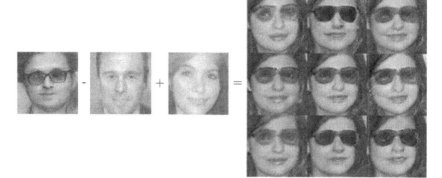

Figure 11.7: Deep Convolutional Generative Adversarial Networks (DCGANs) learn distributed representations that can separate semantically distinct concepts from each other. In this example, a DCGAN has learned one direction in representation space that corresponds to gender and another direction that corresponds to the presence or absence of glasses. Arithmetic can also be performed in this vector space. From left to right, let a be the representation of an image of a man with glasses, b the representation of a man without glasses, and c the representation of a woman without glasses. The vector $d = a - b + c$ now represents the concept of a woman with glasses. The generator maps d to rich images from this class. Images reproduced with permission from Radford et al. (2015).

objective with the usual GAN objective. Makhzani et al. (2015) employs an adversarial cost as a regularizer on the hidden layer representation of a conventional autoencoder, forcing the aggregate posterior distribution of the hidden layer to match a particular synthetic distribution. This formulation closely resembles the VAE. The VAE maximizes a lower bound on the log-likelihood that includes both a reconstruction term and terms regularizing the variational posterior to resemble the model's prior distribution over the latent variables. The adversarial autoencoder removes the regularization term and uses the adversarial game to enforce the desired conditions.

The adversarial network paradigm has also been extended in the direction of supervised and semi-supervised learning. Springenberg (2016) generalizes the convention adversarial network setting to employ a categorical (softmax) output layer in the discriminator. The discriminator and generator compete to shape the *entropy* of this distribution while respecting constraints on its marginal distribution, and an optional likelihood term can add semantics to this output layer if class labels are available. Sutskever et al. (2015) propose an unsupervised criterion designed expressly with the intent of improving performance on downstream supervised tasks in settings where the space of possible outputs is large, and it is easy to obtain independent examples from both the input and output domains. The proposed supervised mapping is adversarially trained to have an output distribution resembling the distribution of independent output domain examples.

11.4.6   Beyond Generative Modeling

Generative adversarial networks were originally introduced in order to provide a means of performing generative modeling. The idea has since proven to be more general. Adversarial pairs of networks may in fact be used for a broad range of tasks.

Two recent methods have shown that the adversarial framework can be used to impose desired properties on the features extracted by a neural network. The feature extractor can be thought of as analogous to the generator in the GAN framework. A second network, analogous to the discriminator, then tries to obtain some forbidden information from the extracted features. The feature extractor is then trained to learn features that are both useful for some original task, such as classification, and that yield little information to the second network. Ganin and Lempitsky (2015) use this approach for domain adaptation. The second network attempts to predict which domain the input was drawn from. When the feature extractor is trained to fool this network, it is forced to learn features that are invariant to the choice of input domain. Edwards and Storkey (2015) use a similar technique to learn representations that do not contain private information. In this case, the second network attempts to recover the private information from the representation. This approach could be used to remove prejudice from a decision making process. For example, if a machine learning model is used to make hiring decisions, it should not use protected information such as the race or gender of applicants. If the machine learning model is trained on the decisions made by human hiring managers, and if the previous hiring managers made biased decisions, the machine learning model could discover other features of the candidates that are correlated with their race or gender. By applying the method of Edwards and Storkey (2015), the machine learning model is encouraged to remove features that have a statistical relationship with the protected information, ideally leading to more fair decisions.

11.5   Discussion

The staggering gains in many application areas brought by the introduction of deep neural networks have inspired much excitement and widespread adoption. In addition to remarkable success tackling difficult supervised classification tasks, it is often the case that even misclassifications the errors made by state-of-the-art neural networks appear to be quite reasonable (as remarked, for example, by Krizhevsky et al. (2012)). The existence of adversarial examples as a problem plaguing a wide variety of model families suggests surprising deficits both in the degree to which these models understand their tasks, and to which human practitioners truly understand their models. Research into such phenomena can yield immediate gains in robustness and resistance to attack for neural networks deployed in commercial and industrial systems, as well as guide research into new model classes which naturally resist such perturbation through a deeper comprehension of the learning task.

Simultaneously, the adversarial perspective can be fruitfully leveraged for tasks other than simple supervised learning. While the focus of generative modeling in the past has often been on models that directly optimize likelihood, many application domains express a need for realistic synthesis, including the generation of speech waveforms, image and video inpainting and super-resolution, the procedural generation of video game assets, and forward prediction in model-based reinforcement learning. Recent work (Theis et al., 2015) suggests that these goals may be at odds with this likelihood-centric paradigm. Generative adversarial networks and their extensions provide one avenue attack on these difficult synthesis problems with an intuitively appealing approach: to learn to generate convincingly, aim to fool a motivated adversary. An important avenue for future research concerns the quantitative evaluation of generative models intended for synthesis; particular desiderata include generic, widely applicable evaluation procedures which nonetheless can be made to respect domain-specific notions of similarity and verisimilitude.

Acknowledgements

The authors of this chapter would like to thank Martin Wattenberg and Christian Szegedy for insightful suggestions that improved the church window plots, and to thank Martin in particular for the name "church window plots." Ilya Sutskever provided the observation that visual stimuli can cause seizures.

11.6   References

P. J. Burt, Edward, and E. H. Adelson. The laplacian pyramid as a compact image code. *IEEE Transactions on Communications*, 31:532–540, 1983.

E. Denton, S. Chintala, A. Szlam, and R. Fergus. Deep generative image models using a laplacian pyramid of adversarial networks. *NIPS*, 2015.

H. Edwards and A. J. Storkey. Censoring representations with an adversary. *CoRR*, abs/1511.05897, 2015. URL `http://arxiv.org/abs/1511.05897`.

J. A. Frederick, D. L. Timmermann, H. L. Russell, and J. F. Lubar. Eeg coherence effects of audio-visual stimulation (avs) at dominant and twice dominant alpha frequency. *Journal of neurotherapy*, 8(4):25–42, 2005.

Y. Ganin and V. Lempitsky. Unsupervised domain adaptation by backpropagation. In *ICML'2015*, 2015.

X. Glorot, A. Bordes, and Y. Bengio. Deep sparse rectifier neural networks. In *JMLR W&CP: Proceedings of the Fourteenth International Conference on Artificial Intelligence and Statistics (AISTATS 2011)*, Apr. 2011.

I. J. Goodfellow. On distinguishability criteria for estimating generative models. In *International Conference on Learning Representations, Workshops Track*, 2014.

I. J. Goodfellow, D. Warde-Farley, M. Mirza, A. Courville, and Y. Bengio. Maxout networks. In S. Dasgupta and D. McAllester, editors, *Proceedings of the 30th International Conference on Machine Learning (ICML'13)*, pages 1319–1327. ACM, 2013a. URL `http://icml.cc/2013/`.

I. J. Goodfellow, D. Warde-Farley, M. Mirza, A. Courville, and Y. Bengio. Maxout networks. In *ICML'2013*, 2013b.

I. J. Goodfellow, J. Pouget-Abadie, M. Mirza, B. Xu, D. Warde-Farley, S. Ozair, A. Courville, and Y. Bengio. Generative adversarial networks. In *NIPS'2014*, 2014a.

I. J. Goodfellow, J. Shlens, and C. Szegedy. Explaining and harnessing adversarial examples. *CoRR*, abs/1412.6572, 2014b. URL `http://arxiv.org/abs/1412.6572`.

S. Gu and L. Rigazio. Towards deep neural network architectures robust to adversarial examples. In *NIPS Workshop on Deep Learning and Representation Learning*, 2014.

M. Gutmann and A. Hyvarinen. Noise-contrastive estimation: A new estimation principle for unnormalized statistical models. In *AISTATS'2010*, 2010.

R. Huang, B. Xu, D. Schuurmans, and C. Szepesvári. Learning with a strong adversary. *CoRR*, abs/1511.03034, 2015. URL `http://arxiv.org/abs/1511.03034`.

S. Ioffe and C. Szegedy. Batch normalization: Accelerating deep network training by reducing internal covariate shift. 2015.

K. Jarrett, K. Kavukcuoglu, M. Ranzato, and Y. LeCun. What is the best multi-stage architecture for object recognition? In *Proc. International Conference on Computer Vision (ICCV'09)*, pages 2146–2153. IEEE, 2009.

D. P. Kingma and M. Welling. Auto-encoding variational bayes. In *Proceedings of the International Conference on Learning Representations (ICLR)*, 2014.

A. Krizhevsky, I. Sutskever, and G. Hinton. ImageNet classification with deep convolutional neural networks. In *Advances in Neural Information Processing Systems 25 (NIPS'2012)*. 2012.

A. B. L. Larsen, S. K. Sønderby, and O. Winther. Autoencoding beyond pixels using a learned similarity metric. *CoRR*, abs/1512.09300, 2015. URL `http://arxiv.org/abs/1512.09300`.

Y. LeCun, L. Bottou, Y. Bengio, and P. Haffner. Gradient-based learning applied to document recognition. *Proceedings of the IEEE*, 86(11):2278–2324, Nov. 1998.

W. Lotter, G. Kreiman, and D. Cox. Unsupervised learning of visual structure using predictive generative networks. *arXiv preprint arXiv:1511.06380*, 2015.

A. L. Maas, A. Y. Hannun, and A. Y. Ng. Rectifier nonlinearities improve neural network acoustic models. In *ICML Workshop on Deep Learning for Audio, Speech, and Language Processing*, 2013.

A. Makhzani, J. Shlens, N. Jaitly, and I. J. Goodfellow. Adversarial autoencoders. *CoRR*, abs/1511.05644, 2015. URL http://arxiv.org/abs/1511.05644.

T. Mikolov, K. Chen, G. Corrado, and J. Dean. Efficient estimation of word representations in vector space. In *International Conference on Learning Representations: Workshops Track*, 2013.

M. Mirza and S. Osindero. Conditional generative adversarial nets. *arXiv preprint arXiv:1411.1784*, 2014.

T. Miyato, S. Maeda, M. Koyama, K. Nakae, and S. Ishii. Distributional smoothing with virtual adversarial training. In *ICLR*, 2015. Preprint: arXiv:1507.00677.

A. Nguyen, J. Yosinski, and J. Clune. Deep Neural Networks are Easily Fooled: High Confidence Predictions for Unrecognizable Images. *ArXiv e-prints*, Dec. 2014.

N. Papernot, P. McDaniel, X. Wu, S. Jha, and A. Swami. Distillation as a defense to adversarial perturbations against deep neural networks. *arXiv preprint arXiv:1511.04508*, 2015.

N. Papernot, P. McDaniel, I. Goodfellow, S. Jha, Z. B. Celik, and A. Swami. Practical black-box attacks against deep learning systems using adversarial examples. *arXiv preprint arXiv:1602.02697*, 2016a.

N. Papernot, P. McDaniel, S. Jha, M. Fredrikson, Z. B. Celik, and A. Swami. The limitations of deep learning in adversarial settings. In *Proceedings of the 1st IEEE European Symposium on Security and Privacy*. IEEE, 2016b.

A. Radford, L. Metz, and S. Chintala. Unsupervised representation learning with deep convolutional generative adversarial networks. *arXiv preprint arXiv:1511.06434*, 2015.

D. J. Rezende, S. Mohamed, and D. Wierstra. Stochastic backpropagation and approximate inference in deep generative models. In *ICML'2014*, 2014.

J. O. Robinson. *The psychology of visual illusion*. Courier Corporation, 2013.

S. Sabour, Y. Cao, F. Faghri, and D. J. Fleet. Adversarial manipulation of deep representations. *CoRR*, abs/1511.05122, 2015. URL http://arxiv.org/abs/1511.05122.

J. T. Springenberg. Unsupervised and semi-supervised learning with categorical generative adversarial networks. In *International Conference on Learning Representations*, 2016.

N. Srivastava, G. Hinton, A. Krizhevsky, I. Sutskever, and R. Salakhutdinov. Dropout: A simple way to prevent neural networks from overfitting. *Journal of Machine Learning Research*, 15:1929–1958, 2014. URL http://jmlr.org/papers/v15/srivastava14a.html.

I. Sutskever, R. Józefowicz, K. Gregor, D. J. Rezende, T. Lillicrap, and O. Vinyals. Towards principled unsupervised learning. *CoRR*, abs/1511.06440, 2015. URL http://arxiv.org/abs/1511.06440.

C. Szegedy, W. Liu, Y. Jia, P. Sermanet, S. Reed, D. Anguelov, D. Erhan, V. Van-houcke, and A. Rabinovich. Going deeper with convolutions. Technical report, arXiv:1409.4842, 2014a.

C. Szegedy, W. Zaremba, I. Sutskever, J. Bruna, D. Erhan, I. J. Goodfellow, and R. Fergus. Intriguing properties of neural networks. *ICLR*, abs/1312.6199, 2014b. URL http://arxiv.org/abs/1312.6199.

C. Szegedy, V. Vanhoucke, S. Ioffe, J. Shlens, and Z. Wojna. Rethinking the Inception Architecture for Computer Vision. *ArXiv e-prints*, Dec. 2015.

L. Theis, A. van den Oord, and M. Bethge. A note on the evaluation of generative models. arXiv:1511.01844, Nov 2015. URL http://arxiv.org/abs/1511.01844.

R. J. Williams. Simple statistical gradient-following algorithms connectionist reinforcement learning. *Machine Learning*, 8:229–256, 1992.

12   Data Augmentation via Lévy Processes

Stefan Wager
Stanford University
Stanford, USA

swager@stanford.edu

William Fithian
University of California, Berkeley
Berkeley, USA

wfithian@berkeley.edu

Percy Liang
Stanford University
Stanford, USA

pliang@cs.stanford.edu

If a document is about travel, we may expect that short snippets of the document should also be about travel. We introduce a general framework for incorporating these types of invariances into a discriminative classifier. The framework imagines data as being drawn from a slice of a Lévy process. If we slice the Lévy process at an earlier point in time, we obtain additional pseudo-examples, which can be used to train the classifier. We show that this scheme has two desirable properties: it preserves the Bayes decision boundary, and it is equivalent to fitting a generative model in the limit where we rewind time back to 0. Our construction captures popular schemes such as Gaussian feature noising and dropout training, as well as admitting new generalizations.

12.1   Introduction

Black-box discriminative classifiers such as logistic regression, neural networks, and SVMs are the go-to solution in machine learning: they are simple to apply and often perform well. However, an expert may have additional knowledge to exploit, often taking the form of a certain family of transformations that should usually leave labels fixed. For example, in object recognition, an image of a cat rotated, translated, and peppered with a small amount of noise is probably still a cat. Likewise, in document classification, the first paragraph of an article about travel is most likely still about travel. In both cases, the "expert knowledge" amounts to a belief that a certain transform of the features should generally not affect an example's label.

One popular strategy for encoding such a belief is *data augmentation*: generating additional pseudo-examples or "hints" by applying label-invariant transformations to training examples' features (Abu-Mostafa, 1990; Schölkopf et al., 1997; Simard et al., 1998). That is, each example $(X^{(i)}, Y^{(i)})$ is replaced by many pairs $(\widetilde{X}^{(i,b)}, Y^{(i)})$ for $b = 1, \ldots, B$, where each $\widetilde{X}^{(i,b)}$ is a transformed version of $X^{(i)}$. This strategy is simple and modular: after generating the pseudo-examples, we can simply apply any supervised learning algorithm to the augmented dataset. Figure 12.1 illustrates two examples of this approach, an image transformed to a noisy image and a text caption, transformed by deleting words.

Dropout training (Srivastava et al., 2014) is an instance of data augmentation that, when applied to an input feature vector, zeros out a subset of the features randomly. Intuitively, dropout implies a certain amount of signal redundancy across features—that an input with about half the features masked should usually be classified the same way as a fully-observed input. In the setting of document classification, dropout can be seen as creating pseudo-examples by randomly omitting some information (i.e., words) from each training example. Building on this interpretation, Wager et al. (2014) show that learning with such artificially difficult examples can substantially improve the generalization performance of a classifier.

To study dropout, Wager et al. (2014) assume that documents can be summarized as Poisson word counts. Specifically, assume that each document has an underlying topic associated with a word frequency distribution π on the p-dimensional simplex and an expected length $T \geq 0$, and that, given π and T, the word counts X_j are independently generated as $X_j \mid T, \pi \sim$ Pois($T \pi_j$). The analysis of Wager et al. (2014) then builds on a duality between dropout and the above generative model. Consider the example given in Figure 12.1, where dropout creates pseudo-documents $\widetilde{X}$ by deleting half the words at random from the original document X. As explained in detail in Section 12.2.1, if X itself is drawn from the above Poisson model, then the dropout pseudo-examples $\widetilde{X}$ are marginally distributed as $\widetilde{X}_j \mid T, \pi \sim$ Pois($0.5\,T \pi_j$). Thus, in the context of this Poisson generative model, dropout enables us to create new, shorter pseudo-examples that preserve the generative structure of the problem.

(a) Gaussian noise

The colorful Norwegian city of
Bergen is also a gateway to majes-
tic fjords. Bryggen Hanseatic Wharf
will give you a sense of the local cul-
ture – take some time to snap photos
of the Hanseatic commercial buildings, which look like scenery from a
movie set. 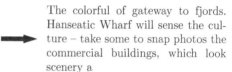 The colorful of gateway to fjords.
Hanseatic Wharf will sense the cul-
ture – take some to snap photos the
commercial buildings, which look
scenery a

(b) Dropout noise

Figure 12.1: Two examples of transforming an original input X into a noisy, less
informative input $\widetilde{X}$. The new inputs clearly have the same label but contain less
information and thus are harder to classify.

The above interpretation of dropout raises the following question: if
feature deletion is a natural way to create information-poor pseudo-examples
for document classification, are there natural analogous feature noising
schemes that can be applied to other problems? In this chapter, we seek to
address this question, and study a more general family of data augmentation
methods generalizing dropout, based on Lévy processes: We propose an
abstract Lévy thinning scheme that reduces to dropout in the Poisson
generative model considered by Wager et al. (2014). Our framework further
suggests new methods for feature noising such as Gamma noising based on
alternative generative models, all while allowing for a unified theoretical
analysis.

From generative modeling to data augmentation. In the above discussion, we treated the expected document length T as fixed. More generally,
we could imagine the document as growing in length over time, with the
observed document X merely a "snapshot" of what the document looks like

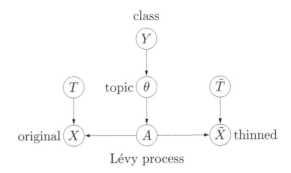

Lévy process

Figure 12.2: Graphical model depicting our generative assumptions; note that we are not fitting this generative model. Given class Y, we draw a topic θ, which governs the parameters of the Lévy process (A_t). We slice at time T to get the original input $X = A_T$ and at an earlier time $\tilde{T}$ to get the thinned or noised input $\tilde{X} = A_{\tilde{T}}$. We show that given X, we can sample $\tilde{X}$ without knowledge of θ.

at time T. Formally, we can imagine a latent Poisson process $(A_t)_{t \geq 0}$, with fixed-t marginals $(A_t)_j \mid \pi \sim \mathrm{Pois}(t\,\pi_j)$, and set $X = A_T$. In this notation, dropout amounts to "rewinding" the process A_t to obtain short pseudo-examples. By setting $\tilde{X} = A_{\alpha T}$, we have $\mathbb{P}[\tilde{X} = \tilde{\mathbf{x}} \mid X = x] = \mathbb{P}[A_{\alpha T} = \tilde{\mathbf{x}} \mid A_T = x]$, for thinning parameter $\alpha \in (0, 1)$.

The main result of this chapter is that the analytic tools developed by Wager et al. (2014) are not restricted to the case where (A_t) is a Poisson process, and in fact hold whenever (A_t) is a *Lévy process*. In other words, their analysis applies to any classification problem where the features X can be understood as time-T snapshots of a process (A_t), i.e., $X = A_T$.

Recall that a Lévy process $(A_t)_{t \geq 0}$ is a stochastic process with $A_0 = 0$ that has independent and stationary increments: $\{A_{t_i} - A_{t_{i-1}}\}$ are independent for $0 = t_0 < t_1 < t_2 < \cdots$, and $A_t - A_s \stackrel{d}{=} A_{t-s}$ for and $s < t$. Common examples of Lévy processes include Brownian motion and Poisson processes.

In any such Lévy setup, we show that it is possible to devise an analogue to dropout that creates pseudo-examples by *rewinding* the process back to some earlier time $\tilde{T} \leq T$. Our generative model is depicted in Figure 12.2: (A_t), the information relevant to classifying Y, is governed by a latent topic $\theta \in \mathbb{R}^p$. Lévy thinning then seeks to rewind (A_t)—importantly as we shall see, without having access to θ.

We should think of (A_t) as representing an ever-accumulating amount of information concerning the topic θ: In the case of document classification, (A_t) are the word counts associated with a document that grows longer as t increases. In other examples that we discuss in Section 12.3, A_t will represent the sum of t independent noisy sensor readings. The independence

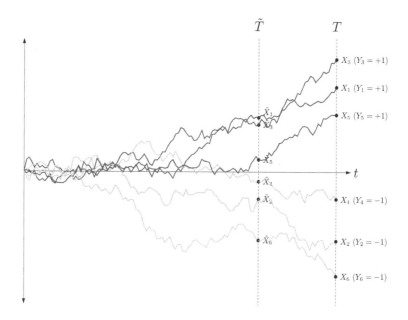

Figure 12.3: We model each input X as a slice of a Lévy process at time T. We generate noised examples $\widetilde{X}$ by "stepping back in time" to $\tilde{T}$. Note that the examples of the two classes are closer together now, thus forcing the classifier to work harder.

of increments property assures that as we progress in time, we are always obtaining new information. The stopping time T thus represents the *information content* in input X about topic θ. Lévy thinning seeks to improve classification accuracy by turning a few information-rich examples X into many information-poor examples $\widetilde{X}$.

We emphasize that, although our approach uses generative modeling to motivate a data augmentation scheme, we do not in fact fit a generative model. This presents a contrast to the prevailing practice: two classical approaches to multiclass classification are to either directly train a discriminative model by running, e.g., multiclass logistic regression on the n original training examples; or, at the other extreme, to specify and fit a simple parametric version of the above generative model, e.g., naive Bayes, and then use Bayes' rule for classification. It is well known that the latter approach is usually more efficient if it has access to a correctly specified generative model, but may be badly biased in case of model misspecification (Efron, 1975; Ng and Jordan, 2002; Liang and Jordan, 2008). Here, we first seek to devise a noising scheme $X \rightarrow \widetilde{X}$ and then to train a discriminative model on the pseudo-examples $(\widetilde{X}, Y)$ instead of the original examples (X, Y). Note that even if the generative model is incorrect, this approach will incur limited bias as long as the noising scheme roughly preserves class boundaries — for example, even if the Poisson document model is incorrect, we may still be justified in classifying a subsampled travel document as a travel document. As a result, this approach can take advantage of an abstract generative structure while remaining more robust to model misspecification than parametric generative modeling.

Overview of results. We consider the multiclass classification setting where we seek to estimate a mapping from input X to class label Y. We imagine that each X is generated by a mixture of Lévy process, where we first draw a random topic θ given the class Y, and then run a Lévy process (A_t) depending on θ to time T. In order to train a classifier, we pick a thinning parameter $\alpha \in (0, 1)$, and then create pseudo examples by rewinding the original X back to time αT, i.e., $\widetilde{X} \sim A_{\alpha T} \mid A_T$.

We show three main results in this chapter. Our first result is that we can generate such pseudo-examples $\widetilde{X}$ without knowledge of the parameters θ governing the generative Lévy process. In other words, while our method posits the existence of a generative model, our algorithm does not actually need to estimate it. Instead, it enables us to give hints about a potentially complex generative structure to a discriminative model such as logistic regression.

Second, under assumptions that our generative model is correct, we show that feature noising preserves the Bayes decision boundary: $\mathbb{P}[Y \mid X = x] = \mathbb{P}[Y \mid \widetilde{X} = x]$. This means that feature noising does not introduce any bias in the infinite data limit.

Third, we consider the limit of rewinding to the beginning of time $(\alpha \to 0)$. Here, we establish conditions given which, even with finite data, the decision boundary obtained by fitting a linear classifier on the pseudo-examples is equivalent to that induced by a simplified generative model. When this latter result holds, we can interpret α-thinning as providing a semi-generative regularization path for logistic regression, with a simple generative procedure at one end and unregularized logistic regression at the other.

Related work. The trade-off between generative models and discriminative models has been explored extensively. Rubinstein and Hastie (1997) empirically compare discriminative and generative classifiers models with respect to bias and variance, Efron (1975) and Ng and Jordan (2002) provide a more formal discussion of the bias-variance trade-off between logistic regression and naive Bayes. Liang and Jordan (2008) perform an asymptotic analysis for general exponential families.

A number of papers study hybrid loss functions that combine both a joint and conditional likelihood (Raina et al., 2004; Bouchard and Triggs, 2004; Lasserre et al., 2006; McCallum et al., 2006; Liang and Jordan, 2008). The data augmentation approach we advocate in this chapter is fundamentally different, in that we are merely using the structural assumptions implied by the generative models to generate more data, and are not explicitly fitting a full generative model.

The present work was initially motivated by understanding dropout training (Srivastava et al., 2014), which was introduced in the context of regularizing deep neural networks, and has had much empirical success (Ba and Frey, 2013; Goodfellow et al., 2013; Krizhevsky et al., 2012; Wan et al., 2013). Many of the regularization benefits of dropout can be found in logistic regression and other single-layer models, where it is also known as "blank-out noise" (Globerson and Roweis, 2006; van der Maaten et al., 2013) and has been successful in natural language tasks such as document classification and named entity recognition (Wager et al., 2013; Wang and Manning, 2013; Wang et al., 2013). There are a number of theoretical analyses of dropout: using PAC-Bayes framework (McAllester, 2013), comparing dropout to "altitude training" (Wager et al., 2014), and interpreting dropout as a form of adaptive regularization (Baldi and Sadowski, 2014; Bishop, 1995; Helmbold and Long, 2015; Josse and Wager, 2014; Wager et al., 2013).

12.2 Lévy Thinning

We begin by briefly reviewing the results of Wager et al. (2014), who study dropout training for document classification from the perspective of thinning documents (Section 12.2.1). Then, in Section 12.2.2, we generalize these results to the setting of generic Lévy generative models.

12.2.1 Motivating Example: Thinning Poisson Documents

Suppose we want to classify documents according to their subject, e.g., sports, politics, or travel. As discussed in the introduction, common sense intuition about the nature of documents suggests that a short snippet of a sports document should also be classified as a sports document. If so, we can generate many new training examples by cutting up the original documents in our dataset into shorter subdocuments and labeling each subdocument with the same label as the original document it came from. By training a classifier on all of the pseudo-examples we generate in this way, we should be able to obtain a better classifier.

In order to formalize this intuition, we can represent a document as a sequence of words from a dictionary $\{1, \ldots, d\}$, with the word count X_j denoting the number of occurrences of word j in the document. Given this representation, we can easily create "subdocuments" by binomially downsampling the word counts X_j independently. That is, for some fixed downsampling fraction $\alpha \in (0, 1)$, we draw

$$\widetilde{X}_j \mid X_j \sim \text{Binom}(X_j, \alpha). \tag{12.1}$$

In other words, we keep each occurrence of word j independently with probability α.

Wager et al. (2014) study this downsampling scheme in the context of a Poisson mixture model for the inputs X that obeys the structure of Figure 12.2: first, we draw a class $Y \in \{1, \ldots, K\}$ (e.g., travel) and a "topic" $\theta \in \mathbb{R}^d$ (e.g., corresponding to travel in Norway). The topic θ specifies a distribution over words,

$$\mu_j(\theta) = e^{\theta_j}, \tag{12.2}$$

where, without loss of generality, we assume that $\sum_{j=1}^d e^{\theta_j} = 1$. We then draw a $\text{Pois}(T)$ number of words, where T is the expected document length, and generate each word independently according to θ. Equivalently, each word count is an independent Poisson random variable, $X_j \sim \text{Pois}(T\mu_j(\theta))$. The following is an example draw of a document:

$$Y = \text{travel}$$

$$\theta = [\ \overbrace{0.5}^{\text{norway}}\ ,\ \overbrace{0.5}^{\text{fjord}}\ ,\ \overbrace{1.2}^{\text{the}}\ ,\ \overbrace{-2.7}^{\text{skyscraper}}\ , \ldots]$$

$$X = [\ \overbrace{2}^{\text{norway}}\ ,\ \overbrace{1}^{\text{fjord}}\ ,\ \overbrace{3}^{\text{the}}\ ,\ \overbrace{0}^{\text{skyscraper}}\ , \ldots]$$

$$\widetilde{X} = [\ \overbrace{1}^{\text{norway}}\ ,\ \overbrace{0}^{\text{fjord}}\ ,\ \overbrace{1}^{\text{the}}\ ,\ \overbrace{0}^{\text{skyscraper}}\ , \ldots]$$

Let us now try to understand the downsampling scheme $\widetilde{X} \mid X$ in the context of the Poisson topic model over X. For each word j, recall that $\widetilde{X}_j \mid X_j \sim \text{Binom}(X_j, \alpha)$. If we marginalize over X, then we have:

$$\widetilde{X}_j \mid T, \theta \sim \text{Pois}\left(\alpha T \mu_j(\theta)\right). \tag{12.3}$$

As a result, the distribution of $\widetilde{X}$ is exactly the distribution of X if we replaced T with $\widetilde{T} = \alpha T$.

We can understand this thinning by embedding the document X in a multivariate Poisson process $(A_t)_{t \geq 0}$, where the marginal distribution of $A_t \in \{0, 1, 2, \dots\}^d$ is defined to be the distribution over counts when the expected document length is t. Then, we can write

$$X = A_T, \quad \widetilde{X} = A_{\widetilde{T}}. \tag{12.4}$$

Thus, under the Poisson topic model, the binomial thinning procedure does not alter the structure of the problem other than by shifting the expected document length from T to $\widetilde{T}$. Figure 12.4 illustrates one realization of Lévy thinning in the Poisson case with a three-word dictionary. Note that in this case we can sample $\widetilde{X} = A_{\alpha T}$ given $X = A_T$ without knowledge of θ.

This perspective lies at the heart of the analysis in Wager et al. (2014), who show under the Poisson model that, when the overall document length $\|X\|_1$ is independent of the topic θ, thinning does not perturb the optimal decision boundary. Indeed, the conditional distribution over class labels is identical for the original features and the thinned features:

$$\mathbb{P}[Y \mid X = x] = \mathbb{P}[Y \mid \widetilde{X} = x]. \tag{12.5}$$

This chapter extends the result to general Lévy processes (see Theorem 12.2).

This last result (12.5) may appear quite counterintuitive: for example, if A_{60} is more informative than A_{40}, how can it be that downsampling does not perturb the conditional class probabilities? Suppose x is a 40-word document ($\|x\|_1 = 40$). When $t = 60$, most of the documents will be longer than 40 words, and thus x will be less likely under $t = 60$ than under $t = 40$. However, (12.5) is about the distribution of Y *conditioned on a particular realization* x. The claim is that, having observed x, we obtain the same information about Y regardless of whether t, the expected document length, is 40 or 60.

12.2.2 Thinning Lévy Processes

The goal of this section is to extend the Poisson topic model from Section 12.2.1 and construct general thinning schemes with the invariance property of (12.5). We will see that Lévy processes provide a natural vehicle for such a generalization: The Poisson process used to generate documents is a specific Lévy process, and binomial sampling corresponds to "rewinding" the Lévy process back in time.

Consider the multiclass classification problem of predicting a discrete class $Y \in \{1, \dots, K\}$ given an input vector $X \in \mathbb{R}^d$. Let us assume that the joint distribution over (X, Y) is governed by the following generative model:

1. Choose $Y \sim \text{Mult}(\pi)$, where π is on the K-dimensional simplex.

2. Draw a topic $\theta \mid Y$, representing a subpopulation of class Y.

3. Construct a Lévy process $(A_t)_{t \geq 0} \mid \theta$, where $A_t \in \mathbb{R}^d$ is a potential input vector at time t.

4. Observe the input vector $X = A_T$ at a fixed time T.

While the Lévy process imposes a fair amount of structure, we make no assumptions about the number of topics, which could be uncountably infinite, or about their distribution, which could be arbitrary. Of course, in such an unconstrained non-parametric setting, it would be extremely difficult to adequately fit the generative model. Therefore, we take a different tack: We will use the structure endowed by the Lévy process to generate pseudo-examples for consumption by a discriminative classifier. These pseudo-examples implicitly encode our generative assumptions.

The natural way to generate a pseudo-example $(\widetilde{X}, Y)$ is to "rewind" the Lévy process (A_t) backwards from time T (recall $X = A_T$) to an earlier time $\widetilde{T} = \alpha T$ for some $\alpha \in (0, 1)$ and define the thinned input as $\widetilde{X} = A_{\widetilde{T}}$. In practice, (A_t) is unobserved, so we draw $\widetilde{X}$ conditioned on the original input $X = A_T$ and topic θ. In fact, we can draw many realizations of $\widetilde{X} \mid X, \theta$.

Our hope is that a single full example (X, Y) is rich enough to generate many different pseudo-examples $(\widetilde{X}, Y)$, thus increasing the effective sample size. Moreover, Wager et al. (2014) show that training with such pseudo-examples can also lead to a somewhat surprising "altitude training" phenomenon whereby thinning yields an improvement in generalization performance because the pseudo-examples are more difficult to classify than the original examples, and thus force the learning algorithm to work harder and learn a more robust model.

A technical difficulty is that generating $\widetilde{X} \mid X, \theta$ seemingly requires knowledge of the topic θ driving the underlying Lévy process (A_t). In order to get around this issue, we establish the following condition under which the observed input $X = A_T$ alone is sufficient—that is, $\mathbb{P}[\widetilde{X} \mid X, \theta]$ does not actually depend on θ.

Assumption 12.1 (exponential family structure). *The Lévy process $(A_t) \mid \theta$ is drawn according to an exponential family model whose marginal density at time t is*

$$f_\theta^{(t)}(x) = \exp\left[\theta \cdot x - t\psi(\theta)\right] h^{(t)}(x) \quad \text{for every } t \in \mathbb{R}. \tag{12.6}$$

Here, the topic $\theta \in \mathbb{R}^d$ is an unknown parameter vector, and $h^{(t)}(x)$ is a family of carrier densities indexed by $t \in \mathbb{R}$.

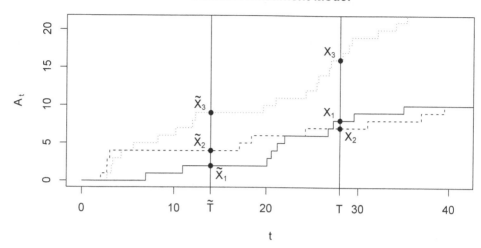

Figure 12.4: Illustration of our Poisson process document model with a three-word dictionary and $\mu(\theta) = (0.25, 0.3, 0.45)$. The word counts of the original document, $X = (8, 7, 16)$, represents the trivariate Poisson process A_t, sliced at $T = 28$. The thinned pseudo-document $\widetilde{X} = (2, 4, 9)$ represents A_t sliced at $\widetilde{T} = 14$.

The above assumption is a natural extension of a standard exponential family assumption that holds for a single value of t. Specifically, suppose that $h^{(t)}(x)$, $t > 0$, denotes the t-marginal densities of a Lévy process, and that $f_\theta^{(1)}(x) = \exp\left[\theta \cdot x - \psi(\theta)\right] h^{(1)}(x)$ is an exponential family through $h^{(1)}(x)$ indexed by $\theta \in \mathbb{R}^d$. Then, we can verify that the densities specified in (12.6) induce a family of Lévy processes indexed by θ. The key observation in establishing this result is that, because $h^{(t)}(x)$ is the t-marginal of a Lévy process, the Lévy–Khintchine formula implies that

$$\int e^{\theta \cdot x} h^{(t)}(x) \, dx = \left(\int e^{\theta \cdot x} h^{(1)}(x) \, dx \right)^t = e^{t \, \psi(\theta)},$$

and so the densities in (12.6) are properly normalized.

We also note that, given this assumption and as $T \to \infty$, we have that A_T/T converges almost surely to $\mu(\theta) \stackrel{\text{def}}{=} \mathbb{E}\left[A_1\right]$. Thus, the topic θ can be understood as a description of an infinitely informative input. For finite values of T, X represents a noisy observation of the topic θ.

Now, given this structure, we show that the distribution of $\widetilde{X} = A_{\alpha T}$ conditional on $X = A_T$ does not depend on θ. Thus, feature thinning is possible without knowledge of θ using the Lévy thinning procedure defined below. We note that, in our setting, the carrier distributions $h^{(t)}(x)$ are always known; in Section 12.3, we discuss how to efficiently sample from the induced distribution $g^{(\alpha T)}$ for some specific cases of interest.

Theorem 12.1 (Lévy thinning). *Assume that (A_t) satisfies the exponential family structure in (12.6), and let $\alpha \in (0, 1)$ be the thinning parameter. Then, given an input $X = A_T$ and conditioned on any θ, the thinned input $\widetilde{X} = A_{\alpha T}$ has the following density:*

$$g^{(\alpha T)}(\tilde{\mathbf{x}}; X) = \frac{h^{(\alpha T)}(\tilde{\mathbf{x}})\, h^{((1-\alpha)T)}(X - \tilde{\mathbf{x}})}{h^{(T)}(X)}, \tag{12.7}$$

which importantly does not depend on θ.

Proof. Because the Lévy process (A_t) has independent and stationary increments, we have that $A_{\alpha T} \sim f_\theta^{(\alpha T)}$ and $A_T - A_{\alpha T} \sim f_\theta^{((1-\alpha)T)}$ are independent. Therefore, we can write the conditional density of $A_{\alpha T}$ given A_T as the joint density over $(A_{\alpha T}, A_T)$ (equivalently, the reparametrization $(A_{\alpha T}, A_T - A_{\alpha T})$) divided by the marginal density over A_T:

$$\begin{aligned}
g^{(\alpha T)}(\tilde{\mathbf{x}}; X) &= \frac{f_\theta^{(\alpha T)}(\tilde{\mathbf{x}}) f_\theta^{((1-\alpha)T)}(X - \tilde{\mathbf{x}})}{f_\theta^{(T)}(X)} \tag{12.8} \\
&= \left(\exp\left[\theta \cdot \tilde{\mathbf{x}} - \alpha T \psi(\theta) \right] h^{(\alpha T)}(\tilde{\mathbf{x}}) \right) \\
&\quad \times \left(\exp\left[\theta \cdot (X - \tilde{\mathbf{x}}) - (1 - \alpha)T\psi(\theta) \right] h^{((1-\alpha)T)}(X - \tilde{\mathbf{x}}) \right) \\
&\quad \times \left(\exp\left[\theta \cdot X - T\psi(\theta) \right] h^{(T)}(X) \right)^{-1},
\end{aligned}$$

where the last step expands everything (12.6). Algebraic cancellation, which removes all dependence on θ, completes the proof. $\qquad\square$

Note that while Theorem 12.1 guarantees we can carry out feature thinning without knowing the topic θ, it does not guarantee that we can do it without knowing the information content T. For Poisson processes, the binomial thinning mechanism depends only on α and not on the original T. This is a convenient property in the Poisson case but does not carry over to all Lévy processes — for example, if B_t is a standard Brownian motion, then the distribution of B_2 given $B_4 = 0$ is $\mathcal{N}(0, 1)$, while the distribution of B_{200} given $B_{400} = 0$ is $\mathcal{N}(0, 100)$. As we will see in Section 12.3, thinning in the Gaussian and Gamma families does require knowing T, which will correspond to a "sample size" or "precision." Likewise, Theorem 12.1 does not guarantee that sampling from (12.7) can be carried out efficiently; however, in all the examples we present here, sampling can be carried out easily in closed form.

Procedure 1. LOGISTIC REGRESSION WITH LÉVY REGULARIZATION

Input: n training examples $(X^{(i)}, Y^{(i)})$, a thinning parameter $\alpha \in (0, 1)$, and a feature map $\phi : \mathbb{R}^d \mapsto \mathbb{R}^p$.

1. For each training example $X^{(i)}$, generate B thinned versions $(\widetilde{X}^{(i,b)})_{b=1}^{B}$ according to (12.7).

2. Train logistic regression on the resulting pseudo-examples:

$$\hat{\beta} \stackrel{\text{def}}{=} \underset{\beta \in \mathbb{R}^{p \times K}}{\text{argmin}} \left\{ \sum_{i=1}^{n} \sum_{b=1}^{B} \ell\left(\beta; \widetilde{X}^{(i,b)}, Y^{(i)}\right) \right\}, \tag{12.9}$$

where the multi-class logistic loss with feature map ϕ is

$$\ell(\beta; x, y) \stackrel{\text{def}}{=} \log\left(\sum_{k=1}^{K} e^{\beta^{(k)} \cdot \phi(x)} \right) - \beta^{(y)} \cdot \phi(x). \tag{12.10}$$

3. Classify new examples according to

$$\hat{y}(x) = \underset{k \in \{1, \ldots, K\}}{\text{argmin}} \left\{ \hat{c}^{(k)} - \hat{\beta}^{(k)} \cdot \phi(x) \right\}, \tag{12.11}$$

where the $\hat{c}_k \in \mathbb{R}$ are optional class-specific calibration parameters for $k = 1, \ldots, K$.

12.2.3   Learning with Thinned Features

Having shown how to thin the input X to $\widetilde{X}$ without knowledge of θ, we can proceed to defining our full data augmentation strategy. We are given n training examples $\{(X^{(i)}, Y^{(i)})\}_{i=1}^{n}$. For each original input $X^{(i)}$, we generate B thinned versions $\widetilde{X}^{(i,1)}, \ldots, \widetilde{X}^{(i,B)}$ by sampling from (12.7). We then pair these B examples up with $Y^{(i)}$ and train *any* discriminative classifier on these Bn examples. Algorithm 1 describes the full procedure where we specialize to logistic regression. If one is implementing this procedure using stochastic gradient descent, one can also generate a fresh thinned input $\widetilde{X}$ whenever we sample an input X on the fly, which is the usual implementation of dropout training (Srivastava et al., 2014).

In the final step (12.11) of Algorithm 1, we also allow for class-specific calibration parameters . After the $\hat{\beta}^{(k)}$ have been determined by logistic regression with Lévy regularization, these parameters $\hat{c}^{(k)}$ can be chosen by optimizing the logistic loss on the original uncorrupted training data. As discussed in Section 12.2.5, re-calibrating the model is recommended, especially when α is small.

12.2.4 Thinning Preserves the Bayes Decision Boundary

We can easily implement the thinning procedure, but how will it affect the accuracy of the classifier? The following result gives us a first promising piece of the answer by establishing conditions under which thinning does not affect the Bayes decision boundary.

At a high level, our results rely on the fact that under our generative model, the "amount of information" contained in the input vector X is itself uninformative about the class label Y.

Assumption 12.2 (Equal information content across topics)**.** *Assume there exists a constant ψ_0 such that $\psi(\theta) = \psi_0$ with probability 1, over random θ.*

For example, in our Poisson topic model, we imposed the restriction that $\psi(\theta) = \sum_{j=1}^{d} e^{\theta_j} = 1$, which ensures that the document length $\|A_t\|_1$ has the same distribution (which has expectation $\psi(\theta)$ in this case) for all possible θ.

Theorem 12.2. *Under Assumption 12.2, the posterior class probabilities are invariant under thinning* (12.7):

$$\mathbb{P}\left[Y = y \mid \widetilde{X} = x\right] = \mathbb{P}\left[Y = y \mid X = x\right] \tag{12.12}$$

for all $y \in \{1, \ldots, K\}$ and $x \in \mathfrak{X}$.

Proof. Given Assumption 12.2, the density of $A_t \mid \theta$ is given by:

$$f_\theta^{(t)}(x) = e^{\theta \cdot x} e^{-t\psi_0} h^{(t)}(x), \tag{12.13}$$

which importantly splits into two factors, one depending on (θ, x), and the other depending on (t, x). Now, let us compute the posterior distribution:

$$\mathbb{P}\left[Y = y \mid A_t = x\right] \propto \mathbb{P}\left[Y = y\right] \int \mathbb{P}\left[\theta \mid Y\right] f_\theta^{(t)}(x) d\theta \tag{12.14}$$

$$\propto \mathbb{P}\left[Y = y\right] \int \mathbb{P}\left[\theta \mid Y\right] e^{\theta \cdot x} d\theta, \tag{12.15}$$

which does not depend on t, as $e^{-t\psi_0} h^{(t)}(x)$ can be folded into the normalization constant. Recall that $X = A_T$ and $\widetilde{X} = A_{\widetilde{T}}$. Substitute $t = T$ and $t = \widetilde{T}$ to conclude (12.12). $\qquad \square$

To see the importance of Assumption 12.2, consider the case where we have two labels ($Y \in \{1, 2\}$), each with a single topic (Y yields topic θ_Y). Suppose that $\psi(\theta_2) = 2\psi(\theta_1)$—that is, documents in class 2 are on average twice as long as those in class 1. Then, we would be able to make class 2 documents look like class 1 documents by thinning them with $\alpha = 0.5$.

Remark 12.1. *If we also condition on the information content T, then an analogue to Theorem 12.2 holds even without Assumption 12.2:*

$$\mathbb{P}\left[Y = y \mid \widetilde{X} = x, \widetilde{T} = t\right] = \mathbb{P}\left[Y = y \mid X = x, T = t\right]. \tag{12.16}$$

This is because, after conditioning on T, the $e^{-t\psi(\theta)}$ term factors out of the likelihood.

The upshot of Theorem 12.2 is that thinning will not induce asymptotic bias whenever an estimator produces $\mathbb{P}\left[Y = y \mid X = x\right]$ in the limit of infinite data ($n \to \infty$), i.e., if the logistic regression (Algorithm 1) is well-specified. Specifically, training either on original examples or thinned examples will both converge to the true class-conditional distribution. The following result assumes that the feature space $\mathcal{X}$ is discrete; the proof can easily be generalized to the case of continuous features.

Corollary 12.3. *Suppose that Assumption 12.2 holds, and that the above multi-class logistic regression model is well-specified, i.e., $\mathbb{P}\left[Y = y \mid X = x\right] \propto e^{\beta^{(y)} \cdot \phi(x)}$ for some β and all $y = 1, ..., K$. Then, assuming that $\mathbb{P}\left[A_t = x\right] > 0$ for all $x \in \mathcal{X}$ and $t > 0$, Algorithm 1 is consistent, i.e., the learned classification rule converges to the Bayes classifier as $n \to \infty$.*

Proof. At a fixed x, the population loss $\mathbb{E}\left[\ell\left(\beta; X, Y \mid X = x\right)\right]$ is minimized by any choice of β satisfying:

$$\frac{\exp\left[\beta^{(y)} \cdot \phi(x)\right]}{\sum_{k=1}^{K} \exp\left[\beta^{(k)} \cdot \phi(x)\right]} = \mathbb{P}\left[Y = y \mid X = x\right] \tag{12.17}$$

for all $y = 1, ..., K$. Since the model is well-specified and by assumption $\mathbb{P}[\widetilde{X} = x] > 0$ for all $x \in \mathcal{X}$, we conclude that weight vector $\hat{\beta}$ learned using Algorithm 1 must satisfy asymptotically (12.17) for all $x \in \mathcal{X}$ as $n \to \infty$. $\quad\square$

12.2.5 The End of the Path

As seen above, if we have a correctly specified logistic regression model, then Lévy thinning regularizes it without introducing any bias. However, if the logistic regression model is misspecified, thinning will in general induce bias, and the amount of thinning presents a bias-variance trade-off. The reason for this bias is that although thinning preserves the Bayes decision boundary, it changes the marginal distribution of the covariates X, which in turn affects logistic regression's linear approximation to the decision boundary. Figure 12.5 illustrates this phenomenon in the case where A_t

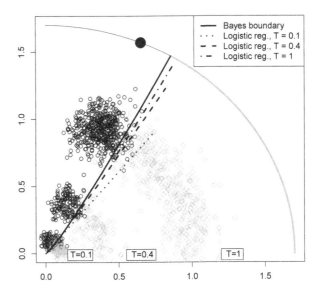

Figure 12.5: The effect of Lévy thinning with data generated from a Gaussian model of the form $X \mid \theta, T \sim \mathcal{N}\left(T\,\theta, \sigma^2 T\, I_{p \times p}\right)$, as described in Section 12.3.1. The outer circle depicts the distribution of θ conditional on the color Y: black circles all have $\theta \propto (\cos(0.75\,\pi/2), \sin(0.75\,\pi/2))$, whereas the grey squares have $\theta \propto (\cos(\omega\,\pi/2), \sin(\omega\,\pi/2))$ where ω is uniform between 0 and 2/3. Inside this circle, we see 3 clusters of points generated with $T = 0.1, 0.4,$ and 1, along with logistic regression decision boundaries obtained from each cluster. The dashed line shows the Bayes decision boundary separating the black and grey points, which is the same for all T (Theorem 12.2). Note that the logistic regression boundaries learned from data with different T are not the same. This issue arises because the Bayes decision boundary is curved, and the best linear approximation to a curved Bayes boundary changes with T.

is a Brownian motion, corresponding to Gaussian feature noising; Wager et al. (2014) provides a similar example for the Poisson topic model.

Fully characterizing the bias of Lévy thinning is beyond the scope of this paper. However, we can gain some helpful insights about this bias by studying "strong thinning"—i.e., Lévy thinning in the limit as the thinning parameter $\alpha \to 0$:

$$\hat{\beta}_{0+} \overset{\text{def}}{=} \lim_{\alpha \to 0} \lim_{B \to \infty} \hat{\beta}(\alpha, B), \tag{12.18}$$

where $\hat{\beta}(\alpha, B)$ is defined as in (12.9) with the explicit dependence on α and B. For each α, we take $B \to \infty$ perturbed points for each of the original

n data points. As we show in this section, this limiting classifier is well-defined under weak conditions; moreover, in some cases of interest, it can be interpreted as a simple generative classifier. The result below concerns the existence of $\hat{\beta}_{0+}$, and establishes that it is the empirical minimizer of a convex loss function.

Theorem 12.4. *Assume the setting of Procedure 1, and let the feature map be $\phi(x) = x$. Assume that the generative Lévy process (A_t) has finitely many jumps in expectation over the interval $[0, T]$. Then, the limit $\hat{\beta}_{0+}$ is well-defined and can be written as*

$$\hat{\beta}_{0+} = \underset{\beta \in \mathbb{R}^{p \times K}}{\operatorname{argmin}} \left\{ \sum_{i=1}^{n} \rho\left(\beta;\, X^{(i)}, Y^{(i)}\right) \right\}, \tag{12.19}$$

for some convex function $\rho(\cdot;\, x,\, y)$.

The proof of Theorem 12.4 is provided in the appendix. Here, we begin by establishing notation that lets us write down an expression for the limiting loss ρ. First, note that Assumption 12.1 implicitly requires that the process (A_t) has finite moments. Thus, by the Lévy–Itō decomposition, we can uniquely write this process as

$$A_t = bt + W_t + N_t, \tag{12.20}$$

where $b \in \mathbb{R}^p$, W_t is a Wiener process with covariance Σ, and N_t is a compound Poisson process which, by hypothesis, has a finite jump intensity.

Now, by an argument analogous to that in the proof of Theorem 12.1, we see that the joint distribution of W_T and N_T conditional on A_T does not depend on θ. Thus, we can define the following quantities without ambiguity:

$$\mu_T(x) = bT + \mathbb{E}\left[W_T \mid A_T = x\right], \tag{12.21}$$

$$\lambda_T(x) = \mathbb{E}\left[\text{number of jumps in } (A_t) \text{ for } t \in [0, T] \mid A_T = x\right], \tag{12.22}$$

$$\nu_T(z;\, x) = \lim_{t \to 0} \mathbb{P}\left[N_t = z \mid N_t \neq 0,\, A_T = x\right]. \tag{12.23}$$

More prosaically, $\nu_T(\cdot;\, x)$ can be described as the distribution of the first jump of $\widetilde{N}_t$, a thinned version of the jump process N_t. In the degenerate case where $\mathbb{P}\left[\mathbb{N}_T = 0 \mid A_T = x\right] = 0$, we set $\nu_T(\cdot;\, x)$ to be a point mass at $z = 0$.

Given this notation, we can write the effective loss function ρ for strong thinning as

$$\rho\left(\beta;\,x,\,y\right) = -\mu_T(x)\cdot\beta^{(y)} + \frac{T}{2}\frac{1}{K}\sum_{k=1}^{K}\beta^{(k)\top}\Sigma\beta^{(k)} \tag{12.24}$$

$$+ \lambda_T(x)\int\ell\left(\beta;\,z,\,y\right)\,d\nu_T(z;\,x),$$

provided we require without loss of generality that $\sum_{k=1}^{K}\beta^{(k)} = 0$. In other words, the limiting loss can be described entirely in terms of the distribution of the first jump of $\widetilde{N}_t$, and continuous part W_t of the Lévy process. The reason for this phenomenon is that, in the strong thinning limit, the pseudo-examples $\widetilde{X}\sim A_{\alpha T}$ can all be characterized using either 0 or 1 jumps.

Aggregating over all the training examples, we can equivalently write this strong thinning loss as

$$\sum_{i=1}^{n}\rho\left(\beta;\,X^{(i)},\,Y^{(i)}\right) = \frac{1}{2T}\sum_{i=1}^{n}\gamma_{Y^{(i)}}^{-1}\left\|\gamma_{Y^{(i)}}\mu_T\left(X^{(i)}\right) - T\Sigma\beta^{(Y^{(i)})}\right\|_{\Sigma^{-1}}^{2}$$

$$+ \sum_{i=1}^{n}\lambda_T(X^{(i)})\int\ell\left(\beta;\,z,\,Y^{(i)}\right)\,d\nu_T(z;\,X^{(i)}), \tag{12.25}$$

up to $\|\mu_T\|_2^2$ terms that do not depend on β. Here, $\frac{1}{2}\|v\|_{\Sigma^{-1}}^{2} = \frac{1}{2}v'\Sigma^{-1}v$ corresponds to the Gaussian log-likelihood with covariance Σ (up to constants), and $\gamma_y = K\left|\{i : Y^{(i)} = y\}\right|/n$ measures the over-representation of class y relative to other classes.

In the case where we have the same number of training examples from each class (and so $\gamma_y = 1$ for all $y = 1, ..., K$), the strong thinning loss can be understood in terms of a generative model. The first term, namely $\frac{1}{2T}\sum_{i=1}^{n}\left\|\mu_T(X^{(i)}) - T\Sigma\beta^{(Y^{(i)})}\right\|_{\Sigma^{-1}}^{2}$, is the loss function for linear classification in a Gaussian mixture with observations $\mu_T(X^{(i)})$, while the second term is the logistic loss obtained by classifying single jumps. Thus, strong thinning is effectively seeking the best linear classifier for a generative model that is a mixture of Gaussians and single jumps.

In the pure jump case ($\Sigma = 0$), we also note that strong thinning is closely related to naive Bayes classification. In fact, if the jump measure of N_t has a finite number of atoms that are all linearly independent, then we can verify that the parameters $\hat{\beta}_{0+}$ learned by strong thinning are equivalent to those learned via naive Bayes, although the calibration constants $c^{(k)}$ may be different.

At a high level, by elucidating the generative model that strong thinning pushes us towards, these results can help us better understand the behavior of Lévy thinning for intermediate value of α, e.g., $\alpha = 1/2$. They also suggest caution with respect to calibration: For both the diffusion and jump terms, we saw above that Lévy thinning gives helpful guidance for the angle of $\beta^{(k)}$, but does not in general elegantly account for signal strength $\left\| \beta^{(k)} \right\|_2$ or relative class weights. Thus, we recommend re-calibrating the class decision boundaries obtained by Lévy thinning, as in Algorithm 1.

12.3 Examples

So far, we have developed our theory of Lévy thinning using the Poisson topic model as a motivating example, which corresponds to dropping out words from a document. In this section, we present two models based on other Lévy processes—multivariate Brownian motion (Section 12.3.1) and Gamma processes (Section 12.3.2)— exploring the consequences of Lévy thinning.

12.3.1 Multivariate Brownian Motion

Consider a classification problem where the input vector is the aggregation of multiple noisy, independent measurements of some underlying object. For example, in a biomedical application, we might want to predict a patient's disease status based on a set of biomarkers such as gene expression levels or brain activity. A measurement is typically obtained through a noisy experiment involving an microarray or fMRI, so multiple experiments might be performed and aggregated.

More formally, suppose that patient i has disease status $Y^{(i)}$ and expression level $\mu_i \in \mathbb{R}^d$ for d genes, with the distribution of μ_i different for each disease status. Given μ_i, suppose the t-th measurement for patient i is distributed as

$$Z_{i,t} \sim \mathcal{N}(\mu_i, \Sigma), \qquad (12.26)$$

where $\Sigma \in \mathbb{R}^{d \times d}$ is assumed to be a known, fixed matrix. Let the observed input be $X^{(i)} = \sum_{t=1}^{T_i} Z_{i,t}$, the sum of the noisy measurements. If we could take infinitely many measurements ($T_i \to \infty$), we would have $X^{(i)}/T_i \to \mu_i$ almost surely; that is, we would observe gene expression noiselessly. For finitely many measurements, $X^{(i)}$ is a noisy proxy for the unobserved μ_i.

We can model the process of accumulating measurements with a multivariate Brownian motion (A_t):

$$A_t = t\mu + \Sigma^{1/2} B_t, \qquad (12.27)$$

where B_t is a d-dimensional white Brownian motion.[1] For integer values of t, A_t represents the sum of the first t measurements, but A_t is also defined for fractional values of t. The distribution of the features X at a given time T is thus

$$X \mid \mu, T \sim \mathcal{N}(T\mu, T\Sigma), \qquad (12.28)$$

leading to density

$$
\begin{aligned}
f_\mu^{(t)}(x) &= \frac{\exp\left[\frac{1}{2}(x - t\mu)^\top (t\Sigma)^{-1}(x - t\mu)\right]}{(2\pi)^{d/2} \det(\Sigma)} \qquad (12.29) \\
&= \exp\left[x^\top \Sigma^{-1}\mu - \frac{t}{2}\mu^\top \Sigma^{-1}\mu\right] h^{(t)}(x),
\end{aligned}
$$

where

$$h^{(t)}(x) = \frac{\exp\left[-\frac{1}{2t}x^\top \Sigma^{-1}x\right]}{(2\pi)^{d/2} \det(\Sigma)^{1/2}}. \qquad (12.30)$$

We can recover the form of (12.6) by setting $\theta = \Sigma^{-1}\mu$, a one-to-one mapping provided Σ is positive-definite.

Thinning. The distribution of $\widetilde{X} = A_{\alpha T}$ given $X = A_T$ is that of a Brownian bridge process with the following marginals:

$$\widetilde{X} \mid X \sim \mathcal{N}\left(\alpha X, \alpha(1 - \alpha)T\Sigma\right). \qquad (12.31)$$

In this case, "thinning" corresponds exactly to adding zero-mean, additive Gaussian noise to the scaled features αX. Note that in this model, unlike in the Poisson topic model, sampling $\widetilde{X}$ from X does require observing T—for example, knowing how many observations were taken. The larger T is, the more noise we need to inject to achieve the same downsampling ratio.

In the Poisson topic model, the features $(X_{i,1}, \ldots, X_{i,d})$ were independent of each other given the topic θ_i and expected length T_i. By contrast, in the Brownian motion model the features are correlated (unless Σ is the identity matrix). This serves to illustrate that independence or dependence of the features is irrelevant to our general framework; what is important is that the *increments* $Z_t = A_t - A_{t-1}$ are independent of each other, the key property of a Lévy process.

Assumption 12.2 requires that $\mu^\top \Sigma^{-1}\mu$ is constant across topics; i.e., that the true gene expression levels are equally sized in the Mahalanobis norm

---

1. By definition of Brownian motion, we have marginally that $B_t \sim \mathcal{N}(0, tI)$.

defined by Σ. Clearly, this assumption is overly stringent in real situations. Fortunately, Assumption 12.2 is not required (see Remark 12.1) as long as T is observed—as it must be anyway if we want to be able to carry out Lévy thinning.

Thinning X in this case is very similar to subsampling. Indeed, for integer values of $\widetilde{T}$, instead of formally carrying out Lévy thinning as detailed above, we could simply resample $\widetilde{T}$ values of $Z_{i,t}$ without replacement, and add them together to obtain $\widetilde{X}$. If there are relatively few repeats, however, the resampling scheme can lead to only $\binom{T}{\widetilde{T}}$ pseudo-examples (e.g. 6 pseudo-examples if $T = 4$ and $\widetilde{T} = 2$), whereas the thinning approach leads to infinitely many possible pseudo-examples we can use to augment the regression. Moreover, if $T = 4$ then subsampling leaves us with only four choices of α; there would be no way to thin using $\alpha = 0.1$, for instance.

12.3.2 Gamma Process

As another example, suppose again that we are predicting a patient's disease status based on repeated measurements of a biomarker such as gene expression or brain activity. But now, instead of (or in addition to) the *average* signal, we want our features to represent the variance or covariance of the signals across the different measurements.

Assume first that the signals at different genes or brain locations are independent; that is, the t-th measurement for patient i and gene j has distribution

$$Z_{i,j,t} \sim \mathcal{N}(\mu_{i,j}, \sigma_{i,j}^2).\tag{12.32}$$

Here, the variances $\sigma_i^2 = (\sigma_{i,1}^2, \ldots, \sigma_{i,d}^2)$ parameterize the "topic." Suppressing the subscript i, after $T + 1$ measurements we can compute

$$X_{j,T} = \sum_{t=1}^{T+1}(Z_{i,j,t} - \bar{Z}_{i,j,T+1})^2, \quad \text{where} \quad \bar{Z}_{i,j,T+1} = \frac{1}{T+1}\sum_{t=1}^{T+1} Z_{i,j,t}.\tag{12.33}$$

Then $X_{j,T} \sim \sigma_j^2 \chi_T^2$, which is a Gamma distribution with shape parameter $T/2$ and scale parameter $2\sigma_j^2$ (there is no dependence on μ_i). Once again, as we accumulate more and more observations (increasing T), we will have $X_T/T \to (\sigma_1^2, \ldots, \sigma_d^2)$ almost surely.

We can embed $X_{j,T}$ in a multivariate Gamma process with d independent coordinates and scale parameters σ_j^2:

$$(A_t)_j \sim \text{Gamma}(t/2, 2\sigma_j^2).\tag{12.34}$$

The density of A_t given σ^2 is

$$f_{\sigma^2}^{(t)}(x) = \prod_{j=1}^{d} \frac{x_j^{t/2-1} e^{-x_j/2\sigma_j^2}}{\Gamma(t/2) 2^{t/2} \sigma_j^{2(t/2)}} \tag{12.35}$$

$$= \exp\left[-\sum_{j=1}^{d} x_j/2\sigma_j^2 - (t/2)\sum_{j=1}^{d} \log \sigma_j^2 \right] h^{(t)}(x),$$

where

$$h^{(t)}(x) = \frac{\prod_j x_j^{t/2-1}}{\Gamma(t/2)^d 2^{dt/2}}. \tag{12.36}$$

We can recover the form of (12.6) by setting $\theta_j = -1/2\sigma_j^2$, a one-to-one mapping.

Thinning.   Because $\widetilde{X}_j \sim \mathrm{Gamma}(\alpha T/2, 2\sigma_j^2)$ is independent of the increment $X_j - \widetilde{X}_j \sim \mathrm{Gamma}((1-\alpha)T/2, 2\sigma_j^2)$, we have

$$\frac{\widetilde{X}_j}{X_j} \mid X_j \sim \mathrm{Beta}\left(\alpha T/2, (1-\alpha)T/2 \right). \tag{12.37}$$

In other words, we create a noisy $\widetilde{X}$ by generating for each coordinate an independent *multiplicative* noise factor

$$m_j \sim \mathrm{Beta}\left(\alpha T, (1-\alpha)T \right) \tag{12.38}$$

and setting $\widetilde{X}_j = m_j X_j$. Once again, we can downsample without knowing σ_j^2, but we do need to observe T. Assumption 12.2 would require that $\prod_j \sigma_j^2$ is identical for all topics. This is an unrealistic assumption, but once again it is unnecessary as long as we observe T.

General covariance.   More generally, the signals at different brain locations, or expressions for different genes, will typically be correlated with each other, and these correlations could be important predictors. To model this, let the measurements be distributed as:

$$Z_{i,t} \sim \mathcal{N}(\mu_i, \Sigma_i), \tag{12.39}$$

where Σ represents the unknown "topic"—some covariance matrix that is characteristic of a certain subcategory of a disease status.

After observing $T + 1$ observations we can construct the matrix-valued features:

$$X_T = \sum_{t=1}^{T+1} (Z_{i,t} - \bar{Z}_{i,T+1})(Z_{i,t} - \bar{Z}_{i,T+1})^{\top}. \tag{12.40}$$

Now X_T has a Wishart distribution: $X_T \sim \text{Wish}_d(\Sigma, T)$. When $T \geq d$, the density of A_t given Σ is

$$f_{\Sigma}^{(t)}(x) = \exp\left\{ -\frac{1}{2}\,\text{tr}(\Sigma^{-1}x) - \frac{t}{2}\log\det(\Sigma) \right\} h^{(t)}(x), \tag{12.41}$$

where

$$h^{(t)}(x) = \left(2^{\frac{td}{2}} \det(x)^{\frac{t-d-2}{2}} \Gamma_d\left(\frac{t}{2}\right) \right)^{-1}, \tag{12.42}$$

$$\Gamma_d\left(\frac{t}{2}\right) = \pi^{\frac{d(d-1)}{4}} \prod_{j=1}^{d} \Gamma\left(\frac{t}{2} + \frac{1-j}{2}\right), \tag{12.43}$$

supported on positive-definite symmetric matrices. If $X = A_T$ and $\alpha T \geq d$ as well, we can sample a "thinned" observation $\widetilde{X}$ from density proportional to

$$h^{(\alpha T)}(\tilde{x}) h^{(T-\alpha T)}(X - \tilde{x}) \propto \det(\tilde{x})^{\frac{2+d-\alpha T}{2}} \det(X - \tilde{x})^{\frac{2+d-(1-\alpha)T}{2}}, \tag{12.44}$$

or after the affine change of variables $\widetilde{X} = X^{1/2} M X^{1/2}$, we sample M from density proportional to $\det(m)^{\frac{2+d-\alpha T}{2}} \det(I_d - m)^{\frac{2+d-(1-\alpha)t}{2}}$, a matrix beta distribution. Here, M may be interpreted as matrix-valued multiplicative noise.

12.4 Simulation Experiments

In this section, we perform several simulations to illustrate the utility of Lévy thinning. In particular, we will highlight the modularity between Lévy thinning (which provides pseudo-examples) and the discriminative learner (which ingests these pseudo-examples). We treat the discriminative learner as a black box, complete with its own internal cross-validation scheme that optimizes accuracy on pseudo-examples. Nonetheless, we show that accuracy on the original examples improves when we train on thinned examples.

More specifically, given a set of training examples $\{(X, Y)\}$, we first use Lévy thinning to generate a set of pseudo-examples $\{(\widetilde{X}, Y)\}$. Then we feed these examples to the R function cv.glmnet to learn a linear classifier on these pseudo-examples (Friedman et al., 2010). We emphasize

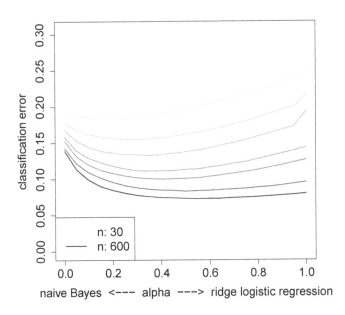

Figure 12.6: Performance of Lévy thinning with cross-validated ridge-regularized logistic regression, on a random Gaussian design described in (12.45). The curves depict the relationship between thinning α and classification error as the number of training examples grows: $n = 30$, 50, 75, 100, 150, 200, 400, and 600. We see that naive Bayes improves over ridge logistic regression in very small samples, while in moderately small samples Lévy thinning does better than either end of the path.

that `cv.glmnet` seeks to choose its regularization parameter λ to maximize its accuracy on the pseudo-examples $(\widetilde{X}, Y)$ rather than on the original data (X, Y). Thus, we are using cross-validation as a black box instead of trying to adapt the procedure to the context of Lévy thinning. In principle, we might be concerned that cross-validating on the pseudo-examples would yield a highly suboptimal choice of λ, but our experiments will show that the procedure in fact works quite well.

The two extremes of the path correspond to naive Bayes generative modeling at one end ($\alpha = 0$), and plain ridge-regularized logistic regression at the other ($\alpha = 1$). All methods were calibrated on the training data as follows: Given original weight vectors $\hat{\beta}$, we first compute un-calibrated predictions $\hat{\mu} = X\hat{\beta}$ for the log-odds of $\mathbb{P}\left[Y = 1 \mid X\right]$, and then run a second univariate logistic regression $Y \sim \hat{\mu}$ to adjust both the intercept and the magnitude of the original coefficients. Moreover, when using cross-validation on pseudo-examples $(\widetilde{X}, Y)$, we ensure that all pseudo-examples induced by a given

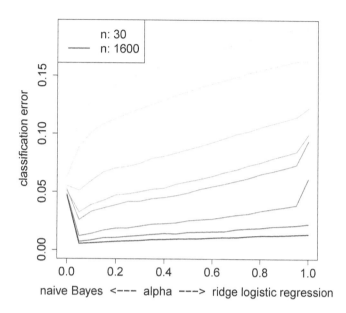

Figure 12.7: Performance of Lévy thinning with cross-validated ridge-regularized logistic regression, on a random Poisson design described in (12.46). The curves depict the relationship between thinning α and classification accuracy for $n = 30, 50, 100, 150, 200, 400, 800$, and 1600. Here, aggressive Lévy thinning with small but non-zero α does substantially better than naive Bayes ($\alpha = 0$) as soon as n is moderately large.

example (X, Y) are in the same cross-validation fold. Code for reproducing our results is available at `https://github.com/swager/levythin`.

Gaussian example. We generate data from the following hierarchical model:

$$Y \sim \text{Binomial}(0.5), \quad \mu \,|\, Y \sim \mathcal{L}_Y, \quad X \,|\, \mu \sim \mathcal{N}(\mu, I_{d \times d}), \qquad (12.45)$$

where $\mu, X \in \mathbb{R}^d$ and $d = 100$. The distribution $\mathcal{L}_Y$ associated with each label Y consists of 10 atoms $\mu_1^{(Y)}, ..., \mu_{10}^{(Y)}$. These atoms themselves are all randomly generated such that their first 20 coordinates are independent draws of $1.1\,T_4$ where T_4 follows Student's t-distribution with 4 degrees of freedom; meanwhile, the last 80 coordinates of μ are all 0. The results in Figure 12.6 are marginalized over the randomness in $\mathcal{L}_Y$; i.e., different simulation realizations have different conditional laws for μ given Y. Figure 12.6 shows the results.

Poisson example.   We generate data from the following hierarchical model:

$$Y \sim \text{Binomial}\,(0.5)\,, \quad \theta \,|\, Y \sim \mathcal{L}_Y, \quad X_j \,|\, \theta \sim \text{Pois}\left(1000\frac{e^{\theta_j}}{\sum_{j=1}^d e^{\theta_j}}\right), \quad (12.46)$$

where $\theta \in \mathbb{R}^d$, $X \in \mathbb{N}^d$, and $d = 500$. This time, however, $\mathcal{L}_Y$ is deterministic: If $Y = 0$, then θ is just 7 ones followed by 493 zeros, whereas

$$\theta \,|\, Y = 1 \sim \left(\underbrace{0, ..., 0}_{7} \,\Big|\, \underbrace{\tau, ..., \tau}_{7} \,\Big|\, \underbrace{0, ..., 0}_{486}\right), \quad \text{with} \quad \tau \sim \text{Exp}(3).$$

This generative model was also used in simulations by Wager et al. (2014); the difference is that they applied thinning to plain logistic regression, whereas here we verify that Lévy thinning is also helpful when paired with cross-validated ridge logistic regression. Figure 12.7 shows the results.

These experiments suggest that it is reasonable to pair Lévy thinning with a well-tuned black box learner on the pseudo-examples $(\widetilde{X}, Y)$, without worrying about potential interactions between Lévy thinning and the tuning of the discriminative model.

12.5 Discussion

In this chapter, we have explored a general framework for performing data augmentation: apply Lévy thinning and train a discriminative classifier on the resulting pseudo-examples. The exact thinning scheme reflects our generative modeling assumptions. We emphasize that the generative assumptions are non-parametric and of a structural nature; in particular, we never fit an actual generative model, but rather encode the generative hints implicitly in the pseudo-examples.

A key result is that under the generative assumptions, thinning preserves the Bayes decision boundary, which suggests that a well-specified classifier incurs no asymptotic bias. Similarly, we would expect that a misspecified but powerful classifier should incur little bias. We showed that in limit of maximum thinning, the resulting procedure corresponds to fitting a generative model. The exact bias-variance trade-off for moderate levels of thinning is an interesting subject for further study.

While Lévy processes provide a general framework for thinning examples, we recognize that there are many other forms of coarsening that could lead to the same intuitions. For instance, suppose $X \,|\, \theta$ is a Markov process over words in a document. We might expect that short *contiguous* subsequences of X could serve as good pseudo-examples. More broadly, there are many forms of data augmentation that do not have the intuition of coarsening an input. For example, rotating or shearing an image to generate pseudo-images appeals to other forms of transformational invariance. It would be enlightening to establish a generative framework in which data augmentation with these other forms of invariance arise naturally.

12.6　Appendix: Proof of Theorem 12.4

To establish the desired result, we show that for a single training example (X, Y), the following limit is well-defined for any $\beta \in \mathbb{R}^{p \times K}$:

$$\rho\left(\beta; X, Y\right) = \lim_{\alpha \to 0} \frac{1}{\alpha} \left(\widetilde{\mathbb{E}} \left[\ell\left(\beta; \widetilde{X}, Y\right) \right] - \log\left(K\right) \right) \tag{12.47}$$

$$= -\beta^{(Y)} \cdot X + \lim_{\alpha \to 0} \frac{1}{\alpha} \widetilde{\mathbb{E}} \left[\log\left(\frac{1}{K} \sum_{k=1}^{K} e^{\beta^{(k)} \cdot \widetilde{X}} \right) \right],$$

where on the second line we wrote down the logistic loss explicitly and exploited linearity of the term involving Y as in Wager et al. (2013). Here $\widetilde{\mathbb{E}}$ denotes expectation with respect to the thinning process and reflects the $B \to \infty$ limit. Because ℓ is convex, ρ must also be convex; and by equicontinuity $\hat{\beta}(\alpha)$ must also converge to its minimizer.

Our argument relies on the decomposition $A_t = bt + W_t + N_t$ from (12.20). Without loss of generality, we can generate the pseudo-features $\widetilde{X}$ as $\widetilde{X} = bt + \widetilde{W}_{\alpha T} + \widetilde{N}_{\alpha T}$, where $\widetilde{W}_{\alpha T}$ and $\widetilde{N}_{\alpha T}$ have the same marginal distribution as $W_{\alpha T}$ and $N_{\alpha T}$. Given this notation,

$$\frac{1}{\alpha} \widetilde{\mathbb{E}} \left[\log\left(\frac{1}{K} \sum_{k=1}^{K} e^{\beta^{(k)} \cdot \left(\alpha b T + \widetilde{W}_{\alpha T} + \widetilde{N}_{\alpha T} \right)} \right) \right]$$

$$= \frac{1}{\alpha} \widetilde{\mathbb{E}} \left[\log\left(\frac{1}{K} \sum_{k=1}^{K} e^{\beta^{(k)} \cdot \left(\alpha b T + \widetilde{W}_{\alpha T} \right)} \right) \Big| \, \widetilde{N}_{\alpha T} = 0 \right] \mathbb{P} \left[\widetilde{N}_{\alpha T} = 0 \right]$$

$$+ \frac{1}{\alpha} \widetilde{\mathbb{E}} \left[\log\left(\frac{1}{K} \sum_{k=1}^{K} e^{\beta^{(k)} \cdot \left(\alpha b T + \widetilde{W}_{\alpha T} + \widetilde{N}_{\alpha T} \right)} \right) \Big| \, \widetilde{N}_{\alpha T} \neq 0 \right] \mathbb{P} \left[\widetilde{N}_{\alpha T} \neq 0 \right].$$

We now characterize these terms individually. First, because N_t has a finite jump intensity, we can verify that, almost surely,

$$\lim_{\alpha \to 0} \frac{1}{\alpha} \mathbb{P} \left[\widetilde{N}_{\alpha T} \neq 0 \right] = \lambda_T(X),$$

where $\lambda_T(X)$ is as defined in (12.22). Next, because $\widetilde{W}_{\alpha T}$ concentrates at 0 as $\alpha \to 0$, we can check that

$$
\lim_{\alpha \to 0} \widetilde{\mathbb{E}} \left[\log \left(\frac{1}{K} \sum_{k=1}^{K} e^{\beta^{(k)} \cdot \left(\alpha b T + \widetilde{W}_{\alpha T} + \widetilde{N}_{\alpha T} \right)} \right) \mid \widetilde{N}_{\alpha T} \neq 0 \right]
$$

$$
= \lim_{\alpha \to 0} \widetilde{\mathbb{E}} \left[\log \left(\frac{1}{K} \sum_{k=1}^{K} e^{\beta^{(k)} \cdot \widetilde{N}_{\alpha T}} \right) \mid \widetilde{N}_{\alpha T} \neq 0 \right]
$$

$$
= \int \log \left(\frac{1}{K} \sum_{k=1}^{K} e^{\beta^{(k)} \cdot z} \right) \, d\nu_T(z; X)
$$

where $\nu_T(\cdot\,; X)$ (12.23) is the first jump measure conditional on X.

Meanwhile, in order to control the remaining term, we note that we can write

$$
\widetilde{W}_{\alpha T} = \alpha \widetilde{W}_T + \widetilde{B}_{\alpha T},
$$

where $\widetilde{B}_t$ is a Brownian bridge from 0 to T that is independent from $\widetilde{W}_T$. Thus, noting that $\lim_{\alpha \to 0} \mathbb{P}\left[\widetilde{N}_{\alpha T} = 0 \right] = 1$, we find that

$$
\lim_{\alpha \to 0} \frac{1}{\alpha} \widetilde{\mathbb{E}} \left[\log \left(\frac{1}{K} \sum_{k=1}^{K} e^{\beta^{(k)} \cdot \left(\alpha b T + \widetilde{W}_{\alpha T} \right)} \right) \mid \widetilde{N}_{\alpha T} = 0 \right] \mathbb{P}\left[\widetilde{N}_{\alpha T} = 0 \right]
$$

$$
= \lim_{\alpha \to 0} \frac{1}{\alpha} \widetilde{\mathbb{E}} \left[\log \left(\frac{1}{K} \sum_{k=1}^{K} e^{\beta^{(k)} \cdot \left(\alpha \left(b T + \widetilde{W}_T \right) \right) + \widetilde{B}_{\alpha T}} \right) \right]
$$

$$
= \bar{\beta} \cdot \mu_T(X) + \frac{T}{2} \left(\frac{1}{K} \sum_{k=1}^{K} \beta^{(k)\top} \Sigma \, \beta^{(k)} - \bar{\beta}^\top \Sigma \bar{\beta} \right),
$$

where $\mu_T(X)$ is as defined in (12.21) and $\bar{\beta} = K^{-1} \sum_{k=1}^{K} \beta^{(k)}$. The last equality follows from Taylor expanding the $\log(\sum \exp)$ term and noting that 3rd- and higher-order terms vanish in the limit.

Bringing back the linear term form (12.47), and assuming without loss of generality that $\bar{\beta} = 0$, we finally conclude that

$$\rho\left(\beta; X, Y\right) = -\beta^{(Y)} \cdot X + \frac{T}{2} \frac{1}{K} \sum_{k=1}^{K} \beta^{(k)\top} \Sigma \, \beta^{(k)}$$

$$+ \lambda_T(X) \int \log\left(\frac{1}{K} \sum_{k=1}^{K} e^{\beta^{(k)} \cdot z}\right) d\nu_T(z; X)$$

$$= -\beta^{(Y)} \cdot \mu_T(X) + \frac{T}{2} \frac{1}{K} \sum_{k=1}^{K} \beta^{(k)\top} \Sigma \, \beta^{(k)}$$

$$+ \lambda_T(X) \int -\beta^{(Y)} \cdot z + \log\left(\sum_{k=1}^{K} e^{\beta^{(k)} \cdot z}\right) - \log(K) \, d\nu_T(z; X),$$

where for the second equality we used the fact that $X = \mu_T(X) + \lambda_T(X) \int z \, d\nu_T(z; X)$. Finally, this expression only differs from (12.24) by terms that do not include β; thus, they yield the same minimizer.

12.7   References

Y. S. Abu-Mostafa. Learning from hints in neural networks. *Journal of Complexity*, 6(2):192–198, 1990.

J. Ba and B. Frey. Adaptive dropout for training deep neural networks. In *Advances in Neural Information Processing Systems (NIPS)*, pages 3084–3092, 2013.

P. Baldi and P. Sadowski. The dropout learning algorithm. *Artificial intelligence*, 210:78–122, 2014.

C. M. Bishop. Training with noise is equivalent to tikhonov regularization. *Neural computation*, 7(1):108–116, 1995.

G. Bouchard and B. Triggs. The trade-off between generative and discriminative classifiers. In *International Conference on Computational Statistics*, pages 721–728, 2004.

B. Efron. The efficiency of logistic regression compared to normal discriminant analysis. *Journal of the American Statistical Association (JASA)*, 70(352):892–898, 1975.

J. Friedman, T. Hastie, and R. Tibshirani. Regularization paths for generalized linear models via coordinate descent. *Journal of Statistical Software*, 33(1):1–22, 2010.

A. Globerson and S. Roweis. Nightmare at test time: robust learning by feature deletion. In *International Conference on Machine Learning (ICML)*, pages 353–360, 2006.

I. Goodfellow, D. Warde-farley, M. Mirza, A. Courville, and Y. Bengio. Maxout networks. In *International Conference on Machine Learning (ICML)*, pages 1319–1327, 2013.

D. P. Helmbold and P. M. Long. On the inductive bias of dropout. *Journal of Machine Learning Research (JMLR)*, 16:3403–3454, 2015.

J. Josse and S. Wager. Stable autoencoding: A flexible framework for regularized low-rank matrix estimation. *arXiv preprint arXiv:1410.8275*, 2014.

A. Krizhevsky, I. Sutskever, and G. E. Hinton. Imagenet classification with deep convolutional neural networks. In *Advances in Neural Information Processing Systems (NIPS)*, pages 1097–1105, 2012.

J. A. Lasserre, C. M. Bishop, and T. P. Minka. Principled hybrids of generative and discriminative models. In *Computer Vision and Pattern Recognition (CVPR)*, pages 87–94, 2006.

P. Liang and M. I. Jordan. An asymptotic analysis of generative, discriminative, and pseudolikelihood estimators. In *International Conference on Machine Learning (ICML)*, pages 584–591, 2008.

D. McAllester. A PAC-Bayesian tutorial with a dropout bound. *arXiv preprint arXiv:1307.2118*, 2013.

A. McCallum, C. Pal, G. Druck, and X. Wang. Multi-conditional learning: Generative/discriminative training for clustering and classification. In *Association for the Advancement of Artificial Intelligence (AAAI)*, 2006.

A. Y. Ng and M. I. Jordan. On discriminative vs. generative classifiers: A comparison of logistic regression and naive Bayes. In *Advances in Neural Information Processing Systems (NIPS)*, 2002.

R. Raina, Y. Shen, A. Ng, and A. McCallum. Classification with hybrid generative/discriminative models. In *Advances in Neural Information Processing Systems (NIPS)*, 2004.

Y. D. Rubinstein and T. Hastie. Discriminative vs informative learning. In *International Conference on Knowledge Discovery and Data Mining (KDD)*, volume 5, pages 49–53, 1997.

S. P. Schölkopf, P. Simard, V. Vapnik, and A. Smola. Improving the accuracy and speed of support vector machines. In *Advances in Neural Information Processing Systems (NIPS)*, pages 375–381, 1997.

P. Y. Simard, Y. A. LeCun, J. S. Denker, and B. Victorri. *Transformation Invariance in Pattern Recognition—Tangent Distance and Tangent Propagation.* Neural networks: Tricks of the trade Springer, 1998.

N. Srivastava, G. Hinton, A. Krizhevsky, I. Sutskever, and R. Salakhutdinov. Dropout: A simple way to prevent neural networks from overfitting. *Journal of Machine Learning Research (JMLR)*, 15(1):1929–1958, 2014.

L. van der Maaten, M. Chen, S. Tyree, and K. Q. Weinberger. Learning with marginalized corrupted features. In *International Conference on Machine Learning (ICML)*, pages 410–418, 2013.

S. Wager, S. I. Wang, and P. Liang. Dropout training as adaptive regularization. In *Advances in Neural Information Processing Systems (NIPS)*, 2013.

S. Wager, W. Fithian, S. I. Wang, and P. Liang. Altitude training: Strong bounds for single-layer dropout. In *Advances in Neural Information Processing Systems (NIPS)*, 2014.

L. Wan, M. Zeiler, S. Zhang, Y. L. Cun, and R. Fergus. Regularization of neural networks using dropconnect. In *International Conference on Machine Learning (ICML)*, pages 1058–1066, 2013.

S. I. Wang and C. Manning. Fast dropout training. In *International Conference on Machine Learning (ICML)*, pages 118–126, 2013.

S. I. Wang, M. Wang, S. Wager, P. Liang, and C. Manning. Feature noising for log-linear structured prediction. In *Empirical Methods in Natural Language Processing (EMNLP)*, 2013.

13   Bilu-Linial Stability

Konstantin Makarychev   komakary@microsoft.com
Microsoft Research
Redmond, WA, USA

Yury Makarychev   yury@ttic.edu
Toyota Technological Institute at Chicago
Chicago, IL, USA

This chapter describes recent results on Bilu-Linial stability, also known as perturbation resilience. It offers an overview of the subject and presents algorithms for stable and weakly stable instances of graph partitioning and clustering problems, including Max Cut, Minimum Multiway Cut, k-center, and clustering problems with separable center-based objectives.

13.1   Introduction

In this chapter, we survey recent research on instance stability and perturbation resilience. Many discrete optimization problems in machine learning, operations research, and other areas are NP-hard. For many of them, not only the exact but even a good approximate solution cannot be found efficiently in the worst case. At the same time, instances appearing in real life can often be solved exactly or almost exactly. This raises the following question:

Why are real-life instances often significantly easier than worst-case instances?

To formally study this question, we must define a model for real-life instances. The two most popular approaches are either to assume that a real-life instance has certain structural properties, or to assume that it is generated in a random or semi-random process. Both approaches are very natural and have led to the discovery of many interesting results. In this chapter, we study the former approach, focusing on stable instances of clustering and graph partitioning problems. We refer the reader to several papers describing the latter approach (Blum and Spencer, 1995; Feige and Kilian, 1998; Mathieu and Schudy, 2010; Makarychev et al., 2012, 2014a, 2013, 2015; Feige et al., 2015).

Instance stability, or perturbation resilience, was introduced by Bilu and Linial (2010). Informally, an instance is Bilu-Linial stable if the optimal solution does not change when we perturb the instance.

Definition 13.1. *Consider an instance of a graph partitioning problem, a graph $G = (V, E, w)$ with a set of edge weights w_e. An instance $G' = (V, E, w')$ is an α-perturbation ($\alpha \geq 1$) of G if $w(e) \leq w'(e) \leq \alpha w(e)$; that is, if we can obtain the perturbed instance from the original by multiplying the weight of each edge by a number from 1 to α (the number may be different for every edge).*

Now, consider an instance $\mathfrak{I} = (V, d)$ of a clustering problem, where V is a set of points and d is a metric on V. An instance (V, d') is an α-perturbation of (V, d) if $d(u, v) \leq d'(u, v) \leq \alpha d(u, v)$; here, d' does not have to be a metric. If, in addition, d' is a metric, then d' is an α-metric perturbation of d.

Definition 13.2. *An instance $\mathfrak{I}$ is α-stable if every α-perturbation of $\mathfrak{I}$ has the same optimal solution as $\mathfrak{I}$.*

Adhering to the literature, we will refer to α-stable instances of graph partitioning problems as "Bilu-Linial stable" and to α-stable instances of clustering problems as "α-perturbation resilient". Additionally, for clustering problems, we will consider a weaker, and perhaps somewhat more natural, notion of α-metric perturbation resilience.

Definition 13.3. *An instance (V, d) of a clustering problem is α-metric perturbation resilient if every α-metric perturbation of (V, d) has the same optimal solution as $\mathfrak{I}$.*

Why is it reasonable to assume that many real-life instances are stable? As Bilu and Linial (2010); Balcan et al. (2009); Bilu et al. (2013) argue, the reason is that often the optimal solution "stands out" among all other solutions — it is significantly better than all other solutions, and, therefore, the optimal solution remains the same even if we slightly perturb the instance. Also, we are often interested not in optimizing the objective function per se, but rather in finding the "true" clustering or partitioning.

Problem	Main Results	Reference
Max Cut & 2-correlation clustering	$O(\sqrt{\log n} \log \log n)$ (incl. weakly stable instances) SDP gap and hardness result	Makarychev et al. (2014b)
Min Multiway Cut	4, (incl. weakly stable instances)	Makarychev et al. (2014b)
Max k-Cut	hardness for ∞-stable instances	Makarychev et al. (2014b)
sym./assym. k-center	2 hardness for $(2-\varepsilon)$-pert. resil.	Balcan et al. (2015)
s.c.b. objective	$1 + \sqrt{2}$ $(2 + \sqrt{3}, \varepsilon)$ for k-median 2, assuming cluster verifiability	Balcan and Liang (2016) Balcan et al. (2015)
s.c.b., Steiner points	$2 + \sqrt{3}$	Awasthi et al. (2012)
min-sum objective	$O(\rho)$ and $(O(\rho), \varepsilon)$, where ρ is the ratio between the sizes of the largest and smallest clusters	Balcan and Liang (2016)
TSP	1.8	Mihalák et al. (2011)

Table 13.1: The table summarizes some known results for Bilu-Linial stability. It shows a number α if there is an algorithm for α-stable/perturbation resilient instances; it shows (α, ε) if there is an algorithm for (α, ε)-perturbation resilient instances. "s.c.b." is a shortcut for a clustering problem with a separable center-based objective.

If the optimal solution changes drastically when we slightly perturb the weights, then by solving the problem exactly, we will likely not find the true clustering since we often know the values of edge weights or distances only approximately. Therefore, if the instance is not stable, we are not interested in solving it in the first place.

Nevertheless, the definition of Bilu-Linial stability is somewhat too strict. Perhaps, it is more natural to require that the optimal solution to a perturbed instance be "ε-close" but not necessarily equal to the optimal solution for the original instance. This notion is captured in the definitions of α-*weak Bilu-Linial stability* and (α, ε)-*perturbation resilience* (we present a formal definition of weak Bilu-Linial stability for Max Cut in Section 13.2.3).

Let us now briefly describe the research on Bilu-Linial stability. We refer the reader to Table 13.1 for the list of known results. The notion of instance stability was introduced by Bilu and Linial (2010). They offered the first evidence that stable instances are much easier than worst-case instances; specifically, they gave an exact algorithm for $O(n)$-stable instances of Max Cut. This result was improved by Bilu et al. (2013), who designed an algorithm for $O(\sqrt{n})$-stable instances. Makarychev et al. (2014b) developed a general approach to analyzing stable instances of graph partitioning problems, showing that if there exist a convex relaxation and a rounding scheme for a problem satisfying certain properties, then

- the convex relaxation for stable instances of the problem is integral;
- there are polynomial-time algorithms for stable and weakly stable instances of the problem;
- the algorithm for stable instances is robust — it either solves the problem or certifies that the instance is not stable.

In particular, this result applies to $O(\sqrt{\log n} \log \log n)$-stable and weakly stable instances of Max Cut, and 4-stable and weakly stable instances of Minimum Multiway Cut. Moreover, the results for Max Cut are essentially tight; see (Makarychev et al., 2014b) for details.

Awasthi et al. (2012) initiated the study of perturbation resilience of clustering problems. They defined a wide class of clustering problems with separable center-based objectives, including such problems as k-center, k-means, and k-median, and presented an algorithm for solving 3-perturbation resilient instances of such problems. Additionally, in a more general setting, where Steiner points are allowed, they gave an algorithm for $(2 + \sqrt{3})$-perturbation resilient instances, and showed that there is no polynomial-time algorithm for 3-perturbation resilient instances with Steiner points.

Later, Balcan and Liang (2016) improved the result of Awasthi et al. (2012) for clustering problems with separable center-based objectives (without Steiner points), by showing that $(1+\sqrt{2})$-perturbation resilient instances can be efficiently solved. In addition, they gave an approximation algorithm for $(2 + \sqrt{3}, \varepsilon)$-perturbation resilient (weakly stable) instances. They also presented an algorithm for clustering with the min-sum objective, as well as sub-linear algorithms for clustering problems.

Most recently, Balcan et al. (2015) designed algorithms for 2-perturbation resilient instances of symmetric and asymmetric k-center and obtained a matching hardness result. They also considered clustering instances with separable center-based objectives satisfying the cluster verifiability condition. This condition requires that there be a polynomial-time algorithm that, given a set S, determines which is of the following statements holds true:

(1) $S = C_i$ for some i,   (2) $S \subset C_i$ for some i,   (3) $S \supset C_i$ for some i

(where $C_1, \ldots, C_k$ is the optimal clustering); under the promise that one of these statements is true. Balcan et al. (2015) showed how to solve 2-stable instances satisfying this condition.

There has also been research on algorithms for stable instances of other problems. Mihalák et al. (2011) gave an algorithm for 1.8-stable instances of the Travelling Salesperson Problem (TSP). Balcan and Braverman (2010) studied the problem of finding the Nash equilibrium under stability assumptions. Also of much interest are the papers by Ostrovsky et al. (2006) and Balcan et al. (2009), which study notions of stability closely related to Bilu-Linial stability. Finally, let us mention that Leontev gave a similar definition of stability for combinatorial optimization problems in 1975. However, his motivation for studying instance stability was different from the motivation of Bilu and Linial; and the questions studied in his paper (Leontev, 1975) and a number of subsequent papers are not related to the questions addressed in this survey.

13.1.1   Organization

We describe several results for stable instances of graph partitioning and clustering problems. We begin with a general definition of graph partitioning problems in Section 13.2.1. Then, we prove that convex relaxations for γ-stable instances of graph partitioning problems, which satisfy certain assumptions, are integral (for the appropriate choice of γ), and, therefore, these instances can be solved in polynomial time. In Section 13.2.2, we apply this theorem to the Minimum Multiway Cut problem to show that 4-stable instances of the problem have an integral LP relaxation. In Section 13.2.1, we also state a general theorem for *weakly* stable instances of graph partitioning problems (Theorem 13.1, part II). However, we omit the proof in this survey. Instead, in Section 13.2.3, we prove a special case of the theorem, presenting an algorithm for γ-weakly stable instances of Max Cut (for $\gamma \geq c\sqrt{\log n} \log \log n$).

Then we proceed to clustering problems. In Section 13.3.1, we give an algorithm for 2-metric perturbation resilient instances of k-center (due to Balcan et al., 2015). Then, in Section 13.3.2, we give the definition of clustering problems with a center-based objective and present an algorithm for solving $(\sqrt{2}+1)$-metric perturbation resilient instances of such problems (due to Balcan and Liang, 2016).

13.2   Stable Instances of Graph Partitioning Problems

13.2.1   Relaxations for Stable Instances Are Integral

In this section, we study stable instances of graph partitioning problems. We show that under certain conditions convex relaxations (e.g., linear programming and semidefinite programming relaxations) for stable instances of graph partitioning problems are integral. In particular, the result of this section implies that 4-stable instances of Minimum Multiway Cut and $c\sqrt{\log n \log \log n}$-stable instances of Max Cut have integral convex relaxations.

The result applies to a wide class of graph partitioning problems. Let us start with defining graph partitioning problems — our definition will include such problems as Min Cut, Max Cut, Minimum Multiway Cut, Minimum Balanced Cut, Minimum Multicut, and many others.

Definition 13.4. *In a graph partitioning problem, we are given a graph* $G = (V, E, w)$ *with positive edge weights* $w(e)$. *Our goal is to remove a subset of edges* $E_{cut} \subset E$ *that satisfies certain conditions, which depend on the specific problem at hand, so as to minimize or maximize the weight of cut edges. Specifically, in a minimization problem, we minimize* $\sum_{e \in E_{cut}} w(e)$; *in a maximization problem, we maximize* $\sum_{e \in E_{cut}} w(e)$.

Consider a few examples that show how our definition captures standard graph partitioning problems; for each problem, we will state the requirements on the set E_{cut}. The global Min Cut problem is a minimization problem, in which we require that the set of edges E_{cut} consist exactly of all the edges between some set A and its complement $\bar{A}$ (both sets A and $\bar{A}$ must not be empty). Max Cut is a maximization problem, in which we similarly require that E_{cut} consist of all the edges between sets A and $\bar{A}$. Minimum Multiway Cut is a minimization problem, in which we require that every two terminals s_i are s_j in a given set of terminals $\{s_1, \ldots, s_k\}$ be disconnected in $G - E_{cut}$.

We show an interesting connection between Bilu-Linial stability and *rounding algorithms or schemes* for convex relaxations of graph partitioning problems. First, let us briefly discuss how rounding schemes are used in solving graph partitioning problems. We write a linear programming (LP) or semidefinite programming (SDP) relaxation for the problem. The relaxation has two types of feasible solutions. First of all, the relaxation has feasible *integral* solutions, which are in one-to-one correspondence with feasible solutions to the graph partitioning problem (we will refer to solutions of the graph partitioning problem as combinatorial solutions). Secondly, the relaxation has solutions that do not correspond to any combinatorial solutions. We solve the relaxation and find an optimal *fractional* solution, which might not be integral. However, since there is an integral solution corresponding to the optimal combinatorial solution, the optimal fractional solution value must be at least the optimal combinatorial value for a maximization problem and at most the optimal combinatorial value for a minimization problem. Now we use a (randomized) *rounding scheme* to transform a fractional solution to a combinatorial solution.[1] Most linear and semidefinite programming relaxations for graph partitioning problems are metric-based. Let us give a very general definition of a metric-based fractional solution.

Definition 13.5. *We say that x is a metric-based fractional solution of value* $\mathrm{val}(x)$ *for a graph partitioning problem if there is a polynomial-time algorithm that given x finds a distance function* $d : E \to [0,1]$ *such that*

$$\mathrm{val}(x) = \sum_{(u,v) \in E} w(u,v)\, d(u,v).$$

We say that distance d is defined by solution x.

Assume that there is a polynomial-time (optimization) algorithm $\mathcal{A}$ *that, given an instance of the problem, finds a metric-based fractional solution x of value* $\mathrm{val}(x)$,

$\mathrm{val}(x) \geq \mathsf{OPT}$	*for a maximization problem,*
$\mathrm{val}(x) \leq \mathsf{OPT}$	*for a minimization problem,*

where OPT *is the value of the optimal combinatorial solution. Then we say that x is an optimal fractional solution found by the optimization algorithm* $\mathcal{A}$.

A standard example of an algorithm $\mathcal{A}$ is an LP or SDP solver that finds an optimal solution to an LP or SDP relaxation of a graph partitioning problem. Then an optimal fractional solution x is just an optimal LP or SDP solution to the relaxation.

Definition 13.6. *Consider a graph partitioning problem and an optimization algorithm* $\mathcal{A}$ *as in Definition 13.5. We say that a randomized algorithm* $\mathcal{R}$ *is a rounding scheme (w.r.t.* $\mathcal{A}$*) if, given an optimal fractional solution x for an instance of the problem, it returns a feasible solution to the instance.*

---

1. We note that "rounding algorithms" are often very non-trivial; they do not merely round real numbers to integers as their name might suggest.

Now note that, by combining an optimization procedure $\mathcal{A}$ and (polynomial-time) rounding scheme $\mathcal{R}$, we get a randomized approximation algorithm (see Algorithm 13.1). The mere existence of a rounding scheme,

---

Algorithm 13.1 Approximation algorithm based on optimization procedure $\mathcal{A}$ and rounding scheme $\mathcal{R}$

1:   Run $\mathcal{A}$ on the input instance $\mathcal{I}$ and get an optimal fractional solution x.
2:   Run $\mathcal{R}$ on x and get a feasible solution to $\mathcal{I}$.

---

however, does not guarantee that the approximation algorithm based on it performs well. Let us say that we have a minimization problem. One of the most common ways to ensure that the approximation algorithm has an approximation factor of α is to use a rounding scheme $\mathcal{R}$ satisfying the following condition: given an optimal fractional solution x, $\mathcal{R}$ returns a random solution E'_{cut} such that

$$\Pr\left((u,v) \in E'_{cut}\right) \leq \alpha d(u,v), \tag{13.1}$$

where d is the distance defined by x. Observe that, then, the expected cost of the solution E'_{cut} is

$$\mathbb{E}\left[w(E'_{cut})\right] = \sum_{(u,v) \in E} w(u,v) \Pr\left((u,v) \in E'_{cut}\right)$$
$$\leq \alpha \sum_{(u,v) \in E} w(u,v)\, d(u,v) = \alpha\, \mathrm{val}(x) \leq \alpha \mathsf{OPT}.$$

That is, in expectation, the algorithm finds a solution of cost at most $\alpha\mathsf{OPT}$, and thus has an approximation factor of α. Now consider the complementary optimization problem of *maximizing* the weight of uncut edges, $w(E \setminus E'_{cut})$. Note that an optimal solution to the original problem is also an optimal solution to the complementary problem, since the sum of their objectives, $w(E'_{cut}) + w(E \setminus E'_{cut}) = w(E)$, depends only on the instance and not on the solution E'_{cut}. However, the problems might be very different in terms of multiplicative approximability — a good approximation algorithm for one of them is not necessarily good for the other. It is not hard to see that in order to get a β approximation algorithm for the complementary problem, we can use a rounding procedure $\mathcal{R}$ satisfying the following condition,

$$\Pr\left((u,v) \notin E'_{cut}\right) \geq \beta^{-1}(1 - d(u,v)). \tag{13.2}$$

We stress that conditions (13.1) and (13.2) are completely independent, and a rounding procedure may satisfy one of them and not the other.

Makarychev et al. (2014b) showed that if there is a rounding scheme $\mathcal{R}$ satisfying both conditions (13.1) and (13.2), then the relaxation for $(\alpha\beta)$-stable instances is integral, and, consequently, there is a robust exact algorithm for $(\alpha\beta)$-stable instances.

Theorem 13.1 (Makarychev et al. (2014b)). *I. Consider a graph partitioning problem. Suppose that there is a rounding scheme that, given a graph $G = (V, E, w)$ and an optimal fractional solution x, returns a feasible solution E'_{cut} such that for some $\alpha \geq 1$ and $\beta \geq 1$ (α and β may depend on n),*

> ***For a cut minimization problem,***
> 1. $\Pr\left((u, v) \in E'_{cut}\right) \leq \alpha d(u, v),$
> 2. $\Pr\left(u \notin E'_{cut}\right) \geq \beta^{-1}(1 - d(u, v)).$
>
> ***For a cut maximization problem,***
> $1'.$ $\Pr\left((u, v) \in E'_{cut}\right) \geq \alpha^{-1} d(u, v)$
> $2'.$ $\Pr\left((u, v) \notin E'_{cut}\right) \leq \beta(1 - d(u, v))$

where distance d is defined by the fractional solution x.

Then distance d is integral for $(\alpha\beta)$-stable instances of the problem; specifically, for every edge $(u, v) \in E$

$$d(u, v) = \begin{cases} 0, & \text{if } (u, v) \notin E^*_{cut}, \\ 1, & \text{if } (u, v) \in E^*_{cut}, \end{cases}$$

where E^*_{cut} is the optimal combinatorial solution.[2] Consequently, there is a robust polynomial-time algorithm for $(\alpha\beta)$-stable instances.

II. Furthermore, there is an algorithm for $(\alpha\beta + \varepsilon, N)$-weakly stable instances of the problem that finds a feasible solution $E'_{cut} \in N$ (for every $\varepsilon > 0$).

The theorem also holds for graph partitioning problems with positive and negative weights if we require that all four properties 1, $1'$, 2 and $2'$ hold.

In this survey, we are going to prove only part I of Theorem 13.1. Since the proofs of Theorem 13.1 for minimization and maximization problems are completely analogous, let us only consider a minimization problem. Before we proceed with the proof itself, we prove the following auxiliary lemmas.

Lemma 13.2 (Bilu and Linial (2010)). *Consider a γ-stable instance of a minimization graph partitioning problem. Suppose E^*_{cut} is the optimal*

---

2. In particular, given d, we can find E^*_{cut}: $E^*_{cut} = \{(u, v) : d(u, v) = 1\}$.

combinatorial solution. Then, for any combinatorial solution E'_{cut}, we have

$$\gamma \, w(E^*_{cut} \setminus E'_{cut}) < w(E'_{cut} \setminus E^*_{cut}).$$

Proof. Consider the following γ-perturbation of w: $w'(u,v) = \gamma w(u,v)$ for $(u,v) \in E^*_{cut} \setminus E'_{cut}$; and $w'(u,v) = w(u,v)$ otherwise. Since the instance is is γ-stable, we have $w'(E^*_{cut}) < w'(E'_{cut})$. Write,

$$\underbrace{w'(E^*_{cut} \setminus E'_{cut}) + w'(E^*_{cut} \cap E'_{cut})}_{w'(E^*_{cut})} < \underbrace{w'(E'_{cut} \setminus E^*_{cut}) + w'(E^*_{cut} \cap E'_{cut})}_{w'(E'_{cut})}.$$

Thus, $w'(E^*_{cut} \setminus E'_{cut}) < w'(E'_{cut} \setminus E^*_{cut})$. Using the definition of w', we get the desired inequality: $\gamma \, w'(E^*_{cut} \setminus E'_{cut}) < w'(E'_{cut} \setminus E^*_{cut})$. □

Lemma 13.3. *If the distance d defined by a fractional solution x is not integral, then the rounding algorithm returns a solution E'_{cut} different from the optimal combinatorial solution E^*_{cut} with non-zero probability.*

Proof. Note that if $d(u,v) < 1$ for some edge $(u,v) \in E^*_{cut}$, then $(u,v) \notin E'_{cut}$ with probability at least $\beta^{-1}(1 - d(u,v)) > 0$, and hence $E^*_{cut} \neq E'_{cut}$ with non-zero probability. So let us assume that $d(u,v) = 1$ for every $(u,v) \in E^*_{cut}$. Since the cost of the optimal combinatorial solution is at least the cost of the optimal fractional solution x, we have

$$\sum_{(u,v) \in E^*_{cut}} w(u,v) \geq \mathrm{val}(x) = \sum_{(u,v) \in E} w(u,v) \, d(u,v)$$

$$= \sum_{(u,v) \in E^*_{cut}} w(u,v) + \sum_{(u,v) \in E \setminus E^*_{cut}} w(u,v) \, d(u,v).$$

Therefore,

$$\sum_{(u,v) \in E \setminus E^*_{cut}} w(u,v) \, d(u,v) \leq 0,$$

and $d(u,v) = 0$ for every $(u,v) \in E \setminus E^*_{cut}$. □

Proof of Theorem 13.1. Consider an $(\alpha\beta)$-stable instance of the problem. Let d be the distance defined by an optimal solution. We are going to prove that d is integral. Assume to the contrary that it is not. Let E'_{cut} be a random combinatorial solution obtained by rounding d, and let E^*_{cut} be the optimal combinatorial solution. Since d is not integral, $E'_{cut} \neq E^*_{cut}$ with non-zero probability.

From $(\alpha\beta)$-stability of the instance (see Lemma 13.2), we get that

$$(\alpha\beta)w(E^*_{cut} \setminus E'_{cut}) < w(E'_{cut} \setminus E^*_{cut}) \text{ unless } E^*_{cut} = E'_{cut},$$

and therefore (here we use that $\Pr(E^*_{cut} \neq E'_{cut}) > 0$),

$$(\alpha\beta)\mathbb{E}\left[w(E^*_{cut} \setminus E'_{cut})\right] < \mathbb{E}\left[w(E'_{cut} \setminus E^*_{cut})\right]. \tag{13.3}$$

Let

$$\mathsf{LP}_+ = \sum_{(u,v)\in E^*_{cut}} w(u,v)(1 - d(u,v)),$$

$$\mathsf{LP}_- = \sum_{(u,v)\in E\setminus E^*_{cut}} w(u,v)\, d(u,v).$$

From conditions 1 and 2 in the statement of the theorem, we get

$$\mathbb{E}\left[w(E^*_{cut} \setminus E'_{cut})\right] = \sum_{(u,v)\in E^*_{cut}} w(u,v)\Pr((u,v) \notin E'_{cut})$$

$$\geq \sum_{(u,v)\in E^*_{cut}} w(u,v)\beta^{-1}(1 - d(u,v)) = \beta^{-1}\mathsf{LP}_+,$$

$$\mathbb{E}\left[w(E' \setminus E^*)_{cut}\right] = \sum_{(u,v)\in E\setminus E^*_{cut}} w(u,v)\Pr((u,v) \in E'_{cut})$$

$$\leq \sum_{(u,v)\in E^*_{cut}} w(u,v)\,\alpha\, d(u,v) = \alpha\,\mathsf{LP}_-.$$

Using inequality (13.3), we conclude that $\mathsf{LP}_+ < \mathsf{LP}_-$. On the other hand, from the formulas for LP_+ and LP_-, we get

$$\mathsf{LP}_+ - \mathsf{LP}_- = w(E^*_{cut}) - \sum_{(u,v)\in E} w(u,v)\, d(u,v) \geq 0,$$

since the value of the fractional solution is at most the value of the integral solution. We get a contradiction, which concludes the proof.   □

13.2.2   An LP Relaxation and Rounding Scheme for Minimum Multiway Cut

In this section, we show that the linear programming relaxation for 4-stable instances of Minimum Multiway Cut is integral. To this end, we present an LP relaxation for Minimum Multiway Cut and a rounding scheme satisfying the conditions of Theorem 13.1. Recall the definition of the Multiway Cut problem.

Definition 13.7. *An instance of Minimum Multiway Cut consists of a graph $G = (V, E, w)$ with positive edge weights w_e and a set of terminals $T = \{s_1, \ldots, s_k\} \subset V$. The goal is to partition the graph into k pieces*

$S_1, \ldots, S_k$ *with* $s_i \in S_i$ *so as to minimize the total weight of cut edges*

$$E_{cut} = \{(u, v) \in E : u \in S_i, v \in S_j \text{ for } i \neq j\}.$$

The problem has been actively studied since it was introduced by Dahlhaus et al. (1994). There has been a series of approximation algorithms for it (Cualinescu et al., 1998; Karger et al., 2004; Buchbinder et al., 2013); the current state-of-the-art approximation algorithm by Sharma and Vondrák (2014) gives a 1.30217 approximation.

We use the LP relaxation of Cualinescu et al. (1998). In this relaxation, we have a variable $\bar{u} = (u_1, \ldots, u_k) \in \mathbb{R}^k$ for every vertex $u \in V$. Let $e_1, \ldots, e_k$ be the standard basis in $\mathbb{R}^k$ and $\Delta = \{x : \|x\|_1 = 1, x_1 \geq 0, \ldots, x_k \geq 0\}$ be the simplex with vertices $e_1, \ldots, e_k$.

$$\text{minimize } \frac{1}{2} \sum_{(u,v) \in E} w(u, v) \|\bar{u} - \bar{v}\|_1 \tag{13.4}$$

subject to:

$$\bar{s}_i = e_i \qquad\qquad \text{for every } i,$$
$$\bar{u} \in \Delta \qquad\qquad \text{for every } u \in V.$$

Every feasible LP solution defines a metric on V: $d(u, v) = \|\bar{u} - \bar{v}\|_1/2$. Note that the objective function equals $\sum_{e \in E} w(u, v) \, d(u, v)$. Let us now present a randomized rounding scheme for this LP relaxation.

Theorem 13.4 (Makarychev et al. (2014b)). *Consider a feasible LP solution* $\{\bar{u} : u \in V\}$ *and metric* $d(u, v) = \|\bar{u} - \bar{v}\|_1/2$. *There is a randomized algorithm that finds a partition* $S_1, \ldots, S_k$ *of* V *and a set* E_{cut} *such that*

- $s_i \in S_i$ *for every* $i \in \{1, \ldots, k\}$ *(always)*,
- $\Pr((u, v) \in E_{cut}) \leq \frac{2d(u,v)}{1+d(u,v)}$ *for every* $(u, v) \in E$. *In particular,*

$$\Pr((u, v) \in E_{cut}) \leq 2d(u, v) \quad \text{and} \quad \Pr((u, v) \notin E_{cut}) \geq \frac{1 - d(u, v)}{2}.$$

The rounding procedure satisfies the conditions of Theorem 13.1 with parameters $\alpha = \beta = 2$, *and, therefore, the LP relaxation for 4-stable instances of Multiway Cut is integral.*

Proof. We use the rounding algorithm by Kleinberg and Tardos (2002). The algorithm starts with empty sets $S_1, \ldots, S_k$ and then iteratively adds vertices to sets $S_1, \ldots, S_k$. It stops when each vertex is assigned to some set S_i. In each iteration, the algorithm chooses independently and uniformly at random $r \in (0, 1)$ and $i \in \{1, \ldots, k\}$. It adds each vertex u to S_i if $r \leq \bar{u}_i$ and u has not yet been added to any set S_j.

Algorithm 13.2 Rounding Algorithm for Minimum Multiway Cut

1: $S_1 = \varnothing, \ldots, S_k = \varnothing$
2: $R = V$ ▷ R is the set of unpartitioned vertices
3: **while** $R \neq \varnothing$ **do**
4:     $r \in_U (0,1); \; i \in_U \{1, \ldots, k\}$
5:     $S_i = S_i \cup \{u \in R : \bar{u}_i \geq r\}$
6:     $R = R \setminus \{u \in R : \bar{u}_i \geq r\}$
7: **end while**
8: **return** $S_1, \ldots, S_k$ and $E_{cut} = \{(u,v) \in E : u \in S_i, v \in S_j \text{ for } i \neq j\}$.

First, note that we add every vertex u to some S_i with probability $\sum_{i=1}^{k} \bar{u}_i / k = 1/k$ in each iteration (unless u already lies in some S_j). So eventually we will add every vertex to some set S_i. Also note that we cannot add s_i to S_j if $j \neq i$. Therefore, $s_i \in S_i$.

Now consider an edge (u,v). Consider one iteration of the algorithm. Suppose that neither u nor v is assigned to any set S_j in the beginning of the iteration. The probability that at least one of them is assigned to some S_i in this iteration is

$$\frac{1}{k} \sum_{i=1}^{k} \Pr(\bar{u}_i \geq r \text{ or } \bar{v}_i \geq r) = \frac{1}{k} \sum_{i=1}^{k} \max(\bar{u}_i, \bar{v}_i)$$

$$= \frac{1}{k} \sum_{i=1}^{k} \left(\frac{\bar{u}_i + \bar{v}_i}{2} + \frac{|\bar{u}_i - \bar{v}_i|}{2} \right) = \frac{1}{k} \left(1 + \frac{\|\bar{u} - \bar{v}\|_1}{2} \right) = \frac{1 + d(u,v)}{k}.$$

The probability that exactly one of them is assigned to some S_i is

$$\frac{1}{k} \sum_{i=1}^{k} \Pr(\bar{u}_i < r \leq \bar{v}_i \text{ or } \bar{v}_i < r \leq \bar{u}_i) = \frac{1}{k} \sum_{i=1}^{k} |\bar{u}_i - \bar{v}_i| = \frac{\|\bar{u} - \bar{v}\|_1}{k} = \frac{2d(u,v)}{k}.$$

We get that in one iteration, the conditional probability that u and v are separated given that at least one of them is assigned to some set is $2d(u,v)/(1 + d(u,v))$. Therefore, the probability that u and v are separated in some iteration is $2d(u,v)/(1 + d(u,v))$. Thus the probability that (u,v) is cut is at most $2d(u,v)/(1 + d(u,v))$.   □

13.2.3 Weakly Stable Instances of Max Cut

Bilu-Linial stability imposes rather strong constraints on an instance of a graph partitioning problem. Can these constraints be relaxed? In this section, we give a definition of a more robust notion — a notion of weak stability. Then we present an algorithm for weakly stable instances of the Max Cut problem. Note that using Theorem 13.1 from the previous section, one can show that a certain SDP relaxation for Max Cut is integral for γ-stable instances of Max Cut with $\gamma \geq c\sqrt{\log n \log \log n}$. However, the SDP does not have to be integral for weakly stable instances of Max Cut. Let us now recall the definition of Max Cut.

Definition 13.8 (Max Cut). *In the Max Cut Problem, we are given a weighted graph $G = (V, E, w)$. Our goal is to partition the set of vertices into two sets S and $\bar{S}$ so as to maximize $w(E(S, \bar{S}))$.*

Max Cut is an NP-hard problem (Karp, 1972). The approximation factor of the best known algorithm due to Goemans and Williamson (1995) is 0.878. It cannot be improved if the Unique Games Conjecture holds true (Khot et al., 2007). We now give the definition of weak stability for Max Cut.

Definition 13.9. *Consider a weighted graph $G = (V, E, w)$. Let $(S, \bar{S})$ be a maximum cut in G, N be a set of cuts that contains $(S, \bar{S})$, and $\gamma \geq 1$. We say that G is a (γ, N)-weakly stable instance of Max Cut if for every γ-perturbation $G' = (V, E, w')$ of G, and every cut $(T, \bar{T}) \notin N$, we have*

$$w'(E(S, \bar{S})) > w'(E(T, \bar{T})).$$

The notion of weak stability generalizes the notion of stability: an instance is γ-stable if and only if it is $(\gamma, \{(S, \bar{S})\})$-weakly stable. We think of the set N in the definition of weak stability as a neighborhood of the maximum cut $(S, \bar{S})$; it contains cuts that are "close enough" to $(S, \bar{S})$. Intuitively, the definition requires that every cut that is sufficiently different from $(S, \bar{S})$ be much smaller than $(S, \bar{S})$, but does not impose any restrictions on cuts that are close to $(S, \bar{S})$. One natural way to define the neighborhood of $(S, \bar{S})$ is captured in the following definition.

Definition 13.10. *Consider a weighted graph G. Let $(S, \bar{S})$ be a maximum cut in G, $\delta \geq 0$, and $\gamma \geq 1$. We say that G is a (γ, δ)-weakly stable instance of Max Cut if G is $(\gamma, \{(S', \bar{S}') : |S \Delta S'| \leq \delta n\})$-weakly stable. In other words, G is (γ, δ)-weakly stable if for every cut $(T, \bar{T})$ such that $|S \Delta T| > \delta n$ and $|S \Delta \bar{T}| > \delta n$, we have $w'(E(S, \bar{S})) > w'(E(T, \bar{T}))$.*

We prove the following analog of Lemma 13.2.

Lemma 13.5. *Consider a (γ, N)-weakly stable instance of Max Cut $G = (V, E, w)$. Let $(S, \bar{S})$ be a maximum cut in G. Then, for every cut $(T, \bar{T}) \notin N$:*

$$w(E(S, \bar{S}) \setminus E(T, \bar{T})) > \gamma \cdot w(E(T, \bar{T}) \setminus E(S, \bar{S})). \tag{13.5}$$

Proof. Fix a cut $(T, \bar{T}) \notin N$. Consider the following γ-perturbation of w: $w'(u, v) = \gamma w(u, v)$ for $(u, v) \in E(T, \bar{T}) \setminus E(S, \bar{S})$; and $w'(u, v) = w(u, v)$

otherwise. Since G is a γ-weakly stable instance, and $(T, \bar{T}) \notin N$, we have

$$w'(E(S, \bar{S})) > w'(E(T, \bar{T})).$$

Write,

$$
\begin{aligned}
w'(E(S, \bar{S})) &= w'(E(S, \bar{S}) \setminus E(T, \bar{T})) + w'(E(S, \bar{S}) \cap E(T, \bar{T})); \\
w'(E(T, \bar{T})) &= w'(E(T, \bar{T}) \setminus E(S, \bar{S})) + w'(E(S, \bar{S}) \cap E(T, \bar{T})).
\end{aligned}
$$

Thus, $w'(E(S, \bar{S}) \setminus E(T, \bar{T})) > w'(E(T, \bar{T}) \setminus E(S, \bar{S}))$. Using the definition of w', we get inequality (13.5). $\qquad \square$

We are now ready to state the main result.

Theorem 13.6 (Makarychev et al. (2014b)). *There is a polynomial-time algorithm that, given a (γ, N)-stable instance of Max Cut, returns a cut from N if $\gamma \geq c\sqrt{\log n} \log \log n$ (for some absolute constant c). The set N is not part of the input and is not known to the algorithm.*

Overview of the algorithm. The algorithm starts with an arbitrary cut $(S_0, \bar{S}_0)$ and then iteratively improves it: first, it finds a cut $(S_1, \bar{S}_1)$ that is better than $(S_0, \bar{S}_0)$, then a cut $(S_2, \bar{S}_2)$ that is better than $(S_1, \bar{S}_1)$, etc.

$$(S_0, \bar{S}_0) \to (S_1, \bar{S}_1) \to (S_2, \bar{S}_2) \to \cdots \to (S_t, \bar{S}_t);$$

finally, it gets a cut $(S_t, \bar{S}_t)$ that it cannot improve. This cut necessarily belongs to the set N, and the algorithm outputs it. The key component of the algorithm is a procedure Improve that, given a cut $(S_i, \bar{S}_i) \notin N$, finds a better cut $(S_{i+1}, \bar{S}_{i+1})$ (if $(S_i, \bar{S}_i) \in N$, the procedure may either find an improved cut or output that $(S_i, \bar{S}_i) \in N$).

Now, we are going to present Improve. We note that we also must show that the improvement process finishes in polynomially many steps, and, thus, the running time is polynomial. In this survey, we assume for simplicity that all edge weights are polynomially bounded integers. Then the weight of every cut is a polynomially bounded integer; therefore, the weight of the cut increases by at least 1 in each iteration, and the algorithm terminate after polynomially many iterations. In the paper (Makarychev et al., 2014b), the theorem is proved without this simplifying assumption.

Before we describe the procedure Improve, we recall the definition of Sparsest Cut with non-uniform demands.

Definition 13.11 (Sparsest Cut with non-uniform demands). *We are given a graph $H = (V, E_c, \mathrm{cap})$ with non-negative edge capacities $\mathrm{cap}(u, v)$, a set of demand pairs E_d, and non-negative demands $\mathrm{dem}: E_d \to \mathbb{R}_{\geq 0}$. Our goal is to find a cut $(A, \bar{A})$ so as to minimize the ratio between the capacity of* *the cut edges and the amount of separated demands*

$$\text{minimize} \quad \sum_{\substack{(u,v)\in E_c \\ u\in A,\, v\in \bar{A}}} \text{cap}(u,v) \Big/ \sum_{\substack{(u,v)\in E_d \\ u\in A,\, v\in \bar{A}}} \text{dem}(u,v).$$

We call this ratio the sparsity of the cut $(A, \bar{A})$.

We use the approximation algorithm for Sparsest Cut by Arora et al. (2008) that gives a $(C_{\mathrm{sc}}\sqrt{\log n}\log\log n)$-approximation (where C_{sc} is an absolute constant).

Theorem 13.7. *Let $\gamma = C_{\mathrm{sc}}\sqrt{\log n}\log\log n$. There is a polynomial-time algorithm* Improve *that, given a (γ, N)-weakly stable instance of Max Cut and a cut $(T, \bar{T}) \notin N$, finds a cut $(T', \bar{T}')$ of greater value,*

$$w(E(T', \bar{T}')) > w(E(T, \bar{T})).$$

Proof. Define an auxiliary Sparsest Cut instance $G_{aux} = (V, E_c, \text{cap})$ on V:

$$E_c = E(T, \bar{T}) \qquad\qquad \text{cap}(u,v) = w(u,v)$$
$$E_d = E \setminus E(T, \bar{T}) \qquad\qquad \text{dem}(u,v) = w(u,v).$$

Now run the approximation algorithm for Sparsest Cut by Arora et al. (2008) and find an approximate cut $(A, \bar{A})$. Let $T' = (T \cap A) \cup (\bar{T} \cap \bar{A})$. If $w(T', \bar{T}') > w(T, \bar{T})$, return the cut $(T', \bar{T}')$; otherwise, output that $(T, \bar{T}) \in N$.

We need to show that if $(T, \bar{T}) \notin N$ then $w(T', \bar{T}') > w(T, \bar{T})$. Let $(S, \bar{S})$ be the maximum cut. First, we prove that there is a sparsest cut with sparsity at most $1/\gamma$ in the auxiliary graph. Let $A^* = (S \cap T) \cup (\bar{S} \cap \bar{T})$. Since $(T, \bar{T}) \notin N$, we have by Lemma 13.5:

$$w(E(S, \bar{S}) \setminus E(T, \bar{T})) > \gamma \cdot w(E(T, \bar{T}) \setminus E(S, \bar{S})).$$

Note that $E(A^*, \bar{A}^*) = E(S \cap T, S \cap \bar{T}) \cup E(S \cap T, \bar{S} \cap T) \cup E(\bar{S} \cap T, \bar{S} \cap \bar{T}) \cup E(S \cap \bar{T}, \bar{S} \cap \bar{T})$ (see Figure 13.1), and

$$E(S, \bar{S}) \setminus E(T, \bar{T}) = E_d \cap E(A^*, \bar{A}^*)$$
$$E(T, \bar{T}) \setminus E(S, \bar{S}) = E_c \cap E(A^*, \bar{A}^*).$$

The sparsity of the cut $(A^*, \bar{A}^*)$ is therefore at most

$$\frac{\text{cap}(E_c \cap E(A^*, \bar{A}^*))}{\text{dem}(E_d \cap E(A^*, \bar{A}^*))} = \frac{w(E(T, \bar{T}) \setminus E(S, \bar{S}))}{w(E(S, \bar{S}) \setminus E(T, \bar{T}))} < \frac{1}{\gamma}.$$

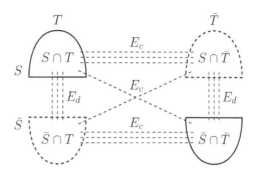

Figure 13.1: The figure shows sets S, $\bar{S}$, T, $\bar{T}$, and their pairwise intersections. Set E_c consists of horizontal and diagonal edges; set E_d consists of vertical edges, as well as edges within $S \cap T$, $S \cap \bar{T}$, $\bar{S} \cap T$, $\bar{S} \cap \bar{T}$; set $E(A^*, \bar{A}^*)$ consists of horizontal and vertical edges.

Hence, the sparsity of the cut $(A, \bar{A})$ returned by the approximation algorithm is less than $(C_{\mathrm{sc}}\sqrt{\log n} \log \log n) \times (1/\gamma) \leq 1$. That is, $\mathrm{dem}(E_d \cap E(A, \bar{A})) > \mathrm{cap}(E_c \cap E(A, \bar{A}))$. We get

$$w(E(T', \bar{T}') \setminus E(T, \bar{T})) = \mathrm{dem}(E_d \cap E(A, \bar{A})) >$$
$$> \mathrm{cap}(E_c \cap E(A, \bar{A})) = w(E(T, \bar{T}) \setminus E(T', \bar{T}')).$$

and, consequently,

$$w(T', \bar{T}') = w(E(T', \bar{T}') \setminus E(T, \bar{T})) + w(E(T', \bar{T}') \cap E(T, \bar{T})) >$$
$$> w(E(T, \bar{T}) \setminus E(T', \bar{T}')) + w(E(T', \bar{T}') \cap E(T, \bar{T})) = w(T, \bar{T}).$$

Thus, the weight of the cut $(T', \bar{T}')$ obtained by the improvement algorithm Improve is greater than the weight of the cut $(T, \bar{T})$. This finishes the proof. □

13.3 Stable Instances of Clustering Problems

13.3.1 Metric Perturbation Resilient Instances of k-Center

In this section, we present an algorithm by Balcan et al. (2015) that solves 2-metric perturbation resilient instances of k-center. In fact, we prove that any α-approximation algorithm for k-center finds the optimal solution of an α-metric perturbation resilient instance of k-center. Therefore, we can use known 2-approximation algorithms for k-center to solve 2-metric perturbation resilient instances of the problem (see Hochbaum and Shmoys

(1985), and Dyer and Frieze (1985)). Recall the definition of the k-center problem.

Definition 13.12. *Consider a set of vertices V, a metric d on V, and a parameter k. Given a set of points ("centers") $c_1, \ldots, c_k$ in V, define a clustering $C_1, \ldots, C_k$ by assigning each vertex u to the closest center among $c_1, \ldots, c_k$:*

$$C_i = \{u : d(u, c_i) \leq d(u, c_j) \text{ for every } i \neq j\}$$

(we break the ties arbitrarily). We say that c_i is the center of cluster C_i. The cost of the clustering is the maximum distance between a point and the center of the cluster it belongs to.

$$\text{cost} = \max_{i \in \{1,\ldots,k\}} \max_{u \in C_i} d(u, c_i).$$

In the k-center problem, our goal is to find a clustering of minimum cost given V, d, and k.

Note that given a set of centers we can efficiently find the corresponding clustering, and given a clustering we can efficiently find an optimal set of centers for it. In this section, however, it will be more convenient for us to view a solution for k-center as a clustering rather than a set of centers. The reason for that is that in the definition of the perturbation resilience, we do not want to require that the set of centers not change when we perturb the distances — that would be a very strong requirement (indeed, it might not be even satisfied by instances with $k = 1$; furthermore, there would be no 2-perturbation resilient instances). Instead, we require that the optimal clustering $C_1, \ldots, C_k$ not change when we perturb the distances.

Remark 13.1. *In this section, we consider perturbations d' of the metric d satisfying $d(u, v)/\gamma \leq d'(u, v) \leq d(u, v)$ for all u,v instead of perturbations satisfying $d(u, v) \leq d'(u, v) \leq \gamma\, d(u, v)$ as in Definition 13.3. We can do so as long as the clustering problem is invariant under rescaling of all distances by the same positive factor, i.e. the clustering for d is the same as the clustering for αd for every $\alpha > 0$. All clustering problems we consider in this section satisfy this property.*

Balcan et al. (2015) obtained their result for 2-perturbation resilient instances of k-center. Most recently, Makarychev and Makarychev (2016) strengthened this result, by showing that it also holds for α-*metric* perturbation resilient instances.

Theorem 13.8 (Balcan et al. (2015); see also Makarychev and Makarychev (2016)). *An α-approximation algorithm for k-center finds the optimal clustering of an α-metric perturbation resilient instance of k-center.*[3]

Proof. Consider the optimal clustering $C_1, \ldots, C_k$ and the clustering $C'_1, \ldots, C'_k$ found by the approximation algorithm. We are going to show that they are identical. Let r^* be the value of the clustering $C_1, \ldots, C_k$. Let $\{c'_1, \ldots, c'_k\}$ be an optimal set of centers for the clustering $C'_1, \ldots, C'_k$. Since the algorithm gives an α-approximation, $d(u, c'_i) \leq \alpha r^*$ for every $u \in C'_i$.

Define a new distance d' as follows

$$d'(u, v) = \begin{cases} d(u, v)/\alpha, & \text{if } d(u, v) \geq \alpha r^*, \\ r^*, & \text{if } d(u, v) \in [r^*, \alpha r^*], \\ d(u, v), & \text{if } d(u, v) \leq r^*. \end{cases}$$

We first prove that d' satisfies the triangle inequality. Define a function $f(x)$ as follows: $f(x) = 1/\alpha$ for $x \geq \alpha r^*$; $f(x) = r^*/x$ for $x \in [r^*, \alpha r^*]$, and $f(x) = 1$ for $x \leq r^*$. Observe, that $d'(u, v) = f(d(u, v))\, d(u, v)$; $f(x)$ is a nonincreasing function; $x f(x)$ is a nondecreasing function. Consider three points u, v, w and assume without loss of generality that $d'(u, w) \geq \max(d'(u, v), d'(v, w))$. We need to prove that $d'(u, w) \leq d'(u, v) + d'(v, w)$. Note that since $x f(x)$ is a nondecreasing function, $d(u, w) \geq \max(d(u, v), d(v, w))$ and $f(d(u, w)) \leq \min(f(d(u, v)), f(d(v, w)))$. Thus,

$$d'(u, v) + d'(v, w) = f(d(u, v))d(u, v) + f(d(v, w))d(v, w) \geq$$
$$\geq f(d(u, w))\big(d(u, v) + d(v, w)\big) \geq f(d(u, w))d(u, w) = d'(u, w).$$

The last inequality follows from the triangle inequality $d(u, v) + d(v, w) \geq d(u, w)$ for the metric d.

Next, we check that $d'(u, v)$ is an α-perturbation, i.e. $d(u, v)/\alpha \leq d'(u, v) \leq d(u, v)$ (see Remark 13.1). We have, $f(x) \in [1/\alpha, 1]$, and, thus, $d'(u, v)/d(u, v) = f(d(u, v)) \in [1/\alpha, 1]$.

By the definition of α-metric perturbation resilience, $C_1, \ldots, C_k$ is the unique optimal clustering for d'. However, the optimal set of centers for d' may be different from $c_1, \ldots, c_k$. Denote it by $c''_1, \ldots, c''_k$. We prove that the cost of the clustering $C_1, \ldots, C_k$ is the same for metrics d and d'. Let

$$r(C_i) = \min_{c \in C_i} \max_{u \in C_i} d(u, c).$$

---

3. Note that the algorithm finds the optimal clustering $C_1, \ldots, C_k$ but not necessarily an optimal set of centers $\{c_1, \ldots, c_k\}$; however, an optimal set of centers can be easily deduced from $C_1, \ldots, C_k$.

Since the cost of the clustering $C_1, \ldots, C_k$ equals r^* w.r.t. d, we have $r(C_i) = r^*$ for some i. Fix this i. By the definition of $r(C_i)$, for every $c \in C_i$ there exists $u \in C_i$ such that $d(u, c) \geq r(C_i) = r^*$. Particularly, for $c = c_i''$, there exists u such that $d(u, c_i'') \geq r^*$. Then $d'(u, c_i'') \geq r^*$ as well. Hence, the cost of the clustering $C_1, \ldots, C_k$ for the metric d' is at least r^*. (It cannot be larger than r^*, since $d'(u, v) \leq d(u, v)$ for all u and v.)

To conclude the proof, we observe that the cost of the clustering $C_1', \ldots, C_k'$ with centers $c_1', \ldots, c_k'$ also equals r^* w.r.t. the metric d'. Indeed, for $u \in C_i'$, we have $d(u, c_i') \leq \alpha r^*$, and, therefore, $d'(u, c_i') \leq r^*$. Thus, $C_1', \ldots, C_k'$ is an optimal clustering for d'. Therefore, it must be equal to the clustering $C_1, \ldots, C_k$. $\qquad\qquad\qquad\qquad\qquad\qquad\qquad\qquad\qquad\qquad\qquad\qquad$ □

13.3.2   Clustering Problems with Separable Center-based Objectives

In this section, we present an algorithm by Balcan and Liang (2016) that solves $(\sqrt{2}+1)$-metric perturbation resilient instances of clustering problems with separable center-based objectives.[4]

Definition 13.13. *In a clustering problem, we are given a set of vertices (points) V and a distance function d on V. Our goal is to partition the vertices into clusters so as to minimize a cost function, which depends on the clustering problem.*

Following Awasthi et al. (2012), we define the notion of a clustering problem with *a center-based objective*. (We note that the definition in Awasthi et al. (2012) makes several implicit assumptions that we make explicit here.)

Definition 13.14. *Consider a clustering problem. We say that it has a center-based objective if the following three properties hold.*

1. Given a subset $S \subset V$ and distance d_S on S, we can find the optimal center $c \in S$ for S, or, if there is more than one choice of an optimal center, a set of optimal centers $\mathrm{center}(S, d_S)$. (In the former case, $\mathrm{center}(S, d_S) = \{c\}$).

2. The set of centers does not change if we multiply all distances between points in S by α. That is,

$$\mathrm{center}(S, \alpha d_S) = \mathrm{center}(S, d_S).$$

---

4. The original result by Balcan and Liang (2016) applies to $(\sqrt{2}+1)$-perturbation resilient instances; recently, Makarychev and Makarychev (2016) showed that their algorithm also works for $(\sqrt{2}+1)$-*metric* perturbation resilient instances.

Also, the optimal clustering does not change if we multiply all distances between points in V by α.

3. *Let $C_1, \ldots, C_k$ be an optimal clustering of V (the clustering of minimum cost). For every i, let $c_i \in \mathrm{center}(C_i, d|_{C_i})$ be an optimal center for C_i (here, $d|_{C_i}$ is the restriction of d to C_i). Then each point $p \in C_i$ is closer to c_i than to any other center c_j, $d(p, c_i) < d(p, c_j)$.*

A clustering-objective is separable if we can define individual cluster scores so that the following holds.

1. *The cost of the clustering is either the maximum or sum of the cluster scores.*

2. *The score $\mathrm{score}(S, d|_S)$ of each cluster S depends only on S and $d|_S$, and can be computed in polynomial time.*

Many standard clustering problems, including k-center, k-means, and k-median, have separable center-based objectives.

We will assume below that the instance is α-metric perturbation resilient with $\alpha = 1 + \sqrt{2}$. Denote the optimal clustering by $C_1, \ldots, C_k$. Fix an optimal set of centers $c_1, \ldots, c_k$ for the clustering ($c_i \in \mathrm{center}(S, d_S)$). Define the radius of cluster C_i as $r_i = \max_{u \in C_i} d(c_i, u)$. For every point u, denote the ball of radius r around u by $B(u, r)$: $B(u, r) = \{v : d(u, v) \le r\}$.

We start with proving some basic structural properties of the optimal clustering $C_1, \ldots, C_k$.

Lemma 13.9 (Awasthi et al. (2012); Makarychev and Makarychev (2016)). *Clusters satisfy the following α-center proximity property: for all $i \neq j$ and $p \in C_i$,*

$$d(p, c_j) > \alpha d(p, c_i).$$

Proof. Suppose that $d(p, c_j) \le \alpha d(p, c_i)$. Let $r^* = d(p, c_i)$. Define a new metric d' as follows: for all u and v,

$$d'(u, v) = \min(d(u, v), d(u, p) + r^* + d(c_j, v), d(v, p) + r^* + d(c_j, u)).$$

The metric $d'(u, v)$ is the shortest path metric on the complete graph on V with edge lengths $len(u, v) = d(u, v)$ for all edges (u, v) but the edge (p, c_j). The length of the edge (p, c_j) equals $len(p, c_j) = r^*$. Observe that since the ratio $d(u, v)/len(u, v)$ is at most $d(p, c_j)/r^* \le \alpha$ for all edges (u, v), we have $d(u, v)/d'(u, v) \le \alpha$ for all u and v. Hence, d' is an α-metric perturbation of d (see Remark 13.1).

Let us now show that d' is equal to d within the cluster C_i and within the cluster C_j.

Lemma 13.10. *For all $u, v \in C_i$, we have $d(u, v) = d'(u, v)$, and for all $u, v \in C_j$, we have $d(u, v) = d'(u, v)$.*

Proof. I. Consider two points u, v in C_i. We need to show that $d(u, v) = d'(u, v)$. It suffices to prove that

$$d(u, v) \leq \min(d(u, p) + r^* + d(c_j, v), d(v, p) + r^* + d(c_j, u)).$$

Assume without loss of generality that $d(u, p) + r^* + d(c_j, v) \leq d(v, p) + r^* + d(c_j, u)$. We have

$$d(u, p) + r^* + d(c_j, v) = d(u, p) + d(p, c_i) + d(c_j, v) \geq d(u, c_i) + d(c_j, v).$$

Since $v \in C_i$, we have $d(v, c_i) < d(v, c_j)$, and thus

$$d(u, p) + r^* + d(c_j, v) > d(u, c_i) + d(c_i, v) \geq d(u, v).$$

II. Consider two points u, v in C_j. Similarly to the previous case, we need to show that $d(u, v) \leq d(u, p) + r^* + d(c_j, v)$. Since now $u \in C_j$, we have $d(u, c_j) < d(u, c_i)$. Thus,

$$\begin{aligned} d(u, p) + r^* + d(c_j, v) &= \big(d(u, p) + d(p, c_i)\big) + d(c_j, v) \\ &\geq d(u, c_i) + d(c_j, v) > d(u, c_j) + d(c_j, v) \geq d(u, v). \end{aligned}$$

$\square$

By the definition of α-metric perturbation stability, the optimal clusterings for metrics d and d' are the same. By Lemma 13.10, the distance functions d and d' are equal within the clusters C_i and C_j. Hence, the centers of C_i and C_j w.r.t. metric d' are also points c_i and c_j, respectively (see Definition 13.14, item 1). Thus, $d'(c_i, p) < d'(c_j, p)$, and, consequently,

$$d(c_i, p) = d'(c_i, p) < d'(c_j, p) = r^* = d(c_i, p).$$

We get a contradiction, which finishes the proof. $\square$

Lemma 13.11 (Awasthi et al. (2012); Balcan and Liang (2016)).

1. *All points outside of C_i lie at distance greater than r_i from c_i. Thus, $C_i = B(c_i, r_i)$.*

2. *Each point p in C_i is closer to c_i than to any point q outside of C_i. Furthermore, for every $p \in C_i$ and $q \notin C_i$, we have $\sqrt{2}\, d(p, c_i) < d(p, q)$.*

3. *For every two distinct clusters C_i and C_j,*

$$d(c_i, c_j) > \sqrt{2} \max(r_i, r_j).$$

Proof. We will prove items in the following order: 3, 1, and finally 2.

3. Let p be the farthest from c_i point in C_i. Then $r_i = d(c_i, p)$. By Lemma 13.9, $d(p, c_j) > \alpha d(p, c_i) = \alpha r_i$. By the triangle inequality,

$$d(c_i, c_j) \geq d(p, c_j) - d(p, c_i) > \alpha r_i - r_i = \sqrt{2} r_i.$$

Similarly, $d(c_i, c_j) > \sqrt{2} r_j$.

1. Consider a point $q \notin C_i$. Assume that $q \in C_j$. Then

$$d(c_i, c_j) \leq d(c_i, q) + d(q, c_j) \overset{\text{by Lemma 13.9}}{\leq} d(c_i, q) + d(c_i, q)/\alpha = \sqrt{2} d(c_i, q).$$

Combining this inequality with the inequality $d(c_i, c_j) > \sqrt{2} r_i$ from item 3, we get that $d(c_i, q) > r_i$.

2. Assume that $q \in C_j$. If $d(c_j, q) \geq d(c_i, p)$, we have

$$d(p, q) \geq d(c_i, q) - d(c_i, p) \overset{\text{by Lemma 13.9}}{>} \alpha d(c_j, q) - d(c_i, p) \geq \sqrt{2} d(c_i, p).$$

If $d(c_j, q) < d(c_i, p)$, we similarly have

$$d(p, q) \geq d(c_j, p) - d(c_j, q) \overset{\text{by Lemma 13.9}}{>} \alpha d(c_i, p) - d(c_j, q) \geq \sqrt{2} d(c_i, p).$$

$\square$

Now we sketch the algorithm of Balcan and Liang (2016). The algorithm consists of two stages. During the first stage, the algorithm employs a greedy approach: it starts with a trivial clustering of V, in which each vertex belongs to its own cluster. Then it repeatedly finds and links two "closest" clusters. The algorithm runs until it gets one cluster that contains all of the vertices. (Importantly, the algorithm does not stop when it gets k clusters — these k clusters are not necessarily optimal!) The result of the first stage of the algorithm is a binary decomposition tree $\mathcal{T}$ of V: the leaves of the tree are singleton clusters; internal nodes of $\mathcal{T}$ are intermediate clusters, obtained during the execution of the first stage; the root of $\mathcal{T}$ is V. We will show that each cluster C_i in the optimal clustering appears in the decomposition tree $\mathcal{T}$. During the second stage, the algorithm uses a simple bottom-up dynamic program to identify all clusters C_i in $\mathcal{T}$.

For the algorithm to succeed, it is important to use the right distance between clusters. We shall now define *the closure distance* to be used.

Definition 13.15. *We say that a point $x \in A$ is an r-central point for a set $A \subset V$ if it satisfies*

- *Coverage condition: $A \subset B(x, r)$.*

• *Padding condition: Every point p in $B(x,r)$ is closer to x than to any point outside of $B(x,r)$; that is, if $d(p,q) \leq d(p,x) \leq r$, then $d(q,x) \leq r$.*

Definition 13.16. *The closure distance $D_S(A_1, A_2)$ between two sets $A_1 \subset V$ and $A_2 \subset V$ is equal to the minimal r such that $A_1 \cup A_2$ has an r-central point.*

Note that the closure distance is well-defined since every point in $A_1 \cup A_2$ is r-central for $r = \text{diam}(V) = \max_{u,v \in V} d(u,v)$.

Now we formally present Algorithm 13.3 (see the figure). It is clear that

---
Algorithm 13.3 Clustering Algorithm

1:    Create n singleton clusters — one for each vertex in V. Add them to $\mathcal{C}$.   ▷ Stage 1
2:    Initialize a tree $\mathcal{T}$. Add all singletons from $\mathcal{C}$ to $\mathcal{T}$.
3:    **while** $|\mathcal{C}| \neq 1$ **do**
4:        Find two closest clusters A and B in $\mathcal{C}$ w.r.t. the closure distance.
5:        Merge A and B:
6:            Replace A and B with $A \cup B$ in $\mathcal{C}$.
7:            Add node $A \cup B$ to $\mathcal{T}$ and make it the parent of A and B.
8:    **end while**
                                                                      ▷ Stage 2
9:    Using bottom-up dynamic programming, find among all clusterings $(C'_1, \ldots, C'_k)$ of V, in which all C'_i appear in the decomposition tree $\mathcal{T}$, the clustering of minimum cost.
10:    **return** clustering $(C'_1, \ldots, C'_k)$.
---

the algorithm runs in polynomial time. To prove the correctness of the algorithm, we need to show that every cluster C_i from the optimal clustering appears in the decomposition tree.

Lemma 13.12. *Consider two subsets A_1 and A_2 of C_i. Assume that $c_i \in A_1 \cup A_2$. Then $d_S(A_1, A_2) \leq r_i$.*

Proof. We show that c_i is an r_i-central point for $A_1 \cup A_2$. Indeed, by Lemma 13.11, item 1, $C_i = B(c_i, r_i)$. Thus $A_1 \cup A_2 \subset C_i = B(c_i, r_i)$. Now consider $p \in B(x_i, r_i)$ and $q \notin B(x_i, r_i)$. We have $p \in C_i$ and $q \notin C_i$, and from Lemma 13.11, item 2, we get that $d(p,q) < d(c_i, p)$.   □

Lemma 13.13. *Assume that a set A contains points from both C_i and the complement of C_i. If a point x is Δ-central for A then $\Delta > r_i$.*

In particular, the closure distance between non-empty sets $A_1 \subset C_i$ and $A_2 \subset V \setminus C_i$ is at least r_i.

Proof. Consider two cases. First, assume that $x \in C_i$. Consider an arbitrary point $q \in A \setminus C_i$. Let C_j be the cluster q lies in (then, $j \neq i$). Since x is Δ-central for A and $q \in A$, we have $d(x,q) \leq \Delta$. By Lemma 13.11, item

2, $d(q, c_j) < d(q, x)$. From the definition of a central point, we get that $d(c_j, x) \leq \Delta$. By Lemma 13.9, $d(c_i, x) \leq \Delta/\alpha$. Therefore,

$$d(c_i, c_j) \leq d(c_i, x) + d(x, c_j) \leq \Delta/\alpha + \Delta = \sqrt{2}\Delta.$$

On the other hand, $d(c_i, c_j) > \sqrt{2}\, r_i$ by Lemma 13.11, item 3. We conclude that $\Delta > r_i$.

Now assume that $x \notin C_i$. Consider a point $p \in A \cap C_i$. Since x is a Δ-central point for A, we have $d(x, p) \leq \Delta$. By Lemma 13.11, item 2, point p is closer to c_i than to x. Thus by the definition of a central point, $c_i \in B(x, \Delta)$. On the other hand, by our assumption, $x \notin C_i = B(c_i, r_i)$. We get that $r_i < d(c_i, x) \leq \Delta$. This concludes the proof.

Now consider $A_1 \subset C_i$ and $A_2 \subset V \setminus C_i$. Applying the lemma to the set $A_1 \cup A_2$, we get that $D_S(A_1, A_2) \geq r_i$. □

Lemma 13.14. *Consider a cluster C_i in the optimal clustering.*
1. Let C be a cluster/node in the decomposition tree $\mathcal{T}$. Then

$$C \subset C_i, \quad C_i \subset C, \quad or \quad C \cap C_i = \varnothing. \tag{13.6}$$

2. C_i appears in the decomposition tree $\mathcal{T}$.

Proof. 1. We prove that the statement holds for all sets C in $\mathcal{C}$ by induction. Initially, all clusters C in $\mathcal{C}$ are singletons, and therefore, satisfy condition (13.6). Now suppose that we proved that condition (13.6) holds until some iteration, in which we merge clusters A and B, and obtain a cluster $C = A \cup B$. We need to prove that C also satisfies the condition. Note that C satisfies condition (13.6) in the following 3 cases:

- Neither A nor B intersects C_i. Then $C \cap C_i = \varnothing$.
- Both sets A and B are subsets of C_i. Then $C \subset C_i$.
- One of the sets A and B contains C_i. Then $C_i \subset C$.

The only remaining case is that one of the sets is a proper subset of C_i and the other does not intersect C_i; let us say $A \subset C_i$ and $B \subset \bar{C}_i$. We will show now that this case actually cannot happen.

Since A is a proper subset of C_i, there is another cluster $A' \subset C_i$ in $\mathcal{C}$. Furthermore, if $c_i \notin A$, then there is A' in $\mathcal{C}$ that contains c_i. By Lemma 13.12, point c_i is r_i-central for $A \cup A'$, and therefore $d_S(A, A') \leq r_i$. On the other hand, by Lemma 13.13, $d_S(A, B) > r_i \geq d_S(A, A')$. Therefore, A and B are not two closest clusters in $\mathcal{C}$ w.r.t. the closure distance. We get a contradiction.

2. Consider the smallest cluster C in $\mathcal{T}$ that contains C_i. If C is a singleton, then $C = C_i$. Otherwise, C is the union of its child clusters A and B. By item 1, both A and B are subsets of C_i, and so $C \subset C_i$. Therefore, $C = C_i$. $\square$

13.4   References

S. Arora, J. Lee, and A. Naor. Euclidean distortion and the sparsest cut. *Journal of the American Mathematical Society*, 21(1):1–21, 2008.

P. Awasthi, A. Blum, and O. Sheffet. Center-based clustering under perturbation stability. *Information Processing Letters*, 112(1):49–54, 2012.

M.-F. Balcan and M. Braverman. Approximate Nash equilibria under stability conditions. Technical report, 2010.

M.-F. Balcan and Y. Liang. Clustering under perturbation resilience. 2016. To appear.

M.-F. Balcan, A. Blum, and A. Gupta. Approximate clustering without the approximation. In *Proceedings of the Symposium on Discrete Algorithms*, pages 1068–1077. Society for Industrial and Applied Mathematics, 2009.

M.-F. Balcan, N. Haghtalab, and C. White. Symmetric and asymmetric k-center clustering under stability. *arXiv preprint arXiv:1505.03924*, 2015.

Y. Bilu and N. Linial. Are stable instances easy? In *Innovations in Computer Science*, pages 332–341, 2010.

Y. Bilu, A. Daniely, N. Linial, and M. Saks. On the practically interesting instances of maxcut. In *Proceedings of the Symposium on Theoretical Aspects of Computer Science*, pages 526–537, 2013.

A. Blum and J. Spencer. Coloring random and semi-random k-colorable graphs. *Journal of Algorithms*, 19(2):204–234, 1995.

N. Buchbinder, J. S. Naor, and R. Schwartz. Simplex partitioning via exponential clocks and the multiway cut problem. In *Proceedings of the Symposium on Theory of Computing*, pages 535–544, 2013.

G. Cualinescu, H. Karloff, and Y. Rabani. An improved approximation algorithm for multiway cut. In *Proceedings of the Symposium on Theory of Computing*, pages 48–52, 1998.

E. Dahlhaus, D. S. Johnson, C. H. Papadimitriou, P. D. Seymour, and M. Yannakakis. The complexity of multiterminal cuts. *SIAM Journal on Computing*, 23:864–894, 1994.

M. E. Dyer and A. M. Frieze. A simple heuristic for the p-centre problem. *Operations Research Letters*, 3(6):285–288, 1985.

U. Feige and J. Kilian. Heuristics for finding large independent sets, with applications to coloring semi-random graphs. In *Proceedings of the Symposium on Foundations of Computer Science*, pages 674–683, 1998.

U. Feige, Y. Mansour, and R. Schapire. Learning and inference in the presence of corrupted inputs. In *Proceedings of the Conference on Learning Theory*, pages 637–657, 2015.

M. X. Goemans and D. P. Williamson. Improved approximation algorithms for maximum cut and satisfiability problems using semidefinite programming. volume 42, pages 1115–1145, 1995.

D. S. Hochbaum and D. B. Shmoys. A best possible heuristic for the k-center problem. *Mathematics of operations research*, 10(2):180–184, 1985.

D. R. Karger, P. Klein, C. Stein, M. Thorup, and N. E. Young. Rounding algorithms for a geometric embedding of minimum multiway cut. *Mathematics of Operations Research*, 29(3):436–461, 2004.

R. M. Karp. Reducibility among combinatorial problems. Springer, 1972.

S. Khot, G. Kindler, E. Mossel, and R. O'Donnell. Optimal inapproximability results for max-cut and other 2-variable CSPs? *SIAM Journal on Computing*, 37 (1):319–357, 2007.

J. Kleinberg and E. Tardos. Approximation algorithms for classification problems with pairwise relationships: Metric labeling and Markov random fields. *Journal of the ACM (JACM)*, 49(5):616–639, 2002.

V. Leontev. Stability of the traveling salesman problem (in Russian). volume 15, pages 1293–1309, 1975.

K. Makarychev and Y. Makarychev. Metric perturbation resilience. 2016.

K. Makarychev, Y. Makarychev, and A. Vijayaraghavan. Approximation algorithms for semi-random partitioning problems. In *Proceedings of the ACM symposium on Theory of computing*, pages 367–384, 2012.

K. Makarychev, Y. Makarychev, and A. Vijayaraghavan. Sorting noisy data with partial information. In *Proceedings of the Conference on Innovations in Theoretical Computer Science*, pages 515–528, 2013.

K. Makarychev, Y. Makarychev, and A. Vijayaraghavan. Constant factor approximation for balanced cut in the pie model. In *Proceedings of the Symposium on Theory of Computing*, pages 41–49, 2014a.

K. Makarychev, Y. Makarychev, and A. Vijayaraghavan. Bilu—Linial stable instances of Max Cut and Minimum Multiway Cut. In *Proceedings of the Symposium on Discrete Algorithms*, pages 890–906, 2014b.

K. Makarychev, Y. Makarychev, and A. Vijayaraghavan. Correlation clustering with noisy partial information. In *Proceedings of the Conference on Learning Theory*, pages 1321–1342, 2015.

C. Mathieu and W. Schudy. Correlation clustering with noisy input. In *Proceedings of the Symposium on Discrete Algorithms*, pages 712–728, 2010.

M. Mihalák, M. Schöngens, R. Šrámek, and P. Widmayer. On the complexity of the metric tsp under stability considerations. In *SOFSEM 2011: Theory and Practice of Computer Science*, pages 382–393. Springer, 2011.

R. Ostrovsky, Y. Rabani, L. J. Schulman, and C. Swamy. The effectiveness of lloyd-type methods for the k-means problem. In *Proceeding of the Symposium on Foundations of Computer Science*, pages 165–176, 2006.

A. Sharma and J. Vondrák. Multiway cut, pairwise realizable distributions, and descending thresholds. In *Proceedings of the Symposium on Theory of Computing*, pages 724–733, 2014.

Printed in the United States
by Baker & Taylor Publisher Services